D1624489

CATHOLICISM AND AMERICAN FREEDOM

ALSO BY JOHN T. McGREEVY

Parish Boundaries:
The Catholic Encounter with Race in the Twentieth-Century Urban North

CATHOLICISM AND AMERICAN FREEDOM

A History

JOHN T. McGREEVY

W. W. NORTON & COMPANY
NEW YORK LONDON

Printed in the United States of America
First Edition

Manufacturing by the Maple-Vail Book Manufacturing Group
Book design by BTDnyc
Production manager: Amanda Morrison

Library of Congress Cataloging-in-Publication Data

McGreevy, John T.
Catholicism and American freedom : a history / by John T. McGreevy.—1st ed.
p. cm.
Includes bibliographical references and index.
ISBN 0-393-04760-1
1. Catholic Church—United States—History. 2. Liberty—Religious aspects—Catholic Church—History. 3. Christianity and politics—Catholic Church—History. 4. Christianity and politics—United States—History. 5. United States—Church history. I. Title.
BX1406.3 .M36 2003
282' .73—dc21 2002154389

W. W. Norton & Company, Inc., 500 Fifth Avenue, New York, N.Y. 10110
www.wwnorton.com

W. W. Norton & Company Ltd., Castle House
75/76 Wells Street, London W1T 3QT

1 2 3 4 5 6 7 8 9 0

CONTENTS

Introduction
THE ELIOT SCHOOL REBELLION, BOSTON, 1859
7

Chapter One
EDUCATION AND THE NINETEENTH-CENTURY CATHOLIC REVIVAL
19

Chapter Two
CATHOLICISM, SLAVERY, AND THE CAUSE OF LIBERTY
43

Chapter Three
CATHOLIC FREEDOM AND CIVIL WAR
68

Chapter Four
THE NATION
91

Chapter Five
THE SOCIAL QUESTION
127

Chapter Six
AMERICAN FREEDOM AND CATHOLIC POWER
166

Chapter Seven
DEMOCRACY, RELIGIOUS FREEDOM, AND
THE NOUVELLE THÉOLOGIE
189

Chapter Eight
LIFE (I)
216

Chapter Nine
LIFE (II)
250

Chapter Ten
A CONSISTENT ETHIC AND SEXUAL ABUSE
282

Notes
297

Photo Credits
407

Acknowledgments
408

Index
411

Introduction

THE ELIOT SCHOOL REBELLION, BOSTON, 1859

I

On Monday morning, March 7, 1859, the instructor Sophia Shepard began the new week at Boston's Eliot School by asking ten-year-old Thomas Whall to recite the Ten Commandments. Beginning the school day by reading Scripture and reciting the Ten Commandments was customary, indeed required by law, at all Massachusetts public, or common, schools. More unusual was Miss Shepard's insistence that Whall and the other boys in her classroom individually recite the Protestant, or King James, Bible version of the commandments. Typically, the Catholic students would mutter a different version of the commandments—avoiding the Protestant second commandment, which cautioned against the worship of any "graven image"—and the substitution would be lost in the general din.[1]

On this day Whall refused Miss Shepard's request. His father, young Thomas announced, had insisted that he refuse to recite the Protestant version of the commandments. During a series of meetings over the next three days, Whall, Whall's father, the principal, and members of the school committee tried to resolve the matter. The principal hinted that differences between Catholic and Protestant versions of the commandments did not trouble him, but a local school committee member, Micah Dyer, once a supporter of Boston's anti-Catholic Know-Nothing Party, insisted on adherence to the letter of the law.[2]

Thomas Whall's family attended St. Mary's Church in Boston's North End. There Thomas listened to the Jesuit Father Bernardine Wiget urge the several hundred boys in the Sunday school not to recite any Protestant prayers, so as to be saved from "infidelity and heresy." At a subsequent meeting parishioners passed twenty resolutions, including one "recommending that the children should be taught not to be ashamed, but to be proud of their holy religion, and, therefore, to bless themselves whenever they should be called upon to recite prayers, and at that time to recite their own Catholic prayers."[3] Wiget also threatened, apparently, to read from the altar the name of any boy who agreed to recite the Protestant version of the commandments in the Eliot School.[4]

The next day, Monday, a week after the first incident, Miss Shepard again asked Whall to recite the commandments from the King James Bible. He again refused. This time an assistant to the principal, McLaurin F. Cooke, stepped into the classroom and informed the class, "Here's a boy that refuses to repeat the Ten Commandments, and I will whip him till he yields if it takes the whole forenoon." And so Cooke did, beating Whall's hands with a rattan stick for half an hour until they were cut and bleeding. During breaks in the beating, other boys yelled at Thomas not to give in. One account suggests Thomas fainted.

The school principal then ordered all boys not willing to recite the Ten Commandments in the King James version to leave the school, and about one hundred Catholic boys were discharged. On Tuesday three hundred boys were discharged for the same offense. On the following Monday the Catholic boys brought copies of the "Catholic commandments" to school, but they were again discharged. Some boys took to ripping the Protestant Ten Commandments out of their readers.

Whall and his father sued Assistant Principal Cooke for use of excessive force. Cooke's attorney used the trial to ask, "Who is this priest who comes here from a foreign land to instruct us in our laws?" He added that "the real objection is to the Bible itself, for, while that is read daily in our schools, America can never be Catholic."[5] The court's ruling, handed down by Judge Sebeus Maine, vindicated Cooke, arguing that Bible reading without comment "is no interference with religious liberty." Whall's refusal to recite the Protestant version of the Ten Commandments threatened the stability of the public school, "the granite foundation on which our republican form of government rests."[6]

Comment about the case—immediately dubbed the Eliot School Rebellion—dominated the local newspapers, and reports spread across the nation. Young Whall, a victim of "inhuman torture," began receiving tributes from Catholic parishes and schools around the country: a goblet from the Cathedral schools of Covington, Kentucky, and gold medals from Nativity in New York City and St. Mary's in Alexandria, Virginia.[7]

Non-Catholic reaction was divided. Major national papers such as the *New York Tribune* criticized school authorities for creating a "religious martyr," and the *Boston Daily Advertiser* flatly termed Whall's punishment "intrinsically wrong and unjust." The *Boston Weekly Messenger* more cautiously viewed the situation as "perplexing and delicate."[8]

The *Boston Daily Atlas and Bee*, on the other hand, the city's most important Republican Party newspaper, concluded, "We are unalterably, sternly opposed to the encroachments of political and social Romanism, as well as to its wretched superstition, intolerance, bigotry and mean despotism—as much so as we are to the monster institution of human slavery and for the same reasons."[9] Amos A. Lawrence, a prominent Boston businessman and a leading supporter of the abolitionist John Brown, noted "trouble with the Catholics in the Boston schools" in his diary. "Father Wiget," he continued, "(an ignorant or bigoted priest, or both) forbids his Sunday School scholars to repeat the 10 commandments in school in the usual form, also the Lord's prayer. . . . If Protestant Christianity is to be abandoned in our public educational system, we shall convert the schools of the Puritans into heathen temples, or what is next to that."[10]

A number of Boston ministers addressed the topic, and most condemned Catholic aggression. One minister warned his congregation that Wiget was a "Jesuit of the ultra-Roman stamp." Another reissued an anti-Catholic polemic he had written four years previously, noting its relevance in a city where "a single foreign priest has introduced anarchy into one of our public schools. . . ."[11]

Reverend Arthur Buckminster Fuller, pastor of a Unitarian church near St. Mary's, began by recommending that the "general and common doctrines of Christianity" not be banished from the common schools. Fuller had run for local office on the Republican ticket in 1857, and he continued his sermon, intriguingly, with an emphasis on slavery, what as a candidate he had once called the "sum of all villainies."[12] "On these western shores, too," he said, "in our own land, Romanism allies itself with every false and anti-republican institution which is yet tolerated in our glorious

MASTER THOMAS J. WHALL, THE HERO OF THE ELIOT SCHOOL.

Thomas Whall, hero of the Eliot School Rebellion, from the *Irish Illustrated Nation* of April 30, 1859. Whall is wearing medals sent to him by admiring Catholics across the country, and standing next to a goblet sent by Catholics in Covington, Kentucky. The inscription on the goblet pays tribute to the "Filial Piety, manly Fortitude and Heroic Faith Under Torture at the Eliot School, Boston, March 14, 1859."

country. . . . Intemperance and slavery would quickly be overcome if Romanism ceased to exert her influence to uphold them both. . . ." Should Catholics achieve political power in the United States, Fuller concluded, "[o]ur national government, now so fearfully subservient to the shameful slave power, would then be no less under the dominion of a standing army of priests and friars."[13]

II

Reverend Fuller's fears were not simply religious bigotry. True, Protestant migrants to the British North American colonies had nurtured a powerful anti-Catholicism since the seventeenth century. When William Brewster sailed for the New World on the *Mayflower* in 1620, he lugged along the just-published English translation of the Venetian historian Paulo Sarpi's slashing attack on the Council of Trent and the papacy.[14] In 1775 Thomas Paine remarked that inhabitants of the "popish world at this day by not knowing the full manifestation of spiritual freedom, enjoy but a shadow of political liberty."[15]

The alliance with Catholic France during the Revolutionary War, and the heroism of such figures as the marquis de Lafayette, briefly made such statements impolitic.[16] When Alexander Hamilton urged the New York state assembly to allow Catholics full voting rights in 1787, he spoke of the "little influence possessed by the Pope in Europe" and the needless "vigilance of those who would bring engines to extinguish fire which had many days subsided."[17]

Catholic loyalty to the new nation also quieted fears. John Carroll, the first American bishop and cousin to Charles Carroll, a signer of the Declaration of Independence, delivered two heartfelt tributes upon the death of George Washington. Carroll also stressed that all sincere Christians, not just Catholics, might have eternal life and encouraged the election of bishops as opposed to their appointment by the Vatican.[18] Boston's first Catholic bishop, Jean Cheverus, fled France after refusing to take an oath in support of the revolutionary civil constitution in 1792, but his unassuming manner made him a beloved figure in the city of the Puritans.[19]

Hostility to Catholicism began to swell again in the 1830s on both sides of the Atlantic, as German and, especially, Irish Catholic immigrants made their way to Liverpool, Glasgow, New York, Philadelphia, and Boston. In Boston, in 1834, a mob destroyed an Ursuline convent. In New

York, two years later, a group of reformers and abolitionists arranged for the publication of Maria Monk's *Awful Disclosures of Hotel Dieu Nunnery*, an exposé of life in a Canadian convent that, though wholly fictitious, nonetheless became the best-selling American book of the nineteenth century before *Uncle Tom's Cabin*.[20]

Reverend Fuller tried to distance himself from this more virulent anti-Catholic strain. "We are opposed to Romanism, but not to Romanists," he emphasized; "it is their system, not their characters. . . ." Recalling Bishop Cheverus, he stressed, "There are devout and good men and women among them [Catholics] and always have been such, whom we truly love or their memory revere."[21] Later, during the Civil War, Fuller would serve as chaplain for a Massachusetts regiment with many Catholic soldiers, and he claimed to preach only on uncontroversial themes—although he did, admittedly, "endeavor to aid [Catholic soldiers] in their religious inquiries which naturally arise in their minds, and in that work 'the word of God is quick and powerful.'"[22]

III

Rather than the last gasps of the Reformation, Reverend Fuller and Father Wiget enacted a Boston variant on a nineteenth-century struggle shaping religion and politics in Europe, Latin America, Canada, and the United States. Fuller's comparison of Catholics to slaveholders opens an important window onto nineteenth-century Atlantic liberalism, just as Wiget's attack on public (but Protestant) education and his ability to rally the Catholics of Boston's North End identify him as an actor in the contemporary Catholic revival.

Historians have only begun to investigate the revival's disruptive effects.[23] On reaching full force in the early nineteenth century, the revival affected large regions of France, Belgium, Germany, and Italy and swept across Ireland and into the United States, Canada, parts of Latin America, and Australia. Mass attendance became more regular, and religious vocations (especially among young women) grew steadily. "Ultramontanism," the term most associated with the revival, is shorthand for a cluster of shifts that included a Vatican-fostered move to Thomistic philosophy, a more intense experiential piety centered on miracles and Vatican-approved devotions such as that of the Sacred Heart, an international outlook suspicious of national variations within Catholicism, and a heightened respect for church authorities ranging from the pope to parish priests. All this was nurtured in the world of Catholic parishes, schools, and associations, whose members understood themselves as arrayed against the wider society.[24]

Like their European counterparts, Catholic intellectuals in the United States influenced by the revival defined themselves against dominant ideas of freedom. Liberal politicians, editors, and intellectuals, Catholics argued, placed too much emphasis on individual autonomy, glibly invoking, in the words of one New Orleans priest, that "most misunderstood" word, "liberté."[25] Opposition to liberal notions of autonomy informed Catholic hostility to immediate slave emancipation, nonsectarian education, and laissez-faire economics.

When confronted with this Catholic resurgence, liberals revitalized long-standing anti-Catholic tropes.[26] Standard theological charges—purgatory was absurd and transubstantiation foolish—reappeared, but liberal reformers also stressed the cultural consequences of Catholicism's seeming disregard for individual autonomy. Political liberty (the individual voter), material prosperity (the individual economic actor in a free market), and intellectual progress (thinking on one's own) all seemed at risk. Maryland's Henry Winter Davis, later a Republican senator, divided American Catholics into those "worthy of their Republican fathers" and "ultra-montanists or papists" in 1856. A rumor swept the country that same year, reaching the Senate floor, that Lafayette on his deathbed had warned that "if ever the liberties of [the United States] are destroyed it will be by Catholic priests."[27]

Reverend Fuller held a similar view. He insisted that an older, more congenial Boston Catholicism had vanished, replaced by "an organization hostile to liberty, seeking the overthrow of the dearest rights of Americans and freedmen the world over." The church had been a primary force for reaction in the European revolutions of 1847 and 1848, Fuller reminded his listeners, and here he referred to his late sister, Margaret Fuller, the most prominent American enthusiast for the 1848 Italian revolt against papal rule. He also cited the British historian Thomas Macaulay's warning that the "progress of the Catholic revival" meant that the church had renewed its authority over much of the European peasantry since the French Revolution. Father Wiget, learning English at Jesuit-run Georgetown University, in Washington, D.C., after being forced to flee Switzerland during the first of the European revolutions in 1847, copied excerpts from Macaulay's essay into his student notebook.[28]

IV

This book sketches the interplay between Catholic and American ideas of freedom, beginning in the 1840s when an unprecedented wave of European immigrants made Catholicism the single largest religious denomination in the United States. It is *a* history, not *the* history, but it moves from nineteenth-century debates over education, slavery, and nationalism to twentieth- and twenty-first-century discussions of social welfare policy, democracy, birth control, abortion, and sexual abuse.

This interplay between Catholic and American remains poorly understood. In part this is because many influential modern Catholic thinkers—Jaime Balmes from Spain, Joseph Kleutgen, Heinrich Pesch, Karl Rahner, and Bernhard Häring from Germany, Matteo Liberatore from Italy, John Henry Newman from England, Charles Montalembert, Jacques Maritain, Yves Congar, Marie-Dominique Chenu, and Henri de Lubac from France, Bernard Lonergan from Canada, Gustavo Gutiérrez from Peru, and Karol Wojtyla (John Paul II) from Poland—did not always (or ever) write in English or work in the United States.[29]

At the same time, historians of the United States seem to have agreed with an 1861 *New York Times* editorial announcing that "intelligent minds in every country" thought Catholic belief a "fast-vanishing quality."[30] In contrast to colleagues studying Europe and Latin America, historians of the United States have evinced little interest in the ideas sustaining Catholic institutions (thousands of churches, the world's largest private school system, the nation's largest network of social welfare agencies, the nation's largest chain of private hospitals) and communicants. Most historians know less about American Catholic intellectual life, even less about important figures such as Orestes Brownson and John Courtney Murray, than about a "republican" tradition already in decline by the late eighteenth century, or a socialism distinguished in the United States by its brevity.[31]

Measuring the Catholic contribution to American intellectual life also entails assessing the role played by Catholicism (and anti-Catholicism) in the American intellectual imagination. The topic is understudied, in part because anti-Catholicism directed against Catholic individuals declined sharply after the 1920s, even as more subtle (and often anti-Catholic) prejudices against hierarchy and authority continued to shape American intellectual life.[32] The trick is to capture two traditions in motion, not one: to explore American ideas about Catholicism along with the predispositions (at times blinders) framing the mental landscape of American Catholics.

But readers must make their own assessment. Better to begin at the beginning. After all, why was there so much Catholicism in the United States, and what did it mean?

CATHOLICISM AND AMERICAN FREEDOM

Chapter One

EDUCATION AND THE NINETEENTH-CENTURY CATHOLIC REVIVAL

I

To begin with Father Bernardine Wiget is appropriate, since, as he confessed in a midnight letter to his Jesuit provincial, he was at the "bottom of it all."[1] Wiget was born in the town of Schwyz, capital of the Swiss canton of the same name. He took the classical course at the Jesuit college, where he joined the sodality and developed what his obituary writer called a "truly filial devotion to the Blessed Mother of God."[2]

Wiget then entered the Jesuit order and studied at the Jesuit seminary in Fribourg from 1840 to 1847. At Fribourg the Jesuits stressed the degeneracy of the modern world, especially its focus on individualism and ignorance of the virtue of obedience.[3] Connected to the seminary was a controversial boarding school enrolling the sons of many French royalist families. The French historian and nationalist Jules Michelet warned his readers that "if you have a Jesuit heart, pass that way, that is to the side of Fribourg; if you are upright and straightforward come here, this is France!"[4]

Swiss liberals expelled the Jesuits from the country during the 1847 Swiss civil war, the first of the conflicts that would sweep over Europe during the next two years. (Events in Switzerland established a pattern: liberal governments also expelled the Jesuits from Italy, Spain, Germany, and France between 1859 and 1880.)[5] When the armies of the Swiss

Protestant cantons overwhelmed the Catholic forces, troops smashed the doors of the Jesuit seminary. Fearing for their lives, small groups of Jesuits, including Wiget, adopted disguises and fled. Ultimately the beleaguered Jesuit provincial ordered eighty-eight members of Wiget's Jesuit province to depart for the United States.[6] Writing in 1849, Wiget recalled his shock at realizing the hollowness of Swiss liberty, once thought to be as permanent as the "eternal mountains."[7]

Wiget's experience is emblematic, not in dramatic detail but in indication of direction. As late as 1847 conflict between Catholicism and the liberal reform movements sweeping Europe did not seem inevitable. Prominent Catholics such as Vincenzo Gioberti in Italy, Daniel O'Connell in Ireland, and Charles Montalembert in France viewed the church as a source—not an opponent—of political liberty, and Montalembert found the conservatism of Swiss Jesuits especially off-putting.[8] Upon O'Con-

Father Bernardine Wiget, S.J., n.d.

nell's death, in 1847, supporters carried his heart to Rome, where the Italian priest and nationalist Gioacchino Ventura eulogized him for having united "true religion and true liberty."[9]

This hope that Catholicism might foster, not inhibit, liberty had also reached the United States. As early as 1831 Alexis de Tocqueville convinced himself that he had discovered a new Catholic style, terming Catholicism a powerful contributor to the "maintenance of a Democratic Republic in the United States." Another visitor, Harriet Martineau, informed her British readers, "The Catholic religion is modified by the spirit of the time in America; and its professors are not a set of men who can be priest-ridden to any fatal extent."[10]

Pius IX seemed to confirm a connection between Catholicism and liberty when he began his pontificate in 1846 and 1847 with a series of reform gestures, including amnesty for political prisoners and endorsement of a constitution for the Papal States. Leading citizens of New York and Philadelphia applauded his actions, and the Louisiana legislature hailed the pope as an "instrument destined by Divine Providence to accomplish the political regeneration of Italy." The *New York Tribune* correspondent Margaret Fuller informed a friend that the pope was a "thoughtful noble-minded man."[11]

Catholics in France cautiously welcomed the formation of the new French government after the February revolution of 1848, and German Catholics participated in the new Frankfurt parliament of that year. By the middle of 1848, however, many European Catholics had begun to recoil from the liberal nationalism sweeping the Continent, a nationalism often anti-Catholic and anticlerical. Particular targets of Austrian, Swiss, Italian, and Hungarian nationalists were the men's religious orders, precisely because members of the orders emphasized loyalty to the pope above national allegiance and had frequently allied themselves with monarchies and conservative governments. Some of the Jesuits who fled Switzerland with Father Wiget landed in the Savoy region of Italy, where at night they heard crowds chanting, "Down with the Jesuits!"[12]

The most far-reaching events occurred in the Papal States. In November 1848, assassins murdered the pope's handpicked prime minister, Pellegrino Rossi, and the Papal States government was overthrown, to popular acclaim. Pius IX fled to the nearby Kingdom of the Two Sicilies, and from that point rejected any compromise with what were, in his chastened view, tainted liberal principles. Trailing behind the French army,

Pius IX returned to Rome in 1849 and again assumed control of the Papal States, but he also began forging a close relationship with Jesuits sympathetic to his increasingly reactionary views.[13]

A parallel reorientation took place in the United States, where many citizens welcomed news of the February revolution in France. Few Americans were sympathetic to attacks on private property, but oratory on liberty and progress had an inspiring, even familiar, ring. Boston reformers sent a message to Paris in 1848 applauding the "birth of European liberty."[14]

Pius IX's opposition to European reformers in 1848 and 1849 elicited howls of betrayal, most prominently from Margaret Fuller. Fuller's dispatches from Italy reflect a mounting disgust that culminated when she claimed, "Not only Jesuitism must go, but the Roman Catholic religion must go. . . . The influence of the clergy is too perverting, too foreign to every hope of advancement and health."[15]

American Catholics also paid close attention to the ebb and flow of European events; as in Europe, in America the equation of revolution and anti-Catholicism became conventional Catholic wisdom, endlessly repeated in sermons and pamphlets. "At the outbreak of 1848, hundreds of priests were murdered by the democrats, simply because they were priests, and churches were desecrated because they were churches," exaggerated the *Boston Pilot*. "The popular revolutions in Europe in 1848," another writer explained, "were all anti-Catholic in their origin. Offspring of the great French revolution, they sought to destroy Catholicity in all its works, to sap it in the hearts of the people, to hurl its protectors from the thrones and the high places."[16]

The most immediate consequence of the European revolutions was to thrust European conflicts into American politics. If exiled Jesuits constituted one small stream of immigrants to the United States immediately after 1848, disappointed European radicals formed a far more powerful current. (Or as one Missouri Jesuit explained to a colleague in Belgium, "the anti-catholic spirit" was now cultivated by "German and Swiss radicals, red-refugees from France, Italy and Hungary [and] infidels of all varieties.")[17]

These radicals carried with them a deep suspicion of ultramontane Catholicism. In St. Louis, Heinrich Bornstein became the editor of the *Anzeiger des Westens*, the newspaper with perhaps the largest circulation (in German or English) in Missouri. Bornstein and other German radicals despised organized religion as a matter of principle, but their hatred of Catholicism had a special fervor. In 1852 Bornstein published an anti-Catholic novel, *The Mysteries of St. Louis*, that echoed in many respects his friend Eugène Sue's wildly popular (and also anti-Catholic) *The Wandering Jew*, published in Paris in 1844. The villains of Bornstein's novel, serialized in the *Anzeiger des Westens*, included decadent priests from St. Louis University, the local Jesuit college and a destination for many of the exiled Swiss Jesuits who accompanied Father Wiget as he fled Fribourg in 1847.[18]

Other German-speaking radicals shared these views. When a rumor reached frontier Wisconsin in 1849 that some of the Jesuits expelled from Switzerland might move to Milwaukee, one editor of a German newspaper wrote, "Now we are even to be confronted with . . . these indefatigable enemies of democracy and enlightenment, who have stood by despotism everywhere in Europe and therefore were chased out of the country by the citizens as soon as they felt themselves somewhat free. Do they have to be sent directly to Wisconsin, so that they can poison the blossoming young republic in its childhood?"[19] One of the most prominent German exiles, Karl Heinzen, sailed to the United States on one of the ships carrying the Swiss Jesuits, a fact he morbidly noted in his diary. Later, as the editor of *Der Pioneer*, he would attack the "anti-republican, anti-democratic, highly dangerous Roman Hierarchy."[20]

Such fears meshed with the growing sense among important American Protestants that a European "revival of the worst forms of Popery" had direct links to "kindred movements of the Romish priesthood in the United States."[21] Theodore Dwight, scion of one of New England's most prominent families, helped arrange for the publication of a virulently anti-Catholic tract, Maria Monk's *Awful Disclosures of Hotel Dieu Nunnery*, in 1836 and contributed articles to many Protestant publications. Dwight later published an admiring account of Italian liberals attempting to overthrow papal rule, and in 1850, after introducing himself to Giuseppe Garibaldi in New York, edited Garibaldi's intensely anti-papal memoirs. By that time Dwight described Catholic forces across the globe as the "enemies of human liberty."[22]

American Protestants also promoted the activities of two prominent European exiles, Louis Kossuth and Alessandro Gavazzi. A leader of the unsuccessful Hungarian independence movement, Kossuth saw his fame precede him, and he attracted enormous audiences during an American lecture tour, with politicians across the country erecting statues and naming streets in his honor. On the U.S. Senate floor Charles Sumner urged his colleagues to welcome Kossuth because "it will inspire all in other lands who are engaged in the contest for freedom; it will challenge the disturbed attention of despots. . . ."[23]

Many conservative American politicians and writers scoffed at the euphoria surrounding Kossuth's visit, but American Catholics were especially disdainful. Bishop John Hughes of New York linked Kossuth with anti-Catholic European revolutionaries, identifying him with "all that I have known of his class, as arch-enemies of the Catholic Church and of the peace of mankind."[24] An exiled Jesuit conducting a parish mission in rural Missouri in 1852 expressed pride that he had raised a cross in a town square to mark the first parish mission, since a few days earlier town "radicals" had shot off cannons in honor of the "notorious Kossuth."[25]

Kossuth's supporters—aware, as one St. Louis politician put it, that "the Catholics here are *Anti-Kossuth*, to a man"—quickly responded.[26] One Massachusetts minister observed that opposition to Kossuth from the "Jesuits of Rome and Vienna" was hardly surprising, "but the political relations of an American Catholic, we had supposed, were somewhat different from those of a foreign Jesuit."[27] Kossuth himself noted in St. Louis that Jesuits taught at St. Louis University, and complained that they were "warmly advocating the cause of Despotism."[28]

The speaking tour of Alessandro Gavazzi demonstrated the same dynamic. Gavazzi, too, had played an important role in the 1848 revolutions as a nationalist Italian priest and chaplain of Garibaldi's army. (He had held Garibaldi's arm when the two men entered Rome on the heels of an exiled Pius IX.) Following the defeat of Italian military forces, Gavazzi left the priesthood and, like Kossuth, embarked on a speaking tour. A group of leading Protestant ministers arranged for Gavazzi to give a series of addresses in Canada and the United States, which he did when not prevented from speaking by Catholic mobs.[29]

Gavazzi's lectures blended classic anti-Catholic imagery—nuns allegedly imprisoned in convents, the horrors of the Inquisition—with appeals to Americans that they not allow the dismissal of the King James Bible from the public schools or the development of a parochial school system. He emphasized the increasingly foreign character of American Catholicism. "Twenty years ago," he argued, "the Papists in your country were . . . only native Americans. But, now, after so many hundred Jesuits have come to America from Europe; now, after so many hundred thousand Roman Catholics have emigrated to this country, to be silent on the Popish system is no longer a duty, indeed it is a crime."[30]

Gavazzi also spurred opposition to the American tour of the Italian archbishop Gaetano Bedini. Bedini arrived in the United States in 1853, nominally to visit American bishops, but actually charged with reporting to the Vatican on the state of American Catholicism and mediating disputes between bishops and lay parish trustees.[31] During the Italian revolution of 1848 Bedini had served as papal legate in Bologna, and Gavazzi accused him of having permitted the torture and execution of the Italian patriot and priest Ugo Bassi.

Bedini and his Catholic defenders denied the charge (the evidence is ambiguous), but accusations that Bedini carried the "blood of the Italian patriots" on his garments reverberated throughout the secular and religious press.[32] In Pittsburgh the newspaper that would become the city's Republican Party journal viewed Bedini's visit as an "outrage" to "every sentiment of liberty and humanity."[33] In Cincinnati, Friedrich Hassaurek, a German exile and editor of a local German newspaper, the *Hochwächter*, roused the populace with a series of incendiary editorials. Ultimately, several hundred citizens marched through the streets with banners proclaiming "No Priests, No Kings, No Popery."[34]

Hung in effigy several times, and the intended victim of an assassination attempt, Bedini stole away from the United States under cover of darkness after a seven-month North American visit. "He will surely complain," Bishop Francis Kenrick of Philadelphia gloomily predicted, "of inhospitable shores, wild men and unrighteous rulers."[35]

II

The most important components of the Catholic revival were philosophical, theological, and organizational: the rehabilitation of philosophy in the tradition of Saint Thomas Aquinas, a more intense piety focused on the suffering Jesus and the miraculous, and an emphasis on Catholic parishes, schools, and organizations as refuges in an increasingly secular, even hostile, world. Allied to these changes was a conscious effort to offer alternative definitions of such terms as "freedom" and "progress."

Father Wiget's connection to the philosophical component of the

Catholic revival was direct. At the Jesuit seminary in Fribourg, one of Wiget's instructors was another young Jesuit, Joseph Kleutgen, the most important neo-Thomist Catholic philosopher of the nineteenth century. Kleutgen did not publish his major works until the 1850s, but he had already become convinced, along with a group of Neapolitan Jesuits, that a destructive individualism permeated modern philosophical thought. This individualism, or focus on autonomy, began in a theological sense with Martin Luther's rejection of church authority and in a philosophical sense with the subjectivity of Descartes. Its inevitable products were attacks on ecclesiastical authority and revolution. The only solution was a return to an Aristotelian, or more properly Thomist, communal vision of church, state, and society.

Kleutgen and the Neapolitan Jesuits initially represented a minority position within the world of Catholic philosophy, but Pius IX became closer to the Jesuits after the revolutions of 1848, encouraging the foundation of a Jesuit-edited journal, *Civiltà Cattolica*, which became influential throughout the Catholic world. In the United States, in Father Wiget's Boston, Jesuit seminarians studied from a Latin text written by Matteo Liberatore, one of the Neapolitan Jesuits editing *Civiltà Cattolica*.[36]

Wiget also sympathized with the Catholic piety fostered during the revival.[37] His actions in St. Mary's parish in Boston suggest a new Catholic style, one that led to tensions among Catholics themselves and between Catholics and non-Catholics. The impetus for this new style was European, not American, and in this respect the Catholic United States remained a provincial outpost of a European center. Leading bishops, including Martin Spalding (Louisville and Baltimore), Francis Kenrick (Philadelphia and Baltimore), and Patrick Lynch (Charleston), studied in Roman seminaries. In the United States these bishops devoted themselves to standardizing the liturgy according to Roman rites, wrestling property and authority away from lay parish trustees, and fostering such Roman-approved devotions as devotion to the Sacred Heart and the rosary. Attacks by these bishops on Gallicanism, or the notion that national customs might trump Roman regulations, were especially evident at the 1866 episcopal meeting in Baltimore, when a long list of Roman procedures became integrated into American canon law. Following the meeting, Archbishop Spalding of Baltimore boasted to his friend from student days in Rome, the Irish cardinal Paul Cullen, "that with perhaps one exception, there is not in the entire American Episcopate, a single element or vestige of *Gallicanism*—Thank God! We are Roman to the heart. . . ."[38]

Ordinary priests, nuns, and laypeople became Roman to the heart, through a less bureaucratic process. The primary mechanism in both the European and the American Catholic revival of the nineteenth century was the parish mission, one or two weeks of precisely timed Masses, instructions, recitations of the rosary, and benedictions of the blessed sacrament. These activities culminated in confession, the central moment of the mission for the individual penitent. Frequently, men and women traveled twenty miles in the darkness, lining up at three in the morning to make a confession that might bring them forgiveness and the hope of eternal life.[39]

The Jesuits, especially, including several of the 1848 exiles, became leading mission directors, traipsing from hamlet to hamlet in order to bring the sacraments to a widely dispersed population. One Jesuit who fled Austria in 1848, Francis X. Weninger, preached an astonishing 519 missions during his career. A Catholic writer reported in 1858 that missions had been given in "almost every ecclesiastical province and diocese; both in our overflowing city churches, and also in the country parishes both large and small."[40]

In contrast to Bishop John Carroll, who favored an irenic approach in the late eighteenth century, the shock troops of the Catholic revival took a polemical stance. Only close adhesion to the hierarchical church protected believers in a sinful environment, these Catholics warned, and the church alone could provide assurance of salvation. Catholic college presidents lectured their students on the "all important virtue" of obedience.[41] The leader of the American Redemptorists, scarred by battles with Belgian liberals, explained, "It betrays weakness to confine ourselves to the defensive. We are children of the Church and of the truth; our adversaries are heretics or unbelievers; it is, then, our duty to take the offensive and to expose to the public the erroneous doctrines of Protestantism and impiety."[42]

Proponents of this new Catholic style also cultivated a fascination with the miraculous. Alleged apparitions of Mary and various saints dot the Catholic literature of the period, as do reports of miraculous healings. Accounts of Lourdes, the most important Catholic apparition site of the nineteenth century, appeared in Catholic papers in New Orleans and New

York as early as October 1858, less than two months after news of the apparition circulated widely in France, and Bernadette's vision at Lourdes remained a source of interest throughout the late nineteenth century.[43] Father Wiget became especially devoted to Mary, and later in his career he led massive processions to a Marian shrine in Rock Springs, Maryland.[44]

The particular form of Catholic identification with God is also crucial. One component of the Catholic revival was the emphasis on a more loving, forgiving God, and a much appreciated clerical sympathy in the confessional.[45] Even so, the Catholic Jesus of the mid-nineteenth century was a suffering Jesus, the Jesus of the Passion more than Jesus the teacher or the risen Lord. The usefulness of suffering, the conviction that it served as part of human redemption, sustained a range of devotions associated with the Catholic revival; it was one reason for the devotions' enormous popularity in Ireland and Germany immediately after the famine and economic distress of the 1840s.[46]

The extant body of Catholic sermons is evocative on this point. One German Redemptorist told his New York City parishioners in 1854, "[M]editate upon your suffering Jesus. . . . Let us place ourselves, now, my very dear brethren, by the side of him who is suffering for us in the Garden of Olives. Let us contemplate him in his agony and covered with blood, and ask ourselves, who is this sufferer?"[47] A Boston Jesuit and colleague of Father Wiget informed his audience, "God can give us no greater proof of His love than by sending afflictions—I am aware that this proposition may seem false or exaggerated but I trust to be able to convince you of its truth." A New York Paulist entitled one sermon "Joy Born of Affliction."[48]

Devotional texts published as part of the Catholic revival, and often read silently during the Latin Mass, urged meditation on the suffering endured by Jesus on his way to the cross. Recitation of the rosary, also a common practice during the Mass, included a long section on the sorrowful mysteries of Jesus. The custom of participating in the stations of the cross, meditating on Christ's suffering through fourteen carvings or paintings within Catholic churches, became more common during Lent and on Fridays during the 1840s and 1850s. Devotion to the Sacred Heart, using a picture of a heart with a crown of thorns and a bleeding wound, spread from France throughout the Catholic world, publicized by

Jesuits convinced of the devotion's importance in a world dominated by "cold egoism and materialism."[49]

The contrast between these emphases in the Catholic revival and developments in Protestant theology was dramatic. In the North, liberal Protestant theologians such as William Ellery Channing and Horace Bushnell rejected a Calvinist view of human suffering as an inevitable and necessary sacrifice to a sovereign God. Instead, Protestants ranging from evangelicals like George Cheever, Gilbert Haven, and Joseph Thompson to liberals such as Theodore Parker increasingly understood suffering as a marker of human failing, a cruelty to be remedied by social reform.[50] Cheever lamented that Italian Catholic peasants "seemed to have the idea that their sufferings in this life, if rightly endured, would be considered as a sort of penance, in consideration of which they would gain eternal life in the world which is to come."[51]

Catholic devotional practices seemed a distraction from real Christian work or, as one *North American Review* writer speculated, a hypocritical attempt by church leaders "to obtain [power] through fear of mental or spiritual suffering in this world to come." Theodore Parker bemoaned "ignorant and squalid people, agape for miracles, ridden by their rulers and worse ridden by their priests, met to adore some relic of a saint."[52]

Grimly realistic Catholic crucifixes and paintings of suffering saints seemed especially offensive. One visitor to an American convent regretted the "endless pantomimes of pain" decorating the walls, and Charles Eliot Norton noted, "A Protestant is often shocked by representations of the crucified Saviour, carved or painted of the size of life, and in a style which betrays the utmost brutality of conception and the deadness of all true reverence."[53]

Some Catholics, too, mistrusted aspects of the ultramontane style. The division between liberal and ultramontane Catholics was never as clear in the United States as in France and Germany, in part because most American Catholic institutions were founded as the ultramontane style crystallized, and in part because the missionary bishops, priests, and nuns eager to work in the United States tended to have strong ultramontane sympathies.[54] But European Catholic immigrants brought conflicts among Catholics to the United States, especially in areas where strong national sympathies clashed with a more Roman vision. In Buffalo's St. Louis parish, Alsatian parishioners cast a skeptical eye not only upon the local bishop and new Roman devotions but also on Father Francis Weninger, the Jesuit asked to broker a settlement between lay trustees and the bishop.[55] Italian exiles in New York published a newspaper critical of Pius IX and Catholic leaders.[56]

The sharpest conflicts occurred in French Catholic Louisiana, where Creoles resisted the reforming efforts of Bishop Antoine Blanc, the product of a Lyon Catholic seminary that would become a center of the French Catholic revival, and a wave of Jesuits sent to Louisiana from the Lyon province of the order.[57] Blanc found his staunchest allies among the city's Irish immigrants, not among his French compatriots. One Creole editor accused Bishop Blanc and the editor of the *Propagateur Catholique*, Father Napoleon Perché, of taking the side of "the Ultra-Montanists, against the Gallican Church." The editor explained, "The Irish Catholics are, almost to a man, papists. The French Catholics are generally anti-Papal. Hence, the French Creoles of this city are true Americans; the Papal Irish are not; and cannot be, until they abjure, as the French have abjured, the tyranny of the Jesuit and other orders of Papal Priests."[58] Some Louisiana Creoles even joined the southern wing of the Know-Nothing, or American, Party because they endorsed the party's attacks on *foreign* Catholics. "If the Louisiana Catholics are not Roman Catholics," observed one American party supporter on the floor of the House of Representatives, "they do not come within the objection raised by the American party."[59]

To Bishop Blanc and his associates, the Creoles seemed dangerously lax in their religious practices, and they distinguished between "latitudinarian" Catholicism in Louisiana and "strict" Catholicism elsewhere. One 1856 pastoral letter written by Blanc criticized "[self]-styled Catholics" who "quarrel with such doctrines as do not exactly suit their taste and prejudices," and the Jesuit Francis Weninger complained of the "stupendous indifference" of the Creoles.[60] Blanc and other conservative Catholics led a successful attack on the reading of the King James Bible in the public schools in the early 1850s, and made an additional (unsuccessful) plea for government funding of parochial schools. But as Blanc confessed to New York's Bishop Hughes, he battled "more with Catholic infidels than with Protestant."[61] Or as one New Orleans Catholic explained privately, "This city, tho' Catholic in name is in reality not so. . . . The Catholics themselves are what may be termed liberals, and a vast number of them are Catholics in sentiment, tho' not, I am sorry to say, in practice."[62]

Similar tensions are evident in Father Wiget's Boston. An 1855 census revealed that 29 percent of the city's residents were Irish natives, and an Irish American majority loomed on the demographic horizon.[63] "Soon," Theodore Parker complained a few months after the Eliot School Rebellion, "Boston will be a Catholic city . . . and we know what use a few demagogues can make of the Catholic voters."[64] The North End neighborhood, home to St. Mary's parish and the Reverend Fuller's church, boasted the city's densest concentration of Catholics, packed into tenements near the wharves. In one letter to his Jesuit provincial, Wiget boasted that "there are almost exclusively only Catholics living in the N[orth] and W[est] end."[65]

The steadily growing Catholic population almost certainly fueled Fuller's dismay. Shortly after his sermons attacking Wiget and Catholics' behavior during the Eliot School Rebellion, Fuller resigned his pastorate. As one newspaper account put it, "The time is near at hand when the Protestant churches at the North [End] must seek some other spot, if they would perpetuate their existence."[66]

Wiget, on the other hand, consolidated a small empire. A central component of the Catholic revival was the formation of new Catholic institutions designed to protect Catholics from hostile influences in the host society. After his arrival at St. Mary's in 1856, Father Wiget formed a youth group, or sodality, for boys, and by 1858 the sodality counted over eight hundred members, including Thomas Whall. Wiget's description of the sodality as the most impressive organization in "Catholic Boston" is self-interested, and his reports to his superiors alternate between false modesty about his accomplishments and glee that he had thwarted the efforts of Protestant missionaries. Still, the meetings and catechism sessions he organized did generate intense enthusiasm, and he saw the sodality as a way to "increase the Roman influence on our young men here."[67]

In 1858 a young sodalist, John Kelly, died. Wiget quickly organized sodalists to carry the body from the Kelly household to the church for a wake. He then arranged for four hundred sodalists, all wearing holy medals, to carry Kelly's body from Boston's North End to Mt. Auburn Cemetery in Cambridge, causing considerable comment as they prayed the rosary and sang hymns during their journey.[68]

Wiget's decision to assume control of John Kelly's funeral reflected a widespread desire of Catholic reformers in Ireland and the United States to pull what they termed "Paddy funerals" out of the home and into the more decorous confines of the church. As Wiget put it, he "hoped to see the mode in which Wakes are too often carried on, remedied by the influence of the Sodality."[69]

Equally important, the formation of the sodality itself, the wearing of medals, the carrying of rosaries, and the forced march to Cambridge exemplified the more visibly pious style favored by advocates of the Catholic revival. One year before the Eliot School Rebellion, Wiget insisted, to the dismay of the same schoolteachers at the Eliot School who would punish Thomas Whall, that all Catholic schoolchildren be excused to attend Mass on Ash Wednesday.[70] Within a decade priests at St. Mary's parish would be distributing Lourdes water to ill parishioners—an important international marker of the Catholic revival.[71] Devotion to the Sacred Heart, another marker of the revival, would flourish at St. Mary's and parishioners would pack the church upon the formal dedication of the parish to the Sacred Heart in 1873.[72]

Church architecture told a parallel story. The Jesuits at St. Mary's inherited a modest structure trapped on a cramped Boston side street, but when they assembled funds to construct a replacement building in 1877, they completed "one of the most purely Roman structures in the city," a self-conscious echo of the sixteenth-century Baroque masterpiece that served as a symbolic headquarters for the Jesuits, Il Gesù. (When the American novelist William Dean Howells visited Il Gesù in Rome, he decided that the "soul shrinks dismayed.") At the consecration of another Boston church designed by the Jesuits, one priest boasted of "New England boys and girls . . . merrily weaving the beautiful garlands to decorate our Lady's beautiful shrine which lies almost under the shadow of Bunker Hill monument." Wiget himself spent the late 1860s in a futile effort to build a small-scale version of the cathedral of Cologne in Washington, D.C.[73]

Wiget's activities in Boston did not endear him to his pastor, the seventy-seven-year-old John McElroy, an American native and one of the last American Jesuits not exposed to the reshaping of the Jesuits in the context of the European Catholic revival. McElroy's lengthy career made him a legendary figure, but his training, in a religious order still recovering from its papal suppression between 1773 and 1814, was haphazard. (McElroy completed his preparations for the priesthood in twenty-two months, instead of the standard twelve years, and he remained one of the few Jesuits incapable of corresponding in Latin, which served as an organizational lingua franca.)[74] In a single letter to their provincial, McElroy described Wiget as "indiscreet," "impulsive," and "impetuous"; he asked the provincial to prohibit Wiget from organizing any more funeral processions, since "it is not the custom here" and "a boy may die every week."[75] Wiget, in turn, complained that McElroy thought evening benediction and novenas "would do more harm than good." McElroy, Wiget moaned, "[h]ates anything like the shadow of a change"; the sodalists "have as little to do with Fr. McE. as possible."[76]

Along with Thomistic philosophy, a theological worldview that emphasized obedience and suffering, and new Catholic organizations, Catholics also developed an alternative history of human progress and freedom. The core liberal position—that Protestantism advanced human progress and freedom while Catholicism retarded it—had long been a staple of religious polemic. A young John Stuart Mill wrote of learning from his father that the Reformation had been the "great and decisive contest against priestly tyranny for liberty of thought."[77] In 1821 John Adams queried another former president, Thomas Jefferson, as to whether "a free Government [can] possibly exist with a Roman Catholic Religion."[78]

The decisive moment in modern history, American reformers argued, had been the independence exhibited by such religious and scientific figures as Martin Luther, John Calvin, and Galileo. "The solitary man," concluded Theodore Parker, "a Luther, a Paul, a Jesus—he outweighs millions of cowardly souls."[79]

More specifically, free access to the Bible and the checking of church authority had given the most important push to human progress since before the Middle Ages. As one contributor to the *North American Review* asked, "What progress did [the mind] make for the many centuries before Luther proclaimed freedom of thought and the God-given, inalienable right of private judgment?"[80] Leading American Jews also hailed Luther and the Reformation, ruefully comparing their own medieval heritage to "the Catholic world—complete intellectual stagnation degenerating into cabbalistical mysticism or the most futile and resultless polemics."[81]

Economic development, similarly, depended upon Catholicism's absence. Protestant travelers and scholars constantly emphasized booming industry in Belfast as opposed to lethargy in Dublin and the wealth of the United States as opposed to the poverty of Mexico. "Why is Spain so much more degraded than Holland," asked the Andover professor Edwards Amasa Park, "Portugal than Denmark, Ireland than Scotland?"[82]

Father Wiget's Switzerland played an important role in this discussion. American and British visitors habitually contrasted the prosperous appearance of the Protestant cantons with the more bedraggled Catholic Swiss counterparts or the Italian Catholic villages just across the border. When one minister crossed from Geneva into Italy, he immediately concluded, "The people who drink the stream of Romanism, and live on that side, are lean, poor, and ignorant." An 1851 American visitor to Switzerland noted in her diary, "We have seen only one or two priests, as this is altogether a Protestant community—which readily accounts for the general prosperity of the country."[83]

By that time the Boston minister Thomas King could note that it had almost become a cliché to describe Catholicism as "the ally of tyranny, the opponent of material prosperity, the foe of thrift, the enemy of the railroad, the caucus, and the school."[84] The most popular and important histories of the period traced a similar arc. John Lothrop Motley's *The Rise of the Dutch Republic* and William Prescott's histories of Spain and Mexico, despite the protests of leading American Catholics, assumed an inextricable connection between Catholicism, the Inquisition, and cultural decline.[85]

Theodore Parker offered a summary statement in 1854. "The Roman Catholic Church," he argued, "claims infallibility for itself, and denies spiritual freedom, liberty of mind or conscience, to its members. It is therefore the foe of all progress; it is deadly hostile to Democracy." He continued, "She is the natural ally of tyrants and the irreconcilable enemy of freedom. Individual Catholics in America as elsewhere, are inconsistent, and favor the progress of mankind. Alas! Such are exceptional; the Catholic Church has an iron logic, and consistently hates liberty in all its forms—free thought, free speech."[86]

How could Catholics respond to these charges? The challenge, as Bishop Hughes summarized it, was to refute the claim that "freedom would have been greatly enlarged, were it not for obstacles presented in the way of its progress by the Church."[87]

Catholics turned Protestant chronology on its head, developing a powerful counternarrative that resonated throughout the Catholic world in much the same way that Marx and Engels's economic analysis inspired socialists, or chronicles of progress attracted liberals. A crucial aid in this project was an 1842 volume entitled *Protestantism and Catholicity Compared in their Effects on the Civilization of Europe*. The author, Father Jaime Balmes, was a longtime battler against liberalism in his native Spain.[88]

Protestantism and Catholicity Compared quickly went through several editions in various European languages. The Catholic convert and polemicist Orestes Brownson termed it "*the* book for our times," Catholic newspapers recommended it to their readers, and even twentieth-century American bishops slipped references to the "celebrated" Balmes into their pastoral letters.[89] The introduction to the American edition explicitly noted the volume's importance for refuting Protestant claims that the Reformation "freed the intellect of man from a degrading bondage, [gave] a nobler impulse to enterprise and industry, and sow[ed] in every direction the seed of national and individual prosperity."[90]

The rhetorical strategy adopted by Balmes was simple. He cautiously accepted the definition of progress favored by Catholic opponents—higher levels of education, political liberty, the development of science—and claimed these achievements for Catholicism. Do not accept the false claim, he warned his readers, that "innovators of the sixteenth century proclaimed the freedom of thought." Instead, remember the founding of Oxford and Bologna in the Middle Ages, the freedom given to the European serfs, and the medieval origins of political liberty. By destroying religious unity, the Reformation hastened the development of absolutist regimes and the destruction of political liberty. Indeed, "the progress which has been made since Protestantism, has been made not by it, but in spite of it." The logical conclusion of the Protestant attack on religious authority lay in Robespierre and the violent final days of the French Revolution.[91]

American Catholics echoed these arguments. Bishop Martin Spalding claimed trial by jury, habeas corpus, and fair taxation for Catholics. "Protestantism has boasted much," he concluded, "but it has really done little for the cause of human freedom." Spalding also refuted the proposition, heard "over and over again," that "Protestant countries are much more free, more enlightened, more industrious, more enterprising, more prosperous, more moral, and more happy, than those which have remained faithful to the Catholic religion." The Catholic Swiss, Spalding explained, simply lived on less fertile mountain land than their Protestant compatriots.[92]

Beneath these polemics lay distinctive views of human freedom. When seventeenth- and eighteenth-century liberals in England and the United States extolled "liberty," they usually referred to political or public liberty, the independent freeholder determined to withstand the blandishments of parliament and crown.[93] These liberals worried about Catholicism because it seemed conducive to tyranny in the form of absolute monarchy, and might lead to the elimination of representative political institutions. In 1689 the New York City militia revolted against a colonial government unfaithful to the "true protestant Religion" and leading the colony into "Tyranny, popery and slavery."[94] The English radicals John Trenchard and Thomas Gordon, avidly read by American colonists, warned in 1720 against Catholic priests "who aim at tyranny" and "find their interest in the loss of publick liberty."[95]

By the middle of the nineteenth century this distinctly political understanding of freedom and liberty had become more capacious. Liberals on both sides of the Atlantic, notably England's John Stuart Mill, who published *On Liberty* in 1859, now understood freedom as an autonomous self, exempt from external constraint. The individual as negotiator of contracts, as voluntary (and equal) marriage partner, and as owner of himself and his labor must serve as the starting point for a progressive social order. In the United States, Ralph Waldo Emerson famously extolled "self-reliance" (and later complained of "Romish priests, who sympathize, of course, with despotism").[96]

Catholics understood freedom differently. If nineteenth-century liberals idealized human autonomy, Catholics habitually referred to communities. Drawing on Aristotle as mediated through Saint Thomas Aquinas, Catholics saw moral choice and personal development as inseparable from virtues nurtured in families and churches. Jaime Balmes argued, "Man is not alone in the world, nor is he born to live alone," and Bishop Hughes agreed, stating that "man is, by his nature, a being of society; [and] the evidences of this accompany him from the moment of his birth until he goes to the grave, indicating clearly that his position is in society."[97]

What bothered Catholics was freedom as freedom to choose, diversity of opinion for diversity's sake. This sort of freedom, without the virtue or character to make proper choices, was dangerous. One Catholic editor bluntly contrasted European liberals and Catholics: "They say that true liberty is a freedom from right as well as from wrong; we assert that it is freedom only from wrong."[98] A Maryland Jesuit entitled an 1852 Fourth of July sermon "On Liberty," conceding that "human liberty is a great gift," but regretting that "so many to their great injury abuse it."[99]

This understanding of freedom, Catholics hastened to add, did not preclude support for constitutional democracies.[100] Both American and European ultramontanes, including Jesuits at *Civiltà Cattolica* and Jaime Balmes, admired the American founders. Seen through Catholic eyes, the American Revolution was hardly a revolution at all, and the eighteenth-century language of virtue and ordered liberty favored by George Washington, Thomas Jefferson, and John Adams remained compelling. Father J. W. Cummings referred to the "so-called" American Revolution and found comparisons between American patriots and European liberals "the greatest insult to our noble and glorious country."[101]

Erroneous understandings of freedom—Bishop Spalding wrote of the "demoniacal shout of liberty"—threatened the foundations of society, as evidenced so clearly during the French revolutions of 1789 and 1848.[102] And such views might ultimately lead to the rejection of God, the church, the family, or other aspects of the natural law imprinted on every human heart. "The true liberty of human society," Pope Leo XIII announced, in an 1888 encyclical that summarized neo-Thomist thinking on the subject, "does not consist in every man doing what he pleases. . . ." Rather, genuine liberty "supposes the necessity of obedience to some supreme and eternal law."[103]

III

Catholics' uneasiness with a liberal emphasis on individual autonomy inevitably shaped discussion of the Eliot School Rebellion and related educational issues.[104] In predominantly Catholic countries, notably France and Italy and, later, almost every country in Latin America, Catholics and anticlerical liberals engaged in protracted struggles over the nature of public education. In the German regions of Prussia and the Rhineland, the presence of a large Catholic minority also ensured tension, and in the English-speaking Protestant North Atlantic the German and Irish Catholic diaspora of the 1840s thrust the religious problem onto center stage. In Glasgow and Toronto, as in Boston, Catholic immigration led to debates about the reading of prayers from the King James Bible.[105] As one American Catholic writer put it in 1850, the battle over religion and education is "the fierce contest in Ireland; the same in France; the same in Belgium; the same in Prussia and the petty States of Germany; the same in Bavaria, the same in Austria; the same in Piedmont. . . ."[106]

The basic positions rarely varied. Liberals urged either a more secular educational program or at least one that did not stress divisive catechetical material. Schools should train citizens, liberals argued, not indoctrinate worshipers. German liberals unsuccessfully promoted a system of secular education during the turmoil of 1848; French liberals in the early 1850s urged the elimination of religious training in state-supervised schools.[107]

The education issue became especially volatile in the United States. Even more than their European counterparts, American liberals relied upon schools to produce citizens worthy of a democratic republic.[108] Theodore Parker claimed that the common school system was "the most original thing which America has produced" and that without common schools "[p]ublic lectures would be as rare in Boston, as in Montreal, Halifax, or even New Orleans and Naples."[109]

That white southerners and Catholics did not support public schools, as Parker suggested in his disparaging reference to New Orleans and Naples, confirmed a shared backwardness. American abolitionists frequently informed northern audiences of the low value that white southerners placed on education, counting the few classrooms in Alabama and Mississippi. The most important American educational reformer, Boston's Horace Mann, emphasized the point, arguing that "it is as impossible for free, thorough, universal education to coexist with slavery as for two bodies to occupy the same space at the same time. Slavery would abolish education, if it should invade a free state; education would abolish slavery, if it *could* invade a slave state."[110]

Even more than white southerners, Catholics threatened the common school system. In its northern strongholds, the very town squares graced by the first common schools, Catholics pressed the knotty question of what prayers and devotional practices were acceptable in publicly funded institutions. This discussion had begun in the late 1830s, as Presbyterians, Lutherans, and orthodox Calvinists countered Horace Mann's common school with a plan for a variety of denominational systems run under church auspices but funded with tax revenues.

Most Protestants, however, eventually accepted the argument of Mann and other educational reformers that the schools could remain both

Christian and nonsectarian—that common formulas like the Ten Commandments or daily Bible readings preserved the crucial principle of private judgment.[111] Use your private judgment to choose a denominational home, students were told, but only after instruction in general Christian principles. One of Mann's contemporaries, Ohio's Calvin Stowe, emphasized that "religious principles" could be "abstracted" from denominational forms in much the same way that the study of human anatomy applied to humans from all cultures.[112]

Mann himself contrasted Protestant and Catholic approaches to education. "When Protestantism arose," he wrote, "freedom of opinion for each, and tolerance for all, were the elements that gave it vitality and strength. The avowed doctrine of Catholicism was, that men could not think for themselves. . . ." Jesuit colleges, in particular, substituted the "painted glass of a creed" for "quickening the mental vision."[113] Theodore Parker was more blunt. "The Catholic Church opposes everything which favors democracy and the natural rights of man," he concluded. "It hates our free churches, free press, and above all, our free schools."[114]

In response Catholics challenged the common schools on several fronts. Requiring use of the King James Bible, they claimed, established a state religion and violated the ideal of tolerance that Protestants claimed to hold so dear. Textbooks in nominally secular subjects such as history, Catholics correctly pointed out, displayed a strong Protestant bias, combining rhapsodic treatments of Martin Luther and John Calvin with jabs at "popery."[115]

At the same time, Catholics disagreed with Horace Mann's premise that teaching a common morality implied no particular religious creed. Catholics viewed the Mass, private prayer, and devotional exercises as foundational for basic morality, not superfluous additions. "Educational work is an essentially moral work," explained Father Napoleon Perché, and since morality depended upon religion "the work of education is a principally religious work."[116] An 1850 synod of Missouri priests resolved, "Education necessarily implies the cultivation of the will as well as of the mind, and the acquisition of moral and religious habits; without which the most brilliant talents and the most varied intellectual acquirements become only instruments of evil."[117]

The initial Catholic challenge to the common schools occurred in the early 1840s when Bishop John Hughes of New York briefly organized a separate political party to press for financial assistance for parochial schools. In Philadelphia, in 1844, a struggle over whether to recite the Protestant version of the Ten Commandments in the common schools exploded into a series of bloody riots.[118]

The tempo quickened in the early 1850s. The bishops at their 1840 meeting encouraged parents to send their children to Catholic schools; in 1852 one episcopal committee report complained about the "radical disease of the Public School System."[119] By that point legislators in almost every state with a significant Catholic population—including Massachusetts, Kentucky, Pennsylvania, Ohio, Maryland, Michigan, New York—were embroiled in fights over whether to aid Catholic schools or eliminate the King James Bible and Protestant hymns from the common schools. Protestants appalled by what they saw as a "a revival of the worst forms of Popery" viewed these challenges as coordinated, but a more persuasive explanation is simply a growing sense in Catholic circles that control of education would become, as one Montreal Catholic editor put it, "*the* question of the XIX century."[120]

These educational battles must be understood as a consequence of the broader Catholic revival. Catholic control of Catholic institutions—as opposed to Catholic participation in state institutions—became a marker of the revival in Europe and North America during the 1840s and 1850s, where fierce battles raged over the organization of primary schools, as well as over seminary and university appointments. This struggle occurred within Catholicism, too, as the conciliatory style of such bishops as Toronto's Michael Power and Dublin's Daniel Murray, both of whom accepted nonsectarian education, fell into disfavor. By contrast, a wave of more ultramontanist bishops, including Toronto's Armand de Charbonnel, Dublin's Paul Cullen, and Philadelphia's Francis Kenrick, demanded public support for Catholic institutions.

In Toronto, Edgerton Ryerson, an admirer of Horace Mann and the founder of Canadian public education, became frustrated by Catholic attempts in the 1850s to win financial support for parochial schools. "In the days of the venerable Bishop McDonell and the excellent Bishop Power, there was no such clamor against our Common Schools," he complained, "no such efforts to separate Roman Catholics and their children from Protestants. . . ." He continued, "It is to the Charbonnels and Bruyeres—the infusion of a new foreign element into our country since the days of Bishops McDonnell and Power—that our Roman Catholic fellow citizens owe the cloudy, civil and social prospects that are darkening the future of themselves and their children."[121]

Exactly the same complaints were registered in Boston. As early as 1854 a writer for a national magazine, the *Independent*, reported that a Boston Jesuit, one of Wiget's fellow Swiss exiles working at Holy Trinity parish, had begun the construction of a parochial school. "As would be expected of a Jesuit," the writer warned, "he aims to keep the children and youth of his congregation away from the public schools and under his exclusive influence."[122] When some Catholics voiced criticism of the Boston public schools, one frustrated Boston resident responded, "[O]ur city is educating children of Catholic parentage without practical difficulty, except as occasionally some foreign priest unacquainted with our institutions, attempts to create a prejudice against them."[123]

From the moment he arrived in Boston in 1856, Father Wiget urged the opening of a large Catholic school at St. Mary's parish, a view dismissed by his pastor, Father McElroy, who had already opened a tiny school for Catholic girls. "God knows," Wiget complained, "what kinds of difficulties Fr. McElroy will throw in my way." McElroy's "*too great prudence*" frustrated Wiget. "Happily," McElroy was in New York when Wiget urged the children of the Eliot School not to say the Protestant version of the Ten Commandments.[124]

Bishop John Fitzpatrick of Boston, himself a graduate of the city's famed (public) Latin school and someone who circulated among the city's elite, built few Catholic schools during his tenure. In 1858 an anonymous Boston priest complained to a Roman cardinal that Fitzpatrick had evinced no interest in "truly Catholic schools," and one bishop confessed to a colleague two months after the Eliot School Rebellion that some thought Fitzpatrick "not sound on the school question."[125]

Father McElroy and Bishop Fitzpatrick responded to the Eliot School crisis only after some prodding, and when Fitzpatrick finally sent an eloquent letter to the Boston school committee, he did not demand public funding of parochial schools, merely an end to reading from the King James Bible in public schools. (One sympathetic Protestant commentator wondered whether even this statement resulted from a "Jesuitical edict from across the water . . . forcing the Romish Bishop among us to pronounce himself in a way he might personally have wished to avoid or postpone.")[126] A frustrated Wiget agreed, complaining to his Jesuit provincial that McElroy and Fitzpatrick, the two most prominent figures in Boston Catholicism, were "sores on the Cath. Public."[127] Wiget also criticized the public comments of another prominent Boston priest, the American native Father George Haskins, who urged Catholic schoolchildren to return to the Eliot School. "Is it right to act as Fr. Haskins preaches?" Wiget asked, "Can the Eliot school boys join in worship with the protestant school boys, recite the protest. Commandments, all explicitly condemned as wrong[?]"[128]

In an effort to prevent another crisis, the Boston school committee arranged in 1860 to have the teacher, not the students, read from Scripture and recite the Ten Commandments at the beginning of each school day.[129] But Wiget's goal was a Catholic school, not a less hostile common school. (Several years later Wiget petitioned Congress to obtain a "pro rata of the school taxes" for Catholics and other religious minorities.)[130] At the time Wiget's sudden popularity allowed him to realize his plans in St. Mary's parish, even if his pastor and his bishop remained unenthusiastic. Within a few weeks of Thomas Whall's beating, he had transformed a small "Latin" school for prospective seminarians into a parochial grade school for boys. "Father Wiget," as one of his supporters put it, "saw that the whole system of education in Boston was the most complete and most ingenious system that could be devised for perverting Catholic youth."[131] A year after the Eliot School Rebellion, St. Mary's Institute enrolled 1,150 young boys, and Wiget enjoyed marching them two by two from the school to the church on religious holidays, in full view of startled non-Catholic spectators.[132]

Chapter Two

CATHOLICISM, SLAVERY, AND THE CAUSE OF LIBERTY

I

As Catholics across the country offered tributes to Father Wiget and Thomas Whall, the most prominent American Catholic intellectual held back. Orestes Brownson had bulled his way from rural Vermont into the center of Boston reform circles in the 1830s through equal measures of audacity and brilliance, publishing his own journal when no one else would print each of the roughly 150,000 words he penned each year. A charter member of the Transcendentalist club, Brownson knew (and feuded with) New England's leading intellectual lights, including William Ellery Channing, Henry David Thoreau, Ralph Waldo Emerson, and Theodore Parker. Stopping only for games of chess with his sons, he read and wrote late into each evening, and delighted in debating the merits of federalism or the plausibility of miracles for hours on end. "Brownson never will stop & listen," complained Emerson in his journal, "neither in conversation, but what is more, not in solitude."[1]

Brownson's religious views were idiosyncratic. He dabbled in (and, inevitably, wrote about) Methodism, Presbyterianism, free thought, Unitarianism, and Universalism. (Theodore Parker once informed a correspondent that he did not know Brownson's current religious views, since he had "not heard from him for eight days.")[2]

In 1844 he converted to Catholicism, and *Brownson's Quarterly Review*, always a one-man show, became a vehicle for discussion of his

Orestes Brownson, the most influential American Catholic intellectual of the nineteenth century, n.d.

new religious loyalties. Brownson's prominence ensured that he would quickly become the one American Catholic writer widely read outside Catholic circles. But many onetime admirers drifted away, put off by Brownson's conversion and his increasingly vehement distaste for individualism and liberal reform. The current age, Brownson argued in 1849, "sympathizes with every rebel," and even some Catholics have "yielded too much to the radical spirit of the age, and too often made common cause with the so-called liberals, whose principles are subversive of all order."[3] When Louis Kossuth visited the United States, Brownson lectured against the idea that Kossuth represented the party of liberty. "No *Catholic*," Brownson concluded, "is or can be a Red Republican or Socialist."[4]

Beginning in the mid-1850s Brownson's views changed. An unforeseen consequence of the emergence of a politically conservative Catholic ultramontanism in the 1840s was the simultaneous development of a liberal Catholic movement, one that Brownson eventually chose to champion. The term "movement" is perhaps misleading, since Charles Montalembert, Augustin Cochin, Henri-Dominique Lacordaire, and Bishop Félix Dupanloup in France, Lord Acton, Richard Simpson, and John Henry Newman in England, Brownson in the United States, and Ignaz von Döllinger in Germany signed no joint manifestos. But these Catholics applauded one another's writing in France's *Le Correspondant*, Britain's *The Rambler*, and *Brownson's Quarterly Review* in the United States, and members of the group sustained an episodic correspondence.[5] Broadly, they shared a devotion to political liberty, and an uneasiness with the direction taken by Vatican authorities in the years after 1848. Lord Acton reported to Döllinger in 1862 that Brownson's decision to "fight until death against [Vatican] obscurantism" echoed the view of liberal Catholics in England and a friend of Montalembert's told Brownson that "Catholics of the same turn of mind should support each other in all countries."[6]

The first hints of change in Brownson's position became evident in an 1854 essay on the anti-Catholic Know-Nothing movement. Brownson dutifully criticized religious bigotry, but he also complained that Irish Catholics failed to recognize the importance of assimilation to American mores. Writing as "an American citizen whose ancestors were among the first settlers of the country," Brownson urged Irish Catholic coreligionists to become "nationalized as well as naturalized, and merge themselves in the great American people."[7] "Our great difficulty in getting our religion fairly presented to the American mind," he informed one correspondent, "is the real dislike of the American people and character felt by a large portion of our bishops & clergy. . . ."[8]

Brownson correspondingly took aim at the parochial school as an institution that delayed the assimilation of Catholic immigrants. Several of his own children attended parochial schools and Catholic colleges, but Brownson stressed that the New England common schools, for all their faults, did not "corrupt the faith of our children." After all, he slyly noted, "[t]he children of Italy had received none but a Catholic education, and yet we found the Peninsula, in 1848, overrun with Italians ready to war to the death on the Pope and Catholicity."[9] Five years later, at the height of the turmoil associated with the Eliot School Rebellion, Brownson wondered whether defenders of Catholic schools wanted "to keep Catholics a foreign colony in United States."[10]

After Brownson's initial comments on nativism and the school question, a wave of attacks appeared in the Catholic press.[11] Brownson stood his ground. As he informed one critic, Bishop Michael O'Connor of Pittsburgh, "Here in Boston I know our children go to the public schools with the permission of the bishop, and with no harm to their faith or piety, as I am assured by those who are best able to judge."[12]

Nonetheless, these disputes made Boston uncomfortable. Or as Brownson put it, "This diocese is becoming more and more Irish."[13] In 1855 Brownson moved to Elizabethtown, New Jersey, across the Hudson River from New York City.

Among New York's attractions was a group of like-minded priests that included Father Isaac Hecker and Father Jeremiah Cummings, "the friends," Brownson explained, "on whom I have chiefly to rely."[14] Neither man possessed Brownson's intellectual range, but both favored the development of a church not beholden to European models. Cummings thought the focus on parochial schools misguided, and angered Archbishop Hughes by closing a parish school and marching the children of his parish to the local public school. He also urged bishops to recruit American-born candidates for Catholic seminaries, and not rely on "cheap priest factories" eager to dump second-rate European clerics on American shores.[15] Hecker, another convert and eventually the founder of the Paulist order, would dedicate his career to the idea that the United States might prove a singularly propitious site for Catholic aspirations.[16]

Equally important, Brownson developed contacts with prominent European liberal Catholics. When nineteen-year-old John (and future Lord) Acton visited the United States, Brownson engaged him in several days' worth of intense conversation. (Acton described Brownson as learned but "rough, uncouth, much given to grimacing when talking.")[17] Soon thereafter Brownson sent his son Henry to study in Munich with Döllinger, Acton's mentor. And Acton later urged Brownson to study the relationship between Catholicism and democratic governments even as Brownson referred to the "great questions in which we both took so deep an interest."[18]

During this same period Brownson pondered an invitation from John Henry Newman to lecture at the newly founded Catholic University in Dublin. (Newman made an identical offer to Döllinger.)[19] In 1856 *Brownson's Quarterly Review* carried a favorable notice of the new English liberal Catholic periodical *The Rambler*, explaining, "We must no longer be encumbered with the obsolete forms of the Middle Ages."[20]

Driving this identification with European liberal Catholicism was Brownson's frustration at being pinned between an "anti-Catholic sentiment . . . shared to a greater or less extent by the majority of our countrymen" and coreligionists creating the impression that a Catholic must make "himself a foreigner in the land of his birth."[21] Here Brownson's contact with the leading French liberal Catholic, the aristocratic Charles de Montalembert, became especially important. Brownson and Montalembert began a correspondence in the early 1850s that took on heightened intensity at the end of the decade.[22] As early as 1854 Montalembert complained to Brownson about Louis Veuillot, editor of France's *L'Univers*, the country's most influential ultramontane paper. Montalembert detested Veuillot's enthusiasm for the French ruler Louis Napoleon, and his "daily denunciations of every [kind?] of rational freedom, not only in France but throughout Europe and America."[23]

In 1855 Montalembert lauded *Brownson's Quarterly Review* and informed Brownson that a group of liberal Catholics had taken control of *Le Correspondant* to offer an alternative to "that vortex of fanaticism and servility, the *Univers*." Commentary on *Brownson's Review*, Montalembert promised, would frequently appear in *Le Correspondant*.[24] Brownson replied to Montalembert, "[Y]our sympathy and approval are very dear to me," and published a glowing review of the first issues of *Le Correspondant*.[25]

Brownson also began to regret his harsh tone during the 1848 revolutions. Perhaps his animosity toward reform, Brownson now conceded, had gone "too far."[26] The current situation, he concluded, was quite different. Montalembert agreed with Brownson that Catholics must "sift and extract, as you do, what is true and just out of Liberalism and Socialism instead of consigning the invincible spirit of modern humanity to a blind and sweeping proscription."[27] In a later meditation Brownson noted, "[I]n 1848 we had to do our best to prevent hot-headed men from treating democracy as a Catholic dogma; now we have to labor even further to prevent them from committing us as Catholics to the cause of despotism."[28]

To the dismay of many readers, Brownson went even further, declaring in 1859 that he sympathized with advocates of Italian unity. Even as Catholics across the United States gathered to express sympathy for the pope and to warn of the "anti-Christian principles" of Italian liberals, Brownson feared that Vatican control of the Papal States would doom the pope's subjects to "hopeless slavery." For good measure Brownson echoed liberal Catholics in France and Germany by registering his suspicion of ultramontane devotions such as that of the scapular, a piece of cloth worn beneath one's shirt, and the miraculous medal in honor of the Immaculate Conception, both of which, in Brownson's view, shifted attention away from God.[29]

Complaints to Vatican officials led to inquiries about Brownson's orthodoxy. (Rumors even circulated, in a deft Catholic touch, that Brownson "*publicly*" chose to disregard the ban on eating meat on Fridays, "in hotels, at banquets, etc.")[30] Bishop James Wood of Philadelphia declared *Brownson's Quarterly Review* no longer a "Catholic Review." Archbishop Hughes compared Brownson's positions to the condemned views of the early nineteenth-century French Catholic Félicité Lamennais, but he also cautioned Roman authorities against public censure since notoriety would "give [Brownson] the opportunity to cause more trouble."[31]

Crucially, Brownson's changing religious stance moved in tandem with his views on political and moral questions. Early in his career Brownson had declared his distaste for slavery, but he attacked abolitionists with greater vigor. In 1845 he described abolitionism as destructive "of the state, of government, of religious institutions, of all social organizations, and of all law but the law of every man unto himself."[32]

Into the 1850s Brownson defended the fugitive slave law requiring northerners to return escaped slaves to their owners—"That law is constitutional, and the Constitution authorizes nothing repugnant to the Divine law"—and he allowed a Boston priest writing for *Brownson's*

Quarterly Review to contrast favorably the plight of American slaves with that of Hungarian peasants.[33]

But as with more strictly religious questions, Brownson's tone shifted. In the late 1850s he continued to caution against immediate emancipation, but he insisted that southern aggressiveness on the slavery question had become the real problem. "[S]lavery," he concluded, "is regarded by the civilized world as an odious institution."[34] The majority opinion in the 1857 *Dred Scott* decision, theoretically permitting slavery in the northern states, appalled him.[35]

Many Catholic readers found Brownson's new sympathy for antislavery positions inexplicable. A Baltimore Catholic journal expressed surprise that "so eminent a controversialist as Dr. Brownson" would align himself with abolitionists who "pronounce the opinion of the Court in *Dred Scott* to be flat 'Popery.'"[36] Brownson explained to Montalembert, "I have nothing encouraging to write you of my own country. I am under a cloud now because I refuse to defend slavery as a natural right, and have received also my 'warning' from a portion of the Catholic public." Brownson signed the letter, "Yours in the cause of liberty."[37]

II

How should Catholics think about slavery? Uneasiness about liberal individualism proved as powerful in shaping Catholic views on slavery as in affecting the conflict over education. Like almost all Christians, Catholics in the early nineteenth century faced few restrictions on their ability to own slaves. Masters must permit slave marriages, Catholic theologians agreed, and educate their slaves in the rudiments of the faith, but slavery itself, as confirmed by Aristotle and Saint Paul, did not violate either the natural law or church teaching. In a theological tradition that distinguished itself from Protestantism by claims of constancy, any shift in the Catholic position on slavery faced formidable obstacles.[38]

As with educational issues, the disjunction between Catholics and liberals on the slavery question did not emerge in full force until the 1840s. The first American bishop, John Carroll of Baltimore, disliked abolitionist agitation and noted that "many eminent & holy missioners in S. America & Asia" had worked with slave populations without urging their emancipation. Still, Carroll claimed to have freed his own slaves (although the evidence is ambiguous) and regretted the "evils" he saw.[39]

A handful of European Catholic theologians criticized slavery in the early nineteenth century, and the decision by the Maryland province of the Jesuits to sell its slaves in 1838 angered some Jesuits who thought it immoral to sell slaves to Protestant masters, abandoning the responsibility to ensure a Catholic education for slaves.[40] In some ways, too, Catholics seemed more accepting of African Americans than white Protestants did. Both white and African American Protestants chided their coreligionists by noting that Roman Catholic churches in the South rarely segregated worshipers: the church's "consolations are open alike to black and white, bond and free."[41]

In the early nineteenth century, many Latin American countries abolished slavery with minimal controversy. In 1839 Pope Gregory XVI published an apostolic letter banning Catholic participation in the slave trade, although he did not prohibit Catholics from owning slaves. That same year Charles Montalembert expressed his horror of American slavery, and along with Félix Dupanloup, the liberal bishop of Orléans, Montalembert would lead the Catholic component of the successful campaign to abolish slavery in French colonial possessions in the late 1840s.[42] Most important, Ireland's Daniel O'Connell attacked Irish Americans tolerant of American slavery in 1843.[43]

All this made an alliance between Catholics and antislavery activists seem possible. In Boston, Wendell Phillips denounced "Prejudice against Catholics among abolitionists" and, after reading Gregory XVI's letter, the "first papal bull which was ever read in Faneuil Hall," led a crowd of abolitionists in three cheers for the pope. In distant Brazil a Protestant missionary mistakenly interpreted the papal letter as ordering Brazilian Catholics "to free the slaves which they severally possess, or cease to call themselves Roman Catholics."[44]

One abolitionist recalled that Catholic opinion on the slavery question seemed open into the early 1850s:

> It was still doubtful which side of the slavery question the Roman church would take. O'Connell was in the zenith of his power and popularity, was decidedly anti-slavery, and members of Catholic churches chose sides according to personal feeling, as did those of other churches. It was not until 1852, that abolitionists began to feel the alliance between Romanism and slavery; but from that time, to

be a member of the Roman church was to be a friend of "Southern interests."[45]

In fact, the trend of American Catholic opinion was already clear. The editor of the *New York Freeman's Journal* first expressed disbelief that O'Connell could have uttered such words, and then chastised abolitionists, a "mischievous set of fanatics," for threatening to overturn the Constitution.[46] Irish Catholics across the country wrote O'Connell, urging him to reconsider his views, and in Savannah, Georgia, Irish Catholics published a statement lamenting "that he [O'Connell] has learned his lessons on Southern institutions from Northern Abolitionists, the dire enemies of real liberties, and the notorious enemies of Ireland's religion."[47]

Recent commentary on the O'Connell episode has highlighted Irish Americans' recalcitrance on the slavery issue, emphasizing the desire of working-class immigrants to deflect competition from African American workers, and to capture the material and psychological benefits of identifying themselves as white. The Catholic Church, in this view, did little more than "reflect the racial attitudes of its members."[48]

These criticisms focus on Irish American racism, and some Catholic leaders, such as New York's Archbishop Hughes, did feel that Africans were "as dark in their spirit as in their complexion." And Catholic newspapers such as the *New York Freeman's Journal* casually displayed the hostility to African Americans endemic to the period, occasionally using the term "nigger."[49]

Still, the argument that Irish Catholics opposed immediate emancipation solely out of psychological and economic self-interest neglects uneasiness about abolition found among German and French Catholics, as well as opposition to abolition among affluent Catholics not vulnerable to competition from African American labor. Studies of membership lists for American abolitionist organizations in the 1830s find few Catholics, and not one prominent American Catholic urged immediate abolition before the Civil War.[50] A small number of French Catholic missionaries called for immediate slave emancipation, but abolitionists in France and the French Caribbean in the 1840s, the Dutch colony of Curaçao in the 1850s, Cuba in the 1860s, and Brazil in the 1880s bemoaned the reluctance of Catholics to join their cause.[51] Of course, most Americans rejected the idea of immediate slave emancipation up until the Civil War, although most white northerners eventually endorsed Abraham Lincoln's pledge to block any expansion of slavery. But the Methodist, Presbyterian, Episcopalian, and Baptist churches had important antislavery wings, while the Catholic did not.

Catholic opposition to abolition cannot be reduced to the particular American racial dynamic. Many Catholic intellectuals around the world accepted slavery as a legitimate, if tragic, institution. This acceptance rested upon the pervasive fear of liberal individualism and social disorder that so shaped Catholic thought during the nineteenth century, along with the anti-Catholicism of many abolitionists.

Some of the first European advocates of slave emancipation in the late eighteenth century confirmed Catholics' suspicions that abolition was a misguided radicalism. France's Abbé Henri Grégoire, for example, became perhaps the most important leader of the nascent abolition movement in France in the 1790s, and he sent the American bishop John Carroll a copy of one of his attacks on slavery, a cause that filled his "religious soul." Ultramontane Catholics detested Grégoire, however, for his allegiance to the revolutionary French government that would persecute and slaughter less conciliatory Catholics in the 1790s.[52] Even Gregory XVI's 1839 decision to condemn only the slave trade, not slavery itself, stemmed in part from abolitionism's association with a European liberalism that papal advisers considered anti-Catholic and revolutionary.[53]

In the United States, Catholics' fears of disorder led to the calculation that societal stability outweighed any benefit to be gained from immediate emancipation. Abolitionists, one writer explained, should follow the example of Peter Claver, the seventeenth-century Jesuit who ministered to passengers on the slave ships in Cartagena, without "incit[ing] them to revolt."[54] Other Catholics invoked Jaime Balmes, who argued that Catholicism deserved credit for the elimination of slavery in medieval Europe. But opponents of slavery in the Middle Ages, American Catholics explained, had moved incrementally, avoiding the chaos inevitable when abolition occurred in a slave society.[55] In 1827 one Maryland Jesuit defined the belief that all men were free as a "compound of Presbyterianism, Baptistism, Quakerism and Methodism. It is a brother to the great Protestant principle that arose out of the pretended Reformation of England, viz. 'Every man has a right to read and interpret the Scriptures, and consequently, to form his religion on them according to his own notion.'"[56]

Bishop Francis Kenrick of Philadelphia, author of the first textbook in Catholic moral theology published in the United States, in 1843, shared this point of view. Kenrick's studies during his years in Rome alerted him to new currents in Catholic theology and philosophy, and his analysis of slavery seems similar to that of Italian neo-Thomists. The Jesuit Luigi Taparelli d'Azeglio, one of the most influential Italian neo-Thomists, noted that slavery in the abstract might be permissible, although he speculated that in lands "where legal slavery has not been done away with" slaveholders rarely adhered to Catholic guidelines. But he also stressed that "certain philanthropic declarations against slavery in its general meaning" had led to a "false idea of an inalienable right to freedom."[57]

Kenrick made similar distinctions when analyzing American slavery: ownership of a slave's labor was permissible, but not treatment of the slave as a thing. The slave trade was wrong, slaves must be allowed to partake of the sacraments and educated in the faith, and lynching was abhorrent. Nonetheless, Kenrick concluded, slavery existed as part of the social order in the American South, and those who attempted to overturn the social order often made conditions worse.[58] Kenrick's 1851 translation of Saint Paul's letter to Philemon contained a preface that disdained "vain theories of philanthropy to the prejudice of social order" and encouraged the return of fugitive slaves to their rightful owners.[59]

Ultramontane Catholics like Kenrick and Hughes, in contrast to liberal Catholics such as O'Connell, Dupanloup, and Montalembert, tended to see slavery as one among many hierarchical relationships. Hughes compared the master to the father, emphasizing that the "difference in the relations and obligations of those who own slaves, and those who are masters of hired servants, or the parents of children, is rather one of degree than of kind. . . ."[60] A writer for the *Boston Pilot* attacked the argument that "slavery is, in itself, intrinsically evil. This is nonsense, and it is so patent that we have never seen even a respectable attempt to prove it. In itself, slavery simply involves the right of one man to the proceeds of another. The *principle* of slavery is involved in apprenticeship, in imprisonment, in peonage, and in other forms of servitude."[61]

The contrast with Catholic views on the economy is striking. Liberal Catholics such as Daniel O'Connell condemned Catholic complicity in slavery but feared that trade unions and minimum-wage laws might restrict economic freedom.[62] Ultramontane Catholics, on the other hand, wary of immediate slave emancipation, offered fierce critiques of laissez-faire economics. As a labor radical prior to his conversion to Catholicism, Orestes Brownson published his most famous essay in 1840, an impassioned analysis of the effects of modern capitalism on workers that bears comparison in its eloquence to the writings of the young Karl Marx.[63] After comparing the situation of workers and slaves, he decided that "as to actual freedom one has just about as much as the other."[64]

Similarly, as early as 1844 Bishop Hughes lamented the "mockery of freedom" evident in an economic system that pitted the "starving laborer" against the "bloated capitalist."[65] (Later Hughes would contrast the plight of northern workers and southern slaves, concluding, "I should sooner remain in Southern bondage than avail myself of the opportunity of Northern freedom.")[66] Bishop Kenrick encouraged workers, at a time when this was a daring recommendation, to unite in associations and demand a minimum wage.[67]

The same Catholics also found it difficult to distinguish the suffering endured by slaves from other forms of human agony. Elizabeth Clark has demonstrated the importance of this conceptual leap, which in the United States typically occurred among Protestants who had abandoned Calvinist verities on the importance of Christ's atonement and the inevitability of human suffering. If human suffering is not foreordained or necessary, these Protestants asked, what about the suffering endured by innocent slaves?[68]

Catholic theology during the nineteenth-century revival did not follow this path. Father J. W. Cummings dismissed as nonsense the claim that "all men are born free."[69] Boston's Father Wiget, of Eliot School Rebellion fame, wrote to his provincial that the slaves in Charles County, Maryland, were "a happy lot of people compared to the poor Irish in Boston. These [Irish] are equal to slaves in ignorance & hundred other ways, have no master to take care of them in sickness & old age, no kind mistress to teach their children their prayers & to keep them in the Church."[70] Father John McMullen, educated in Rome and later bishop of Davenport, Iowa, readily conceded that the plight of a child born into slavery was tragic, and he approved of slavery's abolition. But even in the 1860s McMullen compared slave children to poor children, noting that all children suffered in some fashion. In particular he denied that "it is man's free power to select a state of life more or less exempt from the grievances attending human existence."[71]

Catholics' acceptance of slavery certainly included racism, but did not wholly depend upon it. In fact, the Vatican's insistence on the validity of interracial marriage and its opposition to rigid segregation laws made Roman authorities relatively tolerant of racial mixing and opposed to biological notions of racial inferiority. Augustin Martin, bishop of Natchitoches, Louisiana, published a pastoral in 1861 that declared African Americans fit for slavery because of the biblical curse of Ham, and not worthy of a "freedom which they are unable to defend and which will kill them." The pastoral made its way to Rome, where in a response approved by the Congregation of the Index, the Vatican informed Martin that several of his assertions were unacceptable. Especially troubling was Martin's supposition of "a natural difference between the Negroes whom he calls children of Canaan, and the Whites, [who] he says . . . are the privileged ones of the great human family." African American slaves, the Vatican insisted, remained an integral part of the human family saved by Jesus Christ, not simply "poor children."[72]

Similarly, Catholics in both the North and the South scoffed at claims of polygenesis, that African Americans represented not just another race but another species. One Mississippi bishop specifically urged local Jesuits to criticize the "abominable idea of the plurality of races," and Savannah's Bishop Augustin Verot, a staunch defender of slavery, later urged the world's bishops to denounce theories positing a spurious "white humanity" and "Negro humanity."[73]

A discussion of slavery in the *Propagateur Catholique* during the war's first year captures the complexity of Catholic thought on the issue. The New Orleans paper had already published Bishop Verot's rejection of immediate slave emancipation. Verot exhorted slave owners to conform their practices to Catholic doctrine, regretted sexual outrages perpetrated by masters, and lambasted "unreasonable, unchristian and immoral" owners willing to tear apart slave families on the auction block and enslave free persons of color. But Verot also ridiculed the "allegation of agrarians and anarchists that 'all men are born free and equal'" and defended slavery by means of scriptural and ecclesiastical sources.[74]

Another New Orleans newspaper criticized Verot for failing to mention that only Africans, not whites, should be enslaved. A writer for the *Propagateur Catholique* jumped to Verot's defense, and even as Confederate soldiers gave their lives in battle, insisted that if Holy Scripture condoned slavery it surely condoned the "subjection of white to white." Taking a position held only by the most daring white Protestants, the *Propagateur*

Catholique declared that the enslavement of whites is "approved in the Bible and supported by the patriarchs [church fathers]." The "legitimacy of slavery [is not] uniquely in the color of the skin," because such "fantastic theories" merely "flatter our pride." After all, "the Negroes are men" regardless of skin color and head size.[75]

In short, Catholics dismissed notions that Africans were biologically inferior to other humans, insisted that slaves be permitted to marry and receive an education, frequently expressed doubts about the morality of slavery as it existed in the nineteenth century, and almost never defended slavery as an unqualified good. But most Catholics accepted slavery in principle, with even twentieth-century theologians declaring slavery "not in itself intrinsically wrong."[76] Fearful of social disorder and unwilling to distinguish the suffering of slaves from other human miseries, Catholics lumped immediate slave emancipation with a religious and political radicalism that threatened the foundations of society.

III

Daniel O'Connell's specific appeal to his American brethren suggested another reason for Catholics' uneasiness about slave emancipation—the anti-Catholic (and often anti-Irish) orientation of many abolitionists. O'Connell urged Irish Americans not to support slavery, even if it was true "that there are amongst the Abolitionists many wicked and calumniating *enemies* of Catholicity and the Irish."[77]

William Lloyd Garrison upbraided O'Connell for giving credence to the claim that abolitionists are "bigoted against Catholicism," and scholars have followed Garrison's lead, highlighting the broadly antiauthoritarian character of American abolition, and its ripple effects for those interested in women's rights and other reforms, not abolitionist anti-Catholicism.[78] And abolitionists did direct a steady stream of invective toward Protestant as well as Catholic clergy. When Garrison used the term "priestcraft," he included "self-styled 'Evangelical' clergy who are as bigoted, proscriptive, and self-inflated as the Pope himself."[79] When Bishop Hughes attacked Daniel O'Connell, Massachusetts abolitionists regretted that he had shown "the spirit of Popery to be as bigoted, tyrannical and pro-slavery as that of New England Protestantism."[80]

Yet a powerful strain of explicit anti-Catholicism did shape the antislavery movement.[81] Comparisons of Catholicism and slavery were not new—the earl of Shaftesbury declared in 1679, "Popery and Slavery, like two sisters, go hand in hand, sometimes one goes first, sometimes the other, in a door, but the other is always following close at hand"—but the intensity of the nineteenth-century American slavery debate and the rapid growth of a Catholic Church unwilling to condemn slavery made it newly compelling.[82]

By the late 1840s antislavery activists frequently denounced slavery and Catholicism as parallel despotic systems, opposed to education, free speech, and political liberty in predictable synchronicity. Protestants who tolerated slavery betrayed their principles, abolitionists believed, while Catholics who tolerated slavery applied them. Catholic leaders in Italy forbade distribution of the Bible to their people, just as southern slaveholders stopped the distribution of the Bible to slaves. Catholics relied upon oral instruction in catechism classes, just as slaveholders used oral instruction to prevent slave literacy. Slaveholders exerted unlimited control over female slaves, just as priests allegedly exercised sexual and emotional power over female penitents in the confessional. Slave quarters were likened to the "dungeons of the Popish Inquisition."[83] Popular exposés of women (allegedly) attempting to flee convents bore a startling resemblance to narratives describing efforts of slaves to flee the South.[84]

One Ohio abolitionist, after comparing himself to Martin Luther, offered this summary:

> In this country, popery finds its appropriate ally in the institution of slavery. They are both kindred systems. One enslaves the mind, the other both mind and body. Both deny the Bible to those under their control—both discourage free inquiry. . . . By its penances, masses for the dead, indulgences etc. popery extorts money without rendering an equivalent; slavery robs men of all their earnings, their wives and children.[85]

The list of anti-Catholic abolitionists in the first stages of the American movement is impressive. The first abolitionist martyr, Elijah Lovejoy, murdered in 1836 for his opposition to slavery, spent much of 1835 warning of the Catholic menace.[86] George Bourne became, simultaneously, a leading antislavery and anti-Catholic agitator, writing attacks on Romanism and scurrilous convent narratives even as he became a crucial influence on Garrison's *Liberator*.[87] The abolitionist Angelina Grimké noted,

"The Catholics are universally condemned, for denying the Bible to the common people, but, *slaveholders must not* blame them, for *they* are doing the *very same thing*, and for the very same reason, neither of these systems can bear the light which bursts from the pages of that Holy Book."[88]

Tensions between Catholics convinced that abolitionists would sacrifice social order on the altar of emancipation and abolitionists who viewed Catholicism as a spiritual slavery were mutually reinforcing. They became more apparent after 1848 not only because of the European revolutions but because the slavery question moved to the center of American political life. In that year the Free Soil Party became the first major antislavery political party, and congressmen fiercely debated whether slavery would be permitted in the territories won in the Mexican-American war.[89]

Widespread antislavery sentiment in the 1850s often included an anti-Catholic undercurrent, as suggested by the careers of a wide range of American antislavery activists, including Harriet Beecher Stowe, her brother Edward Beecher, Frederick Douglass, Joseph Thompson, and George Cheever. The anti-Catholicism of the Beecher family began with father Lyman's warnings about papal advances in the West during the 1830s, and extended to daughter Harriet's *Uncle Tom's Cabin.* (In the novel Uncle Tom conspicuously escorts Catholic Eva to Methodist meetings, liberating her from the religious and political decadence of the Catholic, slave-owning St. Clare family.)[90] Harriet's brother Edward Beecher also attacked slavery, even as he published an 1855 manifesto on the papal conspiracy.[91]

Frederick Douglass, too, displayed a casual anti-Catholicism, attacking the "cunning illusions" of Catholic leaders.[92] Thompson and Cheever became editors for the country's most prominent religious weekly, the *Independent*, and, like many evangelicals opposed to slavery, switched back and forth from the dangers of slavery to the dangers of Catholicism.[93] In one 1859 address Thompson noted that "Freedom is grappling with Slavery," even as he worried that "Romanism is taking advantage of our religious freedom to oust religious instruction from common schools. . . ."[94]

Cheever's fear of Catholicism crystallized during two European trips in the 1840s. In Fribourg, Switzerland, Cheever bumped into a group of Jesuit seminarians out for a walk, a group that might have included Father Wiget, and was provoked to wonder whether despotic Jesuits might once again retrieve "pitiless axes and instruments of torture."[95] In 1854 Cheever wrote a popular treatise on the importance of keeping the Bible in the public schools. That same year he used similar language in attacking slavery. "At the South," he warned, "the slaveholders and slave-laws forbid the teaching of the Bible; at the North, [so do] the Romanists and Romish laws." When Supreme Court Justice Roger Brooke Taney announced the *Dred Scott* decision in 1857, Cheever immediately concluded that Taney's Catholicism made him sympathetic to slavery. He also compared the ambitions of southern slaveholders to those of Spain's Philip II, with his "thumb screws and boot for the tortures of the Inquisition."[96]

Foreign abolitionists made similar assessments. The British evangelical and antislavery advocate Hugh McNeile wrote of the "perfect consistency" involved in working for the suppression of "slavery and popery."[97] Richard D. Webb, the Irish correspondent for the *National Anti-Slavery Standard*, compared "the rampant, audacious, insolent Ultramontanism of the Romish clergy" with the "kindred system of chattel slavery."[98] The Mexican liberal Matías Romero pondered the "striking similarity which exists between the Church party of Mexico and the Slavery party in the United States."[99] In Canada, Toronto's George Brown helped found the Anti-Slavery Society of Canada and serialized *Uncle Tom's Cabin* in the country's most influential newspaper, the *Toronto Globe*. In 1855 a *Globe* editorial concluded, "In Canada the Roman Catholic hierarchy is the slave power. It holds us subjects in bondage as slavish as the Southern taskmaster."[100]

Catholics responded to agitation over the slavery question with an entirely different vocabulary, a lexicon developed while observing the European revolutions. The *Boston Pilot* explained that Catholics attacked European liberals for the same reasons that they repudiated "Garrison abolitionism."[101] J. W. Cummings argued, "Those who talk about the 'rights of human nature and the inalienable rights of man,' ought to consider the evil done by the application of their principles. How far these men have gone in the late revolutions in Europe is now a matter of historical record. They have cut throats, overthrown altars, subverted thrones. . . ."[102]

The frustration expressed by Catholics sympathetic to abolition suggests their isolation. Vermont's John Lambert explained to *Pittsburg Catholic* readers, "[A]s a Catholic Christian . . . I cannot but feel for the whole human race who are suffering in bondage and oppression." (The editor of the *Pittsburg Catholic* admonished Lambert, declaring, "[W]e did not believe in the existence of such a thing as a Catholic Free-Soiler. . . .") At the 1855 meeting of the Massachusetts Anti-Slavery Society, Henry Kemp responded to an anti-Catholic aside. According to the minutes Kemp announced that "various Popes" had "condemned slavery, and called upon the faithful everywhere in the name of Almighty God, to put it entirely away from them. Hence he [Kemp] considered Archbishop Hughes, and all the professed Catholics of America, who sympathize with, and aid the Slave power, as *excommunicated heretics*. He thought himself about the only representative of the true Catholic Church in this country."[103]

IV

Three developments sharpened the conflict between Catholics and antislavery activists. First, a series of challenges to the fugitive slave law of 1850, requiring northerners to hand over escaped slaves to their southern owners, electrified one segment of northern public opinion. The most celebrated cases occurred in Boston. In 1854, one group of antislavery activists broke into the city's courthouse in a futile, and bloody, attempt to free one slave, Anthony Burns, and quickly identified "vagabond Irishmen" as the Bostonians most willing to support enforcement of the Fugitive Slave Act.[104]

Second, a wave of anti-Catholic riots swept through the North. Churches throughout the region were destroyed, and street brawls were frequent. Mobs preventing enforcement of the Fugitive Slave Act, and mobs torching Catholic churches were distinct, but some men participated in both, demonstrating the fluidity of anti-Catholic and antislavery rhetoric.[105] Perhaps the most eccentric (but also revealing) figure in this regard was John Orr. Five feet four, with a long black beard and a mustache and wearing a white robe with a hat bearing the slogan "Rule Britannia, Hail Columbia and Down with the Mother of Abominations," Orr became known as the Angel Gabriel, for his habit of blowing a small horn when he arrived in a neighborhood to harangue the natives on the topic of Catholic iniquity. (Orr began his career as an anti-Catholic agitator in Scotland and ended it preaching anti-Catholicism in British Guiana, another marker of the transatlantic quality of the phenomenon.)[106]

Orr provoked crowds into burning several Catholic churches in New

Hampshire, New York, Maine, and Massachusetts, and one of his New York City addresses drew a crowd of ten thousand. At the same time, as in one 1854 visit to Rochester, New York, he declaimed not only against Catholics but "at Slavery, at the Fugitive Slave Law, &c., &c."[107]

Similarly, in Ellsworth, Maine, a mob tarred and feathered Father John Bapst, one of Wiget's fellow Swiss exiles. Respectable Protestants decried the attack on Bapst (the abolitionist *Liberator* termed it a "dastardly outrage"), and Bapst himself thought regret over the attack would "be extremely useful to the cause of the Church in Maine."[108] Still, one Maine politician chose the occasion to complain that "Popery and American slavery seemed united in the effort to sustain and strengthen each other."[109]

That abolitionists and anti-Catholic rioters alike defied the law, and that the partisans of one cause often supported the other, made Catholics only more suspicious of extralegal protests. A Maryland Jesuit chose to deliver a sermon in 1854 on "duty of citizens to their government" and against "rejection of all rule."[110] A New York Catholic editor worried that both the "anti-popery crusade" and the "anti-Slavery propagandism" were "full of danger to our institutions."[111]

A third issue, debate over the 1854 Kansas-Nebraska Act, which allowed residents of Kansas and Nebraska to choose whether to permit slavery in their respective territories, also pitted Catholics against antislavery activists. To Catholics, constantly defending themselves against accusations of meddling in politics or taking orders from Rome, the fact that three thousand antislavery Protestant ministers (Catholics preferred "political parsons") signed a protest against the act smacked of hypocrisy. In both the North and the South, Catholics boasted of their fidelity to constitutional principle. At the Monroe, Michigan, Fourth of July celebration in 1854, James Sheeran informed his listeners that "the liberties of the country are in danger, not indeed from invading enemies, but from domestic foes, who are gnawing at the very vitals of our political institutions, and we have to stand almost alone in their defense." The New Orleans Catholic Thomas Semmes proudly noted that his church had "incurred the censure of red-republicans of Europe," even as "the signature of no Catholic clergyman is affixed to the remarkable remonstrance presented to Congress by three thousand preachers, against the passage of the Nebraska bill."[112]

The uproar caused by the fugitive slave law, the wave of anti-Catholic riots, and the fear of an aggressive South generated by the Kansas-Nebraska debate made 1854 and 1855 the pivotal moments in the political crisis of the 1850s. Motives and behaviors varied—many abolitionists emphasized that hostility toward Catholicism must not supersede the larger problem of slavery, some anti-Catholic northerners despised the radicalism of the abolitionists, and some white southerners shared northern Protestants' concerns about Catholicism.[113]

Still, the decisive development was the movement of northern evangelical Protestants out of the collapsing Whig Party into the anti-Catholic (and in the North largely antislavery) American Party, which first supplanted the Whigs in 1854 as the main rival to the Democrats. Almost as quickly, the new Republican Party swept aside the American Party in 1856, taking the first major step toward the election of Abraham Lincoln in 1860.[114]

The brief triumph of the American Party, and then the movement of many of its members into the Republican Party, ensured that a broad array of politicians, ministers, and editors would begin complaining, in the words of the Pennyslvania congressman David Wilmot, about "the alliance between an ancient and powerful Church and the slave interests of America."[115] (Or as the New York congressman Bayard Clark explained to his colleagues, "As in the empires of the Old World, Jesuitism allies itself with 'kingcraft,' so in the New, it strikes hands with slavery.")[116] A number of antislavery Know-Nothings forced a showdown on the issue at American Party conventions, and one group of Massachusetts lodges resolved that "there can exist no real hostility to Roman Catholicism which does not embrace slavery, its natural co-worker in opposition to freedom and republican institutions."[117]

In Michigan the state legislature passed a personal liberty law in 1855 aimed at nullifying the Fugitive Slave Act, along with a church property bill checking the power of Catholic bishops. In Massachusetts the American Party swept the 1854 elections. Once installed, the newly elected representatives harassed Catholic nuns with convent "inspections," while outlawing racial segregation in Boston schools and making the Fugitive Slave Act unenforceable in Massachusetts. The same men also insisted on codifying the custom of reading the King James Bible that Thomas Whall and Father Wiget challenged four years later.[118]

Orations given at the height of the turmoil in Massachusetts incessantly compared Catholicism and slavery, typified by the congressional candidate Anson Burlingame's complaint that Catholicism and slavery "are in alliance by the necessity of their nature, for one denies the right of a man to his body, and the other the right of a man to his soul."[119] The Reverend Eden B. Foster bluntly concluded that "Slavery and Romanism [are] a two-edged dagger with which to stab liberty to the heart."[120]

Theodore Parker, the most prominent radical minister in Massachusetts, was almost elected chaplain for the Know-Nothing–dominated state legislature in 1855. In an 1854 sermon on dangers threatening the "Rights of Man in America," Parker blended anti-Catholic prejudice with frustration over Catholics' uneasiness about slave emancipation:

> The Catholic worshiper is not to think, but to believe and obey; the priest not to reason and consider, but to proclaim and command; the voter is not to inquire and examine, but to deposit his ballot as the ecclesiastical authority directs. . . . The Catholic clergy are on the side of slavery. They find it is the dominant power, and pay court thereto that they may rise by its help. They love slavery itself; it is an institution thoroughly congenial to them, consistent with the first principles of their Church. . . . I am told there is not in all America a single Catholic newspaper hostile to slavery; not one opposed to tyranny in general; not one that takes sides with the oppressed in Europe.[121]

In contrast to Protestant voters divided among the political parties, Catholics from all ethnic backgrounds favored the Democrats, and scholarly scrutiny of nineteenth-century voting behavior has conclusively identified religion as central to voter choice.[122] Irish Catholics became more fervently Democratic during the 1850s, a fact emphasized by Republicans who noted that only white southerners voted Democratic with any comparable regularity. (The *Chicago Tribune* referred to the "Catholicized Slaveocratic party" and the "Union between Irish priests and bishops and the leaders of the Democracy.") One Michigan study estimates that 95 percent of Irish Catholics supported the Democrats between 1854 and 1860.[123]

German Catholics also supported Democrats more frequently than German Protestants or German radicals did, although the pattern varied by state.[124] The German Catholic press contained frequent denunciations of what Milwaukee's *Der Seebote* called "the infernal ingredients of this loathsome Republican monstrosity"—or, as *Der Seebote* put it, "Temperance men, abolitionists, haters of foreigners, sacrilegious despoilers of churches, killers of Catholics."[125]

Tellingly, some of those German Catholics who did join the Republican Party were more liberal Catholics, even Catholics involved in disputes with church authorities. In Osage County, Missouri, Dr. Bernhard Bruns became a leading Radical Republican in the 1860s, following his involvement in several ecclesiastical controversies. Johann B. Stallo, alternately described as a freethinker and a Catholic, defended parish trustees of Cincinnati's Holy Trinity Church in a legal squabble with the local archbishop, and later served as a Republican delegate to the 1860 convention that nominated Abraham Lincoln.[126]

Most Republican leaders in the late 1850s focused on the fear of an expanding slave power, and Lincoln himself made no anti-Catholic comments during either his 1858 senatorial race or his 1860 presidential campaign. But genuine Republican opposition to nativism, which might alienate German Protestants, did not preclude opposition to Catholicism at the state and local levels. As Bishop John Timon of Buffalo warned one correspondent, "There seems to be an anti-Catholic twang in much of what they write and say. A moderate anti-Catholic party with a concealed warfare would do us much more harm than the brutal force and open warfare of the KN [Know-Nothings]."[127]

Prominent German liberals and anti-Catholics such as the newspaper editors Friedrich Hassaurek in Cincinnati, Heinrich Bornstein in St. Louis, and Bernhard Domschke in Milwaukee became leaders in the Republican Party. Timothy Day, an Ohio congressman worried about Catholic influence, explained to Hassaurek that "hatred of Jesuitism" should unite Germans and native-born Americans, and by 1856 Hassaurek was offering Milwaukee citizens a lecture on "Slavery and Jesuitism."[128]

Republican newspapers used the same explosive language. The *Chicago Tribune* warned its readers that it was not "the foreign element" that threatened the Republic but the "papal portion of that element." Understandably, the "Republican Party, which is the avowed and mortal enemy of chattel bondage, is not less the opponent of partisan schemes of political Catholicism. It could not as the defender of human rights everywhere be otherwise."[129] In Pittsburgh the editor of the *Post-Gazette* wondered how anyone could allow the "curse of slavery . . . to extend over the free territory of Nebraska . . . and . . . see nothing to oppose in the temporal and spiritual despotism of the Pope."[130]

In parallel fashion, southern estimations of Catholicism shifted. The few southerners opposed to slavery in the 1840s and 1850s, like their northern abolitionist counterparts, often displayed an anti-Catholic bias. One southern abolitionist, Moncure Conway, wrote a series of articles on "Jesuitism," even as he urged Virginia to follow the lead of Massachusetts in common school education.[131] The most notorious southern critic of slavery, Hinton Rowan Helper, argued, "There is so little difference between Slavery, Popery and Negro-driving Democracy, that we are not at all surprised to see them going hand in hand in their diabolical works of inhumanity and desolation."[132]

More influential southerners moved in the opposite direction, and the brief tenure of the southern Know-Nothing, or American, Party in the mid-1850s provided leading southerners an opportunity to express their admiration for Catholics unwilling to support immediate slave emancipation. Ex-President John Tyler congratulated Catholic priests for setting "an example of non-interference in politics which furnishes an example most worthy of imitation on the part of the clergy of the other sects at the North."[133] Georgia's Senator Alexander Stephens, in an address widely reprinted in Catholic newspapers, made this announcement in 1855:

> But I think of all the Christian denominations in the United States the Catholics are the last that Southern people should join in attempting to put under the ban of civil proscription. For as a church they have never warred against us or our peculiar institutions. No man can say as much of the New England Baptists, Presbyterians or Methodists: the long role of abolition petitions with which Congress has been so much excited and agitated for years past come not from the Catholics; their pulpits in the North are not desecrated every Sabbath with anathemas against slavery.[134]

Southern intellectuals went even further. One writer for the *Southern Quarterly Review* cited Jaime Balmes in defense of gradual emancipation and against the current "insane appetite for universal and unrestricted freedom."[135] Others reevaluated the individualism associated with the Protestant principle of private judgment. "We quarrel not with the reformation of Luther and Calvin," said one *De Bow's Review* contributor in 1860, but with "the 'right of private judgment' engrated on it by infidels and fanatics. . . . Finally the conservatives have been roused into action. In religion, the admiration generally expressed for the Catholic church as a political institution . . . is a most important point, and symptom of a salutary reaction."[136]

Precisely because defenders of slavery defended the idea of an organic, less individualist society, important southern intellectuals such as Thomas Dew, Henry Hughes, George Frederick Holmes, and George Fitzhugh found Catholicism alluring. Dew regretted the effect of Catholic authoritarianism on free inquiry, but he also admired Catholicism's ability to avoid the "feebleness and anarchy which would have resulted from schism."[137] Hughes became enamored of corporatist thought, and Holmes flirted with conversion to Catholicism, admired Aristotelian defenses of slavery, and worried that the "rejection of spiritual authority" lay at the root of social problems.[138] Fitzhugh admired the Catholic refusal to accept divorce and remarriage and believed that Catholicism had provided a salutary check on laissez-faire economics during the medieval period.[139] "We have no quarrel with the Reformation," he announced in 1857, but then proceeded to a detailed attack on the excesses of private judgment. Sadly, he concluded, northerners opposed to slavery "did nothing more than carry into practice the right of private judgment, liberty of speech, freedom of the press and of religion."[140]

IV

The start of the Civil War, in April 1861, marked a new beginning for Orestes Brownson. He quickly became the leading Catholic supporter of the Union war effort, renewing contact with old friends such as Charles Sumner, the Massachusetts Senator and leading Republican, and lecturing on the crisis up and down the eastern seaboard.[141] He discussed strategy at the White House with President Lincoln.[142]

Brownson's influence became such that a longtime sparring partner in the New York press, the editor Horace Greeley, reprinted a sprawling Brownson essay on the war in the nation's most influential newspaper, the *New York Daily Tribune*. (Frederick Douglass reprinted the same essay in his monthly journal.) Greeley admitted that Brownson wrote from the "stand-point of a Catholic philosopher and theologian," but recommended the essay to "thinking men of every persuasion."[143]

Other responses were less flattering. The tricornered dynamic evident in the 1850s—liberal intellectuals and politicians convinced of Catholicism's hostility to freedom and progress, ultramontane Catholics determined to resist liberalism's insistence on individual autonomy in all spheres, and a loose assemblage of liberal Catholics tacking between the two groups—did not evaporate with the attack on Fort Sumter. (Even as he praised Brownson, for example, Horace Greeley privately identified the "Northern Democracy and the Catholic priesthood" as key aids to the Confederacy.)[144]

Ultimately, discussions of freedom within American society would overlap with discussion of freedom in the church. Brownson and liberal Catholic allies would connect the two subjects, assuming that those favoring slave emancipation would favor other liberal Catholic aims. And in fact only two prominent Catholics, Brownson and Archbishop John Purcell of Cincinnati, would demand immediate slave emancipation as early as 1862, and both would do so in part because of ties with European liberal Catholics. A virtually unknown advocate of emancipation, the New Orleans priest Claude Maistre, also worked in a Louisiana milieu torn by disputes between ultramontane and liberal Catholics.

Brownson's prominence in these theological and political disputes took a personal toll. The chaos of the war and Brownson's fierce support of the Union halved the subscriber base that guaranteed his sustenance, and he announced in 1861 that all subscribers must pay for each issue before they received it. (Searching for new sources of income, he also inquired about the possibility of becoming a college professor at the University of Notre Dame.)[145]

In June 1861, after delivering a commencement speech at St. John's College (now Fordham University) on the political situation, Brownson endured a rebuke from Archbishop Hughes and found himself abandoned as the other guests moved on to a celebratory dinner. A year later Jesuit friends in Boston refused to allow Brownson to enter their house. Brownson's former confessor, Father Charles Gresselin, took the occasion to explain, "You were announced in all the newspapers of the city as coming to give a lecture in behalf of abolitionism. For us to reject that theory is no moral or political sin. Many of the friends of the Union . . . reject it."[146]

Chapter Three

CATHOLIC FREEDOM AND CIVIL WAR

I

While Brownson urged Catholics to support the Union war effort, the country's second-most important Catholic editor, James McMaster, sat in prison. After President Lincoln suspended the writ of habeas corpus in the first weeks of the war, Secretary of State William Seward ordered all newspapers critical of the administration, including McMaster's *New York Freeman's Journal*, to cease publication. McMaster responded by immediately starting another newspaper, the *New York Freeman's Appeal*, which did not endear itself to administration officials by describing the Union war effort as "New England Despotism gone mad."[1]

After perusing an issue of the *New York Freeman's Appeal*, Secretary Seward immediately ordered McMaster's arrest for "editing a disloyal newspaper."[2] McMaster gloried in his martyrdom, ordering the marshal to handcuff him and using his six-week imprisonment in New York harbor's Fort Lafayette (without trial) as proof that the Lincoln administration condoned tyranny. (McMaster's wife, Gertrude, on the other hand, a mother worried about the sustenance of their children, pleaded for her husband's release and promised not to allow the printing of anything "obnoxious" to the "administration of the Government.")[3] When released, McMaster signed a loyalty oath, but not before filing a protest "against the demand made on me to take the oath." Government officials

James McMaster, editor of the *New York Freeman's Journal* from 1848 to 1886, ca. 1860s.

prohibited McMaster from publishing the *New York Freeman's Journal* until April 1862.[4]

McMaster's arrest was only the most dramatic episode in a colorful career.[5] Born James MacMaster, he entered General Theological Seminary in New York in 1842, studying to become an Episcopalian priest. There he encountered the writings of England's John Henry Newman, then on the brink of conversion to Catholicism from Anglicanism. McMaster began a correspondence with one of Newman's closest associates, John Dalgairns, and carefully followed the twists and turns of Newman's Anglo-Catholic Oxford movement. Dalgairns assured his American correspondent that the situation of thoughtful Protestants "across the Atlantic" was the same as McMaster's own, and both McMaster and Dalgairns, like Newman, eventually converted to Catholicism.[6]

McMaster then left New York City and enrolled in a Redemptorist seminary in Belgium, where he stopped short of the priesthood but developed an enduring loyalty to the ultramontane spirit of the Redemptorist order. After returning to New York, he became editor of the *New York Freeman's Journal* in 1848. His model was *L'Univers*, the most influential of the ultramontane European Catholic newspapers, and in McMaster's view, a "fearless independent organ."[7] Louis Veuillot, the editor of *L'Univers,* termed the *Freeman's Journal* the "best edited, best informed" Catholic paper in the United States, and McMaster proudly placed this blurb on his editorial page.[8] Just as Veuillot's *L'Univers* was read throughout France, McMaster's *Freeman's Journal* had a national circulation, as evidenced by McMaster's extensive correspondence and agents across the country selling the paper on his behalf.

McMaster's style also mimicked Veuillot's. Combative and sarcastic, with an inexhaustible (and characteristically nineteenth-century) capacity for theological argument, McMaster never let the inadequacies of his education overcome his determination to defend Catholic doctrine, as least as he understood it. One account of McMaster in the seminary describes him rushing into a fellow student's room when learning that the student doubted church doctrine on a certain point, planting his six-foot-two, hawk-nosed frame in the center of the room, and demanding, "Where are your grounds?"[9]

At first Brownson and McMaster seemed natural allies.[10] The Swiss revolution that led to Father Wiget's expulsion appeared to McMaster, as it did to Brownson, a "severe comment on Protestant progress." McMaster joined Brownson in castigating the "lawless liberalism" making "havoc of society in Europe."[11]

When Brownson began edging into the orbit of European liberal Catholics in the mid-1850s, however, McMaster expressed his disapproval. He derided Brownson's view that "it is safe to allow our children to be associated with Protestant children in schools where every lesson that is taught has the smack of heresy," and Brownson's criticism of the Irish struck McMaster as Anglo-Saxon snobbery.[12] (McMaster, by contrast, dropped the first—tellingly Scottish—*a* in MacMaster when he began editing the *New York Freeman's Journal*, with its large Irish readership.) Brownson's new allies, including Montalembert, seemed to McMaster nothing more than a "neo-Gallican coterie," and he thought French liberal Catholics should be ashamed of their opposition to the "faithful soldiers of the Catholic cause who have clustered around the *Univers* newspaper."[13]

Brownson, in turn, thought both Veuillot and McMaster should conduct themselves "with more consideration" for other Catholics.[14] When Veuillot wrote Brownson, informing him that despite their disagreements he considered him a "good and courageous" Catholic, Brownson responded coolly. He urged Veuillot to temper his support of authoritarian rulers, so as not to embarrass those Catholics who "live under republican and constitutional governments."[15]

McMaster also disagreed with Brownson's interpretation of the political crisis. In contrast to Brownson, who became increasingly sympathetic to attacks on slavery and slaveholders in the years before the Civil War, McMaster admired Stephen Douglas, the Illinois Democrat who favored allowing voters to decide whether slavery would be permitted in a given state or territory. (As early as 1853 McMaster published a wishful rumor that Douglas had converted to Catholicism.)[16] In 1859 Douglas privately thanked McMaster "for the defense you have made of my public career."[17]

Like many Catholics, McMaster thought it foolish for white southerners to proclaim slavery as a "divine right," and he applauded the church's role in the gradual elimination of European slavery, but he saw no pressing need for immediate slave emancipation. "There has never been a day," he emphasized, "in which Catholics, in the communion of the Church, and uncensured by her, have not held slaves."[18] During the tense days of 1859 and 1860, he pleaded with southern secessionists "not to throw away their future, and all the bright aspirations of American liberty, for the sake of four millions of black slaves." At the same time, and more frequently, he expressed his dismay with the "narrow dogmatism of anti-slavery preachers" in the North and the "moral butchery" advocated by Republicans and abolitionists.[19]

II

The meaning of the war for either the liberal Catholicism of Brownson or the ultramontane Catholicism of McMaster was not immediately clear. In the first months of the conflict, northern Catholics rallied to the support of the Union, and southern Catholics proved equally loyal to the Confederacy. Priests volunteered as chaplains on both sides of the Mason-Dixon line, and nuns cared for the wounded soldiers of both armies. Particular units dominated by Catholic soldiers—New York's Sixty-ninth Militia, the Tenth Louisiana Volunteer Regiment—earned reputations for valor.[20]

Northern bishops such as New York's John Hughes regretted that southern Catholic leaders did not resist the pressure to secede, and the editor of the *Boston Pilot*, despite disappointment with "northern fanatics," announced, "We have hoisted the American Stars and Stripes over THE PILOT Establishment and there they shall wave till the 'star of peace' returns."[21] Southern bishops such as Patrick Lynch of Charleston and John Quinlan of Mobile defended secession, and the election of Lincoln prompted the editor of Charleston's *U.S. Catholic Miscellany* to drop the "obnoxious words" "United" and "States" from the paper's masthead.[22]

In the North, Catholic patriotism had the virtue of dampening, for a time, anti-Catholicism among northern liberals and Republicans. In Boston members of Father Wiget's popular sodality served in the Union army, and the North End Irish suffered severe casualties at Antietam and Fredericksburg, showing, as one St. Mary's parishioner later put it, "the patriotism that is ours."[23] The attendance of leading Massachusetts citizens at the funeral of one fallen soldier and former sodality leader, Captain Nathaniel B. Shurtleff Jr., a Catholic convert tutored by Wiget, and the decision by the governor to lower the state house flag in Shurtleff's honor, marked a new acceptance. Wiget's former pastor Father McElroy admitted his uneasiness with Shurtleff's religious intensity. But he rejoiced that "respectable citizens, including several *parsons*," attended Shurtleff's funeral Mass, a service "deeply interesting to hundreds who had never witnessed [Catholic] religious observances."[24]

Catholics in both the North and the South continued to employ the arguments developed over the past fifteen years of assaults on liberalism. Southern Catholics had the easier task, repeating attacks on abolitionists and Yankees made by many Catholics in the 1850s.[25] Northern Catholics drew upon the same vocabulary but redirected its focus. Jefferson Davis and Robert E. Lee, they charged, were no better than Italians attempting to overthrow papal rule. As Father James Keogh explained, "The principle of private judgment must produce disruption in civil as well as in religious society. . . . Why was it wrong and cruel in the Pope to gather together an army of volunteers to keep down his mutinous subjects, if it be noble and patriotic, as it undoubtedly is, to volunteer to suppress an uprising which is supported by the greater portion of the Southern people?"[26]

A current of northern Catholics' uneasiness about the Union effort, however, also became evident. Appalled by the European revolutions of 1848 and stung by the school fights of the 1850s, many Catholics were sympathetic to the charge that the nationalism of the Lincoln administration bordered on dictatorship. The Wisconsin Democrat, and prominent Catholic, Edward G. Ryan warned in 1862 that "blind submission to the Administration of the government is not devotion to the country or the Constitution. The administration is not the government."[27]

McMaster's view of the Lincoln administration—as enamored of tyranny "as any Asiatic or Turkish despot"—was venomous, but other Catholic editors, including Peter Deuster of Milwaukee's *Der Seebote*, James J. Faran of the *Cincinnati Enquirer*, Denis Mahoney of the *Dubuque Herald*, and John Mullaly of New York's *Metropolitan Record*, made similar attacks.[28] The most violent disputes came in response to the draft. In Minnesota, German Catholics seemed especially reluctant to serve in the Union armies after a state draft, and in Wisconsin, German and Luxembourger Catholics were at the forefront of resistance to that state's draft, in part because the draft call highlighted the unavailability of Catholic chaplains for particular units.[29]

President Lincoln's controversial authorization of a federal draft in March 1863 caused further unease. Catholic leaders did not condone violent opposition to the draft, and some Catholic leaders, including Archbishop Hughes, defended Lincoln's decision. Still, in New York, Pennsylvania's coal country, and Boston, Irish Catholics, especially, resisted implementation of the draft, and the conflict in New York became transformed into a murderous attack on African Americans that left 105 dead.[30] In Boston a rare Irish Catholic Republican, Colonel Patrick R. Guiney, complained of "unarmed traitors" in Boston's heavily Catholic North End.[31]

More symbolic Catholic resistance to American nationalism was also evident. While some bishops, including Hughes, ordered American flags flown from the steeples of churches, other Catholics described themselves as "pained" to see "Flags hung on the cross of Christ."[32] One Ohio priest angered many in his congregation by refusing to "hoist the flag on the church." He explained to James McMaster, "I want the House of God to be one clean spot on earth, uncontaminated by politics, where every sinner may . . . bow his proud head before God."[33]

The most dramatic episodes occurred when Union troops attempted to ensure that a short prayer requesting that the nation "be preserved in Union" be recited after Mass. The practice had been initiated by Bishop John Carroll in the late eighteenth century, but became controversial in the 1860s. In Martinsburg, West Virginia, Father Thomas Becker substituted the word "Confederacy" for "Union," much to the displeasure of federal troops then occupying the town. (Becker was briefly jailed and then freed upon the request of Baltimore's Archbishop Kenrick.)[34] In Natchez, Mississippi, Bishop William Elder also rejected the plea of Union military commanders to include in the Mass prayers "expressive of a proper spirit" toward President Lincoln.[35] Elder had quietly supported secession in 1861, shocked by "concentration of all power in the Presid't alone on the grounds of necessity."[36]

Union soldiers arrested Elder in 1864, for "encouraging the people under his authority in treasonable practices," even as he insisted that his refusal reflected only his "unwillingness to use [his] sacred ministry . . . in support of any political views."[37] As soldiers escorted Elder across the Mississippi River to the Union camp at Vidalia, Louisiana, Catholic parishioners knelt in support. With the help of friends in Washington, D.C., the order was rescinded and Elder released, but not before the Catholic press had publicized the incident as yet another example of a "great and crying injustice."[38]

A Missouri dispute near the end of the war captured this Catholic reluctance to follow a Republican lead. In January 1865 a state constitutional convention dominated by Radical Republicans passed a law taxing church property and making it a crime for any minister to conduct marriages or preach unless he swore he had never "directly or indirectly" supported the rebellion.[39] The chief advocate of the new constitution, the Republican (and former Know-Nothing) Charles Drake, denounced opposition coming from "a church, the great mass of whose members *in St. Louis* have, from the first, been universally understood to be disloyal. I say the great mass; for there are many Roman Catholics here who were undoubtedly loyal and patriotic; but that body has been, and is, pervaded by a rebellious and treasonable spirit. . . ."[40]

A number of Protestant ministers, mostly Methodists and Baptists, joined Catholics in refusing to take the test oath, but the arrest of a

Catholic priest, Father John Cummings, became the crucial test case and the occasion for Archbishop Peter Kenrick to order priests not to take the oath. As the Jesuit Pierre De Smet explained, "our authority does not emanate from the State, and we cannot, without compromising the ecclesiastical state, consent to take such an oath."[41]

A bitterly divided U.S. Supreme Court eventually voided the Missouri law, angering Republicans, including Justice Samuel Miller, who argued, "To suffer treasonable sentiments to spread here unchecked is to permit the stream on which the life of the Nation depends to be poisoned at its source."[42] The Missouri politician Frank Blair, by contrast, urged his brother, Senator Montgomery Blair of Maryland, to support Father Cummings. "It will be a great political occasion," he explained, "in which you can serve yourself with the great body of Catholics of Maryland & the whole country. . . ."[43]

III

A more general fear lay beneath Catholic protests against specific exercises of federal power: that Republican leaders would turn against Catholics after winning the war. The *New York Times*, after all, defined both popery and slavery as "incompatible with the spirit of the age [and] liberty and civilization" and "doomed" to "speedy destruction."[44]

James McMaster returned to this fear constantly, and another Catholic newspaper, New York's *Metropolitan Record*, warned that Republican radicals planned to "make war upon Catholicity as well as slavery." Abolitionists, especially, would not acknowledge the Constitution as "binding on them; and should they succeed . . . they will then turn round on Popery, and try to abolish it as a still more heinous abomination, crying to their God for vengeance."[45]

As the war dragged on, Catholics' suspicion of Republicans' motives increased. Writing from Wisconsin, a priest informed a Bavarian friend in 1863 of his worry that a "general persecution of the Catholic Church" might occur. He elaborated, "The constitution of the country has become a dead letter; the president has absolute power. The Catholics take a determined stand for the Constitution, but they do not stand for a government that wants to tyrannize everything without a constitution. . . ."[46] These fears reached Rome—where the director of the North American College (a Catholic seminary) wondered "if the Republican party triumph[s] over the South, the Church will be persecuted . . ."—and Munich, where a German theologian predicted that "as soon as the rebellion in the southern states was ended [the Republicans] would immediately attack the Catholic church."[47]

Charles Sumner and other Republicans dismissed Catholics' fears as nonsensical.[48] But many Republicans did doubt Catholics' loyalty. In tiny Keokuk, Iowa, a Republican newspaper editor complained, "There are not politicians or presses so earnest in the advocacy of slavery as the Catholic politicians and press, and there is no class of people so fierce in the support of slavery as the masses of the Catholics in this country."[49] The *New York Tribune* warned in 1864 that the "the great body of the Roman Catholic priesthood of this country are the ardent and active partisans and upholders of Human Slavery, and do not sympathize with the Republic in the war, which the Slave Power has wickedly waged against it. . . ."[50]

Significantly, liberal Catholics made similar accusations, although unlike non-Catholic liberals they did not see their religion as inherently inconsistent with liberty or national loyalty. As early as October 1861 Brownson noted that most Catholic newspapers did not wholeheartedly support the Union cause and that the Catholic clergy, "the greater part of whom have been born or educated abroad," had "Southern sympathies." One of Brownson's St. Louis correspondents congratulated him on his honesty: "I have grieved over the fact that there are so many secessionists amongst priests who have been sworn to support the general government. It looks to me like perjury."[51]

Brownson's fury deepened as the death toll mounted. In 1863 he mocked the "mischievous fiction that it was the determination of the Republicans, when they had put down the Southern slaveholders, to turn round and put down the Catholic religion in this country." And he blamed the draft riots on Irish Catholics and the Democratic Party.[52] (Upon reading this article, Bishop Martin Spalding of Louisville complained to his diary that Brownson's accusations were "mischievous and wicked, denouncing Catholics as disloyal, because they will not in a body run mad with this insane abolitionism.")[53]

Support of emancipation also allied Brownson with French liberal Catholics. French liberals launched the most vigorous European attacks on slavery, and French liberal Catholics occasionally had to evade complaints that they exaggerated the Catholic role in prior emancipations.[54]

Edouard Laboulaye, for example, became chair of the French Anti-Slavery League, and the most prominent French supporter of the Union effort and emancipation. One letter written by Laboulaye and other French liberals defending the Union armies was immediately translated into French and German by the New York Loyal Publication Society, and reprinted in the *New York Times, New York Herald,* and *New York Tribune.* Laboulaye was also a liberal Catholic who asked all governments to respect religious liberty and urged the Vatican to adapt to the conditions of the nineteenth century. (For such views, Laboulaye endured intense criticism from followers of Louis Veuillot.)[55]

In fact the article in which Brownson first urged emancipation of the American slaves took the form of a review of Augustin Cochin's recently published two-volume work on emancipation and slavery. Cochin, too, was integral to the circle of liberal Catholics in France, a friend of Montalembert and Dupanloup, both of whom had already attacked slavery.[56] Brownson arranged for the translation of Cochin's volumes into English and endorsed Cochin's plea that all Christians unite in the campaign for slavery's abolition.[57] Cochin, in turn, praised Brownson and privately urged him, as someone "already so well and favorably known in France," to contribute to the mouthpiece of French liberal Catholics, *Le Correspondant.*[58] Brownson's daughter, Sarah, published a letter in the *National Anti-Slavery Standard* in 1863, asking abolitionists to remember that Cochin, Dupanloup, and American Catholics opposed to slavery represented the true "Catholic spirit" even if the "Catholic papers of this country [are] generally pro-slavery in the worst sense."[59]

Non-Catholic French liberals taunted Catholic compatriots for defending the party of slavery.[60] "It can not be dissembled," wrote one contributor to the premier organ of French liberalism, *Le Journal des Débats,* "that French public opinion in general and Catholic opinion have always been favorable to the cause of the South and to the cause of slavery, and men like Mgr. Dupanloup and Mr. Augustin Cochin, who dare to protest against that sinful tendency, are very rare in the Church and the Catholic party." The same author conceded that "Catholic opinion" was not "favorable to the institution of slavery, itself" or the mistreatment of slaves. But the church still loved "charity more than liberty" and "guardianship more than emancipation."[61]

Montalembert himself, in a pointed phrase, regretted that "all the enemies, open or secret, political or theological, of liberty have been for the

South. It would be useless and puerile to deny that the United States [i.e., the North] count a certain number of adversaries amongst the Catholics. . . ." He added that "with the exception of the learned and eloquent Dr. Brownson we shall not discover amongst the Catholics of the United States any champion of the emancipation of the blacks. . . ."[62]

The pattern of liberal Catholics endorsing the Union cause and the abolition of slavery, and ultramontanes' worrying about the radicalism of a Protestant-led Republican Party, became familiar in both the United States and Europe. Only a handful of American Catholic bishops supported immediate emancipation, along with some liberal Catholics in Brownson's circle. (As late as 1866, after the death of one abolitionist bishop, Josue Young of Erie, Pennsylvania, a local paper professed astonishment that Young, "unlike most of the members of his Church," had been "Ultra-Radical in Politics.")[63] Only one Jesuit, Francis Weninger, publicly defended emancipation, perhaps because he had personally witnessed the horror of a New Orleans slave auction. Even Weninger, though, wondered whether "bigoted Puritans" might turn upon Catholicism at war's end.[64]

Like Catholics in the United States, Catholics in Europe did not endorse slavery as a positive good. And European Catholics wistfully credited their American coreligionists with more antislavery sentiment than they possessed; one Munich theologian, J. Margraf, misread the Savannah bishop Augustin Verot's plea for a more humane slavery as a veiled call for abolition. (Margraf conceded that American Catholics had not taken the lead in abolitionist agitation, but described them as quietly building the "pre-conditions for the moral improvement and external independence of the slaves.")[65]

At the same time Catholics in Switzerland, Canada, and Germany cautioned against the excesses of mass democracy and understood, in the words of J. Margarf, why American Catholics could not ally themselves with the "radical abolition" party. Or as Margraf explained, American Catholics could not trust a "party that threw Catholicism and slavery together in a completely unjust manner (No slavery no popery!)"[66] Similarly, some European ultramontanes thought the argument of Charleston's Bishop Patrick Lynch—"Whatever may be one's theoretical ideas on Freedom and Slavery, and the Dignity of Man, it is not allowable to shut our eyes to the dangers which meet us when from Theory we would descend into realities"—worthy of serious consideration. Montalembert, by contrast, immediately scorned Lynch's "perversion of the moral sense and sacerdotal conscience."[67]

Irish radicals in the United States and Ireland, such as Thomas Francis Meagher and John Cairnes, tended to support immediate emancipation, while ultramontanes, such as the Irish cardinal Paul Cullen, feared that the Republicans mimicked the behavior of Italian nationalists. Catholics in Ireland, even more than their compatriots in the United States, soured on the Union cause during the final two years of the war. Confederate leaders specifically advised Irish agents like Father John Bannon to distribute copies of McMaster's *New York Freeman's Journal*, and emphasize northern hostility to "foreigners" and "Catholics." By 1864 Bannon could report that "the clergy . . . all now sympathize with the South as the friend of civil and religious liberty, and pray for her success as for the preservation of the only conservative political element in America. . . ."[68]

English Catholics proved a partial exception to this pattern. Here, too, ultramontane voices such as those of the editors of the *Tablet* disparaged Lincoln as an exemplar of the "Liberal Party," striving along with Garibaldi and one of Britain's leading liberals, Richard Cobden, for "an increase of power and the suppression of [their] enemies." Brownson's demand for immediate abolition seemed positively dangerous, not least because "[a]ll men may have incurred the penalty of liability to various ills, one of which may be slavery." The editors "rejoiced" to learn that most American Catholics rejected Brownson's views.[69] More liberal English Catholics, however, like English elites generally, also expressed uneasiness about the Union effort and slave emancipation. Lord Acton only slowly became convinced of the need for abolition, and sent a letter of praise to Robert E. Lee as late as 1866.[70] When a Catholic enthusiastic about Augustin Cochin's work queried Newman, the future cardinal responded in 1863 that a slave owner, like a father or a military commander, was a despot. But the institution itself was not "intrinsically evil," and therefore "we can meet [it] according to what is expedient, giving different rules, according to the particular case." Even Newman, however, conceded the power of Cochin's argument and complained that "it is so large a subject and it is so difficult to put one's ideas in order." Two days later he admitted that he had not made it to the "bottom of the question."[71]

Archbishop Hughes placed himself in this transatlantic discussion by publishing an anonymous (although widely recognized) rejoinder to

Brownson's declaration of support for emancipation, emphasizing that Catholics fighting for the Union did not expend "blood and treasure" to "satisfy a clique of abolitionists in the North."[72] Hughes explained to Secretary of State Seward that he had responded to "an untimely article in *Brownson's Quarterly Review*," adding, "If I had not corrected the reviewer's position, he would have done vast mischief, without, I think, intending it, to the struggle in which the country is now engaged."[73] Hughes was more direct with Secretary of War Simon Cameron. "The Catholics," he told Cameron, "so far as I know, whether of native or foreign birth, are willing to fight to the death for the support of the constitution, the Government and the laws of the country. But if it should be understood that, with or without knowing it, they are to fight for the abolition of slavery, then, indeed, they will turn away in disgust from the discharge of what would otherwise be a patriotic duty."[74]

Brownson received some support in the Catholic press, but most editors sided with Hughes, the *Boston Pilot* terming his attack an "irrefutable and scathing denunciation."[75] Criticism of Hughes, however, soon appeared. *Le Journal des Débats* carried an article that attacked Hughes for accepting slavery, and pointedly criticized another Parisian journal edited by Louis Veuillot, *Le Monde*, which published Hughes's response to Brownson. A writer for *Le Journal des Débats* concluded that "it is fitting that the [conservative Catholic] party which hurls the anathema against the highest principles and most precious accomplishments of modern societies, the party which has denounced freedom of the press, freedom of thought, freedom of conscience as inventions of Hell," becomes the "patron of slavery."[76] Antislavery advocates publicized the controversy, with the French correspondent for the *New York Tribune* describing Veuillot's journal as "the most illiberal and retrograde of all Paris journals, the consistent enemy of political, civil and religious freedom everywhere and in every form."[77]

This public squabble placed Hughes in a quandry, since Secretary of State Seward had asked him to serve as an informal ambassador for the Union cause in France, and sympathy for slavery would not endear him to French leaders. When Hughes arrived in Paris, he met with Augustin Cochin and seems to have denied writing the article he had, in fact, written. Cochin printed a summary of this conversation in *Le Correspondant*, reporting that Hughes had not "signed" the article and optimistically concluding that such disputes should not mar the "unanimity" of all Christians on the "principle" of emancipation.[78] (Hughes also tried to persuade Cochin, however, not to trust the writings of American abolitionists. "[William Ellery] Channing, for instance," he explained, "was a Socinian, if not an infidel. [Theodore] Parker did not hesitate to preach or write against the divinity of our Lord.")[79]

Brownson responded to Hughes's efforts in a letter to Montalembert:

> His Grace wrote, that is, dictated, the article in question, of that there is no doubt, and it was written for the express purpose of checking the anti-slavery sentiment of the country, and to bring the pro-slavery prejudices almost universal among the Irish Catholics of this country to bear in crushing me & my Review. The Archbishop is a man whose word cannot be relied on, and he remembers to speak the truth only when truth best serves his purpose.[80]

Even as Brownson complained to Montalembert, a more public controversy exploded in New Orleans.[81] There the free Afro-Creole Catholic population had become increasingly antagonistic to the ultramontane views of the New Orleans archbishop Antoine Blanc and the *Propagateur Catholique* editor Father Napoleon Perché. (Perché frequently reprinted essays by Louis Veuillot.)[82]

White Catholic Creoles supported the Confederacy throughout the war, but the arrival of Union armies in New Orleans in May 1862 electrified the city's Afro-Creole Catholic residents. Afro-Creoles quickly began a newspaper, *L'Union*, which as its name suggests supported the Union armies and emancipation, and began to criticize the local Catholic clergy on theological and political grounds. The archdiocesan newspaper, claimed a writer for *L'Union,* too often promoted dubious miracles, and Catholic priests generally "oppose progress, because progress so diminishes their power."[83] Catholic clergy failed to follow the lead of British abolitionists or even of the French Catholic bishop Félix Dupanloup.[84] How could it be that as "Confederates we were good Catholics and as Unionists we are impious"?[85]

A New Orleans priest, Claude Maistre, allied himself with the Afro-Creoles. Maistre's preaching on the importance of emancipation in 1862 and 1863 and subsequent conflicts with white Catholics on the subject alienated the city's new archbishop, Jean-Marie Odin. Odin used the lingering suspicion caused by prior controversies in Maistre's checkered career to order him away from his largely Afro-Creole congregation in 1863. The more pressing reason, though, as Odin suggested in a letter to the Congregatio de Propaganda Fide in Rome, was Maistre's "preaching the love of liberty and independence and exciting them [his congregation] even to insurrection against their masters."[86]

Maistre refused to obey Odin and simply moved out of the parish. Many of his Afro-Creole parishioners moved with him and aided in the construction of a new church building for his (now schismatic) congregation. Between 1863 and 1865 Maistre described slavery as a "monstrous injustice," celebrated Mass in honor of John Brown, and led the public mourning at Abraham Lincoln's death.[87]

The most far-reaching Catholic controversy on the slavery question began in Cincinnati. There Archbishop John Purcell and his brother, Father Edward Purcell, the editor of the *Cincinnati Catholic Telegraph*, began to insist on the moral necessity of emancipation. Prior to the war Archbishop Purcell had devoted only occasional attention to the slavery question. In an 1838 speech he had condemned "slavery in the abstract" while emphasizing "prudential motives" that hindered abolition.[88] In 1842 he criticized the *Propagateur Catholique* in New Orleans for carrying an advertisement for a "mulatre" to purchase or to rent. "It is not necessary," the *Catholic Telegraph* editorialized, "to be an abolitionist to condemn a practice so repugnant to Catholic feelings."[89] As late as April 1861 the tone of the *Catholic Telegraph*'s pleas for national unity remained conservative enough for a bishop more sympathetic to President Lincoln to regret the *Telegraph*'s "aid of treason."[90]

Nonetheless, Purcell moved decisively to support the northern armies after secession, ordering the Stars and Stripes to hang above his cathedral and visiting Ohio troops in Union camps. Over the next two years Purcell's support for the Union turned into advocacy of emancipation. This position required courage, since most Irish and German Catholics in Ohio supported peace Democrats eager to negotiate a settlement with the Confederates.[91] In one speech that summarized his thinking, Purcell began by explaining why, unlike most Catholics, he would vote the Republican ticket. The reason was slavery, which he described as "an unchristian evil, opposed to the freedom of mankind, and to the growth and glory of a

Archbishop John B. Purcell of Cincinnati, 1863.

Republican country." He continued, "The Catholic Church has ever been the friend of human freedom. It was Christ's mission to set men free, and Christian people disregard his precepts and principles and example, when they seek to uphold or perpetuate involuntary human servitude."[92]

Why did Purcell support abolition? Support from his brother, also a priest, and also "a *little* inclined to abolitionism" was crucial.[93] That William Rosecrans, the brother of Archbishop Purcell's auxiliary bishop, Sylvester Rosecrans, served as a Union general also may have been important.[94] General Rosecrans distanced himself from the term "abolitionist," but he also argued that the "traditions of the religion" he professed prohibited him from following James McMaster and becoming an "apologist of the legal slave laws of our own land by which man and woman are made cattle."[95]

Purcell's seminary training with the Sulpicians in Paris, his distaste for Gothic architecture, his willingness to lecture in Protestant churches, and his criticism of the Jesuits also suggest a liberal Catholic temperament.[96] In 1834 Purcell regretted, in a letter to a fellow bishop, Gregory XVI's attack on liberty of conscience. In 1849 he urged Brownson to temper his attacks on liberalism, to remember the moderate "spirit and traditions" of Boston's first bishop, Bishop Cheverus.[97] As late as 1875 he reassured John Henry Newman that the abrasive James McMaster did not speak for all American Catholics.[98]

An indicator of Purcell's views on slavery was the *Catholic Telegraph*'s endorsement of Bishop Dupanloup's pastoral on the subject. (Purcell later joined the French bishop in battling against the declaration of papal infallibility.)[99] Purcell met Dupanloup in Rome in 1862, and it seems likely that the two discussed American slavery, since Dupanloup, inspired by Cochin, had just issued a pastoral urging emancipation. Even if "the abolition party has rendered itself odious," Dupanloup explained, "our religion is the religion of the free man."[100]

Dupanloup's letter, like Cochin's book, received a warm welcome from American liberals. French bishops were unaccustomed to tributes from American politicians, but Pennsylvania's Thaddeus Stevens, perhaps the most determined congressional opponent of slavery, lauded Dupanloup, the "great and good and wise bishop," before his Senate colleagues.[101]

Purcell quickly followed Dupanloup's lead. The editors of the *Catholic Telegraph* in Cincinnati defended Dupanloup and the idea of freedom for all races, since "[s]upernatural and moral freedom will never take place without the natural and the physical."[102] In October 1862 Purcell publicly endorsed immediate emancipation because southerners often refused to educate their slaves or allow them to marry.[103] By the following year Purcell had become more insistent. He ordered a reprinting of Daniel O'Connell's 1843 attack on American slavery and placed an original, signed copy of O'Connell's address on display at the *Catholic Telegraph* office.[104] "We have said and we now repeat it," explained the *Catholic Telegraph*, "that slavery and the Catholic Church could never get along well together." One Ohio correspondent congratulated the paper for attacking the view, held by many Catholics, "that the Church of God favors the enslavement of one portion of the human family by another." Such Catholics "quote Scripture and the *Freeman's Journal* alternately to establish the *divinity* and *constitutionality* of the barbarous institution of slavery."[105]

Significantly, Purcell also saw French liberal Catholics as allies. Beginning in September 1863 the *Catholic Telegraph* gave extended coverage to a Catholic congress held that summer at Malines, Belgium.[106] At Malines, Montalembert had given the two most important speeches of his life, ringing pleas for the church to reconcile itself to the modern world of freedom and democracy. In one brief reference he also invoked his late friend Lacordaire, by declaring that whoever tolerated "servitude" for black or white did not struggle in the "sacred cause" of mankind.[107] (Lacordaire had also attacked the "scourge" of slavery in the United States upon his election to the elite Académie Française in 1861.)[108]

Purcell highlighted Montalembert's attack on slavery before a Cincinnati audience, claiming that in Belgium "the denunciation was received with unanimous plaudits, not one of that distinguished Catholic assembly but responded with undistinguished approval."[109] Brownson had already hailed Purcell's "moral grandeur," and in a review of Montalembert's speech he thanked the "liberal Catholics of France, the only Catholics in Europe who sympathize with the loyal people of the Union in their war against the slavery rebellion."[110]

Republicans and abolitionists heaped praise upon Purcell, with the *New York Evening Post* mistakenly concluding that the "best and most respectable priests in that Church, as well as the great mass of the laity are true to the Union and to the cause of human freedom."[111] Many American Catholics, however, reacted less enthusiastically. James McMaster established the dominant tone. A series of scorching editorials and letters in the *New York Freeman's Journal* columns attacked Purcell and those who "trail their sacerdotal vestments in the carnage of fratricidal war."[112] McMaster admitted that Dupanloup's "Catholic principles" had not driven him to the "unbridled rant of the New England preachers and infidel lecturers" but professed shock that Dupanloup would describe all men as "free." (And McMaster added, "Dupanloup's Pastoral on American slavery has met very little consideration among the Catholics in France. . . .") Instead, the spiritual slavery common to all humans "can be done away with only by the Redemption through Christ," and physical emancipation is best achieved through "quiet interior work on masters and slaves."[113]

Writers in the *New York Freeman's Journal* also cited Jaime Balmes and Archbishop Kenrick's moral theology as proof of the need for gradual abolition, denied the authority of Daniel O'Connell to speak on the slavery question, and described abolitionism as "anti-Catholic": "All its affiliations and developments are anti-Catholic. It is akin to the Red-Republicanism of Europe."[114] "We know it is hard for a man to bear perpetual servitude," concluded one reader, but it is also "hard that one man should live forever in poverty and rags, without any fault of his, whilst others revel in ease and luxury."[115]

Private sentiments were no less severe. Father Wiget rejected the argument of Bishop Dupanloup. "Father Rector," a Jesuit diarist reported in 1862, referring to Wiget, "says it [Dupanloup's pastoral letter on slavery] is wrong in many places, and unworthy [of] a Catholic bishop; that Dupanloup knows nothing about the facts of the case; that our Savior and St. Paul never preached universal emancipation, and that it is a forced conclusion to derive such doctrine from the text, 'Do unto others etc.'"[116] The vicar of the New Orleans archdiocese thought that Dupanloup and other French liberal Catholics eager to address the topic were ignorant. They are "blind men," he told his bishop, "who speak of colors."[117]

One of the most prominent American bishops, Martin Spalding of Louisville, later archbishop of Baltimore, felt compelled to take action. Spalding blamed the war on the "hypocritical preachers of the North, with their cant about the Bible & Slavery." In 1862 he led the fight against a Union loyalty oath for Kentucky residents. In November of that year, he endured a dinner with the Union general William Rosecrans. The general, Spalding observed, kept "thrusting on us the odious subject of abolition." On January 1, 1863, noting in his diary that Lincoln's Emancipation Proclamation had officially taken effect, Spalding complained of "three to four millions of half-civilized Africans to murder their Masters & Mistresses! And all this under the pretense of philanthropy! . . . Puritanism, with its preachers & Common Schools, has at length ruined the country, as we all foresaw & predicted it would."[118]

After Archbishop Purcell's *Catholic Telegraph*, published just across the Ohio River from his Louisville diocese, began carrying what Spalding called "straight-out abolition" articles, the Louisville bishop drafted an analysis of the situation. Following a consultation with Archbishop Kenrick of Baltimore, who also disagreed with Purcell's attempt to "claim for the Church the credit for opposing slavery in the past centuries," Spalding mailed his analysis to the Congregatio de Propaganda Fide in Rome.[119]

Spalding's letter explicitly criticized Purcell and "those very politicians who now clamor so much against the *rebellion*." Abolitionists remained the "most devoted friends of Kossuth, Garibaldi, and nearly every other wicked charlatan of our times." After the war northern leaders possessed by an almost "satanic" hatred of Catholicism would soon turn against the church.[120]

Published as the musings of "A Kentucky Priest" in *L'Osservatore Romano*, the semiofficial Vatican newspaper, Spalding's letter signaled renewed interest in the Vatican position on the struggle.[121] From the beginning of the war, Vatican officials maintained a studied neutrality, but the Jesuits at *Civiltà Cattolica* traced the origins of the conflict to a mania for liberty and disrespect for authority endemic in liberal political culture. That Italian nationalists then besieging the papacy and seizing convents and monasteries viewed a blood-soaked United States as an exemplary republic seemed a bitter irony.[122]

The increasingly drastic measures taken by the Lincoln administration further alienated Roman observers. Pius IX, according to one 1864 British observer, "could not conceal from me that all his sympathies were with the Southern confederacy," and an American diplomat claimed that the Jesuits opposed negotiations with Garibaldi even "as they are and were, with few exceptions [opposed] to the cause of the Union."[123] Immediate emancipation appeared to Vatican officials a provocative gesture sure to prolong the war and prevent a peaceful resolution to the admittedly grave problem of slavery. In perhaps the surest sign of the Vatican's disfavor, a writer for *L'Osservatore Romano* compared the Republicans, or "radicali," to French revolutionaries and characterized Republicans as "inflamed by puritan and abolitionist fanaticism and motivated by a poisonous hatred."[124]

The pope wrote well-publicized letters to Archbishop Hughes in New York and Archbishop Odin in New Orleans, urging a negotiated settlement, and had a perfunctory exchange with Jefferson Davis. The American minister to Italy, George Perkins Marsh, was pleased to note that Italian nationalists used the papal correspondence with Davis to demonstrate "sympathy" between "the great enemy of African liberty in America, and the great enemy of all liberty in Europe."[125]

IV

By the mid-1860s volleys between liberal Catholics, anti-Catholic nationalists, and ultramontane Catholics flew back and forth across the Atlantic. As early as 1863, musing on the subject of Catholicism, Ralph Waldo Emerson declared, "When the liberals of Europe join in desiring to strip the Pope of his temporalities, they are led by a just instinct. It is the political character of the Roman Church that makes it incompatible with our institutions, & unwelcome here."[126] A year later, perched on the opposite side of a widening ideological divide, the Missouri Jesuit Pierre De Smet explained to a Belgian acquaintance that American abolitionists and Republicans "belong indeed to the [French revolutionary] class of '93." He added, "One must acknowledge that the liberalism of our young America exceeds that of its elder brothers in Europe."[127]

In Rome and the United States liberal Catholicism lost ground. Following his celebrated plea for a free church in a free state at the 1863 Malines conference, Montalembert received a private letter from the Vatican sharply critical of his remarks, and Vatican officials also released a statement denouncing a group of German Catholic theologians insisting on the right to scientific freedom.[128] In response a discouraged Lord Acton ended the *British and Home Foreign Review*, and Brownson termed the Vatican letter to the German theologians "replete with the spirit of fear."[129]

James McMaster, by contrast, applauded papal criticism of "Catholic savants."[130] More generally, he seemed energized by the last years of the war and by the prospects for a new electoral surge by the Democratic Party. Dismissing accusations from Republicans that he was a "copperhead Jesuit," McMaster used the columns of the *New York Freeman's Journal* to praise efforts to negotiate an end to the war.[131] He made contact with leading Democrats (often Catholics) and traveled the country baiting Republicans and criticizing attempts to suppress his journal.[132] By the end of the war, he was again attacking "Puritan ruled schools" and publishing warnings about a "Puritan venom" that would soon "naturally turn upon the Catholic Church."[133]

Brownson's plight was more poignant. Each issue of *Brownson's Quar-*

terly Review—134 pages in October 1863, 128 pages in January 1864—became an agony, as health problems ranging from blurred vision to gout slowed his labor. Most painfully, Brownson's gnarled hands found it difficult, after so many pages, so many words, to grasp a pen. He also feared for two sons serving in the Union army, and another son about to volunteer.[134] By 1864 Brownson's financial and physical condition was such that friends rallied to purchase him a lifetime annuity.[135]

Later, after the war, Brownson would again change course, reverting to a more ultramontane position and falsely claiming, "A *liberal* Catholic I am not, never was, save in appearance for a brief moment, and never can be."[136] At the time, however, the costs of Brownson's liberal allegiances were very real. On July 11, 1864, his son William Brownson died in a stagecoach accident en route to enlisting in the Union army. Six weeks later his son Ned Brownson was killed while rallying Union troops at Reams' Station, Virginia. Brownson had already announced in January that his review would no longer treat strictly theological questions, but after the death of his two sons, "both true patriots, both ardent lovers of liberty," he halted publication of the review altogether.[137]

In an essay entitled "Explanations to Catholics," published in the final issue of *Brownson's Quarterly Review*, Brownson lashed out at his opponents. (As a French admirer put it, the grieving father's words were "bathed in tears.")[138] He began by regretting the influence of the Jesuits in the United States, "a society so destitute of loyalty that it could look on with indifference and see the nation rent asunder." He went on to attack Vatican rule in the Papal States, blind obedience to Thomas Aquinas, and clerical resistance to change. "A good orthodox Catholic," he concluded, can still believe that "definitions are reformable."[139]

James McMaster did not comment on the final issue of *Brownson's Quarterly Review*, perhaps because he had recently dismissed Brownson's "ludicrous changes and inconsistencies" and identified him as "in the hands of an Abolition clique, mainly supported by the Red republicans of 1848."[140] A New York Jesuit wrote to his French colleagues that "no one regrets" Brownson's decision to end the *Review*.[141]

Other observers were more sympathetic. Brownson's place in the liberal Catholic imagination had by 1865 become such that a young German theologian who had never visited the United States, Franz Xaver Kraus, could confide to his diary that Roman authorities seemed determined to persecute Catholic intellectuals hoping to reconcile the church with the "modern world," and then list Lacordaire, Montalembert, Dupanloup, Acton, Döllinger, and Brownson.[142]

Brownson's old friend Charles Montalembert also expressed his grief at Brownson's "loss of two noble sons." He then regretted that on the question of the American Civil War and other issues "contemporary Catholics are led astray by their fanatical and *slavish* mouthpieces." Montalembert guessed that *Brownson's Quarterly Review* had been suppressed by the same "men who are now omnipotent throughout almost all Catholic Europe, and whose only task or aim is to denounce and to smother every honest and straightforward Catholic." Montalembert included himself among the denounced and smothered, as well as Bishop Dupanloup, Ignaz von Döllinger, Lacordaire, and Brownson. All were "devoted children and soldiers of truth . . . struck down, wounded to the heart by the poisoned shafts of the new Inquisitors."[143]

Chapter Four
THE NATION

I

Ulysses S. Grant gave the most publicized speech of his presidency in Des Moines, Iowa, on October 29, 1875, before a reunion of three thousand veterans of the Union Army of Tennessee. The notoriously taciturn Grant rarely spoke at such gatherings, and the assembled soldiers were startled when their former commander, seated on the platform with other wartime notables, accepted the invitation of William T. Sherman to address the crowd. According to one account, Grant's hands shook as he moved to the podium, and he dropped the pages on which he had scrawled his notes. Sherman and the other former generals scurried to retrieve the pages, and Grant then began to speak. He first urged his former comrades not to permit even one dollar "to be appropriated to the support of any sectarian school." Such aid might destroy the public schools, Grant argued, "the promoter of that intelligence which is to preserve us as a nation." He also warned, ominously, "If we are to have another contest in the near future of our national existence, I predict that the dividing line will not be Mason and Dixon's but between patriotism and intelligence on the one side, and superstition, ambition and ignorance on the other."[1]

The code word "superstition" needed little interpretation, and audience members understood that Grant referred to a Catholic church that he saw as increasingly aggressive. Newspaper editors across the country commented on the speech, and one of Grant's first biographers chose to reprint the address in full.[2]

Grant knew that the Catholic issue had already become crucial in that fall's most fiercely contested election, Ohio's gubernatorial campaign. Rutherford B. Hayes, the Republican candidate for governor, soon to be catapulted into the presidency, had hammered his Democratic opponents for allowing Catholic priests access to state prisons and asylums. Hayes confided to his diary, "I think the interesting point is *to rebuke the Democracy by a defeat for subserviency to Roman Catholic demands.*"[3] Hayes added that the "history of all modern nations" warned against Catholic aggression. "Look at Germany," he cautioned, "at Italy, at Belgium, and heed the warning they give."[4] Another Ohio Republican, and future president, James Garfield, worried about a Catholic assault on "modern civilization" and concluded that "our fight in Ohio is only a small portion of that battle field."[5]

The editor of *Harper's Weekly* offered his own perspective on politicians "willing to permit American priests to enter upon the political field as the . . . allies of slavery." "Every ultramontane," he concluded, "is a Democrat and every ultramontane and Democratic victory means the plunder of industrious citizens."[6] In St. Louis, Washington University's president, William Greenleaf Eliot, a longtime battler against Catholic influence in the St. Louis public schools, expressed his horror at a local priest's demand that Catholics support political candidates friendly to the church. "This," Eliot wrote in his diary, "is war to the knife."[7]

In his December message to Congress that year, Grant urged the passage of a constitutional amendment, drafted by Senator James Blaine of Maine, banning government aid to religious schools. Grant also urged taxation on "vast amounts of untaxed church property," a transparently anti-Catholic measure since only the Catholic Church owned vast amounts of property—in schools, orphanages, and charitable institutions—in addition to the land beneath its churches. Such legislation could protect American citizens from tyranny, Grant argued, "whether directed by the demagogue or by priestcraft."[8] Republican newspapers immediately applauded Grant's initiative, and Grant received a wave of congratulatory letters. "The Catholics will rave," Senator Justin Morrill of Vermont conceded, "but I suppose there is not one who has ever voted for free-men, free-schools, or the Republican party in war or peace."[9]

Discussion of religion in the schools continued through the summer of 1876.[10] The Blaine amendment passed the House with ease, but Democratic legislators blocked the bill in the Senate. In the debate before the final defeat of the bill, the Vermont Republican George Edmunds declared that Catholics belonged to a church that denied "liberty of conscience."[11] The Indiana Republican Oliver P. Morton compared opponents of the bill to Confederates.[12] Later that fall James Garfield attributed Democratic gains in the November elections to the "combined power of rebellion, catholicism and whiskey." "We shall have a hard, uncomfortable struggle," he concluded, "to save the fruits of the great war."[13]

II

Congressman Garfield's brooding diary entry marked an uneasiness about Catholicism's disruptive force in the newly reconfigured nation—a fear, as the reformer Francis Ellingwood Abbott put it, that Catholicism remained "hostile to every fundamental principle of the United States constitution and of modern civilization."[14] In the first decade after the war, leading Republican politicians, ministers, and editors—including Grant, Garfield, and Hayes, George William Curtis and Eugene Lawrence at *Harper's Weekly*, E. L. Godkin of the *Nation*, Joseph Medill of the *Chicago Tribune*, and the editors of the *New York Times*—all emphasized the Catholic threat. They worried that an authoritarian church continued to stand against liberal reform, that an international church threatened national unity, and that Catholicism might slow scientific and intellectual progress.

For reformers concern about Catholicism was nothing new. Most reformers traced their activist roots to the antislavery struggle and frequently recalled Catholic hostility to that once unfashionable cause. The poet John Greenleaf Whittier explained in 1873, "I am not blind to the hostility of leading influences in the Catholic Church to republicanism and religious and political liberty. As an abolitionist I have seen the Bishops and priests oppose the abolition of slavery while a large body of their people were persecuting and abusing the poor blacks in our cities."[15] The author Lydia Maria Child, in a letter read to the final meeting of the American Anti-Slavery Society, also linked slavery and Catholic influence. Slavery had been eliminated, Child conceded, but reformers now had to

Thomas Nast cartoon from *Harper's Weekly,* March 19, 1870. Catholic priests and bishops, instead of Confederates, fire upon Fort Sumter and try to destroy public education and the nation.

worry about Catholic immigrants "led blindfolded by a church hostile to every form of Protestant faith, and strongly opposed to free institutions and the dissemination of knowledge."[16]

The enormously influential political cartoonist Thomas Nast, working for the leading Republican journal, *Harper's Weekly*, sketched Catholics in place of Confederates at Fort Sumter and would frequently warn of growing Catholic influence in American society.[17] *Miss Columbia's Public School*, a fiction by Charles Henry Pullen, illustrated by Nast, begins with a battle between white southern and white northern schoolboys over the rights of an African American classmate that ends only with the southerners' surrender in the "fourth round." But attention then turns to Jesuits "prowling" the halls, mischievous "Tammany" children, an infallible pope, and drunken Irishmen. These threats to the public school, too, are mastered by a schoolyard coalition of "liberal Catholics," "Protestants of all nationalities," "Hans" (a German boy), Jews, "infidels and heretics," and even the "heathen Chinee."[18]

The focus on individual autonomy that animated abolitionists in the

1850s continued to nurture a concomitant anti-Catholicism. When Catholics urged restrictions on Chinese immigration to California, for example, a Methodist minister, Otis Gibson, concluded that Catholic attacks on the rights of Chinese immigrants made sense for a church "historically known to be opposed to free, civil and religious institutions in all lands, known to be openly, bitterly and persistently opposed to the system of public schools, the open bible, the free press and free speech." At congressional hearings Gibson complimented the Chinese for having "no hierarchy" and called Catholics "decidedly" more dangerous than the Chinese for American democracy.[19]

Tensions between Catholicism and women's rights advocates also became more visible. Just as abolitionists compared the slaveholder to the priest, women's rights advocates linked the despotic husband with the pope. "We must take scripture in its proper connexion," wrote Elizabeth Wilson as early as 1849, "what absurdities could we not prove by scripture if we would take detached passages. POPERY, DOMESTIC SLAVERY, POLITICAL DESPOTISM, and this ARISTOCRACY OF SEX."[20]

The expression of such sentiments became more frequent after the war as suffragists attempted to win the vote for women, not simply for African American men. In 1869 Elizabeth Cady Stanton explained that "it is not possible for a foreigner and a Catholic to take in the grandeur of the American idea of individual rights, as more sacred than any civil or ecclesiastical organizations." She elaborated, "The human mind is ever oscillating between the extremes of authority and individualism; and if the former—the Catholic idea—finds lodgment in the minds of this people, we ring the death-knell of American liberties."[21] Other writers for suffragist publications referred to the "idolatrous perversions of the Romish faith" and asserted that "in all ages and climes, where it has a foothold, the Roman Catholic church has been the deadly opponent of progress and freedom. . . ."[22]

In fact, Catholics did not always oppose women's suffrage, and many non-Catholic intellectuals did. (Boston's Francis Parkman, using a logic popular with French and South American liberals, warned that suffrage for women meant power for priests, since Catholic women would follow clerical commands with "edifying docility and zeal.")[23] Ultimately, in Boston and Berlin, Catholic leaders encouraged Catholic women to vote after the passage of the first suffrage laws, in part out of practical concern that Catholic interests be protected in competitive political arenas.[24]

Still, through most of the late nineteenth century, Catholics, including many Catholic women, did resist an individualist language of women's rights.[25] The Catholic argument against woman's suffrage and marriage law reform rested less upon biblical proof texts than its Protestant counterpart did (although Denver's bishop remained convinced that the apostle Paul demonstrated that only "old maids" desired suffrage).[26] Instead, as in the slavery debate of the 1850s, Catholics argued, "The social unit is the family, not the individual." Of unmarried women, only nuns, women organized in a corporate body, received unqualified Catholic approval.[27]

A second and more important source of hostility to Catholicism after the war did not derive from suffragists. Instead, it rested on a heightened sense of American nationalism, a conviction that the crucible of battle had forged a nation where once had stood a rickety Union. Driven by the exigencies of war, congressional Republicans had funded an army of one million men, distributed land through the Homestead Act, issued a national currency, and exerted greater federal control over the country's banking system.[28] As contemporaries frequently observed, the experience of the United States paralleled that of Prussia, where war with Austria and then France led to a unified Germany, and that of Italy, where the collapse of the Papal States allowed the emergence of a single political entity in 1870. Abraham Lincoln became the American Bismarck, the prairie Cavour.[29]

Unsurprisingly, the years immediately following the war witnessed a rhetorical deluge on national themes, including the establishment of the most important journal of liberal opinion in the postwar period, inevitably entitled the *Nation*. And like their European counterparts, American nationalists became increasingly wary of Catholic intentions. The catalyzing event was the Vatican's release of the Syllabus of Errors in December 1864, with its famous concluding denial that "the Roman Pontiff can and should reconcile himself to and agree with progress, liberalism and modern civilization."[30]

The chaotic preparation of this document is now understood (Pius IX seems never to have read the final version), and its origins as a modest salvo against a genuinely anticlerical Italian nationalism. But an important target for syllabus supporters in the Vatican became a liberal nationalism ascendant on both sides of the Atlantic.[31]

Scornful reaction to the Syllabus of Errors dominated the European

Thomas Nast cartoon from *Harper's Weekly*, February 19, 1870. Even as Queen Victoria (*far right*), Otto von Bismarck (*second from right*), and other European leaders applaud the separation of church and state, Catholics in the United States try to bring church and state together through funding of parochial schools and Catholic charities.

press in early 1865. In the United States the Civil War provided a distraction, and Archbishop Martin Spalding nervously reassured Americans that papal condemnation of European "radicals and infidels" implied no criticism of "our noble Constitution."[32] Still, the idea that American Catholics, like southern Confederates, threatened the foundations of the nation-state became a truism in some religious and intellectual circles. Either American Catholics must deny Vatican claims, one minister explained, or they must "renounce their allegiance as citizens."[33] A writer for the *Independent* was more blunt: "The comprehensive lesson from the [Syllabus of Errors] is that *Romanism is incompatible with Republican institutions*. Like slavery, it is a hostile element lodged within the nation, gnawing and burning it like a caustic."[34]

These fears only became more widespread in the late 1860s and 1870s.[35] Just before President Grant urged Congress to bar any aid to religious schools, Grant's pastor and confidant, Minister J. P. Newman, bluntly warned that the nation found itself in a battle with the "uncompromising claims of a politico-religious hierarchy, whose head is in Rome, whose body is in America." As Grant listened from his pew, Newman paid tribute to the German chancellor Otto von Bismarck, former British prime minister William Gladstone, and "another in America," united "against a common foe."[36]

The most intense battles occurred in Germany, where Bismarck inaugurated the so-called Kulturkampf in the early 1870s, harassing Catholic institutions, banning members of most religious orders from German soil, and imprisoning priests and bishops.[37] During the same years Italian nationalists engaged Vatican authorities in a bitter debate over the role of Catholicism in the new nation, a standoff destined to endure for two generations. French liberals passed a stream of anticlerical laws after attaining power in 1879.[38]

In Britain leading liberals viewed Catholicism as a formidable enemy, and Gladstone composed a hugely popular pamphlet, *The Vatican Decrees*, denying that British Catholics could simultaneously be loyal to the papacy and to the nation. (Bismarck congratulated Gladstone for "encountering the same foe" and standing "shoulder to shoulder.") British liberals took to pondering whether Catholic Ireland threatened national stability in the same way that Bavarian and Polish Catholics threatened a unified Germany.[39] In North America, Canadian politics periodically erupted with intense arguments over funds for Catholic schools, and fears of French Catholic disloyalty, while Mexican liberals also understood the checking of Catholic influence as one of their central tasks.[40]

The career of Goldwin Smith, British liberal, American professor, and Canadian newspaper editor, suggests the international fusion of anti-Catholicism and liberal nationalism. When Smith first visited the United States, in 1864 as an Oxford don, he became convinced, after consultation with Charles Eliot Norton and other leading American reformers, that "the priests go with the Oligarchical party [Democrats] against the reformer Republicans on the usual ground of antipathy to real freedom." When visiting Illinois, he regretted the "bitterness and superstition of Catholicism."[41] In 1870, now teaching at Cornell University, Smith excitedly told a friend that Germany's victory in the Franco-Prussian War marked the triumph of the "future over the past" and the "Gettysburg of Europe." Later, in Toronto, Smith worried about Catholicism's ennervating effect on Canadian prosperity.[42]

Other Americans shared these sentiments. New York publishers rushed to reprint Gladstone's *Vatican Decrees*, and the leading American church historian, Philip Schaff, added a commentary to one edition regretting the Vatican's "direct antagonism to the liberal tendencies of the age"[43] James Garfield stayed up late in the evening worrying about what he termed the "papal assault on secular schools in France and Germany," and the American minister to Italy George P. Marsh explained to a friend, "Our Popish friends are growing more and more bellicose. Nothing short of blood will satisfy them."[44]

The American reception of the Kulturkampf is also suggestive. Republican organs such as the *New York Times*, *Harper's Weekly*, the *New York Tribune*, and the *Chicago Tribune* approved of Bismarck's strategy, and the sources of American information themselves were partisan.[45] The German correspondent for the *Nation* during much of this period was Friedrich Kapp, a Republican Party leader in the United States after fleeing Germany in 1848, and a prominent anti-Catholic Liberal after his return to Berlin. During the 1850s, while in the United States, Kapp had shared the anti-Catholicism of other German American liberals, and after his return to Germany he informed *Nation* readers in 1871 that the stringent measures advocated by Bismarck were justified. He also warned Americans that Catholic "tactics and craft are as yet not fully understood by the people of the United States, where the Irish element is the rank and file, which are pushed back and forward, like the pawns on a chessboard at the will of the players in Rome."[46]

The American ambassador to Germany at the height of the Kulturkampf, the historian George Bancroft, sent a steady stream of missives to the State Department defending Bismarck's "firmness and moderation." Bancroft first noted the parallels between American and German history, concluding, "The men who fought successfully for our Union opened the way for the renovation of Germany." He then added, "It is well understood in Germany that during our civil war the sympathies of the ultramontane Catholics were strongly enlisted for the southern insurgents." Indeed, "the selfsame malign [Catholic] influence is at work in Spain, in France, in Rome, in Italy, in Southern Germany, and in Austria. Nay it extends to England and North Germany and the United States."[47]

A decade after Bismarck and Pope Leo XIII negotiated a settlement to the German crisis, the most influential American political scientist of the period, Columbia University's John Burgess, continued to ponder Catholic aggression. (Burgess, like so many American scholars, had studied in Germany with the professorial architects of German anti-Catholic policies.) To Burgess, "the unnational Jesuit order" deserved exile, and the Prussian state needed to turn the Catholic Church into a "modern national institution." Fortunately, "[m]odern thought, science, and education are destructive to the tenets of Romanism. If the clergy of that church are to be not only exposed but compelled to such disciplines, there will soon be few upon whom the hierarchy can rely."[48]

Similar fear of Catholic ambitions informed Americans' approval of Italian unification. John Greenleaf Whittier described one New York meeting in honor of the unified Italy as a check on "American ecclesiastics."[49] William Lloyd Garrison wrote, "The overthrow of the despotic power of the Pope, in regard to civil liberty and the rights of conscience, removes the most formidable barrier which has ever been erected against free thought, free speech, free inquiry, and popular institutions."[50]

Self-conscious theorists of American nationalism in the 1860s and 1870s, like their European counterparts, also instinctively mistrusted Catholicism. Both the nation and its administrative arm, the state, seemed vulnerable to attack from an international church determined to establish and control its own hospitals, orphanages, and, especially, schools. Revealing in this regard was Francis Lieber, Columbia professor, legal scholar, president of the New York Loyal Publication League during the

Civil War, and promoter of free trade.[51] Lieber wrote an important analysis of American nationalism after the war, and exerted a decisive influence on the period's most famous piece of oratory on the subject, the Massachusetts senator Charles Sumner's "Are We a Nation?," as well as Elisha Mulford's *The Nation*.[52]

In varying degrees these figures all expressed a fear of Catholic influence. Sumner regretted the "condition of Rome under papal power," and Mulford explained American Catholics' hostility to the northern war effort as part of a necessary "antagonism of Roman ecclesiasticism to the nation."[53] The fatal sin of the Jesuits, in Lieber's view, remained hostility "to national organic unity and to nationalism in its varied manifestations." Lieber also became convinced, as he informed Congressman James Garfield, that "the danger which threatens us from Catholicism is immense."[54]

The sources of Lieber's fears included two of Europe's most distinguished scholars, Germany's Johann Caspar Bluntschli, and France's Edouard Laboulaye. Lieber worked with the two men on international legal codes, and he peppered them with questions about the role of Catholicism in European politics. "You lately mentioned the Catholics," he told Bluntschli in 1868. "What is their position in Germany? Have the Catholics only become more intense, Ultramontane, and bolder in their religious materialism, or are they also increasing in numbers, as is the case in this country?"[55]

Laboulaye and Bluntschli confirmed Lieber's fears. Laboulaye conceded that the problem was complex but described some French bishops as "fanatics and ambitious," while Bluntschli, as Lieber excitedly told Charles Sumner, warned of the "fierce anti-national, anti-liberty spirit of present Romanism, or Ultramontanism, or Jesuitism,—it is all the same."[56] In 1865, in a letter congratulating the United States for abolishing slavery, Bluntschli emphasized to his American friend that he was writing pamphlets to counteract "ultramontane and religious intolerance." He also bemoaned ultramontane Catholicism's habit of preying upon "the uneducated, the natural need for authority and the tradition and acquired beliefs of the masses."[57]

Predictably, Lieber defended Bismarck's attacks on Catholicism, noting to James Garfield that "Bismarck has manfully declared war against the Ultramontanes." He again related Bluntschli's concerns to Garfield, warning that "for the first time in all history Southern German Catholics have become Ultramontane and the Gallican church exists no more." A few months before his death Lieber confided to Bluntschli his fears about the "baneful influence" of Catholicism in the United States and the "dark future it is preparing." Bismarck had a "duty" to expel Jesuits and "dangerous-mischief doers."[58]

Other scholars and public figures expressed similar fears. The onetime abolitionist and *Independent* editor Joseph P. Thompson compared German Catholics to Confederates, both groups "insisting upon a virtual share of sovereignty as a condition of its allegiance." "The deeper question," Thompson explained, "[is] whether the Nation shall exist—the nation in its entirety and its integrity—with its patriotic consciousness, with its self-ordered institutions, its laws, its schools, its arts and sciences, its community of ideas and interests." "In the United States," he told a British audience, "[Catholicism] would destroy our free school and our religious liberty; in Great Britain it would destroy the unit of your empire; in France it would bring back the Bourbon to the throne, in Italy and Germany it would cause disruption, contention, [and] incessant war."[59]

Underwriting the belief that Catholicism threatened national identity was a more profound, less fully articulated concern: that Catholicism stood opposed to modernity wholesale. The Catholic Middle Ages, in particular, became regarded in the nineteenth century as a cultural trough between the glorious achievements of the ancient Greeks and the modern dawn heralded by Renaissance humanism and the Reformation. The scholar most influential in defining the term "Renaissance," the Swiss historian Jacob Burckhardt, referred to the Middle Ages in 1860 as a time of "faith, illusion and childish prepossession."[60] When Brown University students learned about the Renaissance from their instructor that same year, they were informed that the "habit of inquiry" begun during the Renaissance was not only the "great preparation for the Reformation" but the most important challenge to "the ignorance, the brute force, the feudal insubordination of the middle age."[61]

More specific anxieties—that Catholicism threatened intellectual and economic progress—fed into this larger narrative. That they took on greater importance in the 1870s reflects a heightened sense among liberals that the nation (a political community), and not the church (a religious community), must claim primary loyalty from its members. In turn, and in part as a response, Catholic leaders took a more radical stance on the matter of whether the institutional church could serve as a source of authoritative truth claims. The 1870 declaration by the First Vatican Council that a pope might speak infallibly on matters of faith and morals seemed calculated to shock in this regard. Drafted by conservative bishops and Jesuits, the dogma of infallibility challenged a liberalism that conservative Catholics understood as ceding religious truth to either the scientific method or intellectual fashion.[62] A New York City Jesuit put it more bluntly in an 1870 sermon, expressing his hope that the declaration of infallibility had "killed the spirit of Liberalism among Catholics."[63]

When Catholics referred to "dogmatic" church teachings non-Catholics bristled. James Turner has sketched how late nineteenth-century intellectuals saw "private judgment" as ballast against the corrupting weight of institutional religion, and cultivated a disdain for the traditional Christian virtues of meekness and, perhaps especially, obedience.[64] Ralph Waldo Emerson deemed the claim of papal infallibility as "gross" as "anything in the history of barbarous tribes."[65] The scholar and editor Charles Eliot Norton visited Rome during the First Vatican Council, in 1870, and watched in St. Peter's as the bishops voted the crucial constitution, *De Fide*. The world, he informed readers of the *Nation*, had become divided "between the principle of authority and that of freedom in matters of opinion, between faith and scepticism, between supernaturalism and science, between obscurantism and intelligence." Pius IX realized this, Norton explained, and was marshaling his forces in the battle against Rome's "two most deadly enemies, scientific intelligence and political freedom."[66]

In contrast to intellectuals in the 1840s, those of the late nineteenth century rarely defended Protestant theology as such. Instead, they claimed that the Reformation, despite its sectarian zealotry, had spawned the best aspects of the modern world. Luther's theology—deemed "inconsiderable" by a leading American Protestant theologian during celebrations of the four hundredth anniversary of Luther's birth in 1883—was less consequential than the "social developments," "liberties," and "science" stemming from Luther's advocacy of private judgment.[67]

The argument that Catholicism literally impoverished nations unlucky enough to wallow under its dominion also received much attention, particularly through a widely noticed translation of the Belgian economist Emile de Laveleye's *Protestantism and Catholicism, in Their Bearing upon the Liberty and Prosperity of Nations*. Using the "scientific impartiality of the physiologist and naturalist," de Laveleye concluded, "Protestant

States are incomparably more advanced than Catholic." A Catholicism fascinated by miracles and pilgrimages lay "outside the atmosphere of modern thought."[68] For French readers de Laveleye wrote glowingly of American public schools and their decision not to teach "dogma." Fortunately for the United States, he asserted, Catholic priests were still "relatively few in number."[69]

Johann Caspar Bluntschli, Francis Lieber's friend, edited the German translation of de Laveleye's book and enthusiastically endorsed its claims.[70] And Max Weber's celebrated claim that there was an intimate relationship between Protestantism and capitalism must also be understood as a variant of this literature. Weber cited de Laveleye's arguments about Catholicism's backwardness, and his work, too, rested in part upon a European polarization between liberals and Catholics.[71] Weber, like many German liberals, criticized the German Catholic Center Party and expressed distaste for the continued influence of Catholicism on German peasants. In 1903 he argued that the constitutive features of modernity, especially capitalism and free political institutions, depended upon the emergence of a Calvinist asceticism. Weber's thesis became important in American intellectual life only after its translation into English in 1930, but the same convictions about Catholicism's enervating effect existed on both sides of the Atlantic.[72]

One footnote in Weber's *Protestant Ethic and the Spirit of Capitalism* linked Protestantism, autonomy, and experimental science. The contention that Catholicism inhibited science carried weight because of science's new standing as the most rigorous, honest form of intellectual inquiry, uncorrupted by ecclesiastical bias.[73] In the early 1870s prominent scientists such as John William Draper of the United States, John Tyndall of Britain, and Rudolf Virchow of Germany agreed that Catholicism and science were locked in mortal combat. Virchow coined the term "Kulturkampf," or struggle of civilizations, to describe the battle between German liberals and Catholics, and Tyndall emphasized that "free and cultivated minds" could never study science if Catholic priests exercised "dominant power."[74]

Draper's *History of the Conflict between Science and Religion* was especially influential, with fifty printings and translations into ten languages.[75] Draper described science as "undermining the dogmas of the papacy."[76] George Bancroft sent a copy of Draper's book to Bismarck, pointing with admiration to the author's "determined purpose to defend the policy of Germany in its conflict with the Vatican."[77]

Another American admirer of science, the Cornell president Andrew Dickson White, wrote *A History of the Warfare between Science and Religion* even as he fought "priestly influence" in Tammany Hall and found European Catholic piety appalling.[78] The *Nation* editor E. L. Godkin maintained that Catholic piety and the "intellectual habits" of scientists were incompatible. There are, Godkin concluded,"no pious Catholic scientific men of any note, and never will be if the Catholic clergy can help it."[79] A writer for the *Princeton Review* held that Catholic colleges, by their very nature, "can scarcely hold their own in physical or psychical science. The general substitution of scholastic for inductive logic would close every laboratory in the land. . . ."[80]

Massachusetts provided a final marker of the sentiment that Catholicism and science remained incompatible. Into the early twentieth century Harvard Law School refused to admit graduates of most Jesuit colleges as regular students. Harvard's president, Charles William Eliot, described the policy as a painful necessity, since the fixed Jesuit curriculum, with so few electives, denied "the increasing sanctity of the individual's gifts and will-power." Equally important, Jesuit enthusiasm for Latin and Greek left room for only a "trifling concession made to natural science."[81]

III

Catholics moved in precisely the opposite direction. If for many nineteenth-century American liberals the Middle Ages seemed a bleak interregnum of clerical tyranny (despite efforts by a small number of aesthetes like Henry Adams to detach medieval cathedrals, Saint Francis of Assisi, and Dante from their Catholic moorings), Catholics claimed the period as their own. Through Gregorian chant, Thomistic philosophy, and Gothic architecture, Catholics vowed to recover past glories. Midway into the twentieth century, students at New York's Jesuit-run Fordham University read, as a required text, an unsophisticated American product of Catholic medievalism entitled *The Thirteenth: Greatest of Centuries*.[82]

Seen through Catholic eyes, liberal nationalism seemed less the logical end point of human history than the destroyer of medieval Christian unity. Catholic cautions about the pretensions of the modern nation-state appeared as early as the 1840s when Italian reformers challenged Vatican control of the Papal States, and French liberals seemed determined to quarantine French Catholicism from Roman influence. Catholics agreed with their opponents that modern nationalism derived from the Reformation, but found this an unattractive lineage. An influential treatment by the Italian Jesuit Luigi Taparelli d'Azeglio described Catholicism's mission as one of curing the new illness of "national egoism" and "exaggerated nationalism."[83]

Similar views saturated the American Catholic community. A prominent Redemptorist priest worried in 1872 about the tendency of congressmen to no longer use the words " 'Republic,' or 'Federal Government,' or 'United States.'" Instead, "[i]t was '*Nation*,' 'Empire', etc., etc., *usque ad nauseam*, from beginning to end. To a reflecting mind, this language has an ominous significance."[84] An Italian Jesuit who began his career in Turin but ended it in California sarcastically explained to James McMaster, "[Y]ou know the State is every thing & every thing should be for the benefit of the State, cost what it may. Thanks to heaven, we have succeeded in this glorious 19th century in getting rid of that old-fogish maxim that the State is made for men."[85]

Catholics directed their ire, first, at coreligionists for foolishly favoring all "things national, then political, then Catholic."[86] But their primary animus was directed at European liberals. One Jesuit stationed in Italy informed an American colleague in 1877, "The Republican Party [in Italy] wishes centralized government which tends to absorb all in the God-State: power, wealth, science, religion. Such is the tendency of the party which triumphed over the Sonderbund in Switzerland, of Bismark [*sic*] in Germany. This is the purpose seen in Italy: Despotism presents itself under the mask of liberty. The times are sad and this is the hour of travail for our sanctification."[87]

In the United States there were frequent rallies and editorials in support of German Catholics. "About the sad condition of the church in Germany," a Wisconsin bishop wrote a Bavarian colleague in 1875, "we are well informed by our excellent catholic press."[88] At a Cincinnati meeting, a priest recently arrived from Germany persuaded one thousand German American Catholics to battle the "anti-clerical Colossus of Liberalism."[89]

Meetings to support Pius IX in his battles against Italian liberals also occurred across the country. By 1870 the provincial of the Maryland Jesuit province could inform his superior, "The afflictions of the Holy

Father have made ultramontanes of all of us here. . . ."[90] In 1878 an Italian priest in Chicago refused to celebrate a Mass in honor of King Victor Emmanuel, since under the king's leadership "the temporal dominion of the Supreme Pontiff had been taken away and religious orders had been suppressed." Attacks on the priest quickly appeared in an Italian American newspaper, which the priest dismissed as the rantings of a "diabolical, Garibaldian rag."[91]

Over time American Catholics inevitably shifted their attention away from European liberals and toward Republican politicians in the United States. One prominent Catholic writer argued that President Grant's 1875 plea for a ban on aid to church-related institutions proved that "[o]ur enemies in this country lack only the power to do here, what Bismarck and his friends are trying to do against us in Europe; and should the power be given them, they will do it in a more summary and shameless manner than their European models."[92] An Iowa German Catholic newspaper succinctly concluded that Grant had "inaugurated the Kulturkampf," and a California Jesuit lectured a Portland audience on affinities between "Liberalism in Belgium and Know-Nothingism in the United States."[93]

European Catholics used similar language when commenting upon events in the United States. The influential Italian Jesuit Matteo Liberatore had long admired the American Constitution, especially the division of power between the federal government and the states. In 1876, however, with one eye on Italy, Liberatore warned that the United States had "turned away from its original principles and moved toward liberal ones." He especially regretted that the "radical party" led by President Grant seemed dedicated to "compulsory education without God" and a "war on Catholicism." The French Catholic commentator Claudio Jannet warned that Republican Party "radicals have declared open war on Catholicism" and accused Grant, in his speech to the Army of Tennessee in Des Moines, of following Bismarck's lead.[94]

A steady stream of exiles also stiffened American Catholics' resolve. The Jesuit faculty at the nation's most influential Catholic seminary, in Woodstock, Maryland, for example, continually restocked itself with refugees. Father Camillo Mazzella taught dogmatic theology at Woodstock for eleven years after fleeing Naples ahead of Garibaldi's troops. Mazzella's Latin textbook *De religione et ecclesia*, defending the right of the state to promote the one true religion, went through five American editions, and he returned to Rome in 1878 and became perhaps the most influential curial cardinal.[95] Father Joseph Duverney left Switzerland for the United States after the Sonderbund of 1847–48, and Father Charles Maldonado arrived at Woodstock after Spanish liberals closed the Grand Central Seminary at Salamanca. "Persecution is again in vogue," wrote one contributor to an in-house Jesuit journal, "and in spite of the reiterated boast of liberal civilizers that its days were run."[96]

Similarly, Mexican Catholics and priests moved north of the Rio Grande after the victory of the anticlerical liberal party in 1867, reinforcing the already conservative tendencies of the French missionary bishops painfully erecting a Catholic infrastructure in Texas. One sympathetic bishop expressed his sympathy for "these poor people fleeing the excesses of the Liberals and Mexican heresy."[97] Thousands of German priests, nuns, and brothers fled to the American Midwest, with one group of Franciscan nuns departing Paderborn, where Bismarck had imprisoned their ultramontane bishop, and landing in Dubuque, Iowa, where they immediately began to staff parochial grade schools throughout the region.[98]

Divisions between Catholics and liberals extended to politics. During southern Reconstruction congressional Republicans declined to confiscate the property of white rebels, but instead chose to build schools for freed slaves and extend suffrage to African American males. Ultimately, congressmen hoped to plant what they considered the fundamental institutions of northern society—free labor markets, public education, and the ballot—in the reconstructed South. Freed slaves and ex-Confederates would inhabit a world much like the New England and midwestern small towns that loomed so large in the Republican imagination. "My dream," one Republican explained in 1866, "is of a model republic, extending equal protection and rights to all men. . . . The wilderness shall vanish, the church and school-house will appear; . . . the whole land will revive under the magic touch of free labor."[99]

At the same time many Republicans argued that the North, too, needed reconstruction. New York, Boston, Chicago, San Francisco, and other cities possessed large, heavily Catholic immigrant populations, and striking gains by the Democratic Party in local elections after the war suggested an untutored or, worse, manipulated electorate. One prominent minister explained in 1868 that "the Jesuit is master of the Great Metropolis," and *Harper's Weekly* argued, "The dependence of the Democratic party at this moment is upon the Ku-Klux feeling both in the Northern and Southern States, and upon the Roman Catholic vote."[100]

One of the nation's most influential ministers, Henry Bellows, chair of the U.S. Sanitary Commission during the war, warned in 1869 of the "immense political power" that Catholics were obtaining in the United States, using the hierarchy "to centralize and move its forces with the most solid front upon our political parties."[101] After an 1871 march by Irish and American Protestants erupted into a deadly Protestant-Catholic riot, the *New York Times* commented, "Two out of four of our City rulers are bigoted Roman Catholics, the men who prop up the City Government are Roman Catholics, and now it is decided that Protestants have only such rights as Catholics choose to accord them." "We live," the *Times* sorrowfully concluded, "under the rule of priests and rowdies."[102] Members of New York's elite Council of Political Reform feared citizens "led by a highly cultivated priesthood, nearly all of whom were educated under a foreign theocratic despotism."[103]

Similar fears were voiced across the country. A Republican editor in Indianapolis explained, "We are publishing no news in saying that the Catholic Church of this country is Democratic wholly. . . . There is not one Catholic in five hundred . . . who is not a Democrat."[104] Rutherford B. Hayes complained in 1875 that "the sectarian [Catholic] wing of the Democratic party rules that party to-day in the great commercial metropolis of the nation. It holds the balance of power in many of the large cities of the country. Without its votes, the Democratic party would lose every large city and county in Ohio, and every Northern State."[105] When the young Woodrow Wilson enrolled in a course called "Civil Government" at Princeton University in 1878, he took careful notes on the problem of papal authority. The subject was vital, his instructor explained, "not only in European but also in American politics."[106]

Such attacks only strengthened Catholic allegiance to the Democrats. In 1874 Orestes Brownson denied that "any Catholic or honest and intelligent man" could support the "so-called Republican party."[107] A Pennsylvania abbot explained to a European colleague, "They [the Republicans] consist mainly of German liberals and radicals with a mixture of fanatics and are responsible for the sad conditions we are living in now."[108]

In much of Europe the standoff between Catholics and liberals resulted in independent Catholic political parties. Bishops reacted ambivalently to these ventures, but Catholic parties became central to political life in Belgium, the Netherlands, Austria, and Germany. Frequently, as in Germany, Catholic parties competed directly (and successfully) with socialist parties for the allegiance of newly enfranchised workers, founding parallel trade unions, newspapers, social clubs, and charitable agencies.[109]

American Catholics often expressed their admiration of these Catholic parties and speculated about the possibility of comparable political vehicles in the United States. German American Catholics, in particular, kept close tabs on the activities of the German Catholic Center Party and cheered its electoral successes.[110] In the 1880s and 1890s Center Party leaders continually crossed the Atlantic to address their American Catholic supporters, and a corresponding stream of German Americans traveled to Germany. At the 1896 meeting of the Central Verein in Detroit, the delegates gathered beneath enormous portraits of Pope Leo XIII, George Washington, the local bishop, and the Center leader, Ludwig Windthorst.[111]

The failure to establish an American Catholic political party parallels the failure to establish a durable American workers' party along the lines of the German Social Democrats or British Labour. In most of Europe the creation of Catholic and socialist parties occurred simultaneously with the extension of the ballot. Catholic and socialist party members competed with each other to recruit new voters in rural areas and industrial towns, a much easier task than luring already mobilized voters out of partisan cocoons. In the United States, Irish American Catholics, in particular, had already clambered to the top rungs of the Democratic Party, and saw little advantage in third-party endeavors.[112]

Instead of a Catholic party, the late nineteenth-century United States witnessed the birth of the modern Democrats, dependent on two separate wings—one white, Protestant, and southern and the other white, heavily Catholic, and northern. The basic contours of the party had been evident before the Civil War, but rural Protestants in the North became more likely to vote Republican over the course of the nineteenth century, leaving Catholics as the crucial northern Democratic constituency. Intra-Catholic hostility between Irish and Italian Catholics, or Irish and French Canadian Catholics, occasionally led to Republican apostasy, but even Italians and French Canadians often fled a Republican Party too closely associated with anti-Catholic attacks.[113]

Affiliation did not guarantee influence. Despite Republican claims, clerical influence on the Democratic Party and its northern political machines was rarely direct, and the refusal of Democratic politicians such as Grover Cleveland to favor aid to parochial schools angered Catholic leaders. The Catholic press, in fact, boasted of the scrupulously apolitical character of their clergy, especially when compared with Protestant ministers openly supporting Republican candidates. One Democratic candidate for mayor in Chicago proudly asked a crowd of supporters in 1883, "You who go to the Church hard by [Holy Family], or over to the Cathedral of the Holy Name, or St. Jarlath's, did you ever hear the priests talk politics? [Cries of 'never.'] When they get up they preach Jesus Christ and Him Crucified. Isn't that so? [Cries of 'yes.']"[114]

In addition, the sources of Catholic and white southern hostility to liberal nationalism differed. Unlike white southerners, Catholics imbibed from European coreligionists a specific anxiety about state attacks on religious institutions, and an intellectual tradition that insistently warned against individualism in the familial and economic realms. Nonetheless, the extent to which Catholic commentators on Reconstruction and Republican reform echoed their white southern counterparts is striking. Catholic editors such as James McMaster joined white southerners in opposing many Reconstruction programs, and a few voices, including McMaster's, questioned the capacity of African Americans—"be they rich or poor"—to exercise the ballot.[115]

Catholics and southerners alike constantly warned of an expanding federal state. The Georgetown student newspaper concluded in 1870, "The events which have marked the course of our domestic politics during the past few years, show how slight is the barrier which divides a mighty republic from an unprincipled despotism."[116] The Chicago politician William J. Onahan admonished the graduates of the University of Notre Dame in 1876 to recognize a common impulse behind persecution of Catholics in Europe and America. Catholic students should resist a "theory now so widely prevalent and enforced of the unqualified supremacy of the State, [which] makes [it] an earthly deity and requires of us to bow down and worship it."[117]

The easy entrance of Catholics into southern society immediately following the Civil War is also suggestive. The poet laureate of the postwar South, and the region's best known Catholic, was Father Abram Ryan. Ryan first published the most popular poem in southern history, an ode to the Confederacy entitled "The Conquered Banner," in the Catholic *New York Freeman's Journal*.[118] Jefferson Davis thanked James McMaster for mailing him a copy of another of Ryan's ballads in 1867, along with several issues of the *Freeman's Journal*. Davis added his gratitude that "justice and Constitutional right is and can be so boldly vindicated as it now is in your periodical."[119]

Finally, Catholics also challenged widespread assertions that they disparaged science. No other word than "science," complained one Catholic editor, is "so unintelligently nor so flippantly abused." Defenders of Lourdes accused their critics of a naïve positivism, or as one writer suggested, "we find that sectarians and unbelievers are generally more credulous and more easily imposed on than ourselves."[120] In Rome an Italian Jesuit launched an attack on John William Draper's *History of the Conflict between Science and Religion*, and in St. Louis another Jesuit, F. P. Garesché, disputed Draper's assumption of conflict between science and religion, adding, gratuitously, that the work was one of the "trashy books of modern history."[121]

IV

Opposing views on reform, nationalism, and intellectual progress collided with extraordinary force in discussion of public education. The desire for a state monopoly on education escalated in tandem with nineteenth-century nationalism throughout Europe, with schools increasingly understood as the crucible of citizen formation. In the United States the relationship of religion to education was always charged, but a new wave of controversy swept the country after the Civil War. No other issue so quickly generated both anti-Catholicism and Catholic belligerence, and at the state and local levels debates over education blazed their way through electoral politics.

The discussion began with southern Reconstruction. Virginia, Tennessee, and Mississippi were readmitted to the Union only after promising to establish public school systems, and northern teachers, primarily women, poured into the South in an effort coordinated by the Freedmen's Bureau and the American Missionary Association to nurture new schools. Even as efforts to reconstruct the South waned in the 1870s, reformers continued to hope that the schoolhouse would transform Native Americans (on reservations throughout the West) and Mormons (gathered in

Utah) into model citizens. One Republican Indian commissioner declared in an annual report, "Education is to be the medium through which the rising generation of Indians are to be brought into fraternal and harmonious relationship with their white fellow-citizens. . . ."[122]

This focus on public education as the means of producing loyal citizens tended to carry an anti-Catholic animus, and leading educators often expressed their gratitude that public schools were "unfavorable to dogmatic religion."[123] Two prominent reformers interested in the Indian issue, Thomas Morgan and Daniel Dorchester, became infuriated with Catholics' requests for government funding of parish schools and Catholic agencies on the reservations. (Morgan would describe such requests as "un-American, unpatriotic, and a menace to our liberties.")[124] Republicans also worried that Mormons adopted bad Catholic habits by vesting financial control of the church in a hierarchical body, and expressing little enthusiasm for public education.[125]

Already by the early 1870s this sort of controversy had become inescapable, and Catholic candidates for public office, such as the New York gubernatorial candidate Francis Kernan, knew that newspaper editors and political opponents would be "very solicitous as to your position on the school question."[126] Delegates to state constitutional conventions in the years after the Civil War considered the issue at length. In Illinois, Republican delegates expressed shock that some colleagues considered it "sectarian in this country to read the [King James Bible version of the] ten commandments and the sermon on the mount," while Democrats refuted the charge that Catholics aimed to "overthrow the free institutions of this country." "Sometimes," J. P. Carberry explained to delegates at the Ohio State Constitutional Convention, ". . . when you scratch a non-Catholic's professed liberalism, you find a bigot beneath his coat." Republicans responded that Catholics feared "self-reliant teaching" and "trusting their children."[127]

A turning point in the national discussion occurred when Senator Henry Wilson of Massachusetts, a former Know-Nothing and later Grant's vice-president, made a well-publicized 1871 call for a "new departure" for the Republican Party. The destination was the schoolhouse, and Wilson urged members of the "great national party" to develop a national educational policy. He acknowledged the boldness of this break with American traditions of local control of education, but explained that the virtue of national systems of education was evident in the Franco-Prussian War, where German soldiers crushed "ignorant, priest-ridden and emasculated" French opponents.[128]

Catholics reacted to Wilson's proposal with horror. The Catholic defense of parochial education began in the 1840s and 1850s, but the general tendency toward ultramontanism within the church since that time had only strengthened the Catholic conviction that religion and education must not be separated. Pius IX had given a Vatican imprimatur to such views by chastising leaders of the duchy of Baden in 1864 for removing state schools from Catholic control, and American Catholics frequently referred to this directive.[129]

American Catholics also emphasized that many European countries, including Germany, used tax revenues to support Catholic schools along with those of other religious denominations. The refusal of American liberals to contemplate such funding, even as they urged national control of education, infuriated Catholics. Even moderates like Father Isaac Hecker were moved to describe Senator Wilson as "at the head of a set of fanatics who are in a conspiracy to destroy our political system of government and religious freedom."[130]

Catholic theologians began to debate whether parents unwilling to send their children to available Catholic schools, or pastors unwilling to build them, could be denied the sacraments. One prominent Redemptorist sympathetic to this view defined public schools as "positivae noxiae," or positively dangerous.[131] James McMaster used a well-placed Roman intermediary to prod Vatican authorities on the matter, and a Vatican commentary appeared in November 1875, two weeks before President Grant's request that Congress prohibit any aid to religious schools. The Congregatio de Propaganda Fide instructed American bishops that "evils of the gravest kind are likely to result from the so-called public schools," and it allowed the enrollment of children in public schools only for reason of "sufficient cause." In 1884 the American bishops formally endorsed similar principles, using the labor of American nuns as the cornerstone of their efforts to increase access to parochial education. By 1895, remarkably, an overwhelmingly working-class Catholic population had built some four thousand Catholic schools, which enrolled 755,038 children, an increase of 50 percent in a decade.[132]

V

The clash between liberals viewing education as central to national cohesion and Catholics committed to education as a parental prerogative guaranteed, ironically, the secularization of the public schools. Into the late 1860s, state and local court decisions, including the judgment provoked by the 1859 Eliot School Rebellion, permitted reading from the King James Bible. Horace Mann's reasoning was still persuasive: Bible readings and hymns could be at once religious and nonsectarian. One of Mann's successors as Massachusetts education secretary argued in 1866 that "the state has the right and it is consequently her duty to recognize and teach Christianity in the schools—not the dogmas of sects, but the great duty of love to God and man, as set forth in the Bible, the word of God."[133]

Undermining this view after the war was the new importance of national unity and a consequent willingness to sacrifice religious education in public schools to that goal. By the early 1870s, for the first time, most American intellectuals conceded that the United States could not use public institutions to foster Christianity, a task made impossibly divisive by the massive increase in the Catholic population, along with growing numbers of Jews and nonbelievers.

Controversies in New York and Cincinnati clarified the issue. In New York, Boss Tweed and his Tammany Hall allies persuaded the New York state legislature to permit religious schools to claim portions of an excise tax in the late 1860s. Because enrollment in Catholic schools dwarfed that in any other denominational system, Catholics claimed the bulk of the funds.[134] New York City's government also assisted an array of orphanages, again primarily Catholic. Allegations of shady real estate transactions between the archdiocese and city hall completed the portrait of what *Putnam's Magazine* termed "Our Established Church." "In no European country," a writer for *Putnam's* exclaimed, ". . . has the clergy of a Catholic establishment its hand more nearly closed upon the whole system of public education than here in New York."[135]

Francis Lieber rallied leading citizens of New York to oppose aid to "sectarian schools" and drafted a pamphlet attacking Catholic influence on elected politicians.[136] No further monies were issued to Catholic schools, and a reform coalition unseated Boss Tweed in 1871, but rallies against any aid to Catholic education marked the city's political life for the next decade. In Brooklyn a large crowd listened to speakers describe those in favor of aid to parochial schools as a "band of foreign priestly conspirators, with no sympathy for the American Government, or its system of education, secretly plotting the destruction of both."[137]

Crucially, the New York squabble did not prompt leading citizens and intellectuals to reassert the importance of Christian instruction. Instead, attacks on Catholic aggression now emphasized the importance (and inevitability) of nonsectarian American institutions. Perhaps the most influential exponent of this view was the New York minister Henry Bellows. Conceding, "When [taking the Bible out of the public schools] was first proposed I felt horror-stricken," Bellows argued that "duty to the unsectarian character of our civil institutions demands that this exclusion should be made." Catholic attacks threatened a nation "which morally depends upon the community of feeling and the homogeneity of culture produced by an unsectarian system of common schools."[138]

The Cincinnati "Bible War" of 1869–70, concluding with the decision of the Cincinnati school board to end use of the King James Bible in public school classrooms, had a similar effect.[139] A number of local Protestants urged legislators and judges to reverse the school board decision. A leading advocate of this view was the local Unitarian minister Amory Dwight Mayo, later editor of the National Journal of Education. Mayo organized resistance to the school board's decision to ban Bible reading and described Catholic priests as an "aristocracy" eager for the "ignorance of their people."[140]

Mayo also felt obliged, however, to urge his supporters to avoid the "ultra-secular" parties.[141] The most notable aspect of the Cincinnati dispute was the strong support, among Republican politicians and liberal intellectuals, for acceding to Catholic demands. In fact, some Protestants, Jews, and atheists joined Catholics in congratulating the school board for its decision to jettison Bible reading. A frustrated Mayo described this position as "narrower and more intolerant than that of the Archbishop," but leading public figures disagreed.[142] The country's most prominent minister, Henry Ward Beecher, intervened in the Cincinnati debate with an address, "The Common School as an Element of National Unity," and prominent rabbis such as Cincinnati's Max Lilienthal (who defined the struggle as between "free America" and "priest-serving Rome") urged support for wholly secular public schools, not nominally Christian ones.[143] Major newspapers and journals announced opposition to any

Bible reading, with the *Nation* asking for "truly secular education simply" and the *Chicago Tribune* declaring it impossible to "teach any form of theology" in the public schools.[144]

Less publicized disputes also demonstrated the new emphasis placed on education as a marker of national unity. New Mexico possessed only the rudiments of a public education system in the 1870s, and local politicians proudly referred to the region as a "Catholic land" inhabited by a "Catholic people."[145] The secretary of the territory, W. G. Ritch, ruefully admitted in 1874 that Catholic schools "supplant measurably at least, the public schools of their respective localities."[146] Almost all school textbooks were printed on the press of one of the region's most important Spanish-language newspapers, *Revista Católica*, edited by Italian Jesuits.[147] These Jesuits, exiles from Naples, were determined, as one of them put it, to resist "the ignorant call for non-sectarian schools (understand by this phrase schools with no religion and no God) uttered by the very persons who ought to protect and favor education." Politicians must recognize "that New Mexicans are an eminently religious and Catholic people and that their faith is their energy, their unity, their dignity."[148]

In 1875 Secretary Ritch drafted a school bill that, for the first time, banned aid to Catholic schools and explicitly described public schools as a key to the modernization of the region. Jesuit priests unsuccessfully lobbied against the bill in the state legislature and directed editorial volleys at territorial officials (all appointed Republicans) in the pages of *Revista Católica*. (One editorial attacked the policy of "centralizing everything in the abstract name of the State.") In response, Ritch argued, tellingly, "We did not come to New Mexico to compromise our manhood as an American citizen. . . ."[149]

Similarly, in Cambridge, Massachusetts, in 1879 a local priest, Thomas Scully, sparked an uproar that continued for two years by announcing that parishioners unwilling to send their children to parochial schools would be denied absolution in the confessional and rejected at the communion rail. "In every part of the Catholic world," Scully maintained, "the battle is going on, and I say thank God for it." The more liberal sectors of the Boston press immediately attacked Scully, and one minister concluded "that to divide *citizenship* anywise in this country is a civil crime."[150]

William T. Harris, superintendent of schools in St. Louis and then United States commissioner of education, and after Horace Mann the most important nineteenth-century educational leader, best articulated this transition from Protestant to secular education. Harris disdained anti-Catholic diatribes, but he also rejected Catholic efforts to gain government funding for parochial schools.[151] More radical than Mann, Harris defined theological and moral instruction as distinct enterprises and denied that "religion is the basis of morality."[152] In 1876 Harris agreed with President Grant that no "religious dogmas" should be taught in American public schools, and he added that no Bible should be read in them. Public schools should assist students unfortunate enough to be "reared under a narrow-minded and exclusive system." A teacher promulgating religious dogmas in a public school "must perforce develop a habit of thinking" so authoritarian that it would frustrate the mathematics or science instructor guiding the same students. Classroom attention to religious belief might eliminate "critical acuteness and independent thinking from the mind of the pupil."[153]

VI

Virtually all Catholic leaders rejected Harris's distinction between moral and religious education. The division among Catholics rested on different grounds: whether some compromise might be struck between Catholics and public authorities, or whether Catholics should simply demand public funding for their schools. Here, as during the Civil War, liberal Catholics came into public view, eager to demonstrate loyalty to the nation-state and uneasy with the confrontational stance taken by many American Catholic leaders and the Vatican.

That dissatisfaction with hard-line opposition to Catholic involvement with public schools existed was obvious. More Catholic students attended public schools than Catholic schools throughout the period, and enrollment decisions did not simply reflect the paucity of Catholic facilities. Some parents were unconvinced that Catholic schools offered an education equivalent to that of the public schools, an especially delicate issue when only one spouse was Catholic.[154] One Milwaukee Catholic journal complained about "so-called Catholic parents" dodging responsibility for parochial education, and James McMaster bemoaned the indifference of priests and Catholic parents "on a question so vital."[155]

Some Catholic liberals tried to link Catholic and public schools. Intriguingly, an early effort occurred in Cincinnati, where Archbishop

John Purcell had distinguished himself as a supporter of local Republicans and an opponent of slavery. Using as leverage the twelve thousand children already enrolled in Cincinnati's Catholic schools, compared with twenty-seven thousand in the public schools, Purcell and Catholic members of the public school board proposed a consolidation of the two systems.[156]

Liberals remained opposed to Catholics' receiving tax dollars, but even such normally hostile voices as the *New York Times* praised Purcell's "moderation, liberality and practical statesmanlike views" and his effort to "prove that Catholicity and Republicanism are not necessarily antagonistic powers."[157] The opposition from Purcell's fellow Catholics was actually more venomous. Editors such as James McMaster accused Purcell and his brother, Father Edward Purcell, of abandoning "Catholic orthodoxy" for "pieces of silver." A number of Cincinnati German Catholic pastors voiced opposition to any merger for fear that the German language and German religious customs might wither in the consolidated systems.[158]

The most consequential intra-Catholic dispute over education occurred in New York. Meeting regularly to discuss issues of the day, a small group of clerics terming themselves the Accademia had by the late 1860s become disenchanted with the drift of Catholic leadership.[159] The leaders of the Catholic revival, and their habit of measuring modernity against medieval glories, elicited no enthusiasm. One Accademia member, Father James Burtsell, complained that the Jesuits wished to "fossilize us with the habits of the middle ages. Especially in this New York province, the superiors are Frenchmen of very cramped minds, who denounce our institutions as they would denounce the revolution of 1793."[160]

The same group of liberal priests had earlier favored the abolition of slavery, to such an extent that one member jokingly referred to the "Abolition-Roman priests."[161] After the war two members of the Accademia, Fathers Sylvester Malone and Thomas Farrell, shocked a Virginia bishop during a southern visit by preaching in favor of Radical Reconstruction and attacking papal infallibility.[162] Malone became known as "an intense Republican, outspoken in every campaign," and Farrell spoke with equal candor. At an 1869 address attended by several Republican politicians, Farrell regretted that some Catholics remained "prejudiced against the abolitionists, who had been the best friends the free laboring population ever had in this country." He also criticized the Inquisition and urged religious freedom in Spain.[163] Two years later he attacked papal rule in Italy, leading the *New York Times* to describe him as a lone American representative of "the position which thousands of his fellow-priests take in Italy and Germany—that of a reasonable, progressive, liberal Romanist."[164] The *New York Herald* celebrated Farrell as a check on the "absurd aims of the ultramontanes."[165]

These divisions extended to the schoolhouse. Farrell and Father Edward McGlynn refused to build a parochial school in St. Stephen's on New York's Lower East Side (perhaps the largest Irish American parish in the country, claiming over twenty thousand members in the 1870s), and McGlynn found the withdrawal of the Bible from the public schools a satisfactory compromise. (McGlynn's battles with church authorities, as we shall see, were only beginning.) He emphasized his desire to be a "truer American" and criticized Catholics willing to import the "miserable theological hatred and bickerings" of Europe to the United States. In response James McMaster applied to McGlynn the "unenviable" label of "*liberal* Catholic."[166] Another member of the group, Father Patrick F. McSweeney, used a posting in remote Poughkeepsie as an opportunity to devise an ingenious solution to the education problem. McSweeney arranged for the local school board to fund two parish schools, with the informal understanding that the school board hire qualified Catholics (Sisters of Charity) as instructors. In turn, he promised "[n]o religious exercises to be held, nor religious instruction given during the school hours." Similar experiments also developed in Georgia and Connecticut. McSweeney's successor in Poughkeepsie, another member of the Accademia, Father Patrick Nilan, continued the program into the 1890s.[167]

The Poughkeepsie plan eventually attracted the attention of the foremost Catholic liberal of the late nineteenth century, St. Paul archbishop John Ireland. The line connecting Ireland, a onetime French seminarian, to Bishop Dupanloup, Montalembert, and the French liberal Catholics of the mid-nineteenth century was direct.[168] Like those European liberal Catholics, Ireland believed that Catholicism and modern nationalism might coexist, urging Catholics to cultivate "the sacred stigmata of patriotism."[169] Like other liberal Catholics, Ireland had supported the Union during the Civil War (he served as a Union army chaplain), and he resisted the drift toward racial segregation that marked the succeeding decades. He termed the African American "national" parish in St. Paul a temporary expedient and urged the legalization of interracial marriage, prompting French-speaking Afro-Creole Catholics in New Orleans to lionize the archbishop during their own struggle against religious and public segregation.[170]

At the same time Ireland indulged in a kind of Catholic nativism, describing an "Irish-American, a German-American, or a French-American" as an "intolerable anomaly."[171] When an international coalition of Catholics led by the German Center Party member Peter Paul Cahensly and Italian bishop Giovanni Battista Scalabrini expressed fear that Catholic immigrants were losing their faith in the United States and urged the appointment of bishops from varied backgrounds, a Catholic newspaper editor sympathetic to Ireland printed the headline "Foreign Countries Seeking to Rule the Church in America."[172] Ireland and his allies responded by distorting what Scalabrini termed this "practical" request.[173] Ireland's friend Cushman K. Davis, a Republican from Minnesota, took to the Senate floor to warn of German Catholics' attempts to "denationalize American institutions and plant as many nations as there are people of foreign tongues in our midst."[174]

Ireland found the Poughkeepsie attempt to meld Catholic and public education intriguing, perhaps especially because non-Catholics from the town privately informed him that the plan had enabled Poughkeepsie residents to forget "old prejudices."[175] Ireland authorized his own version of the Poughkeepsie experiment in the tiny Minnesota towns of Faribault and Stillwater, and declared before the annual convention of the National Education Association his standing as a "friend and advocate of the state school."[176]

These were fighting words. More conservative Catholics, convinced that Ireland and his supporters sacrificed the faith to a craven nationalism, waged war through pamphlets, letters to Rome, and manipulation of the secular press. Led by the Jesuits Salvatore Brandi and René Holaind, New York's Archbishop Corrigan, and the influential German editors Father Herman Heuser and Arthur Preuss, conservatives demanded public funding of wholly independent parochial schools. The editors of the *Buffalo Volksfreund* argued that "the chief error of Archbishop Ireland rests in his views about America, Americans, and [the] American Church. America is no nation, no race, no people like France, Italy, or Germany."[177]

Liberals, led by Ireland and Father Thomas Boquillon at Catholic University, agreed that wholly secular education was unsatisfactory, but pleaded for some form of cooperation between public authorities and the church. The dispute veered between theological disputes and a nasty ethnic politics. (Liberal Catholics repeatedly hinted that Germans seeking to preserve parochial education in their native tongue, for example, were reluctant American patriots.)[178]

The loudest fireworks exploded between 1891 and 1893, but the fault lines endured for a generation between Catholics scornful of what Archbishop Corrigan termed "*ultra*-Americanism" and Catholics eager to demonstrate loyalty to the nation-state and more sympathetic to the achievements of modernity.[179] Liberal Catholics in France, Germany, and Italy, notably the French priest Félix Klein and the German theologian Franz Xaver Kraus, defended Archbishop Ireland and advocated their own version of Catholic nationalism. In close touch with Ireland's clerical supporters, Kraus published a string of supportive articles in the influential *Allgemeine Zeitung* emphasizing his (and Ireland's) eagerness to bridge the gap separating "Religion and Science, Church and State, Papacy and Imperium."[180]

Conservatives also rallied their forces. The largest German Catholic newspaper, the *Kölnische Zeitung*, attacked "North American Nativism" after hearing from outraged German American Catholics. The Italian Jesuit Brandi, returned to Rome from the United States to edit *Civiltà Cattolica*. From this influential platform he attacked Ireland's educational plans. He wrote to another conservative polemicist, "I am happy to inform you (confidentially) that Archbishop Ireland is now well known in Rome as a liberal and revolutionary bishop. I have had occasion to speak of him to Cardinals Rampolla, Monaco and Mazzella."[181] The German theologian Joseph Schroeder, then at Catholic University in Washington, kept bishops in the United States, Germany, and Rome posted on events and reminded a colleague not to accept "*Liberalism*, under any conditions, under no mask, and also not under that of Americanism."[182]

VII

Bitter disagreements about education, between Catholics and American liberals and among Catholics themselves, obscured a warming climate. Leading American intellectuals began uttering soothing remarks about their Catholic neighbors in the late 1870s, abandoning the heated language so evident after the war. As early as 1878 E. L. Godkin of the *Nation* marveled at Pius IX's "remarkably successful efforts to strengthen the purely spiritual authority of the Papacy." "The Pope was perhaps,"

Godkin admitted, "more a man of his time than he seemed to most of us ten years ago. . . ."[183] A generation later, in 1911, President William Howard Taft, Vice-President James Sherman, the Speaker of the House of Representatives, members of the cabinet and the United States Supreme Court, and a large delegation from Congress would travel to Baltimore via chartered train to honor Baltimore's Cardinal Gibbons on the fiftieth anniversary of his ordination to the priesthood.[184]

As in Europe, in America a relaxation of tension between Catholics and intellectuals coincided with a surge of labor unrest. Given a choice, leading citizens preferred a predominantly Catholic working class to a potentially socialist one. President Taft admired the Catholic Church as "one of the bulwarks against socialism and anarchy in this country" and Charles Eliot Norton hoped the church might check the "anarchic religion of the unchurched multitude."[185]

The patriotism of Catholic leaders, especially liberal Catholics such as Archbishop Ireland, also had an effect. Theodore Roosevelt defended one New York Catholic Republican, emphasizing that the man was a "staunch upholder of the public schools" and part of the "wing [of the Catholic Church] which is liberalized and Americanized, and is always the object of the inveterate hostility of the ultramontane section."[186] Ireland's attack on the Democratic Party in 1894—especially the notion that "[the Democratic Party] alone is the partisan of religious liberty, while it accuses the Republicans of harboring intentions of persecuting Catholics"—drew grateful Republican attention.[187]

A shift in tone was even evident on the school question. While still opposed to government aid to parochial schools, late nineteenth-century liberals worried about government corruption and, unconcerned about the fate of African Americans languishing in inadequate public schools in the South, could agree with Catholics that schooling should remain a local (not a federal) matter. Henry Blair of New Hampshire—Radical Republican, admirer of Horace Mann—spent much of the 1880s attempting to win support for federal aid to public education. Catholic opposition to the bill in its various incarnations was such that one of Blair's supporters, New York's John Jay, warned of "ultramontanes" bent on "destroying the common schools."[188] Blair himself unleashed a diatribe on the Senate floor urging the expulsion of the Jesuits from the United States; two years later he castigated "jesuitical opposition" and the "unreconstructed Southern aristocracy."[189]

Instead of rallying liberal forces, Blair's remarks provoked only scorn. Establishment organs such as the *Washington Post* and *New York Times* dismissed Blair's accusations, and leading college presidents agreed with Catholics that federal involvement in educational policy was unnecessary and counterproductive.[190]

Similarly, in Boston, when a handful of ministers and city officials attempted to revive specious inspections of the parochial schools (a favorite Know-Nothing tactic in the 1850s), eminences such as President Charles W. Eliot of Harvard and President Francis A. Walker of the Massachusetts Institute of Technology testified on behalf of Catholics. When visiting Rome as a young man, Eliot had admitted to his mother, "I hate Catholicism as I do poison, and all the pomp and power of the Church is depressing and mortifying to me." But in 1889 he refused to condone Protestant bullying, even if he viewed Catholic schools "with some apprehension."[191]

When Republicans proved intolerant, they suffered at the ballot box. In Wisconsin and Illinois, Republicans passed compulsory education laws in the late 1880s that eliminated foreign-language instruction in some subjects, a sore point with German Catholics and Lutherans eager to preserve their native tongue. Democrats quickly rallied Catholics and Lutherans against these efforts—one Wisconsin Catholic bishop explained, "They are all of a class, these laws, whether in Wisconsin, Illinois, or Massachusetts"—and rode the issue to an overwhelming triumph in the 1890 election.[192]

As establishment anti-Catholicism ebbed, anti-Catholicism as a social phenomenon crested, with the openly anti-Catholic American Protective Association [APA] registering over one million members in the early 1890s.[193] Many were recent Canadian and British immigrants, possessing ties to the fiercely anti-Catholic Orange order. Some of the anti-Catholic leaders were associates of Dwight Moody and other evangelical leaders. In Boston they preached in less prestigious pulpits and endured taunts of "fanatics" and "so-called Protestants" in the Brahmin press.[194] One prominent Hartford minister called the organization "un-American, unpatriotic, and un-Christian."[195]

For many APA members and evangelicals, uneasiness about Catholicism became inseparable from efforts to protect a fading world of political and individual autonomy. When these reformers attacked "monopolies" during the 1880s and 1890s, they often jumped from

Roman Catholicism to Tammany Hall and predatory corporations. Josiah Strong's popular 1886 tract, *Our Country*, contained a full chapter on Catholic excesses, and he termed Gladstone and Bismarck the "greatest living statesmen" for their stand against Rome. But Strong also argued that "power is being gathered more and more into the hands of conscienceless monopolies."[196] The founder of the APA, Henry Bowers, began his career crusading against local business interests, and Worcester, Massachusetts, APA members complained about the "rich and soi-disant educated."

The more graphic attacks launched by APA newspapers and speakers in the 1890s suggested desperation. APA meetings—like those of the Know-Nothings four decades earlier—often included fraudulent tales of ex-nuns escaping convent imprisonment, fevered warnings about priests stockpiling arms in rectory cellars, and forged papal encyclicals putatively calling for a Catholic uprising. Perhaps the most prominent figure on the APA lecture circuit, Justin D. Fulton, watched in horror as Irish and French Canadian Catholics poured into New England's small towns to work in local factories. Such uneasiness was widely shared, but Fulton's use of creaky theological arguments—against purgatory, for example—made him an anachronism. Fulton even speculated about a secret cable connecting the White House with the residence of Baltimore's Archbishop Gibbons.[197]

The third-party Populist movement drew from the same evangelical and individualist soil. While never a dominant theme in the Populist press, warnings of Catholic leaders in collusion with corrupt politicians held strong appeal for men and women concerned about the independent farmer in an age of railroad monopolies and grain trusts. In North Carolina, Populist editors and ministers frequently switched from attacks on political "bossism" to assaults on a Catholic hierarchy claiming "infallibility in political principles." A leading Texas Populist, Charles W. Macune, served a stint as an editor of an APA newspaper, and APA members touted the Populist hero Tom Watson for the organization's presidential ticket.[198]

By 1896 the APA had become an empty shell, killed, according to the *Independent*, by "reputable Protestants."[199] In that year's presidential campaign, Republican William McKinley, who twenty years before had advised candidates to appeal to voters who "hate the Catholics," distanced himself from the APA, especially after some of its members charged him with appointing too many Catholics to high office. (McKinley's campaign manager, the businessman Mark Hanna, gleefully noted that such attacks made "papists of us.")[200]

By that time, too, more influential mainstream Protestant reformers had begun to reach across religious divides. The intensely communal and international vision fostered by nineteenth-century ultramontane Catholics became more appealing to a new generation of non-Catholic intellectuals and reformers struggling to understand a society racked by poverty and labor unrest. Catholics might have opposed immediate slave emancipation, but Catholic cautions about the new industrial economy in the late nineteenth century seemed insightful. Prominent ministers such as Lyman Abbott and Washington Gladden, along with Richard T. Ely and other reform-minded economists, dismissed the APA as irrelevant in the early 1890s, even as they expressed admiration for Pope Leo XIII's criticism of economic liberalism, especially in *Rerum Novarum,* an 1891 papal encyclical that became the foundation document of Catholic social thought. Gladden, using language that would have shocked liberals a generation earlier, publicly admired the pope's "large intelligence and quick human sympathy."[201]

Chapter Five
THE SOCIAL QUESTION

I

The details of the composition of *Rerum Novarum* are unusually well documented. In the late 1880s Pope Leo XIII, nearing the age of eighty, announced his desire to prepare an encyclical on the social question. In July 1890 another Italian octogenarian, the Jesuit Matteo Liberatore, submitted a first draft. That fall Cardinal Tommaso Zigliara made a significant revision. A third draft resulted from scrutiny by Liberatore and another Jesuit, Cardinal Camillo Mazzella. The pope himself monitored a series of subsequent versions, dictating emendations and correcting the Latin. During the two weeks preceding the encyclical's release, on May 15, 1891, Vatican officials canceled all papal appointments as Leo XIII scrutinized the final text.[1]

The shared assumptions of these Vatican collaborators are illuminating. Liberatore had spearheaded the neo-Thomist philosophical revival that so shaped Catholic thought in the late nineteenth century, using forty-two years as an editor at *Civiltà Cattolica* as a bully pulpit. The claim that a reinvigorated Thomism might serve as the foundation for a Catholic approach to modern problems was initially a minority view, even among Catholics, but it attracted a number of soon-to-be influential patrons, including Gioacchino Pecci. Pecci became Pope Leo XIII in 1878 and urged Catholic bishops in his first encyclical to study the "streams of wisdom flowing inexhaustibly from the precious fountainhead of the Angelic Doctor [Thomas Aquinas]."[2]

More practically, the pope quickly made cardinals out of staunch Thomists such as Zigliara and Mazzella and placed them in key curial positions.[3] One seminarian studying in Rome informed Baltimore's Archbishop James Gibbons in 1881 that "scholasticism's star is now in the ascendant throughout the eternal city. The majority of professors not bred up as Thomists have been forced to vacate their chairs in favor of the Neapolitian schools of philosophy and theology. . . ."[4]

Papal concern about the conditions of industrial workers was unsurprising. Catholic peasants flocked to the North Atlantic sites of industrial development, and in the heavily Catholic industrial towns of Westphalia and the Rhineland, the cities along the eastern coast and the Great Lakes of the United States, eastern France, and a swath stretching from Belfast to Glasgow and Manchester, Catholics formed a significant percentage of the urban working class. In much of France and, later, Italy and Spain, many workers rejected a church they saw as irrelevant to this new industrial milieu, or incapable of providing pastoral care. But in other areas an array of Catholic parishes and associations sustained the allegiance of workers more successfully than parallel efforts by religious competitors. In Berlin, London, and New York, Protestant ministers marveled at Catholics' loyalty. By 1890, Catholics numbered 76 percent of churchgoers in Boston, 68 percent of churchgoers in Chicago and New York, 58 percent in St. Louis, and 56 percent in Cleveland.[5] An American Protestant activist exaggerated, but the tone is itself telling, when he warned his colleagues in 1887 that "the Protestant churches, as a rule, have no following among the workingmen. Everybody knows it."[6]

The initial Catholic response to the plight of industrial laborers relied upon private charity. France's Frédéric Ozanam, founder of the St. Vincent de Paul Society in Paris in 1833, having discovered a new clientele of bewildered families struggling to find work and shelter, mobilized thousands of middle- and upper-class Catholic men and women to assist these families, and his example inspired Catholics across the world. The first American chapter of the St. Vincent de Paul Society was formed in St. Louis in 1845, the same year as the first German chapter in Munich, the first Scottish chapter in Edinburgh, and the first Mexican chapter in Mexico City. Within twenty years dozens of American chapters existed, some led by figures with close ties to heavily Catholic political machines.[7]

A second strand of Catholic interest in the "social question" came from Catholic women. In both Europe and the United States the number of women joining religious communities jumped dramatically in the last decades of the nineteenth century, and by 1920 ninety thousand women, many of them foreign born, served in American religious orders.[8] The massive American Catholic investment in parochial schools staffed by nuns exhausted much of these women's energy, but Americans nuns, like their European counterparts, also developed expertise in areas more closely connected to social welfare. Nuns provided training and skills for young women, sometimes in institutions founded prior to Jane Addams's far better known efforts at Hull House in Chicago, and Catholic laywomen began a modest settlement house movement in various locations across the country.[9] Most remarkably, Catholic nuns ran almost all of the four hundred Catholic hospitals extant in the United States in 1910, hospitals typically located in urban areas and near large populations of Catholic immigrants.[10]

Catholic nuns also built the country's most extensive orphanage network. In New York by 1875, Protestant agencies, officially deemed "nonsectarian," had shipped an estimated forty thousand children, most of

Mother Superior M. Clodesinde, with residents of the Angel Guardian orphanage, Chicago, Illinois, 1895–97.

them Catholic, to non-Catholic homes outside the city. (New York's foremost child welfare expert, Charles Loring Brace, encouraged such programs, even as he warned against the "chilling formalism of the ignorant Roman Catholic.") In response New York Catholic nuns built an orphanage network capable of housing twenty thousand children annually, and fought to ensure that indigent Catholic children would be placed in Catholic institutions. (An identical struggle between Protestants and Catholics took place in Germany.)[11]

The language used by St. Vincent de Paul volunteers visiting poor families or nuns welcoming children in their orphanages and patients in their hospitals rarely moved beyond traditional notions of charity. Still, close contact with the urban poor distinguished Catholic leaders from many contemporary policymakers, and fostered a jaundiced view of economic "laws" explaining poverty as a consequence of bad choices. One Catholic lecturer explained in 1889, "It will not do to attribute the condition of the poor to themselves—to their improvidence, idleness, and intemperance."[12]

The observation now seems unremarkable, but the historian Thomas Haskell suggests that one of the most momentous shifts of the nineteenth century was from a formalist understanding of the human self, in which self-denial, temperance, and education were the solutions to economic distress, toward an antiformalist understanding that stressed social explanations for individual crises.[13] The guiding principle of mid-nineteenth-century liberals, freedom of contract, effectively served the cause of slave emancipation and laissez-faire. But freedom of contract seemed irrelevant to workers unable to procure wages at subsistence levels. Instead, Catholics joined other reformers in urging a "living wage."[14]

Precisely because they rejected the tenets of political, economic, and theological liberalism, ultramontane Catholics found a social understanding of political economy congenial. Matteo Liberatore urged the development of associations or guilds for workers and employers and lauded the Catholic Middle Ages as a period less dominated by the relentless pursuit of individual self-interest. Between 1887 and 1889 Liberatore published a series of essays in *Civiltà Cattolica* critical of Adam Smith and economic liberalism. "Free competition," he concluded, "is a terrible weapon, most effectual to crush the weak and reduce whole populations to economic slavery under a rod of iron wielded by the potent rulers of social wealth."[15]

Similarly, a leading French Catholic polemicist lamented the "dogma of the free expansion of individual forces, the domination of capital, [and] the exploitation of the worker and the speculation of usury."[16] The central figure in the nineteenth-century German Catholic revival, Bishop Wilhelm von Ketteler of Mainz, even more emphatically warned against an economic system that, in his words, placed the "daily bread necessary to sustain the worker and his family . . . at the complete mercy of the caprice of the market place."[17]

In the United States, Orestes Brownson attacked "political economists [who] consider man only as a producing, distributing, and consuming machine."[18] The *Catholic World* later observed, "The theory of 'competition' as a solution of social and industrial disorder is as baseless as it is immoral." Adam Smith's political economy "makes the individual the unit of society. The true unit of society is the family. . . ."[19]

Rerum Novarum depended upon this ultramontane social vision. Political liberty and democracy are absent from the text, and Leo XIII would soon emphasize his uneasiness with American defenses of religious freedom. Yet the tone of the document—issued by a papacy regarded by nineteenth-century liberals as a citadel of reaction—was remarkable. Leo XIII began with an attack on the "misery and wretchedness pressing so unjustly on the majority of the working class." Unions received a papal blessing, as did, remarkably, government intervention in the economy when employers offered wages "insufficient to support a frugal and well-behaved wage earner."[20]

II

The debt the drafters of *Rerum Novarum* owed to European Catholic social thought was obvious.[21] In the United States *Rerum Novarum* marked a beginning. Still consumed with the task of building institutions for an immigrant population, only a handful of American Catholic leaders concerned themselves with debates on political economy. "The few learned men who are to be found in the Catholic communion of this country," complained one St. Louis writer, "are almost completely isolated. . . ."[22]

Catholics could not form religiously exclusive trade unions in such a diverse society, and even Catholic participation in the most important union of the 1870s and 1880s, the Knights of Labor, worried clerics concerned that nonsectarian fraternal organizations and unions might diminish Catholic influence. Baltimore's Cardinal Gibbons prevented a Vatican condemnation of the Knights of Labor in 1887, but he did so only after explaining that many officers in the organization remained "devout Catholics."[23]

The most important American social reformer of the late nineteenth century, a lapsed Episcopalian named Henry George, encountered fierce Catholic resistance to his popular single-tax crusade. George's claim that only a massive tax on land could restore social harmony triggered discussions of the social question in the United States, and his 1879 book, *Progress and Poverty*, sparked debate around the world. George did not call for the abolition of private property, only for a confiscatory tax on the "unearned" rent resulting from increased population and greater urban density. But he did call slave ownership and the current system of private property "different forms of the same robbery."[24]

George made several successful foreign tours and quickly won a fervent following in Ireland. In 1879, the year *Progress and Poverty* was published, the Irish harvest was the worst in fifteen years, and the resulting hunger recalled famine horrors. Agitation on the land question drew together Irish radicals and moderates, and these activists founded the Land League, which began a campaign to reduce or, later, withhold rents. American Catholic newspapers published extended accounts of the Land League campaign, and both Charles Stewart Parnell, Ireland's most important political figure, and Michael Davitt, the Land League's leading strategist, used American speaking tours to drum up support for the league. Roughly one thousand branches of the Land League took root in America, and several million dollars of donations flowed east across the Atlantic.[25]

American Catholic bishops, like their Irish counterparts, gave the league considerable support. Almost every American bishop and various groups of Catholic laymen urged special collections for Irish relief, with the Vincennes bishop Francis Chatard regretting the "poverty with which the people of Ireland are striken."[26] In Ireland itself Bishop Thomas Nulty of Meath seemed to argue for land nationalization, defining land as "common property of the people of that country, because its real owner, the Creator who made it, has transferred it as a voluntary gift to them."[27]

Nulty's radicalism on the land question was unrepresentative of the Irish hierarchy and unpopular with the Vatican, and even Nulty apparently wanted a wider distribution of land more than nationalization.[28]

Still, the land question became all-absorbing in Ireland, and a delighted George frequently quoted Nulty as he tried to lure Irish and Irish American Catholics into his movement.[29] The Irish statesman Charles Stewart Parnell seemed for a time to be in George's camp, and the most important strategist of the Land League, Michael Davitt, modeled his own program after George's.[30]

Parnell broke with Davitt in May 1882 and horrified George by negotiating a settlement with British authorities. Later that summer, while on an American tour, Davitt, too, began to equivocate, recognizing that new taxes on land might alienate Catholic tenant farmers desiring more widespread ownership of land, not less. A disgusted George described Davitt's moderation as "a pitiable exhibition of weakness."[31]

The collapse of the Land League ended the Irish phase of George's movement, but the fruits of the Irish agitation circled back to the United States. Already a clerk at New York City's Appleton's publishing firm had lent a copy of George's *Progress and Poverty* to his "beloved priest," Edward McGlynn, who read it as "a poem of philosophy, a prophecy and prayer," noting, "I had never found so clear an exposition of the cause of the trouble, involuntary poverty, and its remedy, as I found in that monumental work."[32] McGlynn then served as pastor of St. Stephen's parish on the city's Lower East Side, where he was locally famous for his support for Reconstruction in the South and for his opposition to parochial schools. McGlynn had assisted the Sisters of Charity in establishing St. Stephen's Home for Children in the early 1870s, where listening to the "never-ending procession of men, women, and children coming to my door begging not so much for alms as for employment" must have prepared the ground for his sympathetic reading of George's book.[33]

McGlynn's oratorical ability made him a popular figure in the Irish American community, and a natural to address the New York crowd gathered on July 11, 1882, to hear Michael Davitt in support of the Land League. McGlynn's remarks created an immediate controversy, since he regretted the reluctance of the Catholic clergy to "come out of their pulpits and come a little nearer to the people." After all, "Christ himself was but an evicted peasant." He announced that he "stood on the same platform as Henry George and Bishop Nulty of Meath. [Applause]." The no-rent strategy of the Land League simply recognized that the "landlords never owned the land and therefore no rent could be due them."[34]

A startled James McMaster quickly responded in the *New York Free-*

man's Journal, comparing McGlynn to French revolutionaries and dismissing the "schemes of Henry George and Michael Davitt."[35] Bishop Chatard of Vincennes and the auxiliary bishop Michael Corrigan of New York sent clippings from the New York papers to Cardinal Giovanni Simeoni in Rome, and Simeoni promptly dispatched a letter denouncing statements attributed to McGlynn that "contained propositions openly opposed to the teachings of the Catholic Church."[36] A month later a second letter arrived in New York from Rome, asking Cardinal John McCloskey to suspend McGlynn from priestly functions should he prove unable to refrain from political speeches. McGlynn apologized to McCloskey in a halfhearted way, but three years later he gave an interview in which he simultaneously emphasized the importance of church doctrine and the limits of property rights. In 1885 he evaded a query about yet another impolitic address.[37]

The explosion occurred in 1886. In April, Auxiliary Bishop Corrigan became Archbishop Corrigan, eager to exercise his new authority. That fall Henry George began one of the nineteenth century's most dramatic political campaigns, running for mayor of New York City against a Tammany Hall Democrat, Abram Hewitt, and a young Republican, Theodore Roosevelt. McGlynn became George's most prominent local supporter and a conduit from George's initial base among labor activists to the city's huge Irish working class. Corrigan demanded that McGlynn not accompany George on the hustings, and McGlynn refrained from delivering speeches. But he still traveled at George's side, delivering his single-tax blessing—"Our Father, who art in Heaven, Thy kingdom come, Thy will be done—*on earth*—as it is in Heaven"—to adoring crowds. A furious Corrigan permitted his vicar general, Thomas Preston, to compose a letter to a Tammany Hall official, with a simultaneous release for the local newspapers. Preston informed Tammany leaders that, "although we never interfere directly in elections," the "great majority of the Catholic clergy in this city are opposed to the candidacy of Mr. George. They think his principles unsound and unsafe, and contrary to the teachings of the church. . . ."[38]

George lost a close election (amid serious allegations of Tammany voter fraud), and his influence subsequently waned. Corrigan continued the fight, dragooning a local Jesuit, according to one source, and asking him to "pick out the best arguments and authorities against the George theory." The resulting pastoral letter, under the dubious heading of "faith," decried "unsound principles and theories which assail the rights of property."[39]

Corrigan successfully pressed Vatican authorities for McGlynn's (ultimately temporary) excommunication, and urged that *Progress and Poverty* be placed on the Index of Forbidden Books. More moderate bishops in the United States, Britain, and Ireland, eager to avoid newspaper headlines and convinced, in the words of Dublin's Archbishop William J. Walsh, of the "irrelevancy" of Corrigan's scattershot attacks on George, cautioned against hasty condemnation. Baltimore's Cardinal Gibbons, for example, urged the Vatican to let George's theory "die by itself." In a suave compromise the Vatican pushed Corrigan to the brink of apoplexy by placing *Progress and Poverty* on the Index of Forbidden Books, but ordering American bishops not to publicize the matter. "What's the use of it, if you can't publish it!" complained one of Corrigan's allies, Bishop Bernard McQuaid of Rochester.[40]

Immediately after receiving a copy of *Rerum Novarum* in 1891, Corrigan informed reporters that the pontiff had spoken "directly on errors that for a time and to some extent at least found acceptance in New York." (One opponent of Corrigan dryly noted that the archbishop's interpretation landed in the newspapers "even before the public has seen the encyclical.")[41] Eager for attention, Henry George agreed with his enemy. The encyclical, he excitedly told his son, is "aimed at us & us alone almost."[42] George dropped all other activities for three months after *Rerum Novarum*'s release, writing a widely distributed 118-page pamphlet congratulating Leo XIII for recognizing the "momentous seriousness" of the social problem, but regretting the pope's inability to see the necessity of the single-tax.[43]

George and Corrigan's mutual self-interest in reading *Rerum Novarum* as a commentary on the single tax did not mean both men were wrong.[44] The section of the encyclical on the importance of private property emphasized the challenge posed by European socialists, but the phrasing of paragraph 10—denying the view that "it is unjust for any one to possess outright either the land on which he has built or the estate which he has brought under cultivation"—did seem to evoke *Progress and Poverty*.[45]

One drafter of the encyclical, Cardinal Camillo Mazzella, had lived in the United States in exile for eleven years, becoming a close friend of Corrigan and Father Preston. In Rome, Mazzella and another drafter of the encyclical, Cardinal Tommaso Zigliara, sat on the commission that examined the McGlynn case. Mazzella's report on McGlynn included a summary of George's work, and Mazzella sat on the commission that (quietly) placed *Progress and Poverty* on the Index of Forbidden Books.[46]

Corrigan's vendetta against McGlynn—including the hiring of private detectives to investigate rumors of an illegitimate child—should not obscure the fact that Henry George's single tax did clash with an emerging Catholic social vision. Catholic single-taxers could rightly argue that Thomas Aquinas was less fervent in his defense of private property than Archbishop Corrigan implied, but the disagreement between Henry George and Pope Leo XIII rested upon broader grounds.[47]

The difference was one of approach. Despite his radicalism on the land question, George remained an economic liberal at heart, and he disdained trade unions, protective tariffs, and even limitations on work hours for women and children. These "superficial" measures seemed to George futile, even dangerous, since only a tax on land could level uneven economic playing fields. Then "unrestricted competition" would flourish, without the corruption and risk to individual freedom posed by a government bureaucracy attempting to administer a social welfare state.[48]

The importance of individual autonomy also seeps through George's evaluation of Catholicism. While hardly a standard anti-Catholic—George's wife was Catholic, and he sustained a long, friendly correspondence with an Irish priest enamored of the single tax—the McGlynn episode convinced George that Catholicism might prove incompatible with American freedom. After the 1886 mayoral campaign, George denounced Corrigan's "outrageous attempt to use the power of Rome in American politics." Such actions revealed a church "utterly inconsistent with free institutions." That Corrigan could at once discipline McGlynn and attend the funeral of the editor James McMaster, "during the war, a blatant enemy of the American Union," demonstrated for George the danger of a "power which coerces a most important and influential body of citizens."[49] Opposition to land reform on the part of Catholic prelates was unsurprising, since only McGlynn and the priests who supported George had been "intense haters of slavery when the retrograde clique were apologists of the peculiar institution."[50]

During the period of his excommunication, McGlynn also luxuriated in anti-Catholic tropes, declaiming that the church always seemed to be "opposing rational liberty, or the development of nationalities, or the advance of science." Later he mocked the "higher-archy" and announced, "I am not a Roman Catholic. I am an American Catholic."[51] McGlynn warned the readers of the *North American Review* that a "Germanized" and foreign Catholic Church might destroy the public school, the "palladium of our liberties, and the safeguard of American institutions."[52]

The Catholic social program put forward by Leo XIII started from different premises. If George's proposals had, at root, a vision of the autonomous individual, orthodox Catholic reformers moved in another direction. Hierarchical authority within the church remained unquestioned, and a series of miniature hierarchies, including the pastor within the parish, the father within the family, and the employer within the firm, remained cornerstones of the Catholic vision. Private property remained sacrosanct, and the American correspondent for *Civiltà Cattolica* insisted that workers desired their own houses, not the "elimination of property nor the right to possessions."[53]

Whereas Henry George dreamed of a nation filled with autonomous producers, unfettered by predatory corporations and an aggressive state, Leo XIII and other Catholic reformers envisioned an economy shaped by associations for employers and workers. The German Jesuit Victor Cathrein, the most important European moral theologian of the late nineteenth century, emphasized that liberalism failed by valorizing only "the individual and his independence, and almost entirely disregard[ing] his social relations."[54]

A remarkable number of Catholic intellectuals rushed to criticize George and, in so doing, articulated more clearly the distinctive characteristics of Catholic social thought. In Germany, Cathrein wrote an extended commentary on *Progress and Poverty*, and American Jesuits translated and reprinted Cathrein's "plain and convincing" articles in pamphlet form.[55]

In the United States, William Kerby, the mentor for two generations of Catholic sociologists at Catholic University, wrote his 1897 Louvain dissertation on American socialism and Henry George.[56] Arthur Preuss, editor of the *Fortnightly Review* in St. Louis, published a series of articles attempting to demonstrate that Catholicism and the single tax were "diametrically opposed to one another."[57] Father John A. Ryan, the central figure in the development of American Catholic social thought in the first half of the twentieth century, read *Progress and Poverty* as a Minnesota seminarian in the early 1890s. His first articles on the social question expressed a cautious admiration of George, but he also insisted on the importance of "state responsibility" while "the modern principle of *laissez faire* obtains in the commercial world."[58] Later Ryan faulted George for not defending private property with sufficient vigor and urged, instead of the "radical proposals of the Single Taxers," public housing and progressive taxation.[59]

III

Ryan's criticisms of Henry George meshed with the evolving views of non-Catholic reformers. Whereas during the debate over slavery in the 1850s a divide separated Catholics from liberals, Catholics and liberals in the early twentieth century agreed that the classical liberal economic vision of a minimal state and an open economic playing field had proved unworkable, and both came to advocate greater support for trade unions and the regulatory state. An undercurrent of tension also existed during this period around issues of censorship and sexual ethics, and the question of Catholicism's relationship to a democratic culture. Only in the 1930s would this undercurrent become more visible, taking a form that would shape the relationship of Catholicism and American liberalism for the rest of the century.

That common ground existed at all is surprising, since Catholics and liberals now worked from starkly different philosophical premises. For liberals the late nineteenth century saw an overturning of established modes in both philosophy and political reform. Philosophers such as William James and John Dewey scorned a priori truths and urged wider recognition of the fact that people discover their values in the flux of daily life, confronting particular problems and deducing general principles from these confrontations. Men like Galileo and Descartes, Dewey explained in 1916, deserved admiration because they possessed an "interest in discovery" and not an "interest in systematizing and 'proving' received beliefs."[60]

This same experimental spirit and rejection of authority guided not only pragmatic philosophers but also the editors gathered in the offices of the *New Republic*, and the lawyers and judges inspired by Oliver Wendell Holmes Jr. Holmes, in fact, described "jurists who believe in natural law" as being "in that naïve state of mind that accepts what has been familiar and accepted by all men everywhere."[61] Papal attempts to quash modernist theology were futile, explained the young journalist Walter Lippmann in 1914, because "there is no compromise possible between authority and the scientific spirit."[62]

In this new epistemological setting theology produced no data. John Dewey distanced himself from the Protestantism of his youth in the 1890s, and contemporaries such as the philosophers Horace Kallen and Morris Cohen rejected orthodox Judaism.[63] For these philosophers specific theological claims (Christian or Jewish) only masked arbitrary authority. "Faith in the continued disclosing of truth through directed co-operative human endeavor," Dewey asserted, "is more religious in quality than is any faith in a completed revelation."[64]

A necessary corollary to this conception of knowledge was the movement of elite universities away from religious moorings. Religion as an extracurricular activity continued to receive support; campus ministers were appointed and cavernous chapels built. But religion was no longer central to university intellectual life.[65] In the founding documents of the American Association of University Professors, claims to religious truth were deemed unscientific, and one initial proposal limited membership to all faculty teaching at institutions belonging to the American Association of Universities, "with the exception of the Catholic University." One duty of the professor, in fact, was to enable students to "think about heresies."[66]

Catholic intellectuals provided the most sustained opposition to these views. This resistance stemmed from Leo XIII's insistence in 1879 that Catholic theology work from Thomistic premises, a papal shove to a scholastic revival already immensely important for European and American Catholic intellectual life.[67] As early as 1874, German Catholic seminarians in Wisconsin and Jesuit scholastics in Maryland learned from their instructors of "the importance of St. Thomas' doctrine and his influence in the Church."[68]

If for William James truth famously meant nothing more than "the conduct it dictates or inspires," Catholics insisted that truth existed independent of particular investigators.[69] James and Dewey might roll their eyes at attempts to derive codes of conduct from abstract principles, but Catholic scholars gloried in the effort. The first English-language ethics textbook for American Catholic college students, written by the St. Louis Jesuit Walter H. Hill, began with the assertion "Truths that spring necessarily from the very nature of man and of human society, never change. . . ."[70] The pragmatists, from the Catholic point of view, seemed cavalier in their willingness to have "individual experience" trump objective notions of right and wrong.[71]

Over time Catholic philosophy departments and law schools became centers of natural law inquiry, and medieval studies centers were eventually founded at Louvain, Toronto, and Notre Dame. In the United States, Catholic colleges required virtually a second major (usually six courses) in Thomistic philosophy. As a result of this enormous educational effort, high school principals, labor organizers, and literary critics claimed to ground their lives and work in the ideas of Aquinas. For liberals "medieval" served as a pejorative epithet—the reformer Jane Addams instructed her readers in 1911 that a "grotesque Ecclesiasticalism" preceded the Renaissance. For Catholics, Thomistic philosophy became an architectonic discipline.[72]

The leading figures in American intellectual life paid little attention to their Catholic critics, isolated in underfunded seminaries and Catholic colleges. When Catholic scholars ventured out to philosophy conferences, they discovered that papers on Thomism were usually placed in the "historical" section of conference programs, a classification, as one Catholic noted, not intended to "flatter the adherents of Scholasticism."[73]

Still, the founders of American pragmatism habitually referred to Catholic authoritarianism as the logical opposite of their own rejection of a priori absolutes. Charles Peirce's famous 1877 essay "The Fixation of Belief," often identified as the first pragmatist salvo, invoked the First Vatican Council and contrasted a scientific approach to problems with the "method of authority" used in "the most priestridden states." (In a less measured draft, Peirce used the phrase "methods of despotism.") Peirce admired Abbè Gratry, a French liberal Catholic critical of the papal claim of infallibility, and he concluded that "[i]n Rome, especially," authoritarian methods had "been practised from the days of Numa Pompilius to those of Pius Nonus." A year later Peirce explained, "When the method of authority prevailed, the truth meant little more than the Catholic faith."[74]

William James defined pragmatism as "an alteration in the 'seat of authority' that reminds one almost of the protestant reformation," and a philosophy unlikely to appeal to "papal minds."[75] James cautioned against attacks on American Catholics, and his investigation of religious experience described Catholic mysticism in a friendly, if bemused, manner. Still, James's definition of religion as "the feelings, acts and experiences of individual men in their solitude" gave little solace to adherents of an institutional church. The single most important intellectual influence on James, the French philosopher Charles Renouvier, spent much of the 1870s and 1880s denouncing French Catholic schools, belief in the apparition at Lourdes, and papal infallibility, once confiding to James that "our clericals have fallen into such a state of imbecility."[76] James himself once explained to a correspondent, "I doubt whether the earth supports a more genuine enemy of all that the Catholic Church *inwardly* stands for than I do—*ecrasez l'infame* is the only way I can feel about it."[77]

A 1926 survey of leading academics was littered with fears that Thomistic philosophy served only as a pretext for an authoritarian institution to impose particular theological views. Harvard's Ralph Barton Perry complained that, for Thomists, Aquinas had "become an authority in the sense in which free-thinking and autonomous intellect can acknowledge no authority." Yale's A. K. Rodgers warned that Thomists seemed incapable of engaging in an "open-minded search for truth"; John Dewey frankly added that, since most philosophers had been "brought up in the Protestant tradition," they "identified Scholasticism with the theological dogmas which they do not accept."[78] (As late as 1960, remarkably, the academic honor society Phi Beta Kappa chose to deny the University of Notre Dame membership, in part because required philosophy "courses are rather too wholly and specifically Thomistic in content and orientation to provide a sufficiently liberal education on the philosophical level.")[79]

Philosophical differences, however, did not prevent political cooperation. Catholics and American liberals might differ as to *why* Henry George's plan should be rejected as impracticable, or *why* the state must check the ability of employers to exploit their workers, but they could unite on shared goals. Or as Father John A. Ryan explained to a group of New York social workers, "Since we are all working for the common good, we should aim to emphasize those elements that are common in our social doctrines, and to minimize all differences that are not based on essential principles."[80]

Catholics inspired by Leo XIII and pragmatic philosophers both identified economic liberalism as the enemy. Daniel Rodgers has traced how the reaction against unregulated free markets first entered American reform circles through cadres of graduate students studying at German universities, often under the tutelage of Adolph Wagner and Gustav

Schmoller, the leading economists at the University of Berlin. When these American economists and reformers—including Richard T. Ely, Florence Kelley, John Graham Brooks, and Henry Carter Adams—returned to the United States, they carried with them a German-bred suspicion of laissez-faire and a desire to prod the state to establish enhanced social insurance programs and regulatory measures.[81]

Catholics drew from the same wells. Catholic University's William Kerby, the Loyola sociologist Father Frederick Siedenberg, Father William Engelen, the labor activist Father Peter Dietz, and others studied in Germany between 1890 and 1910, and Kerby and Siedenberg took courses from Schmoller and Wagner. ("It is clear," advised one of Kerby's professors at Catholic University, "that you will find the best facilities for your advancement in Berlin or Leipzig.")[82] German American Catholic priests traveled to Aachen to study how German Catholics dealt with the "social question," and one German American priest lobbied for minimum-wage laws for women as part of a "Catholic program of reform" similar to that developed by the "Catholic school" in Europe.[83]

The most important Catholic social theorist of the early twentieth century, the German Jesuit Heinrich Pesch, also studied with Schmoller and Wagner and became a fierce opponent of the "unrestrained nature of the free economic system based on economic individualism."[84] In one of his first publications Pesch unfavorably contrasted Henry George's reforms with those proposed by Leo XIII.[85]

The career of the Catholic University professor Father John A. Ryan best reflected this Catholic-liberal rapprochement.[86] Ryan worked from a standard-issue scholastic template, and even his studies of wages and consumption contained excursions into Thomistic thickets. His ability, like that of almost all Catholic intellectuals of the period, to read Latin, French, German, and, often, Italian alerted him to ferment throughout Catholic Europe.

In one 1908 homage Ryan lauded European Catholics' cognizance of the "just claims of the poor and weak."[87] Ryan especially admired the work of Heinrich Pesch, terming his monumental *Lehrbuch der Nationalökonomie* "the most comprehensive treatise ever put forth in the name of political economy" and a successful effort to define "solidarity" as a Catholic principle more compelling than "individualism and Socialism."[88]

Ryan's recommendations—that employers provide a "living wage" capable of supporting a (male) breadwinner and his family "in a manner consistent with the dignity of a human being," and that the state regulate the working hours of women and children—placed him on the moderate left wing of American social reform.[89] Like so many early twentieth-century reformers, Ryan viewed economics and theology as being of a piece. I am "pursuing a postgraduate course in moral theology," he told Richard T. Ely, a liberal Protestant and the country's most important reform economist, "together with courses in economics." In a combination of academic duties unlikely today, Ryan taught both moral theology and economics at Catholic University, arguing that "economic inquiry is . . . intended to serve solely as a basis for ethical conclusions."[90]

Ryan's first major study included an introduction by Ely, and Ely privately urged wide distribution of Ryan's work, noting, "The Catholics have some quite strong and pronounced views on various social and economic problems, and these views are of interest to others as well as to Catholics."[91] When Ryan later sent a copy of one his many pamphlets to the reformer and Harvard Law School dean Roscoe Pound, the eminent

Father John A. Ryan, 1930.

jurist congratulated him for not thinking solely in terms of the "individual." Ryan, in turn, agreed with Pound's criticism of courts' "guaranteeing to the individual an excessive amount of freedom, particularly freedom of contract."[92]

As a seminary professor in St. Paul, Minnesota, Ryan drafted one of the first state minimum-wage laws. After moving to Washington in 1915, he became an active member of the American Civil Liberties Union, a collaborator with Florence Kelley in her effort to establish minimum-wage laws for women, and the Catholic whose name was inevitably on a bewildering number of progressive mailing lists. One of Ryan's many protégé's, Father Edwin O'Hara, led the successful Oregon campaign to pass the nation's most comprehensive minimum-wage legislation for women. Working with Ryan and the National Consumer League, O'Hara demanded that "a living wage shall be regarded as the first charge of industry; it shall rank with the rent and interest and take precedence over profits and dividends."[93]

In 1919 Ryan drafted a plan for postwar Reconstruction issued under the name of bishops on the Administrative Committee of the National Catholic War Council. Although they conceded, "It is not to be expected that as many or as great social changes will take place in the United States as in Europe," the bishops still demanded old-age and unemployment insurance, labor participation in management, a minimum wage, and municipal heath clinics. Workers, the bishops recommended, should learn "the folly of excessive selfishness and senseless individualism." Heavy taxation had the salutary effect of forcing a "small class of privileged capitalists . . . to return a part of their unearned gains to society."[94] The editors of the *New Republic* responded to the bishops' proposals with delight, and a commentator for the *Nation* speculated that, as in Germany, Catholics and secular reformers might establish a new "kinship."[95]

And yet the achievements of Ryan and other Catholic reformers were atypical. First, the absence of specifically Christian trade unions, again in contrast to much of continental Europe, limited the contact of Catholic clerics with the labor movement before the mass industrial unions of the 1930s. Catholics did hold many high union offices, especially in the American Federation of Labor, but the most obvious legacy of early Catholic involvement in the union movement was not the development of Catholic social thought but Catholic leadership in the struggle against socialism. The Fall River, Massachusetts, bishop William Stang, for example, agreed with "many thoughtful men outside the Catholic Church [who] have come to the conclusion that nothing can prevent the spread of Socialism or save society from destruction except the Church of Rome."[96] In Milwaukee, the largest American city with a socialist government, Catholics and socialists engaged in bitter polemical warfare, and a disproportionately high number of those Polish Catholics drawn to the socialist party also joined the schismatic Polish National Catholic Church.[97] In New York City socialist organizers complained that they could not organize "Catholic workmen owing to the strong anti-Socialist attitude of the Catholic clergy."[98]

American socialists responded in kind. In Britain and Australia, Labour Party leaders rarely broke into antireligious diatribes, and Catholic leaders, in return, condoned the entrance of Catholic workers into socialist political parties.[99] American socialism was more sectarian, and its leaders begged Catholic workers to abandon a "superstition . . . based upon tyranny and oppression."[100] A leading Texas socialist, William Hickey, constantly returned to the subject of Catholic iniquity, and J. A. Wayland, the founder of the *Appeal to Reason*, the most important socialist newspaper in American history, also founded the most popular anti-Catholic journal of the early twentieth century, *The Menace*, which claimed a circulation of one million in 1914.[101] Even nonsocialist radicals such as the Minnesota congressman Charles Lindbergh Sr., father of the pilot, would urge congressional investigation of the Catholic Church, whose leaders "in all lands and at all times" have been the "ally of oppression."[102]

Second, the absence of an American Catholic political party limited Catholic influence. Teaching in Washington, D.C., and serving as Social Action Division director for the newly formed National Catholic Welfare Conference (NCWC) elevated Ryan to the status of Washington insider, including "the very pleasant custom" of Thanksgiving dinner each year at the home of Justice Louis Brandeis.[103] But Ryan was unusual. Already burdened by an instinctive desire to turn political questions into metaphysics, Catholic social thought in the 1910s and 1920s became even more loosely tethered to the practical world of reform. Even Ryan mournfully concluded, "We have many institutions, such as hospitals and asylums, for the relief of actual want and suffering, but few if any for the *prevention* of these and other social evils."[104]

Information was not the problem. Less than a decade after *Rerum*

Novarum's release, German American Catholics in the Midwest, a San Francisco priest supportive of local unions, and a St. Paul judge could routinely invoke the encyclical.[105] (The judge refused to order an injunction against a plumbers strike, explaining, "[I]f all the owners of capital and all the owners of labor would pay heed to the simple and beautiful lessons of justice taught in the encyclical from which I have quoted there would be no labor troubles, for the occasions from which they arise would cease to exist.")[106] By the 1920s the president of the American Federation of Labor could casually agree to deliver a lecture on *Rerum Novarum*, and Franco-American activists in Woonsocket, Rhode Island, would refer to the encyclical frequently.[107]

The difficulty lay in implementation. A Minnesota Catholic scholar might insist that "the spirit of the Catholic Church and the spirit of Capitalism cannot permanently co-exist," but how would a more corporatist American society develop?[108] In Europe politicians and intellectuals of all sorts urged a corporatist reconstruction of society after World War I, giving Heinrich Pesch's grid of vocational groups, modest state intervention, and a limited free market a rough plausibility.[109] Political parties dominated by Catholics played an important role in this effort, and the influence of Catholic social thought on the German Center Party, France's Parti Démocrate Populaire and Italy's Partito Popolare was palpable.[110]

In the United States free-market capitalism was more entrenched. (A prominent French priest, when visiting the United States in 1918, was horrified by the worker's "mind-numbing" role as a cog in the industrial machine.) Herbert Hoover's vision of cooperation between business and government offered only a faint echo of European reform, and Hoover hatched his plans in a Republican Party with few Catholic members.[111]

This problem of irrelevance was particularly sharp in the German American Catholic subculture. As early as the 1860s German American Catholics founded American branches of German workers' associations and developed life insurance, health, and unemployment programs modeled on those developed in the Rhineland. But ritual invocations of Bishop Ketteler at annual banquets of the German American Central Verein in the late nineteenth century did not make Ketteler's attacks on laissez-faire more relevant to a political universe controlled by Democrats and Republicans.[112]

In the twentieth century the problem became more acute. In Germany, Catholic social thought powerfully influenced the views of Konrad Adenauer, a leading Center Party politician before World War II, and West Germany's most important political figure after 1945.[113] In the United States, German Catholic activists struggled to influence more than one another. The difficulty was not simply that these German Americans addressed a dwindling German-language constituency. Instead, the Jesuit Joseph Husslein's sympathy for medieval guilds and his glum view of the "selfish spirit of rationalistic capitalism that sprang into being after the Reformation" made him an exotic.[114] Another Jesuit, William Engelen, who before moving to the United States knew Pesch in Germany, also placed himself on the margins of American political culture in his description of liberalism as a "reprehensible" system.[115]

Finally, the Democratic Party remained an unlikely vehicle for Catholic reform. The party did develop a more social emphasis in the first two decades of the twentieth century, modifying traditional Democratic faith in limited government and local autonomy. A leader in this shift, a young New York Catholic politician named Al Smith, created a series of social welfare programs as a New York state assemblyman and then governor. But Smith developed his ideas in concert with an eclectic mix of Democratic reformers, not Fordham Jesuits.[116]

And as Smith himself learned, the wave of anti-Catholicism that swept the country in the early 1920s would also engulf the Democrats. An anti-Catholic Ku Klux Klan enrolled roughly two million members and controlled several state governments by 1924, and Protestant evangelicals and pentecostals became even more fiercely anti-Catholic. In Georgia, before and after his election to the U.S. Senate in 1920, the onetime Populist radical Tom Watson published a stream of attacks on Catholicism, for hostility to "republican institutions," alliance with the "moneyed power," and sympathy for African Americans.[117] Watson's senatorial colleague, the Alabama Democrat Thomas Heflin, spent much of the decade fulminating against the "Roman hierarchy and the political machine" and promoting talks by "escaped" nuns.[118] Voters in Oregon approved a law prohibiting Catholics from enrolling children in parochial schools, and threats of similar measures roiled Michigan politics. (Bewildered Catholics called such measures a "new Bismarck Kulturkampf.")[119]

William McAdoo, the leading Democratic candidate for the presidential nomination in 1924, refused to condemn the Klan, for fear of alienating the party's white southern wing. (One despairing Catholic Democrat informed McAdoo's campaign manager "that the report of McAdoo's sympathy or tolerance of the Klan is being persistently circulated among the Catholics of this country. Nearly every Catholic paper in the country has mentioned it.")[120] At the Democratic convention in 1924, the party imploded in a debate over whether to approve a platform plank critical of the Klan.[121]

Sympathy for Catholics came from an unexpected quarter. The first decades of the century saw the flowering of a self-consciously tolerant American intelligentsia more welcoming of diverse immigrant cultures and willing to accept Jews within its ranks.[122] This tolerant sensibility crystallized in opposition to the campaign for immigration restriction, the Ku Klux Klan, and Protestant fundamentalism. The immediate effect was to delegitimize insinuations that Catholicism was incompatible with democracy. (H. L. Mencken thought the Catholic hierarchy "not over-burdened with men of wisdom and discretion" but preferred ridiculing "Methodist and Baptist witchburners.")[123] As late as 1937 the literary critic Van Wyck Brooks pondered whether to publicly announce his concern about "Political Catholicism." "But how?" Brooks asked. "What's the best method?—short of raising the Ku Klux bogey and the latent hatred of popery all over the country."[124]

This liberal sympathy proved especially important as Al Smith began angling for the 1928 Democratic presidential nomination. Beyond explicitly religious periodicals Smith's Catholicism provoked little establishment opposition, although veiled comments about Catholicism even crept into endorsements. ("Happily," Felix Frankfurter concluded, "Smith has not set, doctrinaire 'principles' but possesses a mind free for new experience and responsive to its directions." The philosopher E. C. Lindeman described Smith as "the pragmatist in politics. His mind is not encumbered with *a priori* generalizations.")[125] Still, for most intellectuals Smith became a symbol, as one *Nation* editorial put it, "of tolerance in American life—racial, religious, and social tolerance, accepting into the American family the city-dwellers who have come to us within the last century." During the presidential campaign Reinhold Niebuhr chided Protestants opposed to Smith on religious grounds for engaging in tiresome polemics. Felix Frankfurter argued that a vote for Smith implied "an unequivocal rejection of any sectarian allegiance as a disqualification for the presidency," while John Dewey emphasized his disgust with the "narrow bigotry" so pervasive in American public life.[126]

These sentiments stirred the Brahmin essayist John Jay Chapman, one of the few commentators to express concern about the Catholic threat, into action. "Our plain people have been murmuring and muttering long enough," Chapman complained. "Have we not college presidents, historians, theologians, preachers, writers on all subjects, and especially on social subjects? . . . Are our intellectuals otherwise engaged?"[127]

Chapman's feeble attempt to rally "Protestant intellectuals" suggests his isolation from an intellectual world suspicious of denominational chauvinism. The sole attempt to meet Chapman's challenge was an open letter in the *Atlantic Monthly* to Smith from Charles Marshall, a previously obscure New York lawyer. Marshall, too, noted the "strange reticence" concerning the religious issue in public debate. He plunged forward, asking whether Smith, like the authors of nineteenth-century papal encyclicals, denied American notions of religious freedom. Marshall also wondered how Smith would mediate claims between a state that claimed the right to determine educational standards and a church that viewed education as integral to moral formation.[128]

Smith's initial reaction—"I never heard of these bulls and encyclicals and books"—became part of American political folklore. Following consultation with his advisers and a New York priest, Smith drafted a more measured reply, which the *Atlantic Monthly* then rushed by special trucks from Boston to New York for prompt distribution, and which major newspapers reprinted in full.[129] He dismissed Marshall's questions since in his own experience conflicts between religion and public policy had been nonexistent. Catholic practice—loyalty to the nation, service during the war—outweighed bickering "over dogmatic principles."[130]

Smith's reply generated an enthusiastic response. A few Catholics privately expressed reservations about Smith's dismissal of papal texts, with one Kentucky Catholic wondering if Smith was a "dangerous radical in religion," but non-Catholic liberals were jubilant.[131] "It should forever make it impossible for the form of a public man's religious faith to become a political issue in this country," wrote the editors of *Outlook*, while Walter Lippmann described it as "a landmark in the history of toleration" and "a great document of genuine historic importance." Even the previously skeptical *New Republic* conceded that Smith's reply left "nothing to be desired." Indeed, the exchange between Marshall and Smith "should deprive every American citizen of any reasonable ground for refusing to support him on the pretext of his Catholicism."[132]

Unfortunately, kind words carried little electoral weight. In retrospect

Smith's chances against the popular Hoover were slim, but anti-Catholicism proved the decisive issue for voter behavior, the factor more than any other that ensured his defeat. Prominent southern ministers led a fierce campaign against Smith on the basis of his opposition to temperance and his Catholicism, and traditionally Democratic states such as Texas, Oklahoma, and Florida swung into the Republican column. In a postelection report to the apostolic delegate, officials from the National Catholic Welfare Conference explained that "the Catholics of this country feel that the Republican party and the Republican leaders, at least tacitly, allowed this anti-Catholic campaign."[133]

IV

The gloom of the late 1920s, with Catholic politicians such as Al Smith stymied by popular prejudice and Catholic social thought unable to gain a hearing, quickly dissipated. A harbinger of change was the release of Pius XI's encyclical *Quadragesimo Anno*, in May 1931. Drafted by the German Jesuit Oswald von Nell-Breuning, with the later assistance of some French Jesuits, the encyclical in its title marked forty years since Leo XIII's *Rerum Novarum*. Taught by Heinrich Pesch, Nell-Breuning was part of a circle of German Catholic activists eager to integrate theology and the social sciences in the combustible atmosphere of Weimar Germany. In 1930–31 the group, dubbed the Königswinterer Kreis, met monthly to discuss social policy. Nell-Breuning, sworn to secrecy by the pope, used these occasions to float ideas for what would become *Quadragesimo Anno*.[134]

Released at the height of the global depression, and drenched in German Catholic corporatism, *Quadragesimo Anno* was not an inevitable extension of *Rerum Novarum*. Where *Rerum Novarum* dwelt on the rights of property owners, *Quadragesimo Anno* emphasized the "social character of ownership." Both documents allowed an important role for capitalist enterprise, but *Quadragesimo Anno* stressed that "the right ordering of economic life cannot be left to a free competition of forces. For from this source, as from a poisoned spring, have originated and spread all the errors of individualist economic teaching." Whereas Leo XIII recommended workers' associations, Pius XI drew upon Heinrich Pesch and insisted that "corporations" with worker and employer representatives jointly direct particular industries.[135]

In ordinary times such an uncompromising, even utopian, document would have landed with an awkward thud on American shores. But the worldwide depression hammered the United States more severely than any other industrial nation, and by 1931 even Catholic bishops, such as Cincinnati's John T. McNicholas, were informing audiences that "one of the crimes of our country is the concentration of inconceivable wealth in the hands of a comparatively small group."[136]

More radical Catholic movements also bloomed in this economic climate. In France, Emmanuel Mounier and an energetic circle of young French intellectuals founded the influential magazine *Esprit*, preaching the need for a Catholicism opposed to a dehumanizing capitalism and Soviet communism. The most important radical Catholic movement in American history, the Catholic Worker, was founded in 1933, a year after the first issue of *Esprit*, and drew inspiration from Mounier. (Peter Maurin, a French transplant and Mounier disciple, was one of the two founders of the Catholic Worker.) The Catholic Worker's other founder, Dorothy Day, became the guiding force behind its weekly newspaper, which reached 185,000 readers by 1940.[137]

A superb journalist, Day specialized in portraying the human costs of unemployment, poverty, and despair. She placed less emphasis than mainstream Catholic figures like Father John A. Ryan on government programs and more on direct aid to the poor, and the utopian and pacifist strands within the Catholic Worker movement would become more pronounced in the 1940s. In the 1930s, however, Day joined coreligionists in focusing on the plight of workers and provided sympathetic coverage of the decade's most important strikes. In its first issues the *Catholic Worker* chose to reprint *Quadragesimo Anno*.[138]

To their surprise, Catholics also found an unexpected champion. Just before the 1932 election the Democratic presidential candidate, Franklin Roosevelt, sent a giddy tremor through Catholic circles by quoting *Quadragesimo Anno* before a large Detroit crowd. The encyclical, Roosevelt explained, was "just as radical as I am" and "one of the greatest documents of modern times."[139]

Roosevelt's determination to avoid religious squabbles—during the Al Smith controversy he had informed the editor of the *Atlantic Monthly*, "I can't see the point of discussing 50 year old dicta of Pius the Ixnth [*sic*] in relation to American public officials of 1927 who happen to be Catholics"—and his casual acquaintance with Catholic social thought proved an irresistible mix. One New York Catholic journalist excitedly informed Father Ryan that Roosevelt's victory would mean a "knowledgeful friend and intelligent champion of the social and economic doctrines recommended to us by Authority and experience."[140]

The cornerstone program of Roosevelt's first term, the National Recovery Administration (NRA), confirmed this optimistic view. The NRA established trade associations for the major industries that permitted companies to agree on common pricing and production strategies. Trade associations were required to negotiate with labor unions, and accept an undefined level of government supervision.[141]

This focus on economic planning meshed with the vision outlined by Pius XI. Some Catholics complained about the limited role for organized labor in the NRA structure, but Bishop Karl Alter of Toledo expressed the dominant sentiment when he decided that Roosevelt's first inaugural "breathes the spirit of our Holy Father's recent encyclical."[142] John A. Ryan described Pius XI and FDR as both rejecting "laissez-faire, eco-

Dorothy Day, ca. 1930s.

nomic liberalism and so-called rugged individualism" and eagerly accepted an invitation to serve on the NRA Industrial Appeals Board. Another Catholic writer viewed Roosevelt as moving toward "the Solidarism advocated by Father [Heinrich] Pesch in his National Oeconomie over forty years ago."[143]

V

That Catholic and liberal intellectuals viewed economic planning, not economic growth, as the most logical antidote for the depression, that they stressed the importance and legitimacy of trade unions, and that they supported Franklin Roosevelt marks the early 1930s as a high point for the Catholic-Liberal alliance.

Another cluster of issues signaled conflict. As long as American reformers focused on economic reforms, Catholics proved loyal allies. But important components of progressive activism lay in the cultural sphere, as suggested by liberal campaigns for more explicit sex education in the schools, less rigorous censorship of books and films, and greater access to birth control.[144]

Here lay a fundamental difference. The Catholic vision of social reform, unlike the dominant non-Catholic alternative, saw no connection between social reform and individual autonomy. Employers should pay a living wage because it was just, John A. Ryan explained, and because such an ideal derived from the "received doctrines of the Church."[145]

Non-Catholic reformers such as John Dewey thought received doctrines irrelevant. Dewey claimed no hostility to religion, and many of the most active reformers of the period were Protestant ministers, but pragmatic openness had unstated limits. Most obviously, no church or minister should be allowed to make social policy upon what Dewey termed the "crutch of dogma, of beliefs fixed by authority."[146] Walter Rauschenbusch, perhaps the foremost advocate of the Social Gospel, insisted in 1917 that theology is either "despotic or democratic."[147]

Open any Catholic text written in the late nineteenth and early twentieth centuries, and a different vision jumps out. Catholic writers saturated their prose with disparaging references to what John A. Ryan termed a "perverse individualism" and its effect on social cohesion.[148] Starting with the Reformation and continuing through the French Revolution, Catholics explained, a "false individualism" had culminated in the extremes of wealthy and powerful "men with absolute right to use their possessions as they please" and "robbers" willing to eliminate private property. An Iowa German Catholic enthusiastic about *Rerum Novarum* identified "corporative organization" as the only check against the "heretical principles of Liberalism which is the father of Individualism."[149]

This mistrust of individualism in all spheres led to Catholics' favoring the minimum wage *and* barriers to divorce, economic planning *and* film censorship. Joseph Husslein, S. J., pleaded for "opposition to divorce and birth control legislation" because he worried about the effect of liberal individualism on the family; in the same breath Husslein argued against economic individualism and for "beneficient legislation for working men and women."[150]

Even Catholic radicals such as Dorothy Day rejected the sexual experimentation so important to the Greenwich Village bohemian milieu of her youth. When her radical friends learned of Day's conversion to Catholicism in the late 1920s, they wondered, tellingly, if she had lost interest in sex. Day, for her part, mocked reformers convinced that contraception would solve all "the troubles in the world." The socialist Emma Goldman's advocacy of free love struck Day as "promiscuous." Instead, she encouraged Catholics to find love not by tossing aside conventions such as marriage but within the elemental bonds formed by submission to God and family.[151]

A family ideal, in fact, remained at the core of Catholic social thought. John A. Ryan's demand for a living wage for male workers was at once an economic reform and a defense of traditional gender roles since Ryan judged it "imperative that the wife and mother should not engage in any labor except that of the household." Fathers exhausted from overwork, and mothers forced to labor outside the home, could hardly devote proper attention to raising their children.[152] "Avaricious and arrogant" employers, another priest later complained, should not force wives to leave the "incipient domestic circle" and make the home an "adjunct to the shop or factory."[153]

After initial hesitation many Catholic activists did endorse women's suffrage.[154] (Still, German and Irish Catholics in the Midwest and Irish Catholics in New England persistently voted against suffrage referenda into the early twentieth century.)[155] Even liberal Catholics, however, urged Catholic women not to mimic "feminine adherents of extreme theories." Far better to demand higher wages for all citizens, along with protection for women forced to labor outside the home.[156]

When Alice Paul and the National Women's Party demanded an end to protective legislation for women and an equal rights amendment to the Constitution in the early 1920s, Catholics, along with most Democrats, responded with alarm. Agnes Reagan, representing the National Conference of Catholic Women, informed a congressional committee, "To demand identical rights for men and women is absolutely unreasonable. . . . The differences of function—the results of natural law—imply essential differences in rights and duties. The preservation of these rights justifies special legislation."[157]

Catholics also found themselves at the center of censorship debates. Back in 1873 Protestant moralists led by Anthony Comstock, not Catholics, had persuaded Congress to prohibit the mailing of obscene literature and contraceptive devices, and upper-crust New Yorkers and Bostonians, not Catholics, first headed local societies dedicated to the suppression of vice and the scouring of bookstores for indecent material. In the first decades of the twentieth century, however, Progressive Era reformers found Comstock's equation of innocence and purity off-putting, and Comstock's reliance on religious absolutes clashed with an increasingly powerful sense that scientific investigation, not Victorian moralism, must serve as the foundation of public policy.[158]

Ensconced in the same northern cities that served as centers of artistic innovation, Catholics replaced aging Protestant ministers as the guardians of public morality. Catholics decried the "repeal of reticence" that accompanied widespread public discussion of sexuality, and the liberal conceit that, as Father John Burke put it, "knowledge is virtue and ignorance is sin."[159]

The result was a series of conflicts. When Chicago reformers instituted a course of sex education in the public schools in 1913–14, Catholics argued that information about sex in a nonreligious atmosphere would inevitably demolish "every vestige of supernatural restraint."[160] Young people, one priest explained, needed instruction in morals, not simply hygiene, and reminders of "the nature, the enormity, the ravages of sin."[161]

In Boston, Catholics on the city licensing board continued the oversight of theater productions and booksellers begun by the Brahmin Watch and

Ward Society.[162] By 1929 the American Civil Liberties Union head Roger Baldwin could complain of the "extraordinary combination of the Catholic, Puritan, and Victorian spirit," and Horace Kallen later lamented the indignities suffered by Boston artists under the tyranny of a "female Catholic sodality."[163] Leaders of the lingering remnants of such societies as the New York Society to Suppress Vice began asking Catholic priests, not Protestant ministers, to assist in the removal of offensive books from public library shelves.[164]

Catholic influence culminated at the movies. The relatively decentralized publishing industry offered at best a moving target, and the very attempt to label books as obscene heightened their allure. The extraordinary popularity of films made them a more dangerous medium—the *National Catholic Welfare Conference Bulletin* warned in 1919 that "the influence of motion pictures upon the lives of our people is greater than the combined influence of all our churches, schools, and ethical organizations"—but the consolidation of the motion picture industry in the 1920s also presented an opportunity.[165] Catholic priests and bishops began contemplating strategies to influence films at the point of production; one Jesuit emphasized that organized Catholic activity might bear fruit "since Catholics are an influential part of the population of all large cities."[166]

The Jesuit Daniel Lord led the campaign. Lord drafted a production code in 1929 that ultimately served as the guidebook for all films produced by major studios. During the first years of the code's operation, from 1929 to 1934, Lord and the code's supporters struggled to enforce their will on studios eager to expand their audiences through suggestive scripts. Futile protests against films that condoned premarital sex or portrayed happy criminals made Lord and other Catholics eager for more effective measures. By 1933 Lord had enlisted the aid of the Catholic bishops, who authorized the formation of the Legion of Decency in 1934, and encouraged millions of Catholics to take the decency pledge against attending movies identified as objectionable. (Philadelphia's Cardinal Dougherty briefly forbade local Catholics from attending *any* films.)

Catholic pressure on the box office pushed reluctant studio executives to the bargaining table, and by the mid-1930s a Production Code Administration used guidelines drafted by Father Lord to review and censor all Hollywood films, arguably the most influential cultural products in the world. Lord's casual use of natural law terminology in the production code—"the law which is written in the hearts of all mankind"—and his conviction that the task of art remained that of "lifting men to higher levels" suggested his Catholic training. So too did his refusal to approve any cinematic treatments of abortion, venereal disease, homosexuality, and birth control.[167]

VI

Understandings of gender and sexuality would eventually become the central dividing line between Catholics and American liberals, and divisive within Catholicism as well. The most important topic, initially, was birth control, and here too, as on economic matters, *Rerum Novarum* is suggestive. Matteo Liberatore's first draft for the encyclical included a sentence denouncing the "detestable act" of contraception and called on the pope to stop its growth in Christian countries. In a later version one of the encyclical's editors scratched out Liberatore's sentence, not because of doubts about contraception's immorality, but with the following question jotted in the margin: "Is it appropriate to remark upon such depravity?"[168]

In itself condemnation of contraception in the late nineteenth century was unremarkable, since most religious leaders maintained a united front on the subject until the 1920s.[169] Leslie Tentler has brilliantly demonstrated that a distinctive Catholic campaign against contraception emerged only haltingly in the first decades of the twentieth century, scaling the formidable hurdle of Victorian reticence about sexual matters.[170]

As contraceptive practices, including the use of condoms and withdrawal, became more widespread, Catholic leaders overcame their initial hesitation. Sexual intercourse, Catholic philosophers began to explain, like freedom itself, had particular ends. And the primary end of intercourse remained procreation. Attempts to interfere with this end through contraception violated the natural law.[171]

This set of assumptions—that the primary end of sexual intercourse was procreation, that inhibition of that end distorted the primary purpose of the sexual act, and that contraception itself violated the natural law—fueled Catholic activism. In both the United States and Europe, Catholic clergy began to worry that the allure of smaller families came at risk to Catholic souls. Here the distinctive Catholic practice of confession was also crucial. Until the 1920s and 1930s most Protestant and Jewish leaders also opposed contraception, but their discussion of the issue, at best intermittent, had an ethereal air. For Catholics, by contrast, birth control posed acute problems. Since many Catholic adults attended confession monthly, or even weekly, and since all Catholics were asked to attend confession after having committed serious sins, Catholic priests routinely confronted the issue as a matter of intense practical concern.

As on economic issues Father John A. Ryan spearheaded American activism on family matters. As early as 1906 Ryan disparaged attempts to encourage low-paid workers to limit their offspring. Such efforts, he argued, pinned the blame for insufficient wages on the individual and obscured the "responsibility of society and the necessity of social action." Alternatively, he castigated "self-centered" men unwilling to marry, since "only in the family is it possible for the majority of men to develop those social feelings that are essential for the welfare of a democratic society."[172] In Germany Heinrich Pesch also urged the implementation of a family wage in order to avoid "white death" or the "decrease in the number of people caused by unnatural birth prevention," and French Catholic activists pondered the relationship between the birthrate and the "crisis of production."[173]

In 1916 Ryan urged priests to overcome their inhibitions and publicly address the problem of contraception. Already, he warned, many Catholics found church teaching impracticable. "Despite the optimistic and boastful language that we sometimes affect when contrasting the conduct of our people in this matter with that of the people without the fold," he concluded, "we are forced to acknowledge in our colder moments that large sections of the Catholic population are considerably tainted." Catholics needed "intelligent instruction" because use of birth control leads to "loss of reverence for the marital relation" as well as "softness, luxury and materialism."[174] In 1919, probably at Ryan's urging, the same bishops who surprised liberals by calling for a minimum wage and various social insurance programs earlier in the year attacked the "selfishness" and the "crime" of defeating the "obvious purpose" of sexual intercourse.[175]

Ryan's call for public articulation of Catholic teaching reflected a misplaced confidence that Catholic couples would alter their behavior once properly instructed, but he also reacted to the issue's new prominence. More than any other person, Margaret Sanger, arrested in 1914 for offering contraceptive advice in a newspaper, had brought contraception and birth control into public discussion. Sanger's mother remained a devout Catholic, but her father, an impoverished Irish radical, cultivated his daughter's anger at a Catholic Church opposed to progressive causes. (He named Sanger's younger brother Henry George McGlynn.)[176]

Sanger and other birth control activists understood Catholic leaders as valuable foils, since Protestant and Jewish leaders inevitably expressed reluctance about joining a Catholic-led crusade. And Catholics obliged. Public awareness of Catholic opposition to contraception became widespread after 1921, when New York police broke up a public meeting of the American Birth Control Conference. Allegations that the police acted at the behest of New York's Cardinal Patrick Hayes remained unproven, although plausible. Hayes did take the occasion to issue a pastoral letter, read out loud at each Sunday Mass in over three hundred New York churches, with this conclusion: "Children troop down from Heaven because God wills it. . . . Woe to those who degrade, pervert, or do violence to the law of nature as fixed by the eternal decree of God Himself!"[177]

Quick to define the contest as Catholics versus the enlightened, Sanger immediately informed readers of the *Birth Control Review*, "[Y]ou can no longer remain neutral. You must make a declaration of independence, of self-reliance, or submit to the dictatorship of the Roman Catholic hierarchy."[178] "The R.C.'s are certainly taking their stand against this subject & me," Sanger wrote to a friend, ". . . but it may serve to awaken the Protestant element, in time to save the country later on."[179] The *New Republic* echoed Sanger, explaining, "Birth control is obnoxious to men and women of obscurantist mind." To insist, like Archbishop Hayes, on "'natural law' where there is no natural law is the first necessity of a doctrinaire institution."[180]

The next decade saw an escalation of the debate. As early as 1921 Mary Ware Dennett of the National Birth Control League explained to her supporters, "[S]ince Dr. Ryan of the National Catholic Welfare Council has sent instructions to all Catholic Women's organizations to oppose the birth control movement and they are faithfully responding, we too must now be heard."[181] By 1923 Dennett could tell sympathetic congressmen that the only "organized opposition" came from "the Catholics."[182]

Always more combative, Sanger mocked Catholics by recommending that the United States admit more Italian immigrants, but only if the Italian government agreed to promote widespread birth control.[183] In 1928 Sanger broke with her progressive allies by favoring the Republican Herbert Hoover over the Democrat Al Smith. A Catholic member of a New

York parents' group, she claimed, had prohibited the American Birth Control League from participating in a New York educational exhibition. "This conflict brings into the open," she warned, "the menace of intolerant tyranny in the educational institutions of the United States. If such power is to be given national scope, through a Presidential aspirant, its disastrous effect on the future of American civilization will be incalculable."[184] The *Birth Control Review* explicitly identified Catholics as the primary obstacle to reform:

> No one can deny that the Catholic opposition is the keystone of all the opposition of Birth Control. . . . It explains why social workers believe in Birth Control while social agencies do not officially endorse it; why intelligent doctors concede the need for it, both in curative and preventative medicine while the American Medical Association refuses to declare itself . . . why politicians and political parties do not take a stand. There are, in each case, Catholic supporters, patients, voters, who must not be antagonized.[185]

Catholics did speak on the subject of birth control with increasing frequency, struggling to keep pace as the issue ricocheted through labor unions, civic groups, and settlement houses. "One of the questions we have been apathetic about," explained Agnes Reagan of the National Council of Catholic Women, "is birth control. We did not talk about it, but now we have got to talk about it."[186] Catholics queried the postmaster general to ensure that he agreed with restrictions on mailing birth control devices, and contacted European Catholics in the hope of preventing the League of Nations from distributing birth control information. "I would like to hear you are going [to a Denver conference of Social Agencies]," the Reverend John Burke of the NCWC wrote to a colleague, "for I fear the Birth Control propagandists will seek its support."[187] A year later Burke referred to the "constant fight against Federal legislation that would promote the propaganda of Birth Control."[188]

In these early years few Democrats risked Catholics' wrath by supporting or sponsoring legislation on birth control. When Catholics complained to President Franklin Roosevelt about federal workers' encouraging the use of birth control in Puerto Rico, Roosevelt quickly made it clear that "Federal Government officials" in his administration would refrain from "teaching Birth Control."[189] The situation was much the same in Britain and New Zealand, where Catholic opposition checked the efforts of Labour Party activists to loosen restrictions on access to birth control. In Germany, too, Catholics in the Center Party agreed with many economic policies of the Social Democrats, but disagreed on the matter of birth control.[190]

Still, a handful of Republicans and maverick Democrats, encouraged by Sanger, Dennett, and other leaders of the birth control movement, sponsored bills to increase access to birth control. In their response Catholics relied upon two arguments. First, they stressed that the problem was insufficient wages, not overpopulation. In one pamphlet aimed at workers, the National Catholic Welfare Conference argued, "Society should be reorganized. It should be reorganized so every willing worker will as a matter of fact, get enough work and wages to live comfortably."[191] Or as Father John Burke informed one birth control advocate, "Instead of working for a living wage that would enable a man to maintain his wife and family in plenty, you are working to have him number his children in light of his income."[192]

Second, couples using birth control merited condemnation. According to John Ryan, couples employing contraceptive techniques indulged in a "love of material goods and a self-indulgence." Even as the most severe depression in American history enveloped Catholic families, Father Ignatius Cox warned in 1930, "People of even the lower middle classes today think necessary things which were luxuries only of the rich a few years ago."[193] A distinguished Catholic anthropologist, Father John Cooper, saw attempts by parents to limit their families to three children as a "rationalization" for "self-centeredness" and "egoism."[194]

Women bore the brunt of this rhetorical attack. Father Cox calmly advised women not to subscribe to the "foolish fear" that their husbands must have a "big salary before thinking of children." Each additional child, Cox assured Catholic mothers, promised additional happiness.[195] Father Daniel Lord equated married women using birth control with prostitutes.[196]

A culmination to a decade's worth of discussion on human sexuality occurred in 1930 and 1931. The Universalist and Unitarian churches adopted reports approving the use of birth control, as did the Central Conference of American Rabbis. The Federal Council of Churches, the most prominent umbrella group for mainline Protestants, gave its blessing to "careful and restrained" use of contraceptives by married couples.[197] The most important shift, one that generated worldwide publicity, occurred among Anglicans, whose bishops in 1930 voted to permit the use of contraception among married couples with "a morally sound reason."[198]

Catholics responded to these developments with alarm. In the United States, Father Charles Coughlin, just emerging as the most influential American radio voice, told his millions of listeners that the Federal Council of Churches had abandoned natural law and "traded and bartered [Protestant church members] to the god of political economy."[199] Even the editors of *Commonweal*, a Catholic journal founded by laypeople in 1924 and usually associated with the more liberal end of the Catholic spectrum, saw Protestants' acceptance of birth control as the "liquidation of historical Protestantism by its own trustees." Contraceptives, the editors claimed, were risky to women's health, and greater access to the devices would increase sexual activity outside of marriage.[200]

The direst warnings came from Rome. There the Continent's most influential moral theologian, Arthur Vermeersch, S.J., set to work immediately after the Anglican declaration. A Belgian native, Vermeersch spent two decades in the chair of moral theology at the Gregorian University in Rome, training priests and advising bishops and popes. Like John A. Ryan, Vermeersch worked to develop the social doctrine enunciated in *Rerum Novarum* and advocated various measures to increase economic equality.[201] One of Ryan's colleagues reported from Rome that Vermeersch claimed to be "teaching moral theology practically and doing the same thing that Dr. John Ryan is doing at Washington."[202]

Also like Ryan, Vermeersch had long been convinced, in the words of one 1909 article, that contraceptive use constituted a "grave moral peril."[203] Vermeersch helped draft a pastoral letter on the subject issued that year by the Belgian bishops, and subsequent letters issued by the German, French, and Austrian hierarchies followed a similar template.[204] In 1930 Vermeersch, along with the German Jesuit Franz Hürth, helped compose the papal encyclical *Casti Connubii*. The encyclical consolidated Catholic teaching in the strongest terms. Procreation remained the final, and most important, end of sexual intercourse. No reason, "however grave," justified use of contraceptives, an act "intrinsically against nature."[205]

Released within four months of each other, each written in a prophetic, uncompromising tone, *Casti Connubii* and *Quadragesimo Anno* stretched Catholic teaching to its severest limits. Each document, the one on marriage and the other on the economy, called for wages to match needs. John A. Ryan, predictably, delighted in the passages in *Casti Connubii* that urged government officials to "do their utmost to relieve the needs of the poor."[206] Another American commentator considered the "strongest passages" in *Casti Connubii* to be those which "reassert the obligation incumbent upon employers to give the worker a wage which will enable him to live in accordance with his rights as a human creature."[207]

VII

Until the late 1930s tensions between Catholics and liberals on cultural matters seemed manageable. Catholics remained crucial to the fortunes of the Democratic Party, and the increasing importance of heavily Catholic trade unions to Democratic electoral prospects cemented this alliance. Chicago, Pittsburgh, Boston, and other major cities boasted Catholic mayors during the mid-twentieth century, and Catholic political chieftains such as the Bronx's Ed Flynn served as Democratic strategists and presidential advisers.[208]

Just as Catholics made up a large percentage of the American working class in the North, so too did Catholics include many of the most prominent trade union leaders, including Philip Murray, James Carey, and John Brophy, three founders of the Congress of Industrial Organizations. (Murray's "industrial council" plan, the period's most important union-led effort to gain workers greater responsibility for corporate management, self-consciously followed the model enunciated in the papal encyclicals. According to legend, Murray kept a copy of *Rerum Novarum* in his office for quick reference, and he certainly enjoyed invoking *Quadragesimo Anno*.)[209] Priests across the country spent the 1930s encouraging their parishioners to join unions, and some, like Pittsburgh's Charles Rice, Detroit's Frederick Siedenberg, and Buffalo's John Boland, served on regional labor boards and played key roles in workplace negotiations. Catholic labor schools sprouted up across the country, as priests offered tutorials in parliamentary procedure and Catholic social thought to ambitious union stewards, and the American Catholic Trade Unionists established chapters in a number of northern cities.[210] Detroit's Archbishop Edward Mooney published a 1939 article with the revealing title "Duty of the Catholic Worker to Join Organized Labor."[211]

John A. Ryan's seventieth-birthday celebration, held at a Washington hotel in 1939, drew a crowd of six hundred, including labor leaders, Democratic Party officials, thirty congressmen, two cabinet secretaries, and three Supreme Court justices. The church, explained one dinner speaker, was not "reactionary and unprogressive." Instead, Catholics simply rejected "the doctrine of laissez-faire taught in the system of nineteenth century liberalism." President Franklin Roosevelt sent Ryan a telegram, read out loud at the dinner, congratulating him for advocating the "cause of social justice and the right of the individual to happiness through economic security."[212]

And yet, even as Ryan basked in these accolades, the terrain was shifting. Within the Roosevelt administration, the intractability of the economic crisis had already sapped the enthusiasm of planning advocates. In desperation the president and his advisers stumbled into a program of deficit spending in the late 1930s, roughly along lines suggested by the British economist John Maynard Keynes. The language of common good and social welfare, so prominent in early New Deal pronouncements, became replaced by efforts to increase consumer buying power.[213] Ryan's forlorn 1938 request that economic planning and redistribution of wealth take precedence over "new inventions to produce new luxuries" meant little when measured against this individualist economic current.[214]

The almost miraculous success of deficit spending as an economic stimulant during the war marked a decisive end to discussion in America of economic planning and, in contrast to European countries with strong Catholic or socialist political parties, ensured a less comprehensive American social welfare state.[215] But American Catholic intellectuals only grudgingly acknowledged this growing divide between the program of the Democratic Party and that of Pius XI. Whispers that it might be "difficult to find the true corporatist formula for the modern economy" reached the pages of Roman journals, but American Catholics continued to yearn for the programs of the early New Deal and, in more rhapsodic moments, to condemn the "chronic social sickness" brought on by followers of Adam Smith.[216] As late as 1944 one Jesuit published an attack on "economic liberalism" and asserted that salvation lay only in "cooperative endeavor."[217]

Meanwhile, for many liberal intellectuals, economic inequality paled in importance compared with the threat posed by European fascism. That many Catholics expressed sympathy for fascist governments in Italy and

Spain would come to seem of a piece with opposition to birth control, Father Charles Coughlin's increasingly anti-Semitic radio addresses, a reluctance to support public schools, and an eagerness to censor Hollywood films. That such a church exerted a powerful influence on American culture, long after George Santayana confidently predicted in the *New Republic* in 1916 that American freedoms would act as a "solvent" upon Catholic distinctiveness, was disturbing.[218] In 1938 the editors of the *New Republic* posed the question "Is there a Catholic Problem?" This time, in contrast to Santayana's cool assurance, the answer was yes. In fact, "certain well-defined tendencies and activities in the Catholic Church have recently become so prominent as to force themselves on the attention of thinking Americans and to raise the issue of Catholic political policy to the magnitude of a public question."[219]

Chapter Six

AMERICAN FREEDOM AND CATHOLIC POWER

I

The most unusual best-seller of 1949 and 1950—a volume that began as a series of articles in the *Nation*, garnered a recommendation from the Book of the Month Club, and sold forty thousand copies within three months of publication—was Paul Blanshard's *American Freedom and Catholic Power*. "At every social event I have attended this winter," reported one Harvard professor, "it seems to me that discussion centered on either Blanshard's 'American Freedom and Catholic Power' or on T. S. Eliot's 'The Cocktail Party.'"[1]

Blanshard claimed that "the Catholic problem is still with us." His solution was the formation of a "resistance movement" to counter the "antidemocratic social policies of the hierarchy and . . . every intolerant or separatist or un-American feature of those policies." Blanshard's second treatment of the matter, *Communism, Democracy, and Catholic Power*, defined Catholicism and Soviet communism as parallel threats to American democracy.[2]

Neither book was a cautious monograph. Blanshard described nuns as belonging to "an age when women allegedly enjoyed subjection and reveled in self-abasement," blamed Catholics for producing the bulk of white criminals, and termed the parochial school "the most important divisive instrument in the life of American children."[3]

Blanshard correctly assessed the intellectual mood. Already Lewis

Mumford had warned that "the Catholic Church by acting as a bloc" might destroy the "separation of powers established in the Constitution of the United States," and Reinhold Niebuhr had lamented the chasm "between the presuppositions of a free society and the inflexible authoritarianism of the Catholic religion." Even as John Dewey cautioned against a "reactionary world organization," the Washington minister A. Powell Davies, a founding member of Americans for Democratic Action, worried that "people tired of doing their own thinking" might choose either Roman Catholicism or Stalinism.[4]

Following the publication of *American Freedom and Catholic Power*, Dewey praised Blanshard's "exemplary scholarship, good judgment, and tact." Albert Einstein and Bertrand Russell commented favorably, and Harvard's McGeorge Bundy termed the book's publication "a very useful thing."[5] The philosopher Horace Kallen congratulated the editor of the *Nation*, Freda Kirchwey, on the "bang-up job you had Blanshard do on the church. Ever more power to you!"[6]

Scholarly reviewers were equally enthusiastic. One prominent sociologist admired Blanshard's "objectivity" and "calm but razor keen analy-

Paul Blanshard signing copies of his books, Chicago, 1951.

sis."[7] The Johns Hopkins philosopher George Boas described the church as a "most bitter opponent of the liberal tradition" and compared the "dual loyalty" of American Catholics to that of American communists. Professional philosophers, he advised, should become familiar with Blanshard's work "in detail."[8] Representatives from Princeton and Massachusetts Institute of Technology wrote Blanshard at the height of the controversy surrounding *American Freedom and Catholic Power*, urging him to save drafts of his work, which they assured him would be of "substantial historical interest."[9]

These archival efforts seem premature, since few scholars have investigated mid-twentieth-century fears of Catholic power.[10] And yet discussion of Catholicism, along with criticism of racial segregation and opposition to fascism and communism, helped define the terms of postwar American liberalism. These terms included the insistence that religion, as an entirely private matter, must be separated from the state, and that religious loyalties must not threaten intellectual autonomy or national unity.

These concerns became evident in the mid-1930s, when Catholics seemed sympathetic to authoritarian regimes in Europe and Latin America, and culminated a decade later as Catholics requested aid to parochial schools. Whereas in the 1850s Protestants worried about democracy's fate might also have scorned Catholic devotion to Mary, now a more ecumenical group of Protestants, Jews, and nonbelievers prided themselves on avoiding theological wrangling. During one warmly received Harvard address Blanshard expressed pleasure that "the new movement against Catholic aggression is rising not on the fringes, the lunatic fringes of religion and fanaticism, but right in the hearts of American University leaders."[11]

II

A vital backdrop for fear of Catholic power was the acceptance of anthropological notions of culture. Instead of the term's late nineteenth-century suggestion of personal development, "culture" by the 1930s meant the webs of meaning supporting seemingly disparate practices in a particular society. Robert Lynd explained that culture is "the things that a group of people inhabiting a common geographical area do, the ways they do things and the ways they think and feel about things, their material tools and their values and symbols."[12] Each piece in a culture connected to the larger puzzle; values learned in one place necessarily shaped the whole. Lynd and his wife, Helen, subtitled *Middletown*, their influential survey of Muncie, Indiana, *A Study in Modern American Culture*. Ruth Benedict's best-selling *Patterns of Culture* explicitly compared American mores with those of seemingly more primitive peoples.[13]

Pervasive Catholic separatism—on philosophical matters and in schools, hospitals, and social organizations—posed an "integration" problem. How would Catholics become democrats? To respond as Al Smith did when challenged in 1928, that Catholics would remain loyal citizens, was to miss the point. Democracy was a culture, not a set of propositions. Catholics obviously lived *among* Americans, but were they *of* them? That this question intrigued leading liberal intellectuals is suggested by John Dewey's wartime investigation of Philadelphia's Polish community during World War I. Dewey regretfully concluded that Polish Americans lay in thrall to a "corrupt" Catholic Church. Priests presided over political meetings; parishes sent delegates to national conventions.[14]

Paul Blanshard, then a graduate student at Columbia, briefly worked as part of Dewey's team, and Paul's brother Brand, later a prominent Yale philosopher, stayed for the entire summer. Brand Blanshard's final report was not circumspect. "The test of any institution or society" he wrote, "is . . . the extent to which it enables and encourages every member of it to enjoy complete freedom of growth." Polish Catholicism failed. "It is a world which is simply not our world, a world in which independent criticism and disinterested science is and must remain unknown, a world which still abounds with the primitive concepts and fancies of the middle ages." The church's influence presented a "many-sided and in some ways impossible barrier to the real democratization of the communities it controls."[15]

Other authors also highlighted these themes. Pining for the days of Baltimore's Cardinal Gibbons, who allegedly saw the church as "simply and essentially American," the French social scientist André Siegfried warned his American colleagues, "The Catholic Church is thus a thing apart in the heart of the American body politic . . . in the long run it remains distinct and does not fuse."[16] The University of Chicago Divinity School professor and church historian Winfred E. Garrison explained, "No more serious error can be made in judging the spirit, the attitudes and the methods of Roman Catholicism in the United States at the present time than the assumption that it has been permeated and transformed in some subtle fashion by the spirit of American institutions."[17]

Garrison's tone was irenic, assuring his readers "that this is not designed to be in any sense an anti-Catholic book." For the most part, he rehearsed familiar arguments about potential Catholic threats to religious liberty. But he worried that "tired minds and timid minds" might abdicate the "responsibility of deciding upon difficult questions." A *New Republic* editorial laid out the alternatives in a stark fashion:

> The real conflict is not between a Church and State or between Catholicism and Americanism, but between a culture which is based on absolutism and encourages obedience, uniformity and intellectual subservience, and a culture which encourages curiosity, hypotheses, experimentation, verification by facts and a consciousness of the processes of individual and social life as opposed to conclusions about it.[18]

III

For most American liberals, the importance of economic planning and the redistribution of wealth receded in the late 1930s, replaced by concern for individual freedom. Propelled by a constant distinction made between fascist repression and the American devotion to civil liberties, this new focus on freedom jump-started the campaign for civil rights for African Americans and set a new agenda for American liberalism, even as it prompted new questions about the relationship of Catholicism and democracy.[19]

The first dispute had occurred over Mexico, where President Plutarcho Calles led an unprecedented enforcement of measures directed against the church in the 1920s, including the replacement of Catholic schools with a secular educational system, a series of restrictions on the activity of priests, and the transfer of church property titles to the state. Eventually, government armies had fought Catholic peasants, or *Cristeros*, in a guerrilla war marked by savagery on both sides.[20]

Many American liberals had sympathized with the Mexican government. John Dewey observed that "the church can hardly escape paying the penalty for the continued ignorance and lack of initiative which it has tolerated if not cultivated."[21] The future U.S. senator Ernest Gruening referred to the "fanatical bigotry" of the Mexican church. Gruening acknowledged the harshness of the Mexican government's actions, but defended such measures as "the fruit of the Mexican church's own past and present performance."[22]

American liberals also criticized Catholic pressure groups. As early as 1916, editors of the *New Republic* had attacked Catholics for evaluating Woodrow Wilson's Mexican policy "not in its national, but in its religious aspect." In 1927 prominent Democrats demanded that Al Smith formally renounce any possibility of the Vatican's influencing United States policy on Mexican affairs.[23]

In response American Catholics supported their religious brethren. To Catholics the attacks on priests and church property signaled a lawless regime, and a surge of Mexican Catholic refugees across the Rio Grande testified to the horrors of religious persecution.[24] In 1934 the archbishop of Los Angeles organized a forty-thousand-person rally in defense of the "lowly and the unprotected [who] are being persecuted." Spontaneous cheers of "Viva Christo Rey!," the cry of Catholic forces in Mexico, swept the crowd, and marchers carried banners invoking the aid of Our Lady of Guadalupe.[25]

That American liberals could ignore the actions of the Mexican government seemed inexplicable to Catholics. "It is heartrending," wrote one American bishop, "to know that men like [the prominent New York liberal minister Harry] Fosdick and [the Harvard president A. Lawrence] Lowell are willing to stand sponsor for the crime and injustice of the Calles regime." The priest in charge of the American Catholic lobbying effort in Washington, D.C., complained to the American ambassador to Mexico "of the general attitude of the American press. [And] how ridiculous it was for American liberals and American liberal newspapers to support Calles, who had destroyed liberty."[26]

Even as the Mexican crisis eased, Catholic willingness to accommodate European fascist regimes created greater controversy. Pope Pius XI, aided by his secretary of state, Cardinal Eugenio Pacelli, the future Pius XII, viewed the compromise and bargaining inherent to democratic politics with suspicion, and favored concordats devoted to protecting Catholic interests over the cultivation of independent Catholic political parties. In Germany, Hitler's cunning manipulation of Pacelli, combined with the Vatican's naïveté about the ability of a negotiated agreement to check Nazi aggression, led to a German-Vatican concordat in July 1933. This agreement—aimed at protecting Catholic institutions and organizations in exchange for an end to Catholic "political" activity—muted official German Catholic opposition to the Nazi regime.[27]

In Italy church leaders condoned the evisceration of Father Luigi Sturzo's Catholic political party, the Partito Popolare, because of their conviction that Benito Mussolini and Italian Fascists would prove better able to resolve ongoing land and legal disputes.[28] In 1929 Pius XI signed a concordat with Mussolini abandoning papal land claims beyond Vatican City in exchange for assurances that the Fascist government would permit Catholic youth organizations and reintroduce religious instruction into the schools.

Many American intellectuals also fell under Mussolini's spell during the 1920s and 1930s, but American Catholic bishops, often former Roman seminarians with personal experience of hostility between the Vatican and the Italian state, were especially prone to marvel at Mussolini's ability to defuse church-state tension.[29] Boston's Cardinal O'Connell called the Italian "transformation" a "wonder"; New York's Cardinal Hayes remarked that Mussolini had shown himself "unusually favorably disposed to the progress of the Catholic Church."[30] Even prelates vigorously critical of Hitler and the Nazis, such as Chicago's Cardinal George Mundelein, regretted as late as 1938 that "the Government of Mussolini was not treated with equity in the [American] press."[31]

The Spanish civil war became the pivotal episode.[32] For American Catholics, even liberals such as Father John A. Ryan, the culpability of the Spanish Loyalists, who had murdered priests and nuns and destroyed churches during the civil war, was obvious. They supported, in the words of the leaders of the American Jesuits, General Francisco Franco's attempt to resolve the "chaos caused by those who had attempted to establish a Communist State in Catholic Spain." (In turn, the generalissimo thanked the Jesuits for assisting in the effort to "eliminate for all times from our soil the hordes of Moscow.")[33]

Most American intellectuals, by contrast, found it inconceivable that men and women of good will could support Franco's armed revolt. "We cannot help being disturbed," wrote the authors of a 1937 manifesto entitled *American Democracy v. Spanish Hierarchy*, "by the fact that no leaders of the Catholic Church in America have raised their voices in repudiation of the position taken by the Spanish hierarchy."[34]

Few American liberals condoned the slaughter of priests and nuns by

Loyalist soldiers, but they repeatedly emphasized the inevitability of anticlerical passion in a culture with tight connections between bishop and landlord. In one battlefield dispatch Waldo Frank noted that Loyalist refugees had taken over an abandoned seminary, humbly eating porridge "where perhaps three years ago the plump candidates for the priesthood heard the exposition of the *Summa* of Aquinas."[35]

The cumulative effect of the divide between Catholics and liberals over Mexico, Italy, and, especially, Spain meant that extended analysis of connections between Catholicism and fascism appeared throughout the liberal press. Reinhold Niebuhr's conclusion that "the Catholic Church has cast its lot with fascistic politics" echoed Lewis Mumford's regret that "the Church has chosen to ally itself with democracy's chief enemy, fascism."[36]

For many liberals Father Charles Coughlin's popularity within the United States seemed a domestic counterpart to European and Latin American demagogues. Liberals acknowledged that influential Catholics desired to muzzle the radio priest, and they applauded Father John A. Ryan's 1936 radio address criticizing Coughlin, a speech given front-page coverage in the *New York Times*. (Ryan chided "frightened liberals who think that Father Coughlin is going to set up a Fascist State," but he also lambasted Coughlin's economic proposals.)[37]

Coughlin's turn to openly anti-Semitic appeals in the late 1930s, and the formation of virulently anti-Semitic Christian Front groups inspired by Coughlin, heightened liberal fears.[38] One prominent Jewish leader, Rabbi Julius Morgenstern, conveyed these concerns to the Catholic bishop Francis Kelley. Certainly "many within the ranks of Catholicism" had attacked Coughlin, Morgenstern conceded, but the experience of the United States in the 1920s and Central Europe in the 1930s confirmed that "religious prejudice" remained a "dangerous thing."[39] In 1939 Supreme Court Justice Felix Frankfurter, the journalist Max Lerner, and the Roosevelt aide Benjamin Cohen convened a small group of Jewish leaders to discuss American anti-Semitism. One topic of discussion, according to the minutes, was the insularity of the "Catholic group, both the hierarchy and the laymen."[40]

That Catholics inevitably leaned toward fascism also seemed confirmed by their recalcitrance on civil liberties issues. When Mayor Frank Hague banned allegedly communist speakers from Jersey City, New Jersey, for example, outraged liberals pointed to Hague's Catholicism.[41] The Dartmouth sociologist John Mecklin bluntly explained in 1938, "The

Catholic church has little sympathy with the democratic idea of free speech." Catholics had sustained a "medieval conception of liberty" despite living in American cities imbued by a "democratic way of life."[42] In 1945 the critic Edmund Wilson darkly attributed difficulties in persuading bookstores to stock his sexually explicit novel, *Memoirs of Hecate County*, to New York's Cardinal Spellman. Three years later Wilson termed Catholicism a "retrograde and repressive force" and regretted that its power had increased since Al Smith's 1928 presidential campaign.[43]

Even academic freedom seemed at risk. The Harvard sociologist Talcott Parsons, one eye on Boston's Catholic pols, nervously worried that "it may well be interpreted as an obligation of Harvard professors to take especial care in what they say publicly about the Catholic Church, because of the possible repercussions through political channels on the university."[44] More combatively, Sidney Hook urged Edward Shils at the University of Chicago to rally professors "who will not accept the authority of the Catholic hierarchy." Along with Stalinism, Sidney Hook declared, the sympathy of some University of Chicago leaders for Thomism and the "authority of the Catholic hierarchy" posed the "gravest threat to academic freedom on campus."[45]

The removal of the philosopher Bertrand Russell from his post at New York's City College in 1940 became an important cause célèbre. An Episcopalian bishop led the charge against Russell, but most observers attributed the actual termination of Russell's contract to influential Catholic politicians convinced that Russell's views on sexuality and marriage made him an enemy of "common decency." The Jesuit weekly, *America*, set the tone, describing Russell as a "desiccated, divorced and decadent advocate of sexual promiscuity" and contrasting his character with that of the Fordham-educated judge John E. McGeehan, who had upheld the revocation of Russell's appointment. Archbishop Francis Spellman questioned the "wisdom of subsidizing the dissemination of falsehood under the guise of liberty," and a local Jesuit bemoaned that the term "liberal" now seemed to require sympathy for the "irreligious viewpoint."[46]

Russell privately blamed Catholic influence for his plight, and his friends Horace Kallen and John Dewey quickly put together a volume of essays on the case. "You need have no scruples," Kallen told one contributor, the Yale law professor Walter Hamilton. "You are dealing with a bully [Judge McGeehan] who spoke not for himself but for the whole Catholic hierarchy and used its very language."[47] Kallen described the "ecclesiastical assault on Bertrand Russell" as nothing more than "the current phase of a warfare waged by priestcraft against men of faith and science." Indeed, Kallen wondered whether the Russell affair "concealed an ecclesiastical-political assault on Americanism?"[48]

IV

Defining "Americanism" was exactly the issue. From the mid-1930s to the early 1950s intellectuals concerned about Catholic power labored to demonstrate the non-hierarchical sources of American culture, a project in which Catholicism played a strategic, antithetical role. According to the editors at the *New Republic* and the *Nation*, a broad group of faculty members in the humanities and social sciences, and many influential figures in Reform Judaism and mainline Protestantism, Catholic authoritarianism might quash the scientific spirit, produce adults incapable of psychological autonomy, and have a disastrous effect on national unity because of the growing number of children enrolled in Catholic schools.

These liberals avoided defending democracy in philosophical terms. Instead, in an argument that meshed with the growing interest in culture, liberals insisted that all-encompassing philosophical definitions, such as those made by Catholics devoted to a natural law approach, led to German-style authoritarianism. Sidney Hook, for example, conceded that many Catholics opposed the Nazis, but insisted that "that doesn't make them democrats in a cultural and religious sense."[49] John Dewey concluded his 1939 essay *Freedom and Culture* with the recommendation that Americans not mimic their fascist or communist opponents; the more appropriate task was to cultivate a democratic style directly opposed to "external authority, discipline, uniformity and dependence upon The Leader."[50] Privately, Dewey warned against a "policy of 'appeasement' [toward the church.]"[51]

The *Encyclopaedia of the Social Sciences*, one of the great intellectual projects of the era, used the same language, defining intolerance as "the refusal to appraise social programs in a tentative, experimental manner." The most obvious example of intolerance was Catholicism, since "a religious institution claiming universal validity and essential changelessness for its doctrine of salvation is necessarily intolerant." Or as Horace Kallen explained, only "the methods, the conception [and] the implications of the sciences" could produce a Catholicism compatible with "democracy and loving kindness."[52] "The only religion appropriate to the democratic faith," Charles Morris, a University of Chicago philosopher, announced, "is a non-dogmatic religion."[53]

Fortunately, American democracy rested on "non-dogmatic" premises. Cited as supporting evidence in this regard was Thomas Jefferson. A veneration of Jefferson unlikely among intellectuals today (few scholars in the 1940s, for example, were troubled by Jefferson's ownership of slaves) found expression in Jefferson's appearance on the nickel beginning in 1938, the inauguration of a massive Princeton project to catalog the Jefferson papers, the installation of a series of Jefferson murals in the new Library of Congress building, and the lavish ceremonies dedicating the Jefferson Memorial in Washington in 1943.[54]

Jefferson, his admirers insisted, "took religious individualism for granted, disdaining even to discuss it publicly and recommending to others a similar independence and quietness of spirit. This is true and typical of religious enlightenment." Scholars retrieved Jefferson's Virginia Statute for Religious Freedom, which led to the disestablishment of the Anglican Church, from relative obscurity. (The 1940 volume *The Living Thoughts of Thomas Jefferson*, edited by John Dewey, reprinted the statute under the heading "Intellectual Freedom and Progress.")[55] In the Jefferson Memorial a copy of the statute runs along the second wall; above all else in the dome is the statement "I have sworn upon the altar of God eternal hostility against every form of tyranny over the mind of man."[56] As Horace Kallen argued, "Every schoolboy knows the Declaration of Independence and the Bill of Rights. The Virginia Statute of Religious Liberty should be no less familiar."[57]

Interpretation of the Reformation proved even more important. By linking democratic traditions to the Protestant reformers, scholars clearly distinguished Catholic from American. Since the intellectual community now included significant numbers of Jews and nonbelievers, specific theological claims received less emphasis than a more ecumenical enthusiasm for autonomy, science, and dissent. Indeed, the emergence of the term "Judeo-Christian" in the 1940s served to link the prophetic, anti-institutional emphases found in Protestantism and Judaism.[58] Jews were essentially "democratic in worship," concluded Joseph L. Blau, and shared with Protestantism a common "individualism in religious teaching."[59] Or as Harvard's Howard Mumford Jones put it, "Our culture is a Protestant, and not a Catholic culture; it is a Protestant culture begun in dissent and retaining dissent as its chief characteristic."[60]

American historical surveys between the late 1930s and the 1950s provide an entry into this impulse. One group of scholars met in 1945 to investigate "which of the communions had effectively fostered liberty and brotherhood, and which had been antagonistic." They concluded that "it was no accident that democracy should have run half its course in modern history before it invaded a Roman Catholic country."[61] William Warren Sweet, the dean of American church historians, also emphasized American indebtedness to Puritans and Calvinists for "[a]ll the great concepts for which American democracy stands today."[62] Catholicism threatened these achievements as "the most closely knit and the most powerful pressure group in the nation."[63]

General historical accounts were more nuanced, but made similar arguments. "It may seem strange," began one overview "that an account of American faith should begin with a brief survey of the Reformation in Europe," but "[d]emocracy did not arise out of eighteenth century political and industrial conflicts, as a . . . popular view misconceives." The Quakers advocated equality before the movement of Jefferson's pen, Roger Williams and William Penn lobbied for religious liberty, and the Pilgrims practiced self-government.[64] Henry Steele Commager's influential survey of the "American Mind" concluded that the "theological implications of Puritanism wore off in the course of the eighteenth and nineteenth centuries," but Americans retained a "Puritan inheritance of respect for the individual . . . of recognition of the ultimate authority of reason, of allegiance to principles rather than to persons . . . and to spiritual and moral democracy."[65]

More than one alternative in a philosophical menu, pragmatism became an extension of American culture. Commager described pragmatism as "[p]ractical, democratic, individualistic, opportunistic, spontaneous, hopeful [and] wonderfully adapted to the temperament of the average American." (And he worried that Catholicism might prove "inconsistent with the American principles of liberty and democracy, complete freedom of expression, separation of church and state, and secular control over public education.")[66] Yale's Ralph Gabriel suggested that William James simply "formulated in terms of a sophisticated philosophy the essential ideas and convictions of his countrymen."[67]

Other philosophical systems were suspect. The literary critic Van Wyck Brooks became convinced in 1940 of what he had "*felt* all along, that there is something diabolical in all this modern Thomism" and the editors of the *Literary History of the United States* explained that "no Aristotelian criticism" could ever fathom a body of writing "profoundly influenced" by "democratic living."[68] One group of leading historians soberly warned their colleagues in 1946 to "place absolute systems of thought in their appropriate settings of time and place."[69]

The use of the Reformation to juxtapose Catholicism and democracy is strikingly evident in enthusiasm for the work of Max Weber, which, as we have seen, was powerfully shaped by conflict between Protestants and Catholics in Germany. Talcott Parsons's English translation of Weber's *The Protestant Ethic and the Spirit of Capitalism* appeared in 1930. In 1937, in his monumental *The Structure of Social Action*, Parsons became the first American intellectual to stress Weber's importance for social theory, emphasizing his agreement with Weber's claim that the Reformation marked a turning point for the modern West.[70]

In a 1940 memorandum Parsons outlined the importance of these cultural underpinnings for American democracy. He concluded that "Anglo-Saxon Protestant traditions"—notably a concern for civil liberties and support of experimental science—provided the most substantial barriers to an American fascism. By contrast, Parsons noted an "authoritarian element in the basic structure of the Catholic church itself which may weaken individual self-reliance and valuation of freedom." He knew that some Catholics disliked the attitude taken by the hierarchy on various issues, but he worried that "when confronted with the opposition of 'fascism' and the 'democratic' forces which have a leaning to the left, the policy of the Church has been wavering." As late as 1952 Parsons expressed concern about the "'structural strain' of considerable proportions" produced by the Catholic Church in America, pointing to Quebec as an example of a Catholic society inhospitable to educational and scientific progress.[71]

Parsons also directed a trio of admiring footnotes in *The Structure of Social Action* to the forthcoming work of a Harvard Ph.D., Robert Merton, for whom Parsons had served as a thesis reader. In the most influential essay ever written by an American on the history of science, Merton claimed to confirm Weber's speculation that the Protestant ethic supported not only capitalism but the emergence of modern, experimental science. Calvinist Protestants in seventeenth-century England were willing to replace "cloistered contemplation" with "active experimentation." Merton counted Catholic and Protestant scientists, satisfying himself that Protestants, even in predominantly Catholic France, were more likely to achieve distinction.[72] Parsons began referring to the "Weber-Merton" thesis and the inability of the medieval "schoolmen" to advance scientific knowledge. Merton's mentor, the Harvard historian of science George Sarton, claimed that science in Italy failed to develop because "the Italian climate of that time was not favorable to the development of untrammelled truthseeking."[73]

Again the stakes were considerable. A crucial marker of a democratic culture, liberals agreed, was an enthusiasm for science. Or as Merton argued in a 1942 essay, experimental science rested most comfortably in modern democracies, with their climate of "organized skepticism."[74] Science and democracy, Horace Kallen asserted, were "diverse flowerings from a common root."[75]

Proof that Catholicism hindered science, then, possessed high polemical value. A *New Republic* writer contrasted a Catholicism prone to censorship of ideas with the "scientific humanism animated by Christian ideals that had become the best by-product of Protestantism." The anthropologist Ashley Montague reviewed a "very timely" analysis of the Inquisition for *Isis,* the leading history of science journal. "Catholicism," Montague explained, "is a religion which challenges thought."[76]

The academic mills began to churn. One sociologist charted whether predominantly Catholic or predominantly Protestant countries produced the most inventions. Perhaps Catholic countries did poorly, she speculated, because Catholics obeyed clerical commands, while Protestants evaluated sermons.[77] Two volumes issued by the University of Chicago Press traced the educational background of American scholars. The record for Catholic institutions, the authors concluded, was "singularly unproductive." In science, especially, "the most distinguished accomplishment of our Western civilization," Catholic colleges proved inadequate. The authors pondered whether "Catholicism has permitted comparatively little secularization of outlook among its constituents and has maintained a firm authoritarian structure." Or alternatively, "Catholicism has been a consistent opponent of physical monism, that philosophical tradition under which science has for the most part advanced." Another analyst offered the view that science depended upon a "moral preference for the dictates of individual conscience rather than for those of organized authority." Unfortunately, Catholics seemed to place less emphasis on "critical rationality."[78]

Just as Catholic authoritarianism appeared incompatible with the intellectual autonomy necessary for scientific research, Catholic families, liberals began to argue, might crush psychological independence. Discussion of the family in the 1940s and 1950s frequently contrasted the "democratic companionship" of the successful American family with the authoritarian German model, concluding that the rigid obedience characteristic of German families served as the underpinning of fascism.[79]

Catholic families seemed distant from the tolerant, noncoercive ideal. In their famous 1950 study of the connection between psychological tendencies and political views, *The Authoritarian Personality*, Theodor Adorno and his colleagues clearly included Catholics when they warned of overly restrictive, religious families whose children might channel their frustration into fascist politics. The traits identified by Adorno as suggesting "authoritarian submission" included these: both parents in the family presenting a "unified religious front," acceptance of religion as an "external authority," and the belief that "many important things can never be possibly understood by the human mind."[80] Abraham Maslow's well-known 1954 study of motivation found "self-actualizing" people unlikely to accept "supernatural" religion and "institutional orthodoxy."[81]

Adorno also speculated that Nazism drew sustenance from its origin in heavily Catholic southern Germany, where familiarity with church structures had prepared citizens for National Socialist hierarchies. Alternatively, he alluded to "official" communism and Catholicism as two all-encompassing ideologies, and the enormous secondary literature spawned by *The Authoritarian Personality* carried this theme forward. One study, funded by the Social Science Research Council and the National Institute of Mental Health, forthrightly compared Catholicism and communism, and assumed that adherents of each belief system were "dogmatic." The author, the psychologist Milton Rokeach, singled out Paul Blanshard's analysis of Catholicism as central to his own theoretical approach.[82]

Distinguished commentators such as Seymour Martin Lipset drew upon Adorno's work as well, interpreting the support of some Catholics for Senator Joseph McCarthy as empirical proof of a Catholic susceptibility to authoritarianism. Describing Catholicism as an "extreme moralizing" faith and Catholics as "sexually inhibited" and "vulnerable to status-linked political appeals," Lipset equated these clinical assessments with political views, even though, as he acknowledged, most Catholics remained Democrats.[83]

More specifically, the Catholic prohibition against remarriage within the church after divorce seemed a considerable limitation on human freedom, as did the Catholic demand that non-Catholic spouses agree to raise their children as Catholics. As one prominent analyst put it, "Democracy is a penetrating principle, extending into the most intimate relations of life. . . .Obviously, the Catholic procedure in mixed marriages inhibits this spiritual freedom."[84]

The Harvard social psychologist David McClelland connected Catholic child-rearing habits to economic growth. McClelland claimed that a particular *n* Achievement value measured each person's initiative and self-reliance and, drawing upon Weber, that Catholic families and cultures produced few individuals with high achievement potential.[85]

Confirmation came from a variety of sources. Following a series of studies done on Connecticut families, researchers concluded that parents who insisted that a "*child be able to perform certain tasks well by himself*" would produce children with high *n* Achievement.[86] Protestant families did this work quite well, but Catholic families, McClelland explained, restrained initiative. In fact, "the view toward authority and control which is consciously promoted by the church, has had what is probably an unintended consequence on the child-rearing practices of Catholic parents." The argument rested upon elaborate psychological tests given to children and upon parental surveys asking questions such as "Were all rules handed down in an authoritarian manner, or was family policy decided by everyone concerned?" McClelland even traveled to Germany, where he claimed that Catholic parents were less likely to buy walkers for their sons, and thus foster independence, and more content to stick with playpens.[87]

The implications of this research were enormous. Stagnation in such "Catholic" countries as Spain and Chile became a consequence of not producing high-achievement (male) individuals, a claim McClelland made in testimony before Congress and in research sponsored by the federal government.[88] McClelland delighted in charts comparing consumption of electricity in Catholic and Protestant countries, triumphantly concluding that higher consumption in Norway, as opposed to Ireland, proved his point.[89]

Another notably undemocratic institution, the school, became the site of the most sustained debate over Catholic influence in American culture. The growing number of Catholic schools had worried American liberals in the 1920s, but efforts by the Ku Klux Klan and the Masons to require students to attend public schools seemed more threatening. Oregon voters approved such a measure in 1922, causing liberal groups to rally behind the Catholic challenge of the law's constitutionality. John Dewey argued that the Oregon law "seems to strike at the root of American toleration and trust and good faith between various elements of the population and in each other."[90] When the Supreme Court unanimously overturned the Oregon law in *Pierce v. Society of Sisters*, Felix Frankfurter termed the decision "immediate service on behalf of the essential spirit of liberalism."[91]

This "essential spirit" grew uneasy over the next twenty years. Viewing democracy as a culture meant that the public school became an introduction to democratic habits, not simply a place to acquire skills. The author of one 1937 study worried that Protestant and Catholic views of educational authority rested upon "two totally different philosophies." Pictures of the Last Supper, not Washington crossing the Delaware, decorated Catholic school classrooms. Catholic students memorized the catechism, instead of developing "a recognition of values achieved on the basis of experience."[92]

In 1944 Felix Frankfurter, now on the Supreme Court, confided to his colleague Justice Wiley Rutledge that the Court might "rue the implications of *Pierce,*" and one of Frankfurter's friends, the legal scholar and columnist Max Lerner, noted that *Pierce* marked a "dangerous inroad" on "the nation's stake in having a common democratic education for all its children."[93] A Columbia professor urged states to *require* students to enroll in public schools for at least half of their educational careers.[94]

If even permitting children to attend private schools made liberals uneasy, the possibility of governmental aid to parochial schools provoked outrage. A 1930 Supreme Court decision allowing Louisiana to purchase textbooks for students in parochial schools had created little concern, but comparable proposals at the federal level in the 1940s elicited from John Dewey a prediction that such aid might reverse recent victories over "centuries of systematic stultification of the human mind and human personality."[95]

Catholic leaders, too, had traditionally resisted government intrusion in parochial schools. (One Catholic leader conceded in 1948 that the "average Catholic layperson" remained "under the impression that Catholic school authorities wanted no part of public funds and would not accept public support for fear of public control.")[96] By the 1940s, however, bishops and parish priests understood that property tax increases necessary to fund an expanding public school system would place even more financial pressure on Catholic parents also asked to subsidize parochial schools.

The direction of Catholic arguments shifted. Since students at Catholic colleges received benefits under the GI Bill, Catholic officials asked, why not view governmental aid as assistance to children, not institutions? And since some local school districts already paid for the bus transportation, mathematics textbooks, and school lunches of Catholic schoolchildren, why should federal aid pose special difficulties?[97]

Answers to these questions came in two momentous Supreme Court decisions, *Everson v. Board of Education* (1947) and *McCollum v. Board of Education* (1948). In *Everson* the taxpayer Arch Everson sued his New Jersey township for reimbursing parents of Catholic schoolchildren for bus expenses. In a 5–4 majority ruling written by Justice Hugo Black, the Court sided with the New Jersey township, finding that the busing of Catholic schoolchildren failed to violate, in a metaphor plucked not from the Constitution but from an 1801 Jefferson letter, the "wall of separation between church and State."[98]

Headlines announced the decision in newspapers across the country, and liberals quickly rallied to oppose what one scholar called the "weaken[ing] of American democracy." Law professors pounded out articles attacking aid to parochial schools, making *Everson* the most discussed Supreme Court case of the decade, and prominent journalists such as Max Lerner described themselves as "distressed" by the decision in confidential letters to friends on the Supreme Court.[99]

A group of clergyman and scholars immediately announced the formation of a new lobbying group, saddled with the unwieldy name "Protestants and Other Americans United for the Separation of Church and State" (POAU) and dedicated to outlawing aid to parochial schools as well as to "cultural and spiritual democracy."[100] In Washington the

American Unitarian Association staged an elaborate tribute to Thomas Jefferson's religious views at the Jefferson Memorial, an event attended by four Supreme Court justices and broadcast across the country on NBC radio. The main speaker, the Unitarian leader Frederick May Eliot, pleaded for a Christianity "free of all autocratic ecclesiastical control over the mind and conscience of its individual members." Eliot later confided, "Although I named no names, I have no doubt that what I meant was clearly understood by the members of the hierarchy."[101]

Ironically, as numerous commentators pointed out at the time, Justice Black's use of Jefferson's "wall" metaphor served the losers in *Everson* more effectively than their opponents. In fact, Black's decision to permit the transportation reimbursements contradicted the extraordinary barriers against any government aid to religion established within his own opinion. (And Black promised his skeptical colleagues that he would permit no further aid.)[102]

The Court's 8–1 decision in *McCollum* a year later confirmed this analysis. Vashti McCollum, a Champaign, Illinois, mother, sued to abolish a local "released-time" program that allowed ministers, priests, and rabbis to enter public school classrooms one hour each week. The visiting clerics instructed children whose parents had voluntarily identified them as members of a particular religious group, while other students, including McCollum's son, endured an extra study hall.

Here, too, Black wrote the majority opinion, but this time use of the public school buildings by religious groups constituted an unacceptable establishment. A "wall of separation" had become the new standard, and delighted liberals peppered Justice Felix Frankfurter with requests for copies of the opinion. "I don't need to tell you," Horace Kallen informed Frankfurter, "how relieved and pleased I was to read of the Court's decision in the *McCollum* case."[103] Sympathetic historians agreeably claimed this separation as the original intent of the founders.[104]

Legal scholarship on the two cases is voluminous, since virtually all American jurisprudence on church-state matters stems from these initial applications of the establishment clause of the First Amendment to local matters.[105] Much of this commentary neglects to place *Everson* and *McCollum* within the context of an ongoing discussion about Catholicism and democracy.[106] Several Supreme Court justices, for example, shared a suspicion of Catholic intentions. During oral argument of the *Everson* case, Justice William O. Douglas passed a jocular note to Hugo Black, warning, "If the Catholics get public money to finance their religious schools, we better insist on getting some good prayers in public schools or we Protestants are out of business."[107] Justice Frankfurter gave confidential legal advice to liberals attempting to reverse the removal of the *Nation* from some public school libraries after the publication of Paul Blanshard's articles, and corresponded on religious matters with the Harvard church historian (and former Catholic priest) George La Piana, one of Paul Blanshard's proofreaders and advisers.[108]

Justice Wiley B. Rutledge worried that the *Everson* case was "really a fight by the Catholic schools to secure this money from the public treasury. It is aggressive and on a wide scale. There is probably no other group which is either persistent in efforts to secure this type of legislation or insistent upon it." One of Rutledge's closest friends, the historian Irving Brant, sent Rutledge a draft of forthcoming work on James Madison and religious freedom, and urged him to avoid a "clerical problem in American politics" similar to that of nineteenth-century France. Rutledge thanked Brant for his efforts, promising him that the work on Madison would prove important in the *McCollum* case.[109]

Justice Harold Burton was an active Unitarian and had been the national moderator for the American Unitarian Association even as its publishing arm, Beacon Press, began publishing books arguing for a strict separation of church and state, including Paul Blanshard's efforts. After his 1945 appointment to the Supreme Court, Burton greatly admired his new Washington pastor, A. Powell Davies, who frequently used the pulpit to warn of the danger posed to American society by an aggressive Catholicism.[110]

Appointed to the Court in 1937 as one of the first liberal appointees after Franklin Roosevelt's failed court-packing scheme, Justice Hugo Black had narrowly escaped a forced resignation after a reporter discovered that during the 1920s he had been an active member of Birmingham's virulently anti-Catholic Ku Klux Klan.[111] (Black's campaign manager in his first Alabama Senate campaign recalled, "Hugo could make the best anti-Catholic speech you ever heard.")[112] Black had also played on local anti-Catholic sentiment by vocally opposing his fellow Democrat Al Smith in 1928.[113]

Early in his career Black confessed that next to Thomas Jefferson, no writer had influenced him more than the nineteenth-century scholar John Draper, who depicted Western history as a battle between a church dedicated to "systematic delusion of the illiterate" and scientific progress.[114] Black also expressed enthusiasm for Blanshard's work, painstakingly marking up his copy of *American Freedom and Catholic Power*. As his son recalled, "He suspected the Catholic Church. He used to read all of Paul Blanshard's books exposing the power abuse in the Catholic Church."[115]

This concern about Catholic motives meshed with widespread convictions about the importance of the public school, which in Justice Frankfurter's words had become "the symbol of our democracy and the most pervasive means for promoting our common destiny." Segregation of children into religious groups threatened American unity, since democracy depended upon the mixture of students and, by implication, citizens from all ethnic or religious groups. "You cannot practice democratic living," explained one Columbia professor, "in segregated [Catholic] schools."[116]

Not coincidentally, advocates for the abolition of another kind of segregation, by skin color, made similar arguments. Linking these efforts was the fear that ethnic prejudice (against Jews and African Americans) and authoritarian institutions (the Catholic Church) might weaken American democracy, in much the same way that European democracies had succumbed to atavistic forces in the 1920s and 1930s. Even as Brand Blanshard criticized American Catholicism—privately, he termed it a "stupid creed"—and cheered on his brother Paul's more celebrated efforts, he used his position as chair of Yale's philosophy department to ensure the appointment of the first Jew to the Yale College faculty.[117]

Unity meant more than physical proximity. Not only did Catholic schools isolate students from their non-Catholic peers, but they also shielded young Catholics from the "democratic way of life." Swarthmore's J. Roland Pennock emphasized that children in a democracy "must be taught to submit existing institutions to criticism and to be skeptical of all dogma; [they] must be trained to set store by institutions that provide full opportunity for free expression of critical thought."[118] Sympathy for this position explains Horace Kallen's impassioned plea for the Catholic citizen to abandon the "separatist pull away from [his] non-Catholic neighbor with the suspicions it arouses regarding his loyalty to democracy," as well as the historian Perry Miller's conclusion that Catholicism was antagonistic to both "a free and critical education" and "the democratic way of life."[119]

The theological corollary to this position was also clear. Religion consistent with democratic mores would stress individual choice, self-conscious commitment after a careful survey of the denominational alternatives. The assumption behind the public school, Justice Robert H. Jackson concluded, "is that after the individual has been instructed in worldly wisdom he will be better suited to choose his religion." He added, "Our public school, if not a product of Protestantism, at least is more consistent with it than with the Catholic culture and scheme of values."[120] The reformer Agnes Meyer argued in the *Atlantic Monthly*, "The clear implication in our Constitution [is] that religious truth is an individual quest, that authoritarianism and religion are contradictory terms."[121]

Harvard's James Bryant Conant, the most influential university president of the era, touched upon many of these themes. A chemist himself, Conant expressed confidence in the notion that the Middle Ages produced little valuable science, since the period lacked the "spirit of scientific investigation." The Puritans, by contrast, despite a "narrow, hidebound faith," could claim credit for "religious toleration, representative government, modern science, and universities as we know them."[122]

Harvard's divinity school, especially its dedication to training ministers for the mainline Protestant denominations, seemed to Conant an archaic distraction from the central mission of the university. And one oral history claims Conant so despised the grip of Catholic priests and ward heelers on Massachusetts politics that he favored a contingency plan allowing the university to transfer its administrative offices to Harvard's Dumbarton Oaks campus in Washington, D.C., should threats to academic freedom become intolerable.[123]

Conant also devoted considerable energy to improving the nation's public schools. Precisely the absence of an egalitarian, public educational system, he contended, explained Britain's rigid class structure and German authoritarianism. Thomas Jefferson's retrieval of the notion of public education from the Scottish Enlightenment, even as he jettisoned any hint of a Presbyterian "spiritual tyranny," proved his genius. Secular education was a "common denominator of all religious faiths."[124] In a much publicized 1952 address, Conant blasted private elementary and secondary schools: "To my mind, our schools should serve all creeds. The greater the proportion of our youth who attend independent schools, the greater the threat to our democratic unity. Therefore, to use taxpayers' money to assist such a move is, for me, to suggest that American society use its own hands to destroy itself."[125]

A controversy ensued, with Boston's Archbishop Richard Cushing informing the mayor and the governor of his disappointment with Conant's address and Harvard faculty members rushing to their leader's defense.[126] Paul Blanshard sent the *Harvard Crimson* a telegram announcing his support of Conant.[127]

Criticism of Conant also came from Harvard alumni loyal to Phillips Exeter, Groton, and other private schools. In response Conant privately clarified his position. "My concern," he told the Harvard Corporation member Charles A. Coolidge, "is with the continued *expansion* of private schools. If there were not powerful forces at work favoring a radical change between the present balance between private and public schools, I should never have barged into this thorny area." He also noted, "[T]he Catholic hierarchy and almost all my correspondents (pro and con) were quick to identify the expansive force."[128]

Chapter Seven

DEMOCRACY, RELIGIOUS FREEDOM, AND THE NOUVELLE THÉOLOGIE

I

They were an unlikely pair. One, Jacques Maritain, born in 1882, had been reared in a French Protestant family, converting to Catholicism as a young man, under the charismatic spell of the early twentieth-century French philosopher Henri Bergson. By the early 1930s Maritain had become the world's most distinguished Catholic philosopher, and a central figure in the neo-Thomist revival undergirding Catholic intellectual life. Lecture tours of North and South America made him known beyond the usual European Catholic circles, and even some non-Catholic scholars, impressed by his wide-ranging erudition, found him an intriguing presence. (Maritain's last academic post would be at the Institute for Advanced Study in Princeton, from 1948 to 1956.) "He is able to reach," one New York Catholic editor excitedly told a friend in Switzerland in 1940, "circles until now absolutely closed to all Catholics."[1] During World War II, exiled along with many other European Catholic intellectuals in the United States, Maritain lectured across the country, drafted messages of encouragement for the French resistance, assisted scholars fleeing Nazi occupied Europe, and became the director of the newly formed Ecole libre des Hautes Etudes in New York.[2]

The second figure was the American Jesuit John Courtney Murray. Born in 1904, he entered the Jesuits after high school and remained in the society until his death in 1967. He briefly taught in the Philippines and

Jacques Maritain, early 1950s.

then studied in Rome from 1933 to 1937. Upon his return to the United States, he took a teaching post at the Jesuit seminary in Woodstock, Maryland, home base for the rest of his career.

Jacques and Raïssa Maritain cultivated a certain otherworldliness and fascination with Christian mysticism, and their home in Meudon, south of Paris, became a scholarly retreat center in the 1920s and 1930s. After Raïssa's death, Jacques chose to spend the last dozen years of his life wearing a habit, eating simple meals, and living in community with the Little Brothers of Jesus in Toulouse.[3]

Murray was more urbane. Between classes he shuttled from Washington to New York for meetings and conferences, relaxing by playing the occasional round of golf with his close (and non-Catholic) friend the *Time* magazine publisher Henry Luce, and then joining Luce and his wife, Clare Boothe Luce, a spiritual confidante of Murray's, for cocktails. (The Jesuit vow of poverty, Murray reportedly quipped, was "less a sacred promise than a regrettable fact.")[4]

Maritain's prose rewarded only attentive readers. He circled around abstruse ideas at length, ruminating on the nature of knowledge, the role

John Courtney Murray, S.J. ca. 1940s.

of spirituality in art, and the meaning of the human person. Murray specialized in harder-edged political theory, thrusting short, punchy sentences at rhetorical foes. Maritain's "profound reverence for truth" seemed to Murray admirable, but he once regretted Maritain's "lack of lucidity."[5]

Despite these differences, both men became leaders in a campaign that engaged Catholic intellectuals in Europe and North America, in the 1940s and 1950s, to move Catholic theology and philosophy toward a more nuanced understanding of the challenges posed by modernity. The effort was two-pronged. On one side was the need to confront the individualist (and often anti-Catholic) liberalism of Paul Blanshard and his many supporters in the intellectual community. Maritain disdained Blanshard's "cheap and biased" work, and Murray scorned his use of the term "hierarchy" as an all-purpose slur.[6]

The second battle was within the church. For both Maritain and Murray the political crisis of the 1930s and the Second World War were decisive. For Maritain fascist aggression demonstrated the superiority of democratic regimes and the need for increased Catholic attention to human rights. Similarly, Murray recognized that a war fought in the name of freedom, notably the freedom of religion proclaimed by President Franklin Roosevelt as one of the four basic freedoms, would inevitably make religious liberty a matter of "international concern."[7] He insisted that Catholics must allay doubts as to whether "the Catholic Church can adapt herself vitally, on principle, and not merely on grounds of expediency, to what is valid in American democratic development."[8]

Here the two men recognized each other as allies. Maritain and other European Catholic intellectuals, convinced that religious freedom was a necessary precondition for a successful "struggle against totalitarianism," and embarrassed by conservative Catholics fixated on the virtues of a government-favored Catholicism in Spain, seized upon Murray's work in the late 1940s and early 1950s.[9] Murray, in turn, read Maritain with care and described Latin American criticism of Maritain, often by Catholic defenders of authoritarian regimes, as "vicious."[10]

Both men also cultivated the friendship of Giovanni Battista Montini, a top Vatican official in the 1940s and early 1950s and, later, Pope Paul VI. Montini had long admired Maritain's work, and when Maritain served as French ambassador to the Vatican from 1945 to 1948, the two men dined together frequently.[11] Murray visited Montini, then archbishop of Milan, in 1953 and found him "personally sympathetic with my 'orientations' and rather wanted his hand to be strengthened."[12]

II

Catholics responded to accusations by liberals that their church fostered values inimical to American culture in two ways. First, in legal journals published at Catholic law schools and through such vehicles as the American Catholic Philosophical Association and the Natural Law Institute at the University of Notre Dame, Catholics described themselves as *more* American than mid-twentieth-century liberals, as the rightful descendants of Thomas Jefferson and James Madison. How could liberals convinced that values were contingent venerate the American founders, so many of whom, like Jefferson, believed in "inalienable rights"? Wilfrid Parsons, S.J., explained that "there is vastly more in common between the modern Catholic and the colonial Protestant than between the old colonial Protestant and the modern secularized product of public education." In fact, "by a sort of natural affinity, the modern intelligent Catholic finds himself drawing ever more closely to American cultural origins at the same time that his fellow non-Catholic Americans are disavowing those origins with almost indecent haste."[13]

Two figures venerated by liberal intellectuals, Justice Oliver Wendell Holmes Jr. and John Dewey, came under sustained Catholic attack. Several American Jesuits excoriated Holmes in the early 1940s for his disdain for the natural law, and his blunt claim that ethics depended upon the will of the majority. Francis E. Lucey, S.J., after noting that natural law was "substantially and essentially the philosophy of the Founding Fathers," criticized Holmes by explaining that the "pragmatic test of what works, as the sole criterion of what makes right," had become the "theme song of Nazi storm troopers."[14]

Dewey's position as the dean of American philosophers and educators made him an equally inviting target. His distaste for what one Catholic critic called "anything like a dogma, or fixed principle," made him a dangerous influence.[15] "The utter irony of the situation," complained Georgetown's Father Stephen F. McNamee, "is that the American philosopher [Dewey] who most radically applied the ax to the principles upon which this democratic government, as we know it in the United States, is erected, is openly hailed as *the* philosopher of democracy!"[16]

A few non-Catholics, notably the influential columnist Walter Lippmann, Robert Maynard Hutchins, Richard McKeon, and Mortimer Adler at the University of Chicago and Lon Fuller at Harvard, endorsed Catholic claims, and Catholics sought out these allies because they feared that a reliance on natural law principles would be dismissed as yet another example of papal authoritarianism.[17] One Detroit Jesuit, R. J. Belleperche, wrote Adler that it is usually "taken for granted" that a priest "has no other reason for his Thomism or Aristotelianism except the fact that the Catholic Church has turned a benignant eye upon both systems."[18] Proving Father Belleperche's point, John Dewey, mocking Adler, told a friend in 1935, "It is certainly a wonderful thing to see a go-getting Jew come out as a defender of the dogmas and sacraments of the Roman Catholic church."[19]

III

In one sense, Catholic and non-Catholic disciples of Aquinas made a strong argument. Catholic claims of affinity with the American founders were startling, but the best scholars of the medieval period—Catholic and non-Catholic—had begun to emphasize the medieval roots of such notions as rule of the people and human rights.[20]

In another sense, Catholic attacks on Dewey and Holmes were unconvincing. Catholics, not liberals, had endorsed authoritarian regimes in Spain, Portugal, and Austria. Pope Pius XI, not Franklin Roosevelt, had signed concordats with Hitler and Mussolini. (Felix Frankfurter pointedly reminded one Jesuit that Justice Holmes had attacked the Nazis at a time when "potentates and principalities were still blind to Hitler and indeed trafficked with him.")[21] By the 1940s, when American leaders defined respect for civil liberties as what separated the United States from its fascist opponents, Catholics' ambivalence on such matters—what the American Jesuit John LaFarge ruefully termed the "faint atmosphere of Vichy"—seemed crippling.[22]

This awkward situation spurred the second Catholic response to the accusation that Catholicism fostered authoritarianism: a sustained effort to bind Catholic social thought to democracy, human rights, and religious freedom. This response, in turn, was only one piece of a wider attempt by a remarkable group of European and North American Catholic scholars to encourage their church, in the words of one enthusiast, to open itself to "the modern world" through a "return to the sources."[23]

Leaders in this effort included Jacques Maritain, the French Jesuit Henri de Lubac, the French Dominican priests Yves Congar and Marie-Dominique Chenu, the German Jesuit Karl Rahner, the Canadian Jesuit Bernard Lonergan, and John Courtney Murray. With the exception of Maritain, the only layman and a decade older, each of these men was born between 1895 and 1904, and entered a religious order as a young man. Just reaching the height of their intellectual powers, they were disturbed by what the political crisis of the 1930s and then the Second World War revealed about their church, many of whose members (and leaders) seemed to understand religion as either a pious afterthought to daily life or a reliable bulwark of any social order.[24]

Unbelief appeared to be a consequence of this complacency, fostered by the endless refutations of "modernity" that constituted much of the Catholic theological and philosophical curriculum. That many Catholic theologians and bishops in France and Quebec supported the Vichy government in the early 1940s—even as Maritain labored in support of Charles de Gaulle's Free French forces, de Lubac joined the French resistance, and Congar spent five years in a German prisoner-of-war camp—

was especially disillusioning. In 1944, De Lubac bitterly complained of the "servility" of French bishops to Vichy authorities; Maritain despised "Thomists chanting the litanies of [the Vichy leader Marshal] Pétain."[25]

Already by the late 1930s Chenu, de Lubac, and Congar had embarked on an effort, later dubbed the Nouvelle Théologie, to reinvigorate their church. They relied upon historical inquiry, pivoting toward the past for its own sake, but also as a strategy for developing a more capacious understanding of Catholicism, a realization that authentic Catholic practice in the twentieth century might require a plumbing of Catholic traditions in search of more meaningful forms. Chenu urged Catholics to locate Aquinas in the "intellectual revolution of the thirteenth century," not simply to regurgitate "anti-Protestant polemic" and "baroque scholasticism" from the Reformation period.[26]

De Lubac and Congar paid particular attention to patristics, and de Lubac, especially, viewed the Catholic reliance upon Aquinas as an abandonment of the riches available through study of earlier periods. In his controversial 1946 study, *Surnaturel*, de Lubac focused on the technical question of the relationship between nature and grace, which in his hands evolved into a plea for Catholics to engage the world beyond church walls. He and other French Catholic scholars also began a pathbreaking series of editions of patristic texts, entitled *Sources chrétiennes*.[27]

Various strands of the Nouvelle Théologie drifted across the Atlantic. The New York publishers Sheed and Ward issued translations of several important works, and the small journal *Cross currents*, founded by Joseph Cunneen, an American Catholic GI who stayed in Paris after the war to assess this theological ferment, provided another conduit. (In its first year *Cross currents* published English translations of important essays by de Lubac, Congar, and Karl Rahner, and an essay by John Courtney Murray.)[28] A careful American student of the European scene, the Jesuit Gustave Weigel, offered some cautions, but agreed with the French theologians that standard-issue scholasticism was inadequate. "The Church always teaches the same," Weigel explained, "but this identity permits and demands the use of passing modes arising from the exigencies of history."[29]

European Catholic reformers and their American Catholic followers also fostered a revival of interest in the nineteenth-century British Catholic convert John Henry Newman. Newman's approach to the development of doctrine, closely linked, again, with the study of patristics, looked refreshingly unlike the ahistorical neo-Thomism dominant in seminaries and Catholic universities. And Newman's once scandalous claim that the experience of the faithful might prove decisive in the formulation of doctrine—his 1859 essay on the subject was first reprinted in 1952—seemed one route out of a scholasticism frequently detached from human life. One American Jesuit applauded Newman's skepticism regarding "universals" and worried that contemporary Catholic apologetics tended "to become one with the cause of minor logic: save the syllogism and you save all. Nothing could be more confusing than this misleading relic of eighteenth-century rationalism."[30]

Historians themselves played a role. In both Europe and the United States, mid-twentieth-century scholars sympathetically detailed the evanescent emergence of a more liberal Catholicism in the nineteenth century.[31] A leading European historian of modern Catholicism, the Belgian Roger Aubert, focused on such liberal Catholics as the nineteenth-century French bishop Félix Dupanloup, and both Aubert and an Italian colleague, Father Giuseppe de Luca, studied the life and work of Newman. Aubert also published a surprisingly critical treatment of Pius IX, even as he conducted an admiring correspondence with the most prominent historian of American Catholicism, Monsignor John Tracy Ellis.[32] (Ellis thought Aubert's approach to Catholic history "very encouraging," and Aubert admired Ellis's ability to "understand our time.")[33] Ellis's own, massive biography of Baltimore's Cardinal James Gibbons, along with other publications, stressed the loyalty of Catholics to American ideals.[34]

The American contribution to the strictly theological aspects of this reassessment was minimal. (One French Catholic scholar grimly described American Catholic theology in 1955 as marked by "spiritual and intellectual infantilism.")[35] Nonetheless, one scholar with close ties to the United States, Jacques Maritain, and one American proper, John Courtney Murray, would lead an effort loosely connected to the Nouvelle Théologie, an attempt to defend democracy, human rights, and religious freedom in Catholic terms.

In retrospect, Murray and Maritain agreed, the nineteenth-century Catholic narrative condemning individualism in its religious and economic forms had obscured the merits of political individualism, or democracy. The isolated individual remained for Catholics a tragic figure, and talk of individual rights a distraction from the importance of the common good.[36] Catholic political parties in the early twentieth century competed for the allegiance of voters, but Catholic intellectuals rarely defended democracy in principle. Neither *Rerum Novarum* nor *Quadragesimo Anno* mentioned democracy, and Catholic activists in Europe and Latin America saw reforms like a living wage as independent of any particular political regime.[37]

Catholics' desire for a less individualist society did not make their support for authoritarian regimes inevitable, but widespread suspicion of democracy did permit Catholic leaders to move in that direction. In Portugal, António de Oliveira Salazar graduated from Catholic student groups to become the leader of an authoritarian government that restricted free speech and association. In Austria Chancellors Engelbert Dollfuss and Kurt Schuschnigg dissolved parliament even as they emphasized that the Austrian state would attempt to follow the program outlined in *Quadragesimo Anno*.[38]

Beginning in the late 1930s, however, a group of European Catholic exiles began urging Catholics to recognize the moral importance of democratic politics and civil liberties. These exiles—including the Germans F. A. Hermens, Goetz Briefs, Dietrich von Hildebrand, Heinrich Romnen, Heinrich Brüning, Waldemar Gurian, Franz Mueller, and Theodore Brauer, Spain's Alfredo Mendizábal, Italy's Father Luigi Sturzo, and France's Maritain, Yves Simon, and Paul Vignaux—fled Europe in the 1930s, often for positions in American Catholic universities. (Hermens, Gurian, and Simon, for example, all took posts at the University of Notre Dame.)[39]

That the migration of European Jews in the 1930s powerfully shaped Anglo-American intellectual life is well known, but the parallel Catholic migration has received little scholarly attention.[40] Yet its effects on American Catholic life were significant. Briefs, one of Max Weber's successors at the University of Freiburg, and Romnen had been part of the circle of German Catholics so influential in drafting *Quadragesimo Anno*, and they quickly began publishing in American Catholic journals.[41] Hildebrand joined in the attack on pragmatism, and his writings on marriage gave him prominence among moral theologians.[42] Gurian founded the *Review of Politics*, a journal devoted to political philosophy, and cajoled contributions from such distinguished thinkers as Hannah Arendt and Eric Voegelin.[43]

If these Catholic exiles shared a single sentiment, it was frustration with Catholic leaders unwilling to challenge authoritarian regimes directly. Hildebrand was shocked by the ease with which prominent German Catholics expressed approval of the new National Socialist government in 1933, and Gurian bluntly attacked the German Catholic hierarchy for its timidity. "The church is not an association," Gurian insisted, "which adapts itself to the particular power relationships of the time, but it is the guardian and protector of the moral order for all human beings and all peoples."[44]

In 1941, now at Notre Dame, Gurian mordantly commented that "if St. Thomas lived today he would be for Franco, for Tizo [president of Slovakia, a Catholic priest and a Nazi ally], for Pétain [head of the Vichy government in France]."[45] Gurian's friend and Notre Dame colleague the French philosopher Yves Simon was more caustic. "To do something practical in 1941, in politics, with St. Thomas," Simon told Maritain, "is a joke."[46] When Simon learned that Father Reginald Garrigou-Lagrange, a leading French Thomist and once a mentor of Jacques and Raïssa Maritain, supported the Vichy government, he was appalled. "How disgusting this Garrigou!" he told Maritain. "Were I not so respectful of the sacerdotal character, I would, I think, write him that he is the one I will hold responsible if harm befalls one of my Jewish friends."[47]

Heinrich Brüning, onetime German chancellor and Catholic Center Party leader, fled to the United States steps ahead of the Gestapo in 1935, living incognito in a Long Island Catholic seminary.[48] He felt personally betrayed by the 1933 Vatican concordat with Germany. "As we in Germany all foresaw," he later complained to a Detroit audience, "it gave the Nazis an opportunity, through a purely legalistic interpretation of its terms, to suppress religion in the schools altogether."[49] He also lamented "the outcome of the pro-Franco propaganda about the Catholics all over the world. There is no religious community in the world which as regards political ideals is in such a chaotic state as the Catholics."[50]

Exiled to the United States by Mussolini, Italy's Father Luigi Sturzo, former leader of the Italian political party Partito Popolare, regretted that some Catholic leaders had once believed that "the authoritarian regime is more advantageous to the Church and religion than the constitutional, democratic regime."[51] Privately, Sturzo urged Catholics to stop associating all modern democracies with the legacy of Rousseau, "while smiling towards the fascists and nationalists, conservatives and reactionaries." In 1942 he complained to Maritain that fascism has "poisoned the entire Catholic world."[52]

Maritian became the central figure. During the first years of his career, he devoted himself to technical philosophical problems, while endorsing the standard polemical Catholic narrative linking Protestantism to a destructive individualism. Maritain's 1925 *Three Reformers* identified, in rote Catholic fashion, Luther, Descartes, and Rousseau as the men responsible for the modern world and "all the problems which torment it."[53]

Like many European Thomists suspicious of individualism and ambivalent about democracy who found appeals to authority and order attractive in the 1920s and 1930s, Maritain had briefly supported the Action Française, a French royalist (and, arguably, fascist) group.[54] The Action Française, Yves Simon later recalled, exerted "an almost complete dictatorship over Catholic intellectual circles. Whoever came out as a democrat in these circles was doomed to be the object of an ironical and scornful pity; he was looked down upon as a person behind the times, a survivor of another age."[55]

For Maritain, along with a handful of like-minded Catholic contemporaries, the first turning point came in 1926, when Pius XI condemned the Action Française for its increasingly political and nationalist tone.[56] Many Catholic supporters of the Action Française dismissed Pius XI's charge that the group subordinated religion to politics, but Maritain accepted this papal criticism and, in a major break with onetime allies, ended cooperation with the movement.[57]

The second turning point came in the mid-1930s when Maritain criticized Catholic complicity in European fascism. Maritain found it appalling, as he told Waldemar Gurian, that "the mystique of the Reich has won over German Catholics."[58] More provocatively, Maritain rejected the notion that General Francisco Franco pursued a "holy war" in Spain, leading to a string of angry rebuttals from coreligionists.[59]

Echoes of the Spanish controversy resounded in the United States. Non-Catholic liberals celebrated Maritain's courage, and Maritain privately acknowledged such compliments as more important than "insults from the ministers of General Franco and from their twins."[60] Within Catholic circles Maritain and Heinrich Brüning inspired the *Commonweal* editor George Schuster, a friend of both men, to draft a 1937 statement urging American Catholics not to believe that Franco will "inaugurate a beneficent and progressive social order."[61] Maritain congratulated "our friends at *Commonweal*" after the editorial's appearance, but even this mild criticism of Franco led to blistering attacks from other American Catholic publications and a sharp decline in *Commonweal* subscriptions.[62]

Even as he warned Catholics to beware of alliances with European fascists, Maritain struggled to rehabilitate Thomism, to articulate what Yves Simon termed a "Thomistic treatment of the problem of democracy."[63] Maritain called the battle one between an "antifascist" Catholicism and a "Catholicism of Franco," and he feverishly drafted books and articles on this topic during the late 1930s and early 1940s.[64] Maritain first urged Catholic philosophers not to habitually divide political philosophies into those devoted to the common good and those infected with individualism. The human person, not the individual isolated from community, must become the subject of analysis.[65] Maritain then used history to demonstrate that current Catholic understandings of democracy were not exhaustive. Nineteenth-century European democracies, he conceded, with their frequent anticlerical bias, had too often fallen prey to "individualistic liberalism."[66] As late as 1939 he cautiously requested that the English translation of his latest book be entitled *Politics and Scholasticism*, not *Scholasticism and Democracy*, because "the word democracy, in Europe more than in America, has become so ambiguous. . . ."[67]

By the early 1940s, however, Maritain defended democracy as a system of government morally superior to any alternative. At one time, perhaps, a poorly educated population could accept authoritarian rule, but the "democratic impulse" must now be understood as an "inspiration of the Gospel." "It is necessary to show," he told Yves Simon in 1941, "that Thomism is what is strongest against false democracy. . . . St. Thomas was a democrat, in this sense . . . the Gospel works in history in a democratic direction."[68] Maritain also regretted he had once believed in "a parallelism of action between the people of the Action Française and the Thomistic renaissance." This overlap, he added, "was one of the greatest sadnesses of my life."[69]

Even as he claimed to discover the Christian roots of democracy, Maritain sought to integrate Thomistic philosophy and human rights. Fought in the name of racial tolerance, freedom of speech, and freedom of religion, and concluded in the shadow of the Holocaust, the experience of World War II led to an explosion of interest in the idea of fundamental human rights.

Catholics approached this effusion of "rights talk" with caution. After all, Catholic intellectuals had embraced neo-Thomism in the mid-nineteenth century precisely because it offered a more communal and less individualist view of society.[70] Even liberal Jesuits thought that American scholars championed "individual rights at too great a risk to social stability."[71]

The preoccupation of Catholics with the economic common good also bolstered Catholics inclined to suspect talk of individual rights as camouflage for reactionary defenses of private property. Or as Father John Ryan explained to Harvard Law School's Roscoe Pound, "Today, many of our courts interpret natural law as guaranteeing to the individual an excessive amount of freedom, particularly freedom of contract."[72] On the rare occasions when American Catholics wrote of human rights before World War II, they launched into attacks on "plutocratic capitalism."[73]

Maritain urged a reconsideration. Just as rigid eighteenth-century European concepts of democracy caricatured richer medieval notions of personhood and politics, so too did eighteenth-century notions of absolute human rights mistakenly treat "the individual as a god and making all the rights ascribed to him the absolute and unlimited rights of a god."[74] And yet, in a book whose very title, *The Rights of Man and Natural Law*, startled Catholics weaned on horror stories about the French Revolution, Maritain argued that "the consciousness of the rights of the person really has its origin in the conception of man and of natural law established by centuries of Christian philosophy." Indeed, "by virtue of natural law, the human person has the right to be respected, is the subject of rights, possesses rights."[75] "The error of those Catholics who follow Pétain in France or Franco in Spain," Maritain told the Free French leader Charles de Gaulle in 1941, is an inability to distinguish between the "rights of the human person" and an "old paternalist conception" equivalent to fascism.[76]

Some Catholic scholars found Maritain's uniting of the natural law and human rights, along with his attribution of democratic impulses to Thomas Aquinas, unpersuasive. "What [Maritain] wants apparently," complained one Catholic scholar privately, "is a St. Thomas who, being completely divorced from his life in the thirteenth century, is free to live as a philosopher in the twentieth century and after."[77] Other Catholics worried that a focus on the human person weakened Catholicism's traditional emphasis on the common good.[78]

The more widespread emotion, however, was gratitude. Pius XII himself echoed Maritain's language in two addresses given during the war, one of which noted that "the democratic form of government" now appeared "to many as a postulate of nature imposed by reason itself." (One of Maritain's close friends, the Swiss theologian Father Charles Journet, archly noted "numerous coincidences" between Maritain's words and those of the pope.)[79] In the United States, Maritain lectured at Catholic universities across the country, and one group of Catholic scholars orchestrated an elaborate tribute to Maritain in New York in 1943.[80]

In 1942 Maritain helped coordinate the drafting of a manfesto, "In the Face of the World's Crisis," that crystallized his position. Signed by forty-three European Catholic scholars "sojourning in America" and published in Europe and the United States, the manifesto insisted that democracy was the "issue at stake in the struggle." Maritain worried that the statement was "too tender, unconsciously, to the corporatist state," and non-Catholics such as the young Daniel Bell immediately attacked the statement as "strange new words" from a church that had produced "Petain, Franco and Salazar."[81]

Still, informed readers could hardly fail to notice the statement's emphasis on the dangers posed by antidemocratic regimes, and the dismissal of any attempt to compare this threat with that posed by free-market capitalism. The U.S. State Department recognized Maritain's importance. "One of the dominant themes in Maritain's writings," one analyst wrote in a confidential report, "is the strong natural bond existing between Christianity and Democracy. Such a position, ardently defended by an outstanding liberal Catholic thinker, is of primary importance in such countries as France, Belgium, Spain, Portugal, and Italy, where the official propaganda line represents democracy as bourgeois, decadent, and anti-Christian and tries to use the Catholic Church as a totalitarian tool."[82]

In Europe and Latin America, Maritain's reconciliation of Catholicism and democracy laid much of the intellectual groundwork for the successful Christian Democratic parties after the war, and Maritain exerted considerable influence on such future prime ministers as Chile's Eduardo Frei, France's Robert Schuman, and Italy's Alcide De Gasperi. The first meeting of Christian Democrats from South American countries in Montevideo, Uruguay, in 1947 sent Maritain a telegram thanking him for providing the "ideal solution to our great political and economic difficulties."[83]

Maritain's leading role in the 1947 UNESCO committee of philosophers formed to begin the development of the United Nations Universal Declaration on Human Rights also signaled a new Catholic interest in the subject. (So, too, did the enthusiasm of the Vatican nuncio in Paris, Angelo Roncalli, who as Pope John XXIII would offer the most stirring papal endorsement of human rights in the 1963 encyclical, *Pacem in Terris*.)[84]

A small group of American Catholics working for the National Catholic Welfare Conference (NCWC) lobbied those charged with drafting the Universal Declaration of Human Rights. Along with Maritain, these Catholics cheered efforts to include social welfare provisions in the document, as well as references to the family as the basic unit of society. Caution was still evident—one NCWC official privately complained in 1947 that "modern ideas of rights tend to make rights absolute and tend to under-emphasize or even deny the rights of association"—and arguments over divorce and abortion hinted at future conflict. Even so, a novel Catholic sympathy for an enumeration of human rights, in response to what Maritain called the "savagery of our time," now tethered Catholic intellectuals to an important anchor of contemporary liberalism.[85]

Outside the Catholic milieu respect for Maritain's acumen rarely translated into sympathy for the Thomist particulars. Some American intellectuals still refused to believe that any Catholic philosopher could conduct independent inquiry. Sidney Hook mistrusted Maritain's easygoing manner—"I prefer my poison labeled"—and privately described him as "hierarchical and authoritarian through and through."[86] When Maritain's friends at the University of Chicago attempted to arrange a visiting appointment for him in the philosophy department after the fall of France in 1940, the department chairman refused to pursue the matter. "Professor Maritain's reputation in this part of the world," he explained, "is largely that of an apologist or propagandist for Catholic doctrine."[87]

Still, the experience of living in stable democratic societies affected Maritain and other Catholic exiles deeply. Catholic refugees in London came to admire the British parliamentary tradition and insisted that any form of Catholic corporatism must be compatible, as one French Catholic put it, with a "political regime founded on liberty."[88]

In the United States, Maritain recognized that Catholicism flourished, absent state support. He did find the intellectual level of the American Catholic clergy appalling—"the state of the American clergy makes apostolic work here very difficult"—and he compared Father Coughlin to Catholic-influenced fascist movements in Belgium.[89] But enthusiasm for

Thomism in the United States (with virtually no affinities for fascism) seemed unbounded. Even before Maritain found himself forced to leave France, he encouraged Yves Simon to accept an appointment at the University of Notre Dame. "And who knows?" he wrote. "A living Thomism will perhaps take root more easily over there [the United States] than on our withered soil."[90] A few years later, after settling in the United States, Maritain explained that he now realized "how deeply we love America and have been intoxicated by her soul and her hopes, that great human dream which is permeated with the Gospel infinitely more than the Americans themselves believe."[91]

Maritain became especially enthusiastic about the work of the American reformer Saul Alinsky, a secular Jew who specialized in working with Catholic clergy to develop local community organizations, usually in heavily Catholic urban neighborhoods. (Organizers trained by Alinsky would soon exert a powerful influence on a charismatic young Latino Catholic organizer in California, César Chávez.) Maritain delighted in this merger of Catholicism and democratic activism, and he wrote Alinsky of his admiration for this "new way for *real* democracy, the only way in which man's thirst for social communion can develop and be satisfied, through freedom." "You are a Thomist, dear Saul," he told Alinsky, "a practical Thomist!"[92] In 1958 he arranged an extended meeting between Alinsky and Archbishop Montini in Milan.[93]

IV

Maritain also became an admirer of John Courtney Murray, the one American Catholic intellectual who would exert comparable influence on the wider Catholic world.[94] Studying in Rome during the 1930s, Murray became alarmed by the European crisis. If European Christians should unite to counter fascist foes, and Murray insisted they should, American Christians should do no less.[95] Such alliances required assistance from sympathetic non-Catholics, and Murray began studying the theological problem of intercreedal cooperation. Up until this point, Catholics had been strictly forbidden to participate in most joint ventures with Protestants and Jews, lest such cooperation imply that all religions were equally valid. The few Catholics bold enough to participate in groups like the National Conference of Christians and Jews, including the Columbia University professor Carlton Hayes, faced persistent sniping for perceived laxity. (Hayes told Murray of his wish that Catholic bishops would "frankly accept the *fact* of cultural pluralism among us.")[96] Even liberal bishops such as Toledo's Karl Alter warned priests against interreligious ventures. "We can present our views," Alter explained in 1940, "but not 'cooperatively.'"[97]

Appeals for American unity during the war made Catholic intransigence on interreligious cooperation embarrassing, encouraging Murray in his conviction that the topic deserved a "good deal of attention."[98] In Boston, Father Richard J. Cushing, soon the city's archbishop, privately urged one priest not to restate traditional church cautions against religious cooperation in an article for a popular magazine. "It would be an enlightenment for Catholics," he conceded, "but I am afraid it would antagonize those outside the fold at the very same time when the world needs . . . collaboration among those who call themselves Christians."[99]

Murray spent the late 1940s and early 1950s developing his views on religion and public life. On the one hand, he scorned liberals reflexively opposed to "hierarchy" and "dogmatism," and offered a withering assessment of Justice Felix Frankfurter's attempt to "establish" his own particular theology of church and state in Supreme Court rulings on religion and education.[100] At one off-the-record meeting of religious leaders held in the wake of the 1948 *McCollum* decision, which erected a putative "wall of separation" between church and state, Murray "emphasized that the *McCollum* decision was a victory for secularism and as such should be of great concern to Catholics, Jews and Protestants. He suggested that the 'anti-secularists' should not be distracted by extraneous issues in the consideration of the church-state issue but should always let their consideration be centered around the importance of developing a theory of church and state that will allow religion to be a vital force in American life."[101]

On the other hand, Murray understood that Catholics' acceptance of special privileges from the state in Spain, along with even liberal American Catholics like Father John A. Ryan calmly reaffirming the desirability of such privileges, would suggest to non-Catholics an unscrupulous foe.[102] At the same meeting to discuss the *McCollum* case, the eminent Protestant theologian Reinhold Niebuhr agreed with Murray that the Court had mistakenly relegated religion to the sidelines of public life.[103] But Niebuhr informed Murray, point-blank, of his own uneasiness with the refusal of the Catholic Church to defend religious liberty in principle.

According to the minutes, Niebuhr expressed fear that "the Catholic Church's theory of 'one true church,' which is the very dynamic of Catholic religion, necessarily made Protestants uncomfortable when the Catholic Church appeared to be gaining an increase of power in any particular nation or in any particular phase of a nation's activities, and particularly in the field of education."[104]

Such statements prompted Murray to again turn his attention to Catholic doctrine. Or as Murray privately admitted, "the theory of church and state expressed in Catholic writings on politics could disturb the Protestant mind."[105]

Ultimately, just as Maritain thrust democracy and human rights out from the shadow of nineteenth-century anticlericalism, Murray developed a Catholic defense of religious liberty. That Pope Leo XIII had emphasized the desirability of a formal unity between church and state seemed to Murray understandable in the context of the late nineteenth century. But in a series of dazzling, crisp essays, published in the late 1940s and early 1950s, Murray argued that a state-sponsored religion need not serve as a Catholic ideal. Catholic attacks on the claim of nineteenth-century European liberals—that "religion is a purely subjective and private matter"—should not determine attitudes toward religious liberty in the contemporary United States. Instead of an attempt to diminish the influence of religion, the separation of church and state in the United States allowed religion to flourish without government meddling. Indeed, "there is hardly a point of comparison" between the First Amendment to the U.S. Constitution—"quite defensible in terms of a natural-law concept of the state"—and French anticlerical legislation restricting Catholicism's role in public life.[106]

Both Murray and Maritain urged Catholics to confront the reality of historical development. For Maritain knowledge of human rights increased because of a historical "dynamism which impels the unwritten [natural] law to flower forth in human law, and to render the latter ever more perfect."[107] In 1948 Murray urged American theologians to study the first volumes of *Sources chrétiennes*, the patristic texts edited by Henri de Lubac and colleagues, for insight into "the problem of the development of Christian thought through its historical past."[108] Two years later, in an explosive phrase for Catholics accustomed to understanding theirs as an unchanging church, Murray encouraged Catholics to consider "historical factors" in order to determine what is "principle and what is contingent application of principle."[109]

IV

This extraordinary theological ferment—French Jesuits and Dominicans plumbing the early church for new pastoral and ecclesiastical models, church historians holding up nineteenth-century liberal Catholics as exemplars, Maritain working to bind Catholic social thought to democracy, Murray pressing for revision of church-state doctrine—generated little enthusiasm in Rome. As early as 1942 Marie-Dominique Chenu's pointed attack on standard neo-Thomism, *Une Ecole de théologie: Le Saulchoir*, was placed on the Index of Forbidden Books and Chenu was removed from his post as rector of the leading French Dominican house of studies. Theologians with ties to the Vatican began to challenge perceived excesses in the Nouvelle Théologie; Pope Pius XII demanded, in the 1950 papal encyclical, *Humani Generis*, an end to speculation on certain topics and obedience to papal authority.[110] In the chill of that document's wake, Henri de Lubac was forbidden to teach in his own seminary and Jesuit librarians pulled his books from the shelves.[111] Yves Congar endured what he later described as "an uninterrupted series of denunciations, warnings, restrictive or discriminatory measures and mistrustful interventions."[112]

Forbidden from attending one European conference in 1955, the American historian John Tracy Ellis complained to Roger Aubert, himself the subject of curial suspicion, that the spirit of Pius IX's Syllabus of Errors "is not altogether supplanted."[113] Only the death of Pope Pius XII in 1958 seems to have prevented official Vatican criticism of Maritain's views on the church-state question.[114]

Even John Courtney Murray came under attack. His two leading American opponents, Father Joseph Fenton and Father Francis Connell, were prominent faculty members at the Catholic University, with powerful supporters in Rome. Fenton's suspicion of historically minded theology was such that he accused even Cardinal Newman of demonstrating the "unerring instinct of a minimizer." (Fenton also disagreed with Ellis's interpretation of the "American Catholic tradition" of church and state and allegedly termed another text written in the same vein, Robert Cross's

1958 *The Emergence of Liberal Catholicism in America*, "diabolical.")[115] Connell, for his part, barraged the director of the Holy Office, his friend Cardinal Alfredo Ottaviani, with letters condemning Murray's views, "which cannot be supported by Catholic theology." In response Murray privately complained to Connell that "it is particularly painful when suspicions of unorthodoxy are raised privately, by word of mouth in high places."[116]

By 1955 hostility in Rome toward Murray was such that his Jesuit superiors felt compelled to order him to stop writing on church-state issues. After this decision one friend watched a depressed Murray comb his bookshelves: books on church-state issues would go back to the seminary library; only books on other topics could remain.[117]

V

Ironically, even as Murray's superiors asked him to stop writing on the topic of religious freedom, fears among American intellectuals about Catholic power diminished. Three developments were crucial. First, Catholic leaders came to seem more forward-looking than many white Christians on the era's defining cause, the dismantling of racial segregation in the South. From the late nineteenth century forward, American Catholics had kept their southern churches and schools racially segregated, and a consuming focus on the common good as opposed to individual freedoms left many Catholic intellectuals ill equipped for leadership in the battle for African American civil rights. The country's foremost Catholic liberal, Father John A. Ryan, told African American students and faculty at Howard University in Washington, D.C., in 1943 that legal segregation was morally unacceptable, but he downplayed the need for action on voting rights. "The only moral right possessed by the citizen in the political field is the right to have a government that promotes the common good," he argued. "This end can be obtained without universal suffrage. . . ." A few Howard faculty "sharply dissented" from Ryan's position, and one student asked Ryan how he could reconcile his views with the wartime need for "interracial democracy."[118]

Events at Jesuit-run St. Louis University were also suggestive. Until the early 1940s, university officials had declined to admit African American students. That Missouri's public universities did not admit African American students provided a ready excuse. The St. Louis archbishop John

Glennon agreed with such customs, and Glennon's racial views can be gleaned from periodic complaints about unclean and irresponsible African Americans, particularly those moving into apartments near his cathedral residence.[119]

Controversy over such policies reached the African American press, and Claude Heithaus, S.J., then teaching at St. Louis University, resolved to spark a debate. Heithaus fondly remembered growing up in an integrated parish in South St. Louis as well as the cosmopolitan atmosphere at the University of London, where he received a doctorate in classical archaeology. In a sermon before several hundred students, immediately published in the campus newspaper, Heithaus urged an end to campus segregation. He asked each student to stand (all did) and apologize "for all the wrongs that white men have done to Your colored children."[120]

Neither Archbishop Glennon nor Heithaus's Jesuit superiors viewed this episode favorably. After an extended argument over "social" segregation and the integration of school dances, Jesuit leaders shipped Heithaus and one of his vocal supporters out of St. Louis.[121]

As the controversy developed, leading Catholic theologians waffled. John Courtney Murray favored integration as a matter of charity, but doubted that "the Negro's right to a Catholic education . . . create[s] a right to get it in association with white boys and girls in the same school." Another theologian, Gerald Kelly, worried that mandating immediate integration imposed "obligations that do not exist" on the "Christian conscience." Explosive situations demanded prudence. "If I am not mistaken," he concluded, "the Church herself has applied this principle of prudence to such evils as slavery."[122]

Nonetheless, opponents of racial segregation carried the day. As Yves Simon excitedly wrote to Jacques Maritain, despite a "racist archbishop" and Jesuit superiors willing to "persecute" Father Heithaus, St. Louis University admitted African American students soon after the beginning of the controversy, making the university a regional pioneer. "The future," Simon told Maritain, "goes to those who say, damn, to prudence."[123]

Catholic intellectuals began denouncing racial discrimination and segregation. The pathbreaking American figure was another Jesuit, John LaFarge, who devoted most of his life to battling racial segregation within church and society. LaFarge's 1937 book, *Interracial Justice*, received a glowing notice in *Civiltà Cattolica*, and in 1938 Pope Pius XI, who had read the book, summoned LaFarge to Rome and asked him to work on an encyclical decrying racism and anti-Semitism. (Pius XII chose not to release the encyclical, a decision now enmeshed in an intense debate over his legacy and Catholic conduct during the Holocaust. Nonetheless, the general line of argument did foreshadow a more general Catholic attack on race prejudice after the war.)[124]

Jacques Maritain, as always, also played a role. Concerned about Catholic anti-Semitism in Europe, he quickly found common ground with LaFarge. LaFarge published Maritain's attacks on an "intrinsically inhuman" German racialism and urged the French philosopher to view campaigns against anti-Semitism as part of a larger effort to "teach the Catholic world the principles of justice toward people of other races." Maritain, in turn, called LaFarge's *Interracial Justice* a book of "first importance" and circulated it among his European colleagues.[125]

By the late 1950s ambiguity among Catholic theologians had disappeared. In Europe, Yves Congar described "the idea of 'race'" as meaningless for Catholic theology; in the United States, John Courtney Murray told one correspondent that the sinfulness of segregation was "entirely clear." A Massachusetts Jesuit helped draft a statement for New Orleans Jesuits that defined racial segregation as "seriously immoral."[126]

Vatican officials convinced of the need to eliminate racial distinctions in an international church also registered their displeasure. Upon Archbishop Glennon's death in 1946, Pius XII appointed as his successor Joseph Ritter, known for his rapid desegregation of Catholic institutions while bishop of Indianapolis. One year later Ritter sent a special-delivery letter to each pastor in the St. Louis archdiocese requiring Catholic schools to admit African American Catholic applicants. Such policies were "in keeping with our Catholic teaching and the best principles of our American form of democratic government." Angry white Catholic parents organized a committee with representatives from forty-three parishes to stop integration, but Ritter and the apostolic delegate quashed the revolt by wielding threats of excommunication.[127]

In Louisiana, Archbishop Joseph Rummel denounced parishioners unwilling to allow an African American priest to celebrate Mass. Rummel's boldness received overwhelmingly favorable press attention in the United States and in Rome, where *L'Osservatore Romano*, the Vatican newspaper, explained that "the Church is completely and unalterably opposed to all forms of discrimination—in New Orleans as much as in the Union of South Africa."[128] One year later, in 1958, when some southern bishops balked at the idea of issuing a statement decrying racial segregation and discrimination, Pius XII, just before his death, ordered that the statement be issued "at once."[129]

Catholic leaders now marched in step with the liberal vanguard. "In marked contrast with Protestants," the NAACP leader Walter White explained, Catholics in the District of Columbia had achieved a remarkable "degree of integration."[130] "[O]f course I don't prefer an authoritarian church to a democratic one," Reinhold Niebuhr told one friend in 1957, but he admitted to alternating "between a violent anti-Catholicism and a measure of respect for what they [Catholics] are doing." The Catholic authoritarianism that he found so unattractive, Niebuhr conceded, allowed Catholic bishops to discipline priests and congregations unwilling to integrate Catholic institutions. In most Protestant denominations, by contrast, no one could protect a "poor parson against the manias of his congregation. In this sad world we must pick up virtue wherever we can find it and also recognize weaknesses in our own position."[131]

The second issue easing Catholic acceptance in liberal circles was anticommunism. During the late 1940s critics of Catholicism habitually linked communism and Catholicism. Americans "must no more be caught off guard by the deceptions of the priests and their political tools," one *New Republic* analyst warned, "than by those of the Communists and their stooges."[132] Onetime Librarian of Congress Archibald MacLeish confessed his uneasiness about the "rival authoritarianisms of political Moscow and political Rome," even as the theologian Henry Sloane Coffin bemoaned the "kinship" between "totalitarian Moscow and . . . equally totalitarian Rome. If the one makes us tremble for American liberties, what of the other?"[133] Sidney Hook privately expressed surprise in 1954 that "up and down the country liberal audiences have been throwing into my teeth that Catholic teachers are like communists."[134]

John Wright, then bishop of Worcester, complained about these comparisons. "When the leaders of Protestant clericalism," he warned the activist Agnes Meyer, "are willing to make public statements that in a choice between collaboration with Communist totalitarianism and Roman Catholics, there is *no* choice—then we are living in a time which calls for patience, forbearance and consummate tact—but also for great firmness."[135]

By the late 1950s, however, most liberals conceded that the comparison was overblown. Hook himself, who had in 1940 described Catholicism as "the oldest and greatest totalitarian movement in history," now emphasized the Soviet threat. "All I am saying," he explained to one correspondent still worried about the Catholic hierarchy in 1955, "is that *today the most urgent threat* to your freedom and mine and the freedom of all mankind comes from the Kremlin, not the Vatican. After all, the Pope hasn't got any atomic bombs—neither has Franco or Tito, tyrants both."[136] That same year, in a vastly more influential analysis, the sociologist Will Herberg termed Catholicism an "over-all American religion" professing values similar to Protestantism and Judaism.[137]

Third, and finally, the public posture of American Catholicism shifted into a less combative stance. Prohibited from writing on religious freedom, John Courtney Murray continued to urge Catholics to strike a more temperate balance between Catholic principles and public consensus, and he became a fixture at scholarly conferences on American pluralism. (Murray accepted an offer to spend the 1951–52 academic year at Yale, hoping that "sheer presence in that environment" might do some good.)[138] His open admiration for the American founders, and the sharp distinction he drew between Jefferson and Madison and the anticlerical animus of eighteenth- and nineteenth-century European liberals placed Murray squarely within a scholarly consensus about the distinctive character of American liberalism developed by other prominent scholars such as Harvard's Louis Hartz.[139]

In 1956 Murray cautioned Catholics against overly restrictive censorship of books and films, in an essay that won plaudits from the normally suspicious American Civil Liberties Union. By 1960 Murray's reputation as a political philosopher dedicated to the American experiment was such that his friend Henry Luce could place Murray—recognized for his "lucid, well-modulated concern for the U.S."—on the cover of *Time* as the nation's leading voice on church-state issues.[140] (Murray's longtime foe Father Francis Connell, after meeting with a *Time* correspondent working on the Murray profile, accurately predicted to Father Joseph Fenton, "[The] view which Cardinal Ottaviani and you and myself have championed will be held up to ridicule by some clever writer.")[141]

Catholic liberals also began developing their own criticisms of Catholic conformity. A 1955 essay by the historian John Tracy Ellis castigating American Catholics for neglect of the intellectual life provoked especially intense discussion. Unlike Paul Blanshard, Ellis did not trace intellectual mediocrity to Catholic authoritarianism. Instead, he thought the current state of American Catholic universities a betrayal of the West's most distinguished intellectual tradition.[142] At the same time, waves of Catholic students, especially Catholic graduate students, began receiving degrees from the nation's best universities. One Catholic receiving a Ph.D. from the University of Wisconsin privately complained that "pitifully ill-read" priests held "stereotyped notions of secular colleges as hot-beds of anti-Catholicism."[143]

John F. Kennedy's ability to defuse the religious issue in his 1960 presidential campaign signaled a new armistice. As early as 1958 Murray reported to his Jesuit superior that the office of "Mr. Kennedy" had "approached [him] indirectly some time ago on the question of a statement to be made on the perennially troublesome question: Can a Catholic support, in principle, the religious clauses of the Constitution?"[144]

Murray certainly thought so, although he probably looked askance at Kennedy's disavowal of any religious influence on his political views, in *Look* magazine the next year, which led to unfavorable comment in the Catholic press. (In response Kennedy's father, the onetime ambassador Joseph P. Kennedy, privately complained that the Catholic bishops "don't deserve to have a President.") During the 1960 presidential campaign Catholic intellectuals, including Murray, remained uneasy about Kennedy's rigid distinction between religion and public life.[145]

Still, Kennedy's insistence that religion would not effect his behavior in office disarmed former liberal critics. In a reprise of arguments made during the 1928 Al Smith campaign, and in contrast to the prevailing tone of the 1940s, prominent liberals such as Reinhold Niebuhr and Arthur Schlesinger Jr., maintained that opposition to Kennedy on religious grounds smacked of bigotry.[146] The historian Richard Hofstadter rejected the "absurd" opinion that Smith had lost the 1928 election because of his Catholicism. Hoover's popularity explained the outcome of that campaign, Hofstadter argued, not the "cliché that no Catholic can be elected to the Presidency."[147]

The genuine irrelevance of religion to Kennedy's presidency further diminished fears. In 1958 the Brandeis historian Lawrence Fuchs privately warned that "fundamental and important value differences" distinguished Catholics from other Americans and would produce increasing conflict over the next decade. In 1967 Fuchs termed the evaporation of fears about Kennedy's Catholicism "the triumph of reason."[148]

Meanwhile, attention shifted to Rome. Bishops from around the world would gather for the Second Vatican Council between 1962 and 1965, the most important single event within Catholicism since the Reformation. Attacked during the 1950s, Murray, Maritain, de Lubac, Congar, and Chenu would find themselves vindicated, and the assembled bishops would assume a less defensive stance toward the modern world. (Even a forgotten Paul Blanshard, in Rome observing the Second Vatican Council, would admit that Catholicism "could no longer be described as a monolithic glacier of reactionary thought.")[149]

New tensions, however, quickly emerged. Already conflicts between Catholics and American liberals over the issue of birth control—Reinhold Niebuhr privately scorned Catholics "absolutely caught with [their] ridiculous prohibition of contraception"—were persistent, and this debate exploded within Catholic circles during the 1960s.[150] At the same time American intellectuals and activists began to challenge legal restric-

President-elect John F. Kennedy shakes hands with Father Richard J. Casey after attending Mass prior to his inauguration as president, January 20, 1961.

tions on abortion, a development that pushed liberals toward a more radical defense of individual autonomy, even as Catholics uneasy with changing sexual mores became more determined to protect human life. When the National Federation of Catholic College Students met in the summer of 1964, the assembled students offered a ringing endorsement of the Civil Rights Act then pending in Congress. As one delegate recounted in a letter to her campus adviser, however, the same students felt compelled to issue a general "condemnation of contemporary sexual patterns as proclaimed and practiced by college students."[151]

Chapter Eight
LIFE (I)

I

On August 6, 1964, the Jesuit John Ford approached the lectern in the Chapel of the Immaculate Conception in St. Mary's, Kansas, to preach the funeral sermon of his fellow Jesuit Gerald Kelly. He did so with a sense of purpose, having "dashed out" from Washington, D.C., to Kansas upon learning of Kelly's heart attack, to sit at the hospital bedside of his dying colleague. "He was my very dear friend," Ford would later tell another priest, "and a very great moralist."[1]

Both men entered the Society of Jesus after graduating from Jesuit high schools, Ford in Boston and Kelly in Denver, and spent the rest of their lives in the order. They had met in 1935 in Rome, where along with John Courtney Murray they studied at the Gregorian University. In Rome, Ford and Kelly worked directly under the German Jesuit Franz Hürth, chairholder at the Gregorian, papal adviser, and commonly considered the Catholic world's leading authority on moral theology.

Upon returning to the United States, the two men assumed posts as instructors of moral theology in Jesuit seminaries. Kelly labored at the Missouri Province theologate, in St. Mary's, Kansas; Ford, for most of his career, at the New England Province theologate, in Weston, Massachusetts. Along with Catholic University's Father Francis Connell, Ford and Kelly became the leading Catholic moral theologians in the United States, and among the most influential in the world. We met in Rome, Ford would inform the assembled mourners at Kelly's funeral, "and we have been studying moral theology together ever since."[2]

"Moralist" seems an unprepossessing job description. And yet the importance of moral theology for Catholics was such that Ford and Kelly, despite their current obscurity, should be ranked among the period's most influential American intellectuals, with a reach extending from the confessional to Catholic hospitals, bishops, theological journals, and even the Vatican itself.[3] At Kelly's funeral Ford informed Kelly's friends and family that earlier that summer he had met with Pope Paul VI in Rome. There he gave the pontiff a copy of his latest book, coauthored with Kelly. It was a "great consolation to me," he concluded, "to be able to bring Fr. Kelly on his death bed, the personal thanks of His Holiness, along with his greetings and personal blessing."[4]

Ford's and Kelly's influence, and that of other Catholic moral theologians, began in the darkened wooden boxes where millions of Catholics

Father John C. Ford, S.J., ca. 1960s.

confessed their sins, sometimes on a weekly basis. The stakes were high. Into the 1960s most Catholics believed not only in the possibility of salvation if sins were confessed and forgiven but in the prospect of eternal damnation as well. "God Himself has revealed [hell]," warned Father Connell in a widely used sermon outline, "and we may not reject the word of God merely because our petty intelligence finds His revelation difficult."[5]

Penitents dying in a state of what Catholics called mortal, or serious, sin risked eternal misery. Not every sin was a mortal sin, and the willingness of priests to soften the hard edges of the proscriptive literature in the confessional was well known and appreciated. Even so, the list of mortal sins for Catholics in the 1950s, including the use of contraceptives, skipping Sunday Mass, and drunkenness, was not distinguished by brevity.[6] Absolution for such sins came only in the confessional. Kelly understood, Ford admiringly noted in his funeral homily, that by following the "everyday teaching of the living magisterium of the Church . . . we can know with certainty and in everyday practice what is God's will for us—what we must do and what we must not do in order to be saved."[7]

Ford and Kelly specialized in reinterpreting the arcane terminology of nineteenth-century manuals of moral theology, written by European priests in Latin, for the American scene. Casuistry has come into ill repute, but Ford and Kelly's intellectual curiosity and brisk prose cast the practice in a favorable light, as the effort to apply general moral principles to the dilemmas churned up by daily life.[8] In one examination prepared for his Jesuit students, Ford emphasized that he did not wish to test "*abstract* knowledge." Instead, he wished to measure "the student's ability to *apply correctly* and *prudently* to concrete human situations the law and the moral principles and concepts he has studied for two years."[9] "I have come to the conclusion," Kelly informed his religious superior after a few years of teaching, "that the best way of learning moral [theology] is to solve cases."[10]

In addition to training Jesuits, Ford and Kelly served from 1941 to 1954 as editors for the moral theology section of *Theological Studies*, the premier Catholic theological journal published in the United States. Together, the two men also wrote an influential two-volume analysis of current trends in Catholic moral theology. Kelly simultaneously edited *Review for Religious*, widely read by priests and nuns, and published a guide for teenagers on dating and sex, adapted from the "private notes" of the Gregorian University's Father Hürth, which sold one million copies.[11] In 1947 Kelly drafted the first detailed Catholic code of medical ethics, adopted by hundreds of Catholic hospitals in Canada and the United States, and began publishing a monthly column on the subject for Catholic doctors and hospital administrators.[12]

Each man tackled an extraordinary range of subjects, even as both faithfully adjusted their recommendations to the latest directives from Rome. ("Obviously if we get word of a decision by the H.O. [Holy Office] before the galley proofs are corrected," Kelly explained to a *Theological Studies* editor in 1951, "the foregoing can be changed.")[13] Both Ford and Kelly understood themselves as obligated to assess almost any human action, dispatching problems with clinical efficiency. Both men referred to moral theology as a "science," with Kelly defining his subject as the "science of applying the moral law to the problems of human living."[14]

Like all Catholic moral theologians of the era, the two men occasionally resembled tax lawyers deciphering obscure Internal Revenue Service regulations. Does gargling break the required fast before receiving communion? (No.) What effect does daylight savings time have on the same fast? (It can be taken into account.) Does turtle soup violate the ban on eating meat on Fridays? (Only with a beef, not an oyster, base.)[15]

And yet Ford's and Kelly's writings also displayed a fierce moral seriousness. Should a patient be told she has cancer? (Yes.) Is an alcoholic taking a drink committing a mortal sin? (No.) Can a military officer order the bombing of cities? (No.)[16]

Both the legalism—which Ford and Kelly ruefully recognized as an overemphasis on "sinful deviation"—and the genuine grappling with moral dilemmas reflected their training.[17] The legalism stemmed from immersion in a Catholic ethical tradition strictly subordinate to the practical demands of the confessional, which in the long span from the sixteenth century to the twentieth led to an emphasis on the assessment of individual actions, instead of holistic recommendations for living a Christian life.[18]

The grappling with moral dilemmas arose from the same confessional case method, the same forensic confidence in a moral theologian's ability to parse complex situations into discrete actions. The result was a Catholic literature of unusual sophistication. On the subject of medical ethics, for example, Catholic analysis of just what a doctor or nurse might do, or what rights a patient possessed, was unparalleled. As even the foremost critic of the Catholic approach, Joseph Fletcher, conceded in 1954, "Catholic literature on the morals of medical care is both extensive and painstaking in its technical detail, while Protestant and Jewish literature is practically non-existent."[19]

This Catholic moral universe—of theologians laboring over case studies, seminarians poring over moral theology textbooks in preparation for a lifetime in the confessional, and penitents lined up in churches around the country, silently categorizing their sins as either mortal (serious) or venial (less so)—seemed suddenly vulnerable in the early 1960s. As Ford prepared his homily, he knew that Catholic confidence in a universal and unchangeable natural law, and with it an array of proscriptions and rules, had come under siege.

An immediate source of this vulnerability was sociological. Since the beginning of the nineteenth-century Catholic revival, the importance of the priest as confessor and tribal leader, more in German, Irish, and Polish American parishes than Italian, and more in Italian American parishes than Mexican, rested upon a particular social universe. Its borders were the parish neighborhood, its leaders the priests in the rectory, the nuns in the school, the extended family, and the local ward boss. These parish neighborhood worlds, so powerful that Catholics often identified their neighborhood with a parish name—Holy Cross, St. Ann's, Sacred Heart—became less encompassing in the 1950s, weakened by the GI Bill, which sent millions of Catholic veterans to college, by suburbs beckoning families away from densely populated urban Catholic neighborhoods, and by a rising Catholic intermarriage rate.[20]

The most perceptive American student of these Catholic subcultures, the Jesuit sociologist John L. Thomas, worried that Catholic "group solidarity" might wither when exposed to suburban mores. "It is not so much that religion and moral law are denied or rejected," Thomas explained in 1956; "they are simply judged not pertinent as guiding norms of practical action."[21] The anthropologist Mary Douglas, herself Catholic, later pondered the meaning of a self "progressively detached from the social structure." The result, she warned, might be a "purely ethical religion."[22]

A second vulnerability was intellectual. If in the 1950s Ford's and Kelly's judgments carried oracular weight, the two men felt embattled a decade later. New orientations in Catholic moral theology (notably the historical emphasis and desire to integrate faith and daily life central to the Nouvelle Théologie) assumed far greater prominence, and sex became the primary battleground. What if, scholars began to ask, certain Catholic moral teachings (such as those on birth control) made sense in one historical context and not in another? Should individual sins (especially sexual sins) constitute a primary subject matter of moral theology, or should social problems such as economic inequality and racism? One Illinois bishop privately grumbled that faithful Catholics think the church "stands for only two negatives, no birth control and no meat on Friday."[23]

After Ford and Kelly published the second volume of their *Contemporary Moral Theology*, in 1964, a young Catholic layman, Daniel Callahan, startled the two titans with an acerbic review. (One legend maintains that Kelly suffered his final, ultimately fatal, heart attack seated at his typewriter composing a reply.) Callahan described Ford and Kelly as "loyal civil servants" and "faithful party workers" but "years behind the [theological] revolution now in progress."[24]

II

The initial terms of debate on contraception and abortion were cast in the early twentieth century. For Catholics, Pius XI's 1930 encyclical, *Casti Connubii*, drafted by Arthur Vermeersch and Franz Hürth, John Ford's and Gerald Kelly's Roman mentors, remained decisive. The encyclical described the use of contraceptives as "vicious" and termed all acts of artificial contraception "intrinsically against nature."[25]

Related to this attack on contraception, if logically distinct, was a belief in the sacredness of innocent human life. Although steeped in a neo-Thomism that stressed community goals over individual rights, Catholics consistently defended the principle that each innocent human possessed an inherent right to life. In 1923 Father John A. Ryan complained to the economist Richard T. Ely that eighteenth-century French radicals had exaggerated the importance of rights, which were not autonomous and "are justified and determined by their effects." The one exception, Ryan asserted, was the "right to life."[26] "The Catholic answer," explained John Ford twenty years later, "is the *absolute inviolability* of the right of an innocent human person to life, and the absolute intrinsic evil of the act by which he is deprived of life."[27]

Ford, like almost all Catholic intellectuals of the period, still assumed the existence of a natural law, or what another theologian called an "objective order of universal immutable principles . . . for all men and for all times and circumstances."[28] Well-intentioned inquirers might not accept Catholic doctrine on a topic as obviously dependent upon church authority as the bodily assumption of Mary into heaven. But reasonable people should agree on natural law principles. Early in his career Ford enjoyed identifying such non-Catholics as Mortimer Adler and C. S. Lewis as fellow-traveling defenders of an "absolute moral order."[29] The natural law, insisted Father Connell, was "engraven on the human mind for every intelligent and honest person to read."[30]

Instead of valorizing the natural law, many American intellectuals moved in the opposite direction. They became convinced of the need to allow humans to choose their own ends, to reject any notion of a natural law external to human making. Because couples had to plan their own families, contraceptives should be widely available. Because the desperately ill should be able to plan their own deaths, laws prohibiting euthanasia were archaic taboos. Because science had (seemingly) established links between heredity and intelligence, the state should limit the ability of criminals and the mentally handicapped to have children.

Catholic ethicists found none of this persuasive. "God," explained John Ford, "not man, is the master of human life."[31] Suffering, too, served a purpose, and the most widely used Catholic textbook on medical ethics during the 1940s contained an entire chapter on "the Christian philosophy of suffering." ("It is the duty of the [Catholic] nurse," the author advised, "to explain, when the occasion arises, how suffering fits into the universe.")[32] Mothers bearing eight, ten, even twelve children certainly suffered. Desperately ill patients prevented from ending their own lives suffered too. But while claiming not to "deify pain," theologians such as Gerald Kelly insisted that Americans not ignore "the fact that no one suffers save through the will of God; that through suffering a man can beautify his character, atone for his sins, take a special part in the sublime work of the Redemption."[33]

This cluster of Catholic beliefs became a tightly woven rhetorical package: an objective natural law existed, and contraception violated it; innocent human life deserved unconditional protection; God, not humans, should determine the purpose of sexual acts and the duration of human life; suffering possessed value.

The unwillingness to distinguish among these beliefs explains why

Catholics in the 1930s routinely lumped contraception, forced sterilization, euthanasia, and abortion into the same abhorrent category. The comprehensiveness of the Catholic indictment—*all* contraception was illegitimate, *all* human life must be defended—eviscerated nuance. In 1931 the editors of *Commonweal* pleaded with "all sensible people" to realize that greater access to contraceptives "would be a long step on the road toward state clinics for abortion, for compulsory sterilization of those declared unfit by fanatical eugenicists, and the ultimate destruction of human liberty at the hands of an absolute pagan state."[34] A prominent New York priest declared his opposition, in a single breath, to "Euthanasia, social betterment, contraception for the poor, therapeutic abortions, [and] eugenics by way of sterilization."[35]

With the exception of fights over contraception, this implacable Catholic sexual and medical ethic generated only modest controversy before World War II. The most charged battles were on the subject of eugenics and sterilization. Here the liberal faith in individual autonomy faltered, as many early twentieth-century reformers became convinced that the state needed to limit the reproductive capacities of those deemed unfit.[36] Margaret Sanger herself regretted that "[a]nybody in this vast country is at perfect liberty to become a father or a mother"—including a "mental defective," a "pauper," and those bereft of "common decency."[37] "Birth control," she wrote in 1920, "is nothing more or less than the facilitation of the process of weeding out the unfit, or preventing the birth of defectives or of those who will become defectives."[38]

Advocates of birth control did not always become active members of eugenic groups, and vice versa, since eugenicists promoted birth control among immigrant communities, but chastised upper-class Americans unwilling to produce sufficient progeny. Still, birth control advocates such as Sanger expressed great enthusiasm for laws (passed in twenty-eight states by 1931) permitting the involuntary sterilization of criminals and the insane.[39] Into the 1940s Connecticut Planned Parenthood members trumpeted birth control as a sensible way to avoid "taxation for the insane and the feeble-minded."[40]

The Supreme Court confirmed involuntary sterilization programs as forward thinking when Justice Oliver Wendell Holmes Jr., icon for Progressive Era activists, authorized the forced sterilization of Carrie Buck, a Virginia woman deemed mentally incompetent, with the pungent phrase "three generations of imbeciles are enough."[41] (The Catholic Pierce Butler was the only justice to dissent from Holmes's opinion in *Buck v. Bell*, but Butler gave no reason for his dissent.)[42]

Until the mid-1920s Catholics occasionally used eugenic language themselves, with John Ryan stealing a phrase from Theodore Roosevelt and warning of "race suicide" because of widespread use of birth control.[43] But Catholics also understood that eugenic enthusiasm for sterilization and birth control stemmed in part from fears that Catholics might achieve dominance through the cradle. Two of the most prominent American eugenicists, for example, maintained in a widely used 1918 textbook, "Nothing can be more certain than that, if present conditions continue, Roman Catholics will soon be in an overwhelming preponderance in the eastern United States, because of the differential birth-rate. . . ."[44] In the *Encyclopaedia of the Social Sciences*, Frank Hankins of Smith College chastised parents with several children for "improvidence and unrestrained sexual indulgence." Especially worrisome to Hankins, after calculating birthrates in Massachusetts, Britain, and Germany, was the "rapid multiplication of Catholics as compared with Protestants, Jews and non-believers."[45]

Although a few Catholic theologians, notably in Germany, accepted involuntary sterilization, Catholic opposition to the practice crystallized in the 1920s. John A. Ryan insisted that sterilization, like contraception generally, thwarted the proper end of sexual intercourse. Involuntary sterilization of "defectives" and prisoners also constituted an unacceptable state intervention into the private realm. As he explained in 1926, the "disregard of human sacredness involved in this wholesale killing for a social end [sterilization] would bring about a continuous decline in human sympathy and in the sense of human values generally."[46]

In 1930, in *Casti Connubii,* the same encyclical that condemned contraceptives, Pius XI used even more emphatic language, attacking those "over solicitous for the cause of eugenics" and willing to sterilize so-called "defectives."[47] This Catholic opposition to sterilization extended across the globe. In Britain, France, Quebec, and Latin America, Catholic politicians battled liberals eager to limit the reproductive capacities of the "unfit."[48]

In the United States, the New Orleans archbishop John W. Shaw scorned the notion of a "millennium of supermen and superwomen as perfect specimens of the human animal, bred and reared according to the latest eugenic rules." Instead of forced sterilizations, Shaw suggested, the state might guarantee that the poor were "properly housed and protected against the profiteer."[49] The National Catholic Welfare Conference funded an unsuccessful effort to persuade the Supreme Court to rehear *Buck v. Bell*—"without using the name National Catholic Welfare Council"—and Catholic activists worked to stop sterilization programs in Oregon, Vermont, Texas, and Ohio, where no "organized opposition" existed beyond Catholics.[50]

Catholics relished the debate over involuntary sterilization because it offered a golden opportunity to challenge the pragmatic orthodoxy that values and ethics were contingent. If they were, Catholics asked, what protected the right to procreate, or even human life itself? Liberals such as Felix Frankfurter and Harold Laski might ignore *Buck v. Bell* in tributes to Justice Holmes, or file it under the cheerful heading "On Legislative Freedom."[51] A Detroit Jesuit, by contrast, pointedly asked whether Carrie Buck's daughter had proven to be a "mental defective." (She had not.)[52]

Similarly, Father John Ford, in one of his first scholarly articles, launched a searing attack on Holmes's willingness to jettison the idea of the natural law and his belief that moral principles, such as the sanctity of human life, merely masked judicial preferences. When challenged by Felix Frankfurter, Ford held his ground, responding that Holmes's "strikingly totalitarian" views ultimately rested upon "force and violence in juristic matters."[53]

Euthanasia did not become widely debated in the United States until after World War II. But in the United States and Britain birth control reformers took the lead in sponsoring discussion on the right to end one's own life and, more discreetly, the societal duty to end unproductive lives. The issue was again individual control. Just as a woman should be able to space her pregnancies, so too should an individual have the right to ask a doctor to terminate his or her own life.

The first publicized dispute between Catholics and liberals over euthanasia came in 1915 when a Chicago physician refused to operate to save the life of an allegedly deformed newborn child. The progressive editors of the *New Republic* congratulated the physician for "high courage" and a willingness to challenge "an ancient religious scruple." At a time when many children suffered from inadequate food and housing, the editors found it astonishing that a doctor's "refusal to keep alive a deformed idiot has become a moral issue throughout the nation."[54]

Catholics took an alternative view. A Jesuit priest publicized interviews with doctors who disagreed with the diagnosis of the primary-care physician, suggesting that the alleged deformities were not wholly disabling. A Catholic social worker, Catherine Walsh, baptized the infant and vainly pleaded for his life. "How long," asked a Montana bishop, "will it be until the weak-minded, the deformed, the infirm and the aged will be disposed of according to the same theory?"[55]

A formal campaign to legalize euthanasia began in 1938 with the formation of the Euthanasia Society of America, whose founding members included Margaret Sanger.[56] The leading figure in the society, Charles Potter, had already garnered notoriety for his advocacy of birth control and eugenics, regretting that "Christianity was chiefly responsible for the protection of the unfit, thereby increasing the number of feeble-minded in the world."[57] Potter's views on the dying were equally generous. In 1937 he declared himself appalled by the "social cowardice" that forced Americans to keep alive "congenital idiots, the hopelessly insane, and the incurable sick whose every breath is torture."[58]

Noting the similarities in the arguments made by proponents of birth control, involuntary sterilization, and euthanasia, Catholics warned that the pragmatic criterion of usefulness might move from the right to procreate to the lives of the elderly and the infirm.[59] John Ford chastised intellectuals for forsaking "the absolute *right* of the innocent to life, [because] doing so admits implicitly that the state is the master of the life and death of its subjects."[60]

Abortion generated less controversy before World War II than either sterilization or euthanasia. Despite occasional headline-producing prosecutions of abortionists, the few physicians who suggested even modest changes in the abortion laws received little public attention. Anxious to distinguish its cause from that of abortion reform, the American Birth Control League declared itself "steadfastly opposed to abortion," and Margaret Sanger promised that greater access to birth control would "do away with abortion."[61]

Nonetheless, Catholics had already established themselves as the foremost defenders of an absolute ban on abortion. Prominent Catholic bishops condemned the practice as an "abomination" as early as the mid-nineteenth century, and priests counseled parishioners to avoid doctors eager to recommend "feticide" to Catholic mothers. A nineteenth-century advocate of restrictive abortion laws, Horatio Storer, credited the willingness of Catholic leaders to excommunicate the doctors performing abortions, and the women having them, with saving "to the world thousands of infant lives."[62]

Contingent circumstances, Catholics argued, were irrelevant. Even when a mother in labor risked her own death, directly intending to kill the fetus was not "morally sound."[63] Standard handbooks for Catholic nurses treated the subject in painstaking detail, warning nurses not to violate the "fundamental principles of Natural Law" by assisting doctors willing to perform abortions.[64] One Chicago seminary director explained to his students in the late 1930s that confession and absolution could wash away any sin, but in the absence of confession, abortion remained "so heinous in the sight of God, in the eyes of the Church, that the Church has attached a penalty of excommunication."[65]

III

For John Ford and other Catholic moral theologians, World War II seemed a vindication. In Ford's eyes the mistaken belief that values and ethics were contingent had permitted European fascism and its horrific effects. He lectured Boston lawyers on the folly of asking soldiers chastened by the "horrors and heroism of total war" to accept the position of Justice Holmes, that "fundamentally morality is merely a question of deep-seated preferences." "Do men die for tentative hypotheses?" asked one Georgetown law professor. "Would men die for something that is unreal or indefinite?"[66]

Catholics continued to refer to a universal natural law and defend innocent human life. Ford, remarkably, even extended this argument to military tactics. In 1944, at the height of the war, Ford published a powerfully reasoned forty-nine-page attack on the American and British practice of bombing civilian targets, an essay that became a landmark in the literature of military ethics. So-called "obliteration bombing," Ford explained, violated the "Catholic view that to take the life of an innocent person is always intrinsically wrong, that is, forbidden absolutely by natural law."[67] French, German, and Belgian bishops also protested indiscriminate bombing, and one Italian Catholic, Alfredo Ottaviani, the future cardinal and secretary of the Holy Office, wondered whether *any* modern war remained morally permissible.[68]

After the war Ford condemned the dropping of the atomic bombs on Hiroshima and Nagasaki as "the greatest and most extensive single atrocity of all this period." Another American Jesuit complained that defenders of atomic weapons substituted "national pragmatism" for "the transcendence of the moral order."[69] These denunciations of Allied bombing campaigns had no discernible effect on military strategy, and the intense American Catholic patriotism of the period obscured scholarly dissents. Twenty years later Ford would regret wartime Catholic "complacency and conformity" in the face of a "moral issue that was staring us in the face."[70]

In retrospect, however, the consensus among Catholic theologians that American military leaders should not bomb civilian targets, even when battling Nazi Germany, demonstrated widespread agreement on a basic principle: that innocent life remained sacred, with no good end justifying illicit means. John Courtney Murray congratulated Ford in 1944 for making an "immensely interesting" argument to which he could make "no exception." Father Francis Connell agreed with Ford that "there is apt to be too much rationalizing even among priests in defense of governmental activities, and theologians should make a stand on principles without respect of persons."[71] If asked to drop such a bomb on civilians, Connell suggested, a Catholic aviator must refuse "even if he will be court-martialed and shot."[72]

Catholics also reminded American liberals of Nazi enthusiasm for involuntary sterilization and forced euthanasia, helping to discredit once popular liberal causes. Forced sterilizations declined after the 1940s, and even the Euthanasia Society of America, "after careful consideration," decided not to advocate the taking of life "without consent."[73] After a Vermont doctor drew national attention in 1949 for assisting in a patient's suicide, John Ford accused him of sharing "with our own Justice Holmes (a great admirer of the German philosophers) the idea that there is 'no reason for attributing to man a significant difference in kind from that which belongs to a baboon or a grain of sand.' "[74] Privately, Ford expressed pride that "the Catholic Church will always defend the sanctity of human life against all comers."[75]

Contraception, not euthanasia or sterilization, remained the most polarizing issue. As early as 1936, officials in the National Catholic Welfare Council quietly reported that "the majority opinion of the country is in favor of Birth Control—the people, the legislatures, the Courts."[76] Over the next decade, prompted in part by the stern tone of *Casti Connubii*, Catholic women's colleges withdrew from the American Association of University Women because the organization favored "legalizing the dispensing of information by physicians on contraception"; priests urged African Americans not to promote the "profoundly deleterious practice" of birth control, and bishops tried to prevent the "morally objectionable" custom of commanding officers requiring soldiers to carry condoms when leaving a military base.[77]

Electoral politics were not immune. By 1940 only two states, Massachusetts and Connecticut, restricted the ability to sell and prescribe contraceptives, relying on late nineteenth-century laws written by Protestant moralists. ("The old line non-Catholic population," one Boston Catholic doctor noted, "put these laws on the books.")[78] Because Catholics understood contraception as violating a natural law compelling to all reasonable people, Catholic leaders in both states favored maintaining these laws, even if the restrictions were frequently evaded in practice. (Doctors could prescribe contraceptives for "health" reasons.) Both states possessed powerful, heavily Catholic Democratic parties, able to thwart beleaguered Republicans attempting to modify the laws.[79]

Liberals in Massachusetts decided to try their luck at the ballot box in 1942, gathering signatures for a referendum allowing doctors to prescribe and distribute contraceptives to married women. The leaders of the Boston archdiocese did little active campaigning, but a steady stream of incendiary editorials in the Catholic press helped defeat the measure by a remarkable 58 percent to 42 percent margin.[80]

The battle resumed in 1948. Planned Parenthood supporters, led by MIT's president, Karl T. Compton, again demanded a loosening of restrictions on birth control, in order that the "religious beliefs of some should not be forced upon all. This is an elementary matter of civil liberties in a democracy."[81] This time the Boston archdiocese coordinated a massive countereffort. Priests encouraged parishioners to register to vote, and the archdiocese financed a billboard and radio campaign. Sophistication was not at a premium. What if, one radio advertisement asked, Marie Curie's mother had used contraceptives? Or the mother of Louis Brandeis?[82]

Natural law arguments provided the intellectual ballast. Indeed, the primary slogan of the campaign against the proposed birth control

Publicity for 1948 campaign against the liberalization of Massachusetts birth control laws.

amendment, plastered on local billboards, was "Birth Control Is *Still* against God's Law." Or as a sermon outline distributed to priests for use in the homily on Sunday, October 1, 1948, explained, "the prohibition of Birth Control is not a law peculiar to the church any more than are the laws against murder, theft, perjury or treason." The outline continued, "The Catholic Church does not initiate these laws. They are rooted in our very natures and are written by God in the very heart of every man, woman and child."[83]

The behind-the-scenes director of the archdiocesan effort was the Boston auxiliary bishop John Wright. That Wright—a friend of Jacques Maritain, later bishop of Worcester and Pittsburgh and then a Roman cardinal—directed the effort suggests the importance Catholic leaders placed on the issue. Privately, Wright warned that greater access to birth control rested on a par with "euthanasia, abortion, sterilization and other practices which do not lack defenders in our day."[84] John Ford, teaching in suburban Weston, Massachusetts, in 1948 urged New England Jesuits to "avoid a rhetorical or denunciatory tone." But Father Ford also thought that for a Catholic to vote in favor of greater access to birth control might be a mortal sin.[85] And he brushed aside claims that Catholics imposed their morality on Massachusetts citizens. "The same argument," Ford noted, "is even now being urged in favor of the so-called 'mercy killings' of the aged and helpless; but the civil law still brands so-called 'mercy killings' as murder, and therefore immoral."[86]

On election day Catholics again emerged victorious, with the birth control amendment losing by only a slightly smaller margin than in 1942. The *Boston Pilot*, the archdiocesan newspaper, congratulated "fellow citizens who so wisely saw this whole matter as a community, not a sectarian problem."[87]

IV

Triumph at the Massachusetts polls masked a growing isolation. If for John Ford and other Catholics the experience of World War II confirmed the necessity of adherence to a universal natural law, most American intellectuals understood the European crisis of the 1930s and the war differently. Instead of a uniform moral code, these intellectuals stressed the importance of tolerance and critical debate in a democratic society and warned against unreflective obedience. The "genius" of American life, according to influential scholars such as Daniel Boorstin, was the absence of "dogma" in either politics or religion. "Whatever the dogmatist may feel about it," explained a young Columbia professor, Jacques Barzun, "this relativist-instrumentalist philosophy is the philosophy of free democracy par excellence."[88]

Armed with these convictions, American intellectuals inevitably found the Catholic position on contraception distressing. Already in 1938 a contributor to the *Annals of the American Academy of Arts and Sciences* had framed the contraception debate as one of "freedom of inquiry," emphasizing the importance of physicians' autonomy and speculating that Catholics secretly rooted for a "differential birth rate."[89] After the 1942 Massachusetts birth control referendum, a stunned *New Republic* contributor lashed out against Catholic "destroyers and wreckers of too many of the fundamentals of democracy" employing "the same weapons of attack which they [Catholics] used to destroy democracy in Austria and Spain." A *Nation* counterpart hoped for an "anti-Catholic reaction."[90]

Non-Catholics' incredulity at Catholics' resistance to contraception swelled after the war. Paul Blanshard devoted a chapter to the subject in *American Freedom and Catholic Power*, expressing his eugenic fear that "the feebleminded" were producing "future Americans at a much faster rate than our normal citizens."[91] Less strident voices also joined the fray. When a group of prominent social scientists composed a textbook on social problems, they included a section on "birth control and the Catholic church" that accused Catholic leaders of "defrauding [their] own members" as well as the "rest of the population."[92] "I think it would be wonderful," confided Dr. Mary Steichen Calderone, the medical director of Planned Parenthood, "if the Catholic Church would live up to its great democratic tradition, as evidenced by its stand in the segregation issue for instance, and state clearly and forcefully that birth control is immoral only for Catholics and that other religious groups will be freed from its opposition."[93]

Catholics alternated between counterattacks and, increasingly, a glum recognition that disputes over contraception seemed unresolvable. When the Episcopalian priest James Pike criticized Catholics for not permitting Planned Parenthood chapters to benefit from Community Chest fundraising drives across the country, John Courtney Murray privately accused Pike of a "baneful ethical relativism" but conceded that the issue was "difficult and complicated."[94] In 1952, four years after defeating efforts to loosen birth control restrictions, a leading priest of the Boston archdiocese hoped that Catholics could avoid another electoral battle. "In view of the modern mentality," he wrote, "it is a bit like trying to sweep back the tide. . . ."[95]

This shifting tide included Catholic couples. Public dissent from church teaching on contraception was nonexistent in the United States in the 1940s and 1950s, and birthrates for Catholic women remained higher than those for non-Catholic women, even at the height of the postwar baby boom. Catholic women educated at Catholic colleges, in particular, continued to desire families of five children or more, defying the demographic rule that increased education for women led to decreased fertility.[96]

A quiet anguish, however, was also evident. Even in the early 1930s knowledgeable priests privately admitted that "practically every priest who is close to the people admits that contraception is the hardest problem of the confessional today."[97] After the war, with Catholics following the general pattern of marriage at younger ages, Catholic couples attempting to raise large families faced serious obstacles. Especially difficult was the situation faced by the Catholic woman married at, say, twenty-one, and bearing her fifth child at age thirty. Could she endure four or five more pregnancies? Would her husband's income sustain their family? Could they provide a college education (or pay Catholic school tuition) for their children? In response reform-minded priests and lay Catholics urged couples to avoid "selfishness" by welcoming children and offering prophetic witness to the primacy of human life in a materialist age.[98]

Prophetic witness is by definition not a mass movement. The starkness of the Catholic attack on contraception—Father John A. Ryan once testified before Congress that contraception was "wrong in itself, always and everywhere, regardless of circumstances, conditions or effects"—seemed draconian when measured against the circumstances that might lead couples to use contraceptives.[99] (Ryan's assurance on this matter is especially unsettling, since as he privately admitted, his experience in the confessional was "so slight and so far in the past.")[100] Unsurprisingly, even in the 1940s, one-third of all married Catholics admitted to social scientists that they used contraceptives.[101] John Ford observed in 1948, "*Many* Catholics are emotionally (and even intellectually) inclined to the practice of birth control. They struggle under real and almost overwhelming difficulties."[102]

Partial relief for Catholic couples became available with the so-called rhythm method of birth control, or as Catholic moralists preferred, "periodic continence." By charting a woman's menstrual cycle, Catholic couples could have intercourse during infertile periods, and not violate the ban on "artificial" contraception. In its modern form the method dated only from the early 1930s, when reliable biological information on women's menstrual cycles became available. Until that time some priests had innocently informed couples that the midpoint of the menstrual cycle was a sterile period, exactly the opposite of biological reality. Unsurprisingly, as John Ford and Gerald Kelly ruefully noted, "the public had little confidence" in the method.[103]

Even this new, more reliable rhythm method seemed dubious to strict Catholic moralists. The apostolic delegate in Washington, D.C., acting on instructions from the Vatican, secretly warned the American bishops in 1936 that the rhythm method was an "extreme remedy" suitable only as a last resort for desperate couples. A young John Ford urged priests to avoid "broadcasting" the rhythm method, since the "Catholic ideal of marriage is fertility."[104]

Pius XII eased doubts about the rhythm method in 1951 with a wholehearted papal endorsement, and Catholic moralists during the succeeding decade, including Ford, apologized for prior timidity. Lay couples interested in limiting family size, one Jesuit explained to his peers, were not "selfish, materialistic people distrustful of divine providence."[105] Still, the rhythm method's unreliability when compared with other contraceptives, as well as the requirement that couples abstain from intercourse at the point in the menstrual cycle when a woman most desired intercourse, inevitably limited its appeal.

Ford also recognized another problem. How could Catholics believe that the ban on contraception rested on a natural law accessible to all, when only Catholics seemed to find this interpretation of the natural law plausible? Protestant scholars in the 1940s and 1950s almost uniformly rejected natural law arguments when applied to the subject of contraception, an issue that Reinhold Niebuhr felt should be "touched by freedom."[106] The most distinguished Protestant ethicist, Princeton's Paul Ramsey, agreed. After all, Ramsey asked in 1944, hadn't slave owners justified themselves with recourse to natural law? And opponents of women's suffrage? After listing these two examples, Ramsey proceeded, remarkably, to the "continuing Catholic case of birth control," which he would later term an example of "Catholic absolutism."[107]

In Europe, especially, doubts about the persuasiveness of church teaching became dimly visible. The German theologian Herbert Doms claimed as early as the 1930s that procreation and the expression of marital love should be given equal weight in assessing the meaning of sexual intercourse. A biologist by training, Doms pointed out the inadequacies of nineteenth-century descriptions of human reproduction in theology textbooks and urged a more nuanced articulation of Catholic doctrine. Doms (and other theologians with similar views) did not necessarily favor a change in Catholic teaching on contraception. But arguing that the purpose of marriage was at once procreation and marital love did open the door. If procreation was not the dominant purpose of marriage, did each act of sexual intercourse need to be open to procreation? Doms himself conceded that at some future point the church might favor family limitation, suggesting that the "relative importance of the purposes of marriage is capable of some variation in the course of history."[108]

A handful of scholars explored these questions in theological journals.[109] Vatican officials then entered the debate, prohibiting new printings of Doms's work, and in the process stunting his career. In 1944 the Holy Office, in the words of one satisfied American Catholic theologian, "definitely and conclusively" declared that the "primary end of marriage is the procreation and rearing of children."[110] Privately, Jacques Maritain regretted the Vatican decision and the Catholic ban on contraception, "another of those tragic examples where the church defends a truth by blockading it with ways of thinking that simple human experience has left way behind."[111]

John Ford, by contrast, applauded the Vatican intervention. His own Roman mentor, Father Franz Hürth, had helped draft *Casti Connubii*, and Ford thought Hürth's conviction that procreation remained the primary end of sexual intercourse carried "peculiar weight." "No positive interference," Ford stressed, "with the primary end [of sexual intercourse] is permitted." An official in the family life office of the National Catholic Welfare Conference echoed this view, emphasizing that the "child is the primary purpose of marriage" and not the "'community of love' of husband and wife."[112]

Over time, however, a note of despair crept into the utterances of even the most stalwart defenders of orthodoxy. As early as 1941 one American priest felt compelled to investigate what he called in his book title *The Possibility of Invincible Ignorance of Natural Law*. Ignorance, it turned out, was possible. "The perception of the evil of Birth Control," in particular, "requires the ability to make rather fine distinctions" and might bewilder "acute minds."[113] Ford and Kelly regretted in 1954 that Catholic arguments on contraception were unpersuasive to "the medical profession as a whole." Less than a decade later Kelly abandoned this qualifier, admitting that, "with perhaps some rare exceptions," only men and women of "religious conviction" accepted "the truth" of Catholic teaching on contraception.[114]

Concern about population growth provided a final challenge for Catholic apologists. The immediate postwar period saw an explosion of interest in the problem, with best-selling authors such as the Planned Parenthood director William Vogt urging a "Fifth Freedom—from excessive numbers of children." At the same time John D. Rockefeller III founded (and lavishly funded) the Population Council, beginning a wide-ranging program of research and advocacy that jump-started the study of population issues at numerous foundations and universities.[115]

From the beginning, advocates of population control understood

Catholic teaching on contraception as a primary obstacle, most immediately in the United States, but also in the Caribbean, Latin America, and the Philippines. Vogt accused Catholics of halting "human progress" in the name of "entrenched dogma," and even more moderate officials of the Population Council worried about Catholics with "diametrically opposed points of view."[116] By the late 1950s, instead of simply urging choice for couples, birth control advocates demanded that Catholics adopt "a more realistic and adequate doctrine of responsible parenthood."[117] A distinguished Protestant theologian, John Bennett, wondered whether parents now faced a "moral obligation" to "limit the number of births in a family."[118]

The initial Catholic response to accusations of moral irresponsibility was halting. Into the 1940s John Ford used population data collected during the depression to argue *against* birth control, emphasizing that the "decline of the birth rate in this country, and in other industrial nations, is a source of deep concern to almost all population experts."[119] When American birthrates soared immediately after the war, the utility of this argument diminished, and the Jesuit John L. Thomas conceded that non-Catholics might well view the Catholic perspective on population control "as a cultural residue surviving from an unscientific, agrarian past."[120]

Other Catholics suggested that "over-population" was an indeterminate concept. Much better, argued Giovanni Montini, the future Pope Paul VI, to avoid reliance on contraceptives and redistribute economic resources, a program consistent with the "dignity of conjugal relations."[121] By the early 1960s, in a modest concession, John Ford and Gerald Kelly referred to overpopulation at page 456 of a 459-page book on marriage and sexuality. Here they dismissed concerns about global population as of "little urgency" to the confessor assisting individual penitents. But they also emphasized the need to "increase and distribute resources so that all peoples can live decently."[122]

V

And then a remarkable series of events. A new pope, John XXIII, was elected in 1958 and decided to call an ecumenical council, its opening session scheduled for the fall of 1962. Vatican officials initially hoped to use the council as an opportunity to ratify traditional positions, and the

American bishops certainly expected little from the event.[123] But the gathering of bishops and theologians from around the world set an unpredictable dynamic in motion. Ultimately, the bishops wrested control of the council away from the curia, and the sessions (stretching over three years) became a theological crash course, with what Jesuit seminarians were already dismissing as "ghetto Thomism" losing much of its influence.[124]

What replaced neo-Thomism was less a philosophical or theological system than a sensitivity to historical development and a new openness to the modern world. Yves Congar, Marie-Dominique Chenu, Henri de Lubac, John Courtney Murray, and others returned from ecclesiastical exile and infused the conciliar documents with biblical and patristic emphases, a sensitivity to diverse liturgical forms, and a focus on laypeople. Enveloping the whole was a new sense of the church moving through history, "always in need of being purified" and directly addressing the problems of the current age.[125] One excited priest reported in 1963, "I heard John Courtney Murray say in a dinner talk . . . in Washington in May that Newman's idea of the evolution of dogma might well become one of the key ideas in Vatican Council II."[126]

The adoption of the Declaration of Religious Freedom in 1965 marked the most self-conscious recognition of doctrinal development. By that time the overwhelming majority of bishops favored the principle of religious freedom, precisely because it acknowledged the importance of individual conscience and removed from Catholics the stigma of supporting (even theoretically) intolerant regimes. Even so, as many bishops recognized, recasting Catholic doctrine on the matter of religious freedom raised a broader question. John Courtney Murray, the leading author of the Declaration of Religious Freedom, put it this way: "the fundamental concern of the Council is with the development of doctrine."[127]

By this time ripple effects from the Second Vatican Council had already begun to shape the public posture of Catholics on the birth control question. In Massachusetts, where Catholics had blocked efforts to increase access to contraceptives in 1942 and 1948, an ACLU observer commented as early as 1962 on "an increasing number of statements by liberal, educated Catholics expressing the view that we must 'live and let live' and that no religious group, even if it is the majority group, should impose its views on others."[128] When a young Democratic state legislator, the future Democratic presidential nominee Michael Dukakis, introduced a reform bill in 1965, Boston's Cardinal Richard Cushing agreed not to oppose permitting a "practice that can be considered a case of private morality."[129]

Here again John Courtney Murray played a vital behind-the-scenes role. Then laboring over the Declaration of Religious Freedom at the Second Vatican Council, Murray composed the statement that served as a basis for Cardinal Cushing's position, insisting that it is not "the function of civil law to prescribe everything that is morally right and to forbid everything that is morally wrong." Given that contraceptive devices had "received official sanction by many religious groups within the community," Murray urged Catholics to respect the religious freedom of their fellow citizens.[130]

Pittsburgh's Bishop John Wright, the leader of the successful 1948 Catholic campaign to prevent modification of the birth control law in Massachusetts, grumbled about the new Catholic strategy. Wright warned, presciently, that legislation to allow married couples unlimited access to contraceptives would prove insufficient. Soon legislators would allow the distribution of contraceptives to "teenage girls and the unmarried." In the 1940s, Wright recalled, "incredible though it seems, we thought contraception immoral and thought it bad public policy to place the favor of the law behind it."[131]

John Ford grudgingly accepted the new Catholic tolerance, if only because it was "not worth the trouble and bitterness to fight against the amendment at the present time." But Ford, too, stressed that he now maintained principles that he had followed in the forties, but believed there had "been a substantial change in context." "It all depends," he wearily concluded, "on how much of an evil you think birth control is, and what its effect on the common good might be in the long run."[132]

In Connecticut, as in Massachusetts, Catholic leaders abandoned opposition to modification of the birth control laws. One bishop admitted as early as 1961 that he found it "increasingly difficult" to recruit Catholics willing to testify before the state legislature in favor of keeping the laws, and "even our Catholic legislators and politicians regret this biennial exercise."[133]

By that time, however, Planned Parenthood members had already begun maneuvering a test case through the courts. ACLU lawyers coordinating the effort placed considerable emphasis on recruiting Catholic lawyers to join their team, noting that more and more Catholics favored permitting any birth control methods deemed "spiritually compatible and medically wise."[134] The director of the Catholic Council on Civil Liberties filed a friend-of-the-court brief favoring repeal of the laws, and assured the ACLU, "[O]ur sympathies are with you and the Connecticut defendants."[135]

The U.S. Supreme Court rendered its verdict in 1965, invalidating the Connecticut law in *Griswold v. Connecticut*.[136] The reaction from church officials and the Catholic press was largely favorable, with the editors of *Commonweal* calling the decision "long overdue" and regretting that Catholic leaders in Massachusetts and Connecticut had not come to their senses earlier. "The entire round of court struggles," the editors complained, "was unnecessary, a dubious tribute to the power of a determined minority to impose their moral values on others."[137]

If Catholic leaders conceded that the public sale of contraceptives would not harm the common good, what might that mean for Catholic couples? In an unprecedented development, a wave of articles questioning church teaching on contraception had already appeared in Europe and the United States in the early 1960s, written by priests, laymen, and laywomen.[138] One physician involved in the development of oral contraceptives, Harvard's John Rock, was himself Catholic and had long sparred with church authorities critical of his involvement with the project. (John Ford, for example, told Rock in 1945 that he might feel obligated to deny Rock absolution for the sin of advocating birth control, should such advocacy continue. "I hesitate to tell you," he added, "how strongly some Catholics have spoken about your activities.")[139] Rock toured the country in the early 1960s promoting his well-publicized book, *The Time Has Come: A Catholic Doctor's Proposals to End the Battle over Birth Control*, prompting Ford to wonder whether the Boston archdiocese could somehow limit Rock's frequent television appearances.[140]

For the first time prominent moral theologians joined the side of reform, including the German Redemptorist Bernhard Häring. Häring had witnessed the horrors of Nazism and the war as a German chaplain on the Russian front, where the unusual opportunity to minister to Protestant soldiers and Russian Orthodox villagers had convinced him that denominational differences often obscured the central message of the Gospel.[141]

Why, Häring wondered as he began his scholarly career after the war, did Catholic moral theologians always sound like lawyers advising guilty clients? (Or as one French observer put it, Catholic moral theology seemed mired in "Byzantine discussions on the best way of evading the prescriptions of the church while staying on the right side of the law.")[142] Better to offer advice on how to live a Christian life, to encourage Catholics to respond to the call of Christ. The result was Häring's 1954 *The Law of Christ*, translated into the major European languages and the field's most influential text during the next decade. Häring, too, relied on history, and began his 1,600-page text with a rapid "historical survey of moral theology" that defined his own method as continuous with the practice of moral theology before the manuals of the nineteenth and early twentieth centuries. The importance of individual conscience (Häring invoked Newman) and the insistence that "Christian life may not be viewed solely from the point of formal enactment of law" also distinguished *The Law of Christ*. John Ford and Gerald Kelly thought Häring's treatment illuminating, but they warned against a devaluation of rules and obligations in a world where the "vast majority of Christians will not be spiritual heroes." And Ford and Kelly resented the "frequent carping at the legalism of moral theology."[143]

Häring escaped papal censure for his views, although he later learned that Pius XII's close adviser Franz Hürth had spearheaded an investigation of *The Law of Christ*.[144] In the mid-1960s he chose to publicly reject church teaching on contraception. The entire subject, Häring felt, looked "altogether differently with the passage of time."[145] At the conclusion of two University of Notre Dame conferences on the world population problem in 1965, Häring and a group of Catholic intellectuals, unconvinced by "the arguments from reason customarily adduced to support the conventional position," sent a confidential memo to Rome. The signers agreed that "contraception is not intrinsically immoral, and that therefore there are certain circumstances in which it may be permitted or indeed even recommended."[146] To John Ford, Häring's arguments were nothing more than an "atrocious hodge-podge of ambiguity and obfuscation."[147]

Pope John XXIII withdrew the subject of contraception from general discussion at the Second Vatican Council, but appointed a special commission to study the matter. With the world's bishops altering so many Catholic traditions, from the use of Latin in the liturgy to the role of laypeople, changes in the teaching on contraception became imaginable, even expected. (One confidential survey of 500 devout New Jersey Catholic couples, almost half of whom had four or more children, found that 422 of the couples expected the bishops to allow use of the birth control pill "in some way.")[148] Even John Ford worried, privately, that a "real possibility exists that the Holy See would come with a statement which would require a change of policy. I consider this very unlikely, but it is a possibility."[149]

A young Catholic layman and University of Notre Dame law professor, John Noonan, became the most influential new voice. Like many Catholic intellectuals, Noonan had closely followed John Courtney Murray's effort to reformulate Catholic teaching on church-state issues. (And Noonan also attended a seminar directed by Jacques Maritain at Princeton.) But Noonan wondered whether Murray's elegant reading of the historical record was too reassuring. How could seemingly clear papal pronouncements—Gregory XVI termed freedom of conscience an "absurd and erroneous" opinion in 1832—now be set aside? One day in the late 1940s, Noonan drove from Washington, where he was studying at Catholic University, to Murray's residence at the Jesuit seminary in Woodstock, Maryland, and pursued the issue in a friendly conversation. "I felt the attraction of Murray's position," Noonan recalled, "without being persuaded of it."[150]

The recondite topic of usury, the subject of Noonan's dissertation, allowed him to again consider the problem of doctrinal development. How could a church once willing to condemn lenders now deposit parish collections in banks? Noonan began scouring medieval and Reformation debates on the topic, and this instinctive turn to history is again characteristic of Catholic reformers during this period. Published in 1957 as *The Scholastic Analysis of Usury*—a title guaranteed to repel the casual reader—the book caused little stir. But Noonan emphasized that "no error is more widespread than treatment of the theory [of usury] as if it had been immutable."[151]

Noonan's next subject, contraception, yanked him out of scholarly obscurity. Published in 1965, at the height of the excitement generated by the Second Vatican Council, *Contraception* was an elegantly written 533-page history that received enormous, flattering attention. (A young, and then conservative, Garry Wills flatly termed it a "classic.")[152] Beginning with the ancient Egyptians and ending in the contemporary United States, Noonan again traced a twisting doctrinal path, stressing that any fair reading of the history could not "look at doctrinal development as an automatic unfolding of the divine will." After detailing the emancipation

John T. Noonan Jr., with a copy of his just-published *Contraception*, 1965.

of women, the acknowledgment by many theologians that procreation need not serve as the single, primary end of sexual intercourse, and the widespread support for change expressed by married couples, priests, and bishops, Noonan concluded, "[I]t is a perennial mistake to confuse repetition of old formulas with the living law of the church. The church, on its pilgrim's path, has grown in grace and wisdom."[153]

John Ford was unenthusiastic. Ironically, Ford, a member of the papal birth control commission, had lobbied for Noonan's appointment—"his work will be very valuable to all of us"—to the commission.[154] Before Noonan finished *Contraception*, Ford assumed, as he explained to Bishop John Wright, that Noonan's research would confirm the necessity of a ban on contraception for Catholic couples. The question was a tricky one, Ford conceded, since it is a "fact that the theologians' teaching on conjugal intimacy during the course of the centuries have undergone very considerable development. So it is legitimate to inquire whether further development is not possible and what direction it might take." And indeed, Augustine "actually did reject, in strong terms," the rhythm method. But Ford resisted any "false comparison" between usury and contraception. He even misread Noonan's study of usury, in a telling, yearning error that suggested his emotional stake in the principle of doctrinal consistency, as claiming that "the Church never changed her basic position on usury."[155]

Ford quickly realized his mistake. After receiving the full manuscript of *Contraception*, he pored through it two times, finding it "more and more tendentious, and despite the magnificent array of historical facts, as the book proceeds it gets very one-sided."[156] Another conservative, and close friend, the Georgetown philosopher Germain Grisez, angrily agreed, pointing to the "unbroken tradition which Prof. Noonan's study reveals, however reluctant he is to point up the fact."[157] Soon Ford would be encouraging a Jesuit friend to examine Noonan's work, and was delighted when that Jesuit claimed to find "no parallel" between the church's changing position on usury and its stand on contraception. "To my mind," the Jesuit explained, "for such a parallel to exist there must be a change in the nature of marital relations similar to the change in economic conditions which brought about a difference in the general attitude toward interest."[158]

By this time Ford had immersed himself in a campaign to persuade Pope Paul VI to uphold the traditional teaching. In June 1964, under the aegis of the apostolic delegate to the United States, Archbishop Egidio Vagnozzi, he hurried to Rome for private meetings with three Roman cardinals, Augustin Bea, Alfredo Ottaviani, and Francesco Roberti, as well as Paul VI himself. In these meetings he conceded the failure of the natural law approach. "We lack convincing arguments from natural law," Ford explained in a memo for Archbishop Vagnozzi, forwarded to Paul VI, "which are universally valid and universally admitted."[159]

Instead, Ford stressed the need to conserve papal credibility. "If we disregard the ordinary magisterium of the Church in this matter [contraception]," he explained, "there would be disastrous consequences for moral theology."[160] After meeting with Paul VI, he described himself as being in the "strange position of urging him to uphold the authority of the Papacy."[161]

In November 1965 Ford returned to Rome for more lobbying. "I would like to talk with His Holiness for half an hour," he informed Vagnozzi. ". . . I realize how busy His Holiness is at present, but I am convinced that what I have to say in the present dilemma about contraception needs to be said and that I am in a position to say it."[162] This time Ford's attention centered on the drafting of the final conciliar document, *Gaudium et Spes*. One section of the document discussed Christian marriage, a delicate topic given that the special papal commission on birth control had yet to reach any conclusion. Ford and Bishop John Wright, working in concert, urged the theologians and bishops drafting the section of *Gaudium et Spes* devoted to marriage to praise "parents of large families," avoid the phrase "marital prudence," and emphasize that "responsible" child rearing did not imply that poor couples should avoid having children.[163]

Ford, in particular, urged Paul VI to reiterate the message of *Casti Connubii* in *Gaudium et Spes*. His notes detailing his meetings with the pope suggest Ford's intense convictions on the subject, and the drama of the moment. Called suddenly to the Vatican on the morning of November 22 ("luckily I was at home"), Ford spoke with the pope about the proposed text. "They say *Casti Connubii* is obsolete," Ford complained. The pope replied, "It is not obsolete. *Casti Connubii* e tuttora valido" (is still valid). Ford also emphasized to the pope that "human nature can't change." Meeting on the morning of November 24, with John Wright, Ford agreed that they "damn well better" make clear that the bishops could not "repudiate *Casti Connubii*."[164]

That same day Cardinal Alfredo Ottaviani, the leading conservative at the council, released a letter from Paul VI, drafted by Ford and the papal adviser Archbishop Carlo Colombo, requesting that *Gaudium et Spes* reassert the authority of *Casti Connubii*. (The startled American cardinal chairing the international commission charged with composing *Gaudium et Spes*, Detroit's John Dearden, marked the folder containing his personal copy of the letter "of great historical importance.")[165]

Just how to integrate the papal letter with the working draft caused further discussion on the commission, and moderates successfully steered *Gaudium et Spes* away from the topic of contraception, with Paul VI's ultimate blessing. The final version of *Gaudium et Spes* referred to *Casti Connubii* in one famous footnote, but did not reaffirm procreation as the highest end of marriage. Better, the bishops decided, to await the verdict of the papal commission on the subject.[166]

This ambiguous result disappointed Ford, as did the absence of any condemnation of contraception at the Second Vatican Council. He consoled himself with the thought that he had done "the best I could."[167] The drafters of *Gaudium et Spes*, he privately complained, had developed a new theology of marriage, one that refused to rank procreation above the well-being of the spouses, and the "Pope agreed to what they did, whether realizing how much he had conceded or not."[168]

During the next two years Ford continued to press his case. On the papal birth control commission, which included John Noonan, and which overwhelmingly recommended a change in official church teaching, Ford's became perhaps the most powerful dissenting voice. (The conservative moral theologian Father Francis Connell, worried about the makeup of the commission, lauded Ford as a "staunch defender of truth.")[169] Even after nine of the twelve bishops and fifteen of the nineteen theologians on the commission voted for a change in church teaching, Ford helped draft (and distribute) an unofficial minority report that challenged the majority recommendation for change.[170] When another Jesuit, Richard McCormick, Ford's successor as an editor at *Theological Studies*, expressed the view that *Gaudium et Spes* left open the possibility of a change in church teaching on contraception, Ford retorted, "I do not consider it theologically legitimate or even decent and honest, to contradict a doctrine and then disguise the contradiction under the rubric: growth and evolution."[171]

VII

The release in July 1968 of *Humanae Vitae*, Paul VI's encyclical reiterating Catholic opposition to "artificial" birth control, obviously pleased Ford. The extraordinary hostility with which the encyclical was greeted by Catholic theologians, however, along with a muted episcopal reception, suggested that reaffirming Catholic opposition to contraception had had exactly the diminishing effect on papal teaching authority that Ford had anticipated would follow from permitting contraception.[172] Opposition to *Humanae Vitae*, more vocal and sustained than on any other topic in the history of modern Catholicism, inevitably stimulated study of the very meaning of papal authority, sin, and dissent.

Most Catholic couples rejected the teaching or ignored it. One meticulous Rhode Island survey of Catholic women in 1971 found not a single devout Catholic woman younger than thirty-five (out of seventy-three interviewed) opposed to the use of birth control.[173] Another survey forwarded to the American bishops found a majority of Catholic parents with more than seven children unsympathetic to *Humanae Vitae*.[174]

In the center of the theological mainstream in the 1950s, the confidant of bishops and cardinals, Ford now stood almost alone. Even John Courtney Murray, Ford's onetime classmate and coeditor at *Theological Studies*, had distanced himself from Ford's position. Upon learning of the passage of the Declaration of Religious Liberty in 1965, Ford had congratulated Murray on "a tremendous thing for the Church." But he had also complained that the ongoing debate over contraception showed "very little respect for the previous authoritative teachings of the Church and will very soon lead to a victory by default for the contraceptionists—in this matter I can't bring myself to call them progressivists."[175]

Murray did not reply, but he had already begun framing the issue differently, regretting that Catholic discussion of contraception remained mired in the "conceptualist classicism to which we have for too long been accustomed."[176] The term "classicism" was borrowed from the Canadian Jesuit Bernard Lonergan, who in an enormously influential phrasing described the trajectory of modern Catholicism as that of an institution moving from a classicist worldview to one possessed of "historical consciousness." The classicist worldview understood human nature as "always the same" and applied universal principles to "concrete singularity." Lonergan urged Catholics to begin with the human subject, not an abstract human nature, to use history to scrutinize "how the patterns of living, the institutions, the common meanings of one place and time differ from those of another."[177]

Murray seized upon this formulation, and privately thanked Lonergan for sending him a copy of the essay, for his "own edification."[178] In 1967, in a talk given just before his unexpected death, Murray began to explore what historical consciousness might mean for moral theology. The trick, he concluded, again agreeing with Lonergan, would be to sustain belief in an "objective" truth, while recognizing that truth also remained an "affair of history." On the subject of contraception, Murray added, the church had "reached for too much certainty too soon, it went too far. Certainty was reached in the absence of any adequate understanding of marriage."[179]

Upon reading a report of the talk, Ford immediately asked his old friend for a copy. Murray responded, disingenuously, that he had not given a talk "about birth control," adding, "Heaven forbid that I should get into that subject." Murray then noted, pointedly, the similarities between two documents: "the so-called minority report [on birth control, drafted, as Murray certainly knew, in large part by Ford] and a famous document that I have in my files. It is the letter addressed to the Pope by a group of bishops at the Council, asking him to withdraw the Declaration of Religious Freedom."[180]

As the storm over *Humanae Vitae* enveloped Catholic theologians, Ford recounted a meeting where a group of Jesuit theologians asked him point-blank to explain his views: "How can you maintain a position which is so isolated, with all the 670 theologians (USA) against you, and all the hierarchies saying essentially the same thing as these theologians?" Ford replied by fobbing his questioners "off more or less" and mentioning "the historical fact that whole hierarchies have gone into schism in the past and that maybe we are leading up to a very serious catastrophe in the Church."[181]

Ford became profoundly disillusioned. Catholic universities, including Jesuit institutions, seemed to be abandoning "the promotion of the Catholic religion," and he mistrusted the decision of religious orders such as the Jesuits and the Congregation of Holy Cross to transfer ownership of Catholic colleges and universities to predominantly lay boards of trustees. He complained to highly placed contacts in Rome about the willingness of Jesuit colleges to hire Protestants and Jews to teach required theology courses.[182] He endorsed his friend Cardinal Patrick O'Boyle's threat to expel Washington, D.C., priests publicly critical of *Humanae Vitae*, and Ford's hand seems obvious in O'Boyle's denunciation of priests unwilling to recognize "objective standards" as outweighing individual assessments of a "unique situation." He wrote letters congratulating the occasional bishop, even in distant Bombay, willing to take a "firm stand" in support of *Humanae Vitae*, and he retired from teaching at his beloved Weston seminary, because young Jesuits expressed little interest in his approach to moral theology.[183]

Ford's last major scholarly article attempted to claim *Humanae Vitae* as an infallible papal statement.[184] In 1988, just before his death, he accepted an award "for the defense of the faith" from a conservative group of Catholic scholars. An old friend, the philosopher Germain Grisez, chose the occasion to pay tribute to Ford's ability to persuade Paul VI that he "could not preach a Gospel different than the one he had received." Noting that Ford's work in support of *Humanae Vitae* had led to the severing of many friendships, Grisez complained that Ford had received little respect from the "earthly academy." Ford himself simply recalled his gratitude when he realized that Paul VI would not, could not, change church teaching.[185]

VIII

As the searing internal Catholic debate over contraception culminated in the late 1960s, leaving Paul VI, bishops, theologians, and laypeople emotionally drained, an even more grueling battle was already under way. Just three weeks after Gerald Kelly's funeral in 1964, John Ford had received a suggestive letter. Perhaps, a Catholic physician suggested, "gynecologists, theologians and moralists [should] sit down at a round table and redefine what is meant by abortion."[186]

Ironically, in retrospect, Catholic opposition to the legalization of contraceptives in Connecticut in the 1950s had provided supporters of abortion law reform with an important tool. Without Justice William O. Douglas's claim in *Griswold v. Connecticut* in 1965 that "zones of privacy" protected reproductive decisions, the claim that a right to an abortion logically stemmed from a constitutional right to privacy might have seemed less plausible.[187]

Even more awkwardly, repeated insistence by Catholics that their church should permit contraceptive use by non-Catholics, as a matter of religious freedom and a recognition that immoral actions need not be illegal, provided ammunition for supporters of abortion on demand. If contraception, a divisive religious issue, should be left to the individual conscience, why not abortion? The conservative commentator William F. Buckley thought Catholics should be cautious on the abortion issue, since "the principal meaning of the religious liberty pronouncements of Vatican II is that other men must be left free to practice the dictates of their own conscience." Similarly, the Ohio Democrat John Gilligan announced that he would favor a bill legalizing abortions if a majority of Ohioans felt similarly. "[A]s a Catholic," he explained, "I follow the teachings of my Church as taught by the Vatican Council, that each individual is obliged to follow his own conscience."[188]

When staffers at the National Catholic Welfare Conference proposed formally announcing that Catholic bishops would not try to prohibit citizens from obtaining contraceptives, out of respect for religious pluralism, the theologian Richard McCormick demurred. McCormick agreed with the conciliatory impulse behind the statement, but he thought this particular argument dangerous. "The idea of civic and religious division as constituting the reason for exception to the general principle," he emphasized, "seems very weak to me. We know, for example, that there is going to be, indeed already is, a strong play for widening acceptable indications for abortion. I doubt that we would take the same attitude toward this (where public funds are to be used) that we are trying to take toward contraception. . . . The terms to be juggled, I believe, are: freedom of conscience but only in so far as it is compatible with the public good."[189] The conservative theologian Francis Connell, McCormick's opponent on many issues, agreed. "It must be remembered," he warned, "that even now we must foresee the coming campaign for wider legalization of therapeutic abortion. Are we going to give up without a struggle and say that we don't wish to impose our views on those who differ from us?"[190]

Chapter Nine

LIFE (II)

I

The title of Joseph Fletcher's wry autobiography, *Memoir of an Ex-Radical*, is not self-explanatory. As a young man in the 1920s, he was thrilled by the oratory of Eugene Debs and the courage of Sacco and Vanzetti. During the 1930s Fletcher supported union activists and stuck to his "socialist guns" even after becoming an Episcopalian minister. After World War II he passionately advocated international control of atomic weapons and better relations with the Soviet Union. He became famous, or notorious, as a "Red" clergyman and the subject of State Department scrutiny. He marched with Martin Luther King Jr. at Selma, and wept when southern whites murdered one of his seminary students, a volunteer in the civil rights movement.[1]

What made Fletcher an ex-radical, in his own view, was his abandonment of socialism in the 1950s, along with the prior decision to choose the mundane rhythms of academic life over full-time activism. Beginning in 1944 Fletcher taught at the Episcopal Divinity School in Cambridge, Massachusetts. In 1967 he admitted to finding Christian doctrine—"God, Jesus, revelation, sin, salvation"—essentially "weird and untenable." Anxious to leave a religious milieu, Fletcher moved to the University of Virginia's medical school as an in-house ethicist, and there he remained until his death in 1991.[2]

Fletcher's self-assessment, however, was mistaken. His radicalism came in books and articles, not the occasional visit to a picket line. By delivering a series of lectures at Harvard in 1949 on medical ethics, later published as *Morals and Medicine*, Fletcher helped found the modern discipline of bioethics and ignite the debate over abortion and euthanasia that marked the second half of the twentieth century.[3] In the mid-1960s his best-selling *Situation Ethics*, more than any other single text, popularized the notion that "all laws and rules and principles and ideals and norms are only *contingent*."[4] Indeed, the arc of Fletcher's career, from concern about the "ethics of economic employment" in the 1930s to advocacy of legal abortion in the 1960s and 1970s, tracked that of many liberal intellectuals.[5]

So did Fletcher's view of Catholicism. An Anglo-Catholic of sorts in the 1920s and 1930s, Fletcher knowingly invoked *Rerum Novarum* and Catholic social thought in his first scholarly article. In *Morals and Medicine*, which he described as the first such book "undertaken by non-Catholics," Fletcher carefully distinguished his work from Paul Blanshard's "rather sensational" and "incomplete account of the Catholic

Joseph Fletcher, ca. early 1950s.

views."[6] (Fletcher's editors expressed anxiety "that the book should not seem to be an anti-Catholic book.")[7] During the 1960s Fletcher appeared on panels with Catholic scholars, lectured at Catholic colleges, and sustained friendships with Catholic theologians. He archly reported to one friend in 1967 that he had just dined with "wily Jesuits."[8]

And yet the distances were vast. Fletcher's own work lacked analytical rigor, and the field's first historian gently described Fletcher's scholarship as "theoretically thin."[9] More provocateur than mandarin, Fletcher specialized in distilling the terminology of ethicists and theologians into commonsense dilemmas. What if, he continually asked, "*absolute* prohibition" of certain practices was "morally unjustified, subversive of human dignity, and most seriously of all, spiritually oppressive"? What if no such thing as objective morality existed, only "childish rules" that prevented humans from realizing that "[r]ight and wrong *depend upon the situation*"?[10]

Catholic scholars remained the most articulate and visible opponents of such notions, as Fletcher noted when he described *Morals and Medicine* as a "kind of counterpoint" to the "Roman Catholic literature." The Catholic response was unenthusiastic. One reviewer regretted Fletcher's "allergy to any kind of law" and termed the book "unfair, incomplete and self-contradictory."[11] Gerald Kelly doubted whether the "faithful" should read *Morals and Medicine* "without permission."[12]

II

Is morality subjective or objective? The question permits no simple answer, but a shift toward a more subjective notion of morality helps explain the change in American attitudes toward abortion in the past half century. Broadly, the first decades after World War II witnessed a remarkable growth of interest in human rights and individual autonomy, along with a related sense that personal experience, not hard and fast rules, should determine the morality of particular actions. A cluster of influential books in the 1950s, including David Riesman's *The Lonely Crowd*, William Whyte's *The Organization Man*, and Eric Hoffer's *The True Believer*, along with plays such as *The Crucible* (about the hysteria of the Salem witch trials) and films such as *High Noon* (where only Gary Cooper is willing to defend his town from a band of marauders), warned that mass society and peer pressure might crush the autonomous individual. Perhaps the most widely anthologized short story of the period, Shirley Jackson's "The Lottery" ended with villagers ritually stoning an innocent neighbor, and a surge of postwar interest in Alexis de Tocqueville's *Democracy in America* centered on Tocqueville's claim that public opinion might exert a subtle tyranny. Paul Blanshard's criticisms of Catholicism rested comfortably within this context, particularly Blanshard's assertion that "*any* form of authoritarian control weakens the democratic spirit."[13]

One source of an enhanced sense of individual autonomy emerged from the world of politics and law. Spurred by Allied rhetoric during World War II, and laboring in the shadow of the Holocaust, lawyers, judges, and activists made the decade after 1945 a golden age for those devoted to human and civil rights, drafting the Nuremberg principles of international criminal law, the Genocide Convention of 1948, and the United Nations Universal Declaration of Human Rights. At the same time African Americans demanded civil rights in the Jim Crow South, and colonial peoples across the world demanded self-rule.[14]

Such "rights talk" might seem incompatible with Fletcher's view that moral assessments depended upon the situation.[15] The distinguishing concept was autonomy. When Catholic scholars insisted that it was never lawful to kill innocent people, they assumed that the basic right in question was the "right to life and to bodily integrity from the moment of conception."[16] This right to life trumped the desire to end suffering through assisted suicide, or the desire of a physician to terminate a pregnancy. (Only in the 1960s did Fletcher and other ethicists shift their focus from the rights of the physician to the right of the woman to control her own body.)

From a different vantage point, the right in question was not life, or as Horace Kallen put it in 1956, "existence as such," but the right of the autonomous person to make her own decision, freed from what one legal scholar termed the "morbid, guilt-ridden" doctrines of Christianity.[17] The substantive outcome of any particular decision—whether a patient should be assisted in committing suicide, whether an abortion might be permitted for the sake of the mother's health—mattered less than protecting the autonomy of the decision-making agent. Fletcher described *Morals and Medicine* as supporting "Human Rights in Life, Health, and Death" and the "power of choice" for patients and doctors. Discussion of contraception ("Our Right to Control Parenthood"), artificial insemination ("Our

Right to Overcome Childlessness"), and euthanasia ("Our Right to Die") reiterated the point.[18]

Cambridge University's Glanville Williams became the first prominent legal scholar to reach similar conclusions. In a series of articles in the early 1950s, and then a widely noticed 1956 set of lectures delivered at Columbia University, Williams pleaded for the legalization of assisted suicide and more liberal abortion laws. He rejected the "impossible" Catholic claim that "every life, no matter what its quality or circumstances, is worth living and obligatory to be lived." A "true Christianity," Williams argued, would recognize that "it is impossible to judge others, because one cannot live their lives and experience their inner drives and compulsions; and particularly is this true in matters of sex, marriage, and parenthood."[19]

If law professors stressed rights and the autonomous person, other scholars analyzed the individual decision. In Europe a fascination with existentialism solidified a sense that so-called universal laws and comprehensive moral systems obscured the difficulties faced by individuals in concrete situations. (When Jacques Maritain returned to Paris after the Allied landings in 1944, he was discouraged to see young people enthralled with Jean-Paul Sartre and Albert Camus.)[20]

As European theologians reflected upon the experience of war and occupation, on the black market and the pressure to cooperate with occupying troops, the fragility of external moral codes seemed obvious.[21] The influential Swiss Protestant theologian Karl Barth had long insisted that divine commands did not come packaged in neat ethical systems, and another Swiss Protestant, Emil Brunner, had more bluntly attacked the "rigidly legalistic" moral code associated with Roman Catholicism. (Brunner scorned the Catholic tendency, when confronted with a problem, to "look up the ethical code and find out what is commanded and what is forbidden.")[22]

American Protestant ethicists welcomed this approach, and references to Barth and Brunner soon peppered the scholarly literature.[23] The murder of Dietrich Bonhoeffer, a German Protestant theologian, by the Nazis gave his work an unusual stature, and when a translation of Bonhoeffer's uncompleted *Ethics* appeared in 1955, theologians such as Joseph Fletcher seized upon Bonhoeffer's claim that "the question of the good is posed and is decided in the midst of each definite, yet unconcluded, unique and transient situation of our lives. . . ."[24]

Similar, if more muted, impulses registered in postwar European Catholicism, with German theologians especially eager to explore moral problems guided by the "love of God" and "fraternal charity," not simply natural law rules.[25] The German Jesuit Karl Rahner formally repudiated situation ethics—the "denial of the absolute validity of material norms for the human person"—but wished Catholic moral theologians would refrain from beginning all inquiries with a "syllogistic deduction." Bernhard Häring's influential *Law of Christ*, as we have seen, urged Catholics to understand Christian life as something more inspiring than a balancing of accounts, or a calculation of the sins that might prohibit entrance into heaven.[26]

Pope Pius XII issued a denunciation of "situation ethics" in 1952. Without naming names, he criticized theologians believing that, "in the determination of conscience, each individual finds himself directly with God . . . without the slightest trace of intervention of any law, any authority, any community or cult or religion."[27] In 1956 he amplified this warning, attacking those who believe "that the ultimate determining norm for activity is not the objective right order as determined by natural law" but "some internal judgment and illumination of the mind of every individual by which the mind comes to know what is to be done in a concrete situation."[28]

Gerald Kelly and John Ford thought these papal cautions appropriate. They conceded that Catholic theologians might profit from further consideration of "the charity of Christ from beginning to end."[29] And privately, Kelly expressed his frustration with Pius XII's habit of showering commentary upon every issue in contemporary medical ethics. "He talks so much and writes so much," Kelly noted, "that there is always a real danger of having a thing obsolete before it gets published."[30] Kelly also thought that his former mentor, the German Jesuit and papal adviser Franz Hürth, occasionally traded "theological freedom" for overly rigid "dicta."[31]

Still, Ford and Kelly insisted that humans needed "clear norms." Obeying church teaching did not make someone a "passive" or "negative" Christian. More dangerous was the modern tendency to make the "individual himself his sole norm of action when the chips are down."[32] By the 1960s, however, despite papal admonitions, Catholic scholars began expressing doubts about natural law presuppositions. A young American Catholic theologian, Father Charles Curran, concluded that "Catholic life has often suffered from legalism." An effective moral theology, Curran declared, "places more emphasis on the historical, the particular, the individual, the changing and the relational."[33]

In the United States, Catholic theologians had an additional reason for pondering the importance of individual conscience, as young Catholic men began refusing to serve in the Vietnam era military. In the 1950s, patriotic Catholic leaders such as Chicago's Cardinal Samuel Stritch could advise the Justice Department not to be concerned about Catholic conscientious objectors. "It seems to me," Stritch explained, that if "civil authorities" declared war, "we do not allow personal opinion to override it."[34]

The Catholic component of the 1960s antiwar movement, however, was substantial, with Senators Robert Kennedy and Eugene McCarthy becoming antiwar presidential candidates in 1968, Thomas Merton and Dorothy Day inspiring Catholic pacifists, and priests and nuns sprinkling blood on draft files and denouncing American actions in Vietnam.[35] Catholic theologians and lawyers even pushed a test case to the Supreme Court, where John Noonan argued that Catholics, while not pacifists like Quakers, should have the right not to fight in wars they deemed unjust.[36] Staffers for the United States Catholic Conference agreed, defining the issue as "the inviolability of human conscience."[37]

A further prod to Catholics' reflection on the importance of individual decision making was the declaration of the bishops at the Second Vatican Council that "loyalty to conscience" led to the "right solution" of moral problems. The same conciliar documents invoked "objective norms of morality," but the distinction between following one's own conscience and adapting one's views to each new situation was subtle.[38] Fletcher cheered on Catholics newly protective of the individual conscience, even if he privately disparaged the efforts of Bernhard Häring and others to bring Catholic "ethics up into the twentieth century." "Lots of us agree with you," he confided to one correspondent, "that the so-called aggiornamento in the Roman Church [is] really the same old line in a modern dress and cleaner shirt." A liberal Catholic theologian, Daniel Maguire, explained to Fletcher that he hoped to weaken the "'infallibility' specter" or "at least to nudge it away from those who do ethics."[39]

John Ford had the opposite reaction and prepared for battle with the "false ethic of situationism."[40] What we must defend, Ford held, is the church's duty to "apply the general principles she is entitled to teach to the individual situations which the Christian conscience must decide for itself."[41] After a Notre Dame sociologist informed him of a survey demonstrating widespread unhappiness with the church's teaching on contraception, Ford shot off a reply. "Of course what [Catholic married couples] have to tell us about their married lives is important and relevant to many of the questions which we are now discussing," Ford explained. "Would it be possible," however, he asked, "by searching the whole wide world, to find a more prejudiced group of people to give an opinion on [birth control]?"[42]

When Ford spoke with Paul VI in Rome in 1965, he warned the pope of the dangers of a situational morality. Bernhard Häring, he complained, acted out of compassion but was an existentialist. The new "moralita" was the real threat, and the pope, Ford recounted in his diary, was "very aware of this and *against* it. Wanted the old morality. Told me to *write on this subject*."[43]

III

In his meeting with Paul VI, Ford listed acceptance of abortion and suicide as examples of "intrinsic morality surrendered."[44] Discussion of abortion moved near the center of the public stage only in the mid-1960s, after percolating for two decades in the subdued confines of academic conferences and scholarly monographs. As late as 1959 Alan Guttmacher, later Planned Parenthood's national director, stated, "I deplore the performance of abortion on virtual demand," and Mary Steichen Calderone, medical director of Planned Parenthood, described abortion as the "taking of a life."[45]

The first inklings of change came after the war, as Joseph Fletcher, Glanville Williams, and a handful of lawyers and doctors urged greater tolerance of "therapeutic" abortions, conducted because the mother's life was at risk, or because she seemed unstable or might commit suicide. Strictly speaking, only abortions to save the life of the mother were legal in most states, but a more elastic notion of maternal health became evident. In 1950 National Catholic Welfare Conference staffers learned that the approval of three doctors in many New York City hospitals meant a green light for therapeutic abortions.[46]

Catholic theologians condemned any abortion committed with the direct intent of killing the fetus. (Glanville Williams took particular exception to the Catholic "dogma" that "the foetus has the same right to life as the born child.")[47] If an abortion occurred as doctors attempted to save the life of both the mother and the fetus, Catholic moralists argued, no sin was committed, since the direct intent was not to take innocent life. But all other abortions violated this principle. As early as 1944 John Ford complained that "most so-called therapeutic abortions are not really necessary to the life of the mother," and he and Gerald Kelly only became more insistent on the point. Therapeutic abortions, they reported in 1954, should decrease as new antibiotics made childbirth far less dangerous. Complacency on this matter was foolish, however, because "as long as the principle of legitimate abortion is accepted, the danger of an increasing number of abortions is always present because, as the 'medical indications' decrease, the 'psychiatric indications' tend to increase. The only genuinely progressive policy is the absolute exclusion of direct abortion."[48]

Since Catholics ran several hundred American hospitals, the nation's largest private system, these views had practical consequences. In 1947 the Catholic Hospital Association convened a group of theologians to offer guidelines for administrators. The nuns supervising the majority of these hospitals worried about the occasional staff physician, usually a non-Catholic, who publicly supported Planned Parenthood or hoped to perform therapeutic abortions. This consultation resulted in "Ethical and Religious Directives" drafted by Gerald Kelly, posted on operating room walls and available in a pocket-sized form for "physicians practicing in the hospital."[49] The directives insisted that "[e]very unborn child must be considered as a human person, with all the rights of a human person, from the moment of conception." Indeed, "[d]irect abortion is a *direct* killing of an unborn child, and it is never permitted, even when the ultimate purpose is to save the life of the mother."[50]

For abortion law reformers, by contrast, the hazy legal status of therapeutic abortions, and the idiosyncratic nature of decisions about whether to perform the procedure at all, was infuriating. In 1959 the University of Pennsylvania law professor Louis B. Schwartz, a careful reader of Glanville Williams, persuaded the American Law Institute to endorse a model penal code allowing states to permit abortions if continuation of the pregnancy would impair the "physical and mental health of the mother," if the fetus had a "grave physical or mental defect," or if the pregnancy resulted from rape or incest.[51] The occasional law review article also urged reform, and in 1962, in a case that attracted international attention, Sherri Finkbine, a pregnant mother of four, flew from her home in Phoenix, Arizona, to Sweden for an abortion after learning that the thalidomide pills she had taken might lead to the birth of a child with severe deformities.[52]

A few activists, including Joseph Fletcher, began to make more radical claims. In 1963 Fletcher described abortion as "fertility control." If in a given situation "abortion is the most loving thing possible," he emphasized, "it is the best thing."[53] One of Fletcher's closest friends, the University of California at Santa Barbara biologist Garrett Hardin, drew considerable attention for arguing that "any woman, at any time, should be able to procure a legal abortion for herself *without even giving a reason.* The fact that she *wants* it should be enough."[54]

IV

Efforts to legalize abortion intensified in the late 1960s, making the issue a central one in American politics and weakening the liberal-Catholic alliance welded together by Franklin Roosevelt and his New Deal. In the 1930s Catholic opposition to greater access to contraceptives had caused tension, but not enough to threaten shared enthusiasm for the Democratic Party, New Deal social welfare programs and trade unions. The civil liberties lawyer Morris Ernst, before challenging the 1935 congressional testimony of Father John A. Ryan on contraception, carefully announced, "[O]n many battle fronts in the fight for freedom of the press, for labor, and so forth, I have fought side by side with Father Ryan."[55]

The abortion debate was less amicable. Historians of abortion law reform in the United States tend to view their subject as a sequel to the civil rights movement, with *Roe v. Wade* serving as a *Brown v. Board of Education* for women. Textbooks compare Thurgood Marshall (onetime NAACP lawyer and then Supreme Court justice) and his fight against racial discrimination to Ruth Bader Ginsburg (onetime ACLU lawyer and then Supreme Court justice) and her fight against sex discrimination.

The comparison is not wrong, just incomplete. Women surely demanded equal rights from state legislatures, Congress, and the Supreme Court in the late 1960s and early 1970s, as did other groups, ranging from prisoners to the physically handicapped.[56] The abortion debate marks another sort of pivot. Propelled by their defense of a woman's right to choose, abortion rights activists, and ultimately the Democratic Party, moved toward a liberalism predicated on individual autonomy, and its contemporary legal equivalent, privacy. The achievements of the early civil rights movement—integrated public facilities, protection of voting rights—proved irrelevant in the struggle for legal abortion, forcing judges, lawyers, and activists to erect a different legal foundation. Intermittent discussion of privacy rights extends backward into the nineteenth century, but only debates over contraception and abortion would make "privacy" and "autonomy" keywords in the modern liberal vocabulary. By the 1970s legal scholars would equate privacy, "grounded in notions of individual autonomy," with the right to "choose and adopt a lifestyle which allows expression of [one's] uniqueness and individuality." In *Doe v. Bolton*, the companion case to *Roe v. Wade*, Justice William O. Douglas argued in favor of legal abortion because each individual needs "autonomous control over the development and expression of one's intellect, interests, tastes and personality."[57]

The contrast with the European abortion debate, as Mary Ann Glendon has demonstrated, is striking. With Social Democratic and Christian political parties committed to a more communal understanding of society, France, West Germany, and other European countries did increase access to legal abortion in the 1960s and 1970s, but with restrictions on abortion during later stages of pregnancy, financial assistance for pregnant women wishing to carry their pregnancy to term, and generous maternity benefits. In the United States the language eventually used by the U.S. Supreme Court—defending a woman's "fundamental right to make the highly personal choice whether or not to terminate her pregnancy"—framed the problem as one faced by autonomous individuals, not a responsibility of American society more generally.[58]

What Catholics opposed to abortion discovered in the late 1960s was that they stood, as one California pro-life activist put it, "virtually alone."[59] University professors, liberal lawyers, and editors began favoring the elimination of restrictions on abortion, and for these groups it became a defining issue. When the ACLU took a position in favor of abortion on demand in 1967, one University of Notre Dame Law School professor (and active member) complained that the organization had abandoned the "first principle of secular ethics . . . that life is an absolute value." The same professor admitted that the "medieval attitude" of Catholic leaders on birth control diminished Catholic credibility, but he still found the resolution of "human problems by the destruction of life" appalling. The director of the ACLU replied that he and his colleagues now equated "anti-abortion positions with anti–birth control ones, and the defenders [of restrictions on abortion] with an effort to enact theological positions into law."[60]

The most important new force for change, unpredictable even a decade earlier, was a newly energized women's movement. Conventionally dated from the 1963 publication of Betty Friedan's *The Feminine Mystique*, and the radicalization of women active in the southern civil rights movement, the women's movement of the late 1960s and 1970s did not begin with legal abortion as a goal.[61]

The Feminine Mystique did not mention abortion. Still, Friedan's emphasis on, even obsession with, individual autonomy made legal abortion a congenial cause. Comparing housewives to concentration camp prisoners, Friedan urged women to abandon a "passive, childlike dependency." Instead, women must "live their own lives again according to a self-chosen purpose."[62]

At the second annual convention of the National Organization of Women (NOW), in 1967, Friedan demanded "the right of women to control their reproductive lives" (alienating some Catholic members of NOW in the process), and the issue became a cornerstone of the movement. More radical feminists thought the criticism of Catholic leaders offered by NOW founders inadequate, and launched less inhibited attacks on an institution guided by celibate men eager to regulate women's reproductive lives.[63]

Catholic hopes for a united religious front against legal abortion also crumbled. Optimistic Catholic commentators initially predicted that mainline Protestant opposition to abortion on demand—the Anglicans condemned abortion in the "strongest terms" in 1958, and in 1962 the National Council of Churches declared that "Protestant Christians are agreed" in opposing abortion except in rare circumstances—was unshakable. Protestants will not, the Jesuit law professor Robert Drinan assured his readers, "condone abortion for the mere convenience of the mother."[64]

Activists knew better. Except for Missouri Synod Lutherans, Mormons, members of the Christian Reformed Church, and the occasional Orthodox rabbi, only Catholics seemed willing to defend restrictions on abortion. Anxious to avoid the appearance of a denominational crusade, one California Catholic pro-life activist scoured professional associations for "non-Catholic doctors and lawyers to front the organization."[65] Witnesses testifying before the state legislature, explained one Michigan Catholic lobbyist, "should not identify themselves, or even regard themselves, as representing the Michigan Catholic Conference. They should speak from their professional or personal background and competence."[66]

By the late 1960s several hundred Protestant ministers served as consultants in an underground network that connected women desiring abortions with doctors willing to perform them. A handful of mainline Protestant church leaders and scholars, notably Princeton's Paul Ramsey, opposed legal abortion and warned American liberals not to succumb to an "anti-Catholicism still there beneath the surface in our generally Protestant culture." But Ramsey and his allies were outnumbered by ministers and rabbis emphasizing that abortion reform did not "compel any woman to undergo an abortion" and willing to castigate "medieval-minded laymen and clerics."[67]

Many Catholics felt betrayed. In 1967 an angry John Noonan asked the prominent Protestant theologian Robert McAfee Brown, a sympathetic observer of Catholicism at the Second Vatican Council, why liberals attacked the Catholic church "because it has stood so steadfastly for the rights of the unborn." Some Protestant church leaders, Noonan stressed, are "actively encouraging the destruction of the embryo in particular cases." Brown replied with a tribute to Noonan's research on contraception, before predicting "that Catholics and Protestants are going to be considerably divided at the end of the day on the abortion issue."[68]

Evangelical Protestants generally ignored the issue until the late 1970s. A group of prominent evangelicals, in fact, cautiously endorsed abortion law reform in 1968, and the Southern Baptist Convention leadership made halting steps in the same direction in the early 1970s. When the news service for the Southern Baptist Convention reported the Supreme Court ruling in *Roe v. Wade*, the first sentence, describing the decision as advancing the cause of "religious liberty," seemed directed at Catholics arrogant enough to presume that their own views should be law.[69]

After offering little commentary on abortion in the 1950s and 1960s, philosophers also entered the fray. One of the most influential American philosophers, Harvard's John Rawls, began his scholarly career emphasizing the need to shelter "fundamental liberties" from utilitarian cost-benefit analyses and to conduct public debate by means of a logic accessible to all.[70] Rawls's prose conveyed a timeless confidence—he hoped to define justice for *any* well-ordered society—but he nonetheless stood at the center of postwar liberal currents. His focus on individual rights, so characteristic of the period, would only become more pronounced. "Rights secured by justice," Rawls ultimately argued in his 1971 opus, *A Theory of Justice*, "are not subject to the calculus of social interests."[71]

Rawls himself offered only a brief, much belated comment on abortion (claiming that a woman's right to terminate her pregnancy, at least in the first trimester, outweighed other considerations).[72] The single most widely read scholarly article on the ethics of abortion, however, Judith Jarvis Thomson's 1971 "A Defense of Abortion," defended a woman's "right to decide what happens in and to her body." Thomson, like Rawls, was a passionate defender of individual rights and autonomy, and her essay was published in a scholarly journal edited by Rawls. She understood Catholic arguments against abortion as her main obstacle, and her essay included references to *Casti Connubii* and Pius XII's 1951 address endorsing the rhythm method.[73]

Similarly, Rawls's suspicion of religious arguments became legal orthodoxy. Scholars in the postwar era reflexively pointed to the sixteenth- and seventeenth-century European wars of religion as the consequence of allowing religion into public life, a caution, in Harvard president James Bryant Conant's words, against allowing secular institutions to be "torn asunder by contending theologies led by fanatic men."[74] In 1951 Rawls's first published essay named the Inquisition as an example of a religious institution proceeding without regard for the "canons of inductive procedure."[75]

By the late 1960s and early 1970s, many legal scholars and judges viewed any governmental aid to religious institutions as illegitimate, a position first articulated in Supreme Court decisions in the late 1940s, and now reiterated with messianic fervor. A New York State law allowing public schools to lend used textbooks to religious (usually Catholic) schools came before the Supreme Court in 1968. Justice Hugo Black, an enthusiastic fan of Paul Blanshard in the late 1940s, used the occasion to denounce "sectarian religious propagandists" pointing toward "complete domination and supremacy of their particular brand of religion."[76] In 1971, in *Lemon v. Kurtzman*, its most important decision on the subject since the 1940s, the Supreme Court again resolutely condemned government aid to religious schools. The majority opinion noted the "hazards of religion's intruding into the political arena," and Justice William O. Douglas broke new ground in his concurring opinion with a favorable citation to a 1962 anti-Catholic tract, Loraine Boettner's *Roman Catholicism*, that complained of Roman Catholic "indoctrination" and "propaganda" and Catholic children "told what to wear, what to do, and what to think."[77]

The same emphasis on neutrality shaped the abortion debate. If the federal government could not aid religious schools and institutions, scholars explained, it could not prefer a particular religious (i.e., Catholic) understanding of human life. This argument's success depended upon Catholics' isolation in the abortion debate. Michigan Citizens for Abortion Law Reform announced in 1970, "It is Catholic legislators who oppose reform, Catholic laity and clergy who inveigh against it, Catholics who bombard the legislature with letters and lobbyists; militant, dedicated Catholics making noise far in excess of their numbers."[78]

When Catholic lawyers or doctors testified before state legislatures, their denominational affiliation was automatically deemed newsworthy. (Later, the *Congressional Quarterly Weekly Report* would place an asterisk next to each Catholic legislator when recording votes on abortion-related bills, a custom not practiced when Jews voted in favor of aid to Israel or African Americans in support of affirmative action.)[79] One lawyer complained, "Although my moral opposition to the general subject of abortion may be the result of my Catholic training, I like to feel that my discussion of the proposed bill springs rather from my attitude as a Michigan citizen and a lawyer."[80]

Laurence Tribe, perhaps the country's most influential constitutional lawyer, wove these argumentative threads into a coherent whole. Tribe agreed with John Rawls, his Harvard colleague, that only "ways of reasoning acceptable to all" should inform public debate, and branded Catholic arguments on abortion as impermissible efforts to legislate "religious faith upon which people will invariably differ widely." Involving the state in a woman's decision whether to terminate her pregnancy, Tribe argued, was as ill-advised as permitting governmental aid to Catholic schools.[81] In Senate testimony on abortion, Tribe emphasized that the Supreme Court "has repeatedly urged the importance of avoiding religious political entanglement and fragmentation. . . ."[82]

V

The Catholic understanding of the human person clashed with this new liberal emphasis on autonomy, as well as with the idea that theological arguments were unacceptable in public debate. Since the beginning of the nineteenth-century Catholic revival, Catholics had emphasized the common good more than individual rights, and the dependency of any one person on family, neighborhood, workplace, and church. "The concept of an 'organic' versus an 'atomic' or 'mechanistic' society," one Catholic sociologist explained in 1943, "is the unique contribution of Catholic social thought to the American social panorama."[83]

This intensely social tradition struggled to absorb insights from its liberal counterpart. But just as the work of John Courtney Murray, Jacques Maritain, and others on democracy and religious liberty reached fruition at the Second Vatican Council, the abortion debate shattered this Catholic-liberal rapprochement. Whereas in the 1940s liberals had accused Catholics of producing citizens incapable of loyalty to American institutions, they now accused Catholics of refusing to recognize the moral importance of autonomy. When interviewed, some pro-choice activists named Joseph Fletcher as a primary influence, but even if they did not, these men and women had absorbed Fletcher's message that humans confronted with moral dilemmas must do the most loving thing at the moment, not appeal to an inflexible (and external) moral code.[84]

Here many Catholics drew back. Already in the late 1950s John Courtney Murray was regretting that contemporary American intellectuals, unlike their eighteenth-century predecessors, evinced no interest in the idea of a natural law to which all are bound in "common obedience."[85] In 1963, glancing away from the debate on religious freedom at the Second Vatican Council, Murray had expressed his uneasiness with the "morality of perfect personal autonomy" proposed by John Rawls. "Have we here," Murray wondered, "another speculative effort to find in personal freedom the final root of moral obligations in and toward society?"[86] Even the Declaration of Religious Freedom, Murray assured Pope Paul VI, would rest upon the dignity of the human person, not simply upon "freedom of conscience," a phrase Murray found "dangerous."[87]

Abortion on demand still seemed inconceivable in the early 1960s, perhaps especially to Catholics accustomed to viewing abortion as among the most serious of sins. Murray warned in 1960 of the "barbarian" clothed in a "Brooks Brothers suit" and willing to reduce "all spiritual and moral questions . . . to decision in terms of individual subjective feeling," but he did not mention abortion.[88] As late as 1964, officials in the Chicago archdiocese, after learning of Illinois physicians lobbying to legalize abortions for fetuses diagnosed as abnormal, could vow to scuttle the movement, since it was not "too widespread as of yet."[89]

Three years later all this had changed. Editors of the Catholic journal *America* now predicted that "changes are going to come (and come quickly)," and Catholic intellectuals began shifting gears.[90] Immersed in the vocabulary of sexual ethics, seasoned (or shattered) by the fierce intra-Catholic struggle over contraception, Catholics became leading figures in the abortion debate and the emerging field of bioethics. Daniel Callahan left his position as an editor of *Commonweal* in 1968 to write the single most important study of abortion published before *Roe v. Wade*, entitled simply *Abortion*, and in 1970 he founded the Hastings Center, the leading forum for consideration of bioethical issues.[91] Callahan had favored a change in church teaching on contraception, and after *Humanae Vitae*, he edited a book of essays on the subject dedicated to "Catholic couples who conscientiously decide in favor of contraceptives."[92] Unlike most Catholic intellectuals, Callahan endorsed placing the "final decision [about abortion] in the hands of the pregnant woman," although he also claimed a "bias in favor of protecting incipient human life." (In 1968 Callahan told Joseph Fletcher that he hoped to "criticize quite sharply the traditional Catholic position but also the abortion on demand position.") After *Roe v. Wade*, however, Callahan described the way in which his book had been used by pro-choice advocates as a "personal disaster."[93]

John Noonan began studying the abortion problem in the context of the contraception debate, and he quickly became the most prominent scholarly supporter of the anti-abortion movement. Noonan edited the papers from the first major scholarly conference on the ethical implications of abortion, held at Harvard University in 1967, testified before state legislatures and the U.S. Congress on the subject, and spoke to Catholic groups across the country.[94] "I would like to give a talk on the subject of " 'Abortion in the History of the Church and in the Civil Law,' " he told one Cleveland priest in 1968, "because I think there is now a large organized campaign to promote abortion in this country, and I think it is important for Catholics to be informed about the roots of the Church's opposition."[95]

Father Richard McCormick became one of the most influential theologians writing on abortion, a topic he continually revisited in the late 1960s and early 1970s. "Bone-weary" of the subject in 1974, he still mustered the energy for an incisive survey of the literature because he considered abortion "a paradigm of the way we will face other human problems in the future."[96] During the 1970s and 1980s McCormick would serve as the Rose F. Kennedy Professor in Christian Ethics at Georgetown University's Kennedy Institute of Ethics, the first such institute housed at an American university, founded by two members of America's most prominent Catholic family, Sargent Shriver and Eunice Kennedy Shriver.[97]

Catholics opposed to abortion law reform faced two obstacles. The first was obvious. Public opinion polls in the late 1960s suggested that Catholics were increasingly sympathetic to modest changes in the abortion laws, although more opposed to reform than either Protestants or Jews.[98] Catholic women were as conservative as Catholic men on the issue, and women played as important a role in the struggle to maintain laws restricting abortion as in the effort to abolish them. (The strongest supporters of legal abortion before *Roe v. Wade* were college-educated males, and the typical anti-abortion activist after 1973 was a married, lower-middle class, Catholic woman.)[99]

But women remained absent from positions of Catholic leadership, because only priests and a few laymen had been encouraged to become theologians and because only priests could become bishops. In itself, this gender hierarchy did not destroy the plausibility of the Catholic argument on abortion, as pro-life women attested. (Or it did not if one believed that right and wrong stood independent of individual experience.) And yet the effect was devastating: on one side, in a culture where personal experience seemed crucial to the assessment of moral problems, pro-choice women spoke of the terrors of unwanted pregnancy and the dangers of illegal abortions. On the other side, priests and (male) Catholic lawyers outlined in abstract terminology their opposition to the taking of innocent life. As Daniel Callahan rightly told John Noonan in 1967, the "impasse over [abortion] will not be broken by talking (as Catholics have been prone to talk) only about the right to life. If nothing else, that has been a principle which has precluded the need to look at the evidence, or listen to the testimony of women who want abortions."[100]

Exploiting this weakness, pro-choice activists encouraged pro-choice Catholic women to step into the spotlight. The most effective letters, one

New York pro-choice activist privately stressed, "are those written by Catholic *women* voters." The director of the National Organization to Repeal Abortion Laws recommended that a Massachusetts organizer find a "Catholic woman to organize other Catholics with the same conviction."[101]

Catholic views on contraception were the second obstacle. Most Catholic intellectuals in the late 1960s believed that abortion and contraception were distinct issues: that one could justify a change in church teaching on contraception, on Catholic grounds, without succumbing to a naïve belief in human autonomy that required the legalization of all abortions. When Noonan wrote Paul VI in 1965 urging him to modify church teaching on contraception, he cautioned the pope against sustaining an "unintelligible" ban on contraception that would only confuse "good, educated Catholics." Blanket prohibitions would diminish Catholic credibility on sexual ethics, Noonan warned, weakening a shared Catholic "horror of abortion."[102] Similarly, a Michigan anti-abortion activist urged the state's bishops not to use the abortion debate as an opportunity to revive the denunciatory tone that she and other Catholics had once used when discussing birth control. "In my old age," she confessed, "I blush at my self-righteousness."[103]

Controversy over *Humanae Vitae*, made a united Catholic front on questions of sexual ethics impossible. Even the point man on abortion for the Catholic bishops, Father James McHugh, would recommend in 1970 that national synods of bishops (and not the Vatican) issue statements attacking legal abortion, since such statements "would also indicate a widespread concern and a greater basis of support. In short, it would sidestep some of the problems of *Humanae Vitae*."[104] A foremost Catholic ethicist, Father J. Bryan Hehir, eventually urged "discreet silence" on contraception as part of a program to "distinguish abortion and contraception in the mind of Catholics and in the public mind."[105]

But how? In the cauldron of the late 1960s and early 1970s, Catholics began to make their case. That the discussion often collapsed into protesters thrusting photos of aborted fetuses in front of television cameras should not obscure the idealism of many Catholic anti-abortion activists, motivated by their conviction that a social justice agenda required protection of fetal life. The archdiocese of San Francisco social justice commission declared in 1967 that its members had "consistently supported principles of social justice, and their concrete application, in such community concerns as race relations, elimination of poverty, collective bargaining for farm workers and similar issues concerning human dignity." "We believe it entirely consistent," they continued, ". . . to now urge your opposition to the Beilenson Abortion Bill—this bill abridges the right to life of an unborn child and thereby works a grave injustice."[106] "Contrary to pro-abortion jibes," one Minnesota activist complained, "most people in the right-to-life movement (at least in Minnesota) are 'liberals' in the 1930s and 1960s sense. We expect to right the wrongs of the world, to alleviate human suffering, to overturn social injustices. . . ."[107]

From the beginning of the abortion debate Catholics also warned that abortion on demand would devalue other lives. Eunice Kennedy Shriver worried about "experts" willing to tolerate the destruction of "mongoloid" children diagnosed in the womb, and John Noonan questioned the very notion of "unwanted children." In Indiana the state's Catholic Conference urged Catholics to oppose capital punishment, not just abortion, since the "precious quality of human life has become more apparent to peoples of all faiths."[108]

Reverberations from the Second Vatican Council's insistence on engagement with social problems, and a new emphasis among Latin American Catholics on solidarity with the poor, also strengthened Catholic opposition to legal abortion. In 1965 *Gaudium et Spes* urged Catholics to take responsibility for the modern world, to resist treating Catholic institutions as fortresses, with bishops venturing forth only to demand funding for Catholic schools. After the council dioceses across the country formed Catholic legislative offices, usually located within walking distance of state capitol buildings, in order to press a Catholic agenda. Staffers at these offices assumed that their primary task would be to fight for better housing for the poor, or adequate welfare benefits. Abortion, brusquely defined at the Second Vatican Council as an "abominable" crime, seemed a distant priority.[109]

The surge in abortion-related legislative activity in the late 1960s transformed this situation. A few Catholics, such as the Jesuit law professor and, later, Massachusetts congressman Robert Drinan, attracted attention in the late 1960s with the proposal that Catholics simply abstain from the abortion debate, since to condone any abortion, even for the health of the mother, meant Catholics would be guilty of regulating, and implicitly approving, an abhorrent practice.

Some Catholic legislators gratefully accepted Drinan's caution against regulating abortion in a "religiously pluralistic and morally diverse nation."[110] But the basic thrust of Drinan's argument, allowing the pregnant woman freedom of choice, ran counter to more powerful Catholic currents. For many Catholic activists abortion, like urban poverty or the war in Vietnam, seemed another public issue that Catholics must confront. One of Drinan's critics insisted that Catholics opposed to abortion had an "obligation to protest against injustice and to oppose it actively in the political arena."[111] Certainly, the European bishops and theologians directing the work of the Second Vatican Council, chastened by Catholics' passivity during World War II, worried about irrelevance more than public controversy. *Gaudium et Spes* cautioned Catholics to avoid "one of the gravest errors of our time, . . . the dichotomy between the faith which many profess and the practice of their daily lives."[112]

The understanding of war articulated at the Second Vatican Council also reinforced the growing sense that human life must assume paramount value. The controversial section on modern war in *Gaudium et Spes*, echoing John Ford's 1944 attack on obliteration bombing, invoked the prohibition against direct taking of innocent life.[113] "Too often," reflected Father Richard McCormick in 1966, "the very ones who protest most strongly against all killing in war are the very ones who not only silently tolerate abortions, but plead a liberalization of laws which, on all available evidence, would increase their number. This inconsistency is a curious restriction of humane and liberal thinking."[114]

Latin American influence on the Catholic argument against abortion was less direct, but still significant. The number of American missionaries in Latin America jumped dramatically in the early 1960s, after a Vatican official pleaded with leaders of American religious orders to tithe 10 percent of their priests and nuns to a region with one-third of the world's Catholics, but a "well-known lack of clergy, and indeed of all apostolic workers."[115] Few religious orders met this quota, but the presence in Latin America of several thousand American Catholic nuns and priests by the end of the decade, and a smaller number of lay volunteers through such programs as Papal Volunteers, marked an important American opening to the wider Catholic world. The Jesuits alone sent men from New Orleans to Capinas, in the state of São Paulo, from New England to northeastern Brazil, from Wisconsin to Salta, Argentina, and from New York to Rio de Janeiro.[116] One survey of Peru found representatives from thirty American men's religious orders and forty-eight American women's religious orders by 1967.[117]

The effect on American Catholicism of priests, nuns, and lay volunteers streaming into Peru, Brazil, El Salvador, and Honduras, and then back to the United States, needs more exploration, but the basic trajectory seems clear.[118] These American volunteers arriving in Latin America assumed, or at least their bishops did, that they would work in Catholic schools, parishes, and hospitals similar to those found in Brooklyn, Detroit, and Kansas City. One Sister of St. Joseph, from Nazareth, Michigan, recalled that "everywhere it was a school, or once in awhile a hospital."[119]

Priorities changed when it became clear that Latin America's most pressing need was not the staffing of existing schools or hospitals serving the region's small middle class. Participation in Christian base communities, just forming in the region, strengthened the sense among even conservative priests and nuns that the church must serve as a vehicle for alleviating political and economic oppression, not simply for the distribution of charity. "Is the value of our work here . . . of any real worth," asked one papal volunteer stationed in Brazil, "when it is helping to foster and sustain existing structures (ecclesiastical, political, or otherwise . . .)?"[120]

The same American Catholics encountered the work of Latin American liberation theologians committed to viewing the Gospel from the vantage point of the poor. The most important such figure, Peru's Gustavo Gutiérrez, and the bishop most committed to local base communities, Brazil's Dom Hélder Câmara, briefed visiting American clerics, and conferences devoted to the relationship between the North American and South American churches in the 1960s became steadily more radical in tone. (By 1968 Archbishop Marcos McGrath, an American priest and longtime Latin American missionary serving as archbishop of Panama City, could inform a Philadelphia audience of the need for a "theology of revolution.")[121] Most important, the extraordinary 1968 meeting of the Latin American bishops at Medillín, Colombia, concluded with the bishops critical of "liberal capitalism" and urging "solidarity with the poor."[122]

For many American Catholics the language of liberation and solidarity was revelatory. Beginning in the 1950s a few priests and moral theologians had criticized the exploitation of migrant farm workers by American farmers (often themselves Catholic) and the federal government.[123] In the mid-1960s activist Catholics belatedly rallied in support of César

Chávez's heroic organizing efforts with the United Farm Workers in California's Central Valley. Chávez, himself, however, had received his theological education from the older papal encyclical tradition, not liberation theologians. Like Martin Luther King Jr., Chávez stressed Gandhian nonviolence, while Gutiérrez and other advocates of liberation theology drew to some extent upon Marxian analyses of class struggle.[124]

The practical effect of liberation theology on American Catholic life was modest until the 1980s, when increased immigration, the assassination of San Salvador's Archbishop Oscar Romero and the murder of four American Catholic churchwomen in El Salvador drew the attention of North American Catholics to the region. Still, Gutiérrez spent part of almost every year during the 1970s in San Antonio, where his ideas shaped the agenda of the leading center for Mexican American Catholic pastoral life.[125] And the idea of solidarity with the poor appealed to American Catholic intellectuals, who lavished attention on the movement. In 1970 the most important American Catholic theological journal, *Theological Studies*, published an essay by Gutiérrez even before the Spanish publication of his landmark book, *Teología de la liberación*. Bishop Joseph Bernardin, then general secretary of the National Conference of Catholic Bishops and the United States Catholic Conference, noted as early as January 1970 that American and Latin American bishops needed a deeper understanding of the "Medellín concept of 'liberation'" and "the theological meaning of 'liberation' in general."[126]

This same emphasis on solidarity helped frame Catholic discussion of abortion. As part of the first papal visit to Latin America, Paul VI opened the conference at Medellín with an attack on economic inequality, along with a defense of the just-published *Humanae Vitae* as a "defense of life."[127] To the extent that American Catholics assimilated this emphasis on solidarity with the poor, they edged away from the language of individual and reproductive rights so powerful in the United States, and toward a more communal alternative. Even as non-Catholic liberals placed more emphasis on individual autonomy, Catholics were drawn to a different vocabulary. Solidarity—a term that saturates Catholic writing during this period—became important not just with the poor but with the unborn. Boston's Archbishop Humberto Medeiros invoked Medellín with the phrase "preferential respect due to the poor" in a 1971 address, even as he denounced the increasing availability of legal abortion.[128] Abortion, the theologian Richard McCormick argued, is a "*social* problem," as are "poverty and racism."[129]

Ultimately, then, a rough consensus among Catholic intellectuals opposed to abortion law reform held. The political question—specifically the responsibilities of Catholic officeholders in a society willing to tolerate abortion on demand—would assume greater importance after *Roe v. Wade*, and here debate among Catholics would be fierce.

But the moral question, even as most American liberals became convinced that women needed full reproductive autonomy, elicited only sporadic discussion.[130] Daniel Callahan predicted that abortion "might become the next major topic of internal debate" for Catholics, but the debate never occurred.[131] The impassioned manifestos attacking church teaching on contraception and widespread dissent from within the universe of Catholic scholars, editors, and theologians did not have analogues during the first years of the abortion debate. Father James T. McHugh expressed pride in 1967 that even "liberal and progressive" Catholic journals had broken with secular liberals over abortion, and five years later he stressed that the principle of a right to life was also "the basis of our support of anti-poverty legislation, civil rights legislation."[132] A modest Catholic feminist movement even emerged, disenchanted with secular feminist discussion of abortion as a matter of "property rights" and determined to protect life, "no matter how immature, helpless or different it is from white middle-class adult males."[133]

VI

Catholic opposition to abortion reform had important political consequences. The most immediate was Catholic leadership in a state-by-state campaign that careened across the country between 1967 and 1973. With an instant network of parishes, parish bulletins, newspapers, copy machines, staplers, and, most important, volunteers, Catholic institutions became the grid upon which the anti-abortion movement sprung to life. A single letter from a bishop could reach several hundred priests and, if read at Mass, hundreds of thousands of Catholics.

The first major battles occurred in 1967, as legislators debated abortion law reform bills, usually following American Law Institute guidelines. In New York, Catholic legislators led the successful fight against the bill, and New York's eight bishops issued a pastoral letter, read at every Mass in every parish in the state, that urged legislators to defend the "sanctity of the human right to life."[134] In Arizona that same spring the state's Catholic bishops coordinated an intensive public relations campaign that quashed a similar reform bill, prompting supporters of the bill to invoke the Inquisition. Tucson's Bishop Francis Joseph Green sent a letter to each Catholic parishioner warning of a campaign against the "weak and helpless members of our society."[135]

Abortion reform bills passed in 1967 in Colorado (where sponsors hustled the bill through the legislature despite Catholic opposition) and North Carolina (where Catholics constituted less than one percent of the population). The fight in California that same spring drew more attention. The state's bishops coordinated a campaign against the bill and recruited John Noonan, among others, to testify before the state legislature, but a razor thin majority in the state legislature passed the measure.[136]

These early successes of the abortion law reform movement—in California, Colorado, and North Carolina—did not mean abortion on demand. All three states still allowed abortion not as a woman's right but as the proper decision for a physician given certain circumstances.

By 1970, however, the rallying cry of pro-choice forces had shifted from reform to repeal. And in New York the components for dramatic change fell into place: the nation's most powerful women's movement (with a core of feminists willing to stage protest marches beginning at St. Patrick's Cathedral), New York Catholic lobbyists distracted by exhausting fights over aid to Catholic schools and colleges, and a large Jewish vote overwhelmingly in favor of pro-choice legislation. (Meanwhile, in Pennsylvania, a more cohesive Catholic lobbying effort, a smaller Jewish population, and a less vigorous feminist movement ensured that abortion reform bills in the state legislature never made it out of committee.)[137]

The struggle in New York in 1970 was fierce, and Catholics again led the opposition, but the state assembly passed the nation's most liberal reform bill by one vote in a dramatic late-night session, and the state senate passed the same bill by five votes. (During one preliminary vote, of the twenty-two Catholics in the state senate, eighteen opposed the measure. The Catholics who supported the bill complained of priests making personal attacks from Catholic pulpits.)[138] After Governor Nelson Rockefeller signed the bill into law, thousands of women began streaming into New York City from across the country for abortions, and pro-choice advocates predicted that other states would quickly alter their laws. The National Conference of Catholic Bishops issued a statement decrying "a radical turn of events."[139]

This New York victory, however, was deceptive, as anti-abortion forces took the offensive in the following two years. President Richard Nixon made several gestures in opposition to abortion law reform in 1971 and 1972, including placing restrictions on abortions in military hospitals. (This decision prompted John Noonan to confide to a friend that the "tide may even have turned.")[140] Nixon also promised "careful attention" to the abortion issue when Cardinal Patrick O'Boyle of Washington, D.C., complained of "unfettered feticide" in March 1972, and later that spring

Protesters urging a liberalization of New York State abortion laws, marching in front of St. Patrick's Cathedral in 1967.

the administration released a letter drafted by the presidential aide Patrick Buchanan, signed by the president and sent to New York's Cardinal Terence Cooke, that lauded Catholics' efforts on behalf of "unborn children" as a "noble endeavor."[141]

In New York itself the 1970 reform law came within a whisker of repeal in 1972, saved only by the veto of Governor Rockefeller. By October that same year national columnists such as Shana Alexander of *Newsweek* felt compelled to denounce the "renewed vigor of the reactionary, so-called 'right-to-life' forces," and wonder whether "the Catholic hierarchy may have made abortion its last stand."[142] In the November elections, in North Dakota, an "information" campaign orchestrated by Catholics and Lutherans helped defeat by a 78 percent to 22 percent margin an abortion referendum that would have allowed all abortions in the first five months of the pregnancy.[143]

The results in Michigan that same fall were especially dramatic. Several futile attempts to change Michigan's abortion law in the state legislature—the speaker of the house, one pro-choice activist privately complained, was a "Catholic with twelve kids"—had frustrated abortion rights forces in the late 1960s. (Another activist blamed the "UAW and the Catholic Church.")[144] Abortion rights activists then tried a new tack. By placing a referendum on the ballot allowing abortions for any reason through the twentieth week of pregnancy, activists hoped to demonstrate the existence of a pro-choice majority. At the annual meeting in Detroit, Lee Gidding, director of the National Abortion Rights Action League (NARAL), announced that a Michigan victory would be "terribly significant"; Eleanor Holmes Norton added, "The Michigan vote may well decide the future of the movement."[145]

The campaign developed along familiar lines. The Michigan Abortion Reform Committee emphasized the importance of women's autonomy and health and chastised the Catholic hierarchy for attempting to "impose its religious and moral beliefs upon the citizens of Michigan." Our opposition, one pro-choice activist announced, is "Catholics and a few token non-Catholics."[146]

Catholics developed two responses. The Michigan Catholic Conference provided the bulk of the funding for a nominally nonsectarian group, Voice of the Unborn, that distributed fliers and paid for billboards and television and radio commercials throughout the state. "I strongly believe," one Catholic organizer insisted, "that we need to do more than present 'the Catholic position.' If we limit our public efforts simply to making the position of the Church known, we all but guarantee the passage of the abortion on demand proposal."[147] The group's directors were non-Catholic, but the directors agreed to recognize the "organization, expertise and resources" of the Michigan Catholic Church and run a media campaign stressing the need to respect life.[148]

Within the church the Michigan Catholic Conference sponsored an aggressive outreach campaign, Love and Let Live, complete with sermon outlines for priests on the need to respect life, and speakers sent to every parish carrying slides, outlines, and full-color pictures of healthy and aborted fetuses. "If it is morally permissible for us to say every woman has a right to make her own decision regarding abortion," speakers were instructed to say, "why can't everyone have an equal right to decide whether or not to shoot his neighbor?"[149]

Two months after a poll showed the referendum likely to pass with a large majority, the results of the pro-life campaign were astonishing: a 61.3 percent to 35.7 percent victory for anti-abortion forces. Catholics voted strongly against the measure, and Catholic union members, overwhelmingly Democrats, seem to have been the core of the anti-abortion movement.[150] The director of the Michigan Catholic Conference sent a letter to each priest in the state, noting "stunning and remarkable evidence of the deep-seated regard which the Catholics of Michigan and indeed the majority of the people of Michigan have for the integrity and dignity of each human being."[151] A month after the election staffers at the Michigan Catholic Conference, giddy with victory, began to lobby for increased welfare benefits for poor parents, as part of a "planned, integrated attack on those socio-economic inequities which prompted thousands of women (and men) to consider abortion preferable to protecting the lives of their unborn babies."[152]

VII

The Supreme Court abortion decisions issued on January 22, 1973, *Roe v. Wade* and *Doe v. Bolton*, ended this stage of the abortion debate. By defining abortion as a constitutionally protected privacy right, the Court surprised even pro-choice activists, and it plunged Catholics involved in the anti-abortion movement, buoyant from recent electoral triumphs, into despair. John Noonan bemoaned the "most radical decisions ever issued by the Court," and the Administrative Committee of the National Conference of Catholic Bishops described the opinions as "erroneous, unjust and immoral."[153]

That the nation's highest court had entered the abortion debate meant that federal legislators could no longer avoid the issue. A year after *Roe v. Wade*, four Catholic cardinals made the unprecedented decision to testify before Congress in favor of a constitutional amendment designed to nullify the decision; Philadelphia's Cardinal John Krol again explained, "The right to life is not an invention of the Catholic Church or any other church."[154]

A rift between Catholic and Democratic Party leaders also opened in the abortion issue's wake. Well into the 1960s the Democratic Party arguably stood to the right of the Republicans on issues of sexual morality. Two states with Democratic majorities, Massachusetts and Connecticut, possessed the nation's most restrictive birth control laws, and New England Planned Parenthood members dreamed of the day when Republicans might dominate the state legislature. Republican Party legislators were as likely as Democrats to initiate abortion reform bills in state legislatures, and the national leadership of both parties avoided comment on the issue. During the 1960s the Republican governors of the two largest states, Ronald Reagan of California and Nelson Rockefeller of New York, signed abortion reform bills, and Michigan's Governor William Milliken helped guide that state's abortion reform effort. Those Democrats who did sponsor abortion law reform bills, such as the New York state legislator Michael Blumenthal, endured sharp criticism from Democratic (usually Catholic) colleagues.[155]

When leading Democrats first became aware of the issue's explosive potential—specifically that the Catholic bishops, leaders of a core Democratic constituency, would resist any change in the law—they tiptoed around the subject. As early as the summer of 1964, as Robert F. Kennedy geared up for a Senate campaign in New York, and Edward Kennedy for a Senate campaign in Massachusetts, the Kennedy family quietly convened a group of leading Catholic theologians at the family compound in Hyannis Port, Massachusetts, to discuss the issue. The theologians agreed that some type of abortion reform was inevitable, and a consensus was reached that allowing abortion only in cases of rape, incest, or danger to a mother's life would respect the absence of a moral consensus in a diverse society, yet still protect the overwhelming majority of unborn children.[156]

As the abortion debate began to emerge in New York State politics, Senator Robert Kennedy tried to avoid the subject. Only when a high school student posed the question to him, "being a Catholic," did Kennedy cautiously suggest in 1967 that "changes have to be made."[157] Conservatives such as Father John Ford immediately jumped to the conclusion that Kennedy hoped to assuage liberal political allies and "make straight the path for some of his political ambitions."[158] Kennedy himself, however, did not pursue the matter, and organizers of a major 1967 conference on abortion sponsored by the Joseph P. Kennedy Jr. Foundation privately registered their opposition to "abuses of the abortion liberalization laws" and "abortion on demand."[159]

The major presidential candidates did not discuss abortion in 1968. In the 1972 Democratic presidential primaries, Senator Hubert Humphrey damaged Senator George McGovern's campaign with the accusation that McGovern supported amnesty for draft evaders, the legalization of drugs, and complete freedom of choice on abortion. In fact, McGovern favored allowing state legislatures to decide the issue, and anti-abortion Catholics such as Michael Novak and Ethel Kennedy offered McGovern their support. The country's most outspoken liberal bishop, Detroit's Thomas Gumbleton, emphasized that McGovern "would *not* aid or support the current efforts to liberalize the abortion laws."[160]

McGovern defeated Humphrey, but helped destroy his own campaign with the selection of Missouri's Senator Thomas Eagleton as his vice-presidential nominee, only to drop Eagleton from the ticket after it became public knowledge that Eagleton had undergone shock therapy. Lost in the confusion was the intriguing fact that a Democratic presidential candidate could still select Eagleton, a staunchly pro-life Catholic, as a vice-presidential nominee. Eagleton's replacement was the Kennedy-in-law and longtime Catholic activist Sargent Shriver, whose own stance on abortion was conservative.

Indeed, the number of prominent anti-abortion Catholic Democrats in the early 1970s is striking. Maine's Senator Edmund Muskie, then the leading candidate for the Democratic presidential nomination, confessed in 1971, "I suppose it's related to my religious training, or my church training. . . . I'm concerned about diluting in any way the concept of the sanctity of life. . . ."[161] The Massachusetts congressman, and future Speaker of the House, Tip O'Neill, told one constituent in the summer of 1972, "It is my deep personal conviction that abortion is wrong. . . . It is for this reason that I cannot endorse liberalized abortion."[162] Senator Edward Kennedy of Massachusetts informed a constituent of his "personal feeling that the legalization of abortion on demand is not in accordance with the value which our civilization places on human life." Kennedy added that he hoped his generation would be remembered as "one which cared about human beings enough to halt the practice of war, to provide a decent living for every family and to fulfill its responsibility to its children from the moment of conception."[163]

In the aftermath of *Roe v. Wade*, the issue continued to crisscross party lines. In 1977 a Texas congressman, the Democrat James Wright, noted in his diary that Tip O'Neill would refuse to enlist in the battle against Republican efforts to stop government funding of abortions, because of the "hard line position of the Catholic bishops in Massachusetts." Another leading Catholic Democrat, Indiana's John Brademas, couldn't "get out front because of Notre Dame."[164]

Over time, however, the roster of pro-life Catholic Democrats dwindled. As early as 1972 the Michigan Democratic candidate for the Senate, Frank Kelley, found himself pinned between Catholics eager to have him declare his opposition to abortion and women's groups warning him that if he did so, he would "be publicly denounced by Democratic women all over the State."[165] In 1973 pro-choice activists could still term Senator Edward Kennedy's position on abortion "thoroughly revolting."[166] Two years later, to the applause of liberal commentators, Kennedy led the fight against any effort to restrict federal funding of abortions through the Medicaid program.[167]

In 1980 a major political party nominated a strongly anti-abortion presidential candidate, Ronald Reagan. At the same time Republicans became far more receptive to anti-abortion candidates than the Democrats, and Catholic Republicans, notably Henry Hyde of Illinois, became reliable congressional allies of Catholic bishops on the issue. Within the Democratic Party, women's groups (as opposed to overwhelmingly male, Catholic elected officials) began to play a larger role in the Democratic presidential nominating process than previously, making a self-imposed limitation on legal abortion by a national Democratic Party representative improbable. In 1984 the Democratic Party platform described reproductive freedom as a "fundamental human right."[168] In 1992 Pennsylvania's Governor Robert Casey, the leading pro-life Democrat, was prohibited from speaking on the subject at the Democratic national convention.[169]

Pope John Paul II in Washington, D.C., 1979.

The tenor of the anti-abortion movement would also change, as Protestant evangelicals became active in large numbers in the late 1970s. Those Catholics opposed to abortion now found themselves allied with anti-abortion activists uninterested in supporting trade unions or increasing social welfare benefits.

The resulting situation—with many Catholics, and especially Catholic leaders, to the left of the Democratic Party on economic and military matters, yet opposed to abortion on demand—prompted new formulations. A newly elected pope, John Paul II, harking back to Joseph Fletcher and the debates of the 1950s, would attack "situation ethics" with even more fervor than Pius XII.[170] On his first trip to the United States as pope, in 1979, standing before the Lincoln Memorial in Washington and speaking to a crowd of 175,000, John Paul II would urge Americans to "defend human life against every influence or action that threatens or weakens it."[171]

Chapter Ten

A CONSISTENT ETHIC AND SEXUAL ABUSE

I

Born in 1928, ordained a priest in 1952, Joseph Bernardin spent the first years of his career in Charleston, South Carolina, an unlikely jumping-off point for the ecclesiastical fast track. His abilities attracted the attention of Atlanta's Bishop Paul Hallinan, however, who arranged for Bernardin's ordination as the nation's youngest bishop at the age of thirty-eight, which in turn led to his appointment as general secretary of the National Conference of Catholic Bishops. In 1972 he became archbishop of Cincinnati. Ten years later, he became archbishop, and then cardinal archbishop, of Chicago.

An adroit bureaucrat, Bernardin specialized in mediation. When Washington's Cardinal Patrick O'Boyle suspended nineteen Washington priests for refusing to endorse *Humanae Vitae* in 1968, Bernardin attempted (unsuccessfully) to resolve the matter.[1] When the Vatican tried to replace Seattle's Bishop Raymond Hunthausen because of perceived heterodoxy, Bernardin brokered a settlement. In Chicago, when the migration of Catholics to suburban areas required the closing and consolidation of city parishes and schools, Bernardin organized extensive meetings for parents, parishioners, and clergy.[2]

Bernardin's own ideas about the role of Catholicism in American society must be extracted from what Garry Wills has described as a "disappointingly dull" set of speeches and writings.[3] Submerged beneath the

Cardinal Joseph Bernardin, n.d.

cautious prose, however, was a new Catholic style. For Bernardin and his contemporaries, notably the theologian Father J. Bryan Hehir, who would collaborate with Bernardin closely, the most exciting aspect of the Second Vatican Council was the realization that the church now called them to shape and engage their own societies, not simply fortify Catholic subcultures within them. Instead of the defensive stance cultivated by Catholics since the nineteenth century, Bernardin repeatedly invoked the "powerful" opening words of the final conciliar document, *Gaudium et Spes*—"the joy and hope, the grief and anguish of the men of our time, especially of those who are poor or afflicted in any way, are the joy and hope, the grief and anguish of the followers of Christ."[4]

Catholics participated in the modern world before 1965, of course, but the measured, even optimistic, description of the modern world at the council marked something new. One of Bernardin's mentors, Cardinal John Dearden of Detroit, directed the commission that drafted *Gaudium et Spes*, and after returning from Rome, Dearden told Michigan Catholics that *Gaudium et Spes* meant that "we, the People of God, are intimately bound up with all the concerns of those among whom we live."[5] Bernardin, too, in the first days after the council complained, "There is still too much of a gap between what we do in church on Sunday and what we do the rest of the week."[6]

Bernardin first stepped into the national spotlight during the 1976 presidential campaign, when he directed the bishops' efforts to lobby the candidates on various issues. The Democratic presidential nominee that year, Jimmy Carter, persuaded Catholics in the crucial Iowa caucuses that he had taken the strongest stance of any Democratic candidate against abortion, but later proved unwilling to support a constitutional amendment designed to counter *Roe v. Wade*. The Democratic Party platform, similarly, recognized "religious and ethical" concerns about abortion, but opposed all efforts to "overturn the Supreme Court decision in this area."[7]

Bernardin felt betrayed. Hopeful after contact with Democratic leaders that the party platform would not mention abortion at all, he attributed the final wording to "intense reaction among pro-abortion lobbying groups."[8] "Many who are members of the Democratic Party," Bernardin explained to his fellow bishops, "would, I believe, not agree with the Platform Committee's action on this issue."[9]

The Republican Party shifted in the opposite direction. The 1976 Republican nominee, President Gerald Ford, had an ambivalent record on abortion, and his wife, Betty, persistently voiced her support for bringing abortion "out of the back woods."[10] But Ford and his campaign staff also hoped to lure Catholic voters away from the Democrats. One White House aide urged Ford to take a more aggressive stand after the Democratic convention, "[n]ow that the Democrats have absolutely rejected and insulted the pro-lifers."[11]

Both Ford and Carter agreed to meet a delegation of Catholic bishops that fall. Bernardin headed the delegation and described himself as "disappointed" by Carter's statements on abortion and "encouraged" by Ford.[12] To Bernardin's chagrin, *Time* magazine and other news outlets interpreted these terms as a "clear signal of support for Ford."[13] At an off-the-record meeting of the bishops after the election, New York's Cardinal Terence Cooke felt compelled to defend Bernardin and reject the charge that "our Conference [of bishops] is concerned with only one issue—abortion."[14]

Chastened by this experience, Bernardin resolved to knit the disparate threads of Catholic social thought into a coherent whole. The most publicized effort was the drafting of a pastoral letter on the nuclear arms race. Bernardin served as chair of the bishops' committee that began studying the issue in 1980, and three years of hearings and debate that included theologians, arms control experts, and military officers persuaded even conservative bishops that American nuclear weapons directed at civilians and America's refusal to rule out beginning a nuclear exchange violated the requirement that Catholics protect innocent life. (The final vote on the pastoral, *A Challenge to Peace*, was 238 bishops in favor, 9 opposed.) Reagan administration officials and other conservative Catholics challenged the bishops' conclusions, but the completed document became the era's most influential challenge to American nuclear policy. Bernardin appeared on the cover of *Time* magazine and eminences such as the former diplomat George Kennan called the bishops' letter "the most profound and searching inquiry" conducted on the morality of modern war.[15]

Bernardin would go on to play an important role in the promulgation of another, less influential pastoral letter on economic affairs, urging government officials to increase services for the poor and reduce income inequality.[16] At the same time, in a series of well-publicized lectures that reached the front page of the *New York Times*, Bernardin urged Americans to adopt a "consistent ethic of life."[17] As he frequently noted, the "sustained involvement" of the bishops in the abortion debate had prepared them to see a "direct parallel between the protection of human life in the womb and the preservation of human life in the face of the nuclear threat."[18]

Bernardin soon extended his "consistent ethic" beyond abortion and war. Americans should protect human life by abandoning capital punishment, he argued, and they should make a "substantial commitment to the poor."[19] In 1993 he described a society unwilling to protect "unborn children" as one that "inevitably draw[s] the circle of life too narrowly in other decisions of social and economic policy."[20]

Even the final moments of Bernardin's life pulled him toward his "consistent ethic." Catholic intellectuals had long predicted that legalization of abortion might lead to legalization of euthanasia or physician-assisted suicide. As early as 1966 a Michigan Catholic lawyer had warned the state's Catholic conference to pay "substantial attention" to the "legal springboard from abortion to euthanasia," and a decade later New York's Cardinal Cooke privately warned the bishops, "Public opinion is becoming more permissive on death and dying questions."[21]

Support for physician-assisted suicide did grow in the 1970s and 1980s, spurred by sophisticated medical technology that seemed to threaten unlimited suffering and expense for hospital patients near death.[22] In 1994 the U.S. district court judge Barbara Rothstein fulfilled Catholic prophecies by using Supreme Court abortion decisions as precedent for the claim that an adult possesses a constitutional right to assisted suicide. Physician-assisted suicide, Judge Rothstein explained, was necessary for the promotion of "personal autonomy and basic human dignity." Six of the nation's most distinguished philosophers, including Ronald Dworkin, John Rawls, and Judith Jarvis Thomson, issued a statement insisting that individuals pondering suicide had a "constitutionally protected interest" in being protected from "the imposition of any religious or philosophical orthodoxy."[23]

The most prominent judicial opponent of this position was the longtime Catholic anti-abortion activist and now judge John Noonan, who, when the case came before him on appeal, accused Judge Rothstein and the district court of acting as a "floating constitutional convention" willing to create a right "unknown to the past and antithetical to the defense of human life."[24] (The Supreme Court eventually agreed with Noonan and decided that a state could decide that protection of life outweighed a putative "right to die.")[25] Catholics also led (and largely funded) a successful campaign against a ballot initiative legalizing assisted suicide in Washington. A similar measure passed in Oregon, a state with an unusually small Catholic population.[26]

Bernardin spoke often against the idea that the dying make "free" choices, and warned that poor or lonely patients would feel pressure from their doctors to end their own lives. He lamented a misguided "sense of human autonomy which asserts that an individual's life belongs entirely to the individual, and that each person is free to dispose of that life entirely as he or she wishes."[27] Informed in 1996 that his own death was imminent, he used his last public statement, published four days before his death, to urge the U.S. Supreme Court to recognize that "there can be no moral and legal order which tolerates the killing of innocent human life." If Americans continue to "legitimate the taking of life as policy," he warned, "one has a right to ask what lies ahead for our life together as a society."[28]

II

Even before his death, some components of Bernardin's consistent ethic had become less salient. Less than a decade after the publication of *A Challenge to Peace*, the fall of the Berlin Wall and the breakup of the Soviet Union had diminished fears of a nuclear exchange. At the same time, in the midst of an economic boom, Michael Novak and other Catholic conservatives argued that Catholics had failed to grasp the moral underpinnings of modern capitalism, while placing too much faith in state bureaucracies.[29]

This Catholic sympathy for free-market capitalism was not new. A handful of Catholics, including the *National Review* founder, William F. Buckley, had assisted in the creation of the modern conservative movement in the 1950s. At that time, however, Buckley's libertarian enthusiasm for the free market placed him outside the Catholic intellectual mainstream. The American Jesuit John LaFarge complained to the papal adviser Gustav Gundlach, S.J., in 1952 that Buckley was mistaken in "asserting the absolute rights of Free Enterprise," and an official at the National Catholic Welfare Conference ridiculed Buckley's effort to connect "economic individualism" to "Catholic social teaching."[30] Forty years later Buckley seemed less heterodox. The 1991 papal encyclical, *Centesimus Annus*, while not, as Novak claimed, a "trenchant" attack on the welfare state, did emphasize the importance of free markets and broke with 1930s era Catholic schemes to control wages and prices, let alone the radical denunciation of "unbridled" economic liberalism offered by Pope Paul VI.[31]

The abortion controversy remained. Conservative Catholics complained that Bernardin, by linking abortion, poverty, the arms race, and the death penalty, implied that these issues were of equal gravity. As early as 1984 New York's Cardinal John O'Connor publicly chastised two New York Democratic Catholic politicians, Governor Mario Cuomo and vice-presidential nominee Geraldine Ferraro, for their unwillingness to oppose legal abortion, despite their opposition to capital punishment and support for expanded social welfare programs. O'Connor could not see "how a Catholic in conscience could vote for an individual explicitly expressing himself or herself as favoring abortion."[32]

Ferraro and O'Connor exchanged awkward volleys in the New York newspapers that flattered neither party. Cuomo, then the most popular Democratic politician in the country, graduate of a Catholic college and interested in Catholic theology, made a more formal response. In a well-publicized speech delivered at the University of Notre Dame, reprinted in important journals of opinion such as the *New York Review of Books*, he defended the "prudential political judgement" that the "breadth, intensity and sincerity" of support for legal abortion made it unwise to support challenges to current laws. After all, Cuomo pointedly noted, Catholics understood that church teaching on birth control would not be enacted into law. And he applauded Cardinal Bernardin for reminding Catholics that not only abortion but hunger and joblessness are "diminishing human life and threatening to destroy it."[33]

Cuomo even harked back to an early stage in the Catholic encounter with American liberalism, the battle over slavery. That the bishops had not condemned slavery in the 1850s, when Catholics were "despised by much of the population," seemed reasonable. Nineteenth-century bishops "weren't hypocrites," Cuomo explained; "they were realists." Now Catholics encountered far less hostility, but they still needed to "weigh Catholic moral teaching against the fact of a pluralistic country where our view is in the minority."[34]

Few minds were changed. Catholic anti-abortion activists understood the failure of Catholics to join the nineteenth-century abolition movement as a warning against complacency, not, in Cuomo's words, a "sound practical judgement." The same Catholics wondered why Cuomo, eloquent in his scorn for a wealthy nation unwilling to alleviate the plight of impoverished children, remained mute on the subject of abortion except when challenged by a belligerent cleric.[35]

Cuomo's and Ferraro's assessment of American Catholic opinion did strike a sensitive nerve. "There are a lot of Catholics," Ferraro explained, "who do not share [Cardinal O'Connor's] view of the Catholic church."[36] Catholics were only slightly less likely than other Americans to support legal abortion in the 1980s and 1990s, although most Americans (and most Catholics) favored more restrictions on abortion than permitted in *Roe v. Wade*.[37]

As the obstacles to overturning *Roe v. Wade* became more formidable, Catholic bishops became more combative. John Paul II's description of modern democracies gripped by a "culture of death" and structured by a "war of the powerful against the weak" received widespread attention, and other bishops followed his cue.[38] The Denver archbishop Charles Chaput wondered whether Catholics had been "too polite and timid" in a "culture that grows more estranged from the Gospel with every year." Bernardin's successor in Chicago, Cardinal Francis George, urged Catholics not to surrender truth to "ideological compromise" or a "concern for civility."[39]

Dialogue itself became controversial. A year before his death, Bernardin had inaugurated the Catholic Common Ground project in order to ameliorate intra-Catholic bickering that "seriously undermined" the "great gift of the Second Vatican Council." By the late 1990s the project had taken root, but not before four other cardinals, including New York's John O'Connor, Philadelphia's Anthony Bevilacqua, Washington's James Hickey, and Boston's Bernard Law, in a rare breach of episcopal unity, declined to participate. "Dialogue as a way to mediate between truth and dissent," Law warned, "is mutual deception."[40]

III

And then none of this mattered. Beginning in January 2002, revelations about the protection of pedophile priests rocked the archdiocese of Boston, creating a media firestorm that swept across the country, making the sexual abuse crisis the single most important event in American Catholicism since the Second Vatican Council, and the most devastating scandal in American Catholic history. By June over two hundred priests accused of improper sexual conduct had been pulled out of parishes across the country, the Boston archdiocese teetered on the edge of bankruptcy with potential payments to victims estimated at one hundred million dollars, two bishops and an archbishop had resigned, two accused priests had committed suicide, and one priest had been shot by an alleged sexual abuse victim.[41]

The scandal had been simmering since 1985, when reporters uncovered a string of sexual abuse cases in Louisiana. Victims across the country started to come forward, and the diocese of Dallas and the archdiocese of Santa Fe both paid thirty million dollars in settlements to sexual abuse victims. Most notoriously, James Porter, a onetime priest from the diocese of Fall River, Massachusetts, was found to have molested scores of children during his career, while a succession of bishops shuttled him from one ineffective treatment program to another.[42]

In 1992, dismayed to learn that he had reassigned a putatively "cured" priest guilty of sexual abuse to another Chicago parish, only to have that priest commit new crimes, Bernardin established an archdiocesan commission to scrutinize church records on the subject and founded a lay-dominated board to assess new charges. More dramatically, Bernardin was accused, on national television, of sexually abusing a seminarian in the 1970s. He denied the charge, and the accuser later recanted.[43]

This false accusation created a deceptive calm, shattered a decade later. Relatively few new cases of abuse emerged, especially in dioceses that had established lay-dominated commissions to evaluate all accusations. More shocking were revelations about hundreds of cases between the 1950s and the early 1990s. In Joliet, Illinois, when asked by lawyers in 1995 whether he worried about children's safety around a priest he had brought in from another diocese, who had already been convicted of molesting an altar boy, Bishop Joseph Imesch replied, "I don't have any children."[44] Catholics in Palm Beach, Florida, watched two successive bishops, one in 1999 and one in 2002, resign after admitting improper sexual contact with teenage boys early in their careers. Disclosure of secret diocesan settlements highlighted the absence of adequate financial controls—Cardinal Law's assertion that parish donations would not be used to settle abuse cases was rightly mocked—and the need for lay Catholic oversight of personnel issues.

The most horrific cases were in Boston, where Cardinal Law was found to have transferred a known pedophile, Father John Geoghan, to a new parish as late as 1984, and to have recommended Father Paul Shanley for a position at a Catholic youth center in New York City in 1997, long after Shanley had attracted notoriety as an advocate of the North American Man-Boy Love Association. By the spring of 2002 even prominent Catholic conservatives such as William Bennett and William F. Buckley had demanded Cardinal Law's resignation.

Three aspects of the crisis deserve emphasis. Bishops and priests—not the media—caused the crisis, but commentary occasionally reinforced venerable anti-Catholic tropes. Assertions that celibacy itself was the problem—one *New Yorker* editorial called such a judgment "common sense"—cast an unflattering light on an American culture so saturated in sexual imagery, so quick to equate sexual activity with "health," that any kind of sexual asceticism bordered on the incomprehensible.[45]

The crisis within institutional Catholicism also became more visible. The three most influential American cardinals—Bernard Law in Boston, Edward Egan in New York, Roger Mahony in Los Angeles—became tainted by their callous handling of sexual abuse cases, and the absence of even a candid media strategy revealed a leadership caste, almost all appointed by John Paul II, incapable of creative response. The widely publicized April 2002 meeting in Rome between the American cardinals, Vatican officials, and an ailing John Paul II resulted in a public relations fiasco of conflicting statements. Only at the national meeting of the bishops in Dallas in June, under the leadership of the Belleville, Illinois, bishop Wilton Gregory, did the bishops adopt firm policies prohibiting any priests guilty of sexual abuse from serving in the active ministry.

The final issue is especially delicate. Only a small fraction of the sexual abuse cases involved true pedophiles, or men specifically attracted to children. In this regard the record of the Catholic priesthood was possibly no worse than that of the Boy Scouts or other professions where men routinely work with children. More typically, the cases made public over the past decade involved priests abusing teenage boys. (One knowledgeable commentator put 90 percent of the cases in this category.)[46] The existence of homosexual priests (celibate or not) was hardly news, but homosexual priests as late as the 1940s might not have used the term, since they worked in a society (and certainly a church) where sexual orientation was not consciously perceived as central to personal identity.[47]

The gay awakening of the late 1960s and 1970s created a different climate. One result was a gay clerical subculture, as many priests and seminarians began to understand their own identity in the sexual vernacular of the larger society.[48] A remarkable 1979 letter from Boston's Cardinal Humberto Medeiros to Cardinal Franjo Seper, a top Vatican official, noted the new presence of "widespread" and "open" gay communities in large American cities, with gay men asserting that sexual orientation "is of no consequence to anyone except themselves." Medeiros also expressed concern about the "problem of homosexuality" in Catholic seminaries, "which reflect our local American culture," and asserted that he had weeded out many homosexuals from St. John's seminary in Boston. He assured the Vatican that he would continue to "turn back the number of homosexuals who, for many reasons, are being drawn towards the sacred priesthood."[49]

Identifying homosexuality, per se, as the problem, a favorite tactic of Catholic conservatives, dodged more complicated issues. The data are necessarily vague, but most priests (gay or straight) probably remained chaste, and many gay priests are superb ministers. The more profound issue, as with birth control and women in the 1960s, was the tension between individual experience and received doctrine. At the height of the birth control debate, and on the papal birth control commission, laypeople urged Catholic leaders to alter church teaching that banned artificial contraception because it seemed a doctrine incompatible with work and family life (especially for women) as experienced in the late twentieth century. Hard-liners like John Ford, and ultimately Pope Paul VI, were unsympathetic. "Young married couples," Ford noted privately during the meetings of the papal birth control commission in 1965, "have the advantage of knowing the concrete elements of the problem and the difficulties of the Church's teaching better than anyone else; but they have the disadvantage of being liable to be less objective judges in this matter."[50]

Frustrated by such intransigence, most Catholic couples soon dismissed Catholic teaching on contraception. The comparison is not exact, but the complicated nexus of homosexuality, the priesthood, and sexual abuse offered a variation on the same theme. Just as Catholic couples came to understand their own ideals as distant from, even more authentically Christian than, church teachings, some priests proved incapable of reconciling same-sex attraction with blanket Vatican condemnations of homosexual activity as "disordered" or sinful.

The difference was that couples using birth control had little role in the governing structure of the church, while the pivotal role of priests, and the admiration with which they were viewed, invited hypocrisy. Into the 1980s priests still worked in a trusting Catholic subculture, where parents felt honored by priests' expressing a paternal interest in young men, and where allegations of abuse or homosexual activity were unthinkable. (In Boston, when a boy confided to his mother sexual abuse at the hands of a priest, she slapped him.)[51]

In scholarly forums honest discussion about the importance of understanding clerical sexual identity became more frequent in the 1990s, but most bishops continued to cloak discussion of the issue behind curtains of secrecy. That one of the nation's most accomplished bishops, Milwaukee's

Archbishop Rembert Weakland, felt compelled to purchase the silence of a man with whom he evidently had an affair, with $14,000 in 1980 and $450,000 in 1998, suggests the intensity of the clerical desire to maintain appearances.[52] John Paul II's determination to appoint only bishops adamant in their refusal to contemplate any changes in church teaching on sexual issues only widened the gap between doctrinal claims and a clerical subculture that often ignored (or protected) sexually abusive priests, rather than openly discuss such charged issues as celibacy and sexual orientation.

None of this justified sexual abuse, a crime of power, not passion. But it may help explain why some bishops, aware that vocations to the priesthood had decreased sharply since the 1960s, and aware that many priests struggled with same-sex attraction, seemed endlessly sympathetic to fellow priests, even those guilty of sexual abuse, and blind to the suffering of Catholic young people.

IV

The polarities are stark: on the one hand, an institution enrolling more active members than any other in American society, including prominent leaders in government, the professions, the universities, the trade unions, and all branches of American industry. The same institution is important to the Latino community now taking center stage in American public life, and offers more social services, including soup kitchens, schools, hospitals, and community organizing projects, than any organization besides the federal government. On the other hand, a wounded, fractious church, ripped apart by disputes over sex, gender, and ministry, and incapable of sustaining the loyalty of many of its communicants.

Certainly, history lends little support to the view that Catholics need only conserve their own traditions. The halting Catholic endorsement of slave emancipation in the nineteenth century, and democracy and religious freedom in its successor, stemmed from a belated recognition of the importance of individual human dignity. Similarly, the unhappy conclusion to the harrowing Catholic debate over birth control, and the alienation deepened by the current sexual abuse scandal, suggest the fragility of an institution struggling to distinguish permanent truths from contingent applications.

Still, the contemporary Catholic social ethic, as distinct from the corruption on display in the sexual abuse scandal, retains an attraction for many Catholic and non-Catholic intellectuals.[53] The reluctance of nineteenth-century Catholics to view the nation-state as the end of human history now seems prescient, and a deepening, if still tentative, sense that Catholics of the Americas, from Santiago to Montreal, must pool their efforts suggests the advantages held by a global church.[54] Confirming the importance now placed upon the dignity of the human person in Catholic social thought, John Paul II and Catholic leaders in the Philippines, South Korea, Central Europe, and Latin America defended human rights with remarkable vigor in the 1980s and 1990s.[55]

Within the United States, the long struggle to gain government assistance for parents with children in Catholic schools, the battle with which this book began, seems closer than ever to realization. In June 2002, the U.S. Supreme Court (with three Catholic members voting in the majority) approved such assistance for the first time. Weary rhetoric—Justice Paul Stevens worried in dissent that such aid might make the United States more like the Balkans, Northern Ireland, or the Middle East—cannot conceal widespread admiration for urban Catholic schools and their successes with minority and poor students.[56] A Democratic Party adamant that all abortions remain legal (even up until the last days before birth, even because of preference for a particular gender), joining Republicans in support of capital punishment (even as John Paul II urges Americans to abandon the practice) and willing, in Michigan, to nominate the lawyer of the assisted suicide provocateur Jack Kevorkian for governor, seems unlikely to spark a renewed appreciation for human life. President George W. Bush and his advisers, by contrast, routinely invoke Catholic ideals. Practicing Catholics are increasingly likely to vote for Republicans in presidential elections, but Republican leaders remain indifferent to income inequality in the United States and to the immorality of tax cuts disproportionately benefiting the wealthiest Americans.[57]

The philosopher Charles Taylor's brilliant investigation of our moral resources places current tensions in perspective. Taylor readily admits the importance of modern notions of autonomy and the "free self-determining subject," and he notes that affirmations of universal human rights emerged in spite of Catholic nostalgia for Christendom, not because of it. At the same time Taylor urges Catholics and other people of good will to counter an ethical individualism unwilling to recognize any authority beyond the self, and an economic individualism pliant before the marketplace. A romantic view of individual autonomy, often commingled in the United States with anti-Catholicism, may weaken the solidarity needed to ensure dignity for society's most vulnerable members.[58]

Invocations of solidarity are easy to make but difficult to sustain. In 1857 Bishop Martin John Spalding of Louisville urged his immigrant, poor parishioners not to view themselves as traveling alone in a "gloomy land of pilgrimage." Remember, Spalding advised, that you are joined by other Catholics and the entire communion of saints. All of us, living and dead, are bound "into one society knit by a thousand associations and ties."[59] Perhaps the final assessment of the long Catholic encounter with American ideas of freedom will rest here: on whether twenty-first-century Catholics can convince their fellow citizens, and themselves, that associations and ties with the strangers in our midst satisfy our deepest, most common aspirations.

NOTES

ABBREVIATIONS

Abbreviations used in the endnotes are identified below. Individual pieces of correspondence identified with a Roman numeral, Arabic numeral, and lowercase letter (e.g., III-2-j) are located in the correspondence collection, Manuscripts and Archives, University of Notre Dame.

AAB	Archives of the Archdiocese of Boston.
AASF	Archives of the Archdiocese of San Francisco.
ACCL	American Citizens Concerned for Life Papers, Gerald Ford Presidential Library, Ann Arbor, Michigan.
ACLU	ACLU Papers, Seeley-Mudd Library, Princeton University. Some citations are from the partial microfilm version available at the Harvard Law School.
ACP	Association of Chicago Priests Collection, Manuscripts and Archives, University of Notre Dame.
ACUA	Archives of the Catholic University of America.
ADW	Archives of the Diocese of Worcester.
AL	Amos Lawrence Papers, Massachusetts Historical Society.
AM	Albert Meyer Papers, Joseph Cardinal Bernardin Archives and Records Center, Archdiocese of Chicago.
AP	Arthur Preuss Papers, Manuscripts and Archives, University of Notre Dame.
AS	Arthur Schlesinger Jr. Papers, John Fitzgerald Kennedy Presidential Library.

BW	Bernardine Wiget Papers, Special Collections, Georgetown University.
CFM	Christian Family Movement Collection, Manuscripts and Archives, University of Notre Dame.
CH	Carlton Hayes Papers, Special Collections, Columbia University.
CHA	Catholic Health Association Archives, St. Louis, Missouri.
COMM	Commonweal Papers, Manuscripts and Archives, University of Notre Dame.
DD	David R. Dunigan Papers, Bapst Library, Boston College.
FC	Francis Connell Papers, Redemptorist Archives—Baltimore Province, Brooklyn, New York.
FF	Felix Frankfurter Papers, microfilm edition, Harvard Law School.
FK	Frederick Kenkel Papers, Manuscripts and Archives, University of Notre Dame.
FK-HU	Freda Kirchwey Papers, Schlesinger Library, Harvard University.
FL	Francis Lieber Papers, Huntington Library.
FLETCHER	Joseph Fletcher Papers (unprocessed), Special Collections, University of Virginia Medical School.
FME	Frederick May Eliot Papers, Harvard Divinity School.
FR	Franklin Roosevelt Presidential Papers, Franklin Roosevelt Library, Hyde Park, New York.
FW	Francis Weninger Papers, Missouri Province Archives, St. Louis, Missouri.
GB	George Bancroft Papers, Massachusetts Historical Society.
GF	Gerald Ford Presidential Library, Ann Arbor, Michigan.
GK	Gerald Kelly Papers, Missouri Province Archives, St. Louis, Missouri.
GL	George LaPiana Papers, Harvard Divinity School.
GS	Goldwin Smith Papers, Special Collections, Cornell University.
GS-NCWC	General Secretary's Files, National Catholic Welfare Conference Collection, Archives of the Catholic University of America.
GS-ND	George Schuster Papers, Manuscripts and Archives, University of Notre Dame.
HB	Heinrich Brüning Papers, HUG FP 93.45, Harvard University Archives.
HG	Horace Greeley Papers, microfilm copy, New York Public Library.
HGeorge	Henry George Papers, microfilm copy, New York Public Library.
HK-AJA	Horace Kallen Papers, American Jewish Archives, Cincinnati, Ohio.
HK-YIVO	Horace Kallen Papers, YIVO Institute, New York City.
IB	Irving Brant Papers, Library of Congress.
JAO	John A. O'Brien Papers, Manuscripts and Archives, University of Notre Dame.

JB	Joseph Bernardin Papers, Joseph Cardinal Bernardin Archives and Records Center, Archdiocese of Chicago.
JBC	James Bryant Conant Correspondence, Harvard University Archives.
JC	John Cody Papers, Joseph Cardinal Bernardin Archives and Records Center, Archdiocese of Chicago.
JCM	John Courtney Murray Papers, Special Collections, Georgetown University.
JD	John Dearden Papers, Manuscripts and Special Collections, University of Notre Dame.
JF	John Fitzpatrick Papers, Archives of the Archdiocese of Boston.
JF-BC	John Ford Papers, Bapst Library, Boston College.
JF-HC	John Ford Papers, Special Collections, College of the Holy Cross.
JFK	John F. Kennedy Pre-Presidential Papers, John Fitzgerald Kennedy Presidential Library.
JG	James Garfield Papers, microfilm copy, University of Notre Dame.
JI	John Ireland Papers, microfilm copy, University of Notre Dame.
JLF	John LaFarge Papers, Special Collections, Georgetown University.
JM-AJA	Julius Morgenstern Papers, American Jewish Archives, Cincinnati, Ohio.
JM-MI	Jacques Maritain Papers, Maritain Institute, University of Notre Dame.
JN	John Noll Papers, Manuscripts and Archives, University of Notre Dame.
JP	John T. Pickett Papers, Library of Congress.
JR	John Ryan Papers, Archives of the Catholic University of America.
JTE	John Tracy Ellis Papers, Archives of the Catholic University of America.
JUN	John U. Nef Papers, Special Collections, University of Chicago.
KP	Kernan Family Papers, Special Collections, Cornell University.
LB	Lorraine Beebe Papers, Bentley Historical Library, Ann Arbor, Michigan.
LL	Leo Latz Papers, Joseph Cardinal Bernardin Archives and Records Center, Archdiocese of Chicago.
MA	Melvin Arnold Papers, Harvard Divinity School.
MARC	Michigan Abortion Reform Committee, Bentley Library, University of Michigan.
MA-UC	Mortimer Adler Papers, Special Collections, University of Chicago.
MAUND	Manuscripts and Archives, University of Notre Dame.
MCC	Archives of the Michigan Catholic Conference, Lansing, Michigan.
MF	Mulford Family Papers, Sterling Memorial Library, Yale University.

ML	Max Lerner Papers, Sterling Memorial Library, Yale University.
MP	Maryland Province Collection, Special Collections, Georgetown University.
MSC	Mary Steichen Calderone Papers, Schlesinger Library, Harvard University.
MWD	Mary Ware Dennett Papers, Schlesinger Library, Harvard University.
NARAL	National Abortion Rights Action League Papers, Schlesinger Library, Harvard University.
NCWC	National Catholic Welfare Council Papers, Archives of the Catholic University of America.
NOONAN	John Noonan Papers (unprocessed), Boalt Hall, University of California, Berkeley.
PB	Paul Blanshard Papers, Bentley Library, University of Michigan.
PF	Propaganda Fide Collection, Manuscripts and Archives, University of Notre Dame.
PM	Philip McDevitt Papers, Manuscripts and Archives, University of Notre Dame.
RB	Richard Burtsell Diary, microfilm copy, Manuscripts and Archives, University of Notre Dame.
RE	Richard T. Ely Papers, State Historical Society of Wisconsin.
RFK	Robert F. Kennedy Senate Papers, John Fitzgerald Kennedy Presidential Library.
RM	Richard McKeon Papers, Special Collections, University of Chicago.
RN	Reinhold Niebuhr Papers, Library of Congress.
RP	Roscoe Pound Papers, Harvard Law School.
SAD-NCWC	Social Action Division, National Catholic Welfare Council Collection, Archives of the Catholic University of America.
SH	Sidney Hook Papers, Hoover Institution Archives, Stanford, California.
SS	Samuel Stritch Papers, Joseph Cardinal Bernardin Archives and Records Center, Archdiocese of Chicago.
SW	Sheed and Ward Papers, Manuscripts and Archives, University of Notre Dame.
TG	Thomas Gumbleton Papers, Manuscripts and Archives, University of Notre Dame.
TM	Thomas Mulledy Papers, Georgetown University Special Collections.
TP	Talcott Parsons Papers, Harvard University Archives.
UG	Ulysses S. Grant Papers, Library of Congress.

WFB	William F. Buckley Papers, Sterling Memorial Library, Yale University.
WG	Waldemar Gurian Papers, Manuscripts and Archives, University of Notre Dame.
WGE	William Greenleaf Eliot Papers, Washington University Archives.
WK	William Kerby Papers, Archives of the Catholic University of America.
WM	Willam McAdoo Papers, Library of Congress.
WMSJ	William Markoe Papers, Marquette University Archives.
WR	William Rosecrans Papers, Manuscript and Archives, University of Notre Dame.
WR-LC	Wiley B. Rutledge Papers, Library of Congress.
YS	Yves R. Simon Papers, Simon Institute, Mishawaka, Indiana.

INTRODUCTION: THE ELIOT SCHOOL REBELLION, BOSTON, 1859

1. The most thorough account of the Eliot School Rebellion is Robert H. Lord, John E. Sexton, and Edward T. Harrington, *History of the Archdiocese of Boston, in the Various Stages of Its Development, 1604–1943*, 2 vols. (Cambridge, 1944), 2:585–602. The spelling of the young boy's surname—Whall or Wall—caused confusion at the time and since. Father Wiget emphasized that the correct spelling was Whall, and I have followed his lead. See Wiget to Provincial, March 16, 1859, folder 34, box 76, MP. On controversies over the Bible, see Paul C. Gutjahr, *An American Bible: A History of the Good Book in the United States, 1777–1880* (Stanford, 1999), 113–42.

2. "The Eliot School Rebellion—Continuation of the Examination," *Boston Daily Atlas and Bee*, March 21, 1859, p. 3.

3. "Master Thomas J. Whall," *Irish Illustrated Nation*, April 30, 1859, copy in DD.

4. *Boston Daily Atlas and Bee*, March 30, 1859.

5. *Defense of the Use of the Bible in the Public Schools, Argument of Henry F. Durant, Esq., in the Eliot School Case* (Boston, 1859), 6, 22.

6. *American Law Register* 7 (1859): 417–26.

7. *Boston Pilot*, April 23, 1859, p. 4; ibid., April 30, 1859, p. 4; "True to His Father and to His Faith," *New York Freeman's Journal*, April 2, 1859, p. 4.

8. "*New York Tribune* on the Boston Inquisition," *New York Freeman's Journal*, March 26, 1859, p. 5; *Boston Daily Advertiser*, March 18, 1859, p. 2.

9. "Roman Catholic Oppression," *Boston Daily Atlas and Bee*, April 29, 1859, p. 2.

10. Entry of March 18, 1859, Amos A. Lawrence Diaries, AL.

11. Rev. N. M. Gaylord, in "City and Suburban," *Boston Daily Atlas and Bee,* March 28, 1859, p. 2; Rev. Rufus W. Clark, *Romanism in America* (Boston, [1855], 1859), preface, n.p. Also see "The Bible in Our Schools," *Christian Witness and Advocate* April 1, 1859, p. 34.

12. Richard F. Fuller, *Chaplain Fuller: Being a Life Sketch of a New England Clergyman and Army Chaplain* (Boston, 1864), 94, 127.

13. Rev. Arthur B. Fuller, *Hostility of Romanism to Civil and Religious Liberty: A Discourse Delivered in the New North Church, Boston, April 3rd, 1859* (Boston, 1859).

14. William J. Bouwsma, *Venice and the Defense of Republican Liberty: Renaissance Values in the Age of the Counter Reformation* (Berkeley, 1968), 626.

15. [Thomas Paine], "Thoughts on Defensive War" (1775), in Paine, *Common Sense and Related Writings*, ed. Thomas P. Slaughter (Boston, 2001), 68.

16. Charles P. Hansen, *Necessary Virtue: The Pragmatic Origins of Religious Liberty in New England* (Charlottesville, 1998); Jason Kennedy Duncan, "'A Most Democratic Class': New York Catholics and the Early American Republic" (Ph.D. diss., Univ. of Iowa, 1999).

17. Remarks on an act for Regulating Elections, Jan. 29, 1787, in *The Papers of Alexander Hamilton, vol. 4: Jan. 1787–May 1788*, ed. Harold C. Syrett and Jacob E. Cooke (New York, 1962), 30.

18. On Carroll, see Joseph P. Chinnici, O.F.M., *Living Stones: The History and Structure of Catholic Spiritual Life in the United States* (Maryknoll, N.Y., [1989], 1996), 5–34; James Hennessey, S.J., "An Eighteenth Century Bishop: John Carroll of Baltimore," *Archivum Historiae Pontificiae* 6 [1978]: 171–204. For Carroll on Washington, see *The John Carroll Papers*, ed. Thomas O'Brien Hanly, S.J., 2 vols. (Notre Dame, 1976), 2:292–95, 297–308; for Carroll on salvation, see ibid., 1:87.

19. Lord, Sexton, and Harrington, *History of the Archdiocese of Boston*, 1:761–83.

20. John Wolffe, *The Protestant Crusade in Great Britain, 1829–1860* (Oxford, 1991). On the Ursuline convent, see Nancy Lusignan Schultz, *Fire and Roses: The Burning of the Charlestown Convent, 1834* (New York, 2000). On Maria Monk, see Jenny Franchot, *Roads to Rome: The Antebellum Protestant Encounter with Catholicism* (Berkeley, 1994), 154–61.

21. Arthur B. Fuller, *Hostility of Romanism*, 2.

22. Richard F. Fuller, *Chaplain Fuller*, 192.

23. Raymond Grew terms the conflict between Catholicism and liberalism a "central theme" of nineteenth-century European history. See Grew, "Liberty and the Catholic Church in Nineteenth-Century Europe," in *Freedom and Religion in the Nineteenth Century*, ed. Richard Helmstadter (Stanford, 1997), 197. Also see

Margaret Lavinia Anderson, "The Limits of Secularization: On the Problem of the Catholic Revival in Nineteenth Century Germany," *Historical Journal* 38 (1995): 647–70; David Blackbourn, "The Catholic Church in Europe since the French Revolution," *Comparative Studies in Society in History* 33 (Oct. 1991): 778–90. On Latin America, see Austen Ivereigh, ed., *The Politics of Religion in an Age of Revival: Studies in Nineteenth-Century Europe and Latin America* (London, 2000).

24. Joseph A. Komonchak, "Modernity and the Construction of Roman Catholicism," *Cristianesimo nella storia* 18 (1997): 353–85.

25. "De la liberté," *Propagateur Catholique*, Jan. 30, 1858, p. 1.

26. Marjule Anne Drury, "Anti-Catholicism in Germany, Britain, and the United States: A Review and Critique of Recent Scholarship," *Church History* 70 (March 2001): 98–131.

27. Henry Winter Davis, *The Origin, Principles and Purposes of the American Party* (Baltimore, 1856), 33–34; *Congressional Globe*, Jan. 9, 1856, p. 191; Bishop Martin John Spalding, "Lafayette and Professor Morse," *Metropolitan* 6 (April 1858): 148–55.

28. Wiget Student Notebooks, 1848–1849, Book II, BW. Thomas Babington Macaulay, "Ranke's History of the Popes" (1840), in Macaulay, *Critical and Historical Essays* (New York, 1965), 312.

29. On the provincial quality of much writing on the United States, see Daniel T. Rodgers, "Exceptionalism," in *Imagined Histories: American Historians Interpret the Past*, ed. Anthony Molho and Gordon Wood (Princeton, 1998), 21–40.

30. "The French Press and the Roman Church," *New York Times*, Feb. 2, 1861, p. 4.

31. For a fair-minded assessment of "republicanism," see James T. Kloppenberg, *The Virtues of Liberalism* (New York, 1998), 24–25. On American Catholics, Philip Gleason's work remains the standard. See his "American Catholics and Liberalism," in *Catholicism and Liberalism: Contributions to American Public Philosophy*, ed. R. Bruce Douglass and David Hollenbach (Cambridge, 1994), 45–75; *Keeping the Faith: American Catholicism Past and Present* (Notre Dame, 1987), and *Speaking of Diversity: Language and Ethnicity in Twentieth-Century America* (Baltimore, 1992). Other recent important studies include Eugene McCarraher, *Christian Critics: Religion and the Impasse in Modern American Social Thought* (Ithaca, 2000); Charles R. Morris, *American Catholic* (New York, 1997); Patrick N. Allitt, *Catholic Intellectuals and Conservative Politics in America, 1950–1985* (Ithaca, 1992) and *Catholic Converts: British and American Intellectuals Turn to Rome* (Ithaca, 1997).

32. Ray Allen Billington, *The Protestant Crusade, 1800–1860: A Study of the Origins of American Nativism* (New York, 1938); Franchot, *Roads to Rome*; John Higham, *Strangers in the Land: Patterns of American Nativism, 1860–1925*

(New Brunswick, [1955], 1992); John T. McGreevy, "Thinking on One's Own: Catholicism in the American Intellectual Imagination, 1928–1960," *Journal of American History* 84 (June 1997): 97–131; Mark Massa, S.J., "The New and Old Anti-Catholicism and the Analogical Imagination," *Theological Studies* 62 (Sept. 2001): 549–70. A marvelous study that appeared just as this book went to press, and one I have not been able to take fully into account, is Philip Hamburger, *Separation of Church and State* (Cambridge, 2002).

CHAPTER 1: EDUCATION AND THE NINETEENTH-CENTURY CATHOLIC REVIVAL

1. Wiget to Provincial, March 16, 1859, folder 34, box 79, MP.

2. "Fr. Bernardin F. Wiget," *Woodstock Letters* 12 (1883): 189.

3. Kathleen Ashe, O.P., *The Jesuit Academy (Pensionnat) of St. Michel in Fribourg, 1827–1847* (Fribourg, 1971), 184.

4. Geoffrey Cubitt, *The Jesuit Myth: Conspiracy Theory and Politics in Nineteenth-Century France* (Oxford, 1993), 137.

5. Joachim Remak, *A Very Civil War: The Swiss Sonderbund War of 1847* (Boulder, 1993); William V. Bangert, S.J., *A History of the Society of Jesus* (St. Louis, 1972), 438.

6. Gilbert J. Garraghan, S.J., *The Jesuits of the Middle United States*, vol. 1 (New York, 1938), 524–41.

7. Bernardine Wiget, "La Derniere belle nuit a Fribourg" (1849), box 76, BW.

8. Peter Steinfels, "The Failed Encounter: The Catholic Church and Liberalism in the Nineteenth Century," in *Catholicism and Liberalism: Contributions to American Public Philosophy*, ed. R. Bruce Douglass and David Hollenbach (Cambridge, Eng., 1994), 19–44; Roger Aubert, *Le Pontificat de Pie IX (1846–1878)* (Paris, 1963), 24.

9. Raymond Grew, "Liberty and the Catholic Church in Nineteenth-Century Europe," in *Freedom and Religion in the Nineteenth Century*, ed. Richard Helmstadter (Stanford, 1997), 201.

10. Harriet Martineau, *Society in America*, vol. 2 (London, 1837), 323; Alexis de Tocqueville, *Democracy in America*, trans. George Lawrence (New York, 1988), 287.

11. Howard R. Marraro, *American Opinion on the Unification of Italy, 1846–1861* (New York, 1932), 11; *Proceedings of a Public Meeting of the Citizens of the City and County of Philadelphia, Held Jan. 6, 1848, to Express Their Cordial Approval of the Liberal Policy of Pope Pius IX in His Administration of the Temporal Government of Italy on Monday, Nov. 29, 1847* (Philadelphia, 1848); *Proceedings of the Public Demonstration of Sympathy with Pope Pius IX,*

and with Italy (New York, 1847); Margaret Fuller to Mary Rotch, May 23, 1847, in *"My Heart Is a Large Kingdom": Selected Letters of Margaret Fuller*, ed. Robert N. Hudspeth (Ithaca, 2001), 245.

12. "Autobiography of Father Burchard Villiger," *Woodstock Letters* 32 (1903): 62. Also note Jonathan Sperber, *The European Revolutions, 1848–1851* (Cambridge, Eng., 1994), 123–24.

13. Owen Chadwick, *A History of the Popes, 1830–1914* (Oxford, 1998), 61–94.

14. As noted in Charles Sumner to George Sumner, April 14, 1848, in *The Selected Letters of Charles Sumner*, ed. Beverly Wilson Palmer, vol. 1 (Boston, 1990), 221. For an overview, see Timothy Mason Roberts, "The American Response to the European Revolution of 1848" (Ph.D. diss., Oxford Univ., 1998).

15. Margaret Fuller, *These Sad But Glorious Days: Dispatches from Europe, 1846–1850*, ed. Larry J. Reynolds and Susan Belasco Smith (New Haven, 1992), 321.

16. Robert Francis Hueston, *The Catholic Press and Nativism, 1840–1860* (New York, 1976), 123; "The Catholic Element in the History of the United States," *Metropolitan* 5 (Oct. 1857): 528.

17. Pierre De Smet, S.J., to a father at the Collège Saint-Michel, June 17, 1854, in *L'Ami de la religion* 165 (1854): 613.

18. Henry Bornstein, *The Mysteries of St. Louis: A Novel*, trans. Friedrich Munch (Chicago, 1990).

19. Leonard G. Kroeber, "Anti-Catholic Agitation in Milwaukee, 1843–1860" (M.A. thesis, Marquette Univ., 1960), 56–57.

20. Carl Frederick Wittke, *Against the Current: The Life of Karl Heinzen (1809–1880)* (Chicago, 1945), 53; "The Liberator," from the *Pioneer* of April 20, 1859, in *Liberator*, May 20, 1859, p. 77.

21. "The Annual Meeting," *American and Foreign Christian Union* 4 (June 1853): 254.

22. Theodore Dwight, *The Roman Republic of 1849* (New York, 1851); *The Life of Genl Garibaldi, Written by Himself, with Sketches of His Companions in Arms*, ed. Theodore Dwight (New York, 1859), 12.

23. Charles Sumner, *Recent Speeches and Addresses* (Boston, 1856), 7.

24. John R. G. Hassard, *Life of the Most Reverend John Hughes, D.D., First Archbishop of New York, with Extracts from His Private Correspondence* (New York, 1866), 343.

25. Francis X. Weninger, S.J., *Memoirs: Events of My Life in Europe and America for 80 Years, 1805–1885*, trans. Susan X. Blakely (Columbus, Ohio, 1886), 78–79, box 2B, FW.

26. Michael F. Holt, *The Rise and Fall of the American Whig Party: Jacksonian Politics and the Onset of the Civil War* (New York, 1999), 695.

27. N. M. Gaylord, *Kossuth and the American Jesuits: A Lecture Delivered in Lowell, January 4, 1852* (Lowell, Mass., 1852), 14.

28. "Kossuth at St. Louis," *New York Tribune*, March 24, 1852, p. 6.

29. Basil Hall, "Alessandro Gavazzi: A Barbabite Friar and the Risorgimento," in *Church, Society and Politics*, ed. Derek Baker (Oxford, 1975).

30. *Father Gavazzi's Lectures in New York*, trans. and rev. by Madame Julie de Marguerittes (New York, 1853), 192, 276.

31. James F. Connelly, *The Visit of Archbishop Gaetano Bedini to the United States of America (June 1853–February 1854)* (Rome, 1960), 1–15.

32. Daniel C. Eddy, *The Times and the Men for the Times* (Boston, 1854), 41; Jasper Ridley, *Garibaldi* (New York, 1974), 337.

33. *Pittsburgh Post-Gazette*, March 3, 1854, p. 2.

34. Bruce Levine, "Community Divided: German Immigrants, Social Class, and Political Conflict in Antebellum Cincinnati," in *Ethnic Diversity and Civic Identity: Patterns of Conflict and Cohesion in Cincinnati since 1820*, ed. Henry D. Shapiro and Jonathan D. Sarna (Urbana, 1992), 67–70.

35. Connelly, *Visit*, 95–108; Francis Patrick Kenrick to Peter Richard Kenrick, Jan. 30, 1854, in *The Kenrick-Frenaye Correspondence: Letters Chiefly of Francis Patrick Kenrick and Marc Antony Frenaye, 1830–1862*, ed. F. E. T[ourscher, O.S.A.] (Lancaster, Pa., 1920), 364–65.

36. Gerald A. McCool, *Nineteenth-Century Scholasticism: The Search for a Unitary Method* (New York, 1989), 17–187; John Inglis, *Spheres of Philosophical Inquiry and the Historiography of Medieval Philosophy* (Leiden, 1998), 62–156; David R. Dunigan, *A History of Boston College* (Milwaukee, 1947), 54.

37. Patricia Byrne, C.S.J., "American Ultramontanism," *Theological Studies* 56 (June 1995): 301–38. A perceptive local study is Dale B. Light, *Rome and the New Republic: Conflict and Community in Philadelphia Catholicism between the Revolution and the Civil War* (Notre Dame, 1996).

38. Thomas W. Spalding, *Martin John Spalding: American Churchman* (Washington, D.C., 1973), 221.

39. Jay P. Dolan, *Catholic Revivalism: The American Experience, 1830–1900* (Notre Dame, 1978).

40. Ibid., 44; Orestes Brownson, "Protestant Revivals and Catholic Retreats," *Brownson's Quarterly Review* 3 (July 1858): 289.

41. Weninger, *Memoirs*, 421; Mary M. Meline and Rev. Edward F. X. McSweeny, *The Story of the Mountain: Mt. St. Mary's College and Seminary, Emmitsburg, Maryland* (Emmitsburg, 1911), 463.

42. Pieter Claessens, *The Life of Father Bernard, Missionary Priest of the Congregation of the Most Holy Redeemer: The Apostolate of a Redemptorist* (New York, 1875), 202.

43. "A Reported Apparition," *New York Freeman's Journal*, Oct. 23, 1858, p.

1; "La Grotte de Lourdes, France," *Propagateur Catholique*, Oct. 16, 1858, p. 1. On Lourdes in the United States, see John T. McGreevy, "Bronx Miracle," *American Quarterly* 52 (Sept. 2000): 413–22.

44. "Fr. Bernardin F. Wiget," 189.

45. Margaret Lavinia Anderson, "The Limits of Secularization: On the Problem of the Catholic Revival in Nineteenth Century Germany," *Historical Journal* 38 (1995): 657–61; Ralph Gibson, *A Social History of French Catholicism, 1789–1914* (London, 1989), 247–49, 262–63.

46. Jonathan Sperber, *Popular Catholicism in Nineteenth-Century Germany* (Princeton, 1984), 292–93; Gibson, *Social History*, 242.

47. "Final Discourse: The Agony in the Garden," *New York Freeman's Journal*, March 11, 1854, p. 5.

48. "Edward Holker Welch: The Puritan as Jesuit," in *American Jesuit Spirituality: The Maryland Tradition, 1634–1900*, ed. Robert Emmett Curran (New York, 1988), 300–301; Clarence A. Walworth, "Joy Born of Affliction," in *Sermons Preached at the Church of St. Paul the Apostle New York during the Year 1863* (New York, 1978), 43–57.

49. Ann Taves, *The Household of Faith: Roman Catholic Devotions in Mid-Nineteenth-Century America* (Notre Dame, 1986), 28–45; "Introduction," *Messenger of the Sacred Heart* 1 (April 1866): ix.

50. Elizabeth B. Clark, "'The Sacred Rights of the Weak': Pain Sympathy, and the Culture of Individual Rights in Antebellum America," *Journal of American History* 82 (Sept. 1995): 470–73.

51. George B. Cheever, *Wanderings of a Pilgrim in the Shadow of Mont Blanc* (New York, 1846), 131.

52. "The Romish Hierarchy," *North American Review* 82 (Jan. 1856): 114.

53. Ryan K. Smith, "The Cross: Church Symbol and Context in Nineteenth Century America," *Church History* 70 (Dec. 2001): 74; Charles Eliot Norton, *Notes of Travel and Study in Italy* (Boston, 1859), 210–11.

54. Austin Gough, *Paris and Rome: The Gallican Church and the Ultramontane Campaign, 1848–1853* (Oxford, 1986); Thomas Mergel, "Ultramontanism, Liberalism, Moderation: Political Mentalities and Political Behavior of the German Catholic *Bürgertum*, 1848–1914," *Central European History* 29 (1996): 151–74.

55. David A. Gerber, *The Making of an American Pluralism: Buffalo, New York, 1825–60* (Urbana, 1989), 280–96; Patrick W. Carey, *People, Priests, and Prelates: Ecclesiastical Democracy and the Tensions of Trusteeism* (Notre Dame, 1987), 270–78.

56. "The Archdiocese of New York a Century Ago: A Memoir of Archbishop Hughes, 1838–1858," *Historical Records and Studies* 39–40 (1952): 169–70.

57. J. Edgar Bruns, "Antoine Blanc: Louisiana's Joshua in the Land of Promise

He Opened," in *Cross, Crozier, and Crucible: A Volume Celebrating the Bicentennial of a Catholic Diocese in Louisiana*, ed. Glenn R. Conrad (New Orleans, 1993), 120–21; *A Frenchman, a Chaplain, a Rebel: The War Letters of Père Louis-Hippolyte Gache, S.J.*, trans. Cornelius M. Buckley (Chicago, 1981), 19.

58. "The Jesuits as Educators," *Semi-Weekly Creole*, Oct. 18, 1854, n.p.

59. John David Bladek, "America for Americans: The Southern Know Nothing Party and the Politics of Nativism, 1854–1856" (Ph.D. diss., Univ. of Washington, 1998), 82–83; Congressman William R. Smith, in *Congressional Globe*, Jan. 7, 1856, p. 167; Robert Reinders, "The Louisiana American Party and the Catholic Church," *Mid-America* 40 (Oct. 1858): 218–28.

60. "The Louisiana Know-Nothing Platform," *Southern Standard*, July 15, 1855, p. 2; Pastoral Letter of the Archbishop and Bishops at the First Provincial Council of New Orleans, ibid., Feb. 10, 1856, p. 4; Weninger Latin Relationes, 1852, FW.

61. John Peter Marschall, C.S.V., "Francis Patrick Kenrick, 1851–1863: The Baltimore Years" (Ph.D. diss., Catholic Univ. of America, 1965), 106; Donald E. DeVore and Joseph Logsdon, *Crescent City Schools: Public Education in New Orleans, 1841–1991* ([Lafayette, La.] 1991), 365.

62. Thomas Semmes to Orestes Brownson, March 5, 1855, I-3-l.

63. Oscar Handlin, *Boston's Immigrants [1790–1880]* (Cambridge, [1941], 1959), 244.

64. Theodore Parker to Rev. J. T. Sargent, Sept. 18, 1859, in John Weiss, *Life and Correspondence of Theodore Parker*, vol. 2 (New York, 1864), 354.

65. Handlin, *Boston's Immigrants,* 93–94; Wiget to Provincial, March 16, 1859, folder 34, box 76, MP.

66. Richard F. Fuller, *Chaplain Fuller: Being a Life Sketch of a New England Clergyman and Army Chaplain* (Boston, 1864), 138.

67. Wiget to Provincial, Jan. 19, 1858, folder 6, box 76, MP; Wiget to Fr. Burchard Villiger, n.d. [1858?], ibid.; Wiget to Provincial, March 16, 1859, folder 34, box 76, MP.

68. Wiget to Villiger, Feb. 9, 1858, folder 6, box 76, MP.

69. Extract from the Records of the Sodality of the Immaculate Conception, [1858], 76/6, MP; Emmet Larkin, "The Devotional Revolution in Ireland, 1850–75," *American Historical Review* 77 (June 1972): 625–52.

70. M. F. Cooke to Wiget, Feb. 17, 1858, folder 6, box 76, MP.

71. "An Account of a Miraculous Cure Effected at Boston, Mass. by the Use of the 'Water of Lourdes,'" *Woodstock Letters* 1 (1872): 68–70.

72. "Residence of St. Mary's, Boston, Mass. 1868–1876," *Woodstock Letters* 6 (1877): 37–39.

73. William Augustine Leahy, "Archdiocese of Boston," in *History of the Catholic Church in the New England States,* ed. Very Rev. William Byrne et al.,

vol. 1 (Boston, 1899), 127; "Consecration of the Church of the Immaculate Conception, Boston, Mass.," *Woodstock Letters* 6 (1877): 150–51; "Laying of the Cornerstone of St. Joseph's German Catholic Church, Washington," *Catholic Mirror*, Oct. 31, 1868, p. 2.

74. David R. Dunigan, S.J., *A History of Boston College* (Milwaukee, 1947), 9–10.

75. McElroy to Villiger, July 21, 1858, folder 6, box 76, MP.

76. Wiget to Villiger, Jan. 19, 1858, folder 6, box 76, MP; Wiget to Villiger, Jan. 8, 1858, ibid.

77. John Stuart Mill, *Collected Works of John Stuart Mill*, vol. 1, *Autobiography and Other Literary Essays*, ed. John M. Robson and Jack Stilinger (Toronto, 1981), 45.

78. John Adams to Thomas Jefferson, May 19, 1821, in *The Adams-Jefferson Letters: The Complete Correspondence between Thomas Jefferson and Abigail and John Adams* vol. 2, *1812–1826*, ed. Lester J. Cappon (Chapel Hill, 1959), 573.

79. David Brion Davis, *Slavery and Human Progress* (New York, 1984), 143; Theodore Parker, "A Sermon of the Dangers Which Threaten the Rights of Man in America" (July 2, 1854), in Parker, *Additional Speeches, Addresses, and Occasional Sermons*, vol. 2 (Boston, 1855), 293.

80. "The Romish Hierarchy," *North American Review* 82 (Jan. 1856): 121.

81. Max Lilienthal, "Letter on Reform Addressed to the Rev. I. Leeser" (Nov. 24, 1856), in David Philipson, *Max Lilienthal, American Rabbi: Life and Writings* (New York, 1915), 372; Max Lilienthal, "The Spirit of the Age" (Dec. 4, 1856), ibid., 376.

82. Edwards Amasa Park, *Intellectual and Moral Influence of Romanism* (Boston, 1845), 465.

83. Cheever, *Wanderings of a Pilgrim*, 19; James W. Patton, "Facets of the South in the 1850s," *Journal of Southern History* 23 (Feb. 1957): 17.

84. Thomas King, *The Railroad Jubilee: Two Discourses Delivered in Hollis Street Meeting House, Sunday, Sept. 21, 1851* (Boston, 1851), 32.

85. Philip Benedict, "Between Whig Traditions and New Histories: American Historical Writing about Reformation and Early Modern Europe," in *Imagined Histories: American Historians Interpret the Past*, ed. Anthony Molho and Gordon S. Wood. (Princeton, 1998), 297; Richard Kagan, "Prescott's Paradigm: American Historical Scholarship and the Decline of Spain," ibid., 328–29; Henry Kamen, *The Spanish Inquisition: An Historical Revision* (New Haven, 1997), 305–20. For a Catholic response, see M. J. Spalding, *Miscellanea: Comprising Reviews, Lectures and Essays, on Historical, Theological and Miscellaneous Subjects* (Louisville, 1855), 213–33, 250–97.

86. Parker, "Sermon of the Dangers."

87. John Hughes, "The Church and the World" (1850), in *Complete Works of the Most Rev. John Hughes, D.D., Archbishop of New York: Comprising His Sermons, Letters, Lectures, Speeches, etc.*, ed. Laurence Kehoe, vol. 2 (New York, 1864), 73.

88. Rev. J. Balmes, *Protestantism and Catholicity Compared in Their Effects on the Civilization of Europe* (Baltimore, [1842], 1851). On his influence, see Edgar Hocedez, S.J., "Centenaire de la mort de Balmes," *Gregorianium* 29 (1948): 179–203. On the Catholic narrative, see Robert E. Sullivan, "Modernizing Tradition: Some Catholic Neo-Scholastics and the Genealogy of Natural Rights," in *Religion and the Authority of the Past*, ed. Tobin Siebers (Ann Arbor, 1993), 184–208.

89. Brownson to Father Jeremiah Cummings, Oct. 30, 1849, I-3-i; Bishop James A. McFaul, "Some Modern Problems" (1908)," in *Pastoral Letters, Addresses, and Other Writings*, ed. Rev. James J. Powers (New York, 1916), 265; "Memoir of the Rev. James Balmes," *Metropolitan* 5 (May 1857): 201–8.

90. Balmes, *Protestantism and Catholicity Compared*, iv.

91. Ibid., 27, 419.

92. Spalding, *Miscellanea*, xli, 455, 472–74.

93. Quentin Skinner, *Liberty before Liberalism* (Cambridge, Eng., 1998), 59–101.

94. Address of the Militia to King William III and Queen Mary, June 1689, in *The Glorious Revolution in America: Documents on the Colonial Crisis of 1689*, ed. Michael G. Hall, Lawrence H. Leder, and Michael G. Kammen (Chapel Hill, 1964), 109.

95. "The Leaders of Parties, Their Usual Views" (Feb. 11, 1720), in John Trenchard and Thomas Gordon, *Cato's Letters; or, Essays on Liberty, Civil and Religious, and Other Important Subjects*, ed. Ronald Hamowy, vol. 1 (Indianapolis, 1995), 119. On Trenchard and Gordon's influence, see Bernard Bailyn, *The Ideological Origins of the American Revolution* (Cambridge, 1967), 35–36.

96. Ralph Waldo Emerson to Thomas Carlyle, Sept. 26, 1864, in *The Correspondence of Thomas Carlyle and Ralph Waldo Emerson, 1834–1872*, vol. 2 Boston, 1883), 286.

97. John Hughes, "The Church and the World," 73; Balmes, *Protestantism and Catholicity Compared*, 118.

98. "Hungary," *New York Freeman's Journal*, Sept. 1, 1849, p. 4.

99. Thomas Mulledy, S.J., "On Liberty," July 4, 1852, folder 1, box 4, TM.

100. John Cyrus Rao, "La *Civiltà Cattolica* as a Background for Understanding *Quanta Cura* and the Syllabus of Errors (1850–1865)" (Ph.D. diss., Oxford Univ., 1977), 106.

101. Cummings, "Lecture on the Nature of Law," p. 1.

102. Spalding, *Miscellanea*, 390.

103. *Libertas* (1888), in *The Papal Encyclicals, 1878–1903*, ed. Claudia Carlen, I.H.M. (Raleigh, N.C., 1981), 172.

104. Davis, *Slavery and Human Progress*, 107–15.

105. John McManners, *Church and State in France, 1870–1914* (New York, 1972), 45–54; Peter F. Anson, *Underground Catholicism in Scotland, 1622–1878* (Montrose, 1970), 234; Sr. Dominis Savio Hamer, C.P., "A Phase of the Struggle for Catholic Education: Manchester and Salford in the Mid-Nineteenth Century," *Recusant History* 23 (May 1996): 115.

106. "Education," *New York Freeman's Journal*, March 30, 1850, p. 4.

107. James J. Sheehan, *German Liberalism in the Nineteenth Century* (Chicago, 1978), 68; C. T. McIntire, "Changing Religious Establishments and Religious Liberty in France, Part 1: 1787–1879," in *Freedom and Religion*, ed. Helmstadter, 270.

108. Carl F. Kaestle, *Pillars of the Republic: Common Schools and American Society, 1780–1860* (New York, 1983), 75–103.

109. Theodore Parker, "Education of the People" (1848), in *The Collected Works of Theodore Parker*, ed. Frances Power Cobbe, vol. 9 (London, 1864), 266, 269.

110. Horace Mann, *Slavery: Letters and Speeches* (Boston, 1853), 46.

111. Timothy L. Smith, "Protestant Schooling and American Nationality, 1800–1850," *American Historical Review* 71 (July 1966): 1265–79; R. Laurence Moore, "Bible Reading and Nonsectarian Schooling: The Failure of Religious Instruction in Nineteenth-Century Public Education," *Journal of American History* 86 (March 2000): 1581–99.

112. Calvin Stowe, *The Religious Element in Education: An Address Delivered before the American Institute of Instruction at Portland, Me., August 30, 1844* (Boston, 1844), 21.

113. Horace Mann, "Introduction to Third Volume of the *Common School Journal*," in *Life and Works of Horace Mann*, ed. Mary Mann, vol. 5 (Boston, 1891), 12, 18.

114. Parker, "Sermon of the Dangers," 242–43.

115. Ruth M. Elson, *Guardians of Tradition: American Schoolbooks of the Nineteenth Century* (Lincoln, Neb. 1964), 47–58; Joseph Robert Moreau, "Schoolbook Nation: Imagining the American Community in United States History Texts for Grammar and Secondary Schools, 1865–1930" (Ph.D. diss., Univ. of Michigan, 1999), 116.

116. N. J. Perché, "De l'éducation," *Propagateur Catholique*, April 3, 1858, p. 81.

117. Rev. John E. Rothensteiner, *History of the Archdiocese of St. Louis in Its Various Stages of Development from A.D. 1637 to A.D. 1928*, vol. 2 (St. Louis, 1928), 186.

118. Lloyd P. Jorgenson, *The State and the Non-Public School, 1825–1925* (Columbia, Mo., 1987), 69–110.

119. *The National Pastorals of the American Hierarchy, 1792–1919* (Westminster, Md., [1923], 1954), 124–25, 190–91; Bernard Julius Meiring, "Educational Aspects of the Legislation of the Councils of Baltimore, 1829–1884," (Ph.D. diss., Univ. of California, Berkeley, 1963), 143.

120. "The Annual Meeting," *American and Foreign Christian Union* 4 (June 1853): 246; *New York Freeman's Journal*, Aug. 21, 1852, p. 6.

121. *Controversy between Dr. Ryerson, Chief Superintendent of Education in Upper Canada, and Rev. J. M. Bruyere, Rector of St. Michael's Cathedral, Toronto, on the Appropriation of the Clergy Reserves Funds; Free Schools vs. State Schools; Public Libraries and Common Schools, Attacked and Defended* (Toronto, 1857), 29–30.

122. "The Germans and Their Churches," *Independent*, Feb. 9, 1854, p. 8.

123. James N. Sykes, *Common v. Catholic Schools: A Discourse before the Congregational, Methodist and Baptist Congregations, Delivered Thanksgiving Day, Nov. 24, 1853 at the Meridian Street Church* (Boston, 1853), 25.

124. Wiget to Provincial, March 16, 1859, folder 34, box 76, MP.

125. Thomas H. O'Connor, *Fitzpatrick's Boston, 1846–1866: John Bernard Fitzpatrick, Third Bishop of Boston* (Boston, 1984), 60–63, 115–17.

126. C. A. Bartol, *Religion in Our Public Schools: A Discourse Preached in the West Church, Boston* (Boston, 1859), 5.

127. John McElroy to Provincial, March 23, 1859, folder 34, box 76, MP; Wiget to Provincial, March 16, 1859, ibid.; Fitzpatrick letter reprinted in Robert H. Lord, John E. Sexton, and Edward T. Harrington, *History of the Archdiocese of Boston in the Various Stages of Its Development, 1604 to 1943*, vol. 2 (Cambridge, 1944), 596–99.

128. Wiget to Provincial, March 28, 1859, folder 34, box 76, MP.

129. "The Bible in the Schools," *Boston Pilot*, March 31, 1860, p. 4.

130. Margaret Mary duFief, "A History of St. Aloysius' Parish, Washington, D.C.: 1859–1909" (Ph.D. diss., Georgetown Univ., 1961), 94.

131. "To the Friends of Young Catholics," Aug. 6, 1860, folder 30, box 76, MP.

132. Wiget to Provincial, April 7, 1860, folder 30, box 76, MP.

CHAPTER 2: CATHOLICISM, SLAVERY, AND THE CAUSE OF LIBERTY

1. *The Journals and Miscellaneous Notebooks of Ralph Waldo Emerson*, vol. 8, *1841–1843*, ed. William H. Gilman and J. E. Parsons (Cambridge, 1970), 305. On Brownson, see Arthur M. Schlesinger Jr., *Orestes Brownson: A Pilgrim's*

Progress (Boston, 1939), and Thomas R. Ryan, *Orestes A. Brownson: A Definitive Biography* (Huntington, Ind., 1976). Patrick W. Carey's careful investigation of Brownson's career is now the best starting point. For a comprehensive overview, see *Orestes A. Brownson: A Bibliography, 1826–1876*, compiled and annotated by Patrick W. Carey (Milwaukee, 1996).

2. Theodore Parker to Caroline Healey, April 4, 1843, in John Weiss, *Life and Correspondence of Theodore Parker, Minister of the Twenty-eighth Congregational Society, Boston,* vol. 1 (New York, 1864), 353.

3. Orestes Brownson, "The Licentiousness of the Press," *Brownson's Quarterly Review* (Oct. 1849), reprinted in *The Works of Orestes Brownson*, ed. Henry F. Brownson, 20 vols. (Detroit, 1882–87), 2:138–39.

4. [Brownson], "The Two Worlds, Catholic and Gentile," *Brownson's Quarterly Review* 9 (April 1852): 187–88.

5. Bernard Aspinwall, "Orestes A. Brownson et l'Europe," in *Les Catholiques liberaux au XIXe siècle* (Grenoble, 1974), 147–76. See also C. F. Audley, "Un Catholique du Nouveau Monde," *Le Correspondant* 66 (1865): 165.

6. Lord Acton to Ignaz von Döllinger, June 8, 1862, in *Ignaz von Döllinger Briefwechsel, 1820–1890*, ed. Victor Conzemius, vol. 1 (Munich, 1963), 269; C. F. Audley to Brownson, May 10, 1965, I-4-c.

7. Orestes Brownson, "Know Nothingism; or, Satan Warring against Christ," *Brownson's Quarterly Review* 11 (Oct. 1854): 473.

8. Brownson to Rev. Isaac Hecker, June 1, 1855, in *The Brownson-Hecker Correspondence*, ed. Joseph F. Gower and Richard M. Leliaert (Notre Dame, 1979), 182.

9. Orestes Brownson, "Schools and Education," *Brownson's Quarterly Review* 16 (July 1854): 363–64.

10. Orestes Brownson, "Public and Parochial Schools," *Brownson's Quarterly Review* 21 (July 1859): 351.

11. "Mr. Brownson on Nativism," *New York Freeman's Journal*, July 2, 1854, p. 4; "Letter from Mr. Brownson," *Catholic Mirror*, July 22, 1854, p. 5; "Mr. Brownson," *Pittsburgh Catholic*, Aug. 12, 1854, p. 1623; *New York Freeman's Journal,* Aug. 5, 1854, p. 1.

12. Brownson to Editor of the *Pittsburgh Catholic*, Aug. 1, 1854, I-3-l; also *Pittsburgh Catholic*, Aug. 12, 1854, p. 162.

13. Brownson to Rev. Isaac Hecker, Aug. 29, 1855, in *Brownson-Hecker Correspondence*, 186.

14. Brownson to Montalembert, Dec. 25, 1855, I-3-l.

15. Rev. John Talbot Smith, *The Catholic Church in New York: A History of the New York Diocese from Its Establishment in 1808 to the Present Time*, vol. 1 (New York, 1905), 187; [Fr. Jeremiah Cummings], "Seminaries and Seminarians," *Brownson's Quarterly Review* 23 (Jan. 1861): 115–17.

16. David J. O'Brien, *Isaac Hecker: An American Catholic* (New York, 1992).

17. Josef L. Altholz and Victor Conzemius, "Acton and Brownson: A Letter from America," *Catholic Historical Review* 49 (Jan. 1964): 525–28; Roland Hill, *Lord Acton* (New Haven, 2000), 66.

18. Acton to Brownson, March 7, 1860, I-3-o; Brownson to Acton, March 28, 1860 (incomplete) I-3-o.

19. John Henry Newman to Orestes Brownson, Dec. 15, 1853, in *The Letters and Diaries of John Henry Newman*, vol. 15 (London, 1964), 504–5.

20. "The Rambler," *Brownson's Quarterly Review* 13 (July 1856): 400–402.

21. Brownson, "Know Nothingism," 448, 450.

22. Montalembert to Brownson, March 31, 1850, I-3-j.

23. Montalembert to Brownson, Dec. 28, 1854, I-3-l.

24. Montalembert to Brownson, Nov. 1, 1855, I-3-l.

25. Brownson to Montalembert, Dec. 25, 1855, I-3-l; "Le Correspondant," *Brownson's Quarterly Review* 18 (Jan. 1856): 121–34.

26. Brownson, "Know Nothingism," 484.

27. Montalembert to Brownson, Nov. 1, 1855, I-3-l.

28. Brownson to Montalembert, Dec. 27, 1858, I-4-h. For the battle within the French church over miracles, see Jean-Marie Mayeur, "Mgr Dupanloup et Louis Veuillot devant les 'prophéties contemporaines' en 1874," *Revue d'Histoire de la Spiritualité* 48 (1972): 193–204.

29. "Sympathy with Pope Pius IX," *New York Freeman's Journal*, June 2, 1860, p. 4; "Rights of the Temporal," *Brownson's Quarterly Review* 22 (Oct. 1860): 462–496.

30. A. Hechinger to Henry Brownson, Dec. 22, 1890, III-3-d-4.

31. Ryan, *Orestes A. Brownson*, 606; Hughes to Cardinal Barnabo, Sept. 30, 1861, reprinted in Thomas T. McAvoy, "Orestes A. Brownson and Archbishop John Hughes in 1860," *Review of Politics* 24 (Jan. 1962): 44–46.

32. "Loyal National Repeal Association," *New York Freeman's Journal*, Sept. 20, 1845, p. 91.

33. "The Know-Nothing Platform," *Brownson's Quarterly Review* 17 (Oct. 1855): 480.

34. Orestes Brownson, "The Presidential Election," *Brownson's Quarterly Review* 18 (Oct. 1856): 512–13; idem, "The Incoming Administration—Slavery, the Slave Trade, and Central America," ibid. 19 (Jan. 1857): 101.

35. Orestes Brownson, "The Slavery Question Once More," *Brownson's Quarterly Review* 19 (April 1857): 272–77.

36 "Dr. Brownson and the Supreme Court of the United States," *Metropolitan* 5 (May 1857): 212–13.

37. Brownson to Montalembert, May 24, 1857, I-4-h.

38. John Francis Maxwell, *Slavery and the Catholic Church: The History of*

Catholic Teaching concerning the Moral Legitimacy of the Institution of Slavery (Chichester, 1975). For the United States the basic source remains Madeleine Hooke Rice, *American Catholic Opinion in the Slavery Controversy* (New York, 1944). Especially thoughtful and persuasive, however, is Thomas Murphy, S.J., *Jesuit Slaveholding in Maryland, 1717–1838* (New York, 2001). For a survey focusing on France, see Claude Prudhomme, "L'Eglise catholique et l'esclavage: Une aussi longue attente," in *L'Eglise et l'abolition de l'esclavage*, ed. Guy Bedouelle, O.P., et al. (Paris, 1999), 9–20. A brief, but astute, treatment that recognizes the high theological stakes is John T. Noonan Jr., "Development in Moral Doctrine," in *The Context of Casuistry*, ed. James F. Keenan, S.J., and Thomas A. Shannon (Washington, D.C., 1995), 189–98. For a more extended examination, see Joseph Edward Capizzi, "A Development of Doctrine: The Challenge of Slavery to Moral Theology" (Ph.D. diss., Univ. of Notre Dame, 1998).

39. John Carroll to John Thayer, July 15, 1794, in *The John Carroll Papers*, vol. 2, *1792–1806*, ed. Thomas O'Brien Hanley, S.J., (Notre Dame, 1976), 122–23. On John Carroll and slavery, see *John Carroll Recovered: Abstracts of Letters and Other Documents Not Found in the John Carroll Papers*, ed. Thomas W. Spalding (Baltimore, 2000), 215–20. Also see Robert Emmett Curran, "Rome, the American Church and Slavery," in *Building the Church in America: Studies in Honor of Monsignor Robert F. Trisco on the Occasion of His Seventieth Birthday*, ed. Joseph C. Linck, C.O., and Raymond Kupke (Washington, D.C, 1999), 35–36.

40. Maxwell, *Slavery and the Catholic Church*, 101–10; Murphy, *Jesuit Slaveholding in Maryland*, 187–214.

41. "Colour in the Catholic Church," *National Anti-Slavery Standard*, July 1, 1847, p. 17; James McCune Smith to Horace Greeley, Jan. 29, 1844, in *The Black Abolitionist Papers, vol. 3, The United States, 1830–1846*, ed. C. Peter Ripley (Chapel Hill, 1991), 435.

42. Herbert S. Klein, *African Slavery in Latin America and the Caribbean* (New York, 1986), 250–52; Charles de Montalembert to Fr. Jean Baptiste Henri Lacordaire, O.P., Sept. 20, 1839, in *Lacordaire-Montalembert correspondance inédite, 1830–1861*, ed. Louis Le Guillou (Paris, 1989), 449; Charles de Montalembert, "Emancipation des esclaves" (April 7, 1845) and "Emancipation des noirs dans les colonies" (March 30, 1847), in *Oeuvres de M. le comte de Montalembert*, vol. 2 (Paris, 1860), 59–62, 461–72; Lawrence C. Jennings, *French Anti-Slavery: The Movement for the Abolition of Slavery in France, 1802–1848* (New York, 2000), 213–46.

43. Daniel O'Connell, "Daniel O'Connell and the Committee of the Irish Repeal Association of Cincinnati" (1843) in *Union Pamphlets of the Civil War, 1861–1865*, ed. Frank Freidel, 2 vols. (Cambridge, 1967), 2:802–3. On this episode, see Gilbert Osofsky, "Abolitionists, Irish Immigrants and the Dilemmas

of Romantic Nationalism," *American Historical Review* 80 (Oct. 1975): 889–912.

44. "Grand Meeting in Faneuil Hall," *Liberator*, Nov. 24, 1843, p. 187; *George Pilkington's Reply to a Priest in Brazil Who, by Letter, Kindly Expressed His Desire That He Should Adopt Roman Catholic Views of Religious Truth* (Rio de Janeiro, 1841), 4.

45. Jane Grey Swisshelm, *Half a Century* (Chicago, [1880], 1970), 150.

46. "The Abolitionist," *New York Freeman's Journal*, March 5, 1842, p. 284. For abolitionist reaction, see James Gillespie Birney to the editor of the *Free Press*, April 29, 1842, in *Letters of James Gillespie Birney, 1831–1857*, ed. Dwight L. Dumond, vol. 2 (New York, 1938), 681–84.

47. Thomas Paul Thigpen, "Aristocracy of the Heart: Catholic Lay Leadership in Savannah, 1820–1870" (Ph.D. diss., Emory Univ., 1995), 591.

48. The most influential formulation is David R. Roediger, *The Wages of Whiteness: Race and the Making of the American Working Class* (London, 1991), 133–86, quotation on 140.

49. John Hughes, "Sermon on the Occasion of His Return from Cuba" (1854), in *Complete Works of the Most Rev. John Hughes, D.D., Archbishop of New York: Comprising His Sermons, Letters, Speeches, etc.*, ed. Laurence Kehoe, 2 vols. (New York, 1864), 2:222; "The Nigger," *New York Freeman's Journal*, April 30, 1864, p. 1.

50. John R. McKivigan, *The War against Proslavery Religion: Abolitionism and the Northern Churches, 1830–1865* (Ithaca, 1984), 38; John W. Quist, "'The Great Majority of Our Subscribers Are Farmers': The Michigan Abolitionist Constituency of the 1840s," *Journal of the Early Republic* 14 (Fall 1994): 357.

51. Jennings, *French Anti-Slavery*, 129; Victor Schoelcher, *Histoire de l'esclavage pendant les deux dernières années*, vol. 2 (Paris, [1847], 1984), 215–301; See Philippe Delisle, *Renouveau missionaire et société esclavagiste: Le Martinique, 1815–1848* (Paris, 1997), 99–101; Armando Lampe, *Mission or Submission?: Moravian and Catholic Missionaries in the Dutch Caribbean during the 19th Century* (Göttingen, 2001), 160–64; Arthur F. Corwin, *Spain and the Abolition of Slavery in Cuba, 1817–1886* (Austin, Tex., 1967), 166–68; Joaquim Nabuco, *Abolitionism: The Brazilian Antislavery Struggle*, trans. and ed. Robert Conrad (Urbana, 1977), 19.

52. Abbé Henri Grégoire to John Carroll, Feb. 6, 1815, in Jacques M. Gres-Gayer, "Four Letters from Henri Grégoire to John Carroll, 1809–1814," in *Catholic Historical Review* 79 (Oct. 1993): 703.

53. Claude Prudhomme, "La Papauté face à l'esclavage: Quelle condamnation?" *Mémoire Spiritaine* 9 (1999): 135–60; François Renault, "Aux origines de la lettre apostolique de Grégoire XVI *In Supremo* (1839)," ibid. 2 (1995): 143–49.

54. "The Catholic Church and the Question of Slavery," *Metropolitan* 3 (June 1855): 268.

55. Rev. J. Balmes, *Protestantism and Catholicity Compared in Their Effects on the Civilization of Europe* (Baltimore, 1851), 90–115.

56. Murphy, *Jesuit Slaveholding in Maryland*, 136.

57. Luigi Taparelli d'Azeglio, *Saggio teoretica di dritto naturale: Appogiato sul fatto*, vol. 1 (Rome, [1855], 1949), 360–62.

58. Rev. Joseph D. Brokhage, *Francis Patrick Kenrick's Opinion on Slavery* (Washington, D.C., 1955), 123.

59. Francis Patrick Kenrick, *The Acts of the Apostles, the Epistles of St. Paul, the Catholic Epistles, and the Apocalypse* (New York, 1851), 497. Also see idem to George Bernard Allen, Dec. 5, 1862, in *Records of the American Catholic Historical Society of Philadelphia* 32 (Dec. 1921): 265–66.

60. "The Archbishop's Sermon," *New York Freeman's Journal*, May 26, 1854, p. 1.

61. "Free Soilism," reprinted in *Pittsburgh Catholic*, June 21, 1851, p. 113.

62. Joseph Lee, "The Social and Economic Ideas of O'Connell," in *Daniel O'Connell: Portrait of a Radical*, ed. Kevin B. Nowlan and Maurice R. O'Connell (New York, 1985), 75–78.

63. Orestes A. Brownson, *The Laboring Classes (1840) with Brownson's Defence of the Article on the Laboring Classes* (New York, 1978), 14.

64. Ibid., 10.

65. John Hughes, "A Lecture on the Importance of a Christian Basis for the Science of Political Economy, and Its Application to the Affairs of Life" (1844), in *Complete Works of the Most Rev. John Hughes*, 1:521.

66. "Manuscript Notes by Archbishop John Hughes on the Subject of Slavery" (1861), in *American Catholics and Slavery, 1789–1866: An Anthology of Primary Documents*, ed. Kenneth J. Zanca (Lanham, Md., 1994), 215.

67. James Healy, S.J., *The Just Wage, 1750–1890: A Study of Moralists from Saint Alphonsus to Leo XIII* (The Hague, 1966), 337–38.

68. Elizabeth B. Clark, "'The Sacred Rights of the Weak': Pain Sympathy, and the Culture of Individual Rights in Antebellum America," *Journal of American History* 82 (Sept. 1995): 463–93.

69. Rev. Dr. Cummings, "Slavery and the Union," *New York Freeman's Journal*, May 25, 1850, pp. 1–2.

70. Robert Emmett Curran, S.J., *The Bicentennial History of Georgetown University: From Academy to University, 1789–1989*, vol. 1 (Washington, D.C., 1993), 363.

71. Rev. John McMullen, "Bishop England on Domestic Slavery" (1865?), in Rev. James J. McGovern, *The Life and Writings of the Right Reverend John McMullen, D.D., First Bishop of Davenport, Iowa* (Chicago, 1888), xcv.

72. Maria Genoino Caravaglios, *The American Catholic Church and the Negro Problem in the XVIII–XIX Centuries*, ed. Ernest L. Unterkoefler (Charleston, S.C., 1974), 183–200.

73. Bishop William Elder to Archbishop Jean-Marie Odin, March 24, 1862, VI-2-f-4. On polygenesis, see George M. Frederickson, *The Black Image in the White Mind: The Debate on Afro-American Character and Destiny, 1817–1914* (Middletown, Conn., [1971], 1987), 71–96; Caravaglios, *American Catholic Church*, 202–3.

74. Rev. A. Verot, "Slavery and Abolitionism: Being the Substance of a Sermon Preached in the Church of St. Augustine, Florida, on the 4th Day of January, 1861," *New York Freeman's Journal*, June 18, 1864, p. 1. The second part of the sermon was published ibid., July 9, 1864, pp. 1–2. Michael V. Gannon, *Rebel Bishop: The Life and Era of Augustin Verot* (Milwaukee, 1964), 37.

75. "De la source légitime de l'esclavage," *Propagateur Catholique*, Jan. 18, 1862, p. 1, and Feb. 1, 1862, p. 1.

76. James J. Fox, "Slavery, Ethical Aspect Of," *The Catholic Encyclopedia*, vol. 14 (New York, 1912), 40; Maxwell, *Slavery and the Catholic Church*, 87–88.

77. O'Connell, "Daniel O'Connell and the Committee," 809.

78. William Lloyd Garrison to Daniel O'Connell, Dec. 8, 1843, in *The Letters of William Lloyd Garrison*, vol. 3 *No Union with Slaveholders* 1841–1849, ed. Walter M. Merrill (Cambridge, 1973), 229–30; Lewis Perry, *Radical Abolitionism: Anarchy and the Government of God in Antislavery Thought* (Knoxville, [1973], 1995), 18–54.

79. Garrison to Oliver Johnson, April 9, 1873, in *The Letters of William Lloyd Garrison*, vol. 6, *To Rouse the Slumbering Land*, 1868–1879, ed. Walter M. Merrill and Louis Ruchames (Cambridge, 1981), 273–74.

80. *Eleventh Annual Meeting of the Massachusetts Anti-Slavery Society* (Boston, 1843), 95.

81. Peter Walker, *Moral Choices: Memory, Desire, and Imagination in Nineteenth-Century American Abolition* (Baton Rouge, 1978), 161–66.

82. Shaftesbury, quoted in Michael P. Zuckert, *Natural Rights and the New Republicanism* (Princeton, 1994), 103.

83. [George Bourne], *Picture of Slavery in the United States of America* (Boston, 1838), 151.

84. Jenny Franchot, *Roads to Rome: The Antebellum Protestant Encounter with Catholicism* (Berkeley, 1994), 104–6.

85. *The Life and Writings of Rev. Joseph Gordon*, written and compiled by a Committee of the Free Presbyterian Synod (Cincinnati, 1860), 302.

86. "Elijah P. Lovejoy as an Anti-Catholic," *Records of the American Catholic Historical Society* 62 (Sept. 1951): 172–80.

87. John W. Christie and Dwight L. Dumond, *George Bourne and the Book and Slavery Irreconcilable* (Wilmington, Del., 1969), 83–86, 99–101.

88. Angelina Emily Grimké, "Appeal to the Christian Women of the South" (1836), in *The Public Years of Sarah and Angelina Grimké: Selected Writings, 1835–1839,* ed. Larry Ceplair (New York, 1989), 56.

89. David M. Potter, *The Impending Crisis, 1848–1861*, ed. Don E. Fehrenbacher (New York, 1976), 1–89.

90. Lyman Beecher, *A Plea for the West* (Cincinnati, 1835); Harriet Beecher Stowe, "The Fete of St. Joseph in Rome," *National Anti-Slavery Standard* 20 (April 28, 1860): n.p.; Franchot, *Roads to Rome*, 103. Franchot (pp. 246–55) identifies an undercurrent of attraction to Catholicism in Stowe's later work.

91. Edward Beecher, *The Papal Conspiracy Exposed, and Protestantism Defended in the Light of Reason, History, and Scripture* (New York, [1855], 1977); Robert Merideth, *The Politics of the Universe: Edward Beecher, Abolition, and Orthodoxy* (Nashville, 1968), 120–24.

92. Frederick Douglass, "Pictures and Progress: An Address Delivered in Boston, Massachusetts, on 3 December 1861," in *The Frederick Douglass Papers*, ser. 1, *Speeches, Debates, and Interviews, vol. 3, 1855–1863*, ed. John W. Blassingame and John R. Mckivigan (New Haven, 1985), 461–62. Also see Richard Hardack, "The Slavery of Romanism: The Casting Out of the Irish in the Work of Frederick Douglass," in *Liberating Sojourn: Frederick Douglass & Transatlantic Reform*, ed. Alan J. Rice and Martin Crawford (Athens, Ga., 1999), 115–40.

93. Leo P. Hirrel, *Children of Wrath: New School Calvinism and Antebellum Reform* (Lexington, Ky., 1998), 93–116, 134–54.

94. Joseph P. Thompson, *The College as a Religious Institution: An Address Delivered in Boston, May, 1859, in Behalf of the Society for the Promotion of Collegiate and Theological Education at the West* (New York, 1859), 32.

95. George B. Cheever, *Wanderings of a Pilgrim in the Shadow of Mont Blanc* (New York, 1846), 15.

96. George B. Cheever, *The Right of the Bible in Our Public Schools* (New York, 1854); [Cheever], "The New York Tribune and the Bible in Schools," *Independent*, March 19, 1854, p. 3; Robert M. York, *George B. Cheever: Religious and Social Reformer, 1807–1890* (Orono, 1955), 148; George B. Cheever, *God against Slavery, and the Freedom and Duty of the Pulpit to Rebuke It, as a Sin against God* (New York, 1857), 179–80.

97. Rev. Hugh McNeile, *Anti-Slavery and Anti-Popery: A Letter Addressed to Edward Cropper, Esquire, and Thomas Berry Horsfall, Esquire* (London: 1838), 4.

98. Richard D. Webb, "Letter from Our Dublin Correspondent," *National Anti-Slavery Standard* (Jan. 22, 1859), n.p.

99. Matías Romero, *The Situation of Mexico: Speech Delivered by Señor Matias Romero, Envoy Extraordinary and Minister Plenipotentiary of the Republic of Mexico to the United States, at a Dinner in the City of New York, on the 16th of December, 1863* (New York, 1864), 11.

100. J. M. S. Careless, *Brown of the Globe*, vol. 1, *The Voice of Upper Canada, 1818–1859* (Toronto, 1959), 102–3; *Toronto Globe* quoted in *Provincial Freeman*, Oct. 13, 1855, n.p.

101. "Free Soilism," *Pittsburg Catholic*, June 21, 1851, p. 113.

102. Dr. Cummings, "Slavery and the Union," *New York Freeman's Journal*, May 25, 1850, p. 1.

103. "Free-Soilism," *Pittsburg Catholic*, June 7, 1851, pp. 97–98; *Annual Statement of the Massachusetts Anti-Slavery Society, at the Twenty-third Annual Meeting, January 1855* (Boston, 1855), 41.

104. Albert J. Von Frank, *The Trials of Anthony Burns: Freedom and Slavery in Emerson's Boston* (Cambridge, 1998), quotation in illustration after 160.

105. Ibid., 249.

106. "Gabriel's Wing Clipped," *New York Freeman's Journal*, Sept. 9, 1854, p. 3; "The 'Angel Gabriel,' " ibid., March 24, 1855, p. 2; James E. Handley, *The Navvy in Scotland* (Cork, 1970), 269–70.

107. Ray Allen Billington, *The Protestant Crusade, 1800–1860: A Study of the Origins of American Nativism* (New York, 1938), 306; "About the Angel Gabriel's Preaching," *New York Freeman's Journal*, Aug. 12, 1854, p. 3.

108. "Dastardly Outrage in Ellsworth Me.," *Liberator*, Oct. 27, 1854, p. 171.

109. John Bapst to Bishop John Fitzpatrick, Oct. 20, 1854, folder 1.5, box 1, JF; James H. Mundy, *Hard Times, Hard Men: Maine and the Irish, 1830–1860* (Scarborough, Maine, 1990), 162.

110. Thomas Mulledy, S.J., "Duty of Citizens to Their Government," May 30, 1854, folder 5, box 7, TM.

111. "Some Considerations for Protestants," *New York Freeman's Journal*, April 29, 1854, p. 4.

112. "The Catholic Celebration of the Fourth of July, 1854 in Monroe, Michigan," *New York Freeman's Journal*, July 2, 1854, p. 1; Thomas Semmes, *Harmony between the Spiritual and the Civil Obligations of Catholics: A Lecture Delivered before the Catholic Institute of New Orleans, February 25, 1855* (New Orleans, 1855), 18.

113. Paul Bourke and Donald DeBats, *Washington County: Politics and Community in Antebellum America* (Baltimore, 1995), 149–67.

114. For the best overview, see William E. Gienapp, *The Origins of the Republican Party, 1852–1856* (New York, 1987), 61–237. Also see Tyler Anbinder, *Nativism and Slavery: The Northern Know Nothings and the Politics of the 1850s* (New York, 1992); Michael F. Holt, *The Rise and Fall of the American*

Whig Party: Jacksonian Politics and the Onset of the Civil War (New York, 1999); Richard J. Carwardine, *Evangelicals and Politics in Antebellum America* (New Haven, 1993).

115. David Wilmot, Answers to Campaign Questions, July 10, 1857, in Charles Buxton Going, *David Wilmot, Free-Soiler* (New York, 1924), 736.

116. Speech of Hon. Bayard Clarke, of N.Y., July 24, 1856, Appendix to *Congressional Globe*, [1856], 957.

117. Billington, *Protestant Crusade*, 425.

118. Ronald P. Formisano, *The Birth of Mass Political Parties, Michigan, 1827–1861* (Princeton, 1971), 256–57; John R. Mulkern, *The Know-Nothing Party in Massachusetts: The Rise and Fall of a People's Movement* (Boston, 1990), 105–8, 111.

119. *Oration of Hon. Anson Burlingame, Delivered at Salem, July 4, 1854* (Salem, Mass., 1854), 21.

120. Eden B. Foster, *The Rights of the Pulpit, and the Perils of Freedom: Two Discourses Preached in Lowell, Sunday, June 25th 1854* (Lowell, Mass., 1854), 69.

121. Theodore Parker, "A Sermon of the Dangers Which Threaten the Rights of Man in America" (July 2, 1854), in Parker, *Additional Speeches, Addresses, and Occasional Sermons*, vol. 2 (Boston, 1855), 244; Dean Grodzins, "A Transcendentalist's Know Nothingism: The Anti-Catholic Thought of Theodore Parker" (paper in author's possession), 6.

122. Important summaries include Ronald P. Formisano, "The Invention of the Ethnocultural Interpretation," *American Historical Review* 99 (April 1994): 453–77; Robert P. Swierenga, "Ethnoreligious Political Behavior in the Mid-Nineteenth Century: Voting, Values, Cultures," in *Religion and American Politics: From the Colonial Period to the 1980s*, ed. Mark A. Noll (New York, 1990), 146–71.

123. Editorial, *Chicago Tribune*, Nov. 2, 1858, p. 2; "The Jews and the Democracy," ibid., Dec. 6, 1858, p. 2; Formisano, *Birth of Mass Political Parties*, 305.

124. Walter D. Kamphoefner, "German-Americans and Civil War Politics: A Reconsideration of the Ethnocultural Thesis," *Civil War History* 37 (Sept. 1991): 232–46; Paul J. Kleppner, "Lincoln and the Immigrant Vote: A Case of Religious Polarization," in *Ethnic Voters and the Election of Lincoln*, ed. Frederick C. Luebke (Lincoln, Neb., 1971), 151–74.

125. Sr. Mary Demetria Meyer, O.P., "The Germans in Wisconsin and the Civil War: Their Attittude toward the Union, the Republicans, Slavery and Lincoln" (M.A. thesis, Catholic Univ., 1937), 261.

126. Kamphoefner, "German-Americans," 232–46; "John Bernard Stallo," *National Cyclopaedia of American Biography*, vol. 11 (New York, 1901), 259;

Gilbert J. Garraghan, S.J., *The Jesuits of the Middle United States*, vol. 3 (New York, 1938), 184.

127. John Timon to John B. Purcell, Sept. 17, 1855, II-4-m.

128. Gienapp, *Origins of the Republican Party*, 306, Sr. M. Hedwigis Overmoehle, "The Anti-Clerical Activities of the Forty-eighters in Wisconsin, 1848–1860: A Study in German-American Liberalism" (Ph.D. diss., St. Louis Univ., 1941), 180.

129. "Popery and Slavery," *Chicago Tribune*, Feb. 8, 1856, p. 2.

130. *Pittsburgh Post-Gazette*, March 3, 1854, p. 2.

131. Moncure Conway, *Autobiography: Memories and Experiences of Moncure Daniel Conway*, vol. 1 (Boston, 1904), 119; John d'Entremont, *Southern Emancipator: Moncure Conway, the American Years, 1832–1865* (New York, 1987), 46.

132. Hinton Rowan Helper, *The Impending Crisis of the South: How to Meet It* (New York, [1857], 1860), 172–73.

133. John Tyler to Robert Tyler, July 17, 1854, cited in Philip Morrison Rice, "The Know-Nothing Party in Virginia, 1854–1856," *Virginia Magazine of History and Biography* 55 (1947): 65.

134. *Southern Standard*, June 3, 1855, p. 1.

135. "Slavery and Freedom," *Southern Quarterly Review* 1 (April 1856): 76, 83.

136. "Disunion within the Union," *De Bow's Review* 28 (July 1860): 6.

137. Thomas R. Dew, *A Digest of the Laws, Customs, Manners and Institutions of the Ancient and Modern Nations* (New York, 1852), 378. On this point, see Eugene D. Genovese, *The Slaveholders' Dilemma: Freedom and Progress in Southern Conservative Thought, 1820–1860* (Columbia, S.C., 1992), 6–7; Elizabeth Fox-Genovese and Eugene D. Genovese, "Political Virtue and the Lessons of the French Revolution: The View from the Slaveholding South," in *Virtue, Corruption and Self-Interest: Political Values in the Eighteenth Century*, ed. Richard K. Matthews (Bethlehem, 1994), 202–4.

138. Douglas Ambrose, *Henry Hughes and Proslavery Thought in the Old South* (Baton Rouge, 1996); Neil C. Gillespie, *The Collapse of Orthodoxy: The Intellectual Ordeal of George Frederick Holmes* (Charlottesville, 1972), 153, 211.

139. George Fitzhugh, *Sociology for the South or the Failure of Free Society* (New York, n.d.), 1, 194–95.

140. George Fitzhugh, *Cannibals All! Or Slaves without Masters* (Cambridge, [1857], 1988), 131.

141. Orestes Brownson, "The Great Rebellion," *Brownson's Quarterly Review* 23 (July 1861): 378–402; idem, "Slavery and the War" (1861), in *Union Pamphlets*, 1:128–65; *The War for the Union, Speech by Dr. O. A. Brownson:*

How the War Should Be Prosecuted: The Duty of the Government and the Duty of the Citizen (New York, 1862); Charles Sumner to Orestes Brownson, Oct. 12, 1862, I-4-b.

142. *Lincoln Day by Day: A Chronology, 1809–1865*, vol. 3, *1861–1865*, ed. Earl Schenck Miers (Washington, D.C., 1960), 135.

143. *New York Daily Tribune*, Oct. 9, 1861, p. 4. "Mr. Brownson on Immediate Emancipation," *Douglass' Monthly* 4 (Nov. 1861): 552.

144. Horace Greeley to Sam Wilkeson, Aug. 24, 1861, reel 1, HG.

145. Brownson to Father Edward Sorin, Nov. 5, 1862, I-3-c; Patrick Kenrick to Peter Richard Kenrick, Aug. 23, 1861, in *The Kenrick-Frenaye Correspondence: Letters Chiefly of Francis Patrick Kenrick and Marc Antony Frenaye, 1830–1862*, ed. F. E. T[ourscher, O.S.A.] (Lancaster, Pa., 1920), 462.

146. Fr. Charles Gresselin, S.J., to Brownson, Feb. 19, 1862, I-4-b.

CHAPTER 3: CATHOLIC FREEDOM AND CIVIL WAR

1. "The Freeman's Appeal," *New York Freeman's Appeal*, Aug. 31, 1861, p. 2; Robert S. Harper, *Lincoln and the Press* (New York, 1951), 115–16. On civil liberties, see Mark E. Neely, *The Fate of Liberty: Abraham Lincoln and Civil Liberties* (New York, 1991), 28.

2. William H. Seward to Robert Murray, Sept. 14, 1861, in *The War of the Rebellion: A Compilation of the Official Records of the Union and Confederate Armies*, ser. 2, vol. 2 (Washington, D.C., 1897), 802

3. Gertrude G. McMaster to President Lincoln, Sept. 29, 1861, in *War of the Rebellion*, 803.

4. Ibid., 804.

5. Sr. Mary Augustine Kwitchen, O.S.F., *James Alphonsus McMaster: A Study in American Thought* (Washington, D.C., 1949).

6. John Dalgairns to James McMaster, Oct. 1843, I-1-m.

7. "The French Paper *L'Univers*," *New York Freeman's Journal*, July 24, 1852, p. 4.

8. "A Few Words about Our Journal," *New York Freeman's Journal*, July 5, 1851, p. 4.

9. Rev. Clarence E. Walworth, *The Oxford Movement in America; or, Glimpses of Life in an Anglican Seminary* (New York, [1895], 1974), 11.

10. James McMaster to Orestes Brownson, March 14, 1849, I-3-i.

11. "The Swiss Radicals," *New York Freeman's Journal*, Feb. 19, 1848, p. 268; J. A. McMaster, "The Swiss Revolution," *American Review* 8 (July 1848): 63–80; "Catholicity and National Permanence," *New York Freeman's Journal*, Jan. 5, 1850, p. 4.

12. *New York Freeman's Journal*, Aug. 5, 1854, p. 1; "Mr. Brownson on Nativism," ibid., July 2, 1854, p. 4.

13. *New York Freeman's Journal*, April 30, 1853, p. 4; "M. de Montalembert on England," ibid., Feb. 9, 1855, p. 4.

14. Orestes Brownson to James McMaster, July 10, 1853, in Henry F. Brownson, *Orestes A. Brownson's Middle Life: From 1845 to 1855* (Detroit, 1899), 450.

15. Louis Veuillot to Orestes Brownson, Aug. 28, 1856, I-3-m; Orestes Brownson to Louis Veuillot, Oct. 6, 1856, I-3-m.

16. "The Late Convert at Rome," *New York Freeman's Journal*, Aug. 13, 1853, p. 5; "A Mean Political Trick," ibid., Sept. 1, 1860, p. 4.

17. Stephen A. Douglas to James McMaster, Dec. 3, 1859, I-1-m.

18. "The Twin Relics of Barbarism," *New York Freeman's Journal*, April 7, 1860, p. 4; James McMaster, Lecture on Liberty, n.d., I-2-k.

19. "Christmas Times," *New York Freeman's Journal*, Dec. 29, 1860, p. 4; "The Cry of a Great Country," ibid., June 16, 1860, p. 4; "The Morale of the Struggle," ibid., Aug. 24, 1861, p. 4.

20. Sr. Mary Denis Maher, *To Bind Up the Wounds: Catholic Sister Nurses in the U.S. Civil War* (New York, 1989); William L. Burton, *Melting Pot Soldiers: The Union's Ethnic Regiments* (Ames, Iowa, 1988), 112–54; *A Frenchman, a Chaplain, a Rebel: The War Letters of Pere Louis-Hippolyte Gache, S.J.*, trans. and ed. Cornelius M. Buckley, S.J. (Chicago, 1981), 53–54.

21. John Jay Hughes, "Letter of Archbishop Hughes to Bishop Lynch, of South Carolina" (1861), in *Union Pamphlets of the Civil War, 1861–1865*, ed. Frank Freidel, 2 vols. (Cambridge, 1967), 1:118–27; "The Civil War," *Boston Pilot*, April 27, 1861, p. 4, cited in Thomas H. O'Connor, *Civil War Boston: Home Front and Battlefield* (Boston, 1997), 56.

22. Madeleine Hooke Rice, *American Catholic Opinion on the Slavery Controversy* (New York, 1944), 145; "Pleas for Disunion," *New York Freeman's Journal*, Dec. 8, 1860, p. 4.

23. "Close of St. Mary's Jubilee, North End, Boston." *Boston Pilot*, Oct. 16, 1897, p. 5. On Irish Union soldiers from Boston, see Daniel George MacNamara, *The History of the Ninth Regiment Massachusetts Volunteer Infantry, June 1861–June 1864* (New York, [1899], 2000).

24. Fr. McElroy to Father Paresce, Sept. 30, 1862, folder 27, box 62, MP; Catholique, "The Late Capt. N. B. Shurtleff, Jr.," *New York Freeman's Journal*, Sept. 6, 1862, p. 5.

25. "Disunion—Church and State," *Louisville Guardian*, Nov. 24, 1860, p. 4.

26. Rev. James Keogh, *Catholic Principles of Civil Government: A Lecture* (Cincinnati, 1862), 10–12.

27. Joel H. Silbey, *A Respectable Minority: The Democratic Party in the Civil War Era, 1860–1868* (New York, 1977), 57.

28. "The Ship on the Breakers," *New York Freeman's Journal*, June 8, 1861, p. 4; Frank L. Klement, "Catholics as Copperheads during the Civil War," *Catholic Historical Review* 80 (Jan. 1994): 40–42; idem, *The Copperheads in the Middle West* (Chicago, 1960), 223–24; Joseph George Jr., "A 'Catholic Family Newspaper' Views the Lincoln Administration: John Mullaly's Copperhead Weekly," *Civil War History* 24 (June 1978): 112–32; Sr. Mary Demetria Meyer, O.P., "The Germans in Wisconsin and the Civil War: Their Attitude toward the Union, the Republicans, Slavery and Lincoln" (M.A. thesis, Catholic Univ., 1937); D. A. Mahony, *The Prisoner of State* (New York, 1863).

29. Kathleen Neils Conzen, *Making Their Own America: Assimilation Theory and the German Peasant Pioneer* (New York, 1990), 17; Robert E. Sterling, "Civil War Draft Resistance in the Middle West" (Ph.D. diss., Univ. of Northern Illinois, 1974), 127–30; Peter Leo Johnson, "Port Washington Draft Riot of 1862," *Mid-America* 12 (Jan. 1930): 212–22.

30. Randall M. Miller, "Catholic Religion, Irish Ethnicity, and the Civil War," in *Religion and the American Civil War*, ed. Randall M. Miller, Harry S. Stout, and Charles Reagan Wilson (New York, 1998), 261–96; Iver Bernstein, *The New York City Draft Riots: Their Significance for American Society and Politics in the Age of the Civil War* (New York, 1990); Grace Palladino, *Another Civil War: Labor, Capital, and the State in the Anthracite Regions of Pennsylvania, 1840–68* (Urbana, 1990), 95–120; Thomas H. O'Connor, *Civil War Boston: Home Front and Battlefield* (Boston, 1997), 139–41.

31. *Commanding Boston's Irish Ninth: The Civil War Letters of Colonel Patrick R. Guiney, Ninth Massachusetts Volunteer Infantry*, ed. Christian Samito (New York, 1998), 167, 179–80.

32. James R. Brooke to James McMaster, June 6, 1861, I-l-m.

33. Fr. Joseph T. Jarboe to James McMaster, March 30, 1863, I-l-m.

34. Thomas Joseph Peterman, *The Cutting Edge: The Life of Andrew Thomas Becker* (Devon, Pa., 1982), 49–53.

35. Special Order No. 31, Provost Marshal's Office, June 28, 1864, in *Civil War Diary (1862–1865) of Bishop William Henry Elder, Bishop of Natchez*, ed. Rev. R. O. Gerow, (Natchez, 1960), 122.

36. Willard E. Wright, "Bishop Elder and the Civil War," *Catholic Historical Review* 44 (Oct. 1958): 294.

37. *Civil War Diary of Bishop Elder*, 95, 123.

38. "Justice" to editor, *New York Freeman's Journal*, Aug. 27, 1864, p. 2.

39. William E. Parrish, *Missouri under Radical Rule, 1865–1870* (Columbia, Mo., 1965); Thomas S. Barclay, "The Test Oath for Clergy in Missouri," *Mis-*

souri Historical Review 18 (April 1924): 345–81; Charles Fairman, *History of the Supreme Court of the United States*, vol. 4, *Reconstruction and Reunion, 1864–1868* (New York, 1971), 240–48.

40. Letter by C. D. Drake in *Daily Missouri Democrat*, April 28, 1865, n.p.

41. Letter of Archbishop Peter Kenrick to priests of the St. Louis archdiocese, July 28, 1865, in *Appleton's Annual Cyclopedia* (New York, 1866), 591; Pierre De Smet, S.J., to Gustave [?], Sept. 23, 1865, in *Life, Letters and Travels of Father Pierre-Jean De Smet, S.J., 1801–1873*, vol. 4 (New York, [1905], 1969), 1445.

42. *Cummings v. Missouri*, 4 Wall. 277 (1867): 386.

43. William Ernest Smith, *The Francis Preston Blair Family in Politics*, vol. 2 (New York, 1933), 351.

44. "The Progress of Population," *New York Times*, May 5, 1861, p. 4.

45. "After Slavery Shall Have Been Disposed of Popery Must Be Examined Into," *Metropolitan Record*, Dec. 27, 1862, p. 824; "A Statement of the Way Catholicity Is to Be Looked Into," ibid. March 7, 1863, p. 152; "Daniel O'Connell and the Abolitionists," ibid. Oct. 3, 1863, 626. Also see "The Plot to Establish Despotism," *New York Freeman's Journal*, Jan. 31, 1863, p. 4.

46. Michael Heiss to Rev. Kilian Kleiner, July 4, 1863, in *Salesianum* 11 (April 1916): 20–21.

47. Wm. McCloskey to Bishop F. P. McFarland, May 7, 1864, I-l-b; J. Margraf, *Kirche und Sklaverei seit der Entdeckung Amerika's* (Tübingen, 1865), 213–14.

48. Charles A. Sumner to Orestes A. Brownson, Dec. 27, 1863, in *The Selected Letters of Charles Sumner*, ed. Beverly Wilson Palmer, vol. 2 (Boston, 1990), 216–17; "An Old Slander Revived," *New York Times*, Dec. 21, 1863, p. 4; "What We Find in the Papers," *Harper's Weekly*, Jan. 2, 1864, p. 2.

49. Hubert H. Wubben, *Civil War Iowa and the Copperhead Movement* (Ames, Iowa, 1980), 175.

50. "The Irish Vote," *New York Weekly Tribune*, Nov. 12, 1864, p. 4.

51. "Brownson on the Rebellion" (1861), in *Union Pamphlets*, 1:141; M. L. Linton to Brownson, Oct. 16, 1861, I-4-a.

52. "Are Catholics Pro-Slavery and Disloyal?" *Brownson's Quarterly Review* 25 (July 1863): 371; "Catholics and the Anti-Draft Riots," ibid. 25 (Oct. 1863): 402.

53. Entry for June 1863, in Journal of Martin John Spalding, Bishop of Louisville, April 5, 1860–March 27, 1864, typed transcript by Father Peter E. Hogan, Bardstown-Louisville Papers, MAUND.

54. Barbara Karsky, "Les Libéraux français et l'émancipation des esclaves aux Etats-Unis, 1852–1870," *Revue d'Histoire Moderne and Contemporaine* 21 (1974): 575–90; Lawrence C. Jennings, *French Anti-Slavery: The Movement for the Abolition of Slavery in France, 1802–1848* (New York, 2000), 8–10, 213.

55. Walter D. Gray, "Liberalism in the Second Empire and the Influence of America: Edouard Laboulaye and His Circle," in *Liberty/Liberté: The American and French Experiences*, ed. Joseph Klaits and Michael H. Haltzel (Baltimore, 1991), 71–85; idem, "Edouard de Laboulaye: 'Liberal' Catholic and 'Americanist' during the Second Empire," *Cithara* 3 (May 1964): 3–16; Frank Freidel, "The Loyal Publication Society: A Pro-Union Propaganda Agency," *Mississippi Valley Historical Review* 26 (Dec. 1939): 372.

56. Charles Poinsatte and Anne Marie Poinsatte, "Augustin Cochin's *L'Abolition de l'esclavage* and the Emancipation Proclamation," *Review of Politics* 46 (July 1984): 410–27; Guy Bedouelle, O.P., "L'Abolition de l'esclavage et les libéraux catholiques français: Le Cas d'Augustin Cochin," in *L'Eglise et l'abolition de l'esclavage*, ed. Guy Bedouelle, O.P., et al. (Paris, 1999), 63–70.

57. Augustin Cochin, *The Results of Emancipation*, trans. Mary L. Booth (Boston, 1863), xi.

58. Augustin Cochin, "L'Esclavage et la politique des Etats-Unis," *Le Correspondant* 46 (Feb., 1859): 198, 221–22; Mary Booth to Brownson, April 2, 1864, I-4-c; Mary Booth to Brownson, April 7, 1863 I-4-b.

59. Sarah M. Brownson to editor, *National Anti-Slavery Standard*, May 8, 1863, n.p.

60. Seymour Drescher, "Servile Insurrection and John Brown's Body in Europe," *Journal of American History* 80 (Sept. 1993): 512.

61. John Lemoinne, in *Le Journal des Débats*, May 8, 1865, p. 1.

62. Count de Montalembert, *The Victory of the North in the United States* (Boston, 1866), 5.

63. Rev. Charles A. Costello, "The Episcopate of the Right Rev. Josue M. Young, Bishop of Erie, Pennsylvania—1854–1866" (M.A. thesis, Univ. of Notre Dame, 1951), 181.

64. Weninger, *Memoirs: Events of My Life in Europe and America for 80 Years, 1805–1885*, trans. Susan X. Blakely (Columbus, Ohio, 1886), 201–5, box 2B, FW.

65. Margraf, *Kirche und Sklaverei*, 213, 216.

66. George Müller, *Der amerikanische Sezessionskrieg in der schweizerischen öffentlichen Meinung* (Basel, 1944), 131–35; Preston Jones, "Civil War, Culture War: French Quebec and the American War between the States," *Catholic Historical Review* 78 (Jan. 2001): 55–70; Pierre Savard, *Jules-Paul Tardivel, la France et les Etats-Unis, 1851–1905* (Quebec, 1967), 35; Dr. M., "Christenthum und Sklaverei," *Historisch-politische Blätter für das katholische Deutschland* (Munich, 1868), 195; Margraf, *Kirche und Sklaverei*, 214.

67. Bishop Patrick Nelson Lynch, "A Few Words on the Domestic Slavery in the Confederate States of America," ed. David C. R. Heisser, *Avery Review* 3 (Spring 2000): 113, and 2 (Spring 1999): 70; David C. R. Heisser, "Bishop

Lynch's Civil War Pamphlet on Slavery," *Catholic Historical Review* 134 (Oct. 1998): 685, 695; Montalembert, *Victory of the North*, 5.

68. Judah Benjamin to Father John Bannon, Sept. 4, 1863, vol. 22, reel 13, JP; Joseph M. Hernon, "Irish Religious Opinion on the American Civil War," *Catholic Historical Review* 49 (1963–64): 518; idem, *Celts, Catholics & Copperheads: Ireland Views the American Civil War* (Columbus, Ohio, 1968), 105; Philip Tucker, "Confederate Secret Agent in Ireland: Father John B. Bannon and His Irish Mission, 1863–1864," *Journal of Confederate History* 5 (1990): 55–85; Emmet Larkin, *The Consolidation of the Roman Catholic Church in Ireland, 1850–1870* (Chapel Hill, 1987), 243.

69. *The Tablet*, Nov. 8, 1862, p. 713; ibid., Nov. 15, 1862, p. 729.

70. Gertrude Himmelfarb, *Lord Acton: A Study in Conscience and Politics* (Chicago, 1952), 78–83.

71. Newman to T. W. Allies, Nov. 8, 1863, in *Letters and Diaries of John Henry Newman*, vol. 20 (London, 1964), 553–56; Newman to T. W. Allies, Nov. 10, 1863, ibid., 557–58.

72. [John Hughes], "The Abolition Views of Brownson Overthrown," as reprinted in the *Catholic Mirror*, Oct. 12, 1861, p. 3.

73. Hughes to William Seward, Oct. 10, 1861, cited in Rena Mazcyk Andrews, "Archbishop Hughes and the Civil War" (Ph.D. diss., Univ. of Chicago, 1935), 56.

74. Hughes to Simon Cameron, Oct. 2, 1861, cited in Richard Shaw, *Dagger John: The Unquiet Life and Times of Archbishop John Hughes of New York* (New York, 1977), 344.

75. "The Pilot and Archbishop Hughes," *Boston Pilot*, Sept. 6, 1862, p. 4. For support of Brownson, see "Brownson's Review," *Pittsburgh Catholic*, April 26, 1862, p. 68.

76. Louis Alloury, "France," *Le Journal des Débats*, Dec. 25, 1861, p. 1.

77. "Archbishop Hughes in Paris," *New York Daily Tribune*, Jan. 13, 1862, p. 7.

78. "Les Evénements du Mois," *Le Correspondant* 55 (Jan. 1862): 170.

79. Hughes to Augustin Cochin, Jan. 28, 1862, quoted in Benjamin J. Blied, *Catholics in the Civil War* (Milwaukee, 1945), 33.

80. Brownson to Montalembert, April 11, 1862, I-4-b.

81. Steven J. Ochs, *A Black Patriot and a White Priest: André Cailloux and Claude Paschal Maistre in Civil War New Orleans* (Baton Rouge, 2000). Also see Caryn Cossé Bell, *Revolution, Romanticism, and the Afro-Creole Protest Tradition in Louisiana, 1718–1868* (Baton Rouge, 1997).

82. Louis Veuillot, "Melanges religieux, historiques, politiques et litteraires," *Propagateur Catholique*, March 2, 1861, p. 1.

83. "L'Opinion de M. Renan sur les miracles," *L'Union*, March 21, 1864, p. 1; "A Monsieur S.J....ne," ibid., May 5, 1863, p. 1.

84. "Addresse française," *L'Union*, May 19, 1863, p. 1

85. "La Religion accommodée à la politique," *L'Union*, Dec. 6, 1862, p. 1.

86. Archbishop J. M. Odin to Propaganda Fide, Aug. 14, 1863, reel 64, folios 358 and 361, PF; Ochs, *Black Patriot*, 95–115.

87. Ochs, *Black Patriot*, 132–37, 190–201, 234–66; Rev. Maistre, "Priere," *L'Union*, April 16, 1864, p. 1.

88. "Dinner at Mallow—the Catholic Church in America," *Catholic Telegraph*, Oct. 11, 1838, pp. 350–51.

89. Anthony H. Deye, "Archbishop John Baptist Purcell of Cincinnati, Pre–Civil War Years" (Ph.D. diss., Univ. of Notre Dame, 1959), 255.

90. Bishop Josue Young to James F. Meline, April 4, 1861, I-4-a.

91. Frank L. Klement, *The Limits of Dissent: Clement Vallandigham & the Civil War* (Lexington, Ky., 1970), 237, 256.

92. "Archbishop Purcell's Lecture at Mozart Hall Last Sunday Nov. 1," *Catholic Telegraph*, Nov. 4, 1863, p. 860.

93. Fr. Ignatius Reynolds to John Baptist Purcell, May 8, 1850, I-3-i.

94. Deye, "Archbishop John Baptist Purcell," 349.

95. William Rosecrans to Laurence Kehoe, Oct. 8, 1864, WR.

96. Deye, "Archbishop John Baptist Purcell," 304. On the Jesuits, see "The Church and Slavery," *Catholic Telegraph*, April 8, 1863, p. 116; Gilbert J. Garraghan, S.J., *The Jesuits of the Middle United States*, vol. 3, (New York, 1938), 184–85.

97. Purcell to England, Oct. 9, 1834, Irish College Correspondence, MAUND; Deye, "Archbishop John Baptist Purcell," 160; John Baptist Purcell to Orestes Brownson, Jan. 25, 1849, I-3-i.

98. Entry of May 6, 1875, in Canon Peter L. Benoit, "Diary of a Trip to America, Jan. 6, 1875 to June 8, 1875," p. 280, copy in Benoit papers, MAUND.

99. Archbishop John Baptist Purcell, *Pastoral Letter to the Very Reverend Clergy and the Laity of the Archdiocese* (Cincinnati, 1865), 5; James Hennesey, S.J., *The First Council of the Vatican: The American Experience* (New York, 1963), 86–87, 207.

100. Félix Dupanloup to Purcell, March 12, 1865, II-5-c; Pastoral Letter of the Rt. Rev. Felix Dupanloup, Bishop of Orleans, April 6, 1862, in *Records of the American Catholic Historical Society* 25 (1914): 21, 25, 27.

101. *Speech of the Hon. T. Stevens in Reply to the Attack on Gen. Hunter's Letter* (n.p., 1862), 7.

102. A.G.R., "The *Freeman's Journal* on the Bishop of Orleans," *Catholic Telegraph*, June 18, 1862, p. 197.

103. "Lecture of the Most Rev. Archbishop: His 'Impressions in Europe,'" *Catholic Telegraph*, Sept. 3, 1862, pp. 284–85.

104. Daniel O'Connell, *Daniel O'Connell and the Committee of the Irish Repeal Association of Cincinnati* (Cincinnati, 1863).

105. "The Church and Slavery," *Catholic Telegraph*, April 8, 1863, p. 116; M. D. Carr to editor, ibid., June 17, 1863, p. 196.

106. "Catholic Congress at Malines," *Catholic Telegraph*, Sept. 16, 1863, pp. 298–99.

107. Charles de Montalembert, *L'Eglise libre dans l'état libre: Discours prononcés au Congrès Catholique de Malines* (Paris, 1863), 139. On the context, see Roger Aubert, "L'Intervention de Montalembert au Congrès de Malines en 1863," *Collectanea Mechliniensia* 35 (1950): 525–52.

108. Romanus Cessario, O.P., "Lacordaire et les Etats Unis," in *Lacordaire: Son pays, ses amis et la liberté des ordres religieux*, ed. Guy Bedouelle (Paris, 1991), 337.

109. "Archbishop Purcell's Lecture at Mozart Hall," 860.

110. "Civil and Religious Freedom," *Brownson's Quarterly Review* 26 (July 1864), *The Works of Orestes Brownson*, ed. Henry F. Brownson, 20 vols. (Detroit, 1882–87), 20:308; "Are Catholics Pro-Slavery and Disloyal?" *Brownson's Quarterly Review* 25 (July 1863): 377.

111. "The Church and Slavery," *National Anti-Slavery Standard*, May 23, 1863, p. 4; "Roman Catholics and Liberty," reprinted ibid., May 30, 1863, pp. 1–2.

112. "Considerations on Infirmities," *New York Freeman's Journal*, Nov. 28, 1863, p. 4.

113. "An Episcopal Sensation," *New York Freeman's Journal*, June 7, 1862, p. 4; "Our Controversial Friend of New York," *Catholic Telegraph*, July 9, 1862, p. 220.

114. "Pastoral of the Archbishop of Cincinnati," *New York Freeman's Journal*, Feb. 6, 1864, p. 4.

115. Letter from A. O'C, *New York Freeman's Journal*, July 4, 1863, p. 5.

116. Entry of June 6, 1862, in "The Civil War Diary of John Abell Morgan, S.J.: A Jesuit Scholastic of the Maryland Province," ed. George M. Anderson, S.J., *Records of the American Catholic Historical Society* 101 (Fall 1990): 38.

117. Count Alfred de Falloux, *Augustin Cochin*, trans. Augustus Craven (London, 1877), 130, 135; Fr. Stephen Rousselon to Odin, Aug. 23, 1862, VI-2-f.

118. Entries of Nov. 1, 1862 (pp. 33–34), Jan. 1, 1863 (p. 35), June, n.d., 1863 (p. 38), in Journal of Martin John Spalding, Bishop of Louisville, April 5, 1860–March 27, 1864, typed transcript by Fr. Peter E. Hogan, Bardstown-Louisville Papers, MAUND.

119. Entry of April 12, 1863, in Journal of Martin John Spalding, April 5,

1860–March 27, 1864, Bardstown-Louiville Papers, MAUND; Spalding, *Martin John Spalding*, 135, 137, 139; Maria Genoino Caravaglios, *The American Catholic Church and the Negro Problem in the XVIII–XIX Centuries*, ed. Ernest L. Unterkoefler (Charleston, S.C., 1974), 173–74.

120. "Martin John Spalding's Dissertation on the American Civil War," ed. David Spalding, C.F.X., *Catholic Historical Review* 52 (April 1966): 66–85.

121. J. C. Hooker to Richard M. Blatchford, Nov. 21, 1863, in *United States Ministers to the Papal States: Instructions and Despatches, 1848–1868*, ed. Leo Francis Stock (Washington, D.C., 1933), 301.

122. Anthony B. Lalli, S.X., and Thomas H. O'Connor, "Roman Views on the American Civil War," *Catholic Historical Review* 57 (April 1971): esp. 20–31.

123. *The Roman Question: Extracts from the Despatches of Odo Russell from Rome, 1858–1870*, ed. Noel Blakiston (London, 1962), 288; Rufus King to Seward, June 26, 1865, in *United States Ministers to the Papal States*, 344.

124. "America," *L'Osservatore Romano*, Nov. 8, 1862, also cited in Lalli and O'Connor, "Roman Views," 34.

125. George Perkins Marsh to William Seward, Jan. 8, 1864, in *L'unificazione italiana vista dai diplomatici statunitensi*, vol. 4, *(1861–1866)*, ed. Howard Marraro (Rome, 1971), 220.

126. Glen M. Johnson, "Ralph Waldo Emerson on Isaac Hecker: A Manuscript with Commentary," *Catholic Historical Review* 74 (Jan. 1993): 55–56.

127. Pierre De Smet, S.J., to Edmond De Bare, March 15, 1864, Letter Press Book D8, De Smetiana Collection, pp. 212–14, MPA.

128. Owen Chadwick, *A History of the Popes, 1830–1914* (Oxford, 1998), 173–74; John P. Boyle, *Church Teaching Authority: Historical and Theological Studies* (Notre Dame, 1995), 10–42.

129. "Civil and Religious Freedom," *Brownson's Quarterly Review* (July 1864), in *Works*, 20:341.

130. "His Holiness the Pope on the Study of Science," *New York Freeman's Journal*, April 16, 1964, p. 1.

131. "The Next Puritan Warfare," *New York Freeman's Journal*, Jan. 2, 1864, p. 4; See Klement Vallandigham speech ibid., Jan. 24, 1863, pp. 2–4.

132. William Onahan to James McMaster, Sept. 19, 1863, I-1-m; "Editorial Correspondence," *New York Freeman's Journal*, Dec. 19, 1863, p. 4; "Local Attacks on the Freeman's Journal," ibid., Aug. 29, 1863, p. 4.

133. "Common School System," *New York Freeman's Journal*, Nov. 24, 1866, p. 4; "New Orleans Correspondence," ibid., Dec. 3, 1864, p. 1.

134. Orestes Brownson to Henry Brownson, July 9, 1862, III-3-a.

135. Fr. Jeremiah Cummings to Brownson, Nov. 5, 1864 , I-3-c.

136. "Introduction to the Last Series," *Brownson's Quarterly Review* 27 (Jan. 1873), in *Works*, 20:382.

137. "Introduction to the National Series," *Brownson's Quarterly Review* 26 (Jan. 1864): 1–12.

138. C. F. Audley, "Un Catholique du Nouveau Monde," *Le Correspondant* 66 (1865): 172.

139. "Explanations to Catholics," *Brownson's Quarterly Review* 26 (Oct. 1864), in *Works*, 20:361–81.

140. "Mr. Brownson's Review," *New York Freeman's Journal*, July 23, 1864, p. 5.

141. "Amérique?—Etats-Unis," *Lettres de Laval*, March 1865, p. 41.

142. Franz Xaver Bischof, *Theologie und Geschichte: Ignaz von Döllinger (1799–1890) in der zweiten Hälfte seines Lebens* (Stuttgart, 1997), 115.

143. Charles Montalembert to Brownson, Dec. 17, 1864, I-4-c.

CHAPTER 4: THE NATION

1. Quotations are from the (misdated) and typed copy in container 20, Writings by Grant, ser. 10, UG. On the speech, see L. F. Parker, "President Grant's Des Moines Address," *Annals of Iowa* 3 (1897): 179–83; James S. Clarkson, "General Grant's Des Moines Speech: The Circumstances of a Remarkable Utterance," *Century Magazine* 55 (1897–98): 785–88. On anti-Catholicism during this period, see esp. Philip Hamburger, *Separation of Church and State* (Cambridge, 2002), 246–51, 322–28; Ward M. McAfee, *Religion, Race, and Reconstruction: The Public School in the Politics of the 1870s* (Albany, 1998), 192–93; Tyler Anbinder, "Ulysses S. Grant, Nativist," *Civil War History* 43 (June 1997): 130–31.

2. Frank A. Burr, *A New, Original and Authentic Record of the Life and Deeds of General U.S. Grant* (Philadelphia, 1885), 869–72.

3. Entry of Jan. 3, 1875, in *Diary and Letters of Rutherford Birchard Hayes, Nineteenth President of the United States*, vol. 3, *1865–1881*, ed. Charles Richard Williams (Columbus, Ohio, 1924), 274 (emphasis in original).

4. Charles Richard Williams, *The Life of Rutherford Birchard Hayes: Nineteenth President of the United States*, vol. 1 (Columbus, Ohio, 1928), 400.

5. Entry of July 28, 1875, in *The Diary of James A. Garfield*, vol. 3, *1875–1877*, ed. Harry James Brown and Frederick D. Williams (Lansing, 1973), 120.

6. Eugene Lawrence, "Roman Catholic Democracy," *Harper's Weekly*, Oct. 16, 1875, p. 842.

7. William Greenleaf Eliot, Oct. 28, 1875, notebook #9, box 1, WGE.

8. *Compilation of the Messages and Papers of the Presidents 1789–1902*, ed. James D. Richardson, vol. 9 (New York, 1907), 4288–89.

9. Senator Justin Smith Morill to G. G. Benedict, Dec. 19, 1875, cited in Sr. Marie Carolyn Klinkhamer, "The Blaine Amendment of 1875: Private Motives for Public Action," *Catholic Historical Review* 42 (April 1956): 26.

10. For a useful case study, see Samuel T. McSeveney, "Religious Conflict, Party Politics, and Public Policy in New Jersey, 1874–1875," *New Jersey History* 110 (Spring–Summer 1992): 18–44.

11. *Congressional Record*, 44th Cong., 1st sess., Aug. 11, 1876, pp. 5587, 5588. On the Blaine amendment, see Alfred W. Meyer, "The Blaine Amendment and the Bill of Rights," *Harvard Law Review* 64 (April 1951): 939–45; Steven K. Green, "The Blaine Amendment Reconsidered," *American Journal of Legal History* 36 (Jan. 1992): 38–69.

12. *Congressional Record*, Aug. 11, 1876, pp. 5591, 5594.

13. Garfield writing on Nov. 9, 1876, quoted in Theodore Clarke Smith, *The Life and Letters of James Abram Garfield*, vol. 1 (New Haven, 1925), 613.

14. Francis Ellingwood Abbott, "The Catholic Peril in America," *Fortnightly Review* 25 (March 1876): 385–405.

15. John Greenleaf Whittier to an unidentified correspondent, Dec. 1873, in *The Letters of John Greenleaf Whittier*, vol. 3, *1861–1892*, ed. John B. Pickard (Cambridge, 1975), 312.

16. Morrill, in *Congressional Globe*, Jan. 30, 1867, p. 884; D. L. and Maria Child, *National Anti-Slavery Standard*, April 16, 1870, p. 1.

17. Morton Keller, *The Art and Politics of Thomas Nast* (New York, 1968), 159–75.

18. Charles Henry Pullen, *Miss Columbia's Public School; or, Will It Blow Over?* (New York, [1871], 1969), 13, 26, 55.

19. Rev. Otis Gibson, *"Chinaman or White Man, Which?": Reply to Father Buchard Delivered in Platt's Hall, San Francisco, Friday Evening March 14, 1873* (San Francisco, 1873), 16; *Report of the Joint Special Committee to Investigate Chinese Immigration U.S. Senate Forty-fourth Congress* (New York, [1877], 1978), 469; Robert Seager II, "Some Denominational Reactions to Chinese Immigration to California, 1856–1892," *Pacific Historical Review* 28 (Feb. 1959): 49–66.

20. Elizabeth Wilson, *A Scriptural View of Woman's Rights and Duties, in All the Important Relations of Life* (Philadelphia, 1849), 252.

21. Elizabeth Cady Stanton, "The 'Catholic World' on Woman's Suffrage," *Revolution*, April 29, 1869, p. 264.

22. "Christianity and Woman Suffrage," *Woman's Journal*, Aug. 24, 1878, p. 268; T.W.E., "A Suffragist's Reply to a Roman Catholic Bishop," ibid., March 24, 1877, p. 93.

23. Francis Parkman, "The Woman Question," *North American Review* 129 (Oct. 1879): 320.

24. Paula Kane, *Separatism and Subculture: Boston Catholicism*, 1900–1920 (Chapel Hill, 1994), 241–44; Margaret Lavinia Anderson, *Practicing Democracy: Elections and Political Culture in Imperial Germany* (Princeton, 2000), 422.

25. Richard J. Evans, *The Feminists: Women's Emancipation Movements in Europe, America and Australasia 1840–1920* (London, 1977), 237. On Catholic women and suffrage in the United States, see Kathleen Anne Sprows, "New Footsteps in Well-Trodden Ways: Gender, Religion, and Ethnicity in Irish America, 1890–1910" (Ph.D. diss., Univ. of Notre Dame, 1999), 96–97, 182–83.

26. Rt. Rev. J. P. Machebeuf, *Woman's Suffrage: A Lecture Delivered in the Catholic Church of Denver, Colorado* (Denver, 1877), 6.

27. Orestes Brownson, "The Woman Question," *Catholic World* 9 (May 1869): 150.

28. Heather Cox Richardson, *The Greatest Nation of the Earth: Republican Economic Policies during the Civil War* (Cambridge, 1997), 248.

29. Carl N. Degler, "One among Many: The United States and National Unification," in *Lincoln, the War President: The Gettysburg Lectures*, ed. Gabor S. Boritt (New York, 1992), 89–120; idem, "The American Civil War and the German Wars of Unification: The Problem of Comparison," in *On the Road to Total War: The American Civil War and the German Wars of Unification, 1861–1871*, ed. Stig Förster and Jörg Nagler (Washington, D.C., 1997), 53–71.

30. The full text is in A. Freemantle, *The Papal Encyclicals in Their Historical Context* (New York, 1956), 143–52.

31. Owen Chadwick, *A History of the Popes, 1830–1914* (New York, 1998), 168–81.

32. "Pastoral Letter of the Most Rev. Archbishop of Baltimore," *New York Freeman's Journal*, Feb. 18, 1865, p. 1.

33. [T. M. Ellis], "The Encyclical Letter," *Christian Examiner* 78 (May 1865): 401–7.

34. "Picking a Bone with the Pope," *Independent*, Feb. 2, 1865, p. 4.

35. Roger Aubert et al., *The Church in the Age of Liberalism*, trans. Peter Becker (New York, 1981), 248–303. On Britain, see Linda Colley, *Britons: Forging the Nation, 1707–1837* (New Haven, 1992); J. C. D. Clark, "Protestanism, Nationalism, and National Identity, 1660–1832," *Historical Journal* 43 (2000): 249–76; Hugh McLeod, "Protestantism and British National Identity, 1815–1945," in *Nation and Religion: Perspectives on Europe and Asia*, ed. Peter van der Veer and Hartmut Lehmann (Princeton, 1999), 44–70. On Holland, see Frans Groot, "Papists and Beggars: National Festivals and Nation Building in the Netherlands during the Nineteenth Century," ibid., 161–77. On Germany, see Helmut Walser Smith, *German Nationalism and Religious Conflict: Culture, Ideology, Politics, 1870–1914* (Princeton, 1995); Michael Benedict Gross, "Anti-

Catholicism, Liberalism and German National Identity, 1848–1880" (Ph.D. diss., Brown Univ,. 1997). On Italy, see A. C. Jemolo, *Church and State in Italy, 1850–1950*, trans. David Moore (Oxford, 1960), 28–181. On France, see Geoffrey Cubitt, *The Jesuit Myth: Conspiracy Theory and Politics in Nineteenth-Century France* (Oxford, 1993), 143–81.

36. John P. Newman, *Religious Liberty: A Free Church in a Free Country* (Washington, D.C., 1875), 24, 29. Newman's hostility to Catholicism was long-standing. See "President Grant at Church," *New York Herald*, June 7, 1869, p. 6. Also see Ralph E. Morrow, *Northern Methodism and Reconstruction* (East Lansing, 1956), 217–18.

37. David Blackbourn, *Populists and Patricians: Essays in Modern German History* (London, 1987), 143–67.

38. Jemolo, *Church and State in Italy*, 28–181; Cubitt, *Jesuit Myth*, 143–81.

39. J. P. Parry, *Democracy and Religion: Gladstone and the Liberal Party, 1867–1875* (Cambridge, 1986), 423–24; Richard Shannon, *Gladstone*, vol. 2, *1865–1898* (Chapel Hill, 1999), 150; H. C. Matthew, "Gladstone, Vaticanism, and the Question of the East," in *Religious Motivation: Biographical and Sociological Problems for the Church Historian*, ed. Derek Baker (Oxford, 1978), 436–37; Hillary Jenkins, "The Irish Dimension of the British Kulturkampf: Vaticanism and Civil Allegiance, 1870–1875," *Journal of Ecclesiastical History* 30 (July 1979): 356, 374; J. Altholz, "The Vatican Decrees Controversy," *Catholic Historical Review* 57 (Jan. 1972): 597–605.

40. J. R. Miller, "Anti-Catholic Thought in Victorian Canada," *Canadian Historical Review* 66 (Dec. 1985): 474–94; Richard N. Sinkin, *The Mexican Reform, 1855–1876: A Study in Liberal Nation-Building* (Austin, Tex., 1979), 133–45; David Brading, "Ultramontane Intransigence and the Mexican Reform: Clemente de Jesús Munguía," in *The Politics of Religion in an Age of Revival: Studies in Nineteenth-Century Europe and Latin America*, ed. Austen Ivereigh (London, 2000), 115–42.

41. Goldwin Smith, "U.S. Notes," reprinted in Arnold Haultain, *Goldwin Smith: His Life and Opinions* (London, [1913]), 259, 277.

42. Goldwin Smith to Max Müller, Aug. 8, 1870, in reel 2, GS. Undated newspaper editorial with comparison of Quebec and Ireland in reel 4, GS.

43. Philip Schaff, "A History of the Vatican Council," in W. E. Gladstone, *The Vatican Decrees in Their Bearing on Civil Allegiance: A Political Expostulation* (New York, 1876), 65.

44. David Lowenthal, *George Perkins Marsh: Prophet of Conservatism* (Seattle, 2000), 349.

45. Sr. M. Orestes Kolbeck, O.S.F., *American Opinion on the Kulturkampf (1871–1882)* (Washington, D.C., 1942), 28–49.

46. Wolfgang Hinners, *Exil und Rückkehr: Friedrich Kapp in Amerika und*

Deutschland, 1824–1884 (Stuttgart, 1987), 119; [Friedrich Kapp], "The Clerical Defeat: Mr. Bancroft's Resignation," *Nation*, May 11, 1871, p. 319.

47. George Bancroft to Hamilton Fish, Dec. 2, 1871, in *Foreign Relations of the United States*, pt. 1, *(1872)* (Washington, D.C., 1873), 187; George Bancroft to Hamilton Fish, Dec. 4, 1871, ibid.; George Bancroft to Hamilton Fish, March 18, 1872, ibid., 188; Bancroft to Rev. Dr. Samuel Osgood, Feb. 21, 1868, in *The Life and Letters of George Bancroft*, ed. M. A. DeWolfe Howe, vol. 2 (New York, 1908), 203.

48. John W. Burgess, "The 'Cuturconflict' in Prussia," *Political Science Quarterly* 2 (June 1887): 317, 326, 338. On Burgess, see Daniel T. Rodgers, *Contested Truths: Keywords in American Politics since Independence* (New York, 1987), 164–68.

49. John Greenleaf Whittier to Theodore Roosevelt, Jan. 4, 1871, *Letters of John Greenleaf Whittier*, 3:247–48.

50. William Lloyd Garrison to Theodore Roosevelt, Jan. 10, 1871, in *The Letters of William Lloyd Garrison*, vol. 6, *To Rouse the Slumbering Land, 1868–1879*, ed. Walter M. Merrill (Cambridge, 1981), 185.

51. Frank Freidel, *Francis Lieber: Nineteenth-Century Liberal* (Baton Rouge, 1947).

52. Francis Lieber, *The Miscellaneous Writings of Francis Lieber*, vol. 2 (Philadelphia, 1881), 225–43; Charles Sumner, "Are We a Nation?" (1867), in *Charles Sumner: His Complete Works*, 20 vols. (Boston, 1900), 16:3–66, esp. 12; Lieber to Sumner, May 13, 1868, LI 3948, box 48, FL. On Lieber and Mulford, see Elisha Mulford to L. D. Brewster, June 15, 1871, folder 18, box 2, MF. Also see Lieber lectures notes taken by Elisha Mulford, [1867], folder 102, box 12, MF.

53. Charles Sumner, Letter to a Public Meeting at the Academy of Music in New York, Jan. 10, 1871, in *Complete Works*, 18:307–8.

54. Elisha Mulford, *The Nation: The Foundations of Civil Order and Political Life in the United States* (New York, 1870), 375, 377; Francis Lieber, *Fragments of Political Science on Nationalism and Inter-nationalism* (New York, 1868), 12, 7, 9; Lieber to James Garfield, Jan. 30, 1870, ser. 4B, reel 104, JG.

55. Lieber to Johann Bluntschli, Feb. 8, 1868, *Life and Letters of Francis Lieber*, ed. Thomas Sergeant Perry (Boston, 1882), 379.

56. Edouard Laboulaye to Lieber, Oct. 23, 1868, LI 2552, box 16, FL; Lieber to Sumner, April 8, 1868, in *Life and Letters of Francis Lieber*, 382.

57. Bluntschli to Lieber, Oct. 18, 1865, LI 938, box 3, FL; Gross, "Anti-Catholicism," 188–89.

58. Lieber to Garfield, Feb. 26, 1872, ser. 4B, reel 104, JG; Lieber to Garfield, March 6, 1869, ibid., Lieber to Bluntschli, Feb. 19, 1872, in *Life and Letters of Francis Lieber*, 420; [Francis Lieber], "Religion and the Law," *New York Evening Post*, Sept. 24, 1871, p. 4.

59. Joseph P. Thompson, *The Contest with Ultramontanism in Germany* (London, 1874), 3, 12, 26.

60. Burckhardt quoted in Thomas Albert Howard, *Religion and the Rise of Historicism: W. M. L. de Wette, Jacob Burckhardt, and the Theological Origins of Nineteenth-Century Historical Consciousness* (Cambridge, Eng., 2000), 152.

61. Anthony Molho, "The Italian Renaissance, Made in the U.S.A.," in *Imagined Histories: American Historians Interpret the Past*, ed. Anthony Molho and Gordon S. Wood (Princeton, 1998), 268.

62. Chadwick, *History of the Popes*, 161–214.

63. Rev. D. A. Merrick, *Sermons for the Times, Delivered in St. Francis Xavier's Church, New York, 1870–'71* (New York, 1872), 128.

64. James Turner, *Without God, without Creed: The Origins of Unbelief in America* (Baltimore, 1985), 207–11.

65. Note in journal for 1870, in *The Journals and Miscellaneous Notebooks of Ralph Waldo Emerson*, vol. 16, *1866–1882*, ed. Ronald L. Bosco and Glen M. Johnson (Cambridge, [1960], 1982), 151.

66. [Charles Eliot Norton], "The Crisis at Rome," *Nation*, June 2, 1870, pp. 350–51.

67. Frederick Henry Hedge, "Luther and His Work," *Atlantic Monthly* 52 (Dec. 1883): 805.

68. Emile de Laveleye, *Protestantism and Catholicism, in Their Bearing upon the Liberty and Prosperity of Nations: A Study of Social Economy* (London, 1875), 11, 23, 52.

69. Emile de Laveleye, "L'Enseignement aux Etats-Unis," *Revue de Deux Mondes* 96 (Dec. 15, 1871): 892; idem, "La Crise récente en Belgique," ibid. 97 (Jan. 15, 1872): 250; idem, *Le Parti clerical en Belgique* (Brussels, 1874).

70. Thomas Nipperdey, "Max Weber, Protestantism, and the Context of the Debate around 1900," in *Weber's Protestant Ethic: Origins, Evidence, Contexts*, ed. Hartmut Lehmann and Guenther Roth (Cambridge, 1993), 78.

71. Ibid., 77–78.

72. Friedrich Wilhelm Graf, "The German Theological Sources and Protestant Church Politics," in *Weber's Protestant Ethic*, 27–28; Guenther Roth, "Introduction," ibid., 5–7; Blackbourn, *Populists and Patricians*, 143–207; Arthur Mitzman, *The Iron Cage: An Historical Interpretation of Max Weber* (New York, 1970), 67–71.

73. Turner, *Without God, without Creed*, 240–44; David A. Hollinger, "Inquiry and Uplift: Late Nineteenth Century American Academics and the Moral Efficacy of Scientific Practice," in *The Authority of Experts: Studies in History and Theory*, ed. Thomas L. Haskell (Bloomington, Ind., 1984), 142–56; idem, "Justification by Verification: The Scientific Challenge to the Moral

Authority of Christianity in Modern America," in *Religion and Twentieth-Century American Intellectual Life*, ed. Michael J. Lacey (Cambridge, 1989), 116–35.

74. Byron A. Boyd, *Rudolf Virchow: The Scientist as Citizen* (New York, 1991); John Tyndall, "Apology for the Belfast Address" (1874), in Tyndall, *Lectures and Essays* (London, 1903), 48–49.

75. Donald Fleming, *John William Draper and the Religion of Science* (Philadelphia, 1950), 134.

76. John William Draper, *History of the Conflict between Science and Religion* (New York, [1874], 1897), 331.

77. George Bancroft to Otto von Bismarck, Dec. 3, 1874, Bancroft Correspondence, GB.

78. *Autobiography of Andrew Dickson White*, 2 vols. (New York, 1905), 1:111, 551–55; entry of June 1, 1854, in *The Diaries of Andrew D. White*, ed. Robert Morris Ogden (Ithaca, 1959), 27; George M. Marsden, *The Soul of the American University: From Protestant Establishment to Established Nonbelief* (New York, 1994), 113–22; Julie A. Reuben, *The Making of the Modern World: Intellectual Transformation and the Marginalization of Morality* (Chicago, 1996), 58–59.

79. [Godkin] "The Catholic Church and Scientific Education," *Nation*, Jan. 1, 1874, p. 5.

80. Archibald Alexander, "Thomas Aquinas and the Encyclical Letter," *Princeton Review* 56 (March 1880): 245–61.

81. Kathleen A. Mahoney, "Modernity and the Education of American Catholics: Charles W. Eliot, Harvard Law School, and the Jesuits" (Ph.D. diss., Univ. of Rochester, 1995), 87.

82. On American medievalism, see T. J. Jackson Lears, *No Place of Grace: Antimodernism and the Transformation of American Culture, 1880–1920* (New York, 1981), 141–215; Robin Fleming, "Picturesque History of the Medieval in Nineteenth Century America," *American Historical Review* 100 (Oct. 1995): 1062–64. On Catholic medievalism, see Robert E. Sullivan, "Modernizing Tradition: Some Catholic Neo-Scholastics and the Genealogy of Natural Rights," in *Religion and the Authority of the Past*, ed. Tobin Siebers (Ann Arbor, 1993), 184–208; James J. Walsh, *The Thirteenth: Greatest of Centuries* (New York, 1913); Philip Gleason, *Keeping the Faith: American Catholicism Past and Present* (Notre Dame, 1987), 11–35.

83. Fr. Luigi Taparelli d'Azeglio, S.J., "Sur la nationalité," in *Essai théorique de droit naturel basé sur les faits*, vol. 2, translator anonymous (Paris, [1846], 1875), 529.

84. Rev. Michael Müller, C.SS.R., *Public School Education* (New York, [1872], 1873), 144.

85. Fr. Nicholas Accolti, S.J., to James McMaster, May 8, 1874, I-2-a.

86. [OAB], "Father Hyacinthe's Discourses," *New York Tablet*, Jan. 8, 1870, p. 8.

87. John Louis Ciani, "Across a Wide Ocean: Salvatore Maria Brandi, S.J., and the 'Civiltà Cattolica' from Americanism to Modernism, 1891–1914" (Ph.D. diss., Univ. of Virginia, 1992), 63.

88. Heiss to Kleiner, June 19, 1875, reprinted in *Salesianum* 12 (July 1917): 13.

89. "The Catholic Germans of Cincinnati," *New York Freeman's Journal*, Aug. 17, 1872, p. 2.

90. Robert Emmett Curran, S.J., *The Bicentennial History of Georgetown University: From Academy to University, 1789–1989*. vol. 1 (Washington, D.C., 1993), 265.

91. Austin Morini, O.S.M., *The Foundation of the Order of Servants of Mary in the United States of America (1870–1883)*, trans. and ed. Conrad M. Borntrager, O.S.M. (Rome, 1993), 126.

92. Rt. Rev. James O'Connor, "Anti-Catholic Prejudice," *American Catholic Quarterly Review* 1 (Jan. 1876): 17.

93. Sr. Mary De Paul Faber, O.S.F., "*The Luxemburger Gazette*: A Catholic German Language Paper of the Middle West, 1872–1918" (M.A. thesis, Catholic Univ. of America, 1947), 46; "Lecture on the 'Jesuits and Their Persecutors,'" *Catholic Sentinel*, Nov. 17, 1881, p. 1.

94. [Matteo Liberatore, S.J.], "Il liberalismo e gli Stati Uniti di America," *Civiltà Cattolica*, ser. 9, vol. 6 (1876): 272, 534–35; Claudio Jannet, *Les Etats-Unis contemporains; ou, Les Moeurs, les institutions et les idées depuis la Guerre de la Sécession* (Paris, 1876), 366–69.

95. John Ciani, S.J., "Cardinal Camillo Mazzella, S.J.," in *Varieties of Ultramontanism*, ed. Jeffrey von Arx, S.J. (Washington, D.C., 1998), 103–17.

96. "Fr. Joseph Louis Durverney," *Woodstock Letters* 8 (1879): 110–11; "The Late Father Maldonado," ibid. 1 (1872): 194–203; Rev. Patrick J. Dooley, S.J., *Woodstock and Its Makers* (Woodstock, Md., 1927), 30; "Woodstock: Its Surroundings and Associations," *Woodstock Letters* 2 (1873): 55.

97. Bishop Claude DuBuis to Archbishop John Odin, March 2, 1867, copy in Mary Hoffman Ogilvie, "Claude Marie DuBuis: Nineteenth Century Texas Missionary" (M.A. thesis, Univ. of Texas, Austin, 1990), 191.

98. Silas Barth, O.F.M., "The Franciscans in Southern Illinois," *Illinois Catholic Historical Review* 3 (July 1920): 77–87; Sr. Eunice Mousel, O.S.F., *They Have Taken Root: The Sisters of the Third Order of St. Francis of the Holy Family* (New York, 1954), 85–111.

99. Eric Foner, *Reconstruction, 1863–1877: America's Unfinished Revolution* (New York, 1988), 235

100. Arthur Cleveland Coxe, *Practical Wisdom: Planting of a Church: A Ser-*

mon Preached at the Consecration of the Second Bishop of Vermont, Whitsun Week, June 3, 1868 in Christ Church, Montpelier (Diocesan Convention of Vermont, 1868), 18; "Rome at Home and Abroad," *Harper's Weekly*, May 13, 1871, p. 426.

101. H. W. Bellows, "The Mission of America," *Christian Examiner* 86 (Jan. 1869): 71.

102. "The Underlying Issue," *New York Times*, July 19, 1871, p. 4. On the riot, see Michael A. Gordon, *The Orange Riots: Irish Political Violence in New York City, 1870 and 1871* (Ithaca, 1993).

103. Political Reform Document no. 4, in *Sectarian Appropriations of Public Money and Public Property in the City of New York* (1872), 4.

104. Emma Lou Thornbrough, *Indiana in the Civil War Era, 1850–1880* (Indianapolis, 1965), 642–43.

105. William D. Howells, *Sketch of the Life and Character of Rutherford B. Hayes* (New York, 1876), 154.

106. *The Papers of Woodrow Wilson*, vol. 1, *1856–1880*, ed. Arthur S. Link (Princeton, 1966), 427.

107. Orestes Brownson, "Home and Foreign Politics," *Brownson's Quarterly Review* 28 (Jan. 1874): 122.

108. Jerome Oetgen, *An American Abbot: Boniface Wimmer, O.S.B., 1809–1887* (Latrobe, Pa., 1976), 247.

109. Stathis N. Kalyvas, *The Rise of Christian Democracy in Europe* (Ithaca, 1996), 167–221.

110. Joseph Schroeder, "The Impregnable Fortress: Prince Bismarck and the Zentrum," *American Catholic Quarterly Review* 15 (July 1890): 390–421.

111. Sr. Mary Liguori Brophy, *The Social Thought of the German Roman Catholic Verein* (Washington, D.C., 1941), 33.

112. Sean Wilentz, "Against Exceptionalism: Class-consciousness and the American Labor Movement," *International Labor and Working-Class History* 26 (1984): 1–24.

113. Paul Kleppner, *The Third Electoral System, 1853–1892: Parties, Voters, and Political Cultures* (Chapel Hill, 1979), 148–53; Evelyn Sterne, "All Americans: The Politics of Citizenship in Providence, 1840 to 1940" (Ph.D. diss., Duke Univ., 1998), 290.

114. Claudius O. Johnson, *Carter Henry Harrison I: Political Leader* (Chicago, 1928), 201.

115. "Constitutional Convention of New York," *New York Freeman's Journal*, July 20, 1867, p. 4.

116. Curran, *Bicentennial History of Georgetown University*, 302.

117. *Oration of William J. Onahan of Chicago Illinois Delivered at the Thirty-*

second Annual Commencement of the University of Notre Dame, Indiana, Wednesday, June 21, 1876 (Notre Dame, 1876), 5.

118. "The Conquered Banner," *New York Freeman's Journal*, June 24, 1865, p. 8; John C. Bowes, C.M., "Glory in Gloom: Abram J. Ryan, Southern Catholicism, and the Lost Cause" (Ph.D. diss., St. Louis Univ., 1996); Charles Reagan Wilson, *Baptized in Blood: The Religion of the Lost Cause, 1865–1920* (Athens, Ga., 1980), 58–61.

119. Jefferson Davis to James McMaster, Sept. 18, 1867, I-1-n.

120. "Science," *New York Freeman's Journal*, July 6, 1872, p. 8; "The Positivists and Our Lady of Lourdes," *Ave Maria* 8 (Dec. 7, 1872): 787–88.

121. Gabriel Motzkin, "The Catholic Response to Secularization and the Rise of the History of Science as a Discipline," *Science in Context* 3 (1989): 214; Rev. F. P. Garesché, S.J., *Science and Religion: The Modern Controversy: A Lecture Delivered before the Young Men's Sodality of St. Xavier Church* (St. Louis, 1876), 27; idem, "Draper's Conflict between Science and Religion," *Catholic World* 21 (May 1875): 178–200.

122. Frederick E. Hoxie, *A Final Promise: The Campaign to Assimilate the Indians, 1880–1920* (Lincoln, Neb., 1984), 64.

123. James P. Wickersham, "An American Education for the American People," in *Proceedings of the National Teachers' Association, the National Association of School Superintendents, and the American Normal School Association at their Annual Meetings, Held in Indianapolis, Ind., August 1866* (n.p., 1867), 41.

124. Thomas Jefferson Morgan, *Roman Catholics and Indian Education: An Address* (Boston, 1893), 2. Also see Daniel Dorchester, *Romanism versus the Public School System* (New York, 1888).

125. Sarah Barringer Gordon, *The Mormon Question: Polygamy and Constitutional Conflict in Nineteenth-Century America* (Chapel Hill, 2002), 198, 206.

126. George W. Toue to Francis Kernan, Sept. 7, 1872, box 77, KP.

127. *Debates and Proceedings of the Constitutional Convention of the State of Illinois: Convened at the City of Springfield, Tuesday, Dec. 13, 1869* (Springfield, 1870), 1751, 1760; *Official Report of the Proceedings and Debates of the Third Constitutional Convention of Ohio: Assembled in the City of Columbus, on Tuesday, May 13, 1873*, vol. 2 (Cleveland, 1873), 2203, 2196, 2220, 2232.

128. Henry Wilson, "New Departure of the Republican Party," *Atlantic Monthly* 27 (Jan. 1871): 114–15, 119–20.

129. For selections from Pius IX's letter, see Thomas J. Jenkins, *Christian Schools* (London, [1886], 1890), 76–78.

130. Isaac Hecker to Orestes Brownson, Jan. 28, 1871, in *The Brownson-Hecker Correspondence*, ed. Joseph F. Gower and Richard M. Leliaert (Notre Dame, 1979), 299.

131. Gilbert Ahr Enderle, C.SS.R., "The American Moral Theology of Anthony Konings, C.SS.R." (Ph.D. diss., St. Louis Univ., 1995), 112–14.

132. Instruction of the Congregation of Propaganda de Fide concerning Catholic Children Attending American Public Schools, Nov. 24, 1875, in *Documents of American Catholic History*, ed. John Tracy Ellis (Milwaukee, 1956), 416–20; Thomas T. McAvoy, C.S.C., "Public Schools vs. Catholic Schools and James McMaster," *Review of Politics* 28 (Jan. 1966): 19–46; Philip Gleason, "Baltimore III and Education," *U.S. Catholic Historian* 4 (1985): 273–313.

133. White, in *Proceedings of the National Teachers' Association*, 17.

134. Gordon, *Orange Riots*, 205–9.

135. "Our Established Church," *Putnam's Magazine*, July 4, 1869, p. 50.

136. Freidel, *Francis Lieber*, 414.

137. "The School Question," *New York Times*, Oct. 2, 1873, p. 5

138. Henry W. Bellows, *"Church and State in America": A Discourse Given at Washington, D.C. at the Installation of Rev. Frederick Hinckley, as Pastor of the Unitarian Church, January 25, 1871* (Washington, D.C., 1871), 5, 19.

139. Robert Michaelsen, "Common School, Common Religion?: A Case Study in Church-State Relations, Cincinnati, 1869–1870," *Church History* 38 (June 1969): 201–17; F. Michael Perko, "A Time to Favor Zion: A Case Study of Religion as a Force in American Educational Development" (Ph.D. diss., Stanford Univ., 1981), 154–201.

140. *The Bible in the Public Schools: Addresses of Rev. A. D. Mayo and Rev. Thos. Vickers, of Cincinnati* (New York, 1870), 52.

141. Amory Dwight Mayo, "Methods of Moral Instruction in Common Schools," *The Addresses and Journal of Proceedings of the National Education Association, Session of the Year, 1872* (Peoria, 1873), 12.

142. *The Bible in the Public Schools: Addresses of Rev. A. D. Mayo and Rev. Thos. Vickers*, 5.

143. Beecher, in *The Bible in the Public Schools: Opinions of Individuals and of the Press, with Judicial Decisions* (New York, 1870), 3; Max Lilienthal, "Rome or America," *American Israelite* 9 (Feb. 4, 1870): 8–9; idem, "The Contest for Religious Liberty in Cincinnati; or, The Bible Question" (1869), in David Philipson, *Max Lilienthal, American Rabbi: Life and Writings* (New York, 1915) 474–75.

144. "Some Considerations for Protestant Controversialists," *Nation*, April 7, 1870, p. 219; "The Bible in the Schools," *Chicago Tribune*, Dec. 5, 1869, p. 2.

145. Rafael Romero Speech at Colegio de Las Vegas, Aug. 16, 1878, in *New Mexican Spanish Religious Oratory, 1800–1900*, ed. Thomas J. Steele, S.J. (Albuquerque, 1997), 155.

146. Hon. W. G. Ritch, *Education in New Mexico* (Sante Fe, 1875), 7.

147. Edward R. Vollmar, S.J., "La Revista Católica," *Mid-America* 58 (April–July 1976): 85–96.

148. Vito Tromby, S.J., "The New School Building at San Felipe Neri" (1877), in *New Mexican Spanish Religious Oratory*, 171.

149. W. G. Ritch, "Jesuitism in New Mexico" (1878), pamphlet in Huntington Library.

150. "Massachusetts," *New York Freeman's Journal*, Nov. 22, 1879, p. 2; "The Pope and Thomas Aquinas," *Index* 11 (Jan. 8, 1880): 18–19; Cyrus A. Bartol, *Reason and Rome in Education: A Sermon Preached at the West Church, Boston, Sunday, Nov. 23, 1879* (Boston, 1879), 6–7. For a summary, see Robert H. Lord, John E. Sexton, and Edward T. Harrington, *History of the Archdiocese of Boston in the Various Stages of Its Development, 1604 to 1943*, vol. 3 (New York, 1944), 79–85.

151. Kurt F. Leidecker, *Yankee Teacher: The Life of William Torrey Harris* (New York, 1946).

152. *Seventeenth Annual Report of the Board of Directors of the St. Louis Public Schools for the Year Ending August 1, 1871* (St. Louis, 1872), 21.

153. William T. Harris, "The Division of School Funds for Religious Purposes," *Atlantic Monthly* 37 (Aug. 1876): 172–83.

154. Leslie Woodcock Tentler, *Seasons of Grace: A History of the Catholic Archdiocese of Detroit* (Detroit, 1990), 88–91.

155. "Catholic Parents and the School Dilemma," *Milwaukee Catholic Magazine* 1 (Sept. 1875): 195; "Catholic Education," *New York Freeman's Journal*, March 16, 1872, p. 3.

156. Michaelsen, "Common School, Common Religion?" 201–17.

157. "The Roman Catholic Church and Our Public Schools," *New York Times*, Sept. 19, 1869, p. 4.

158. "A Startling Proposal," *New York Freeman's Journal*, Sept. 4, 1869, p. 4; "Very Rev. Edward Purcell in Defence of His Propositions," ibid., Sept. 11, 1869, p. 4.

159. Robert Emmett Curran, S.J., "Prelude to 'Americanism': The New York Accademia and Clerical Radicalism in the Late Nineteenth Century," *Church History* 47 (March 1978): 49–65; idem, *Michael Augustine Corrigan and the Shaping of Conservative Catholicism in America, 1878–1902* (New York, 1978), 172–74.

160. Entries of July 11 and Nov. 26, 1865, in *The Diary of Richard L. Burtsell, Priest of New York: The Early Years, 1865–1868*, ed. Nelson J. Callahan (New York, 1978), 100, 178.

161. Entries of Feb. 10 and Nov. 20, 1865, in *Diary of Richard L. Burtsell*, 5, 333.

162. Manuel Scott Shanaberger, "The Reverend Dr. Edward McGlynn: An Early Advocate of the Social Gospel in the American Catholic Church: An Intellectual History" (Ph.D. diss., Univ. of Virginia, 1993), 96.

163. James G. Blaine to William Henry Harrison, Sept. 16, 1891, in *The Correspondence between Benjamin Harrison and James G. Blaine, 1882–1893*, ed. Albert T. Volwiler (Philadelphia, 1940), 186; "Catholics and Their Difficulties—An Extraordinary Lecture by Rev. Thomas Farrell," *New York Herald*, June 7, 1869, p. 3.

164. "A Bold Priest," *New York Times*, Feb. 19, 1871, p. 4.

165. "Liberalism in the American Catholic Church," *New York Herald*, March 22, 1870, p. 6.

166. "Rev. Dr. McGlynn on Public Education," *New York Freeman's Journal*, Dec. 23, 1871, p. 5; "Rev. Dr. McGlynn on Schools," ibid., 4.

167. Daniel F. Reilly, O.P., *The School Controversy (1891–1893)* (Washington, D.C., 1943), 74–77. On the Poughkeepsie Plan, see Rev. Edward M. Connors, *Church-State Relationships in Education in the State of New York* (Washington, D.C., 1951), 110; Timothy Hughes Morrissey, "Archbishop John Ireland and the Faribault-Stillwater School Plan of the 1890's: A Reappraisal" (Ph.D. diss., Univ. of Notre Dame, 1975), 137–45.

168. Christopher J. Kauffman, *Tradition and Transformation in Catholic Culture: The Priests of Saint Sulpice in the United States from 1791 to the Present* (New York, 1988), 159, 181, 164.

169. John Ireland, "Patriotism" (1894), in Ireland, *The Church and Modern Society* (Chicago, 1896), 143.

170. Marvin R. O'Connell, *John Ireland and the American Catholic Church* (St. Paul, 1988), 268–69; Douglas J. Slawson, "Segregated Catholicism: The Origins of Saint Katharine's Parish, New Orleans," *Vincentian Heritage* 17 (1996): 163.

171. John Ireland, "American Citizenship" (1895), in *Church and Modern Society*, 188–89.

172. *Catholic Citizen*, May 9, 1891, p. 1.

173. Colman J. Barry, O.S.B., *The Catholic Church and German Americans* (Milwaukee, 1953), 131–82; Edward Claude Stibili, "The St. Raphael Society for the Protection of Italian Immigrants, 1887–1923" (Ph.D. diss., Univ. of Notre Dame, 1977), 76–77, 81–89; Scalabrini to Archbishop Michael Corrigan, Aug. 10, 1891, in *For the Love of Immigrants: Migration Writings and Letters of Bishop John Baptist Scalabrini (1839–1905)*, ed. Archbishop Silvano M. Tomasi, C.S. (New York, 2000), 276–78.

174. *Congressional Record*, April 22, 1892, p. 3532.

175. Charles Arnold to Father Patrick Nilan, June 22, 1890, copy in microfilm roll 4, JI.

176. John Ireland, "State Schools and Parish Schools" (1890), in *Church and Modern Society*, 199.

177. Robert Curtis Ayres, "The Americanists and Franz Xaver Kraus: An His-

torical Analysis of an International Liberal Catholic Combination, 1897–1898" (Ph.D. diss., Syracuse Univ., 1981), 132.

178. R. Scott Appleby, "*Church and Age Unite!": The Modernist Impulse in American Catholicism* (Notre Dame, 1992); Robert D. Cross, *The Emergence of Liberal Catholicism in America* (Cambridge, 1958).

179. Corrigan, in Emmett R. Curran, "Conservative Thought and Strategy in the School Controversy, 1891–1893," *Notre Dame Journal of Education* 7 (Spring 1976): 44. Also see Gleason, *Keeping the Faith*, 115–35.

180. Jacques Portes, *Fascination and Misgivings: The United States in French Opinion, 1870–1914*, trans. Elborg Forster (Cambridge, Eng., 2000), 293–307; Ayres, "Americanists and Franz Xavier Kraus," 136. On Italy, see Ornella Confessore, *L'americanismo cattolico in Italia* (Rome, 1984).

181. Ciani, "Across a Wide Ocean," 168.

182. Joseph Gerard Hubert, "'For the Upbuilding of the Church': The Reverend Herman Joseph Heuser, D.D., 1851–1933," vol. 1 (Ph.D. diss., Catholic Univ. of America, 1992), 168; Joseph Schroeder to Bishop Ignatius Horstmann, Oct. 11, 1897, in Joseph M. Lackner, "Bishop Ignatius F. Horstmann and the Americanization of the Catholic Church in the United States" (Ph.D. diss., St. Louis Univ., 1978), 310–13.

183. [Godkin], "Pius the Ninth," *Nation*, Feb. 14, 1878, p. 107.

184. John Tracy Ellis, *The Life of James Cardinal Gibbons: Archbishop of Baltimore 1834–1921*, vol. 2 (Milwaukee, 1952), 549.

185. Taft, quoted in Henry F. Pringle, *The Life and Times of William Howard Taft: A Biography*, vol. 2 (New York, 1939), 834; Turner, *Liberal Education of Charles Eliot Norton*, 399.

186. Theodore Roosevelt to Charles Henry Parkhurst, March 19, 1895, in *The Letters of Theodore Roosevelt*, vol. 1, *The Years of Preparation, 1868–1898*, ed. Elting E. Morison, (Cambridge, 1951), 434; Theodore Roosevelt to Bellamy Storer, Feb. 28, 1899, in *The Letters of Theodore Roosevelt*, vol. 2, *The Years of Preparation, 1898–1900*, ed. Elting E. Morison (Cambridge, 1951), 954.

187. O'Connell, *John Ireland*, 396–97.

188. "John Jay on Blair's Bill," *New York Times*, March 5, 1890, p. 3. Daniel W. Crofts, "The Blair Bill and the Elections Bill: The Congressional Aftermath to Reconstruction" (Ph.D. diss., Yale Univ., 1968); Allen J. Going, "The South and the Blair Educational Bill," *Missouri Valley Historical Review* 44 (Sept. 1957): 267–90; John Whitney Evans, "Catholics and the Blair Educational Bill," *Catholic Historical Review* 46 (Oct. 1960): 273–98.

189. "Passage of the Blair Educational Bill—Mr. Blair's Attacks on the Jesuits," *Woodstock Letters* 17 (1888): 128; Crofts, "Blair Bill," 200.

190. Crofts, "Blair Bill," 151–52.

191. Henry James, *Charles W. Eliot: President of Harvard University, 1869–1909*, vol. 1 (Boston, 1930), 141.

192. Richard Jensen, *The Winning of the Midwest: Social and Political Conflict, 1888–1896* (Chicago, 1971), 139.

193. Donald L. Kinzer, *An Episode in Anti-Catholicism: The American Protective Association* (Seattle, 1964), 178–79, 255–58.

194. Margaret Bendroth, "Rum, Romanism, and Evangelicalism: Protestants and Catholics in Late-Nineteenth Century Boston," *Church History* 68 (Sept. 1999): 641; Lord, Sexton, and Harrington, *History of the Archdiocese of Boston*, 3:101–59; James T. Watt, "Anti-Catholic Nativism in Canada: The Protestant Protective Association," *Canadian Historical Review* 48 (March 1967): 45–58; Timothy J. Meagher, *Inventing Irish America: Generation, Class, and Ethnic Identity in a New England City, 1880–1928* (Notre Dame, 2001), 227.

195. Joseph W. Duffy, "Congregational Clergy and the A.P.A.: The Growth of Religious Tolerance in America," *Connecticut Historical Society Bulletin* 48 (Winter 1983): 15, 20.

196. Josiah Strong, *Our Country* (Cambridge, [1886], 1963), 67, 149; George Marsden, *Fundamentalism and American Culture: The Shaping of Twentieth-Century Evangelicalism, 1870–1925* (New York, 1980), 66–67.

197. Justin D. Fulton, *The Fight with Rome* (New York, [1889], 1977), 3, 106; idem, *Washington in the Lap with Rome* (Boston, 1888), vii.

198. Joseph W. Creech Jr., "Righteous Indignation: Religion and Populism in North Carolina, 1886–1906," 2 vols. (Ph.D. diss., Univ. of Notre Dame, 2000), 1:186–87, 228, 339–40; 2:547. On Macune, see Lawrence Goodwyn, *Democratic Promise: The Populist Movement in America* (New York, 1976), 561–64. Kinzer, *Episode in Anti-Catholicism*, 225.

199. Kinzer, *Episode in Anti-Catholicism*, 133.

200. Ari Hoogenboom, *Rutherford B. Hayes: Warrior and President* (Lawrence, Neb., 1995), 258; Margaret Leech, *In the Days of McKinley* (New York, 1959), 76–77; Stanley L. Jones, *The Presidential Election of 1896* (Madison, Wisc., 1964), 142–44.

201. Washington Gladden, "The Anti-Catholic Crusade," *Century* 47 (March 1894), 790.

CHAPTER 5: THE SOCIAL QUESTION

1. The manuscripts were first published in *L'enciclica Rerum Novarum e il suo temp*, ed. Giovanni Antonazzi and Gabriele de Rosa (Rome [1957], 1991). I rely upon the informative summaries in John Moloney, "The Making of *Rerum Novarum* April 1890–May 1891," in *The Church Faces the Modern World:*

Rerum Novarum and Its Impact, ed. Paul Furlong and David Curtis (Hull, 1994), 27–39. Also see Paul Misner, "The Predecessors of *Rerum Novarum* within Catholicism," *Review of Social Economy* 49 (Winter 1991); 444–64; Jean-Marie Mayeur, *Catholicisme social et démocratie chrétienne: Principes romains, expériences françaises* (Paris, 1986), 47–65.

2. Gerald A. McCool, *From Unity to Pluralism: The Internal Evolution of Thomism* (New York, 1989), 5–39; Marcia L. Colish, "St. Thomas Aquinas in Historical Perspective: The Modern Period," *Church History* 44 (Dec. 1975): 433–49.

3. Claude Prudhomme, "Léon XIII et la curie romaine à l'époque de Rerum Novarum," in *"Rerum Novarum": Ecriture, contentu et réception d'une encyclique* (Rome, 1997), 38–40.

4. Thomas J. A. Hartley, *Thomistic Revival and the Modernist Era* (Toronto, 1971), 34–35.

5. David Blackbourn, "The Catholic Church in Europe since the French Revolution," *Comparative Studies in Society and History* 33 (October, 1991): 785; Hugh McLeod, *Piety and Poverty: Working-Class Religion in Berlin, London, and New York, 1870–1914*, (New York, 1996), 116–17; Kevin J. Christiano, *Religious Diversity and Social Change: American Cities, 1890–1906* (Cambridge, 1987), 172–75.

6. Samuel Lane Loomis, *Modern Cities and Their Religious Problems* (New York, [1887], 1970), 82.

7. Rev. Daniel T. McColgan, *A Century of Charity: The First One Hundred Years of the Society of St. Vincent de Paul in the United States*, vol. 1 (Milwaukee, 1951), 45. On politics, see Dorothy Brown and Elizabeth McKeown, *The Poor Belong to Us: Catholic Charities and American Welfare* (Cambridge, 1997), 26–27.

8. Carol K. Coburn and Martha Smith, *Spirited Lives: How Nuns Shaped Catholic Culture and American Life, 1836–1920* (Chapel Hill, 1999), 2.

9. Suellen Hoy, "Caring for Chicago's Women and Girls: The Sisters of the Good Shepherd, 1859–1911," *Journal of Urban History* 23 (March 1997): 260–94; Deirdre M. Moloney, *American Catholic Lay Groups and Transatlantic Social Reform in the Progressive Era* (Chapel Hill, 2002), 117–66; M. Christine Anderson, "Catholic Nuns and the Invention of Social Work: The Sisters of the Santa Maria Institute of Cincinnati, Ohio, 1897 through the 1920s," *Journal of Women's History* 12 (Spring 2000): 60–88; Margaret M. McGuiness, "A Puzzle with Missing Pieces: Catholic Women and the Social Settlement Movement, 1897–1915" (Notre Dame: Cushwa Center Working Paper Series, ser. 22, no. 2, Spring 1990); Michael E. Engh, S.J., "Female, Catholic and Progressive: The Women of the Brownson Settlement House of Los Angeles, 1901–1920," *Records of the American Catholic Historical Society* 109 (Spring–Summer 1999): 113–26.

10. Christopher J. Kauffman, *Ministry and Meaning: A Religious History of Catholic Health Care in the United States* (New York, 1995), 130; Sioban Nelson, *Say Little, Do Much: Nurses, Nuns and Hospitals in the Nineteenth Century* (Philadelphia, 2001).

11. Charles Loring Brace, *The Dangerous Classes of New York, and Twenty Years' Work among Them* (New York, [1872], 1880), 154; Maureen Fitzgerald, "Irish-Catholic Nuns and the Development of New York City's Welfare System, 1840–1900" (Ph.D. diss., Univ. of Wisconsin, Madison, 1992), 415. For comparable events in Germany, see Edward Ross Dickinson, *The Politics of German Child Welfare from the Empire to the Federal Republic* (Cambridge, 1996), 94–97.

12. Pete L. Foy, *The New Social Order: Paper Read at the Catholic Lay Congress, Baltimore, Nov. 11th, 1889* (St. Louis, 1889), 12.

13. Thomas L. Haskell, *Objectivity Is Not Neutrality: Explanatory Schemes in History* (Baltimore, 1998), 307–17.

14. Amy Dru Stanley, *From Bondage to Contract: Wage Labor, Marriage and the Market in the Age of Slave Emancipation* (Cambridge, 1998), 168; Lawrence B. Glickman, *A Living Wage: American Workers and the Making of Consumer Society* (Ithaca, 1997).

15. Fr. Matteo Liberatore, S.J., *Principles of Political Economy*, trans. Edward Heneage Dering (London, 1891), 194.

16. Mayeur, *Catholicisme social et démocratie chrétienne*, 22.

17. Wilhelm Emmanuel von Ketteler, "The Labor Problem and Christianity" (1864), in *The Social Teachings of Wilhelm Emmanuel von Ketteler, Bishop of Mainz (1811–1877)*, trans. Rupert J. Ederer (Washington, D.C., 1981), 323.

18. Orestes A. Brownson, "Conversations on Liberalism and the Church" (1869), in *The Works of Orestes Brownson*, ed. Henry F. Brownson, 20 vols. (Detroit, 1882–87), 13:17.

19. "The Material Mission of the Church," *Catholic World* 28 (Feb. 1878): 662.

20. *Rerum Novarum* (1891), in *The Papal Encyclicals, 1878–1903*, ed. Claudia Carlen, I.H.M. (Raleigh, N.C., 1981), 241, 253.

21. Paul Misner, *Social Catholicism in Europe: From the Onset of Industrialization to the First World War* (New York, 1991), 204. Still useful is Joseph N. Moody, ed., *Church and Society: Catholic Social and Political Thought and Movements, 1789–1950* (New York, 1953).

22. Merwin Marie Snell, "The Catholic Social-Reform Movement," *American Journal of Sociology* 65 (July 1899): 49.

23. Cardinal Gibbons' Defense of the Knights of Labor, Feb. 20, 1887, in *Documents of American Catholic History*, ed. John Tracy Ellis (Milwaukee, 1956), 464, 471. On the episode, see Henry J. Browne, *The Catholic Church and the Knights of Labor* (New York, [1949], 1976), 182–274.

24. Charles Albro Barker, *Henry George* (New York, 1955). Decisive for my own thinking is Ronald Yanosky, "Seeing the Cat: Henry George and the Rise of the Single Tax Movement, 1879–1890" (Ph.D. diss., Univ. of California, Berkeley, 1993). Henry George, *The Condition of Labor: An Open Letter to Pope Leo XIII* (New York, [1891], 1893), 29.

25. James J. Green, "American Catholics and the Irish Land League, 1879–1882," *Catholic Historical Review* 35 (April 1949): 19–42; Thomas N. Browne, *Irish-American Nationalism, 1870-1890*, (Philadelphia, 1966), 101–32; Eric Foner, *Politics and Ideology in the Age of the Civil War* (New York, 1980), 150–200.

26. "Practical Sympathy with the Irish Sufferers," *New York Freeman's Journal*, Dec. 13, 1879, p. 4.

27. Gabriel Flynn, "Bishop Thomas Nulty and the Irish Land Question," *Records of Meath Archaeological and Historical Society* 7 (1984): 23-24; idem, "Bishop Thomas Nulty and the Irish Land Question: Part II, 1879–1881," ibid. 7 (1985–86): 93–110.

28. Ibid.; Rev. Bernard J. Canning, *Bishops of Ireland, 1870–1987*, (Ballyshannon, 1987), 145.

29. Henry George Jr., *The Life of Henry George* (New York, 1943), 345–48.

30. T. W. Moody, *Davitt and Irish Revolution, 1846–82* (Oxford, 1981), 404–5.

31. Yanosky, "Seeing the Cat," 175.

32. See the remarks of A. J. Steers in "Catholic Workingmen Protest," *Standard*, Jan. 22, 1887, p. 1. Stephen Bell, *Rebel, Priest and Prophet: A Biography of Dr. Edward McGlynn* (New York, 1937), 23. On McGlynn, see Alfred Isacsson, *The Determined Doctor: The Story of Edward McGlynn* (Tarrytown, N.Y., 1990). The best narration of the McGlynn saga remains Robert Emmett Curran, *Michael Augustine Corrigan and the Shaping of Conservative Catholicism in America, 1878–1902* (New York, 1978).

33. Bell, *Rebel, Priest and Prophet*, 23; "The Catholic Charities of New York," *Catholic World* 43 (Aug. 1886): 686–87.

34. "Dr. McGlynn's Speech at the Davitt Reception," *New York Freeman's Journal*, July 15, 1882, p. 2.

35. "God Help Ireland!" *New York Freeman's Journal*, July 15, 1882, p. 4.

36. Isacsson, *Determined Doctor*, 81; Curran, *Michael Augustine Corrigan*, 184.

37. Curran, *Michael Augustine Corrigan*, 188–89.

38. Thomas Preston to John O'Donoghue, Oct. 25, 1886, in Frederick J. Zwierlein, *The Life and Letters of Bishop McQuaid* vol. 3 (Rochester, 1927), 6–7.

39. Pius J. A. Brown, "'Egregius Archepiscopus': A Life of Michael Augustine Corrigan, 1839–1902, Archbishop of New York" (Ph.D. diss., National Univ. of Ireland, 1981), 296; "Pastoral Letter," *Catholic Review*, Nov. 27, 1886, p. 349.

40. Thomas J. Morrissey, S.J., *William J. Walsh, Archbishop of Dublin, 1841–1921: No Uncertain Voice* (Dublin, 2000), 78; Cardinal Gibbons Opposes the Condemnation of the Works of Henry George, Feb. 25, 1887, in *Documents of American Catholic History*, ed. Ellis, 475. On this episode, see Gerald P. Fogarty, *The Vatican and the American Hierarchy* (Stuttgart, 1982), 103.

41. "The Archbishop on the Encyclical," *Catholic Review*, June 20, 1891, p. 2; Entry of June 8, 1891, Diary of Richard Burtsell, reel 2, RB.

42. Henry George to Henry George Jr., June 9, 1891, reel 5, HGeorge.

43. "The Archbishop on the Encyclical," 2; Henry George, *The Condition of Labor: An Open Letter to Pope Leo XIII* (New York, [1891], 1893), 4.

44. C. Joseph Nuesse, "Henry George and 'Rerum Novarum,'" *American Journal of Economics and Sociology* 44 (April 1985): 241–55.

45. *Rerum Novarum* (1891), 243.

46. John Molony, *The Worker Question: A New Historical Perspective on "Rerum Novarum"* (Victoria, 1991), 83, 91, 109.

47. James Nilan, "St. Thomas Aquinas," *Standard,* Jan. 29, 1887, p. 1.

48. George, *Condition of Labor*, 65–67.

49. Henry George, "The Case of Dr. McGlynn," *Standard*, Jan. 8, 1887, p. 1, and Jan. 15, 1887, p. 1.

50. "Ecclesiasticism in Politics," *Standard* (April 30, 1887), p. 4.

51. "Anti-Poverty," *Standard*, July 16, 1887, p. 2; Edward McGlynn, *The Inquisition and the Anti-Poverty Society* (New York, 1889), 572.

52. Edward McGlynn, D.D., "The New Know Nothingism and the Old," *North American Review* 145 (Aug. 1887): 195, 198.

53. "Stati Uniti d'America," *Civiltà Cattolica*, ser. 13, vol. 7 (1887): 252.

54. Victor Cathrein, S.J., *Socialism Exposed and Refuted*, trans. James Conway, S.J. (New York, 1892), 162.

55. "Fr. Cathrein, S.J. vs. Henry George," *New York Freeman's Journal*, March 10, 1888, p. 7; "Buffalo," *Woodstock Letters* 19 (1890): 277; Victor Cathrein, S.J., *The Champions of Agrarian Socialism: A Refutation of Emile de Laveleye and Henry George*, trans. Rev. J. U. Heinzle (Buffalo, 1889); Edward Walsh, S.J., to Fr. Daniel Hudson, C.S.C., July 6, 1887, X-3-e.

56. William J. Kerby, *Le Socialisme aux Etats-Unis* (Bruxelles, 1897), 175–202.

57. Arthur Preuss, "Is the Single Tax an Open Question?" *Fortnightly Review* 11 (May 5, 1904): 278.

58. [John A. Ryan], "The Right to Work," *Northwestern Chronicle*, March 2, 1894, p. 4; John A. Ryan, "Georgism and Justice," ibid., April 24, 1896, p. 4.

59. John A. Ryan, "Methods of Reforming Our Land System," *Catholic World* 96 (Oct. 1912): 7; idem, "Methods of Reforming Our Land System," *Catholic World* 96 (Nov. 1912): 156–69; idem, "Ethical Arguments of Henry George against Private Ownership of Land," ibid. 93 (July 1911): 483–92.

60. John Dewey, "The Individual and the World" (1916), in Dewey, *The Middle Works, 1899–1924,* vol. 9, *1916*, ed. Jo Ann Boydston (Carbondale, Ill., 1980), 303; Daniel J. Wilson, *Science, Community, and the Transformation of American Philosophy, 1860–1930* (Chicago, 1990), 175.

61. Oliver Wendell Holmes, "Natural Law" (1918), in *The Essential Holmes: Selections from the Letters, Speeches, Judicial Opinions, and Other Writings of Oliver Wendell Holmes, Jr.*, ed. Richard A. Posner (Chicago, 1992), 181.

62. Walter Lippmann, *Drift and Mastery* (Englewood Cliffs, N.J., [1914], 1961), 162.

63. Robert B. Westbrook, *John Dewey and American Democracy* (Ithaca, 1991), 78–79; Morris R. Cohen, *A Dreamer's Journey: The Autobiography of Morris Raphael Cohen* (Boston, 1949), 213; Andrew R. Heinze, "Jews and American Popular Psychology: Reconsidering the Protestant Paradigm of Popular Thought," *Journal of American History* 88 (Dec. 2001): 965.

64. John Dewey, *A Common Faith* (New Haven, 1934), 26; Michael J. Buckley, S.J., "Experience and Culture: A Point of Departure for American Atheism," *Theological Studies* 50 (Sept. 1989): 446–57.

65. George M. Marsden, *The Soul of the American University: From Protestant Establishment to Established Nonbelief* (New York, 1994), esp. 150–66. Also see Julie A. Reuben, *The Making of the Modern University: Intellectual Transformation and the Marginalization of Morality* (Chicago, 1996); James T. Burtchaell, *The Dying of the Light: The Disengagement of Colleges and Universities from Their Christian Churches* (Grand Rapids, 1998).

66. Arthur Lovejoy and James W. Bright to John Dewey, April 13, 1914, in John Dewey, *Correspondence of John Dewey,* vol. 1, *1871–1918*, ed. Larry A. Hickman (electronic ed., Center for Dewey Studies, Southern Illinois Univ., Carbondale, 1999); Marsden, *Soul of the American University*, 307.

67. For an overview, see McCool, *From Unity to Pluralism*, 5–39; Philip Gleason, *Contending with Modernity: Catholic Higher Education in the Twentieth Century* (New York, 1995), 105–14.

68. "St. Thomas Day," *Salesianum* 2 (April 1874): 6; Patrick J. Dooley, S.J., *Woodstock and Its Makers* (Woodstock, Md., 1927), 202.

69. William James, *Pragmatism* (Cambridge, 1975), 259.

70. Walter H. Hill, S.J., *Ethics; or, Moral Philosophy* (Baltimore, [1878], 1879), v.

71. William Turner, "Pragmatism," *The Catholic Encyclopedia,* vol. 12 (New York, 1913), 338.

72. Jane Addams, "The Social Situation: Religious Education and Contemporary Social Conditions," *Religious Education* 6 (June 1911): 147. On the American revival of Thomism, see William M. Halsey, *The Survival of American*

Innocence: Catholicism in an Era of Disillusionment, 1920–1940 (Notre Dame, 1980), 138–68.

73. Charles A. Hart, "Neo-Scholastic Philosophy in American Catholic Culture," in *Aspects of the New Scholastic Philosophy*, ed. Charles A. Hart (New York, 1932) 27; L. Keeler, S.J., "Two Philosophical Gatherings," *Gregorianum* 9 (1928): 313.

74. Charles Sanders Peirce, "The Fixation of Belief" (1877), in *Writings of Charles Sanders Peirce: A Chronological Edition,* vol. 3, *1872–1878*, Christian J. W. Kloesel (Bloomington, Ind., 1986), 251; idem, "How to Make Our Ideas Clear" (1878), ibid., 272. On Peirce, Vatican I, and Gratry, see Ian Hacking, *The Taming of Chance* (Cambridge, 1990), 206–7.

75. James, *Pragmatism*, 62. Also see Louis Menand, *The Metaphysical Club* (New York, 2001), 88–89.

76. Charles Renouvier to William James, May 14, 1878, in Ralph Barton Perry, *The Thought and Character of William James,* vol. 1, *Inheritance and Vocation* (Boston, 1935), 668. On Renouvier and Catholicism, see William Logue, *Charles Renouvier: Philosopher of Liberty* (Baton Rouge, 1993), 73–74, 109–10, 132–35, 138.

77. William James to Mrs. Henry Whitman, July 24, 1890, *The Letters of William James*, ed. Henry James (Boston, 1926), 296–97.

78. Responses in John S. Zybura, ed., *Present-Day Thinkers and the New Scholasticism: An International Symposium* (St. Louis, 1926), 29–30, 16, 5.

79. Carl Billman to Dr. Bernard Kohlbrenner, Dec. 16, 1960, 1961–1964 folder, Phi Beta Kappa Collection, MAUND.

80. John Dewey and James H. Tufts, *Ethics* (1908), in John Dewey, *The Middle Works, 1899–1924,* vol. 5, *1908*, ed. Jo Ann Boydston (Carbondale, Ill., 1978), 392; John A. Ryan, "A Practical Philosophy of Work," *Social Thought* 9 (Fall [1920] 1983), 4.

81. Daniel T. Rodgers, *Atlantic Crossings: Social Politics in a Progressive Age* (Cambridge, 1998), 76–119.

82. Msgr. Thomas Bouquillon to William J. Kerby, May 26, 1895, folder 3, box 1, WK. Also see Kerby's course notebook, Anmeldebuch, folder 3, box 1, WK. On Siedenburg, see the entry in *The New Catholic Encyclopedia,* vol. 13 (New York, 1967), 198. On Engelen, see "Fr. William Engelen," *Missouri Province Newsletter*, Dec. 1937, p. 95.

83. Joseph Frey to Frederick Kenkel, May 29, 1912, folder 26, box 3, FK; Rev. Joseph Reiner, S.J., "A Program for Social Legislation," in *Proceedings of the Sixth Biennial Meeting of the National Conference of Catholic Charities* (Washington, D.C., 1920), 7–16.

84. *Heinrich Pesch on Solidarist Economics*, trans. Rupert J. Ederer (Lanham, Md., 1998), 74. Pesch also quoted in *Church and Society*, ed. Moody, 547. On

Pesch, see Richard E. Mulcahy, S.J., *The Economics of Heinrich Pesch* (New York, 1952).

85. Heinrich Pesch, *Liberalismus, Socialismus und christliche Gesellschaftsordnung* (Freiburg, 1901), 309–53, Rupert J. Ederer, trans., copy in author's possession.

86. Francis L. Broderick, *Right Reverend New Dealer* (New York, 1963).

87. Rev. John A. Ryan, "Catholic Social Activity in Europe," *Catholic University Bulletin* 14 (1908): 183, 180.

88. John A. Ryan, "A Great Catholic Work on Political Economy," *Fortnightly Review* 17 (May 1910): 289.

89. John A. Ryan, *A Living Wage: Its Ethical and Economic Aspects* (New York, [1906], 1912), xi–xiii.

90. John A. Ryan to Richard T. Ely, May 15, 1902, box 21, folder 5, RE; Ryan to Ely, May 18, 1901, box 19, folder 3, RE. On progressivism, see Richard Wightman Fox, "The Culture of Liberal Protestant Progressivism, 1875–1925," *Journal of Interdisciplinary History* 23 (Winter 1993): 639–60.

91. Ryan, *Living Wage*, xii; Richard T. Ely to Mr. George P. Brett, May 21, 1901, box 19, folder 3, RE; Richard T. Ely, *Ground under Our Feet: An Autobiography* (New York, 1938), 289–95.

92. Roscoe Pound to John A. Ryan, July 5, 1923, reel 43, RP; John A. Ryan to Roscoe Pound, Oct. 18, 1923, ibid.

93. Timothy Michael Dolan, *"Some Seed Fell on Good Ground": The Life of Edwin V. O'Hara* (Washington, D.C., 1992), 34.

94. Program of Social Reconstruction, Feb. 12, 1919, in *Pastoral Letters of the United States Catholic Bishops,* vol. 1 *1792–1940* (Washington, D.C., 1984), 255–71; Joseph M. McShane, S.J., *"Sufficiently Radical": Catholicism, Progressivism, and the Bishops' Program of 1919* (Washington, D.C., 1986).

95. Editorial, *New Republic*, Feb. 22, 1919, p. 99; Raymond Swing, "The Catholic View of Reconstruction," *Nation*, March 29, 1919, pp. 467, 468.

96. Marc Karson, *American Labor Unions and Politics* (Carbondale, Ill., 1958), 212–84; William Stang, *Socialism and Christianity* (New York, 1905), 27; Ronald W. Schatz, "American Labor and the Catholic Church, 1919–1950," *International Labor and Working Class History* 20 (Fall 1981): 46–53.

97. Robert Lewis Mikkelsen, "Immigrants in Politics: Poles, Germans and the Social Democratic Party of Milwaukee," in *Labor Migration in the Atlantic Economies: The European and North American Working Classes during the Period of Industrialization* (Westport, Conn., 1985), 277–95.

98. Melvin Dubofsky, "Success and Failure of Socialism in New York City, 1900–1918: A Case Study," *Labor History* 9 (Fall 1968): 372.

99. Neil Riddell, "The Catholic Church and the Labour Party, 1918–1931," *Twentieth Century British History* 8 (1997): 165–73; Seymour Martin Lipset and

Gary Marks, *It Didn't Happen Here: Why Socialism Failed in the United States* (New York, 2000), 147–54.

100. Aileen S. Kraditor, *The Radical Persuasion, 1890–1917: Aspects of the Intellectual History and the Historiography of Three American Radical Organizations* (Baton Rouge, 1981), 136.

101. Neil Foley, *The White Scourge: Mexicans, Blacks, and Poor Whites in Texas Cotton Culture* (Berkeley, 1997), 100; David Paul Nord, "The *Appeal to Reason* and American Socialism, 1901–1920," *Kansas History* 1 (Summer 1978): 84; John Higham, *Strangers in the Land: Patterns of American Nativism, 1860–1925* (New Brunswick, [1955], 1992), 180. Also see Bishop John Noll to Richard Ginder, May 24, 1949, file 30, box 2, JN.

102. *Congressional Record*, July 5, 1916, p. 1840; Bruce L. Larson, *Lindbergh of Minnesota: A Political Biography* (New York, 1972), 206–7.

103. John Ryan to Louis Brandeis, Nov. 13, 1934, file 3, box 4, JR; *Letters of Louis D. Brandeis*, vol. 5 *(1921–1941): Elder Statesman*, ed. Melvin I. Urofsky and David M. Levy (Albany, 1978), 155, 341.

104. Ryan, "Catholic Social Activity in Europe," 183.

105. Joseph F. Bruscher, S.J. , "*Rerum Novarum* in the San Francisco Strike of 1901," *American Ecclesiastical Review* 141 (Aug. 1959): 103–16.

106. Mary Lethert Wingerd, *Claiming the City: Politics, Faith, and the Power of Place in St. Paul* (Ithaca, 2001), 102.

107. William Green to John A. Ryan, March 13, 1929, folder 34, box 14, JR; Pierre Anctil, "Aspects of Class Ideology in a New England Ethnic Minority: The Franco-Americans of Woonsocket, Rhode Island (1865–1929)" (Ph.D. diss., New School for Social Research, 1980), 155.

108. Fr. Jeremiah Harrington, *Catholicism, Capitalism or Communism* (St. Paul, 1926), 6.

109. Charles S. Maier, *Recasting Bourgeois Europe: Stabilization in France, Germany, and Italy in the Decade after World War I* (Princeton, 1975).

110. On Catholic political parties, see the relevant essays in *Political Catholicism in Europe, 1918–1965*, ed. Tom Buchanan and Martin Conway (Oxford, 1996).

111. Entry of Nov. 9, 1918, in *Les Carnets du cardinal Baudrillart, 1 août 1914–31 décembre 1918*, ed. Paul Christophe (Paris, 1994), 954; Ellis Hawley, *The New Deal and the Problem of Monopoly* (Princeton, 1966).

112. Sr. M. Irmtrudis Fiederling, O.S.F., *Adolf Kolping and the Kolping Society of the United States* (Chicago, 1941); Joseph Matt, "The German Roman Catholic Central-Verein" (official souvenir of its golden jubilee) (Cincinnati, 1905), 152.

113. Karl-Egon Lönne, "Germany," in *Political Catholicism in Europe*, ed. Buchanan and Conway, 180–81; Charles Williams, *Adenauer: The Father of the New Germany* (New York, 2000), 221–24.

114. Joseph Husslein, *The World Problem: Capital, Labor and the Church* (New York, 1918), 37–41. On Husslein, see Eugene McCarraher, *Christian Critics: Religion and the Impasse in Modern American Social Thought* (Ithaca, 2000), 27–30.

115. See the summary in Philip Gleason, *The Conservative Reformers: German-American Catholics and the Social Order* (Notre Dame, 1968), 130–36.

116. Robert F. Wesser, *A Response to Progressivism: The Democratic Party and New York Politics, 1902–1918* (New York, 1986), 218.

117. *Watson's Jeffersonian Magazine* 3 (April 1909): 250; "Taft and the Growing Power of Romanism," ibid. 3 (Dec. 1909), 980; ibid. 3 (June 1909): 447. On pentecostals, see Grant Wacker, *Heaven Below: Early Pentecostals and American Culture* (Cambridge, 2001), 182.

118. *Congressional Record*, May 8, 1928, p. 8049.

119. Thomas Elton Brown, "Patriotism or Religion," *Michigan History* 64 (July–Aug. 1980): 36–42. Quotation in "Plans of Oregon Bigots Denounced by Father O'Hara," NCWC news release, n.d., file 7, box 14, SAD-NCWC; Thomas J. Shelley, "The Oregon School Case and the National Catholic Welfare Conference," *Catholic Historical Review* 75 (July 1989): 439–57.

120. Arthur F. Mullen to David F. Rockwell, April 26, 1924, file MA 46, WM.

121. David Burner, *The Politics of Provincialism: The Democratic Party in Transition, 1918–1932* (Cambridge, [1968], 1986), 103–41.

122. David A. Hollinger, *In the American Province: Studies in the History and Historiography of Ideas* (Baltimore, 1985), 56–73.

123. H. L. Mencken, *A Carnival of Buncombe* (Baltimore, 1956), 141, 186.

124. Van Wyck Brooks to Lewis Mumford, April 12, 1938, *The Van Wyck Brooks–Lewis Mumford Letters: The Record of a Literary Friendship, 1921–1963*, ed. Robert E. Spiller (New York, 1970), 154.

125. Felix Frankfurter, "Why I Am for Smith," *New Republic*, Oct. 31, 1928, p. 294; E. C. Lindeman, "The Education of Al Smith," ibid., Nov. 7, 1928, pp. 319–20.

126. Richard Wightman Fox, *Reinhold Niebuhr: A Biography* (New York, 1985), 113; "Should Liberals Vote for Smith?" *Nation*, Sept. 26, 1928, pp. 284–85; Frankfurter, "Why I Am for Smith," 292–95; John Dewey, "Why I Am for Smith," *New Republic*, Nov. 7, 1928, pp. 320–21.

127. John Jay Chapman, "America and Roman Catholicism," *Forum* 73 (April 1925): 454.

128. "Mr. Chapman Replies to Mr. Cram," *Commonweal*, Dec. 10, 1924, p. 116; Charles C. Marshall, "An Open Letter to the Honorable Alfred E. Smith," *Atlantic Monthly* 139 (April 1927): 540; Charles C. Marshall, *Governor Smith's American Catholicism* (New York, 1928); Thomas J. Shelley, "'What the Hell Is an Encyclical?': Governor Alfred E. Smith, Charles C. Marshall, Esq., and Father Francis P. Duffy," *U.S. Catholic Historian* 15 (Spring 1997): 87–107.

129. Oscar Handlin, *Al Smith and His America* (Boston, 1958), 3–4.

130 "Catholic and Patriot: Governor Smith Replies," *Atlantic Monthly* 139 (May 1927): 721–28.

131. Benedict Elder to Arthur Preuss, Aug. 22, 1927, file 2, box 1, AP.

132. "The Marshall-Smith Correspondence," *Outlook* 145 (1927): 522; Walter Lippmann to Al Smith, April 11, 1927, in *Public Philosopher: Selected Letters of Walter Lippmann*, ed. John Morton Blum (New York, 1985), 203; "A Good American and a Good Catholic," *New Republic*, April 27, 1927, p. 260.

133. Allan J. Lichtman, *Prejudice and the Old Politics: The Presidential Election of 1928*. (Chapel Hill, 1979); 231–46; Memorandum, Nov. 24, 1928, file 21, box 9, SAD-NCWC.

134. Oswald von Nell-Breuning, S.J., "The Drafting of Quadragesmo Anno," in *Official Catholic Social Teaching*, ed. Charles Curran and Richard A. McCormick (New York, 1986), 60–68; Francis X. Murphy, "Oswald von Nell-Breuning: Papal Surrogate," *America* 165 (Oct. 26, 1991): 293–95; Paul Droulers, *Le Père Desbuquois et l'Action populaire* (Paris, 1980), 152–56.

135. *Quadragesimo Anno* (1931), in *The Papal Encyclicals, 1903–1939*, ed. Claudia Carlen, I.H.M. (Raleigh, N.C., 1981), 422, 429, 430; Geza B. Grosschmid, "Pesch's Concept of the Living Wage in *Quadragesimo Anno,*" *Review of Social Economy* 12 (Sept. 1954): 146–55.

136. John T. McNicholas, O.P., "Justice and the Present Crisis," *Catholic Mind* 29 (Oct. 22, 1931): 475.

137. Mel Piehl, *Breaking Bread: The Catholic Worker and the Origin of Catholic Radicalism in America* (Philadelphia, 1982). On Mounier, see John Hellman, *Emmanuel Mounier and the New Catholic Left, 1930–1950* (Toronto, 1981).

138. Dorothy Day, "Experiences of Catholic Worker Editor in Steel Towns with C.I.O.," *Catholic Worker* 4 (Aug. 1936): 1–2; "Forty Years After," ibid. 1 (Sept. 1933): 10–12.

139. *The Public Papers and Addressses of Franklin D. Roosevelt,* vol. 1, *The Genesis of the New Deal, 1928–1932*, ed. Samuel I. Rosenman (New York, 1938), 778.

140. Roosevelt to Ellery Sedgwick, March 19, 1927, in Edmund A. Moore, *A Catholic Runs for President* (New York, 1956), 72; John McHugh Stuart to Ryan, Oct. 29, 1932, file 12, box 35, JR.

141. Alan Brinkley, *The End of Reform: New Deal Liberalism in Recession and War* (New York, 1995), 36–39.

142. R. A. McGowan, "Reconstructing the Social Order," in *Proceedings of the Ninth Annual Meeting of the American Catholic Philosophical Association* (1933), 188; Alter, quoted in David J. O'Brien, *American Catholics and Social Reform: The New Deal Years* (New York, 1968), 52. Also see Monroe Billington

and Cal Clark, "Catholic Clergymen, Franklin D. Roosevelt, and the New Deal," *Catholic Historical Review* 79 (Jan. 1993): 65–82.

143. John A. Ryan, "New Deal and Social Justice," *Commonweal*, April 13, 1934, p. 658; Joseph Thorning, S.J., "Principles and Practice of the NRA," *Catholic Mind* 32 (Oct. 8, 1934): 363.

144. Henry F. May, *The End of American Innocence: A Study of the First Years of Our Own Time, 1912–1917* (New York, [1959], 1992).

145. Ryan, *Living Wage*, xii.

146. John Dewey, *Democracy and Education* (1916), in Dewey, *Middle Works*, 9:348.

147. Walter Rauschenbusch, *A Theology for the Social Gospel* (New York, 1917), 175.

148. Ryan, *Living Wage*, 313.

149. John J. Keane, "The Catholic Church and Property," *Quarterly Journal of Economics* 6 (1891): 40–41; Sr. Mary De Paul Faber, O.S.F., "*The Luxemburger Gazette*: A Catholic German Language Paper of the Middle West, 1872–1918" (M.A. thesis, Catholic Univ. of America, 1947), 42.

150. Joseph Husslein, S.J., "Women's Influence in Moulding Political Opinion," *National Catholic Welfare Conference Bulletin* 3 (1921): 14.

151. William Miller, *Dorothy Day: A Biography* (San Francisco, 1982), 63, 198; Richard Wightman Fox, "New Baptized: The Culture of Love in America, 1830s to 1950s," in *Religion and Cultural Studies*, ed. Susan L. Mizruchi (Princeton, 2001), 132–35.

152. Ryan, *Living Wage*, 133.

153. Paul L. Blakely, "The Marriage Encyclical and Wages," *America* 44 (Jan. 24, 1931): 386, 385.

154. For a sampling, see Margaret H. Rourke, *Letters and Addresses on Woman Suffrage by Catholic Ecclesiastics* (New York, 1914); Rev. T. J. Brennan, *A Catholic Clergyman's Reasons for Equal Suffrage* (Berkeley, 1911).

155. Superb on Catholics and parallel developments within Dutch Calvinism and German Lutheranism is Jon Gjerde, *Minds of the West: The Ethnocultural Evolution in the Rural Middle West, 1830–1917* (Chapel Hill, 1997), 298–301.

156. John A. Ryan, "Suffrage and Woman's Responsibility," *America* 18 (Dec. 22, 1917): 260–61.

157. Sr. M. Camilla Mullay, "The Feminist Fight for a Federal Equal Rights Amendment with Particular Reference to the Opposition of the National Council for Catholic Women from 1920 to 1950" (M.A. thesis, Catholic Univ. of America, 1961), 19.

158. Nicola Beisel, *Imperiled Innocents: Anthony Comstock and Family Reproduction in Victorian America* (Princeton, 1997), 50–53. For a general his-

tory, see Paul S. Boyer, *Purity in Print: The Vice-Society Movement and Book Censorship in America* (New York, 1968).

159. Agnes Repplier, "The Repeal of Reticence," *Atlantic Monthly* 113 (March 1914): 297–304; Burke, in Frank Walsh, *Sin and Censorship: The Catholic Church and the Motion Picture Industry* (New Haven, 1996), 15.

160. Jeffrey M. Moran, "'Modernism Gone Mad': Sex Education Comes to Chicago, 1913," *Journal of American History* 83 (Sept. 1996): 505.

161. John W. Melody, "Instruction in Sex Hygiene," *Catholic University Bulletin* (June 1913): 475.

162. Paula M. Kane, *Separatism and Subculture: Boston Catholicism, 1900–1920* (Chapel Hill, 1994), 298–313.

163. Horace Kallen, *Art and Freedom,* vol. 2 (New York, [1942], 1969), 897–98; Boyer, *Purity in Print*, 204.

164. Burke to John Sumner, March 30, 1935, folder 18, box 106, GS-NCWC.

165. *National Catholic Welfare Conference Bulletin* 1 (Oct. 1919): 23–24.

166. Edward F. Garesché, "The Parish Priest and Moving-Pictures," *Ecclesiastical Review* 76 (May 1927): 475.

167. The Lord-Quigley code is reprinted in Gregory D. Black, *Hollywood Censored: Morality Codes, Catholics, and the Movies* (New York, 1994), quotations on 305, 303.

168. Moloney, "Making of *Rerum Novarum*," 30.

169. Kathleen Tobin-Schlesinger, "Population and Power: The Religious Debate over Contraception, 1916–1936," 2 vols. (Ph.D. diss., Univ. of Chicago, 1994).

170. Leslie Woodcock Tentler, "'The Abominable Crime of Onan': Catholic Pastoral Practice and Family Limitation, 1875–1919," *Church History* 71 (June 2002): 307–40.

171. For an overview, see John T. Noonan, *Contraception: A History of Its Treatment by the Catholic Theologians and Canonists*, enl. ed. (Cambridge, [1965], 1986), 414–34.

172. Ryan, *Living Wage*, 287.

173. *Heinrich Pesch on Solidarist Economics*, 253; Philippe Lécrivain, S.J., "Les Semaines sociales de France," in *Le Mouvement social catholique en France au XXe siècle*, (Paris, 1990), 157.

174. John A. Ryan, "Family Limitation," *Ecclesiastical Review* 54 (June 1916): 684–85, 690.

175. Pastoral Letter of the Archbishops and Bishops of the United States, Sept. 25, 1919.

176. Ellen Chesler, *Woman of Valor: Margaret Sanger and the Birth Control Movement in America* (New York, 1992), 27.

177. "Archbishop Hayes on Birth Control," *New York Times*, Dec. 18, 1921, p. 16.

178. "Church Control?" *Birth Control Review* 5 (Dec. 1921): 3.

179. Chesler, *Woman of Valor*, 213.

180. "Birth Control and Taboo," *New Republic*, Nov. 30, 1921, p. 9.

181. Mary Ware Dennett to Council of Voluntary Parenthood League and Contributors, Report #18, June 23, 1921, in file 33, box 116, GS-NCWC.

182. Mary Ware Dennett, Congressional Diary, Jan. 26, 1923, reel 12, MWD.

183. Chesler, *Woman of Valor*, 216.

184. "Mrs. Sanger Calls Catholics Bigots," *New York Times*, April 25, 1928, p. 14.

185. Editorial, *Birth Control Review* 14 (May 1930): 131.

186. Reagan, in Jan. 10, 1921, *Providence Evening News*, clipping in folder 33, box 116, GS-NCWC.

187. Rev. John J. Burke to Ignaz Seipel, May 20, 1932, folder 31, box 116, GS-NCWC; James H. Ryan to Laughlin, Jan. 1, 1922, file 1, box 117, GS-NCWC; Burke to Rev. Robert E. Lucey, May 30, 1925, file 3, ibid.

188. Burke to McNicholas, May 6, 1932, folder 22, box 85, GS-NCWC.

189. Franklin Delano Roosevelt, Memorandum for Dr. Ernest Gruening, May 20, 1935, folder "Puerto Rico, January–June 1935," box 23, Federal Appointments, President's Official File 400, FR; Roosevelt to Fr. John J. Burke, April 23, 1935, ibid.; John J. Burke to Franklin Roosevelt, April 1, 1935, ibid.

190. Riddell, "Catholic Church and the Labour Party" 179–82; Atina Grossman, *Reforming Sex: The German Movement for Birth Control and Abortion Reform, 1920–1950* (New York, 1995), 50–51; Christopher Van Der Krogt, "Excercising the Utmost Vigilance: The Catholic Campaign against Contraception in New Zealand during the 1930s," *Journal of Religious History* 22 (Oct. 1998): 321.

191. "Birth Control and the Labor Movement" (1925), folder 3, box 117, GS-NCWC.

192. John J. Burke to Grace Murray, March 6, 1923, file 2, box 117, GS-NCWC.

193. Ryan, *Living Wage*, 284; Fr. Ignatius Cox, S.J., *Birth Control Is Wrong!* (New York, 1930), 10.

194. John M. Cooper, "Contraception and Altruistic Ethics," *International Journal of Ethics* 41 (1930–31): 457–58.

195. Fr. Ignatius Cox, S.J., *The Divine Romance of Marriage* (New York, 19[30?]), 22.

196. Fr. Daniel A. Lord, S.J., *Speaking of Birth Control* (St. Louis, 1930), 7–11.

197. On this crucial period, see Tobin-Schlesinger, "Population and Power," 206–73, quotation on 237. Also see Richard M. Fagley, *The Population Explosion and Christian Responsibility* (New York, 1960), 189–209.

198. Therese Notare, "'A Revolution in Christian Morals': Resolution #15 at Lambeth 1930," *Revue d'Histoire Ecclésiastique* 44 (Jan.–March and April–June 1999): 54–75, 471–501.

199. *Father Coughlin's Radio Sermons* (Baltimore, 1931), 237.

200. "The Birth Control Revolution," *Commonweal,* April 1, 1931, pp. 589–91.

201. Ryan, *Living Wage*, 131; Edgar Hocedez, S.J., *Histoire de la théologie au XIX siècle,* vol. 3, *Le Règne de Léon XIII, 1878–1903* (Brussels, 1947), 333.

202. Francis Haas to Ryan, Sept. 27, 1929, file 15, box 16, JR.

203. Arthur Vermeersch, "Un Grave Péril moral," *Nouvelle Revue Théologique* 41 (1909): 65–72.

204. Noonan, *Contraception*, 420–22.

205. *Casti Connubii* (1930), in *Papal Encyclicals, 1903–1939*, 399.

206. Ibid., 411.

207. Paul Blakely, S.J., "The Marriage Encyclical and Wages," *America* 44 (Jan. 24, 1931): 384–85.

208. On Flynn, see Jane Colleen Hannon, "Saints and Patriots: Catholicism in the Bronx, 1920–1940" (Ph.D. diss., Univ. of Notre Dame, 2000), 36–99.

209. Kenneth J. Heineman, *A Catholic New Deal: Religion and Reform in Depression Pittsburgh* (University Park, Pa., 1999), 121; John C. Cort, "Are We Missing a Bus? Why Not Support the Murray Industry Council Plan?" *Commonweal*, Aug. 14, 1942, p. 392; Philip Murray, "Labor's Stake in the Principle of the Dignity of Man," in *Democracy: Should It Survive?* (Milwaukee, 1943), 87.

210. Neil Betten, *Catholic Activism and the Industrial Worker* (Gainesville, 1976), 73–89; Richard H. Rovere, "Labor's Catholic Bloc," *Nation*, Jan. 4, 1941, pp. 11–14; Peter McDonough, *Men Astutely Trained: A History of the Jesuits in the American Century* (New York, 1992), 98–118.

211. Archbishop Edward Mooney, "Duty of the Catholic Worker to Join Organized Labor," *Catholic Mind* 37 (March 8, 1939): 569–71.

212. Rt. Rev. Msgr. John A. Ryan, *Social Doctrine in Action: A Personal History* (New York, 1941), 277–85.

213. Brinkley, *End of Reform*, 104.

214. Fr. John Ryan, "Economic Planning and the Occupational Group System," ca. 1938, Ryan Addresses file, box 11, JR.

215. H. Wilensky, "Leftism, Catholicism and Democratic Corporatism: The Role of Political Parties in Recent Welfare State Development," in *The Development of Welfare States in Europe and America*, ed. Peter Flora and Arnold J. Heidenheimer (New Brunswick, 1981), 345–82.

216. Louis Chagnon, S.J., "Bulletin de Philosophie Morale," *Gregorianum* 19 (1938): 615; George Barry O'Toole, "Translator's Preface," in Louis Veuillot, *The Liberal Illusion* (Washington, D.C., 1939), 19.

217. Benjamin L. Masse, S.J. *Economic Liberalism and Free Enterprise* (New York, 1944), 8, 28.

218. George Santayana, "The Alleged Catholic Danger," *New Republic*, Jan. 15, 1916, p. 269.

219. "Is There a Catholic Problem?" *New Republic*, Nov. 16, 1938, pp. 32–33.

CHAPTER 6: AMERICAN FREEDOM AND CATHOLIC POWER

1. Gordon Allport to Edward Darling, May 11, 1950, folder 42, box 1, PB. On publishing figures, see Paul Blanshard to George La Piana, August 7, 1949, folder 13, box 36, GL.

2. Paul Blanshard, *American Freedom and Catholic Power* (Boston, 1949), 9, 303; idem, *Communism, Democracy, and Catholic Power* (Boston, 1951).

3. Blanshard, *American Freedom and Catholic Power*, 67, 226, 81, 302.

4. Lewis Mumford, *The Condition of Man* (New York, 1944), 319; Reinhold Niebuhr, *The Children of Light and the Children of Darkness* (New York, 1944), 128; John Dewey, "Implications of S.2499" (1947), in John Dewey, *The Later Works, 1925–1953*, vol. 15, *1942–1948*, ed. Jo Ann Boydston (Carbondale, Ill., 1989), 284–85; A. Powell Davies, "Let's Be Sane about Russia," March 10, 1946, folder 9, box 7, FME.

5. John Dewey to Melvin Arnold, June 7, 1949, folder 24, box 1, PB. The Dewey quotation was used on the dust jacket of *American Freedom and Catholic Power* after the third printing. Bertrand Russell to Paul Blanshard, April 21, 1951, folder 5, box 2, PB; Albert Einstein to Frederick May Eliot, May 22, 1951, folder 11, box 2, PB; McGeorge Bundy in panel discussion entitled "Religion and the Growth of the Free Mind," 125th American Unitarian Association Convocation, May 23, 1950, folder 7, box 1, 125th Anniversary Collection (Andover Library, Harvard Divinity School).

6. Horace Kallen to Freda Kirchwey, Jan. 16, 1948, folder 903, HK-YIVO.

7. Clifford Kirkpatrick, review of Paul Blanshard, *American Freedom and Catholic Power*, in *Annals of the American Academy of Political and Social Science* 267. (Jan. 1950): 244.

8. George Boas, review of *American Freedom and Catholic Power*, in *Philosophical Review* 59 (Jan. 1950): 126–28.

9. John E. Burchard to Blanshard, Sept. 16, 1949, folder 29, box 1, PB.

10. Philip Gleason, *Speaking of Diversity: Language and Ethnicity in Twentieth-Century America* (Baltimore, 1992), 207–28; John T. McGreevy, "Thinking

on One's Own: Catholicism in the American Intellectual Imagination, 1928–1960," *Journal of American History* 84 (June 1997): 97–131; Christopher Shannon, *A World Made Safe for Differences: Cold War Intellectuals and the Politics of Identity* (Lanham, Md., 2001), xviii–xx; David A. Hollinger, *Science, Jews, and Secular Culture: Studies in Mid-Twentieth-Century American Intellectual History* (Princeton, 1996), 158–59. Also see the early and incisive commentary of Edward A. Purcell Jr., *The Crisis of Democratic Theory: Scientific Naturalism & the Problem of Value* (Lexington, Ky., 1973), 202–4.

11. *The Catholic Church and Politics: A Discussion of a Vital Issue*, (Harvard Law School Forum, 1950), folder 17, box 4, MA.

12. Robert S. Lynd, *Knowledge for What?: The Place of Social Science in American Culture* (Princeton, [1939], 1948), 19.

13. Warren I. Susman, *Culture as History: The Transformation of American Society in the Twentieth Century* (New York, 1985), 155.

14. John Dewey to Alice Dewey, July 13, 1918, in John Dewey, *Correspondence of John Dewey*, vol. 1, *1871–1918*, ed. Larry A. Hickman (electronic ed., Center for Dewey Studies, Southern Illinois Univ. Carbondale, 1999); John Dewey, "Confidential Report of Conditions among the Poles in the United States" (1918), in *The Middle Works, 1899–1924*, vol. 11, *1918–1919*, ed. Jo Ann Boydston (Carbondale, Ill., 1982), 262, 286, 303–4. For a good summary of this venture despite the complaint that it has received "inordinate attention" from scholars, see Robert B. Westbrook, *John Dewey and American Democracy* (Ithaca, 1991), 212–23.

15. Brand Blanshard, *The Church and the Polish Immigrant* (n.p., 1920).

16. André Siegfried, *America Comes of Age*, trans. H. H. Hemming and Doris Hemming (New York, 1927), 50–51.

17. Winfred E. Garrison, *Catholicism and the American Mind* (Chicago, 1928), 243.

18. Ibid., 14–15, 200; "More about Catholicism and the Presidency," *New Republic*, May 11, 1927, pp. 315–17.

19. Gleason, *Speaking of Diversity*, 153–206. Also see Alan Brinkley, *The End of Reform: New Deal Liberalism in Depression and War* (New York, 1994), 137–271.

20. David C. Bailey, *¡Viva Cristo Rey!: The Cristero Rebellion and the Church-State Conflict in Mexico* (Austin, Tex., 1974).

21. John Dewey, "Church and State in Mexico" (1926), in John Dewey, *The Later Works, 1925–1953*, vol. 2, *1925–1957*, ed. Jo Ann Boydston (Carbondale, Ill., 1984), 197–98. Also see John Dewey, "Mexico's Educational Renaissance" (1926), ibid., 199–205.

22. Robert David Johnson, *Ernest Gruening and the American Dissenting Tra-*

dition (Cambridge, 1998), 13–16; Ernest Gruening, *Mexico and Its Heritage* (New York, 1928), 281.

23. "Catholicism contra Mundum," *New Republic*, Sept. 2, 1916, pp. 104–5; "More about Catholicism and the Presidency," ibid., May 11, 1927, pp. 315–16; "A Test for Governor Smith," ibid., April 6, 1927, p. 183; Walter Lippmann to Al Smith, March 21, 1927, in *Public Philosopher: Selected Letters of Walter Lippmann*, ed. John Morton Blum (New York, 1985), 201–2.

24. For example, see Letter from Exiled Mexican Bishops meeting in San Antonio to Pope Pius XI, Nov. 20, 1928, in Persecution file, box 17, PM. For a concise summary of Catholic and Vatican involvement in diplomatic negotiations, see Gerald P. Fogarty, *The Vatican and the American Hierarchy from 1870 to 1965* (Collegeville, Minn., 1985), 230–36; James C. Hasdorff, "The *Southern Messenger* and the Mexican Church-State Controversy, 1917–1941," *Journal of Texas Catholic History and Culture* 5 (1994): 25–46; David A. Badillo, "Between Alienation and Ethnicity: The Evolution of Mexican-American Catholicism in San Antonio, 1910–1940," *Journal of American Ethnic History* 16 (Summer 1997): 62–83.

25. "40,000 in Holy Name Union Demonstration to Restore Religious Freedom in Mexico," *Los Angeles Tidings*, Dec. 14, 1934, pp. 54–55.

26. Bishop Philip McDevitt to Fr. John Burke, July 15, 1927, NCWC file, box 17, PM; [Fr. John Burke], Memorandum of Interview with Ambassador Morrow, Oct. 13, 1927, ibid.

27. Stewart A. Stehlin, *Weimar and the Vatican, 1919–1933: German-Vatican Diplomatic Relations in the Interwar Years* (Princeton, 1983), 431–47; William L. Patch Jr., *Heinrich Brüning and the Dissolution of the Weimar Republic* (Cambridge, 1998), 295–305.

28. John Pollard, "Italy," in *Political Catholicism in Europe, 1918–1965*, ed. Tom Buchanan and Martin Conway (Oxford, 1996), 81.

29. On American intellectuals and Mussolini, see John P. Diggins, *Mussolini and Fascism: The View from America* (Princeton, 1972), 5–73.

30. "O'Connell Lauds Mussolini," *New York Times*, Feb. 29, 1924, p. 4; "Hayes Comes Home; Opposes Dry Law," ibid., Feb. 7, 1926, p. 3.

31. Peter R. D'Agostino, "The Scalabrini Fathers, the Italian Emigrant Church, and Ethnic Nationalism in America," *Religion and American Culture* 7 (Winter 1997): 145.

32. Frances Lannon, *Privilege, Persecution and Prophecy: The Catholic Church in Spain, 1875–1975* (Oxford, 1987), 170–224.

33. "American Jesuits Salute Franco," *Woodstock Letters* 68 (1939): 112, 107.

34. *American Democracy vs. the Spanish Hierarchy* (New York, 1937), 6.

35. Waldo Frank, "Spain in War I: The People," *New Republic*, July 13, 1938, p. 271.

36. Reinhold Niebuhr, "The Catholic Heresy," *Christian Century* 54 (Dec. 8, 1937): 1524; Lewis Mumford, "The Call to Arms," *New Republic*, May 18, 1938, p. 41.

37. Rev. John A. Ryan, *Seven Troubled Years, 1930–1936* (Ann Arbor, 1937), 298; "Mgr. Ryan Backs Roosevelt, Attacks Father Coughlin," *New York Times*, Oct. 9, 1936, p. 1.

38. John T. McGreevy, *Parish Boundaries: The Catholic Encounter with Race in the Twentieth-Century Urban North* (Chicago, 1996), 48–50.

39. Julius Morgenstern to Bishop Francis C. Kelley, Dec. 6, 1938, box 6, file 13, JM-AJA.

40. Memorandum of a Discussion at a Conference Called by Justice Felix Frankfurter in Washington, D.C., April 10, 1939, in folder 119, box 3, ser. I, ML.

41. "Liberty in Journal Square," *New Republic*, May 18, 1938, p. 30; Leo H. Lehman, "The Catholic Church and Politics: The Church and Freedom of Speech," ibid., Nov. 16, 1938, pp. 34–36.

42. John M. Mecklin, "Freedom of Speech for Clergymen," *Annals of the American Academy of Political and Social Science* 200 (Nov. 1938): 170–71.

43. Jeffrey Meyers, *Edmund Wilson: A Biography* (Boston, 1995), 314; Edmund Wilson, *The Triple Thinkers: Twelve Essays on Literary Subjects* (New York, 1948), 161.

44. Talcott Parsons, "Academic Freedom" (1939), in *Talcott Parsons on National Socialism*, ed. Uta Gerhardt (New York, 1993), 98.

45. Sidney Hook to Edward Shils, Nov. 19, 1941, folder 34, box 44, SH.

46. Bertrand Russell, *Why I Am Not a Christian*, ed. Paul Edwards (London, 1957), 183; Paul Blakely, S.J., "The Teacher and Caesar's Wife," *America* 63 (April 13, 1940): 6; "Comment," ibid., 2; Clippings of addresses by Archbishop Spellman and Fr. John A. Toomey, S.J., in reel 179, microfilm ed. of ACLU papers.

47. Kallen to Walter Hamilton, Nov. 6, 1940, box 71, file 11, HK-AJA.

48. Patricia Russell to Roger Baldwin, April 3, 1940, reel 179, ACLU; Roger Baldwin to Bertrand Russell, April 3, 1940, ibid.; Horace M. Kallen, "Behind the Bertrand Russell Case," in *The Bertrand Russell Case*, ed. John Dewey and Horace Kallen (New York, [1941], 1972), 30, 53. Also see Caroline Moorehead, *Bertrand Russell: A Life* (New York, 1993), 430–36.

49. Sidney Hook to Katherine Hayden Slater, May 7, 1943, folder 1, box 46, SH.

50. John Dewey, *Freedom and Culture* (New York, 1939), 98.

51. John Dewey to Ernest Hocking, May 16, 1940, copy in folder 7, box 175, SH.

52. *Encyclopaedia of the Social Sciences*, s.v. "Intolerance"; ibid., "Modernism."

53. Charles Morris, in *The Authoritarian Attempt to Capture Education, 1944* (New York, 1945), 142.

54. Merrill Peterson, *The Jefferson Image in the American Mind* (New York, 1960), esp. 355–62.

55. *The Living Thoughts of Thomas Jefferson*, ed. John Dewey (New York, 1940), 98–100.

56. Peterson, *Jefferson Image in the American Mind*, 431.

57. Horace M. Kallen, "Freedom and Authoritarianism in Religion," in *Scientific Spirit and Democratic Faith, 1945* (New York, 1944), 5.

58. Mark Silk, *Spiritual Politics: Religion and America since World War II* (New York, 1988), 40–53.

59. Joseph L. Blau, "'The Freeborn Mind': A Review Article," *Review of Religion* 9 (Nov. 1944): 36–37.

60. Howard Mumford Jones, "The Drift to Liberalism in the American Eighteenth Century" (1936), in Jones, *Ideas in America* (New York, 1965), 120.

61. Henry Sloane Coffin, "Foreword," in James Hastings Nichols, *Democracy and the Churches* (Philadelphia, 1951), 7.

62. William Warren Sweet, *The American Churches: An Interpretation* (London, 1947), 15. See also Roland Bainton, *Studies on the Reformation* (Boston, [1941], 1963), 129.

63. William Warren Sweet, *The Story of Religion in America* (New York, 1950), 441.

64. Ernest Sutherland Bates, *American Faith: Its Religious, Political, and Economic Foundations* (New York, 1940), 9.

65. Henry Steele Commager, *The American Mind* (New Haven, 1950), 165.

66. Ibid., 97, 194.

67. Ralph Gabriel, *The Course of American Democratic Thought: An Intellectual History since 1815* (New York, 1940), 287.

68. Van Wyck Brooks to Sidney Hook, Sept. 24, 1940, folder 34, box 44, SH; Robert F. Spiller et al., eds., *Literary History of the United States*, vol. 1 (New York, 1948), xvi.

69. *Theory and Practice in Historical Study: A Report of the Committee on Historiography* (New York, 1946), 136.

70. Max Weber, *The Protestant Ethic and the Spirit of Capitalism*, trans. Talcott Parsons (London, 1930); Talcott Parsons, *The Structure of Social Action* (Glencoe, Ill., [1937], 1949), 52–53, 500–538. See also idem, "The Circumstances of My Encounter with Max Weber," *Sociological Traditions from Generation to Generation: Glimpses of the American Experience*, ed. Robert K. Merton and Matilda White Riley (Norwood, N.J., 1980), 37–45.

71. Talcott Parsons, "Memorandum: The Development of Groups and Organizations Amenable to Use against American Institutions and Foreign Policy and Possible Measures of Prevention"([1940), in *Talcott Parsons on National Socialism*, 106–7, 130; Benton Johnson and Miriam M. Johnson, "The Integrating of the Social Sciences: Theoretical and Empirical Research and Training in the Department of Social Relations at Harvard," *The Nationalization of the Social Sciences*, ed. Samuel Z. Klausner and Victor M. Lidz (Philadelphia, 1986), 138; Talcott Parsons, "Sociology and Social Psychology," *Religious Perspectives in College Teaching* (New York, 1952), 324, 326.

72. Robert Merton, *Science, Technology, and Society in Seventeenth-Century England* (New York, [1938], 1970), 99–136. The explosion of interest in science conducted under Catholic auspices during the seventeenth and eighteenth centuries has complicated Merton's definition of what constitutes science, as well as the theological underpinnings of his argument. For overviews, see Rivka Feldhay, "The Cultural Field of Jesuit Science," in *The Jesuits: Cultures, Sciences and the Arts 1540–1773*, ed. John W. O'Malley, S.J., et al. (Toronto, 1999), 107–30; J. L. Heilbron, "Science in the Church," *Science in Context* 3 (1989): 9–28; Steven J. Harris, "Transposing the Merton Thesis: Apostolic Spirituality and the Establishment of the Jesuit Scientific Tradition," ibid., 30–66.

73. Talcott Parsons to Eric Voegelin, Aug. 18, 1941, Voegelin file, box 17, HUG 15.2, TP; George Sarton, *Horus: A Guide to the History of Science* (Waltham, Mass., 1952), 33–34.

74. Robert Merton, *Social Theory and Social Structure* (Glencoe, Ill., [1942], 1957), 550–61. See also Hollinger, *Science, Jews, and Secular Culture*, 80–96.

75. Kallen, "Freedom and Authoritarianism in Religion," 3.

76. George West, "The Catholic Issue," *New Republic*, March 1, 1943, p. 278; M. F. Ashley Montague, review of G. G. Coulton, *Inquisition and Liberty*, in *Isis* 30 (Aug. 1939), 559.

77. Isidor Thorner, "Ascetic Protestantism and the Development of Science and Technology," *American Journal of Sociology* 58 (July 1952): 25–33.

78. Robert H. Knapp and Joseph J. Greenbaum, *The Younger American Scholar: His Collegiate Origins* (Chicago, 1953), 47; R. H. Knapp and H. B. Goodrich, *Origins of American Scientists* (Chicago, 1952), 24, 288–89; Bernard Barber, *Science and the Social Order* (Glencoe, Ill., 1952), 136.

79. Ernest W. Burgess, "The Family in a Changing Society," *American Journal of Sociology* 53 (May 1948): 419; Margaret Mead, "Administrative Contributions to Democratic Character Formation at the Adolescent Level," in *Personality in Nature, Society, and Culture*, ed. Clyde Kluckhohn and Henry A. Murray (New York, [1941], 1948), 527–28.

80. T. W. Adorno et al., *The Authoritarian Personality* (New York, 1950), 221, 310, 218.

81. A. H. Maslow, *Motivation and Personality* (New York, 1954), 221.

82. Adorno et al., *Authoritarian Personality*, 734, 230; Milton Rokeach, *The Open and Closed Mind: Investigations into the Nature of Belief Systems and Personality Systems* (New York, 1960), 4.

83. Seymour Martin Lipset, "The Sources of the Radical Right," in *The New American Right*, ed. Daniel Bell (New York, 1955), 201, 230.

84. Charles Clayton Morrison, *Can Protestantism Win America?* (New York, 1948), 73–74; Blanshard, *American Freedom and Catholic Power*, 156–79.

85. Nicholas Lemann, "Is There a Science of Success?" *Atlantic Monthly* 273 (Feb. 1994): 83–98.

86. David C. McClelland et al., *The Achievement Motive* (New York, 1953), 275. See also David C. McClelland, A. Rindlisbacher, and Richard deCharms, "Religious and Other Sources of Parental Attitudes toward Independence Training," in *Studies in Motivation*, ed. David C. McClelland (New York, 1955), 389–97.

87. McClelland et al., *Achievement Motive*, 277; David C. McClelland, *The Achieving Society* (Princeton, 1961), 361.

88. On McClelland and foreign aid, see Ellen Herman, *The Romance of American Psychology: Political Culture in the Age of Experts* (Berkeley, 1995), 139–41.

89. McClelland, *Achieving Society*, 51–53.

90. For Dewey's statement, see David B. Tyack, "The Perils of Pluralism: The Background of the Pierce Case," *American Historical Review* 74 (Oct. 1968): 82.

91. "Can the Supreme Court Guarantee Toleration?" *New Republic*, June 17, 1925, p. 86.

92. Elin L. Anderson, *We Americans: A Study of Cleavage in an American City* (Cambridge, 1937), 80, 97, 110, 113.

93. Frankfurter note of Jan. 22, 1944, cited in Gerald T. Dunne, *Hugo Black and the Judicial Revolution* (New York, 1977), 266; Max Lerner, *Nine Scorpions in a Bottle: Great Judges and Cases of the Supreme Court*, ed. Richard Cummings (New York, [1947], 1994), 195.

94. *New York Times*, Aug. 30, 1949, p. 15.

95. *Cochran v. Board of Education*, 281 U.S. 370 (1930); Dewey, "Implications of S.2499," 284–85.

96. Rev. William E. McManus, "State Aid for Parochial Schools," May 21, 1948, in file 12, box 11, SAD-NCWC.

97. Gilbert E. Smith, *The Limits of Reform: Politics and Federal Aid to Education, 1937–1950* (New York, 1982), 52–56, 138.

98. *Everson v. Board of Education*, 330 U.S. 16 (1947).

99. Prof. John Child quoted in *New York Times*, March 6, 1947, p. 27. Among law professors support for the dissenters in *Everson* was overwhelming. See Robert Drinan, "The Lawyers and Religion," *America*, (March 5, 1949): 593–95;

Thomas Reed Powell, "Public Rides to Private Schools," *Harvard Educational Review* 17 (Spring 1947), 73–84; Max Lerner to Felix Frankfurter, Feb. 20, 1947, folder 131, box 3, ser. I, ML; Max Lerner to Wiley Rutledge, Feb. 20, 1947, folder 348, box 7, ser. I, ML.

100. For a copy of the initial POAU manifesto, see Joseph Martin Dawson, *Separate Church and State Now* (New York, 1948), 199–213.

101. Frederick May Eliot, sermon at the Jefferson Memorial, April 13, 1947, folder 24, box 33, FME; Eliot to Russell R. Bletzer, April 15, 1947, folder 1, box 29, FME.

102. Justice Wiley B. Rutledge Memo after Conference [1946], *Everson* file, box 143, WR-LC.

103. Felix Frankfurter to Arthur Schlesinger Jr., March 12, 1948, Frankfurter file, box P-14, AS; Horace Kallen to Felix Frankfurter, March 9, 1948, file 925, HK-YIVO.

104. *McCollum v. Board of Education* 333 U.S. 203 (1948); John Courtney Murray, S.J., "Law or Prepossessions?" *Journal of Law and Contemporary Problems* 14 (Winter 1949): 31, 37; Irving Brant, "Madison: On the Separation of Church and State," *William and Mary Quarterly* 8 (Jan. 1951): 3–24.

105. Melvin I. Urofsky, "Church and State," in *The Bill of Rights in Modern America: After 200 Years*, ed. David J. Bodenhamer and James W. Ely Jr. (Bloomington, Ind., 1993), 64.

106. For a superb exception, see Philip Hamburger, *Separation of Church and State* (Cambridge, 2002), 422–78.

107. Howard Ball, *Hugo L. Black: Cold Steel Warrior* (New York, 1996), 134.

108. Note especially the comments about Catholicism in La Piana to Frankfurter, Nov. 22, 1948, in *The Felix Frankfurter Papers* (microfilm, 209 reels, University Publications of America, 1987), reel 16, pt. 3. On George La Piana, see Frankfurter to La Piana, n.d. [c. 1951], file 26, box 30, GL; La Piana to Frankfurter, Nov. 18, 1951, ibid. On the *Nation*, see Memo to Lillie Schultz from Freda Kirchwey, July 13, 1948, folder 124, box 7, FK.

109. Justice Wiley B. Rutledge Memo after Conference (1946), *Everson* file, box 143, WR-LC; Irving Brant to Rutledge, Nov. 10, 1947, Rutledge file, box 13, IB; Rutledge to Brant, Nov. 12, 1947, ibid.; Brant to Rutledge, March 11, 1947, ibid.; Brant to Rutledge, March 11, 1947, ibid.; Rutledge to Brant, Nov. 25, 1947, ibid.

110. Harold Burton to Frederick May Eliot, Nov. 6, 1945, B file, box 9, FME; George N. Marshall, *A. Powell Davies and His Times* (Boston, 1990), 170.

111. On Black's anti-Catholic sentiments, see Hamburger, *Separation of Church and State*, 422–34. Anti-Catholic sentiment in Birmingham resulted in a purge of all Catholics from city positions in 1920. See John Higham, *Strangers in*

the Land: Patterns of American Nativism, 1860–1925 (New Brunswick, 1955), 292.

112. Roger K. Newman, *Hugo Black: A Biography* (New York, 1994), 104.

113. *New York Times*, Aug. 18, 1937, p. 6.

114. John William Draper, *History of the Intellectual Development of Europe* (New York, 1863), 409. On Black's enthusiasm for Draper, see Max Lerner, *Ideas Are Weapons: The History and Use of Ideas* (New York, 1939), 260.

115. Gerald T. Dunne, *Hugo Black and the Judicial Revolution* (New York, 1977), 269; Hugo T. Black, *My Father: A Remembrance* (New York, 1975), 104.

116. Frankfurter, in *McCollum v. Board of Education* 333 U.S. 231 (1948); Joseph L. Blau, "Democracy and Parochial Schools," *Jewish Frontier* 21 (April 1954): 13.

117. On the link between debates over Catholic schools and African American segregation, see Mark DeWolfe Howe, *The Garden and the Wilderness: Religion and Government in American Constitutional History* (Chicago, 1965), 138–43. On Brand Blanshard, see Brand Blanshard, "Theology and the Value of the Individual," in *The Scientific Spirit and Democratic Faith, 1945* (New York, 1944), 74–86; Brand Blanshard to Paul Blanshard, June 15, 1951, folder 9, box 2, PB; Dan A. Oren, *Joining the Club: A History of Jews and Yale* (New Haven, 1985), 261–66.

118. J. Roland Pennock, *Liberal Democracy: Its Merits and Prospects* (New York, 1950), 293.

119. *McCollum v. Board of Education* 333 U.S. 231 (1948); Horace M. Kallen, *The Education of Free Men* (New York, 1949), 213; Perry Miller, review of Paul Blanshard, *Communism, Democracy, and Catholic Power*, in *New York Herald Tribune*, June 10, 1951, sec. 6, p. 1.

120. *Everson v. Board of Education* 330 U.S. at 23, 24 (1947).

121. Agnes E. Meyer, "The School, the State and the Church," *Atlantic Monthly* 182 (Nov. 1948): 50.

122. James Bryant Conant, *Science and Common Sense* (New Haven, 1951), 10; James Bryant Conant, "The Advancement of Learning during the Puritan Commonwealth," *Proceedings of the Massachusetts Historical Society* 66 (Oct. 1936–May 1941): 17.

123. James G. Hershberg, *James B. Conant: Harvard to Hiroshima and the Making of the Nuclear Age* (New York, 1993), 578–89; Levering Reynolds Jr., "The Later Years," in *The Harvard Divinity School: Its Place in Harvard University and in American Culture*, ed. George Huntston Williams (Boston, 1954), 212–13; interview with former Harvard president Nathan Pusey, cited in Richard Norton Smith, *The Harvard Century: The Making of a University to a Nation* (New York, 1986), 186.

124. James Bryant Conant, "Education for a Classless Society: The Jefferson-

ian Tradition," *Atlantic Monthly* 165 (May 1940): 597; idem, *Education in a Divided World* (Cambridge, 1949), 62–63; idem, *Thomas Jefferson and the Development of American Public Education* (Berkeley, 1963), 19; Hershberg, *James B. Conant*, 582.

125. A copy of the address is in James Bryant Conant, *My Several Lives: Memoirs of a Social Inventor* (New York, 1970), 665–70.

126. *Boston Globe*, April 14, 1952, p. 1; *Harvard Crimson*, April 18, 1952, p. 1.

127. "Blanshard Backs Conant in Education Argument," *Harvard Crimson*, April 18, 1952, p. 1.

128. Conant to Charles A. Coolidge, April 28, 1952, AASA comments file, box 1, JBC.

CHAPTER 7: DEMOCRACY, RELIGIOUS FREEDOM, AND THE NOUVELLE THÉOLOGIE

1. Gouverneur Paulding to Abbé Journet, May 21, 1940, in *Journet-Maritain Correspondance*, vol. 3, *1940–1949* (Fribourg, 1998), 902–4.

2. Maritain to Yves R. Simon, Aug. 6, 1939, YS. For a concise analysis of Maritain's philosophy in a broad context, see Gary Gutting, *French Philosophy in the Twentieth Century* (Cambridge, Eng., 2001), 94–98. On Maritain's influence during the war, see Renée Bédarida, *Les Catholiques dans la guerre 1939–1945: Entre Vichy et la Résistance* (Paris, 1998), 142–48.

3. Judith D. Suther, *Raïssa Maritain: Pilgrim, Poet, Exile* (New York, 1990), 42–63; Jean-Luc Barré, *Jacques et Raïssa Maritain: Les Mendiants du ciel* (Paris, 1995), 557–63.

4. W. A. Swanberg, *Luce and His Empire* (New York, 1972), 402; Emmet John Hughes, "A Man for Our Season" (1969), folder 1288, box 28, JCM.

5. John Courtney Murray, "Current Theology: Christian Cooperation," *Theological Studies* 3 (Sept. 1942): 421.

6. Maritain to the *Nation*, Feb. 2, 1949, box 1, folder 1, JM-MI; John Courtney Murray, "Paul Blanshard and the New Nativism," *Month* 5 (April 1951): 216.

7. John Courtney Murray, S.J., "Freedom of Religion," *Theological Studies* 6 (March 1945): 87. On the general topic, see Wendy L. Wall, "'Our Enemies Within': Nazism, National Unity, and America's Wartime Discource on Tolerance," in *Enemy Images in American History*, ed. Ragnhild Fiebig-von Hase and Ursula Lehmkuhl (Providence, 1997), 216–23.

8. Joseph A. Komonchak, "'The Crisis in Church-State Relationships in the U.S.A.': A Recently Discovered Text by John Courtney Murray," *Review of Politics* 61. (Fall 1999): 692.

9. Jacques Maritain to P. Garrigou-Lagrange, May 12, 1948, in *Journet-Maritain Correspondence*, 644; Valentine Zuber, "Concorde ou pluralisme? Les Historiens catholiques et l'essor de l'oecuménisme dans la deuxième moitié du XXe siècle," *Revue d'Histoire de l'Eglise de France* 86 (July–Dec. 2000): 387; Joseph A. Komonchak, "The Silencing of John Courtney Murray," in *Cristianesimo nella storia: Saggi in onore di Giuseppe Alberigo*, ed. Alberto Melloni et al. (Bologna, 1996), 664–65; Jacques Maritain, *Man and the State* (Chicago, 1951), 156.

10. John Courtney Murray, S.J., "Current Theology: Freedom of Religion," *Theological Studies* 6 (March 1945): 98; idem to Vincent McCormick, S.J., Sept. 9, 1953, folder 151, box 2, JCM. On Maritain in Latin America, see Austen Ivereigh, *Catholicism and Politics in Argentina, 1810–1960* (New York, 1995), 112–19.

11. Philippe Chenaux, *Paul VI et Maritain: Les Rapports du "Montinianisme" et du "Maritainisme"* (Rome, 1994).

12. John Courtney Murray to John Tracy Ellis, July 20, 1953, folder 62, box 1, JCM.

13. Wilfrid Parsons, S.J., "Philosophical Factors in the Integration of American Culture," in *Phases of American Culture*, ed. Clarence E. Sloane, S.J. (Worcester, Mass., 1942), 15. Also see Wilfrid Parsons, S.J., *Which Way, Democracy?* (New York, 1939), 2–4.

14. Francis E. Lucey, S.J., "Natural Law and American Legal Realism: Their Respective Contributions to a Theory of Law in a Democratic Society," *Georgetown Law Journal* 39 (April 1942): 524; idem, "Jurisprudence and the Future Social Order," *Social Science* 16 (July 1941): 213.

15. James A. McWilliams, "John Dewey's Educational Philosophy," *Modern Schoolman* 22 (March 1945): 147

16. Stephen F. McNamee, "Presidential Address," in *Phases of American Culture*, ed. Sloane, 11.

17. Edward A. Purcell Jr., *The Crisis of Democratic Theory: Scientific Naturalism and the Problem of Value* (Lexington, Ky., 1973), 168–70, 220–22.

18. R. J. Belleperche to Mortimer Adler, April 17, 1934, Belleperche file 1934–1936, box 29, MA-UC.

19. John Dewey to M. C. Otto, May 8, 1935, copy in file 7, box 175, SH.

20. Philip Gleason, *Contending with Modernity: Catholic Higher Education in the Twentieth Century* (New York, 1995), 125–30.

21. Frankfurter to John Ford, S.J., Feb. 3, 1942, Frankfurter file, box 15, JF-HC.

22. John LaFarge to Luigi Sturzo, June 22, 1943, folder 1, box 20, JLF.

23. Roger Aubert, *La Théologie catholique au milieu du XX siècle* (Paris, 1954), 45–46. For an illuminating overview, see Aidan Nichols, O.P., *From Newman to Congar: The Idea of Doctrinal Development from the Victorians to the Second Vatican Council* (Edinburgh, 1990).

24. On the general problem, see Henri de Lubac, S.J., *Catholicism: A Study of Dogma in Relation to the Corporate Destiny of Mankind*, trans. Lancelot C. Sheppard (New York, [1938], 1950.) The broad subject of European Catholic theology in the 1940s and 1950s needs a sophisticated English-language history. For a superb beginning, see Joseph A. Komonchak, "Theology and Culture at Mid-Century: The Example of Henri De Lubac," *Theological Studies* 51 (March 1990): 579–602.

25. Henri de Lubac, *The Drama of Atheist Humanism*, trans. Edith M. Riley (New York, [1945], 1949), esp. 68–73. idem, "La Question des évêques sous l'occupation," *Revue des Deux Mondes* 58 (1944; Feb. 1992): 70; Jacques Maritain to Charles Journet, June 24, 1945, in *Journet-Maritain Correspondance*, 324. On Quebec, see Eric Amyot, *Le Québec entre Pétain et de Gaulle: Vichy, France libre et les Canadiens français, 1940–1945* (Saint-Laurent, Quebec, 1999), 65–68.

26. Marie-Dominique Chenu, *Une Ecole de théologie: Le Saulchoir* (Paris, [1937], 1985), 122, 143, 155.

27. Charles Kannengiesser, S.J., "Fifty Years of Patristics," *Theological Studies* 50 (Dec. 1989): 633–56.

28. Yves Congar, "Attitudes towards Reform in the Church," *Cross currents* 1 (Summer 1951): 78–102; Henri de Lubac, "The New Man: The Marxist and the Christian View," ibid. 1 (Fall 1950): 67–88; Karl Rahner, "The Church of Sinners," ibid. 1 (Spring 1951): 64–74; John Courtney Murray, "Contemporary Orientations of Catholic Thought on Church and State in the Light of History," ibid. 2 (Fall 1951): 15–55. On the magazine, see Joseph Cunneen, "The Dialogue Has Barely Begun," ibid. 50 (Spring–Summer 2000): 51–52.

29. Gustave Weigel, S.J., "The Historical Background of the Encyclical *Humani Generis*" *Theological Studies* 12 (June 1951): 227.

30. John Henry Newman, "On Consulting the Faithful in Matters of Doctrine," *Cross currents* 2 (Summer 1952): 69–97; Walter J. Ong, S.J., "Newman's Essay on Development in Its Intellectual Milieu," *Theological Studies* 7 (March 1946): 3–45.

31. On the United States, see Philip Gleason, *Speaking of Diversity: Language and Ethnicity in Twentieth-Century America* (Baltimore, 1992), 286–89.

32. Roger Aubert, "Monseigneur Dupanloup et le syllabus," *Revue d'Histoire Ecclésiastique* 51 (1956): 79–42, 471–512, 837–915; idem, "Actualité de Newman," *La Revue Nouvelle* 22 (1955): 455–63; John W. O'Malley, *Trent and All That: Renaming Catholicism in the Early Modern Era* (Cambridge, 2000), 89; Roger Aubert, *Le Pontificat de Pie IX (1846–1878)* (Paris, 1952).

33. John Tracy Ellis to Fr. Joseph N. Moody, Dec. 6, 1953, 1953–1954 file, box 6, JTE; Roger Aubert to Ellis, Jan. 31, 1957, 1957–1962 file, box 8, JTE.

34. John Tracy Ellis, *The Life of James Cardinal Gibbons, Archbishop of Baltimore, 1834–1921* (Milwaukee, 1952).

35. Avery Dulles, "Theological Orientations: American Catholic Theology, 1940–1962," *Cristianesimo nella Storia* 13 (1992): 363.

36. Gerald McCool, S.J., "Maritain's Defense of Democracy," *Thought* 54 (June 1979): 134.

37. Raymond Grew, "Liberty and the Catholic Church in Nineteenth-Century Europe," in *Freedom and Religion in the Nineteenth Century*, ed. Richard Helmstadter (Stanford, 1997), 196–232.

38. Tom Gallagher, "Portugal," in *Political Catholicism in Europe, 1918–1965*, ed. Tom Buchanan and Martin Conway (Oxford, 1996), 129–55; Ellen L. Evans, *The Cross and the Ballot: Catholic Political Parties in Germany, Switzerland, Austria, Belgium and the Netherlands, 1785–1985*, (Boston, 1999), 190–91; Laura Gellott, "Defending Catholic Interests in the Christian State: The Role of Catholic Action in Austria, 1933–1938," *Catholic Historical Review* 74. (Oct. 1988) 571–89.

39. Robert E. Burns, *Being Catholic, Being American: The Notre Dame Story, 1934–1952*, vol. 2 (Notre Dame, 2000), 14–28.

40. For an introduction, see Kathleen Mary Connelly, S.C.L., "Catholic Witness: The Political Activities of Five European Christian Democratic Scholars While in Exile in the United States, 1938–1945" (Ph.D. diss., Boston College, 1995).

41. Godfrey A. Briefs, "Goetz Briefs' Life and Work," *Social Order* 9 (May 1959): 196–200; Johannes Schwarte, *Gustav Gundlach S.J. (1892–1963)* (Munich, 1975), 38.

42. Dietrich von Hildebrand, "The Dethronement of Truth," *Proceedings of the American Catholic Philosophical Association* 18 (1942): 3–16. On Hildebrand and marriage, see John T. Noonan Jr., *Contraception: A History of Its Treatment by the Catholic Theologians and Canonists*, enl. ed. (Cambridge, [1965], 1986), 494–95.

43. M. A. Fitzsimons, "The Human Prospect as Seen in *The Review of Politics*, 1939–1992: A Sesquicentennial Reflection," *Review of Politics* 54 (Fall 1992): 509–49.

44. Alice von Hildebrand, *The Soul of a Lion: Dietrich von Hildebrand: A Biography* (San Francisco, 2000), 243–44; Klaus Scholder, *The Churches and the Third Reich*, vol. 2, *The Year of Disillusionment: 1934* (Philadelphia, 1988), 202.

45. Gurian, quoted in Yves R. Simon to Maritain, July 16, 1941, YS.

46. Yves R. Simon to Maritain, July 16, 1941, YS; Yves R. Simon to Maritain, Nov. 6, 1941, YS.

47. Yves R. Simon to Maritain, Sept. 3, 1941, YS.

48. George N. Schuster, "Dr. Brüning's Sojourn in the United States (1935–1945)," in *Staat, Wirtschaft und Politik in der Weimarer Republik: Festschrift für Heinrich Brüning*, ed. Ferdinand A. Hermens and Theodor

Schieder (Berlin, 1967), 449–66; William L. Patch Jr., *Heinrich Brüning and the Dissolution of the Weimar Republic* (Cambridge, 1998), 308.

49. Heinrich Brüning, untitled lecture, Dec. 7, 1941, p. 2, HB.

50. Heinrich Brüning to Schuster, June 2, 1939, file 1, box 1, GS-ND.

51. Luigi Sturzo, "The Roman Question before and after Fascism," *Review of Politics* 5 (Oct. 1943): 499.

52. Luigi Sturzo to Mario Einaudi, March 19, 1941, in *Luigi Sturzo–Mario Einaudi corrispondenza Americana, 1940–1944* (Florence, 1998), 27; Luigi Sturzo to Jacques Maritain, March 8, 1942, file 5, box 18, JM-MI; Luigi Sturzo, "Modern Wars and Catholic Thought," *Review of Politics* 3 (April 1941): 155–87.

53. Jacques Maritain, *Three Reformers: Luther-Descartes-Rousseau* (New York, 1928), 4.

54. Bernard Doering, *Jacques Maritain and the French Catholic Intellectuals* (Notre Dame, 1983), 6–59.

55. Yves R. Simon, *The Road to Vichy, 1918–1938*, trans. James A. Corbett and George J. McMorrow (Lanham, Md., 1988), 42–43.

56. Eugen Weber, *Action Française* (Stanford, 1962), 219–55.

57. Doering, *Jacques Maritain*, 6–59.

58. Maritain to Gurian, July 19, 1935, file 1, box 1, WG.

59. Jacques Maritain to Cardinal Alfred Baudrillart, Sept. 28, 1939, in *Les Carnets du cardinal Baudrillart, 11 Avril 1939–19 Mai 1941*, ed. Paul Christophe (Paris, 1998), 977–80.

60. Maritain to John U. Nef, April 22, 1938, folder 18, box 29, JUN.

61. Doering, *Jacques Maritain*, 85–125; George N. Schuster, "Some Reflections on Spain," *Commonweal*, April 2, 1937, p. 626; idem, "Dr. Brüning's Sojourn in the United States,"459.

62. Maritain, quoted in Julie K [Kernan] to Harry Binsse, July 21, 1938, file 27, box 10, COMM; Rodger Van Allen, *The Commonweal and American Catholicism: The Magazine, the Movement, the Meaning* (Philadelphia, 1974), 60–66.

63. Yves R. Simon, "Thomism and Democracy," in *Science, Philosophy and Religion: Second Symposium*, ed. Lyman Bryson and Louis Finkelstein, (New York, 1942), 258.

64. Maritain to Yves R. Simon, Aug. 6, 1939, YS.

65. Jacques Maritain, *The Person and the Common Good*, trans. John J. Fitzgerald (New York, 1947), 32; McCool, "Maritain's Defense of Democracy," 132–42.

66. Maritain, *Person and the Common Good*, 94.

67. Maritain to Mortimer Adler, Dec. 11, 1939, Maritain 1933–1940 file, box 29, MA-UC.

68. Jacques Maritain, *Christianity and Democracy*, trans. Doris C. Anson (New York, 1944), 58; Jacques Maritain to Yves R. Simon, June 15, 1941, YS.

69. Jacques Maritain to Yves R. Simon, Aug. 31, 1941, YS. On this subject, see Jacques Prévotat, "L'Historien face à la théologie: Le Cas du néo-thomisme de l'Action française," in *Histoire et théologie*, ed. Jean-Dominique Durand (Paris, 1994), 101–22.

70. On the background to Catholic interest in human rights, see Bernard Plongeron, "Anathema or Dialogue?: Christian Reactions to Declarations of the Rights of Man in the United States and Europe in the Eighteenth Century," in *The Church and the Rights of Man*, ed. Alois Müller and Norbert Greinacher (New York, 1979), 39–48. On the nineteenth and twentieth centuries, see J. Bryan Hehir, "Religious Activism for Human Rights: A Christian Case Study," in *Religious Human Rights in Global Perspective: Religious Perspectives*, ed. John Witte Jr. and Johan D. van der Vyver (The Hague, 1996), 97–120.

71. Robert C. Hartnett, S.J., review of Zechariah Chafee, *Free Speech in the United States*, in *Review of Politics* 4 (July 1942): 371.

72. John Ryan to Roscoe Pound, Oct. 18, 1923, reel 43, RP.

73. Virgil Michel, *The Social Question*, pts. 1–8, vol. 1, *Human Rights* (St. Paul, 1936), 9.

74. Jacques Maritain, *The Meaning of Human Rights* (Philadelphia, 1949), 7.

75. Jacques Maritain, *The Rights of Man and Natural Law*, trans. Doris C. Anson (London, 1944), 45, 37.

76. Maritain to Charles de Gaulle, Nov. 21, 1941, in *Cahiers Jacques Maritain* 16–17 (April 1988): 61.

77. Anton Pegis to Mortimer Adler, Jan. 11, 1943, Philosophical Correspondence file, box 29, MA-UC.

78. For an evaluation of the extended dispute between Maritain and Quebec's Charles de Konink, see Mary M. Keys, "Personal Dignity and the Common Good: A Twentieth-Century Thomistic Dialogue," in *Catholicism, Liberalism, and Communitarianism: The Catholic Intellectual Tradition and the Moral Foundations of Democracy*, ed. Kenneth L. Grasso, Gerard V. Bradley, and Robert P. Hunt (Lanham, Md., 1995) 173–95.

79. "Pope's Christmas Message, 1944," *Catholic Mind* 43 (Feb. 1945): 68. Also see "The 1942 Christmas Message of Pope Pius XII," ibid. 41 (Jan. 1943): 45–60; Charles Journet to Jacques Maritain, April 5, 1945, in *Journet-Maritain Correspondance*, 310.

80. Julie Kernan, *Our Friend, Jacques Maritain: A Personal Memoir* (Garden City, N.Y., 1975), 84–101; *The Maritain Volume of the Thomist* (New York, 1943).

81. [Daniel Bell], "Where the News Ends," *New Leader* (1942), clipping in folder 9, box 115, SH. Also see Bell to Sidney Hook, Oct. 7, 1942, folder 6, box 39, SH.

82. To Dr. Fry and Mr. Stanley, from M. Rapaport, J. L. Brown of Foreign Language Section on May 7, 1942, file 3, box 18, JM-MI.

83. Pierre Letamendai, "Eduardo Frei et Jacques Maritain," in *Jacques Maritian et ses contemporains*, ed. Bernard Hubert and Yves Floucat (Paris, 1991), 371.

84. Mary Ann Glendon, "Catholic Thought and Dilemmas of Human Rights," in *Higher Learning & Catholic Traditions*, ed. Robert E. Sullivan (Notre Dame, 2001), 117.

85. Fr. R. A. McGowan to Francis W. Russell, Nov. 1, 1947, file 15, box 52, GS-NCWC; Maritain, *Meaning of Human Rights*, 9.

86. Sidney Hook to Prof. H. A. Overstreet [1942], box 13, file 14, HK-AJA.

87. Charner Perry to Richard McKeon, July 30, 1940, Maritain file, box 48, RM.

88. Wolfram Kaiser, "Co-operation of European Catholic Politicians in Exile in Britain and the USA during the Second World War," *Journal of Contemporary History* 35 (June 2000): 455–57.

89. Maritain to Fr. Charles Journet, July 4, 1940, and Jan. 23, 1940, in *Journet-Maritain Correspondance*, 98, 41.

90. Maritain to Yves R. Simon, [June 1938], YS.

91. Maritain to Alinsky, Aug. 20, 1945, in *The Philosopher and the Provocateur: The Correspondence of Jacques Maritain and Saul Alinsky*, ed. Bernard Doering (Notre Dame, 1994), 11.

92. Maritain to Alinsky, Aug. 20, 1945, in *Philosopher and the Provocateur*, 11. On Alinsky and the Catholic Church, see John T. McGreevy, *Parish Boundaries: The Catholic Encounter with Race in the Twentieth-Century Urban North* (Chicago, 1996), 111–32. On Alinsky and Chávez, see Sanford D. Horwitt, *Let Them Call Me Rebel: Saul Alinsky—His Life and Legacy* (New York, 1989), 520–22.

93. Alinsky to Maritain, Feb. 17, 1958, in *Philosopher and the Provocateur*, 72–73; Chenaux, *Paul VI et Maritain*, 72–74.

94. Komonchak, "Silencing of John Courtney Murray," 657–702. Also see Donald E. Pelotte, *John Courtney Murray: Theologian in Conflict* (New York, 1976), 23–73.

95. John Courtney Murray, "Co-operation: Some Further Views," *Theological Studies* 4 (March 1943): 100–111.

96. Carlton Hayes to John Courtney Murray, March 22, 1943, M-N Correspondence files, box 5, CH.

97. Karl J. Alter to Stephen K. Mahon, Jan. 10, 1940, cited in Carol Bresnahan Menning, "The Professor and the Bishop: Catholics and Catholicism at the University of Toledo before and after the Second World War," *Northwest Ohio Quarterly* 70 (Summer–Autumn 1998): 127.

98. John Courtney Murray, "Christian Co-operation," *Theological Studies* 3

(Sept. 1942): 413–31; idem to Carlton Hayes, Jan. 13, 1942, M-N correspondence file, box 5, CH.

99. Fr. Richard J. Cushing to Bishop Francis McIntyre, Aug. 21, 1943, Religious Freedom file, FC.

100. "A Statement by Fr. Murray," *American Mercury* 69 (Nov. 1949): 637–39, in *Bridging the Sacred and the Secular: Selected Writings of John Courtney Murray*, ed. J. Leon Hooper (Washington D.C., 1994), 308; John Courtney Murray, "Law or Prepossessions," *Law and Contemporary Problems* 14 (Winter 1949): 23–43.

101. Summary of meeting, in Fr. McManus to Msgr. Hochwalt, May 5, 1948, file 23, box 9, SAD-NCWC.

102. A 1940 reiteration of the traditional teaching drew much attention. See John A. Ryan and Francis J. Boland, *Catholic Principles of Politics: The State and Church*, rev. ed. (New York, 1940), 311–21.

103. For his position on *Everson*, see Reinhold Niebuhr, "Separation of Church and State" (1947), reel 6, part III, FF. On *McCollum*, see Niebuhr, "Editorial Notes," *Christianity and Crisis*, March 29, 1948, p. 34. See also "Statement on Church and State" (1948), in *First Things* 26 (Oct. 1992): 32.

104. Fr. McManus to Msgr. Hochwalt, May 5, 1948, file 23, box 9, SAD-NCWC.

105. Murray, quoted in Fr. William McManus to Msgr. Carroll, Nov. 21, 1946, file 10, box 11, SAD-NCWC.

106. John Courtney Murray, S.J., "Leo XIII and Pius XII: Government and the Order of Religion" (1955), in Murray, *Religious Liberty: Catholic Struggles with Pluralism*, ed. J. Leon Hooper (Louisville, 1993), 51; idem, "Governmental Repression of Heresy," *Proceedings of the Catholic Theological Society of America* 3 (1948): 81.

107. Maritain, *Rights of Man and Natural Law*, 40.

108. [John Courtney Murray, S.J.], "Sources chrétiennes," *Theological Studies* 9 (June 1948): 251.

109. Komonchak, "Crisis in Church-State Relationships," 703.

110. Etienne Fouilloux, "Autour d'une mise à l'index," in *Marie-Dominique Chenu: Moyen-Âge et modernité* (Paris, 1997), 25–56.

111. *At the Service of the Church: Henri de Lubac Reflects on the Circumstances That Occasioned His Writings* (San Francisco, 1989), 60–79.

112. Yves M.-J. Congar, O.P., *Dialogue between Christians: Catholic Contributions to Ecumenicism*, trans. Philip Loretz, S.J. (Westminster, Md., 1966), 34.

113. John Tracy Ellis to Roger Aubert, Aug. 8, 1955, 1952–1956 file, box 4, JTE; Jean Pirotte, "Le Sens d'un hommage: Roger Aubert, l'histoire et le métier d'historien," in *Le Cardinal Mercier (1851–1926): Un Prélat d'avant-garde: Pub-*

lications du professeur Roger Aubert rassemblées à l'occasion de ses 80 ans (Louvain, 1994), 17.

114. Etienne Fouilloux, "Du rôle des théologiens au début de Vatican II: Un Point de vue romain," in *Cristianesimo nella storia: Saggi in onore di Giuseppe Alberigo*, ed. A. Melloni et al. (Bologna, 1996), 289–90.

115. John Tracy Ellis to Fr. Edward Cardinal, Nov. 30, 1953, Cardinal folder, box 2, JTE; Ellis to Cardinal, May 10, 1958, ibid.; John Tracy Ellis, "Church and State: An American Catholic Tradition," *Harper's Magazine* 207 (Nov. 1958): 63–67; Robert Cross, *The Emergence of Liberal Catholicism in America* (Cambridge, 1958); Joseph Fenton, "The Components of Liberal Catholicism," *American Ecclesiastical Review* 139 (July 1959): 52.

116. Francis Connell to Cardinal Alfred Ottaviani, Oct. 1, 1953, Ottaviani file, FC; John Courtney Murray to Francis Connell, Jan. 25, 1952, Church-State Writings file, FC.

117. Walter J. Burghardt, "A Half Century of *Theological Studies*: Retrospect and Prospect," *Theological Studies* 50 (Dec. 1989): 772.

118. Rt. Rev. John Augustine Ryan, "The Place of the Negro in American Society," March 2, 1943, copy in "Social Actions—Race Relations, 1929–1947" file, box 89, SAD-NCWC; Mr. Jacob Billikaph to Ryan, March 4, 1943, folder 12, box 2, JR.

119. Donald J. Kemper, "Catholic Integration in St. Louis, 1935–1947," *Missouri Historical Review* 73 (Oct. 1978): 1–22; William Markoe, "Reflections of My Experience in the Field of Race Relations," box 4, ser. 103, WMSJ. The best summary of events at St. Louis University is in Gleason, *Contending with Modernity*, 235–40.

120. Claude H. Heithaus, S.J., "A Challenge to Catholic Colleges," *Interracial Review* 17 (March 1944): 40–41. On Heithaus, see Claude Heithaus, S.J., interview with Marilyn Nickels, June 5, 1973, transcript in Josephite archives, Baltimore, Md.; Paul J. Shore, "The Message and the Messenger: The Untold Story of Father Claude Heithaus and the Integration of Saint Louis University," in *Trying Times: Essays on Catholic Higher Education in the 20th Century*, ed. William M. Shea with Daniel Van Slyke (Atlanta, 1999), 135–52.

121. George Dunne, *King's Pawn: The Memoirs of George H. Dunne* (Chicago, 1990), 90–96.

122. Memorandum [1945], file 585, box 8, JCM; Gerald Kelly "Concerning the Article Why Not Christian Cannibalism?" [ca. 1945], Kelly file, GK.

123. Yves R. Simon to Maritain, Jan. 9, 1945, YS.

124. Georges Passelecq and Bernard Suchecky, *The Hidden Encyclical of Pius XI*, trans. Steven Rendall (New York, 1997). For the latest volley, see Daniel Jonah Goldhagen, "What Would Jesus Have Done? Pope Pius XII, the Vatican, and the Holocaust," *New Republic*, Jan. 21, 2002, pp. 37–38. On LaFarge, see

David W. Southern, *John LaFarge and the Limits of Catholic Interracialism, 1911–1963* (Baton Rouge, 1996). On *Civiltà Cattolica*, see Susan Zucotti, *Under His Very Windows: The Vatican and the Holocaust in Italy* (New Haven, 2000), 17.

125. John LaFarge, S.J., to Jacques Maritain, May 26, 1937, folder 17, box 17, JLF; Jacques Maritain to John LaFarge, S.J., June 26, 1937, ibid.; Jacques Maritain, "The Menace of Racialism," *Interracial Review* 10 (May 1937): 70; "Maritain Speaks Again," ibid. 11 (June 1938): 85.

126. Yves Congar, O.P., *The Catholic Church and the Race Question* (Paris, 1953), 40; John Courtney Murray to Theodore M. Lewis, April 12, 1956, file 139, box 2, JCM; A. W. Crandell, S.J., to John Ford, S.J., Dec. 31, 1954, "Negro Integration" file, box 7, JF-HC. On the statement, see John Robert Payne, "A Jesuit Search for Social Justice: The Public Career of Louis J. Twomey, S.J., 1947–1969" (Ph.D. diss., Univ. of Texas, Austin, 1976): 204–5.

127. Kemper, "Catholic Integration," 1–22; *Our Colored Missions* 33 (Dec. 1947): 181.

128. Steven Ochs, *Desegregating the Altar: The Josephites and the Struggle for Black Priests, 1871–1960* (Baton Rouge, 1990), 426–45; Adam Fairclough, *Race & Democracy: The Civil Rights Struggle in Louisiana, 1915–1972* (Athens, Ga., 1995), 171–78; "Vatican Rejects Segregation Bid," *New York Times*, Aug. 9, 1957, p. 1.

129. McGreevy, *Parish Boundaries*, 91.

130. Walter White, "How Washington's Color Line Looks to Me," *Saturday Evening Post*, April 3, 1954, p. 85.

131. Reinhold Niebuhr to Will Scarlett, March 26, 1957, folder 2, box 33, RN.

132. M. R. Warner, "Varieties of Totalitarian Experience," *New Republic*, July 2, 1951, p. 18.

133. Archibald MacLeish to Henry R. Luce, Aug. 24, 1949, in *Letters of Archibald MacLeish, 1907–1982*, ed. R. H. Winnick (Boston, 1983), 349–50; Henry Sloane Coffin, "American Freedom and Catholic Power," *Christianity and Crisis*, May 2, 1949, p. 49.

134. Sidney Hook to William Lynch, Feb. 17, 1954, folder 1, box 54, SH.

135. Bishop John Wright to Agnes Meyer, Dec. 12, 1951, Bishop's correspondence, M file, ADW.

136. Sidney Hook to Richard K. Washburn, March 10, 1955, in *Letters of Sidney Hook: Democracy, Communism, and the Cold War* (Armonk, N.Y., 1995), 233.

137. Will Herberg, *Protestant-Catholic-Jew: An Essay in American Religious Sociology* (Garden City, N.Y.: 1960), 87.

138. Murray to Fr. Vincent McCormick, n.d., folder 161, box 2, JCM.

139. Compare Murray, *We Hold These Truths, with Louis Hartz, The Liberal*

Tradition in America: An Interpretation of American Political Thought since the Revolution (New York, [1955], 1991).

140. John Courtney Murray, review of Paul Blanshard, *American Freedom and Catholic Power*, in *Catholic World* 169 (June 1949): 233–34; idem, "Literature and Censorship," *Catholic Mind* 54 (Dec. 1956): 665–77; "Statement on Censorship Activity by Private Organizations and the National Organization for Decent Literature" (1957), folder 6, box 776, ACLU; "City of God & Man," *Time*, Dec. 12, 1960, p. 64.

141. Fr. Francis Connell to Fr. Joseph Fenton, Nov. 22, 1960, Church-State Writings file, FC.

142. John Tracy Ellis, "American Catholics and the Intellectual Life," *Thought* 30 (Autumn 1955): 351–88.

143. Donald Kommers to Francis Connell, July 15, 1959, Kommers file, FC.

144. Murray to Fr. Vincent McCormick, July 22, 1958, file 151, box 1, JCM.

145. Fletcher Knebel, "Democratic Forecast: A Catholic in 1960," *Look*, March 3, 1959, pp. 13–17. On Catholic reaction, see Timothy J. Sarbaugh, "Champion or Betrayer of His Own Kind: Presidential Politics and John F. Kennedy's 'LOOK' Interview," *Records of the American Catholic Historical Association of Philadelphia* 105 (Spring–Summer 1995): 54–70; Joseph P. Kennedy to Enrico Galeazzi, March 18, 1959, in *Hostage to Fortune: The Letters of Joseph P. Kennedy*, ed. Amanda Smith (New York, 2001), 682. On the general topic, see Thomas J. Carty, "Cultural and Regional Responses to John F. Kennedy's Catholicism in the 1960 Presidential Campaign" (Ph.D. diss., Univ. of Connecticut, 1999).

146. "Bennett and Niebuhr Repudiate Religious Attack on Kennedy Candidacy," Sept. 9, 1960, press release, box 1018, JFK; Arthur M. Schlesinger Jr., "Catholics in America," *New Republic*, March 21, 1960, pp. 13–14.

147. Richard Hofstadter, "Could a Protestant Have Beaten Hoover in 1928?" *Reporter* 22 (March 17, 1960): 31.

148. Lawrence H. Fuchs, *John F. Kennedy and American Catholicism* (New York, 1967), 182–88; Fuchs to Paul Blanshard, Nov. 21, 1958, folder 34, box 3, PB.

149. *Paul Blanshard on Vatican II* (Boston, 1966), quotation in unpaginated preface.

150. Reinhold Niebuhr to Will Scarlett, Jan. 9, [1960], folder 1, box 33, RN.

151. Patricia Tallon to Sr. Mary David, Sept. 16, 1964, file Mount Affairs, 1952–1964, box 10, National Federation of Catholic College Student Papers, MAUND.

CHAPTER 8: LIFE (I)

1. Ford to Fr. Joseph Fischer, July 8, 1964, Kelly file, MPA; Ford to Joe [?], Aug. 7, 1964, "m" file, box 17, JF-HC.

2. John Ford, S.J., Sermon at the funeral of Gerald Kelly, S.J., Aug. 5, 1964, Kelly file, GK. On Connell, see R. Scott Appleby and John H. Haas, "The Last Supernaturalists: Fenton, Connell, and the Threat of Catholic Indifferentism," *U.S. Catholic Historian* 13 (Winter 1995): 23–48.

3. Margaret Kelly Menius, "John Cuthbert Ford, S.J.: His Contribution to Twentieth Century Catholic Moral Theology on the Issue of Contraception" (Ph.D. diss., St. Louis Univ., 1998).

4. John Ford, Sermon at the funeral of Gerald Kelly.

5. Fr. Francis Connell, C.S.S.R., *Sunday Sermon Outlines* (New York, 1955), 57.

6. Ibid., 85, 96–97.

7. Ford, Sermon at the funeral of Gerald Kelly.

8. For a defense of casuistry that emphasizes its roots in Catholic moral theology, see Albert R. Jonsen and Stephen Toulmin, *The Abuse of Casuistry: A History of Moral Reasoning* (Berkeley, 1988).

9. Some Notes on the Exam "Ad Audeindas Confessiones" [1950s], Audeindas Confessiones, 1940–1962 file, box 18, JF-HC.

10. Kelly to Fr. Provincial, Oct. 17, 1946, Kelly file, GK.

11. Undated Kelly obituary in Kelly file, MPA, for one million figure; Gerald Kelly, *Modern Youth and Chastity* (St. Louis, [1941], 1943), 5.

12. Robert J. Shanahan, S.J., *The History of the Catholic Hospital Association, 1915–1965: Fifty Years of Progress* (St. Louis, 1965), 215. For a collection of Kelly's columns, which first appeared in the journal *Hospital Progress*, see Gerald Kelly, S.J., *Medico-Moral Problems* (St. Louis, 1958).

13. Gerald Kelly to Father Conway, Dec. 30, 1951, Kelly file, GK.

14. Kelly, *Medico-Moral Problems*, 34; John C. Ford, "Chemical Comfort and Christian Virtue," *American Ecclesiastical Review* 141 (Dec. 1959): 363.

15. Gerald Kelly, S.J., "The Communion Fast, I," *Hospital Progress* 34 (Aug. 1953) 56–58; idem, "The Fast before Communion," *Review for Religious* 4 (1945): 113; Casus file (n.d.), box 18, JF-HC.

16. Kelly, *Medico-Moral Problems*, 42–50; John C. Ford, S.J., and Gerald Kelly, S.J., *Contemporary Moral Theology*, vol. 1, *Questions in Fundamental Moral Theology* (Westminster, Md., [1958], 1964), 277–312; John C. Ford, S.J., "The Morality of Obliteration Bombing," *Theological Studies* 5 (Sept. 1944): 261–309.

17. Ford and Kelly, *Contemporary Moral Theology*, 1:43.

18. John Mahoney, *The Making of Moral Theology: A Study of the Roman Catholic Tradition* (Oxford, 1987): 27–36.

19. Joseph Fletcher, *Morals and Medicine* (Princeton, 1954), 16.

20. John T. McGreevy, *Parish Boundaries: The Catholic Encounter with Race in the Twentieth-Century Urban North* (Chicago, 1996), 8–28, 79–84.

21. John L. Thomas, S.J., *The American Catholic Family* (Englewood Cliffs, N.J., 1956), 8–9.

22. Mary Douglas, *Natural Symbols: Explorations in Cosmology* (London, [1970], 1996), 35–36. On Douglas, see Paul Baumann, "Anthropology with a Difference: Mary Douglas at 80," *Commonweal*, Aug. 17, 2001, pp. 11–19.

23. Bishop Martin McNamara to Cardinal Albert Meyer, Jan. 5, 1965, Birth control folder, box 43785.02, AM.

24. Daniel Callahan, "Authority and the Theologian," *Commonweal*, June 5, 1964, p. 322; Richard A. McCormick, S.J., "Moral Theology 1940–1989: An Overview," *Theological Studies* 50 (March 1989); 6.

25. *Casti Connubii* (1930), in *The Papal Encyclicals, 1903–1939*, ed. Claudia Carlen, I.H.M., (Raleigh, N.C., 1981), 399.

26. Fr. John Ryan to Richard T. Ely, Jan. 13, 1923, box 82, folder 2, RE.

27. Ford comment on Kennedy, n.d. [1942?], in Euthanasia file, box 6, JF-HC.

28. E. A. Ryan, S.J., and J. Blett, S.J., "The Nature and Destiny of Man," *Theological Studies* 5 (March 1944): 77.

29. Fr. John Ford, S.J., "Notes on Moral Theology, 1943," *Theological Studies* 4 (Dec. 1943): 562–63.

30. Fr. Francis Connell, *Morals in Politics and Professions: A Guide for Catholics in Public Life* (Westminster, Md., 1946), 140.

31. John C. Ford, S.J., *Mercy Murder* (New York, [1950?]), 6.

32. Charles J. McFadden, O.S.A., *Medical Ethics for Nurses* (Philadelphia, 1946), vii.

33. Kelly, *Medico-Moral Problems*, 118.

34. "The Birth Control Revolution," *Commonweal*, April 1, 1931, pp. 589–91.

35. Fr. Ignatius Cox, S.J., *Mercy Killing Is Murder!* (New York, 1936), 7. On the conflation of abortion and contraception, see Bernard Häring, "Abortion: A Theological Evaluation," in *The Morality of Abortion: Legal and Historical Perspectives*, ed. John T. Noonan Jr. (Cambridge, 1970), 133–35.

36. Michael Willrich, "The Two Percent Solution: Eugenic Jurisprudence and the Socialization of American Law, 1900–1930," *Law and History Review* 16 (Spring 1998): 63–111. Also see Carl N. Degler, *In Search of Human Nature: The Decline and Revival of Darwinism in American Social Thought* (New York, 1991), 42–48.

37. Margaret Sanger, "The Need of Birth Control in America," in *Birth Control: Facts and Responsibilities*, ed. Adolf Meyer (Baltimore, 1925), 27.

38. Sanger, in *Birth Control Review* (May 1919), 12, quoted in David M.

Kennedy, *Birth Control in America: The Career of Margaret Sanger* (New Haven, 1969), 115. Also see Carole R. McCann, *Birth Control Politics in the United States, 1916–1945* (Ithaca, 1994), 59–97.

39. Philip Reilly, *The Surgical Solution: A History of Involuntary Sterilization in the United States* (Baltimore, 1991), 88.

40. Horace Taft to Committee Members (1941), Connecticut Committee to Make Birth Control Legal file, Seeley G. Mudd Library, Yale Univ.

41. *Buck v. Bell*, 274 U.S. at 207 (1927). On Holmes, see Mary L. Dudziak, "Oliver Wendell Holmes as a Eugenic Reformer: Rhetoric in the Writing of Constitutional Law," *Iowa Law Review* 71 (March 1986): 833–67; David A. Hollinger, "The 'Tough-Minded' Justice Holmes, Jewish Intellectuals, and the Making of an American Icon," in *The Legacy of Oliver Wendell Holmes, Jr.*, ed. Robert W. Gordon (Stanford, 1992), 216–28. For a defense of Catholic criticisms of Holmes, see Albert W. Alschuler, *Law without Values: The Life, Work, and Legacy of Justice Holmes* (Chicago, 2000), 204.

42. William E. Leuchtenburg, *The Supreme Court Reborn: The Constitutional Revolution in the Age of Roosevelt* (New York, 1995), 15.

43. Paterfamilias [Ryan], "Race Suicide," *North American Review* 176 (June 1903): 892–900.

44. Paul Popenoe and Roswell Johnson, *Applied Eugenics* (NewYork, 1918), 273.

45. *Encyclopaedia of the Social Sciences*, s.v. "Birth Control."

46. On Germany, see Michael Burleigh, *Ethics and Extermination: Reflections on Nazi Genocide* (Cambridge, 1997), 132, 138–39; Ryan, "The Spiritual Element in Social Work," May 30, 1926, in The Church and Social Questions file, box 11, JR.

47. *Papal Encyclicals, 1903–1939*, nos. 85, 54, 69, and 70.

48. Daniel Kevles, *In the Name of Eugenics: Genetics and the Uses of Human Heredity* (New York, 1985), 118–19; Philip R. Reilly, *The Surgical Solution: A History of Involuntary Sterilization in the United States* (Baltimore, 1991), 118–20; William H. Schneider, "The Eugenics Movement in France, 1890–1940," in *The Wellborn Science: Eugenics in Germany, France, Brazil and Russia*, ed. Mark B. Adams (New York, 1990), 79–84; Nancy Leys Stepan, *"The Hour of Eugenics": Race, Gender, and Nation in Latin America* (Ithaca, 1991), 111–13.

49. Edward J. Larson, *Sex, Race, and Science: Eugenics in the Deep South* (Baltimore, 1995), 108–9.

50. Minutes of the National Council on Catholic Welfare, Sept. 12, 1927, NCWC; James A. Ryan to Burke, Dec. 26, 1922, file 12, box 118, GS-NCWC; Burke to Rev. Wm. Crosby, Feb. 2, 1927, ibid.; Charles F. Dolle to Burke, March 30, 1927, ibid.

51. Harold Laski provided an introduction for the volume *Representative*

Opinions of Mr. Justice Holmes, arr. by Alfred Lief (New York, 1931). *Buck v. Bell* (1927) is included on pp. 67–71. The case is ignored in Felix Frankfurter, *Mr. Justice Holmes and the Supreme Court* (Cambridge, 1938). On Catholics, see Francis E. Lucey, S.J., "Jurisprudence and the Future Social Order," *Social Science* 16 (July 1941): 214.

52. J. E. Coogan, S.J., to Eugenics Record Office, Nov. 12, 1940, cited in Reilly, *Surgical Solution*, 117; Paul A. Lombardo, "Three Generations, No Imbeciles: New Light on *Buck v. Bell*," *New York University Law Review* 60 (April 1985): 61.

53. Rev. John C. Ford, S.J., "The Fundamentals of Holmes' Juristic Philosophy," *Fordham Law Review* 11 (1942): 255–78; Felix Frankfurter to Ford, Feb. 3, 1942, Frankfurter file, box 15, JF-HC; Ford to Frankfurter, Feb. 7, 1942, JF-HC.

54. "The Defective Baby," *New Republic*, Nov. 27, 1915, pp. 85–86.

55. H. S. Spalding, S.J., "The Case of the Bollinger Baby," *American Ecclesiastical Review* 54 (Jan. 1916): 71; John B. Carroll, "The Moral Side of the Bollinger Baby Case," ibid. 54 (April 1916): 319.

56. On euthanasia in the United States, see Stephen Louis Kuepper, "Euthanasia in America, 1890–1960: The Controversy, the Movement, and the Law" (Ph.D. diss., Rutgers Univ., 1981); Valery Garrett, "The Last Civil Right?: Euthanasia Politics and Policy in the United States, 1938–1991" (Ph.D. diss., Univ. of California, Santa Barbara, 1998).

57. "Ask Churches' Aid for a Better Race," *New York Times*, March 31, 1925, p. 7. On Potter, birth control, and eugenics, see Charles Francis Potter, *The Preacher and I: An Autobiography* (New York, 1951), 393–99.

58. Garrett, "Last Civil Right?," 20.

59. William Montavon to Agnes Regan, Oct. 25, 1938, Euthanasia file, box 21, Legal Department series, NCWC; George P. Klubertanz, "The Man Whom Dewey Would Educate," *Modern Schoolman* 16 (March 1939): 59–64.

60. Ford comment on Foster Kennedy [1942?], in Euthanasia file, box 6, JF-HC.

61. David J. Garrow, *Liberty and Sexuality: The Right to Privacy and the Making of* Roe v. Wade (New York, 1994), 270–74; "The Curse of Abortion," *Birth Control Review* 13 (Nov. 1929): 307.

62. "Extravagances and Excesses of the Times," *Catholic Mirror*, Feb. 20, 1869, p. 4; "Residence of St. Mary's, Boston, Mass., 1868–1876," *Woodstock Letters* 6 (1877): 39–40; Horatio R. Storer and Franklin Fiske Heard, *Criminal Abortion: Its Nature, Its Evidence, and Its Law* (Boston, 1868), 74.

63. Dom Thomas Verner Moore, *Principles of Ethics*, 3d ed. (Philadelphia, [1935], 1939), 160. Also see Kathleen M. Joyce, "The Evil of Abortion and the Greater Good of the Faith: Negotiating Catholic Survival in the Twentieth-Century

American Health Care System," *Religion and American Culture* 12 (Winter 2002): 91–121.

64. McFadden, *Medical Ethics for Nurses*, 130, 139.

65. Reynold Hillenbrand, sermon [ca. 1937–41], folder 2, box 4, Reynold Hillenbrand Papers, MAUND.

66. John C. Ford, S.J., "Unity of the Threefold Law," *Catholic Mind* 40 (Nov. 8, 1942): 2–3; Francis E. Lucey, S.J., "Natural Law and American Legal Realism: Their Respective Contributions to a Theory of Law in a Democratic Society," *Georgetown Law Journal* 39 (April 1942): 520.

67. Ford, "Morality of Obliteration Bombing," 272.

68. Roger Smith, "The Witness of the Church," in *Nuclear Weapons and Christian Conscience*, ed. Walter Stein (London, 1981): 110–11.

69. John C. Ford, S.J., "Notes on Moral Theology, 1945," *Theological Studies* 6 (Dec. 1945): 540; Edgar R. Smothers, S.J., "An Opinion on Hiroshima," *America* 77. (July 5, 1947): 380.

70. Ford to Furfey, Aug. 23, 1965, Furfey file, box 8, JF-HC.

71. John Courtney Murray to John Ford, S.J., July 30, 1944, Obliteration Bombing file, box 8, JF-HC; Fr. Francis Connell to Ford, Oct. 18, 1944, ibid.

72. Fr. Francis Connell, *Morals in Politics and Professions: A Guide for Catholics in Public Life* (Westminster, Md., 1946), 47.

73. Kuepper, "Euthanasia in America," 158. On the effect of World War II on eugenicists, see Degler, *In Search of Human Nature*, 202–5.

74. Ford, *Mercy Murder*, 7.

75. Ford, n.t., Jan. 8, 1950, Euthanasia file, box 6, JF-HC.

76. Mr. Heffron to Msgr. Michael J. Ready, Dec. 14, 1936, file 13, box 117, GS-NCWC.

77. Sr. Mary Aloysius Molloy to Ready, Jan. 8, 1937, file 13, box 117, GS-NCWC; John LaFarge to Mabel Keaton Staupers, May 20, 1941, folder 35, box 53, JLF; Archbishop Edward Mooney to Franklin D. Roosevelt, June 8, 1943, file 7, box 13, SS.

78. Joseph Doyle to Eugene Butler, Dec. 13, 1954, Birth Control file, box 19, Dept. of Education, NCWC.

79. Garrow, *Liberty and Sexuality*, 2–130.

80. James M. O'Toole, "Prelates and Politicos: Catholics and Politics in Massachusetts, 1900–1970," in *Catholic Boston: Studies in Religion and Community, 1870–1970*, ed. Robert E. Sullivan and James M. O'Toole (Boston, 1985), 32–35.

81. The Case for Planned Parenthood in Massachusetts [1948], Proponents' Position file, box 21, Chancery Office files, AAB.

82. Proposed Advertising Schedule for Committee Opposing Adoption of Referendum #4, Radio and TV Advertising file, box 212, Chancery Office files, AAB.

83. "Birth Control Is Still against God's Law," Sermon Outline for Sunday, Oct. 1, 1948, in Record Group III G.2., box 21, Chancery Office files, AAB.

84. Bishop John J. Wright to Everett M. Hicks, July 30, 1948, RG III G.2, box 21, Chancery Office files, AAB.

85. Some Notes for Fourth Year Fathers on Birth Control Amendment [1948], Massachusetts file, box 3, JF-HC.

86. No title, [1948], Massachusetts file, box 3, JF-HC.

87. "Finis," *Boston Pilot*, Nov. 6, 1948, p. 4.

88. Daniel Boorstin, *The Genius of American Politics* (Chicago, 1953), 1–7, 133–60; Jacques Barzun, *Of Human Freedom*, rev. ed. (Philadelphia, [1939], 1964), 27. On the general topic, see Edward A. Purcell Jr., *The Crisis of Democratic Theory: Scientific Naturalism and the Problem of Value* (Lexington, Ky., 1973), 197–217.

89. Richard H. Shryock, "Freedom and Interference in Medicine," in *Annals of the American Academy of Political and Social Science* 200 (Nov. 1938): 40.

90. "The Cardinal Stoops to Conquer," *New Republic*, Nov. 30, 1942, p. 712; Eugene L. Belisle, "Church Control versus Birth Control," *Nation*, Nov. 28, 1942, p. 570.

91. Paul Blanshard, *American Freedom and Catholic Power* (Boston, 1949), 152.

92. Kingsley Davis, Harry C. Bredemeier, and Marion J. Levy Jr., *Modern American Society: Readings in the Problems of Order and Change* (New York, 1949), 495.

93. Mary Steichen Calderone to Jack Heber, June 3, 1958, file 203, box 12, MSC.

94. Lillian Bellison, "Planned Parenthood Barred by Council on Catholic Veto," *New York Times*, Jan. 15, 1953, pp. 1, 21; John Courtney Murray to Dean James Pike, Feb. 5, 1953, file 198, box 2, JCM.

95. [Rev. James T. Cotter] to William Carolan, Jan. 9, 1952, Birth Control 1950–1954 file, box 21, AAB.

96. Ronald Freedman, Pascal K. Whelpton, and John W. Smit, "Socio-Economic Factors in Religious Differentials in Fertility," *American Sociological Review* 26 (Aug. 1961): 608–14; Norman B. Ryder, Charles F. Westoff, and Raymond H. Potvin, *College Women and Fertility Values* (Princeton, 1967), 42–44.

97. Anonymous to Fr. Wilfrid Parsons, S.J., March 2, 1933, 1933–34 correspondence file, LL.

98. "How Many Children Shall We Have?" *New Life* 3 (Oct. 20, 1951): 3, in 1951 newsletters file, box 56, CFM. Also see James Terence Fisher, *The Catholic Counterculture in America, 1933–1962*, (Chapel Hill, 1989), 101–29.

99. Statement of Msgr. John A. Ryan, April 10, 1935, in *Hearings before the*

Subcommittee No. 8 of the Committee on the Post Office and Post Roads, House of Representatives, Seventy-fourth Congress (Washington, D.C., 1935), 72.

100. Ryan to Karl Llewellyn, May 19, 1928, file 28, box 20, JR.

101. John Winchell Riley and Matilda White, "The Uses of Various Methods of Contraception," *American Sociological Review* 5 (Dec. 1940): 895; Charles F. Westoff and Larry Bumpass, "The Revolution in Birth Control Practices of U.S. Roman Catholics," *Science* 179 (Jan.–March 1973): 41–42.

102. Some Notes for Fourth Year Fathers on Birth Control Amendment [1948], Birth Control Amendment in Massachusetts file, box 3, JF-HC.

103. John A. O'Brien, "Editor's Foreword," in *Family Planning in an Exploding Population* (New York, 1968), xvi–xvii; John C. Ford, S.J., and Gerald Kelly, S.J., *Contemporary Moral Theology,* vol. 2, *Marriage Questions* (New York, 1964), 385.

104. John Ford, "Notes on Moral Theology, 1944," *Theological Studies* 5 (Dec. 1944): 509; Apostolic Delegate to Bishops, May 23, 1936, in file 22, box 85, SAD-NCWC.

105. John J. Lynch, S.J., "Changing Pastoral Emphases on the Practice of Periodic Continence," in *Catholic Theological Society of America: Proceedings of the Eighteenth Annual Convention* (St. Louis, 1963), 110, 113.

106. Reinhold Niebuhr, *The Nature and Destiny of Man,* vol. 1, *Human Nature* (New York, 1943), 281.

107. Paul Ramsey, "Natural Law and the Nature of Man," *Christendom* 9 (Summer 1944): 377; idem, *Basic Christian Ethics* (New York, 1950), 340–41.

108. Dr. Herbert Doms, *The Meaning of Marriage* (New York, 1939), 197.

109. On Doms, see John T. Noonan Jr., *Contraception: A History of Its Treatment by the Catholic Theologians and Canonists*, enl. ed. (Cambridge, 1986), 496–99; Geoffrey J. Grubb, "The Anthropology of Marriage in Significant Roman Catholic Documents from *Casti Connubii* to *Gaudium et Spes*" (Ph.D. diss., St. Louis Univ., 1986), 128–96.

110. Bernard Häring, *My Witness for the Church*, trans. Leonard Swidler (New York, 1992), 95–96; Fr. Francis J. Connell, C.SS.R., "The Catholic Doctrine on the Ends of Marriage," *Proceedings of the Catholic Theological Society of America* 1 (1946): 35.

111. Jacques Maritian to Charles Journet, Nov. 15, 1948, in *Journet-Maritain Correspondance,* vol. 3, *1940–1949* (Fribourg, 1998), 715. I am indebted to the translation and analysis in Bernard Doering, "Silent Dissenter: Jacques Maritain on Contraception," *Commonweal*, May 18, 2001, p. 18.

112. John C. Ford, S.J., "Marriage: Its Meaning and Purposes," *Theological Studies* 3 (Sept. 1942): 372, 369; Minutes of the Meeting of the Committee on the Proposed Family Symposium, Dec. 6, 1943, in file 14, box 85, SAD-NCWC.

113. Rev. Stanley Berke, *The Possibility of Invincible Ignorance of the Natural Law* (Washington, D.C., 1941), 99.

114. Gerald Kelly, S.J., and John Ford, S.J., "Notes on Moral Theology," *Theological Studies* 15 (March 1954): 72–73; Gerald Kelly, S.J., "Contraception and Natural Law," in *Catholic Theological Society of America: Proceedings of the Eighteenth Annual Convention* (St. Louis, 1963), 28.

115. William Vogt, *Road to Survival* (New York, 1948), 211. For an excellent introduction, see Donald T. Critchlow, *Intended Consequences: Birth Control, Abortion, and the Federal Government in Modern America* (New York, 1999), 1–49.

116. William Vogt, "Your National Director," *Planned Parenthood News Exchange*, Jan.–Feb., 1952, copy in folder 1, box 1142, ACLU; Critchlow, *Intended Consequences*, 22.

117. Richard M. Fagley, *The Population Explosion and Christian Responsibility* (New York, 1960), 186.

118. John C. Bennett, "It May Be a Moral Obligation to Limit Births in a Family," *Washington Post*, Aug. 2, 1959, p. E9.

119. Ford, "Notes on Moral Theology, 1944," 507.

120. John L. Thomas, S.J., "The Catholic Position on Population Control," *Daedalus* 88 (Summer 1959): 450.

121. Monsignor J. B. Montini to Cardinal Siri, [1953], copy in Rev. Anthony Zimmerman, S.V.D., *"Overpopulation": A Study of Papal Teachings on the Problem, with Special Reference to Japan* (Washington, D.C., 1957), 305.

122. Ford and Kelly, *Contemporary Moral Theology*, 2:458–59.

123. J. A. Komonchak, "U.S. Bishops' Suggestions for Vatican II," *Cristianesimo nella Storia* 15 (June 1994): 313–71.

124. Joseph M. Becker, S.J., *The Re-Formed Jesuits*, vol. 1, *A History of Changes in Jesuit Formation during the Decade 1965–1975* (San Francisco, 1992), 290; Joseph A. Komonchak, "Thomism and the Second Vatican Council," in *Continuity and Plurality in Catholic Theology: Essays in Honor of Gerald A. McCool, S.J.*, ed. Anthony J. Cernera (Fairfield, Conn., 1998), 53–73.

125. *Lumen Gentium*, in *Vatican Council II*, ed. Austin P. Flannery, O.P., (Northport, N.Y., 1975), 358.

126. Msgr. John Tracy Ellis to Fr. Edward Cardinal, Sept. 13, 1963, Cardinal file, box 2, JTE.

127. John Courtney Murray, S.J., "The Declaration on Religious Freedom," in *War, Poverty, Freedom: The Christian Response* (New York, 1966), 12. On the declaration, see John T. Noonan Jr., *The Lustre of Our Country: The American Experience of Religious Freedom* (Berkeley, 1998), 331–53.

128. Mrs. Maurice Sagoff to Mr John de Pemberton, Nov. 29, 1962, folder 24, box 1142, ACLU.

129. A Statement of Richard Cardinal Cushing, Archbishop of Boston, March 2, 1965, on House Bill #1401, 1964–1965, Birth control file, box 21, AAB.

130. John Courtney Murray, S.J., "Memo to Cardinal Cushing on Contraception Legislation," in *Bridging the Sacred and the Secular: Selected Writings of John Courtney Murray*, ed. Leon Hooper, S.J. (Washington, D.C, 1994), 82–84.

131. Bishop John Wright to Dr. Joseph Dorsey, Jan. 20, 1965, 1964–1965, Birth control file, box 21, AAB.

132. Ford to Dorsey, Dec. 16, 1964, Dorsey file, box 3, JF-HC.

133. Bishop Vincent J. Hines to Francis Connell, March 7, 1961, Connecticut contraception file, FC.

134. Morris Ernst to Robert B. Fleming, May 15, 1964, Griswold file, box 1142, ACLU. On the legal fight in Connecticut, see Garrow, *Liberty and Sexuality*, 196–269.

135. Robert Fleming to Morris Ernest, May 21, 1964, Griswold file, box 1142, ACLU.

136. *Griswold v. Connecticut* 381 U.S. 479 (1965).

137. "The Connecticut Decision," *Commonweal*, June 1965, pp. 437–38.

138. Jan Grootaers, "Ebb and Flow between Two Seasons," in *History of Vatican II*, vol. 2, *The Formation of the Council's Identity First Period and Intersession October 1962–September 1963*, ed. Giuseppe Alberigo, English version ed. Joseph A. Komonchak (Maryknoll, N.Y., 1997), 530–31.

139. John Ford to John Rock, Feb. 2, 1945, Rock file, box 17, JF-HC.

140. John Rock, *The Time Has Come: A Catholic Doctor's Proposals to End the Battle over Birth Control* (New York, 1963); Ford to Msgr. Lawrence J. Riley, April 5, 1962, Rock file, box 17, JF-HC.

141. Bernard Häring, *Embattled Witness: Memories of a Time of War* (New York, 1976).

142. Roger Aubert, *La Théologie catholique au milieu du XX siècle* (Paris, 1954), 75.

143. Bernard Häring, *The Law of Christ: Moral Theology for Priests and Laity*, vol. 1, *General Moral Theology*, trans. Edwin G. Kaiser (Westminster, Md., 1963), 154, vii; Ford and Kelly, *Contemporary Moral Theology*, 1:91, 82.

144. Häring, *My Witness for the Church*, 36.

145. Bernard Häring, "Responsible Parenthood," *Commonweal*, June 5, 1964, p. 327.

146. George N. Schuster to Rev. Henri de Riedmatten, O.P., March 22, 1965, in folder 27, box 8, JAO. For the conference proceedings, see *The Problem of Population*, vol. 1, *Moral and Theological Considerations*, ed. Donald N. Barrett (Notre Dame, 1964); *The Problem of Population*, vol. 2, *Practical Catholic Applications* (Notre Dame, 1964).

147. Ford to John Wright, Sept. 8, 1964, "W" file, box 17, JF-HC.

148. Rev. James T. McHugh, Family Life Survey Preliminary Report, March 19, 1965, folder 8, box 86, GS-NCWC.

149. John Ford to Bishop John Wright, Sept. 8, 1964, "W" file, box 17, JF-HC; Gerald Kelly, S.J., "Notes on Moral Theology," *Theological Studies* 24 (Dec. 1963): 637.

150. On Noonan, see Kevin Starr, "Judge John T. Noonan, Jr., A Brief Biography," *Journal of Law and Religion* 11 (1995): 151–76; John T. McGreevy, "A Case for Doctrinal Development," *Commonweal*, Nov. 17, 2000, pp. 12–17; Noonan, *Lustre of Our Country*, 29.

151. John T. Noonan Jr., *The Scholastic Analysis of Usury* (Cambridge, 1957), 6.

152. Garry Wills, review of *Contraception*, in *National Review*, Oct. 19, 1965, p. 944.

153. Noonan, *Contraception*, 532.

154. Ford to Fr. Henri de Riedmatten, O.P., Jan. 3, 1965, "de Riedmatten" file, box 17, JF-HC.

155. Ford to Wright, July 23, 1964, "W" box 17, JF-HC.

156. Ford to Germain Grisez, Aug. 31, 1965, Grisez file, box 17, JF-HC.

157. Grisez to Fr. Stanislas de Lestapis, July 26, 1965, Grisez file, box 17, JF-HC.

158. Thomas F. Divine, S.J., to Ford, April 20, 1966, Contraception file, box 3, JF-HC; Ford to Divine, May 1, 1966, ibid.

159. John Ford, S.J., Answer to Question "What Would Be the Doctrinal and Pastoral Tendencies in this Country?" sent to Egidio Vagnozzi, April 6, 1964, folder 5, box 86, General Secretary-NCWC.

160. Ford to Msgr. Henry Cosgrove, July 25, 1965, Cosgrove file, box 17, JF-HC; Ford to Fr. John Pesce, Oct. 31, 1964, "op" file, box 17, JF-HC.

161. Ford to Rev. M. O'Leary, Aug. 3, 1964, "op" file, box 17, JF-HC.

162. Ford to Vagnozzi, Nov. 6, 1965, quoted in Giovanni Turbanti, *Un concilio per il mondo moderno: La redazione della costituzione pastorale "Gaudium et spes" del Vaticano II* (Bologna, 2000), 744.

163. John Wright, critique on De Matrimonio, Pars II, DR, 11.20-2 [n.d], file 8, box 5, JD.

164. Roman Diary, First Audience with Pope, Monday, Nov. 22, Roman Diary file, box 14, JF-HC; Notes on Conversation with Pope Paul VI, Nov. 22, 1965, ibid.; Roman Diary, Wednesday, Nov. 24, ibid. Ford's notes are ambiguous, as is the secondary literature, but he refers to two meetings with the pope, one certainly (and perhaps both) on Nov. 22.

165. Modi proposed by Holy Father of Nov. 23, 1965, file 9, box 5, JD. On this controversy and Ford's role, see Turbanti, *Un concilio*, 744–49; Mgr. J. M. Heuschen, "*Gaudium et spes*: Les Modi pontificaux," in *Les Commissions con-*

ciliaires à Vatican II, ed. M. Lamberigts, Cl. Soetens, and J. Grootaers (Leuven, 1996), 353–58; J. Grootaers, *Actes et acteurs à Vatican II* (Leuven, 1998), 236–45; Robert Blair Kaiser, *The Politics of Sex and Religion: A Case History in the Development of Doctrine, 1962–1984* (Kansas City, 1985), 114–22.

166. *Gaudium et Spes*, in *Vatican Council II*, 955.

167. Ford to Cosgrove, Dec. 8, 1965, Cosgrove file, box 17, JF-HC.

168. Roman Diary, Dec. 3, 1965, Roman Diary file, box 14, JF-HC.

169. Francis Connell to Patrick Cardinal O'Boyle, March 3, 1965, O'Boyle file, CP.

170. On the birth control commission, see Robert McClory, *Turning Point: The Inside Story of the Papal Birth Control Commission, and How* Humanae Vitae *Changed the Life of Patty Crowley and the Future of the Church* (New York, 1995), esp. 109–28.

171. Richard A. McCormick, S.J., "The Council on Contraception," *America* 114 (Jan. 8, 1966): 47–48; John C. Ford, S.J., "More on the Council and Contraception," *America* 114 (April 16, 1966), 557.

172. Mahoney, *Making of Moral Theology*, 259–301; Joseph A. Komonchak, "*Humanae Vitae* and Its Reception: Ecclesiological Reflections," *Theological Studies* 39 (June 1978): 221–57.

173. Leon F. Bouvier and S. L. N. Rao, *Socioreligious Factors in Fertility Decline* (Cambridge, 1975), 165. A few of the less devout women, ironically, expressed opposition to birth control, but the number of Catholic women under thirty-five opposed to birth control was less than 10 percent of the total.

174. Martin H. Work to Bishops, [1968], in box 14, folder 19, JCD.

175. Ford to John Courtney Murray, Oct. 3, 1965, "M" file, box 17, JF-HC.

176. John Courtney Murray to Fr. Francis Hurley, March 27, 1965, file 12, box 95, SAD-NCWC

177. Bernard J. F. Lonergan, *A Second Collection*, ed. William F. J. Ryan, S.J., and Bernard J. Tyrrell, S.J. (Philadelphia, 1974), 3–4, 38.

178. John Courtney Murray to Bernard Lonergan, Nov. 30, 1966, folder 141, box 2, JCM. Also note remarks of Murray in Discussion of Declaration of Religious Freedom, in *Vatican II: An Interfaith Appraisal*, ed. John H. Miller, C.S.C., (Notre Dame, 1966), 581.

179. John Courtney Murray, S.J., "Appendix: Toledo Talk," in *Bridging the Sacred and the Secular*, 335–36.

180. Murray to Ford, May 31, 1967, folder 77, box 1, JCM.

181. Ford to Grisez, Nov. 8, 1968, "G" file, box 17, JF-HC.

182. Memorandum on Ownership and Government of St. Louis University in View of the Contemplated Enlargement of the Board of Trustees [1967?], in "Bombing" file, box 8, JF-HC; Ford to Cardinal Augustin Bea, Feb. 28, 1967, Bea file, JF-HC.

183. Bob Olmstead, "O'Boyle Warns Bishops of New Morality Curse; Acts against Priests," *National Catholic Reporter*, Sept. 25, 1968, 1, 14; Ford to Valerian Cardinal Gracias, Oct. 17, 1968, "G" file, box 17, JF-HC. Ford to Grisez, Nov. 8, 1968, ibid.

184. John C. Ford and Germain Grisez, "Contraception and the Infallibility of the Ordinary Magisterium," *Theological Studies* 39 (June 1978): 258–312.

185. Germain Grisez, "Presentation of the Cardinal O'Boyle Award for Defense of the Faith to John C. Ford, S.J.," Sept. 24, 1988, Honors and Dedications file, Ford Papers, box 2, JF-BC.

186. Maxwell Roland, M.D., to Fr. Richard McCormick, S.J., Oct. 22, 1964, "R" file, box 17, JF-HC.

187. David J. Garrow, "Abortion before and after *Roe v. Wade:* An Historical Perspective," *Albany Law Review* 62 (1999): 833–52.

188. William F. Buckley, "The Catholic Church and Abortion," *National Review*, April 5, 1966, p. 308; "Gilligan Yes, Cloud No on Allowing Abortions," *Catholic Chronicle*, Oct. 16, 1970, p. 1, clipping in Pro-Life Issues drawer, 1960–1970, MCC.

189. Richard McCormick, S.J., to Hurley, March 27, 1965, file 12, box 95, SAD-NCWC.

190. Rev. Francis J. Connell, C.SS.R., Comments on Family Planning and Public Policy Draft, March 23, 1965, file 12, box 95, SAD-NCWC.

CHAPTER 9: LIFE (II)

1. Joseph Fletcher, *Memoir of an Ex-Radical: Reminiscence and Reappraisal*, ed. Kenneth Vaux (Louisville, 1993), 74.

2. Ibid., 85. On Fletcher's student Jonathan Daniels, see Charles Eagles, *Outside Agitator: Jon Daniels and the Civil Rights Movement in Alabama* (Chapel Hill, 1993).

3. Albert R. Jonsen, *The Birth of Bioethics* (New York, 1998), 42–47.

4. Joseph Fletcher, *Situation Ethics: The New Morality* (Philadelphia, 1966), 29.

5. Joseph Fletcher, "The Catholic Revival: An American Viewpoint," *Christendom* 3 (Sept. 1933): 208.

6. Joseph Fletcher, "Catholic Social Reform in the Third Republic," *Stockholm* 3 (1931): 255–64; idem, *Memoir of an Ex-Radical*, 76; idem, *Morals and Medicine* (Princeton, 1954), 19.

7. Herbert S. Bailey Jr. to Fr. Francis Connell, Aug. 31, 1953, Fletcher file, CP.

8. Fletcher to Rory M. Culhane, May 8, 1967, FLETCHER.

9. Jonsen, *Birth of Bioethics*, 45.

10. Fletcher, *Morals and Medicine*, 25; Joseph Fletcher, "The New Look in Christian Ethics," *Harvard Divinity Bulletin*, Oct. 1959, pp. 16, 9.

11. Urban Voll, O.P., review of Fletcher, *Morals and Medicine*, in *Thomist* 18 (Jan. 1955): 94, 101.

12. Gerald Kelly, S.J., "Medico-Moral Notes," *Hospital Progress* 52 (May 1955): 60.

13. This paragraph rests on the superb analysis in Wilfred M. McClay, *The Masterless: Self & Society in Modern America* (Chapel Hill, 1994), 226–68. Also see Paul Blanshard, *American Freedom and Catholic Power* (Boston, 1949), 6.

14. Mary Ann Glendon, *A World Made New: Eleanor Roosevelt and the Universal Declaration of Human Rights* (New York, 2001); Daniel T. Rodgers, *Contested Truths: Keywords in American Politics since Independence* (New York, 1987), 212–25.

15. Thomas L. Haskell, *Objectivity Is Not Neutrality: Explanatory Schemes in History* (Baltimore, 1998), 115–44.

16. Wilfrid Parsons, S.J., *Timeless Rights in Modern Times: Commentaries on the N.C.W.C.'s Declaration of Human Rights* (Washington, D.C., 1948), 9.

17. Horace M. Kallen, "An Ethic of Freedom: A Philosopher's View," *New York University Law Review* 31 (Nov. 1956): 1168; Glanville Williams, *The Sanctity of Life and the Criminal Law* (London, 1958), 58.

18. Fletcher, *Morals and Medicine*, 3, 11; Kallen, "Ethic of Freedom," 1168.

19. Williams, *Sanctity of Life*, 282, 211.

20. Jacques Maritain to Yves R. Simon, Jan. 8, 1945, reprinted in *Cahiers Jacques Maritain* 4 (June 1982): 13.

21. Useful reviews of a large literature include James M. Gustafson, "Context versus Principles: A Misplaced Debate in Christian Ethics," *Harvard Theological Review* 58 (April 1965): 171–202; Robert W. Gleason, "Situational Morality," *Thought* 32 (1957): 533–58.

22. Emil Brunner, *The Divine Imperative: A Study in Christian Ethics*, trans. Olive Wyon (Philadelphia, [1932], 1947), 91.

23. Paul L. Lehmann, "The Foundation and Pattern of Christian Behavior," in *Christian Faith and Social Action*, ed. John A. Hutchison (New York, 1953), 93–116.

24. Dietrich Bonhoeffer, *Ethics*, trans. Neville Horton Smith (London, 1955), 185.

25. Roger Aubert, *La Théologie catholique au milieu du XX siècle* (Paris, 1954), 76.

26. Karl Rahner, *Theological Investigations*, vol. 2, *Man in the Church*, trans. Karl H. Kruger (Baltimore, 1963), 219, 231.

27. Pius XII, "The Moral Law and the 'New Morality,'" *Irish Ecclesiastical Record* 78 (Aug. 1952): 139.

28. "Instruction Concerning 'Situation Ethics,'" *American Ecclesiastical Review* 135 (July 1956): 64–66.

29. John C. Ford, S.J., and Gerald Kelly, S.J., "Notes on Moral Theology, 1953," *Theological Studies* 15 (March 1954): 53.

30. Gerald Kelly to John Ford, Sept. 22, 1957, Legion of Decency file, box 7, JF-HC.

31. Gerald Kelly to John Courtney Murray, June 12, 1956, folder 124, box 1, JCM.

32. John C. Ford and Gerald Kelly, S.J., *Contemporary Moral Theology,* vol. 1, *Questions in Fundamental Moral Theology* (Westminster, Md., 1964), 137–38.

33. Charles Curran, "Dialogue with Joseph Fletcher," *Homiletic and Pastoral Review* 67 (July 1967): 822, 827.

34. Cardinal Samuel Stritch, Observations on Father Ford's Opinion [1957], file 27, box 14, Stritch Papers, AAC.

35. On Catholics and Vietnam, see Patricia F. McNeal, *The American Catholic Peace Movement, 1928–1972* (New York, 1978), 214–93.

36. John T. McGreevy, "The Northern District of California and the Vietnam Draft," *Western Legal History* 2 (Summer–Fall 1989): 269–71.

37. Report of the USCC Advisory Council to the Administrative Board, Sept. 15, 1970, file 5, box 24, JCD.

38. *Gaudium et Spes*, in *Vatican Council II: The Conciliar and Post-Conciliar Documents*, ed. Austin Flannery, O.P. (Northport, N.Y., 1975), 916. On conscience and contraception, see Bernard Häring, "The Encyclical Crisis," *Commonweal*, Sept. 6, 1968, p. 588–94.

39. Daniel Maguire to Joseph Fletcher, n.d. [1968?], FLETCHER; Joseph Fletcher to Frank Rubel, May 17, 1968, ibid.

40. John Ford to Philip Scharper, June 21, 1965, Ford file, box 3, SW.

41. Ford to Msgr. Henry Cosgrove, July 25, 1965, Cosgrove file, box 17, JF-HC.

42. John Ford to Donald Barrett, Oct. 24, 1965, Vagnozzi file, box 17, JF-HC.

43. Notes on Conversation with Pope Paul VI, Nov. 22, 1965, file of same name, box 14, JF-HC.

44. Ibid.

45. Alan Guttmacher, *Babies by Choice or by Chance* (Garden City, N.Y., 1959), 166; Mary Steichen Calderone, "Illegal Abortion as a Public Health Problem," *American Journal of Public Health* 50 (July 1960): 951

46. Allred to Eugene Butler, Nov. 13, 1950, in Birth Control file, box 19, Department of Education, NCWC; Meeting of Nov. 15, 1950, *Minutes of the Annual Meetings of the Bishops of the United States*, p. 22, ACUA.

47. Williams, *Sanctity of Life*, 181–82.

48. Ford, "Notes on Moral Theology, 1944," *Theological Studies* 5 (Dec.

1944): 522; Gerald Kelly and John C. Ford, "Notes on Moral Theology," ibid. 15 (March 1954): 74.

49. Bishop Alter's Report on Certain Moral Problems involving Public Policy, [1947], in reel 147, CHA; Msgr. Donald A. McGowan to Bishop's Representative Oct. 7, 1954, in Code of Ethics file, CHA.

50. "Ethical and Religious Directives for Catholic Hospitals," *Linacre Quarterly* 15 (July–Oct. 1948): 4.

51. Cynthia Gorney, *Articles of Faith: A Frontline History of the Abortion Wars* (New York, 1998), 45–47.

52. Garrow, *Liberty and Sexuality*, 277–89; Herbert Packer and Ralph J. Gampell, "Therapeutic Abortion: A Problem in Law and Medicine," *Stanford Law Review* 11 (May 1959): 415–55.

53. Joseph Fletcher, "A Moral Tension and an Ethical Frontier," *Christian Scholar* 46 (Fall 1963): 256, 260.

54. Garrett Hardin, *Stalking the Wild Taboo* (Los Altos, Calif., 1973), 11.

55. Statement of Morris Ernst, April 10, 1935, in *Hearings before the Subcommittee No. 8 of the Committee on the Post Office and Post Roads, House of Representatives, Seventy-fourth Congress* (Washington, D.C., 1935), 87.

56. Mary Ann Glendon, *Rights Talk: The Impoverishment of Political Discourse* (New York, 1991).

57. The analysis in this paragraph is indebted to Michael Sandel, "Moral Argument and Liberal Toleration: Abortion and Homosexuality," *California Law Review* 77 (May 1989): 521–38, quotation on 523. *Doe v. Bolton* 410 U.S. 211 (1973).

58. Mary Ann Glendon, *Abortion and Divorce in Western Law: American Failures, European Challenges* (Cambridge, 1987), 10–24, quotation on 24.

59. Fr. James Flynn to Alden Bell, Jan. 22, 1966, Abortion Law file, General files, AASF.

60. Thomas L. Shaffer to Mr. John de Pemberton, March 21, 1967, folder 2, box 1145, ACLU; John de Pemberton to Thomas L. Shaffer, March 27, 1967, NOONAN.

61. For a standard history, see Sara Evans, *Personal Politics: The Roots of Women's Liberation in the Civil Rights Movement and the New Left* (New York, 1979).

62. Betty Friedan, *The Feminine Mystique* (New York, [1963], 1983), 304, 309.

63. Judith Hole and Ellen Levine, *Rebirth of Feminism* (New York, 1971), 88–90.

64. Robert F. Drinan, "Contemporary Protestant Thinking," *America* 117 (Dec. 9, 1967): 713–15.

65. Bishop Alden Bell to Archbishop Joseph McGucken, Aug. 10, 1966, Abortion Law file, General files, AASF.

66. Ron Coomes to Jerry, Aug. 15, 1967, Pro-Life Issues drawer, 1960–1970, MCC.

67. Testimony of Paul Ramsey, March 7, 1974, in *Abortion Part I: Hearings before the Subcommittee on Constitutional Amendments of the Committee on the Judiciary, United States Senate, Ninety-third Congress, Second Session, on S.J. Res 119 and S.J. Res. 130* (Washington, D.C., 1974), 350; "Life in the Dark Age," *Christian Century* 89 (May 31, 1972): 624; "Foes of Abortion Assailed by Rabbi," *New York Times*, Feb. 12, 1967, p. 61.

68. John Noonan to Robert McAfee Brown, May 23, 1967, NOONAN; Brown to Noonan, June 2, 1967, ibid.

69. "A Protestant Affirmation on the Control of Human Reproduction," *Christianity Today* 13 (Nov. 8, 1968): 18–19; Gorney, *Articles of Faith*, 188; Donald W. Sweeting, "From Conflict to Cooperation?: Changing American Evangelical Attitudes towards Roman Catholics: 1960–1998" (Ph.D., diss., Trinity Evangelical Divinity School, 1998), 214.

70. John Rawls, "Constitutional Liberty and the Concept of Justice" (1963), in Rawls, *Collected Papers*, ed. Samuel Freeman (Cambridge, 1999), 73.

71. John Rawls, *A Theory of Justice* (Cambridge, 1971), 4.

72. John Rawls, *Political Liberalism* (New York, 1993), 243–44.

73. Judith Jarvis Thomson, "A Defense of Abortion," *Philosophy and Public Affairs* 1 (Fall 1971): 50–51.

74. James Bryant Conant, "Challenge of the Times," *Vital Speeches*, Aug. 15, 1948, p. 644.

75. John Rawls, "Outline of a Decision Procedure for Ethics" (1951), in Rawls, *Collected Papers*, 16; idem, "Constitutional Liberty and the Concept of Justice," 73.

76. *Board of Education v. Allen*, 392 U.S. 251 (1968).

77. *Lemon v. Kurtzman*, 403 U.S. 602, 623, 635 (1971). See Douglas Laycock, "Civil Rights and Civil Liberties," *Chicago-Kent Law Review* 54 (1977): 418–20.

78. Testimony of Citizens for Abortion Law Reform before Michigan State Senate, Feb. 27, 1970, p. 4, Michigan 1969–70 file, box 3, NARAL.

79. As noted in James Tunstead Burtchaell, C.S.C., *Rachel Weeping and Other Essays on Abortion* (Kansas City, 1982), 113. See Mary Eisner Eccles, "Abortion: How Members Voted in 1977," *Congressional Weekly Quarterly Report* 36 (Feb. 4, 1978): 262–67.

80. Arthur F. Barkey to Francis Coomes, Aug. 4, 1967, Pro-Life Issues drawer, 1960–1970, MCC.

81. Lawrence H. Tribe, "The Supreme Court 1972 Term," *Harvard Law Review* 87 (Nov. 1973): 25, 21.

82. Testimony of Laurence Tribe, Oct. 8, 1974, in *Abortion Part III: Hearings*

Before the Subcommittee on Constitutional Amendments of the Committee on the Judiciary, United States Senate, Ninety-third Congress, Second Session, on S.J. Res 119 and S.J. Res. 130 (Washington, D.C., 1974), 393.

83. A. H. Clemens, "The Catholic Sociologist Faces a New Social Order," *American Catholic Sociological Review* 4 (Oct. 1943): 159.

84. Kristin Luker, *Abortion and the Politics of Motherhood* (Berkeley, 1984), 185.

85. John Courtney Murray, *We Hold These Truths: Catholic Reflections on the American Proposition* (New York, 1960), 40.

86. John Courtney Murray, S.J., "The Problem of Mr. Rawls's Problem," in *Law and Philosophy: A Symposium*, ed. Sidney Hook (New York, 1964), 32.

87. John Courtney Murray to Paul VI, May 6, 1965, in Dominique Gonnet, S.J., *La Liberté religieuse à Vatican II: La Contribution de John Courtney Murray, S.J.* (Paris, 1994), 354.

88. Murray, *We Hold These Truths*, 12.

89. Msgr. James V. Moscow to Bishop Cletus F. O'Donnell, Aug. 14, 1964, Abortion file, AM.

90. "The Abortion Question: Life and Law in Pluralistic Society," *America* 117 (Dec. 9, 1967): 706.

91. Daniel Callahan, *Abortion: Law, Choice and Morality* (New York, 1970).

92. Daniel Callahan, "Introduction," in *The Catholic Case for Contraception*, ed. Daniel Callahan (New York, 1968), xi.

93. Callahan, *Abortion*, 19; Callahan, quoted in Paul Ramsey, "Abortion: A Review Article," *Thomist* 37 (Jan. 1973): 206; Jonsen, *Birth of Bioethics*, 20–22.

94. *The Morality of Abortion: Legal and Historical Perspectives*, ed. John T. Noonan Jr. (Cambridge, 1970).

95. Noonan to Rev. Eugene C. Best, Dec. 20, 1968, NOONAN.

96. Richard McCormick, "Notes on Moral Theology: The Abortion Dossier," *Theological Studies* 35 (June 1974): 312–59.

97. Warren Thomas Reich, "Revisiting the Launching of the Kennedy Institute: Re-visioning the Origins of Bioethics," *Kennedy Institute of Ethics Journal* 6 (Dec. 1996): 323–27.

98. Alice Rossi, "American Attitudes on Population Policy—Recent Trends," *Studies in Family Planning* 30 (May 1968): 5–6; Charles Westoff, Emily C. More, and Norman B. Ryder, "The Structure of Attitudes toward Abortion," *Milbank Memorial Fund Quarterly* 47 (Jan. 1969): 11–37.

99. Judith Blake, "Abortion and Public Opinion: The 1960–1970 Decade," *Science* 171 (Feb. 12, 1971): 544; Luker, *Abortion and the Politics of Motherhood*, 194–97.

100. Daniel Callahan to John T. Noonan Jr., Sept. 16, 1967, NOONAN.

101. Lee Gidding to Mary Lou Thompson, Sept. 14, 1970, MA 1968–70 file, box 3, NARAL; Brewster Paley to Mrs. Frank Grasso, Jan. 13, 1971, NY State campaign 1970–71 file, box 4, NARAL.

102. Noonan to Paul VI, Dec. 22, 1965, NOONAN.

103. Madeline White to Ronald Hayes, Sept. 25, 1966, Pro-Life Issues drawer, 1960–1970, MCC.

104. James T. McHugh to John Cardinal Dearden, Sept. 21, 1970, file 9, box 14, JCD.

105. Thomas L. Shaffer to Mr. John de Pemberton, March 21, 1967, folder 2, box 1145, ACLU.

106. Fr. Eugene Boyle to McGucken, June 14, 1967, Legislature: abortion—Legalized Law file, General files, AASF

107. Thomas St. Martin, Memo—Minnesota Concerned Citizens for Life, Aug. 1, 1973, 1973 file, box 11, ACCL.

108. Text of Mrs. Eunice Kennedy opening remarks, Sept. 8, 1967, in International Conference on Abortion, Pro-Life Issues drawer, 1960–70, MCC; John T. Noonan, "Introduction," in *Morality of Abortion*, xvi; *Social and Moral Questions Facing the People of Indiana* (Indianapolis, 1968), n.p.

109. Timothy A. Byrnes, *Catholic Bishops in American Politics* (Princeton, 1991), 35–53; *Gaudium et Spes*, in *Vatican Council II*, 955; Gorney, *Articles of Faith*, 183–87.

110. Marjorie Hyer, "Yano Explains Vote on Abortion," *National Catholic Reporter*, Dec. 11, 1970, p. 14; Robert F. Drinan, "The Morality of Abortion Laws," *Catholic Lawyer* 14 (Summer 1968): 194. On Drinan's influence, see Doug Rossinow, *The Politics of Authenticity: Liberalism, Christianity, and the New Left in America* (New York, 1998), 447; Garrow, *Liberty and Sexuality*, 342–43, 412–13, 421–22.

111. Fr. William C. Hunt, "Theologian Challenges Drinan on Abortion Laws," *National Catholic Reporter*, June 19, 1968, p. 6.

112. *Gaudium et Spes*, in *Vatican Council II*, 943.

113. J. Bryan Hehir, "Church and Population: A Strategy," *Theological Studies* 35 (March 1974): 77–78.

114. Richard McCormick, "Renewal in Moral Theology," *Theological Studies* 27 (Dec. 1966), 644. See also "Human Life in Our Day," statement issued by the National Conference of Catholic Bishops, Nov. 15, 1968, in *Pastoral Letters of the United States Catholic Bishops:* vol. 3, *1962–1974*, ed. Hugh Nolan (Washington, D.C., 1984), 180.

115. Address of Msgr. Agostino Casaroli, Aug. 17, 1961, in Gerald M. Costello, *Mission to Latin America: The Successes and Failures of a Twentieth Century Crusade* (Maryknoll, N.Y., 1979), 275.

116. Peter McDonough, *Men Astutely Trained: The History of the Jesuits in the American Century* (New York, 1992), 268.

117. Report from Centro de Información Católica, [1967], file 12, box 13, JCD.

118. Angelyn Dries, O.S.F., *The Missionary Movement in American Catholic History* (Maryknoll, N.Y., 1998), 179–246.

119. Karen M. Kennelly, C.S.J., "Foreign Missions and the Renewal Movement," *Review for Religious* 49 (May–June 1990): 452.

120. Costello, *Mission to Latin America*, 123.

121. "The Gospel and Revolution," *National Catholic Reporter*, Feb. 28, 1968, p. 3; Virgilio Elizondo, "*Mestizaje* as a Locus of Theological Reflection," in *The Future of Liberation Theology: Essays in Honor of Gustavo Gutiérrez*, ed. Marc H. Ellis and Otto Maduro (Maryknoll, N.Y., 1989), 359–60.

122. Gustavo Gutiérrez, "The Church and the Poor: A Latin American Perspective," in *The Reception of Vatican II*, ed. Giuseppe Alberigo, Jean-Pierre Jossua, and Joseph A. Komonchak, trans., Matthew J. O'Connell (Washington, D.C., 1987), 171–93; *The Church in the Present-Day Transformation of Latin America in the Light of the Council* (Bogotá, 1970), 62, 217.

123. Gina Maria Pitti, "'A Ghastly International Racket': The Catholic Church and the *Bracero* Program in California, 1942–1964," *Cushwa Center for the Study of American Catholicism Working Paper Series*, 33 (Fall 2001): 12–22.

124. Susan Ferriss and Ricardo Sandoval, *The Fight in the Fields: Cesar Chávez and the Farmworkers Movement* (New York, 1997); Gustavo Gutiérrez, *A Theology of Liberation: History, Politics and Salvation*, ed. and trans. Sr. Caridad Inda and John Eagleson (Maryknoll, N.Y., 1973), 308.

125. Virgilio Elizondo, "The Mexican-American Cultural Center Story," *Listening* 32 (Fall 1997): 152; Archbishop Rembert Weakland, "How Medellin and Puebla Influenced North America," *Origins* 18 (April 13, 1989): 757–60.

126. Gustavo Gutiérrez, "Notes for a Theology of Liberation," *Theological Studies* 321 (June 1970): 243–61; Bishop Joseph L. Bernardin, Memo, Jan. 19, 1970, NCCB box 13, file 18, JCD; Notes for a Theology of Liberation, Document #2, Inter-American Bishops' Meeting Miami, Feb. 2–5, 1970 in box 13, file 18, JCD.

127. Paul VI, opening address to Latin American Bishops' Conference, Aug. 24, 1968, in *Church in the Present-Day Transformation of Latin America*, 32.

128. "Archbishop Reaffirms Ethic of Life and Law," *Boston Pilot*, July 10, 1971, p. 7.

129. McCormick, "Abortion Dossier," 359.

130. On Catholics in favor of legal abortion, see Mary Jo Weaver, "Resisting Traditional Catholic Sexual Teaching: Pro Choice Advocacy and Homosexual Support Groups," in *What's Left?: Liberal American Catholics*, ed. Mary Jo

Weaver (Bloomington, Ind., 1999), 93–97; Mary E. Hunt and Frances Kissling, "The *New York Times* Ad: A Case Study in Religious Feminism," *Journal of Feminist Studies in Religion* 3 (1987): 116–27.

131. Daniel Callahan, "Contraception and Abortion: American Catholic Responses," *Annals of the American Academy of Political and Social Science* 387 (Jan. 1970): 110.

132. Fr. James T. McHugh, "Abortion Law Change—A Current Report," March 1, 1967, in Pro-Life Issues drawer, 1960–1970, MCC; James T. McHugh to Bishop Francis F. Reh, July 20, 1972, ibid., 1971–1972, MCC.

133. Sidney Callahan, "Feminist as Anti-Abortionist," *National Catholic Reporter* 8, April 7, 1972, p. 11.

134. George Dugan, "State's 8 Catholic Bishops Ask Fight on Abortion Bill," *New York Times*, Feb. 13, 1967, p. 1.

135. Daniel J. O'Neil, *Church Lobbying in a Western State: A Case Study on Abortion Legislation* (Tucson, 1970), 25, 33–35.

136. Rose Bacon, "How Liberalized Abortion Became Law in One State," *Ave Maria* 106 (July 22, 1967): 16–18; Garrow, *Liberty and Sexuality*, 323–25.

137. Grace Lichenstein, "Abortion Laws Opposed at Rally," *New York Times*, March 29, 1967, p. 35; Rosemary Nossiff, *Before* Roe*: Abortion Policy in the States* (Philadelphia, 2001), 77–126.

138. Bill Kovach, "Abortion Reform Approved, 31–26, by State Senate," *New York Times*, March 19, 1970, p. 39; Bill Kovach, "Abortion Reform is Voted by the Assembly, 76 to 73; Final Approval Expected," ibid., April 10, 1970, p. 1; Francis X. Clines, "Pressures on Assemblymen over Abortion Measure," ibid., April 11, 1970, p. 17.

139. "Statement on Abortion" (April 22, 1970), in *Pastoral Letters of the United States Catholic Bishops*, 3:254. On the struggle in New York, see Gorney, *Articles of Faith*, 88–94; Garrow, *Liberty and Sexuality*, 418–21.

140. Noonan to Iltud Evans, O.P., April 26, 1971, NOONAN.

141. Robert D. McFadden, "President Supports Repeal of State Law on Abortion," *New York Times*, May 7, 1972, pp. 1, 29.

142. Shana Alexander, "The Politics of Abortion," *Newsweek*, Oct. 2, 1972, p. 29.

143. Bishop Justin Driscoll [Fargo] to John Cardinal Dearden, Feb. 13, 1973, box 24, file 20, JCD.

144. Office Memo on Michigan, March 29, 1971, in MI 1971 file, box 3, NARAL; Jack M. Stack to Lorraine Beebe, Nov. 6, 1970, Correspondence 1970, box 2, LB.

145. Mrs. Robert Z. Norman to Richard D. Lamm, May 14, 1972, MI Jan.–June 1972 file, box 3, NARAL; Jerry M. Flint, "Abortion Backers Hopeful of Gains," *New York Times*, Oct. 9, 1972, p. 9.

146. Michigan Catholics for Abortion Law Reform, June 2, 1971, statement, folder 35, box 2, MARC; Minutes of NARAL Annual Meeting, Oct. 6, 7, 8, 1972, folder 70, box 3, MARC.

147. Helen Casey to MCC Board of Directors, Aug. 2, 1972, MCC Respect for Life file, box 1, TG.

148. The Churches' Involvement in a Public Campaign against Abortion, July 10, 1972, Pro-Life Issues drawer, 1971–72, MCC.

149. Love and Let Live Campaign Packet, Pro-Life Issues drawer, 1971–72, MCC.

150. See early polling data, De Vries & Associates, Abortion Reform Study, March 15, 1972, MCC file, box 41, TG.

151. Tom Bergeson to Father, Nov. 9, 1972, Pro-Life Issues drawer, 1971–72, MCC.

152. Joint Proposal of MCC Protection-of-Life and MCC Welfare Reform Coordinators, Dec. 13, 1972, Respect Life file—MCC, box 1, TG.

153. John T. Noonan Jr., "Raw Judicial Power," *National Review*, March 2, 1973, p. 261; "Pastoral Message on Abortion" (Feb. 13, 1973), in *Pastoral Letters of the United States Catholic Bishops*, 3:368.

154. *Abortion Part I: Hearings before the Subcommittee on Constitutional Amendments of the Committee on the Judiciary, United States Senate Ninety-third Congress, Second Session, on S.J. Res 119 and S.J. Res. 130* (Washington, D.C., 1974).

155. On Blumenthal, see Sydney H. Schanberg, "Bill's Backer Loses Post," *New York Times*, Feb. 13, 1967, pp. 1, 50.

156. Jonsen, *Birth of Bioethics*, 290–91.

157. "Kennedy Predicts Abortion Reform," *New York Times*, Feb. 18, 1967, p. 30; Sidney H. Schanberg, "Kennedy Defends View on Abortion," *New York Times*, Feb. 23, 1967, pp. 1, 41.

158. Ford to Grisez, Aug. 30, 1967, Grisez file, box 17, JF-HC.

159. Fred McDonald to Robert F. Kennedy, July 10, 1967, Legis-Subject file—Abortion Conference—Planning, box 1, RFK; Garrow, *Liberty and Sexuality*, 340.

160. "McGovern Seeks Catholic Support," *National Catholic Reporter*, Sept. 1, 1972, p. 1; Thomas Gumbleton, "Vote McGovern," ibid., Oct. 27, 1972, p. 17.

161. Hole and Levine, *Rebirth of Feminism*, 93.

162. John Aloysius Farrell, *Tip O'Neill and the Democratic Century* (Boston, 1999), 520.

163. Kennedy to Mrs. Edward J. Barshak, copy [Aug. 3, 1971], in MA 1971 file, box 3, NARAL; Dr. Jeanne H. Fertel to NARAL headquarters, Oct. 14, 1973, file MA 1973, ibid.

164. Farrell, *Tip O'Neill*, 521.

165. Jean I. King to Frank Kelley, Oct. 31, 1972, file 85, box 3, MARC.

166. Dr. Jeanne H. Fertel to NARAL headquarters, Oct. 14, 1973, file MA 1973, box 3, NARAL.

167. Theo Lippmann Jr., *Senator Ted Kennedy* (New York, 1976), 231.

168. Democratic Party platform in *1984 Congressional Quarterly Alamanac*, 93-B. On Democratic Party reform, see Byron Shafer, *Quiet Revolution: The Struggle for the Democratic Party and the Shaping of Post-Reform Politics* (New York, 1983), 460–91.

169. Peter Steinfels, "Beliefs," *New York Times*, June 3, 2000, p. B6.

170. *Veritatis Splendor* (Washington, D.C., 1993), 53.

171. *Pilgrimage of Peace: The Collected Speeches of John Paul II in Ireland and the United States* (New York, 1980), 169.

CHAPTER 10: A CONSISTENT ETHIC AND SEXUAL ABUSE

1. *The Case of the Washington Priests* (n.p., 1970), esp. 62–65, copy in file 67, box 9, ACP.

2. Peter R. D'Agostino, "Catholic Planning for a Multicultural Metropolis, 1982–1996," in *Public Religion and Urban Transformation* (New York, 2000), 269–91.

3. Garry Wills, "A Tale of Two Cardinals," *New York Review of Books*, April 26, 2001, p. 24.

4. *Gaudium et Spes*, in *Vatican Council II: The Conciliar and Post-Conciliar Documents*, ed. Austin Flannery, O.P. (Northport, N.Y., 1975), 903. On Hehir, see William J. Gould, "Father J. Bryan Hehir: Priest, Policy Analyst, and Theologian of Dialogue," in *Religious Leaders and Faith-Based Politics: Ten Profiles* (Lanham, Md., 2001), 197–223.

5. "Heavy Attendance Greets Project Commitment Debut," *Michigan Catholic*, Feb. 10, 1966, p. 1.

6. Bishop Joseph L. Bernardin of Atlanta to St. Augustine Diocesan Council of Catholic Women [1967], copy in Pro-Life Issues drawer, MCC; Bernardin, "The Pastoral Constitution on the Church in the Modern World: Its Impact on the Social Teaching of the U.S. Bishops" (1985), in *Selected Works of Joseph Cardinal Bernardin*, vol. 2, *Church and Society*, ed. Alphonse P. Spilly (Collegeville, Minn., 2000), 146–47.

7. 1976 Democratic Party Platform, in *Congressional Quarterly Almanac* 32 (1976): 860.

8. Arch. Joseph Bernardin, Memorandum, Democratic Platform Statement on Abortion, June 21, 1976, Pro-Life and Politics file, JC.

9. Bernardin to Bishops, June 22, 1976, Abortion printed material file, box 20, TG.

10. Betty Ford's Recent Statements on Abortion [1976], in Abortion—President's Position file, box 1, Sarah Massengale Papers, GF.

11. Anne Higgins to David Gergen, July 2, 1976, Abortion file, box 1, David Gergen files, GF.

12. On the bishops and the abortion issue in 1976, see Timothy A. Byrnes, *Catholic Bishops in American Politics* (Princeton, 1991), 68–81.

13. "On Abortion, the Bishops v. the Deacon," *Time*, Sept. 20, 1976, p. 11.

14. Confidential Minutes of the Executive Sessions of the General Meeting of the National Conference of Catholic Bishops, Nov. 1976, in NCCB/USCC minutes file, box 41, TG.

15. "God and the Bomb: Catholic Bishops Debate Nuclear Morality," *Time*, Nov. 29, 1982, pp. 68–77; George F. Kennan, "The Bishops' Letter," *New York Times*, May 1, 1983, sec. 4, p. 21. For dissent from the pastoral letter, see Michael Novak, "Moral Clarity in the Nuclear Age: A Letter from Catholic Clergy and Laity," *National Review*, April 1, 1983, pp. 354–58.

16. *Economic Justice for All: A Pastoral Letter on Catholic Social Teaching and the U.S. Economy* (Washington, D.C., 1986).

17. Kenneth A. Briggs, "Bernardin Asks Catholics to Fight Both Nuclear Arms and Abortion," *New York Times*, Dec. 7, 1983, pp. 1, B8.

18. Bernardin, "The Challenge of Peace: Genesis, Principles and Perspectives of the American Bishops' Letter" (1984), in *Selected Works of Joseph Cardinal Bernardin*, 2:45.

19. Bernardin, "The Fact of Poverty Today: A Challenge for the Church" (1985), in *Selected Works of Joseph Cardinal Bernardin*, 2:108.

20. Bernardin, Remarks, Speak Out Illinois, Jan. 21, 1993, National Coalition for Life file, JB.

21. Arthur Barkey to Medical Practices Committee, Michigan Catholic Conference, Oct. 24, 1966, Pro-Life Issues drawer, 1960–1970, MCC; Confidential Minutes of the Executive Sessions of the General Meeting of the National Conference of Catholic Bishops, Nov. 1976, NCCB/USCC minutes file, box 41, TG.

22. Peter G. Filene, *In the Arms of Others: A Cultural History of the Right-to-Die Movement in America* (Chicago, 1998).

23. Ronald Dworkin et al., "Assisted Suicide: The Philosophers' Brief," *New York Review of Books*, March 27, 1997, p. 43.

24. *Compassion in Dying v. Washington* 850 F. Supp. 1461 (1994); *Compassion in Dying v. Washington* 49 F. 3d 591 (1995).

25. *Washington v. Glucksberg* 521 U.S. 702 (1997).

26. Valery Garrett, "The Last Civil Right?: Euthanasia Policy and Politics in the United States, 1938–1991" (Ph.D. diss., Univ. of California, Santa Barbara,

1998), 233–83; Daniel Patrick Hillyard, "Dying Right: The Death with Dignity Movement and the Reform of Oregon's Assisted Suicide Law" (Ph.D. diss., Univ. of California, Irvine, 1999).

27. Bernardin, "Euthanasia in the Catholic Tradition" (1995), in *Joseph Cardinal Bernardin: A Moral Vision for America*, ed. John P. Langan (Washington, D.C., 1998), 125.

28. Bernardin, "Letter to the Supreme Court" (1996), in *Joseph Cardinal Bernardin*, 128–29.

29. Michael Novak, *The Spirit of Democratic Capitalism* (New York, 1982), 239–50.

30. John LaFarge, S.J., to Gustav Gundlach, S.J., May 25, 1952, folder 24, box 16, JLF. Msgr. George Higgins comments on Buckley in *The Yardstick* (Nov. 19, 1951), in folder 193, box 410, WFB. On Catholics and modern conservatism, see Patrick Allitt, *Catholic Intellectuals and Conservative Politics in America, 1950–1985* (Ithaca, 1993).

31. Paul VI, *Populorum Progressio* (1967), in *The Papal Encyclicals, 1958–1981*, ed. Claudia Carlen, I.H.M. (Raleigh, N.C., 1981), 188; Michael Novak, "Wisdom from the Pope," *Washington Post*, May 7, 1991, p. A21.

32. Byrnes, *Catholic Bishops in American Politics*, 119.

33. Mario M. Cuomo, "Religious Belief and Public Morality," *New York Review of Books*, Oct. 25, 1984, pp. 31–37. On the Notre Dame speech, see Garry Wills, *Under God: Religion and American Politics* (New York, 1990), 305–17.

34. Cuomo, "Religious Belief and Public Morality," 34.

35. John T. Noonan Jr., "Development in Moral Doctrine," in *The Context of Casuistry*, ed. James F. Keenan, S.J., and Thomas A. Shannon (Washington, D.C., 1995), 189–98; idem, *A Private Choice: Abortion in America in the 1970s* (New York, 1970). Also see James Tunstead Burtchaell, c.s.c., *The Giving and Taking of Life: Essays Ethical* (Notre Dame, 1989), 260–75.

36. Byrnes, *Catholic Bishops in American Politics*, 121; Burtchaell, *Giving and Taking of Life*, 269.

37. On public opinion, see "Public Backs Abortion, But Wants Limits," *New York Times*, Jan. 16, 1998, pp. A1, A16.

38. *Evangelium Vitae* (1995), in *The Encyclicals of John Paul II*, ed. J. Michael Miller (Huntington, Ind., 1996), 802.

39. Archbishop Charles J. Chaput, "Be Doers of the Word, and Not Hearers Only," address delivered at the Union League, New York City, Oct. 17, 2000, copy in author's possession; Cardinal Francis George, "Catholic Christianity and the Millennium: Frontiers of the Mind in the 21st Century," address delivered at the Library of Congress on June 16, 1999, copy in author's possession.

40. Bernardin, "Catholic Common Ground News Conference" (1996), in

Selected Works of Joseph Cardinal Bernardin, 2:311–12; Bernard Cardinal Law, "Response to 'Called to Be Catholic,'" *Origins* 26 (Aug. 29, 1996): 170; idem, "Reaction to the Catholic Common Ground Project," ibid. 26 (Sept. 12, 1996): 198–206.

41. "Dioceses in 46 States Feel Impact of Sex Scandal," *USA Today*, April 28, 2002, p. A1. For a keen assessment, see Michael Sean Winters, "The Betrayal," *New Republic*, May 6, 2002, pp. 24–28.

42. Superb on the origins and development of the crisis is Peter Steinfels, "The Church's Sex-Abuse Crisis: The Story behind the Stories," *Commonweal*, April 19, 2002, pp. 13–19. Also see Jason Berry, *Lead Us Not into Temptation* (New York, 1992).

43. For a moving description of this episode, see Joseph Cardinal Bernardin, *The Gift of Peace* (Chicago, 1997), 19–41.

44. Todd Lighty and David Heinzmann, "Joliet Bishops at Center of Crisis," *Chicago Tribune*, May 16, 2002, p. 1.

45. Hendrik Hertzberg, "Sins," *New Yorker*, May 1, 2002, p. 36. Insightful on this point in French Catholic history is Thomas Kselman, "The Perraud Affair: Clergy, Church, and Sexual Politics in Fin-de-Siècle France," *Journal of Modern History* 70 (Sept. 1998): 614–15.

46. Philip Jenkins, *Pedophiles and Priests* (New York, 1996); Donald B. Cozzens, *The Changing Face of the Priesthood* (Collegeville, Minn., 2000), 124.

47. George Chauncey, *Gay New York 1890–1940* (New York, 1994).

48. For a case study, see Peter McDonough and Eugene C. Bianchi, *Passionate Uncertainty: Inside the American Jesuits* (Berkeley, 2002), 101–7.

49. The letter is reprinted in: *Gender, Urban Culture and the Making of the Gay Male World,* Investigative Staff of the *Boston Globe, Betrayal: The Crisis in the Catholic Church* (Boston, 2002), 235–42.

50. Reflections of P. Ford on Sessions of May 9 to 12 [1965], Response ad Puncta file, box 14, Ford Papers.

51. Garry Wills, "Scandal," *New York Review of Books*, May 23, 2002, p. 9.

52. Laurie Goodstein, "Accused of Sexual Assault, Archbishop Seeks to Retire," *New York Times*, May 24, 2002, p. A1.

53. For example, with variations, Robert Bellah, "Religion and the Shape of National Culture," *America* 181 (July 21, 1999): 9–14; Bellah et al., *The Good Society* (New York, 1991), 281–83; Margaret O'Brien Steinfels, "Democrats and Catholics," *Dissent* 46 (Fall 1999): 41–44; Alan Wolfe, "Liberalism and Catholicism," *American Prospect*, Jan. 31, 2000, pp. 16–21; William A. Galston, "Catholics and Liberals: Can We Get Along?" *Commonweal*, April 6, 2001, pp. 12–15; Michael J. Baxter, c.s.c., "Catholicism and Liberalism: Kudos and Questions for Communio Ecclesiology," *Review of Politics* 60 (Fall 1998): 743–64.

54. Michael A. Fahey Jr., S.J., "The Synod of America: Reflections of a Non-Participant," *Theological Studies* 59 (Sept. 1998): 486–504.

55. Samuel P. Huntington, *The Third Wave: Democratization in the Late Twentieth Century* (Norman, Okla., [1991], 1993), 72–85; José Casanova, *Public Religions in the Modern World* (Chicago, 1994), 75–134.

56. *Zelman v. Simmons-Harris*, 536 U.S., 122 S.Ct. 2460 (2002); Richard W. Garnett, "The Right Questions about School Choice: Education, Religious Freedom, and the Common Good," *Cardozo Law Review* 23 (March 2002): 1281–1313. On Catholic schools, see Anthony S. Bryk et al., *Catholic Schools and the Common Good* (Cambridge, 1993).

57. George W. Bush, "Report on Our Nation's Commitment to the Poor," *Origins* 31 (May 31, 2001): 46–48; Franklin W. Foer, "The Catholic Teachings of George W. Bush," *New Republic*, June 5, 2000, pp. 18–20; James L. Guth et al., "America Fifty/Fifty," *First Things* 116 (Oct. 2001): 19–26.

58. Charles Taylor, *Sources of the Self: The Making of Modern Identity* (Cambridge, 1989), 395, 495–521; *A Catholic Modernity?: Charles Taylor's Marianist Award Lecture*, ed. James L. Heft (New York, 1999), 13–37; Charles Taylor, "What's Wrong with Negative Liberty?," in *The Idea of Freedom: Essays in Honour of Isaiah Berlin*, ed. Alan Ryan (New York, 1979), 175–93.

59. M. J. Spalding, D.D., *Lectures on the Evidences of Catholicity, Delivered in the Cathedral of Louisville*, 4th ed. (Baltimore [1857], 1866), 217.

PHOTO CREDITS

Page 10: Courtesy of American Antiquarian Society
Page 20: Special Collections, Georgetown University
Page 44: Manuscripts and Archives, University of Notre Dame
Page 69: Manuscripts and Archives, University of Notre Dame
Page 83: Manuscripts and Archives, University of Notre Dame
Page 94: Courtesy of American Antiquarian Society
Page 97: Courtesy of American Antiquarian Society
Page 129: Manuscripts and Archives, University of Notre Dame
Page 143: LC-USZW62-118517, Library of Congress
Page 152: Marquette University Archives
Page 167: Bentley Historical Library, University of Michigan
Page 190: Manuscripts and Archives, University of Notre Dame
Page 191: Georgetown University Archives
Page 214: Corbis Images
Page 217: The Archives of the New England Province of the Society of Jesus, College of the Holy Cross
Page 230: Courtesy of Archives, Archdiocese of Boston
Page 242: Manuscripts and Archives, University of Notre Dame
Page 251: Courtesy of Historical Collections and Services, The Claude Moore Health Sciences Library, University of Virginia
Page 275: LC-USZ62-12278, Library of Congress
Page 281: Courtesy of Catholic News Service
Page 283: Courtesy of Archdiocese of Chicago's Joseph Cardinal Bernardin Archives and RecordsCenter

ACKNOWLEDGMENTS

I am indebted to more persons and institutions than I can possibly remember. The American Council of Learned Societies, Harvard University, the Louisville Institute (led by James Lewis), the University of Notre Dame, and the Institute for Scholarship in the Liberal Arts at Notre Dame gave me time to think. Not only did the Erasmus Institute at Notre Dame do the same, but its director, Jim Turner, read the manuscript with unusual care. Its associate director, Father Robert Sullivan, read successive drafts with characteristic generosity and an acute eye.

The editors and staff of *Commonweal*, especially Paul Baumann and Margaret Steinfels, produced a magazine that never failed to enlighten and gave me room to try out new ideas. The *Journal of American History* published an early version of Chapter Six in their June 1997 issue. At W. W. Norton, Alane Mason's thoughtful editing improved (and shortened) almost every page.

Archivists and librarians across the country—including Jeff Burns, Kevin Cawley, Father Carl Hoegerl, Charles Lamb, Tim Meagher, Nancy Merz, Father Paul Nelligan, John Shepherd, and Sharon Sumpter—were invariably helpful. Rupert Ederer, Gerald Fogarty, S.J., Rick Garnett, Joseph George, John Inglis, Michael Lacey, Kathleen Mahoney, David O'Brien, Tom O'Connor, John Quinn, and Mark Schwehn provided assistance and advice. John Noonan allowed me to look at his own papers, and Anthony Simon helped me understand those of his father. Mel Piehl offered shrewd commentary on an early draft. The energy of my research assistants, Darren Dochuk, Jane Hannon, Katie Kamlowsky, Jim McCartin, John Nagy, and Tom Rzeznik, never flagged. Christian and Silvia Dupont did marvelous translations from the Italian; David Bachrach did the same from the German.

At Harvard, the encouragement of Ellen Fitzpatrick, Bill Hutchison, David Hall, Akira Iriye, William Kirby, and Kevin Van Anglen got me started. Talking about history with Jim Goodman, Pat Kelly, and Ron Yanosky proved so enjoyable, so intoxicating, that I'm still not sure where their ideas end and mine begin. Father J. Bryan Hehir's dazzling lectures pushed me to consider both the role of moral theology in American history and the contribution Catholics might make to our common culture.

At Notre Dame, Scott Appleby's friendship and support as the director of the Cushwa Center for the Study of American Catholicism was invaluable, as was that of his assistant extraordinaire, Barbara Lockwood. Kathy Sprows Cummings, Jay Dolan, Phil Gleason, Suellen Hoy, Tom Kselman, George Marsden, Tim Matovina, Walter Nugent, Chris Shannon, and Paul Weithman sharpened my prose, and Charlotte Ames built the library collections upon which this book stands. Terry Bays, Bill Donahue, Gary Gutting, Anita Houck, Pam Jason, Wes Kort, Daniella Kostroun, Roger Lundin, and Susan Rosa made my semester at the Erasmus Institute a stimulating one.

My parents, Kathleen and Patrick McGreevy, and my in-laws, Carol and the late Jack McManus, never doubted, even if they wondered. Nora, Margaret, Patrick, and Leo McGreevy entered the world while I worked on this book, and I am lucky for it.

Only Jean made this and other dreams real.

INDEX

Page numbers in *italics* refer to illustrations.

Abbott, Francis Ellingwood, 93
Abbott, Lyman, 126
abolitionism, 13, 49–63, 65, 71, 72, 76–78, 80, 81–87, 93
Brownson's position on, 48–49, 77
education and, 38
McMaster's view of, 75
Purcell's support of, 82–85
abortion, 203, 215, 221, 223, 226–27, 230, 248–54, 257–70, 272–88, 294
Abortion (Callahan), 266
academic freedom, 174
Accademia (New York clerics), 119, 120
ACLU (American Civil Liberties Union), 144, 156, 212, 237–39, 260–61
Action Française, 199, 200
Acton, Lord, 45, 46–47, 79, 88
Adams, Henry, 105
Adams, Henry Carter, 142
Adams, John, 33, 37
Addams, Jane, 129, 140
Adenauer, Konrad, 146–47
Adler, Mortimer, 193, 222
Adorno, Theodor, 180
AFL (American Federation of Labor), 144, 146
African Americans, 50, 73, 111, 120
see also racism; segregation; slavery
Afro-Creoles, 81–82, 120–21
Alexander, Shana, 276
Alinsky, Saul, 204
Allgemeine Zeitung, 122
Alsatian-Americans, 29
Alter, Karl, 152, 205
America, 174, 266
American Anti-Slavery Society, 93
American Association of Universities, 139
American Association of University Professors, 139
American Association of University Women, 229
American Birth Control Conference, 159
American Birth Control League, 160, 226
American Catholic Philosophical Association, 192
American Catholic Trade Unionists, 163
American Civil Liberties Union (ACLU), 144, 156, 212, 237–39, 260–61
American Democracy v. Spanish Hierarchy, 172
American Federation of Labor (AFL), 144, 146
American Freedom and Catholic Power (Blanshard), 166–68, 186, 232
Americanism, 175
American Law Institute, 258, 273

American Missionary Association, 112
American Party, *see* Know-Nothing Party
American Protective Association (APA), 124–26
American Revolution, 37
Americans for Democratic Action, 167
Anglicans, 52, 162, 261
Annals of the American Academy of Arts and Sciences, 231
anti-Catholicism, 14–15, 22–25, 72, 75, 91–105, 122, 124, 147, 166–70
  abortion controversy and, 262
  of American Protective Association, 124–26
  Eliot School Rebellion and, 9
  individual autonomy and, 295
  in Mexico, 170–71
  nationalism and, 21, 88
  public schools and, 113
  of Republican Party, 64, 65, 75–76
  sexual abuse scandal and, 290
  Al Smith's campaign and, 150
  of socialists, 145
  of Edmund Wilson, 174
anticlericalism, 21, 37, 108, 170, 171, 173, 200
anti-Semitism, 165, 173, 210
antiwar movement, 256
Anzeiger des Westens, 22, 23
APA (American Protective Association), 124–26
apologetics, 196
Appeal to Reason, 145
architecture, church, 32
Arendt, Hannah, 197
Arizona, abortion controversy in, 274
arms race, 285, 287
art, Catholic, 29
artificial insemination, 253
assisted suicide, 228, 253–54, 286, 294
atheists, and educational issues, 116
Atlantic Monthly, 149, 151, 187
atomic weapons, *see* nuclear weapons
Aubert, Roger, 196, 207
Augustine, St., 243
Australia, 145
Austria, 38, 194, 197
authoritarianism, 175, 178–81, 187, 194, 197, 198, 200, 211, 212, 253
Authoritarian Personality, The (Adorno), 180
authority, principle of, 33, 103, 137–40
autonomy, individual, 136, 153, 252–55, 260–26, 265, 272, 276, 286, 294–95
Awful Disclosures of Hotel Dieu Nunnery (Monk), 12, 23

Baden, duchy of, 114
Baldwin, Roger, 156
Balmes, Jaime, 35–37, 52, 65, 86
Baltimore episcopal councils, 26, 40
Bancroft, George, 100, 104
Bannon, John, 79
Bapst, John, 61
Baptist churches, 52, 74, 262
Barth, Karl, 254
Barzun, Jacques, 231
base communities, Latin America, 271
Bassi, Ugo, 25
Bavaria, 38
Bea, Augustin, 243
Beacon Press, 185
Becker, Thomas, 74
Bedini, Gaetano, 25
Beecher, Edward, 58
Beecher, Henry Ward, 116
Beecher, Lyman, 58
Belfast, Ireland, 33
Belgium, 38
Bell, Daniel, 202
Belleperche, R. J., 193
Bellows, Henry, 109
Benedict, Ruth, 169
benediction of the blessed sacrament, 27
Bennett, John, 236
Bennett, William, 290
Bergson, Henri, 189
Bernardin, Joseph, 272, 282–90, *283*
Bevilacqua, Anthony, 289
Bible, free access to, 33
bioethics, 251, 266
  see also medical ethics
birth control, 153, 154, 157–62, 214, 221–26, 228–49, *230,* 268, 278, 288
  Callahan's position on, 266
  Fletcher's view of, 253
  papal commission on, 245, 292
  and right to privacy, 260
  situation ethics and, 257
Birth Control Review, 159, 160

bishops, meetings of:
at Baltimore, 26, 40
at Dallas, 291
at Medillín, Colombia, 271, 272
Bismarck, Otto von, 98–102, 125
Black, Hugo, 183–86, 263
Blaine, James, 92, 93
Blair, Frank, 75
Blair, Henry, 123–24
Blair, Montgomery, 75
Blanc, Antoine, 30, 81
Blanshard, Brand, 169, 186
Blanshard, Paul, 166–69, *167,* 180, 185, 186, 188, 191, 212, 214, 232, 251, 253, 263
Blau, Joseph L., 176–77
Blumenthal, Michael, 278
Bluntschli, Johann C., 101, 102, 104
Boas, George, 168
Boettner, Loraine, 264
Boland, John, 163
Bonhoeffer, Dietrich, 254
books, censorship of, 155–56, 174, 212
Boorstin, Daniel, 231
Boquillon, Thomas, 121
Bornstein, Heinrich, 22–23, 64
Boston, Mass., 22, 31, 32, 128
American Protective Association in, 124
anti-slavery movement in, 60
birth control issue in, 229–30, 232, 238
censorship in, 155–56
draft resistance in, 73
education conflicts in, 37, 41–42, 46, 124
Eliot School Rebellion in, 7–11
sexual abuse scandal in, 289–92
Ursuline convent destroyed in, 11
Boston Daily Advertiser, 9
Boston Daily Atlas and Bee, 9
Boston Pilot, 22, 53, 59, 72, 80, 231
Boston Weekly Messenger, 9
Bourne, George, 57
Bowers, Henry, 125
Brace, Charles Loring, 130
Brademas, John, 280
Brahmin Watch and Ward Society, 155–56
Brandeis, Louis, 145
Brandi, Salvatore, 121, 122
Brant, Irving, 185
Brauer, Theodore, 197
Brazil, slavery in, 50, 51
Brewster, William, 11
Briefs, Goetz, 197
British and Home Foreign Review, 88
Brooks, John Graham, 142
Brooks, Van Wyck, 148, 178
Brophy, John, 163
Brown, George, 59
Brown, John, 82
Brown, Robert McAfee, 262
Brownson, Orestes, 35, 43–49, *44,* 66–68, 76, 77, 79, 80, 88–90
economic issues and, 131
Hughes and, 80, 81
labor issues and, 54
McMaster and, 70, 71
Purcell and, 84, 85
on Republican Party, 109
Brownson, Sarah, 77
Brownson's Quarterly Review, 43, 45, 47–49, 80, 88–90
Brüning, Heinrich, 197–99
Brunner, Emil, 254
Bruns, Bernhard, 64
Buchanan, Patrick, 276
Buck, Carrie, 223, 225
Buckley, William F., 248, 287, 290
Buck v. Bell, 224, 225
Buffalo, N.Y., 29
Buffalo Volksfreund, 121
Bundy, McGeorge, 167
Burckhardt, Jacob, 102
Burgess, John, 100
Burke, John, 155, 160, 161
Burlingame, Anson, 63
Burns, Anthony, 60
Burton, Harold, 185
Burtsell, James, 119
Bush, George W., 294
Bushnell, Horace, 29
Butler, Pierce, 224

Cahensly, Peter Paul, 121
Cairnes, John, 79
Calderone, Mary Steichen, 232, 257
California, 272, 274
Callahan, Daniel, 221, 266, 267, 273
Calles, Plutarcho, 170, 171
Calvinism, 177, 179
Câmara, Hélder, 271
Cambridge, Mass., 117

Cameron, Simon, 80
Canada, 40, 59, 78, 98, 99
capitalism, 104, 150, 271, 287
capital punishment, 269, 285, 287, 294
Carberry, J. P., 113
Carey, James, 163
Carroll, John, 11, 27, 49, 52, 74
Carter, Jimmy, 284
Casey, Richard J., *214*
Casey, Robert, 280
Casti Connubii, 162–63, 221, 224, 229, 235, 244, 245, 263
Catholic Council on Civil Liberties, 239
Catholic Hospital Association, 258
Catholic political parties, 110
see also Center Party, German
Catholic revival, nineteenth century, 12–13, 25–32, 40, 54, 119
Catholic University, 139, 142, 143
Catholic Worker movement, 151
Catholic World, 131
Cathrein, Victor, 137
celibacy, and sexual abuse scandal, 290–91
censorship, 138, 153–57, 174, 212
Center Party, German, 104, 110, 121, 146, 147, 161
Centesimus Annus, 287
Central Conference of American Rabbis, 161
Central Verein, 110, 146
Challenge to Peace, A (pastoral letter), 285, 287
Channing, William Ellery, 29, 81
Chapman, John Jay, 148–49
Chaput, Charles, 289
Charbonnel, Armand de, 40
Chatard, Francis, 132, 134
Chávez, César, 204, 271–72
Cheever, George, 29, 58–59
Chenu, Marie-Dominique, 194, 195, 207, 214, 237
Cheverus, Jean, 11, 12, 84
Chicago, Ill., 111, 128, *129,* 155, 282, 290
Chicago, University of, 193, 203
Chicago Tribune, 63, 64, 93, 99, 117
Child, Lydia Maria, 93–94
child labor, 143
child-rearing practices, 181
child welfare, 129–30
Chinese immigration, 95
choice, power of, 253
choice, right of, in abortion controversy, *see* right to choose
Christian Democratic parties, 202
Christian Front groups, 173
Christian Reformed Church, 261
church property, taxation of, 74, 92
church-related institutions, public aid to, 107
see also denominational schools
church-state issues, 168, 185, 205–8, 212, 241
in Nast cartoon, *97*
see also denominational schools
Cincinnati, Ohio, 25, 64, 82–85, 116–19
Cincinnati Catholic Telegraph, 82, 84–86
Cincinnati Enquirer, 73
CIO (Congress of Industrial Organizations), 163
civil rights, *see* human rights and civil rights
Civil Rights Act, 215
Civiltà Cattolica, 26, 37, 87, 122, 127, 130, 137, 209
Civil War, 66–68, 71–75, 80, 90
Clark, Bayard, 62
Clark, Elizabeth, 54
classicism, Lonergan's notion of, 246
class struggle, 272
Claver, Peter, 52
Cleveland, Grover, 111
Cleveland, Ohio, 128
Cobden, Richard, 79
Cochin, Augustin, 77, 79, 80–81, 84
Coffin, Henry Sloane, 211
Cohen, Benjamin, 173
Cohen, Morris, 139
colleges and universities, 139, 140, 229, 232, 247
Colombo, Carlo, 244
Colorado, abortion controversy in, 274
Commager, Henry Steele, 177
common good, 196, 201, 265
Common Ground project, 289
common schools, *see* public schools
Commonweal, 162, 199, 200, 223, 239
communism, 166, 168, 172, 173, 180, 211–12
Communism, Democracy, and Catholic Power (Blanshard), 166
competition, 130, 131, 150

Compton, Karl T., 229
Comstock, Anthony, 155
Conant, James Bryant, 187–88, 263
Confederacy, 71–72, 74, 79, 81, 87
confession and absolution, 27, 28, 157–58, 218, 219, 227
Congar, Yves, 194, 195, 207, 210, 214, 237
Congregatio de Propaganda Fide, 114
Congressional Quarterly Weekly Report, 264
Congress of Industrial Organizations (CIO), 163
Connecticut, 229, 238–39, 278
Connecticut Planned Parenthood, 223
Connell, Francis, 207, 208, 212, 216, 218, 222, 228, 245, 249
"Conquered Banner, The" (Ryan), 112
conscience, individual, 237, 240, 241, 256, 265
conscientious objectors, 256
conservative Catholics, 122, 192, 287
  see also ultramontanism
consistent ethic of life, Bernardin's notion of, 285–87
Contemporary Moral Theology (Ford and Kelly), 221
contraception, *see* birth control
Contraception (Noonan), 241–43
Conway, Moncure, 65
Cooke, McLaurin F., 8
Cooke, Terence, 276, 284, 286
Coolidge, Charles A., 188
Cooper, John, 161
corporatist society, 146
Correspondant, Le, 45, 47, 77, 80
Corrigan, Michael Augustine, 121, 122, 134–36
Coughlin, Charles, 162, 165, 173, 203
Council of Political Reform, 109
Cox, Ignatius, 161
Creoles, 30, 81
Cross, Robert, 207
Cross currents, 195
Crucible, The (Miller), 252
Cuba, 51
Cullen, Paul, 26, 40, 79
culture, anthropological notions of, 168–69
culture of death, John Paul II's notion of, 289
Cummings, Jeremiah W., 46, 54, 59
Cummings, John, 75
Cunneen, Joseph, 195
Cuomo, Mario, 287, 288
Curaçao, 51
Curran, Charles, 255–56
Curtis, George William, 93
Cushing, Richard J., 188, 205, 238

Dalgairns, John, 69
Dallas, Tex., 289
  bishops' meeting in, 291
Davenport, Iowa, 54
Davies, A. Powell, 167, 185
Davis, Cushman K., 121
Davis, Henry Winter, 13
Davis, Jefferson, 72, 87, 112
Davitt, Michael, 132–34
Day, Dorothy, 151, *152,* 154, 256
Day, Timothy, 64
Dearden, John, 244, 283–84
death penalty, *see* capital punishment
De Bow's Review, 66
Declaration of Religious Freedom (Vatican II), 237, 238, 246, 247, 265
"Defense of Abortion, A" (Thomson), 263
deficit spending, 164
De Gasperi, Alcide, 202
democracy, 37, 39, 48, 138, 148, 169–71, 174–79, 192, 194, 196–97, 200, 202–4, 293
  public schools and, 182, 186, 187
  relativism and, 231
  science and, 179
Democracy in America (de Tocqueville), 253
Democratic Party, 63, 76, 82, 88
  abortion issue and, 259, 277–81, 284, 287, 288, 294
  anti-Catholic attacks on, 92, 93
  birth control controversy and, 160, 161, 229
  Blaine amendment and, 93
  Catholic allegiance to, 108–11
  economic issues and, 164
  educational issues and, 113, 124
  John Ireland's attack on, 123
  Irish Americans and, 110
  Ku Klux Klan and, 148
  sexual ethics and, 278
  Al Smith's campaign and, 150

Democratic Party (*continued*)
social issues and, 147
trade unions and, 163
Dennett, Mary Ware, 159, 161
denominational schools, 37, 41, 114, 147
authoritarianism in, 175
Blanshard's view of, 166
Brownson's view of, 45–46
democracy and, 186
liberal Catholics and, 46
liberal opposition to, 182
McGlynn's position on, 120
public assistance for, 30, 38, 40, 42, 91, 111, 113–21, 123, 182–85, 263–64, 294
staffed by nuns, 129
transportation reimbursements, 183, 184
Depression, Great, 151, 153
De religione et ecclesia (Mazzella), 107
Descartes, René, 26, 199
De Smet, Pierre, 75, 88
Deuster, Peter, 73
devotions, *see* piety and devotions
Dew, Thomas, 66
Dewey, John, 138–41, 148, 153, 167, 169, 170, 174–76, 182–83, 193, 194
Dietz, Peter, 142
divorce, 154, 181, 203
doctrinal development, 237, 241
Doe v. Bolton, 260, 277
Dollfuss, Engelbert, 197
Döllinger, Ignaz von, 45, 47
Dominican Order, 207
Doms, Herbert, 234–35
Domschke, Bernhard, 64
Dorchester, Daniel, 113
Dougherty, Dennis, 156
Douglas, Mary, 220
Douglas, Stephen, 71
Douglas, William O., 184–85, 248, 260, 264
Douglass, Frederick, 58, 66
draft, federal, 73, 76
Drake, Charles, 74
Draper, John William, 104–5, 112, 185
Dred Scott decision, 49, 59
Drinan, Robert, 261, 269–70
Dublin, Ireland, 33, 40
Dubuque, Iowa, 108
Dubuque Herald, 73
Dukakis, Michael, 237
Dupanloup, Félix, 50, 53, 77, 81, 84–86, 196
Duverney, Joseph, 108
Dwight, Theodore, 23
Dworkin, Ronald, 286
Dyer, Micah, 7

Eagleton, Thomas, 279
Ecole de théologie, Une: Le Saulchoir (Chenu), 207
economic issues, 33–34, 102, 150–54, 287
bishops' pastoral letter on, 285
Bush administration on, 294
corporatist society and, 146
industrialism and, 126
moral theology and, 143
poverty, causes of, 130
Protestantism and capitalism and, 104
Franklin Roosevelt and, 152–53, 164
single-tax crusade, 132
slavery and, 53–54
economic liberalism, 130, 138, 141–42, 154, 164, 287
economic oppression, alleviation of, 271
Edmunds, George, 93
education:
of American scholars, 179
Catholic-liberal conflicts, 122
Eliot School Rebellion, 7–11, 37
foreign language instruction, 124
see also denominational schools; public schools
Egan, Edward, 291
Einstein, Albert, 167
Elder, William, 74
Eliot, Charles William, 105, 124
Eliot, Frederick May, 184
Eliot, William Greenleaf, 92
Eliot School Rebellion, 7–11, 37, 41–42, 115
Ellis, John Tracy, 196, 207, 212
Ellsworth, Maine, 61
El Salvador, 272
Ely, Richard T., 126, 142, 143
Emancipation Proclamation, 86
Emergence of Liberal Catholicism in America, The (Cross), 208
Emerson, Ralph Waldo, 36, 43, 88, 103
Encyclopaedia of the Social Sciences, 175, 224

Engelen, William, 142, 147
England, *see* Great Britain
Episcopalians, *see* Anglicans
episcopal meetings, *see* bishops, meetings of
epistemology, 139
equal rights amendment, 155
Ernst, Morris, 259
Esprit, 151
establishment clause, of First Amendment, 184
"Ethical and Religious Directives" (Kelly), 258
ethics, 193, 225, 227
  legalism and, 219
  textbook on, 139
  see also medical ethics; military ethics; sexual ethics; situation ethics
Ethics (Bonhoeffer), 254
eugenics, 223–26
euthanasia, 222, 223, 225–26, 228, 230, 231, 251, 254, 286
Euthanasia Society of America, 226, 228
evangelicals, 124, 125, 147, 262, 281
Everson v. Board of Education, 183–85
existentialism, 254

Fall River, Mass., 290
family, 131, 154, 158, 159, 203
  democratic vs. authoritarian, 180, 181
Faran, James J., 73
Farrell, Thomas, 119–20
fascism, 164, 168, 170–73, 178, 180, 191, 198, 199
Federal Council of Churches, 161, 162
federal power, Catholics and, 75, 111
Feminine Mystique, The (Friedan), 261
feminism, *see* women's movement
Fenton, Joseph, 207, 212
Ferraro, Geraldine, 287, 288
Finkbine, Sherri, 259
First Amendment, 184, 206
Fitzhugh, George, 66
Fitzpatrick, John, 41
"Fixation of Belief, The" (Peirce), 140
Fletcher, Joseph, 220, 250–54, *251,* 256, 257, 259, 265, 266, 281
Flynn, Ed, 163
Ford, Betty, 284
Ford, Gerald, 284
Ford, John, 216–22, *217,* 224–28, 230–31, 233–36, 238–48, 270, 292
  abortion and, 258, 279
  situation ethics and, 255–57
Fordham University, 105
Fortnightly Review, 137
Fosdick, Harry, 171
Foster, Eden B., 63
France, 224
  abolitionists in, 51, 52, 76–77
  abortion debate in, 260
  American Revolution and, 11
  anticlericalism in, 98
  Catholic revival in, 30
  Catholic social thought in, 146
  economic issues in, 130–31, 158
  educational issues in, 37, 38
  labor issues in, 128
  liberal Catholics in, 21, 45, 47, 48, 77, 85
  liberals in, 106
  reinvigoration of church in, 194, 195
  revolution of 1848, 22
  social issues in, 151
Franco, Francisco, 172, 198–201
Franco-Prussian War, 99, 114
Frank, Waldo, 173
Frankfurter, Felix, 148, 173, 182, 184–86, 194, 205, 225
Freedman's Bureau, 112
Freedom and Culture (Dewey), 175
freedom of choice, in abortion controversy, *see* right to choose
freedom of conscience, 265
freedom of contract, 130, 144, 201
freedom of religion, 192, 194, 205–6, 237, 238, 246–49, 265, 293
free economic system, 141, 142, 145, 202, 287
Free Soil Party, 58
free speech, 174
Frei, Eduardo, 202
French Americans, 51, 146
French Anti-Slavery League, 77
French Canadian Catholics, 99, 110
French Caribbean, 51
French Revolution, individualism and, 153
French revolutions, 35, 37
Friedan, Betty, 261
Fuchs, Lawrence, 213
Fugitive Slave Act, 48, 60–62
Fuller, Arthur Buckminster, 9, 11–13, 31
Fuller, Lon, 193

Fuller, Margaret, 13, 21, 22
Fulton, Justin D., 125
funerals, Catholic, 31–33

Gabriel, Ralph, 177
Gallicanism, 26, 27
Gareschė, F. P., 112
Garfield, James, 92, 93, 99, 101
Garibaldi, Giuseppe, 23, 24, 79, 87
Garrigou-Lagrange, Reginald, 198
Garrison, William Lloyd, 56, 100
Garrison, Winfred E., 169–70
Gaudium et Spes (Vatican II), 244, 245, 269, 270, 283–84
Gavazzi, Alessandro, 23–25
Geoghan, John, 290
George, Francis, 289
George, Henry, 132–38, 142
Georgetown University, 111
German Americans:
  anti-Catholicism of, 22–23, 25, 99
  as Catholics, 102, 106–8, 110, 119, 121, 122, 124, 139
  in Civil War era, 51, 73, 82
  educational issues and, 37, 119, 122, 124
  political parties favored by, 63–64
  social issues and, 142, 146, 147, 154
  women's suffrage and, 154
Germany:
  abortion debate in, 260
  anti-Catholicism in, 98–100
  birth control controversy in, 161
  Catholic intellectuals in, 197
  Catholics and slavery issue in, 78
  Catholic social thought in, 146, 147, 150
  Catholic support of Nazis in, 198
  child welfare work in, 130
  devotion to suffering Jesus in, 28
  economic issues in, 131, 141–42
  educational issues in, 37, 114, 187
  family issues in, 180, 181
  labor issues in, 128
  liberal Catholics in, 48
  liberal movement in, 21, 104, 106
  racism in, 210
  scientific freedom advocated in, 88
  situation ethics in, 255
  unification of, 96
  Vatican concordat with, 171–72, 198
Gibbons, James, 123, 125, 132, 135, 169, 196
GI Bill, 183, 220
Gibson, Otis, 95
Gidding, Lee, 276
Gilligan, John, 249
Ginsburg, Ruth Bader, 259
Gioberti, Vincenzo, 20
Gladden, Washington, 126
Gladstone, William, 98, 99, 125
Glendon, Mary Ann, 260
Glennon, John, 209, 210
Godkin, E. L., 93, 105, 122–23
Goldman, Emma, 154
Gordon, Thomas, 36
government funding, *see* public funding
Grant, Ulysses S., 91–93, 98, 107, 118
Gratry, Abbè, 140
Great Britain, 203, 224, 225
  American slavery issue in, 79
  anti-Catholicism in, 98
  birth control controversy in, 161
  class structure in, 187
  liberal Catholics in, 45, 79
  socialism in, 145
Great Depression, 151, 153
Greeley, Horace, 66, 67
Green, Joseph, 274
Grégoire, Henri, 52
Gregory, Wilton, 291
Gregory XVI, 50, 52, 84, 241
Gresselin, Charles, 67
Grimké, Angelina, 57–58
Grisez, Germain, 243, 248
Griswold v. Connecticut, 239, 248
Gruening, Ernest, 170–71
Guiney, Patrick R., 73
Gumbleton, Thomas, 279
Gundlach, Gustav, 287
Gurian, Waldemar, 197–99
Gutiérrez, Gustavo, 271, 272
Guttmacher, Alan, 257

Hague, Frank, 173
Hallinan, Paul, 282
Hamilton, Alexander, 11
Hamilton, Walter, 174
Hankins, Frank, 224
Hanna, Mark, 126
Hardin, Garrett, 259

Häring, Bernhard, 239–40, 255–57
Harper's Weekly, 92, 93, 99, 108–9
Nast cartoons in, 94, *94,* 97
Harris, William T., 117–18
Hartz, Louis, 212
Harvard divinity school, 187
Harvard Law School, 105
Haskell, Thomas, 130
Haskins, George, 42
Hassaurek, Friedrich, 25, 64
Hastings Center, 266
Haven, Gilbert, 29
Hayes, Carlton, 204, 205
Hayes, Patrick, 159, 172
Hayes, Rutherford B., 92, 93, 109
health care, 144, 146
Hecker, Isaac, 46, 114
Heflin, Thomas, 147
Hehir, J. Bryan, 268, 283
Heinzen, Karl, 23
Heithaus, Claude, 209
Helper, Hinton Rowan, 65
Herberg, Will, 212
Hermens, F. A., 197
Heuser, Herman, 121
Hewitt, Abram, 134
Hickey, James, 289
Hickey, William, 145
High Noon (film), 252
Hildebrand, Dietrich von, 197, 198
Hill, Walter H., 139
History of the Conflict between Science and Religion (Draper), 104, 112
History of the Warfare between Science and Religion, A (White), 105
Hochwächter, 25
Hoffer, Eric, 252
Hofstadter, Richard, 213
Holaind, René, 121
Holmes, George Frederick, 66
Holmes, Oliver Wendell, Jr., 138, 193, 194, 223–24, 227, 228
Holy Cross, Congregation of the, 247
homosexuality, 291–92
Hook, Sidney, 174, 175, 203, 211–12
Hoover, Herbert, 146, 150, 159, 213
Howells, William Dean, 32
Hughes, Henry, 66
Hughes, John, 24, 34, 36, 39–40, 46, 48, 51–54, 56, 60, 67, 72, 73, 79–81, 87
Hull House, 129
Humanae Vitae, 245–48, 268, 272, 282
Humani Generis, 207
human rights and civil rights, 173, 178, 191, 194, 197, 200, 201, 206, 208, 215, 250, 252, 253, 273, 294
UN declaration on, 203
Humphrey, Hubert, 279
Hunthausen, Raymond, 282
Hürth, Franz, 162, 216, 219, 221, 235, 240, 255
Husslein, Joseph, 147, 154
Hutchins, Robert Maynard, 193
Hyde, Henry, 280

Illinois, 113, 124, 266
Imesch, Joseph, 290
immigration, immigrants, 14, 29–31, 108, 121, 125, 148
anti-Catholicism and, 11, 94, 95
assimilation of, 45–46
of Catholic intellectuals, 197
educational controversies and, 37
of European radicals, 22–24
inalienable rights, Jefferson's notion of, 192
Independent, 58, 98, 102, 125
Indiana, 269
Indianapolis, Ind., 109
individualism, 26, 52, 65, 111, 153, 154, 196, 200, 201
economic, 142, 294–95
religious, 176
industrial council plan, 163
industry, 126, 128, 150
infallibility, papal, *see* papal infallibility
Inquisition, 263
Interracial Justice (LaFarge), 209, 210
interracial marriage, 55, 120
interreligious cooperation, 204
"In the Face of the World's Crisis" (manifesto), 202
inventions, 179
Ireland, 28, 38, 79, 98, 132–33, 182
Ireland, John, 120–23
Irish-Americans, 31, 45, 72, 73, 76, 109
abolitionism and, 51, 79, 82
Democratic Party and, 63, 110
educational issues and, 37
French Canadian Catholics and, 110
Italian Catholics and, 110

Irish-Americans (*continued*)
  Kapp's opinion of, 99
  women's suffrage and, 154
Isis, 179
Italian-Americans, 107, 110
Italy, 21, 48, 96, 100, 172
  anti-Catholicism in, 98
  Catholic social thought in, 146
  educational issues in, 37
  nationalism in, 87, 98, 106
  science in, 179

Jackson, Robert H., 187
Jackson, Shirley, 253
James, William, 138–41, 177
Jay, John, 123
Jefferson, Thomas, 37, 176, 183, 184, 187, 192, 212
Jefferson Memorial, 176
Jesuits, 19–25, 32–33, 41, 94, 100, 101, 106–8, 112, 117, 119, 172, 247
  Blair's attack on, 123
  Brownson and, 67, 89
  devotions promoted by, 28, 29
  film censorship by, 156
  Harvard Law School admissions and, 105
  individualism and, 201
  in Louisiana, 30
  Mann's opinion of, 39
  missionaries in Latin America, 270
  moral theology and, 216
  Nouvelle Théologie and, 207
  papal infallibility and, 103
  parish missions conducted by, 27
  Progress and Poverty and, 137
  racial segregation and, 209, 210
  Bertrand Russell and, 174
  slavery issue and, 50, 52
  Thomistic revival and, 26, 139
  Union cause opposed by, 87
Jews, Judaism, 139, 148, 176–77
  abortion and, 261
  birth control controversy and, 157, 158
  educational issues and, 116, 186
  interreligious cooperation of, 204
John Paul II, 281, *281*, 289, 291, 293, 294
John XXIII, 203, 236, 240
Joliet, Ill., 290
Jones, Howard Mumford, 176
Joseph P. Kennedy Jr. Foundation, 279
Journal des Débats, Le, 77, 80
Journet, Charles, 202

Kallen, Horace, 139, 156, 167, 174–76, 179, 184, 186, 253
Kansas-Nebraska Act, 61, 62
Kapp, Friedrich, 99
Kelley, Florence, 142, 144
Kelley, Francis, 173
Kelley, Frank, 280
Kelly, Gerald, 209, 216–19, 221, 222, 233, 235, 236, 240, 252, 255, 258
Kelly, John, funeral of, 31
Kemp, Henry, 60
Kennan, George, 285
Kennedy, Edward, 278, 280
Kennedy, Ethel, 279
Kennedy, John F., 213, *214*
Kennedy, Joseph P., 213
Kennedy, Robert F., 256, 278, 279
Kennedy Institute of Ethics, 267
Kenrick, Francis, 25, 26, 40, 53, 74, 86, 87
Kenrick, Peter, 75
Kentucky, 40, 86
Keogh, James, 72
Kerby, William, 137, 142
Kernan, Francis, 113
Ketteler, Wilhelm von, 131, 146
Keynes, John Maynard, 164
King, Martin Luther, Jr., 272
King, Thomas, 34
Kirchwey, Freda, 167
Klein, Félix, 122
Kleutgen, Joseph, 26
Knights of Labor, 131–32
knowledge, conception of, 139
Know-Nothing Party (American Party), 7, 30, 45, 62, 63, 65, 124, 125
Kölnische Zeitung, 122
Königswinterer Kreis, 150
Kossuth, Louis, 23–24, 45, 87
Kraus, Franz Xaver, 89, 122
Krol, John, 278
Ku Klux Klan, 147–48, 182, 185
Kulturkampf, 98–100, 104, 107

labor issues, 53–54, 123, 125, 126, 128, 130–31, 137, 142–44, 146, 150, 151, 154, 155, 163
  migrant farm workers, 271–72

labor unions, *see* unions, labor
Laboulaye, Edouard, 77, 101
Labour Party (British), 145, 161
Lacordaire, Jean-Baptiste-Henri, 85
LaFarge, John, 194, 209–10, 287
Lafayette, marquis de, 11, 13
laissez faire, principle of, 138, 142, 152, 164
Lambert, John, 59–60
Lamennais, Félicité, 48
land issues, 132–33, 136
  see also single-tax movement
Land League, 132, 133
La Piana, George, 185
Laski, Harold, 225
Latin America, 37, 50, 192, 202, 224, 236, 269–71
latitudinarianism, 30
Laveleye, Emile de, 103–4
Law, Bernard, 289–91
Law of Christ, The (Häring), 240, 255
Lawrence, Amos A., 9
Lawrence, Eugene, 93
law schools, 105, 140
lay parish trustees, *see* trusteeism, lay
Lee, Robert E., 72, 79
legalism, in ethics, 219
Legion of Decency, 156
Lemon v. Kurtzman, 263
Leo XIII, 37, 100, 126–28, 131, 135–37, 139, 141, 142, 150, 206
Lerner, Max, 173, 182, 183
Lewis, C. S., 222
liberal Catholics, 45–48, 67, 77, 79, 85, 86, 123, 206–7, 212
  Brownson and, 89
  educational issues and, 118, 121–22
  in Louisiana, 30
  McMaster's view of, 70
  New York priests as, 119–20
  slavery issue and, 53, 76, 78, 79
  ultramontanism and, 29–30, 88
  women's suffrage and, 154
liberalism, 13, 108, 168
  abortion and, 215, 260
  anticommunism and, 211
  birth control and, 214
  Catholic pressure groups and, 171
  Catholics and, 98, 99, 102, 107, 111, 113, 122, 138, 141, 148, 173, 175, 191–93, 196, 259, 265
  compulsory sterilization and, 224
  dogma of infallibility and, 103
  economic, *see* economic liberalism
  educational issues and, 38, 114–16, 119, 182
  Engelen's description of, 147
  European, 20–24, 48, 109–10, 122, 200
  euthanasia and, 225
  failure of, 137
  fascism and, 164
  individual autonomy and, 260
  Italian, 106
  John F. Kennedy's campaign and, 213
  Mexico and, 108, 170–71
  nationalism and, 105–6, 122
  progress and freedom and, 33, 36
  racial integration and, 211
  right-to-life movement and, 269
  Roosevelt-Catholic alliance and, 153
  sexual issues and, 157
  slavery issue and, 49, 52, 77, 87
  Al Smith's campaign and, 149
  Spanish civil war and, 172
liberal Protestants, 29
liberation theology, 271, 272
Liberator, 57, 61
Liberatore, Matteo, 26, 107, 127, 130, 157
Lieber, Francis, 100–102, 115
life, protection of, 221–28, 254, 260, 266–70, 273, 277–80, 285–87, 294
  see also right to life
Lilienthal, Max, 116
Lincoln, Abraham, 52, 66, 68, 73, 74, 79, 82, 87, 96
Lindbergh, Charles, Sr., 145
Lindeman, E. C., 148
Lippmann, Walter, 139, 149, 193
Lipset, Seymour Martin, 180–81
Literary History of the United States, 178
liturgy, 26
Living Thoughts of Thomas Jefferson, The (Dewey, ed.), 176
living wage, 130, 142, 144, 153, 154, 197
Lonely Crowd, The (Riesman), 252
Lonergan, Bernard, 194, 246, 247
Look magazine, 213
Lord, Daniel, 156–57, 161
Los Angeles, Calif., 291
"Lottery, The" (Jackson), 253
Louisiana, 30, 182, 210, 289

Lourdes, France, 27–28, 32, 112, 141
Lovejoy, Elijah, 57
Lowell, A. Lawrence, 171
Loyalists, Spanish, 172, 173
loyalty oath, in Missouri, 74–75
Lubac, Henri de, 194–95, 206–7, 214, 237
Luca, Giuseppe de, 196
Luce, Claire Booth, 190
Luce, Henry, 190, 212
Lucey, Francis E., 193
Luther, Martin, 26, 33, 103, 199
Lutherans, 124, 261, 276
Luxembourger Catholics, 73
Lynch, Patrick, 26, 72, 78–79
Lynd, Helen, 169
Lynd, Robert, 168–69
Lyon, France, 30

McAdo, William, 147–48
Macaulay, Thomas, 13–14
McCarthy, Eugene, 256
McCarthy, Joseph, 180
McClelland, David, 181–82
McCloskey, John, 134
McCollum v. Board of Education, 183–85, 205
McCormick, Richard, 245, 249, 267, 270, 273
McElroy, John, 32–33, 41, 72
McGeehan, John E., 174
McGlynn, Edward, 120, 133–37
McGovern, George, 279
McGrath, Marcos, 271
McHugh, James T., 268, 273
McKeon, Richard, 193
McKinley, William, 125–26
MacLeish, Archibald, 211
McMaster, Gertrude, 68
McMaster, James, 68–71, *69,* 73, 75, 79, 84, 85, 88, 89, 111–14, 118–20, 133–34, 136
McMullen, John, 54
McNamee, Stephen F., 193
McNeile, Hugh, 59
McNichols, John T., 151
McQuaid, Bernard, 135
McSweeney, Patrick F., 120
Macune, Charles W., 125
Madison, James, 185, 192, 212
Maguire, Daniel, 256
Mahoney, Denis, 73
Mahoney, Roger, 291
Maine, Sebeus, 8
Maistre, Claude, 67, 81
Maldonado, Charles, 108
Malines, Belgium, Catholic congress at, 85, 88
Malone, Sylvester, 119
Mann, Horace, 38, 39, 115
Margraf, J., 78
Marian apparitions and devotions, 27–28
Maritain, Jacques, 189–92, *190,* 194–210, 214, 235, 241, 254
Maritain, Raïssa, 190, 198
marriage, 234–35, 242, 244, 245
  interracial, 55, 120
Marsh, George Perkins, 87, 99
Marshall, Charles, 149
Marshall, Thurgood, 259
Martin, Augustin, 55
Martineau, Harriet, 21
Martinsburg, W.Va., 74
Marxism, liberation theology and, 272
Maryland, 40
Maslow, Abraham, 180
Masons, 182
Mass, patriotic prayers included in, 74
Massachusetts, 40, 62–63, 72
  birth control issue in, 229–31, *230,* 231, 237, 238, 278
  see also Boston, Mass.
Massachusetts Anti-Slavery Society, 60
Maurin, Peter, 151
Mayo, Amory Dwight, 116
Mazzella, Camillo, 107–8, 127, 128, 135–36
Meagher, Thomas Francis, 79
Mecklin, John, 173
Medeiros, Humberto, 272, 291
Medicaid, abortion funding through, 280
medical ethics, 219, 220, 222, 223, 225–27, 250, 251, 255, 286
  see also abortion; birth control; euthanasia
Medill, Joseph, 93
Medillín, Colombia, meeting of bishops at, 271, 272
meekness, virtue of, 103
Memoir of an Ex-Radical (Fletcher), 250
Memoirs of Hecate County (Wilson), 174

Menace, The, 145
Mencken, H. L., 148
Mendizábal, Alfredo, 197
mental incompetence, compulsory sterilization and, 223–26
Merton, Robert, 178
Merton, Thomas, 256
Methodist churches, 52, 74
Metropolitan Record, 73, 75
Mexican Americans, 272
Mexico, 59, 99, 108, 170–71
Meyer, Agnes, 187, 211
Michelet, Jules, 19
Michigan, 40, 62, 147, 262, 264, 276–78, 294
Michigan Abortion Reform Committee, 276
Michigan Catholic Conference, 276–77
Michigan Citizens for Abortion Law Reform, 264
Middle Ages, 102, 105, 119, 130, 193–94
  scientific knowledge in, 179, 187
  study centers of, 140
Middletown (Lynd and Lynd), 169
migrant farm workers, 271–72
military ethics, 227–28, 256, 270, 285
Mill, John Stuart, 33, 36
Miller, Perry, 186
Miller, Samuel, 75
Milliken, William, 278
Milwaukee, Wis., 23, 64, 145, 292–93
minimum-wage issue, 53, 54, 142, 144, 154
Minnesota, 73, 120, 121, 269
miraculous medal, 48
miraculous occurrences, fascination with, 27
Miss Columbia's Public School (Pullen), 94
missionaries, in Latin America, 270–71
Missouri, 22, 24, 74–75
Missouri Synod Lutherans, 261
modernity, Catholicism and, 102, 104, 119, 122, 191, 194, 214
Monde, Le, 80
Monk, Maria, 12, 23
monopolies, attacks on, 124, 125
Montague, Ashley, 179
Montalembert, Charles de, 20, 47–50, 53, 70, 77–79, 81, 85, 88, 90
Moody, Dwight, 124
Mooney, Edward, 163
morality, teaching of, 39, 118
  in pluralistic society, 288
  situation ethics and, 252
Morals and Medicine (Fletcher), 251–53
moral theology, 216–22, 225, 227, 239–40, 248
  contraception and, 244, 245
  Curran's view of, 256
  economics and, 143
  historical consciousness and, 246–47
Morgan, Thomas, 113
Morgenstern, Julius, 173
Mormons, 112–13, 261
Morrill, Justin, 92
Morris, Charles, 176
mortal sin, 218, 220
Morton, Oliver P., 93
motion pictures, 154, 156–57, 212
motivation, Maslow's study of, 180
Motley, John Lothrop, 34
Mounier, Emmanuel, 151
Mueller, Franz, 197
Mulford, Elisha, 101
Mullaly, John, 73
Mumford, Lewis, 167, 173
Mundelein, George, 172
Murray, Daniel, 40
Murray, John Courtney, 189–92, *191,* 194–96, 204–16, 228, 232, 246–47, 265–66
  at Vatican II, 237, 238, 241
Murray, Philip, 163
Muskie, Edmund, 279
Mussolini, Benito, 172
Mysteries of St. Louis, The (Bornstein), 23

NARAL, *see* National Abortion Rights Action League
Nast, Thomas, cartoons by, 94, *94,* 97
Natchez, Miss., 74
Nation, 93, 96, 99, 105, 117, 122–23, 144, 148, 175, 231
  Blanshard's articles in, 166, 167, 185
Nation, The (Mulford), 101
National Abortion Rights Action League (NARAL), 276
National Anti-Slavery Standard, 59
National Birth Control League, 159
National Catholic War Council, 144
National Catholic Welfare Conference (NCWC), 145, 150, 161, 203, 225, 228–29, 235, 249, 257, 287

National Catholic Welfare Conference Bulletin, 156
National Conference of Catholic Bishops, 272, 275, 278, 282
National Conference of Christians and Jews, 204
National Consumer League, 144
National Council of Catholic Women, 160
National Council of Churches, 261
National Federation of Catholic College Students, 215
National Institute of Mental Health, 180
nationalism, 21, 73, 105–6, 111, 122
  anti-Catholicism and, 96, 100–101
  John Ireland's position on, 120, 121
  Italian, 87, 98
  public education and, 112–13, 115
National Organization of Women (NOW), 261
National Organization to Repeal Abortion Laws, 268
National Recovery Administration (NRA), 152–53
National Review, 287
national unity, education and, 117
National Women's Party, 155
Native Americans, and public education, 112–13
nativism, 121, 122
natural law, 138, 140, 193, 201, 220, 221–22, 227, 231
  abortion and, 225
  Catholics' loss of interest in, 255, 265
  contraception and, 157, 159, 229–30, 234, 235, 243
  film censorship and, 156
  protective legislation for women and, 155
Natural Law Institute, 192
Nazism, 171–72, 175, 180, 193, 198, 228
NCWC, *see* National Catholic Welfare Conference
Negroes, *see* African Americans; racism; slavery
Nell-Breuning, Oswald von, 150
neo-Thomism, *see* Thomistic revival
New Deal, 164
New England Planned Parenthood, 278
Newman, John Henry, 47, 69, 79, 84, 195–96, 207, 237, 240
Newman, J. P., 98
New Mexico, 117
New Orleans, La., 86
  Afro-Creole dispute in, 81–82, 120–21
New Republic, 138, 144, 149, 159, 165, 170–71, 175, 179, 211, 225–26, 231
Newsweek, 276
New York City, 36, 46, 128
  abortion controversy in, 274, *275,* 276
  birth control controversy in, 159, 160
  Catholic-Protestant conflict in, 109
  school issues in, 115, 116, 119, 120
  sexual abuse scandal in, 291
New York Daily Tribune, 66
New Yorker, 290–91
New York Evening Post, 85
New York Freeman's Appeal, 68
New York Freeman's Journal, 51, 68–70, 79, 85, 86, 88, 112, 133–34
New York Herald, 77, 120
New York Review of Books, 288
New York Society to Suppress Vice, 156
New York State, 40, 73, 263, 273–75, *275,* 278, 279
  see also New York City
New York Times, 99
  anti-Catholic position of, 93
  on Bernardin, 285
  on Blair, 124
  on Catholics in city government, 109
  on Malone, 120
  popery and slavery compared by, 75
  Purcell praised by, 119
  on Ryan's criticism of Coughlin, 173
  on vanishing Catholic beliefs, 14
New York Tribune, 9, 21, 77, 80, 99
New Zealand, 161
Niebuhr, Reinhold, 148, 167, 173, 205–6, 211, 213, 214, 234
Nilan, Patrick, 120
Nixon, Richard, 275–76
nonviolence and pacifism, 151, 256, 272
Noonan, John T., Jr., 241–43, *242,* 245, 256, 262, 266–69, 274–75, 277, 286
North American Review, 29, 33, 137
North Carolina, 125, 274
North Dakota, 276
Norton, Charles Eliot, 29, 99, 103, 123
Norton, Eleanor Holmes, 276
Notre Dame, University of, 141, 197
Nouvelle Théologie, 195–208, 221

Novak, Michael, 279, 287
NOW (National Organization of Women), 261
NRA (National Recovery Administration), 152–53
nuclear weapons, 228, 285, 287
Nulty, Thomas, 132, 133
nuns, 108, 114, 129, 130, 166

obedience, virtue of, 27, 103
obliteration bombing, 227
O'Boyle, Patrick, 247, 275, 282
O'Connell, Daniel, 20–21, 50–51, 53, 56, 84, 86
O'Connell, William H., 172
O'Connor, John, 287–89
O'Connor, Michael, 46
Odin, Jean-Marie, 82, 87
O'Hara, Edwin, 144
Ohio, 40
old-age insurance, 144
Onahan, William J., 111
O'Neill, Tip, 279, 280
On Liberty (Mill), 36
Orange order, 124
Oregon, 147, 182, 286
Organization Man, The (Whyte), 252
orphanages, Catholic, 129, *129,* 130
  public support for, 115
Orr, John, 60–61
Osservatore Romano, L', 87, 210
Ottaviani, Alfredo, 208, 212, 227, 243, 244
Our Country (Strong), 125
Outlook, 149
Ozanam, Frédéric, 128

Pacem in Terris, 203
pacifism and nonviolence, 151, 256, 272
Paddy funerals, 31
Paine, Thomas, 11
Palm Beach, Fla., 290
papal authority, 246
papal infallibility, 103, 119, 140, 141
  Humanae Vitae and, 248
  Purcell's battle against, 84
Papal States, 21–22, 48, 96, 172
parish missions, 27
Park, Edwards Amasa, 34
Parker, Theodore, 29, 31, 33, 34, 38, 39, 43, 63, 81
Parkman, Francis, 95
Parnell, Charles Stewart, 132, 133
parochial schools, *see* denominational schools
Parsons, Talcott, 174, 178
Parsons, Wilfrid, 192
Parti Démocrate Populaire (France), 146
Partito Popolare (Italy), 146, 172, 198
patriotism, 120, 123
patristics, 195
Patterns of Culture (Benedict), 169
Paul, Alice, 155
Paulists, 28, 46
Paul VI, 192, 204, 217, 236, 243–45, 248, 257, 265, 268, 272, 287, 292
pedophilia, 291
Peirce, Charles, 140
Penn, William, 177
Pennock, Roland, 186
Pennsylvania, 40, 73, 274
pentecostals, 147
Perché, Napoleon, 30, 39, 81
Perry, Ralph Barton, 141
Pesch, Heinrich, 142, 146, 150, 153, 158
Pétain, Philippe, 201
Phi Beta Kappa, 141
Philadelphia, Pa., 40
Phillips, Wendell, 50
philosophy, 138–41
  see also Thomistic revival
Piedmont, Italy, 38
Pierce v. Society of Sisters, 182
piety and devotions:
  Brownson's view of, 48
  nineteenth century Catholic revival and, 12, 25–29, 32
Pike, James, 232
Pioneer, Der, 23
Pittsburg Catholic, 59–60
Pittsburgh, Pa., 25
Pius IX, 21, 22, 26, 30, 87, 96, 103, 106, 114, 122–23, 151, 196, 207
Pius XI, 150, 152, 171, 172, 194, 199, 209, 221, 224
Pius XII, 171, 201–2, 207, 210, 211, 234, 240, 255, 263
Planned Parenthood, 229, 232, 235, 238, 257, 258
pluralism, American, 212
POAU, *see* Protestants and Other Americans

United for the Separation of Church and State
Polish Americans, 145, 169
Polish National Catholic Church, 145
political economy, 142
political individualism, 196
political oppression, alleviation of, 271
Politics and Scholasticism (Maritain), 200
polygenesis, theory of, 55
population control, 235–36, 240
Population Council, 235, 236
Populist movement, 125
Porter, James, 290
Portugal, 194, 197
Possibility of Invincible Ignorance of Natural Law, The, 235
Post-Gazette, 64
Potter, Charles, 226
Poughkeepsie, N.Y., 120, 121
Pound, Roscoe, 143–44, 201
poverty, 130
  abortion issue and, 273, 277
  Bernardin's consistent ethics of life and, 285, 287
  bishops' pastoral letter on, 285
  Catholic Worker movement and, 151
  in Latin America, 269, 271, 272
  liberation theology and, 271
Power, Michael, 40
pragmatism, 139–41, 153, 177, 193
Presbyterian churches, 52
Prescott, William, 34
press:
  Mexican crisis and, 171
  Mussolini's government and, 172
  see also specific newspapers and magazines
Preston, Thomas, 134, 135
Preuss, Arthur, 121, 137
Princeton Review, 105
privacy, right to, 248, 260, 277
private judgment, principle of, 65–66, 72, 103
private property, *see* property rights
private schools:
  Conant's opposition to, 187–88
  see also denominational schools
pro-choice, *see* right to choose
Production Code Administration, 156
Progress and Poverty (George), 132–34, 136, 137
Progressive Era, censorship in, 155
pro-life, *see* right to life
Propagateur Catholique, 30, 55–56, 81, 82
property rights, 132, 134, 135, 137, 138, 154, 201
property taxes, 183
Protestant Ethic and the Spirit of Capitalism, The (Weber), 104, 178
Protestantism, 33–35, 103, 126, 147
  achievement of children and, 181
  capitalism and, 104
  democracy and, 176–78
  individualism and, 199
  public schools and, 187
Protestantism and Catholicism, in Their Bearing upon the Liberty and Prosperity of Nations (de Laveleye), 103–4
Protestantism and Catholicity Compared in their Effects on the Civilization of Europe (Balmes), 35
Protestants, American, 23, 109, 168, 192, 254
  abortion and, 261, 262, 281
  American Party and, 62
  birth control controversy and, 157, 158, 161–62, 229, 234
  censorship and, 155
  child welfare agencies, 129
  denominational schools, 38
  John Dewey and, 153
  educational issues and, 38, 40, 116, 187
  Eliot School Rebellion and, 7–9
  interreligious cooperation of, 204
  liberal theologians, 29
  Missouri test oath and, 74
  racial integration and, 211
  Republican Party and, 111
  slavery issue and, 52, 54, 61
  Al Smith and, 148
Protestants and Other Americans United for the Separation of Church and State (POAU), 183
Prussia, Germany, 37, 38, 96
public funding:
  of abortions, 280
  of church-related institutions, 107, 263
  of denominational schools, 30, 38, 40, 42, 91, 111, 113–21, 123, 182–85, 263–64, 294

public morality, censorship and, 155
public opinion, de Tocqueville's notion of, 253
public schools, 92, 94, 112–19
Bible reading in, 7, 8, 30, 37, 39, 41, 42, 59, 62, 113, 115–18, 120
Canadian, 40
Conant's support of, 187
democracy and, 186
Eliot School Rebellion, 7–11
federal aid to, 123
John Ireland and, 121
de Laveleye's comments on, 104
liberal Catholics and, 46
released-time programs in, 184
religion and, 37–42, 107, 187
secularization of, 115–18
Pullen, Charles Henry, 94
Purcell, Edward, 82, 119
Purcell, John, 67, 82–87, *83,* 119
Puritanism, 177, 187
Putnam's Magazine, 115

Quadragesimo Anno, 150–51, 162, 163, 197
Quakers, 52, 177
Quebec, Canada, 178, 194, 224
Quinlan, John, 72

racism, 51, 54–56, 208–11
Radical Reconstruction, 119
Radical Republicans, 64, 74, 123
Rahner, Karl, 194, 255
Rambler, The, 45, 47
Ramsey, Paul, 234, 262
rationalism, 196
Rauschenbusch, Walter, 153
Rawls, John, 262–65, 286
Reagan, Agnes, 155, 160
Reagan, Ronald, 278, 280
Reconstruction era, 108, 111–13
Redemptorists, 27, 28, 69–70, 114
Reformation, 33, 35, 102, 103, 106, 153, 176–78
relativism, 231, 232
released-time programs, in public schools, 184
religious education, 39, 118
see also denominational schools
religious liberty, *see* freedom of religion
religious orders, men's, 21
Renaissance, 102
Renouvier, Charles, 141
reproductive freedom, 280
see also abortion; birth control
Republican Party, 62–65, 75–76, 78, 96, 107–10
abortion issue and, 280, 284
anti-Catholicism of, 92, 93, 110
birth control issue and, 161, 229
capital punishment and, 294
educational issues and, 113, 116, 117, 124
Eliot School Rebellion and, 9
John Ireland and, 123
Missouri test oath and, 74–75
New York liberal priests and, 119
Osservatore Romano's criticism of, 87
Purcell's support of, 82, 85
sexual ethics and, 278
Al Smith's campaign and, 150
social issues and, 146
Rerum Novarum, 126, 127, 131, 135, 146, 150, 154, 157, 162, 163, 197, 251
Review for Religious, 218
Review of Politics, 197
Revista Católica, 117
revolutions of 1848, 21–22, 38, 47–48
Rhineland, Germany, 37
rhythm method, 233–34, 243, 263
Rice, Charles, 163
Riesman, David, 252
Rights of Man and Natural Law, The (Maritain), 201
right to choose, 259, 260, 265–68, 270, 274, 276, 280
right to die, 286
right to life, 221–23, 253, 258, 260, 261, 267, 273, 274, 276–79
Rise of the Dutch Republic, The (Motley), 34
Ritch, W. G., 117
Ritter, Joseph, 210
Roberti, Francesco, 243
Rock, John, 239
Rockefeller, John D., III, 235
Rockefeller, Nelson, 274, 276, 278
Rodgers, A. K., 141
Rodgers, Daniel, 141
Roe v. Wade, 259, 262, 266, 277, 284, 288, 289

Rokeach, Milton, 180
Roman Catholicism (Boettner), 264
Romero, Matías, 59
Romnen, Heinrich, 197
Roosevelt, Franklin, 151–53, 164, 192
  birth control controversy and, 160
Roosevelt, Theodore, 123, 134, 224
rosary, 26–28
Rosecrans, William, 83–84, 86
Rossi, Pellegrino, 21
Rothstein, Barbara, 286
Rousseau, Jean-Jacques, 198, 199
Rummel, Joseph, 210
Russell, Bertrand, 167, 174–75
Rutledge, Wiley B., 182, 185
Ryan, Abraham, 111–12
Ryan, Edward G., 73
Ryan, John A., 137, 138, 141–45, *143*, 151–54, 158, 159, 161–64, 172, 173, 201, 205, 208, 221, 224, 233, 259
Ryerson, Edgerton, 40

Sacred Heart devotions, 12, 26, 28–29, 32
St. Louis, Mo., 22, 24, 92, 128, 210
St. Louis University, 23, 24, 208–9
St. Mary's Institute, Boston, 42
St. Mary's parish, Boston, 32
St. Paul, Minn., 120
St. Stephen's Home for Children, New York City, 133
St. Stephen's parish, New York City, 120, 133
St. Vincent de Paul Society, 128, 130
Salazar, António de Oliveira, 197
San Francisco, Calif., 268–69
Sanger, Margaret, 158–59, 161, 223, 226
Santa Fe, N.Mex., 289
Santayana, George, 165
Sarpi, Paulo, 11
Sarton, George, 179
Savannah, Ga., 51
Scalabrini, Giovanni Battista, 121
scapular, 48
Schaff, Philip, 99
Schlesinger, Arthur, Jr., 213
Schmoller, Gustav, 142
Scholastic Analysis of Usury, The (Noonan), 241
Scholasticism, *see* Thomistic revival
Schroeder, Joseph, 122
Schuman, Robert, 202
Schuschnigg, Kurt, 197
Schuster, George, 199
Schwartz, Louis B., 258
science:
  authority and, 139, 140
  Catholicism and, 104–5, 112, 175, 179
  Robert Merton's history of, 178–79
  in Middle Ages, 179, 187
  Protestantism and, 178–79
  public policy and, 155
scientific freedom, Vatican criticism of, 88
Scully, Thomas, 117
Seebote, Der, 63, 64, 73
segregation, 50, 55, 120, 186, 208–11
self-reliance, Emerson's notion of, 36
Semmes, Thomas, 61
settlement house movement, 129
Seward, William, 68, 80
sex education, 153, 155
sexual abuse crisis, 289–94
sexual ethics, 138, 154, 155, 215, 221–24, 278
  see also abortion; birth control; marriage
Shaftesbury, Earl of, 57
Shanley, Paul, 290
Shaw, John W., 224–25
Sheeran, James, 61
Shepard, Sophia, 7, 8
Sherman, James, 123
Sherman, William T., 91
Shils, Edward, 174
Shriver, Eunice Kennedy, 267, 269
Shriver, Sargent, 267, 279
Shurtleff, Nathaniel B., Jr., 72
Siedenberg, Frederick, 142, 163
Siegfried, André, 169
Simeoni, Giovanni, 134
Simon, Yves, 197–200, 204, 209
single-tax movement, 132, 134–37
Sisters of Charity, 133
situation ethics, 251–53, 255–57, 265, 281
Situation Ethics (Fletcher), 251
slavery, 48–66, 71, 76–79, 288, 293
  Cincinnati controversy over, 82–85
  education and, 38
  in Latin America, 50
  in New Orleans, 81–82
  see also abolitionism
Smith, Adam, 130, 131, 164

Smith, Al, 147–51, 159, 169, 171, 174, 185, 213
Smith, Goldwin, 99
Social Democrats, 161, 260
Social Gospel, 153
social insurance, 142
socialism, 48, 110, 142, 144, 145
social issues, 126–28, 137, 143–45
  democracy and, 207
  family ideal and, 154
  German Americans and, 142
  individual autonomy and, 153
  Franklin Roosevelt and, 151–52
  in San Francisco, 268–69
  see also child welfare; economic issues; labor issues; property rights; *Rerum Novarum*
Social Science Research Council, 180
social welfare, 129, 136, 147, 203, 288
sodalities, 31–33, 72
solidarity, 142, 269, 271, 272, 295
Sources chrétiennes, 195, 206
Southern Baptist Convention, 262
Southern Quarterly Review, 65
Spain, 128, 181, 192, 194, 199, 205
  civil war in, 172–73
Spalding, Martin, 26–27, 35, 37, 76, 86–87, 98, 295
Spellman, Francis, 174
Stallo, Johann B., 64
Stang, William, 144–45
Stanton, Elizabeth Cady, 95
State Department, U.S., 202
stations of the cross, 28
Stephens, Alexander, 65
sterilization, compulsory, 223–25, 228, 230
Stevens, Paul, 294
Stevens, Thaddeus, 84
Storer, Horatio, 227
Stowe, Calvin, 39
Stowe, Harriet Beecher, 58
Stritch, Samuel, 256
Strong, Josiah, 125
Structure of Social Action, The (Parsons), 178
Sturzo, Luigi, 172, 197, 198
subjectivity, 26, 266
Sue, Eugène, 23
suffering, 28, 29, 54, 222
suicide, 228, 253, 254, 257, 286, 294
Sumner, Charles, 24, 66, 76, 101
Supreme Court, U.S.:
  abortion issue and, 259, 260, 277–78, 286
  antiwar movement and, 256
  birth control issue and, 239
  compulsory sterilization and, 223–25
  Dred Scott decision and, 59
  educational issues and, 182–85, 205, 263–64, 294
  Missouri test oath case and, 75
  privacy rights and, 248
  right to die and, 286
Surnaturel (de Lubac), 195
Sweet, William Warren, 177
Switzerland, 19–20, 34, 35, 78
Syllabus of Errors, 96, 98, 207

Tablet, 79
Taft, William Howard, 123
Tammany Hall, 115, 134
Taney, Roger Brooke, 59
Taparelli d'Azeglio, Luigi, 53, 106
taxation, 144
  Bush administration and, 294
  of church property, 74, 92
  of land, 132
Taylor, Charles, 294
Tentler, Leslie, 157
Teología de la liberación (Gutiérrez), 272
Texas, 108
textbooks:
  on ethics, 139
  in New Mexico, 117
  Protestant bias in, 39
thalidomide, 259
theater, censorship of, 155
Theological Studies, 218, 219, 245, 272
theology, 139
  see also moral theology
Theory of Justice, A (Rawls), 263
therapeutic abortions, 258
Thirteenth, The: Greatest of Centuries, 105
Thomas, John L., 220, 236
Thomistic revival, 12, 25–26, 33, 36, 37, 127–28, 136, 139, 141, 193, 195, 196, 198–201, 203, 204
  academic freedom and, 174
  Van Wyck Brooks's suspicion of, 178
  in Catholic colleges, 140

Thomistic revival (*continued*)
Chenu's attack on, 207
Maritain and, 189
replacement of, 237
right to life and, 221
slavery issue and, 53
Thompson, Joseph P., 29, 58, 102
Thomson, Judith Jarvis, 263, 286
Three Reformers (Maritain), 199
Time Has Come, The: A Catholic Doctor's Proposals to End the Battle over Birth Control (Rock), 239
Time magazine, 212, 284, 285
Timon, John, 64
Tocqueville, Alexis de, 21, 253
tolerance, 148
Toronto, Canada, 37, 40, 59
Toronto Globe, 59
totalitarianism, 211–12
trade associations, 152
trade unions, *see* unions, labor
Transcendentalists, 43
Trenchard, John, 36
Tribe, Laurence, 264
True Believer, The (Hoffer), 252
trusteeism, lay, 26, 30, 64
truth:
church as source of, 103
James's notion of, 139
Murray's view of, 247
Turner, James, 103
Tweed, William Marcy, 115
Tyler, John, 65
Tyndall, John, 104

ultramontanism, 12, 13, 22, 29, 30, 45, 70
American Revolution and, 37
Bluntschli's attack on, 101
Brownson's position on, 89
Catholic education and, 40
in Civil War period, 67, 78, 100
educational issues and, 114
industrial economy and, 126
liberal Catholics and, 47, 48, 88
Lieber's hostility to, 101–2
in New Orleans, 81
slavery issue and, 52, 53, 79
social issues and, 130, 131
Uncle Tom's Cabin (Stowe), 58, 59
unemployment insurance, 144, 146
Union, in Civil War, 71–74, 77, 78, 80
Afro-Creoles' support of, 81
Brownson's support of, 66–68, 76
English view of, 79
French support for, 77–78
John Ireland's support of, 120
Purcell's support of, 82
Union, L', 81
unions, labor, 53, 131–32, 138, 144, 152, 153, 163
Unitarian churches, 161, 184, 185
United Farm Workers, 272
United Nations Universal Declaration on Human Rights, 203
United States Catholic Conference, 256, 272
Univers, L', 47, 70
Universalist churches, 161
universities and colleges, 139, 140, 229, 232, 247
U.S. Catholic Miscellany, 72
usury, 131, 241, 243

Vagnozzi, Egidio, 243, 244
Vatican Council, First, 103
Vatican Council, Second, 214, 236–38, 240, 244, 245, 256, 269, 270, 283
Vatican Decrees, The (Gladstone), 98, 99
Vatican-German concordat (1933), 171–72, 198
venial sin, 220
Ventura, Gioacchino, 21
Vermeersch, Arthur, 162, 221
Verot, Augustin, 55, 78
Veuillot, Louis, 47, 70, 71, 77, 80, 81
Vichy government, 194, 195, 198
Vietnam War, 256
Vignaux, Paul, 197
Virchow, Rudolf, 104
Virginia Statute for Religious Freedom, 176
Voegelin, Eric, 197
Vogt, William, 235–36
Voice of the Unborn, 276
voting rights:
of African Americans, 208
of women, 95, 96, 154

wages, 53, 54, 130, 142, 144, 153, 154, 158, 161, 162
Wagner, Adolph, 141, 142
Walker, Francis A., 124

Walsh, Catherine, 226
Walsh, William J., 135
Wandering Jew, The (Sue), 23
war, *see* military ethics
Washington, George, 37
Washington Post, 124
Washington State, 286
Watson, Tom, 125, 147
Wayland, J. A., 145
Weakland, Rembert, 293
Webb, Richard D., 59
Weber, Max, 104, 178, 181
Weber-Merton thesis, 179
Weigel, Gustave, 195
Weninger, Francis X., 27, 30, 78
Whall, Thomas, 7–9, *10,* 31
White, Andrew Dickson, 105
White, Walter, 211
Whittier, John Greenleaf, 93, 100
Whyte, William, 252
Wiget, Bernardine, 8, 9, 12–14, 19–21, *20,* 31, 32, 41, 42
- McElroy and, 32–33
- Marian devotions of, 28
- slavery issue and, 54, 86
- Thomistic revival and, 25–26

Williams, Glanville, 254, 257, 258
Williams, Roger, 177
Wills, Garry, 241, 282
Wilmot, David, 62
Wilson, Edmund, 174
Wilson, Elizabeth, 95
Wilson, Henry, 113–14
Wilson, Woodrow, 109, 171
Windthorst, Ludwig, 110
Wisconsin, 23, 73, 124
women's issues:
- labor issues, 142–44, 154, 155
- religious communities and, 129
- suffrage, 95, 96, 154
- *see also* abortion; birth control

women's movement, 261, 273, 274
women's rights, Catholicism and, 95–96
Wood, James, 48
Woodstock seminary, Maryland, 107–8
World War II, 194–95, 200
Wright, James, 280
Wright, John, 211, 230, 238, 243, 244

Yale College, Jews on faculty of, 186
Young, Josue, 78

Zigliara, Tommaso, 127, 128, 136